THE FRENCH
REVOLUTION

THE FRENCH REVOLUTION

NESTA H. WEBSTER

THE NOONTIDE PRESS

The French Revolution
by Nesta H. Webster

The Noontide Press
1822½ Newport Bl., Suite 183
Costa Mesa, CA 92627

First published 1919
First Noontide printing 1988

ISBN 0-939482-09-6
Cover design © 1988
by The Noontide Press

Send for our catalog of unusual
and hard-to-find titles

PREFACE

ASTROLOGERS tell us that the history of the world moves in cycles; that from time to time the same forces arise producing eras that strangely resemble one another. Between these eras a close affinity exists, and so it is that we, in looking back to the past from the world crisis of to-day, realize that periods which in times of peace have soothed or thrilled us have now lost their meaning, that the principles which inspired them have no place in our philosophy. The Renaissance is dead; the Reformation is dead; even the great wars of bygone days seem dwarfed by the immensity of the recent conflict. But whilst the roar of battle dies down another sound is heard—the angry murmur that arose in 1789 and that, though momentarily hushed, has never lost its force. Once more we are in the cycle of revolution.

The French Revolution is no dead event; in turning over the contemporary records of those tremendous days we feel that we are touching live things; from the yellowed pages voices call to us, voices that still vibrate with the passions that stirred them more than a century ago—here the desperate appeal for liberty and justice, there the trumpet-call of "King and Country"; now the story told with tears of death faced gloriously, now a maddened scream of rage against a fellow-man. When in all the history of the world until the present day has human nature shown itself so terrible and so sublime? And is not the fascination that amazing epoch has ever since exercised over the minds of men owing to the fact that the problems it held are still unsolved, that the same movements which originated with it are still at work amongst us? "What we learn to-day from the study of the Great Revolution," the anarchist Prince Kropotkin wrote in 1908, "is that it was the source and origin of all the present communist, anarchist, and socialist conceptions."

Indeed Kropotkin goes so far as to declare that " up till now, modern socialism has added absolutely nothing to the ideas that were circulating among the French people between 1789 and 1794, and which it was tried to put into practice in the year II. of the Republic (*i.e.* in the Reign of Terror). Modern socialism has only systematised those ideas and found arguments in their favour," etc. Now since the French Revolution still remains the one and only occasion in the history of the world when those theories were put into practice on a large scale, and carried out to their logical conclusion—for the experiment in Russia is as yet unfinished—it is surely worth while to know the true facts about that first upheaval. So far, in England, the truth is not known ; we have not even been told what really happened. " As to a real history of the French Revolution," Lord Cromer wrote to me a few months before his death, " no such thing exists in the English language, for Carlyle, besides being often very inaccurate and prejudiced, produced merely a philosophical rhapsody. It is well worth reading, but it is not history." Yet it is undoubtedly on Carlyle's rhapsody that our national conceptions of the Revolution are founded ; the great masterpiece of Dickens was built up on this mythological basis, whilst the old histories of Alison and Morse Stephens, and even the illuminating *Essays* of Croker, lack the power to rouse the popular imagination.[1] Thus the legend created by Carlyle has never been dispelled.

During the last few years the French Revolution has become less a subject for historical research than the theme of the popular journalist who sees in that lurid period material to be written up with profit. This being so, accuracy plays no part in his scheme. For the art of successful journalism is not

[1] No English writer was better acquainted with the *dessous des cartes* of the French Revolution than John Wilson Croker. Born in 1780, he talked with people who had taken part in the movement, and spent many years in forming and studying the magnificent collections of revolutionary pamphlets that he afterwards sold to the British Museum. In 1816 the publisher, John Murray, offered him the sum of 2500 guineas to write the complete history of the Revolution, but Croker never found time to do this, and his *Essays*, reprinted from the *Quarterly Review*, are all that he has left us of his stores of knowledge. These, though too controversial to appeal to the general public, throw more light on the hidden causes of the revolutionary movement than any book in the English language.

to illuminate the public mind but to reflect it, to tell it in even stronger terms what it thinks already, and therefore to confirm rather than to dispel popular delusions.

But if the Revolution is to be regarded as the supreme experiment in democracy, if its principles are to be held up for our admiration and its methods advocated as an example to our own people, is it not time that some effort were made to counteract that " conspiracy of history " that in France also, as M. Gustave Bord points out, has hitherto concealed the real facts concerning it ? Shall we not at last cease from rhapsody and consider the matter calmly and scientifically in its effects on the people ? This, after all, is the main issue—how was the experiment a success from the people's point of view? Strangely enough, though it was in their cause that the Revolution was ostensibly made, the people are precisely the portion of the nation that by Royalist and Revolutionary writers alike have been most persistently overlooked — the Royalists occupying themselves mainly with the trials of the monarchy and aristocracy, the Revolutionaries losing themselves in panegyrics on · the popular leaders. Thus Michelet was a Dantoniste, Louis Blanc a Robespierriste ; Lamartine was a Girondiste ; Thiers and Mignet were Orléanistes, not only as historians but as politicians, for their exoneration of the Duc d'Orléans was only a part of their policy for placing his son Louis Philippe on the throne of France,— and consequently to all these men the people were a matter only of secondary importance. So far no one has written the history of the movement from the point of view of the people themselves.

In studying the Revolution as an experiment in democracy, we must clear our minds of all predilections for certain individuals. Just as the author of a treatise on the discovery of tuberculin or on the antidote to hydrophobia devotes no space to recording the sufferings of the unhappy guinea-pigs and rabbits sacrificed in the cause of science, or in dilating on the virtuous private life of Koch or Pasteur, but concerns himself solely with the exact process adopted and the symptoms exhibited by the subjects with a view to proving or disproving the efficacy of the serums employed, so, if we would examine the Revolution as a scientific experiment, King, noblesse, and revolutionary leaders alike must be considered only in their relation to the cause of democracy ; we must concern ourselves with the people only, with the ills from which they suffered, with the means employed for their relief, with the part they themselves played in the great movement, and finally the results that were achieved. By this means alone we shall do justice to that brave and brilliant people by whose side we have fought to-day; we shall come to understand that they were not the blind unreasoning herd portrayed by Taine, the enraged " hyenas " of Horace Walpole, nor yet, as revolutionary writers would have us believe, a nation of slaves brought by long years of oppression to a pitch of exasperation that found a vent in the crimes and horrors of the Revolution.

It is on this last theory that popular opinion in England on the Revolution is founded, and that might, I think, be epitomized thus : " The French Revolution was in itself a purely beneficial movement, inspired by the desire for liberty and justice : unhappily it went too far and produced excesses which, though deplorable, were nevertheless the unavoidable accompaniment to the regeneration of the country." Now this statement is as illogical as it is unjust ; how could a movement that was purely beneficial " go too far " ? How could the desire of the people for liberty and justice be carried to excess and produce cruelty and bloodshed such as the civilized world had never seen before ? If this were true, then the only opinion at which a thinking human being could arrive would be that the French Revolution was the *reductio ad absurdum* of the proposition of democracy, a proposition that, once worked out to its tragic and grotesque conclusion, should have proved for all time that to give power into the hands of the people is to create a tyranny more terrible than any despotism can produce. But it was not so ; it was *not* the desire of the people for liberty and justice that produced these horrors ; it was *not* the movement for reform that " went too far "; the crimes and excesses of the Revolution sprang from totally distinct and extraneous causes that must be understood if justice is to be done to the people of France. It is by the revolutionary writers that the people have been most maligned, for since, as I have pointed out, these writers were not the advocates of the people but of certain revolutionary leaders, their method is to absolve their heroes from all blame and heap the whole responsibility upon the people. For this purpose a legend has been woven around all the great outbreaks of the Revolution and the rôle of the people persistently misrepresented.

Now if we study carefully the course of the revolutionary movement we shall find that the rôle of the people is in the main passive ; only on these great days of tumult do they play an active part. Between these outbreaks the fire of revolution smoulders, at moments almost flickers out, then suddenly for no apparent reason bursts again into flame, and it is only by long and patient search amongst contemporary documents that we can begin to understand the causes of these conflagrations. " The popular Revolution," said St. Just, " was the surface of a volcano of extraneous conspiracies," and consequently the actions of the people seen from the surface only can never be understood. Thus the story of the Revolution, as it is usually told us, with its pointless crimes, its unreasoning violence, and its hideous waste of life, is simply unintelligible—" a tale told by an idiot, full of sound and fury and signifying nothing."

If, then, we would discover the truth about these great revolutionary outbreaks, we must dig down far below the surface, we must trace the connection between the mine and the explosion, between the actions of the people and the causes that provoked them.[1] For, as Mr. Croker truly observed, " It is doubtless a very remarkable—though hitherto very little remarked—feature of the whole Revolution, that not one, not a single one, of the tumults which now had its successive stages, from the Affaire Réveillon to the September massacres, had any real connection with the pretext under which it was executed." These great moments of crisis, five in number, are like the five acts of a tremendous drama ; through them all we see the same methods at work, the same actors under different disguises, the same tangled threads of intrigue leading up to the tremendous cataclysm of the Terror. The Siege of the Bastille—the March on

---

[1] Lord Acton in his *Essays on the French Revolution* apparently caught a stray glimmer of this truth when he wrote these words : " The appalling thing in the French Revolution is not the tumult but the design. Through all the fire and smoke we perceive the evidence of calculating organization. The managers remain studiously concealed and masked ; but there is no doubt about their presence from the first. They had been active in the riots of Paris, and they were again active in the provincial risings." Having delivered himself, however, of this profound reflection, Lord Acton seems to have lost it from sight, for he proceeds to describe all the tumults of the Revolution without any further reference to organization or design— his chief concern being to absolve all the leaders from complicity.

Versailles—the two Invasions of the Tuileries—the Massacres of September—and finally the Reign of Terror—these form the history of the French people throughout the Revolution. The object of this book is, therefore, to relate as accurately as conflicting evidence permits the true facts about each great crisis, to explain the motives that inspired the crowds, the means employed to rouse their passions, and thereby to throw a truer light on the rôle of the people, and ultimately on the Revolution as the great experiment in democracy.

AUTHORITIES CONSULTED

AN immense advantage offered to the historian by the modern and popular way of writing history lies in the fact that he is able to dispense with any reference to the authorities he has consulted. Both public and critics object to notes and quotations which interrupt the flow of the narrative ; therefore notes and quotation marks have gone out of fashion. This convenient plan not only facilitates enormously the author's task, since it enables him to write down anything that comes into his head without troubling to remember where he read it, but also provides the unscrupulous historian with unlimited scope for misrepresentation, for by pandering to this popular prejudice he is able to propound theories absolutely at variance with fact, to attribute to historical personages sentiments they never entertained, and even words they never uttered, and so to present a period in precisely the colours that best suit his purpose.

In this book, however, at the risk of giving to its pages a ponderous appearance, I have reverted to the old-fashioned system of notes, since my object is not to weave fanciful word-pictures around the great scenes of the Revolution, but to tell as simply and clearly as possible what really happened. Now since the whole story of these great revolutionary days is a series of disputed points, no book on the subject is of the slightest historical value that does not give chapter and verse for every controversial statement. Further, it is essential to indicate the political faction to which the authorities quoted belonged, and also the value of their evidence. For to condemn an individual or a party on the word of their enemies, or to absolve them on the testimony of their accomplices, is as absurd as if one were to accept evidence at a trial without inquiring into the identities of the witnesses. Criminology plays no small part in understanding the true causes of the revolutionary outbreaks, and for this purpose contemporaries alone must be consulted, and the identity of these contemporaries must be clearly defined. The following *résumé* will show the political standpoint of the authorities quoted most frequently throughout the course of this book, whilst the policy of those referred to on particular events will be given in the context :—

CONTEMPORARY AUTHORITIES (REVOLUTIONARY)

1. *Histoire de la Révolution par Deux Amis de la Liberté*, in nineteen volumes.—The first six volumes, violently revolutionary in tone and filled with grotesque fables current at the time, have been attributed to the bookseller Clavelin, and to Kerverseau, but this surmise rests on no evidence whatever (see *Bibliographie de la Révolution*, by Maurice Tourneux, i. 3). Montjoie stated that the work was dictated and paid for by the Duc d'Orléans (*Conjuration de d'Orléans*, ii. 97), and it is no doubt strongly Orléaniste in its point of view. After the sixth volume, however, it makes a complete *volte-face* and becomes moderate, even Royalist in opinion, and at the same time less interesting. As an anonymous publication the history of the *Deux Amis* carries none of the weight that attaches to signed work, but since it was on the early part of the series that Carlyle mainly based his account of the first stages of the Revolution, and also his accusations against the Old Régime, it should be read if one would realize how flimsy was the evidence that Carlyle blindly accepted as the truth.

2. The *Moniteur*, a journal edited by Panckoucke, first made its appearance on November 24, 1789. The numbers relating to events anterior to this date were written up afterwards, and the accounts of the great revolutionary tumults in July 1789 are copied verbatim from the *Deux Amis*. Its policy throughout the Revolution is always that of the dominating party—at first Orléaniste, then Girondiste, and finally Montagnard.

3. Prudhomme. — The paper known as *Révolutions de Paris*, published weekly throughout the whole course of the Revolution by this indefatigable journalist, is the most genuinely democratic record of the period, since it attaches itself to no political party, but identifies itself with the revolutionary element amongst the people and supports the demagogues only as representative of the popular cause. Later on, however, Prudhomme realized that he had been duped by these men, and in his *Histoire impartiale des Crimes et des Erreurs de la Révolution Française*, published in 1797, completely gave away his former associates and showed up the intrigues of the Revolution more thoroughly than any Royalist has done. The former work — *Les Révolutions de Paris* — is freely quoted by revolutionary writers ; on the second—*Crimes de la Révolution*—they are strangely silent.

4. The *Histoire Parlementaire*, by Buchez et Roux, contains reports of the debates that took place in the Assembly (mainly abbreviated from the *Moniteur*), and also in the Jacobin Club, besides reprints of various contemporary pamphlets, etc. But the opinion of the authors, strongly biassed in favour of the revolutionary leaders rather than of the people, should be accepted with caution.

CONTEMPORARY AUTHORITIES (ROYALIST)

1. Montjoie.—Félix Christophe Louis Ventre de la Touloubre (1756–1816), known as Galart de Montjoie (or Montjoye), was the author of an *Histoire de la Révolution de France et de l'Assemblée Nationale* which appeared in the Royalist journal *L'Ami du Roi*, of a history of the Orléaniste conspiracy, *Histoire de la Conjuration de Louis Philippe Joseph d'Orléans* (1796), and of an inferior work, *L'Histoire de la Conjuration de Maximilien Robespierre.* Montjoie as an eye-witness of the earlier revolutionary tumults is extremely interesting, but owing to his violent animosity towards the Orléanistes his accusations against them should not be accepted unless confirmed by other contemporary evidence. In most instances, however, this is forthcoming. Both by Taine and by Jules Flammermont, a strongly revolutionary writer, Montjoie is regarded as an important authority on the period.[1]

2. Beaulieu. — Claude François Beaulieu (1754–1827) edited several papers during the Revolution, and, according to Dauban, was the author of the *Diurnal*, of which Dauban reprinted a large part in *La Demagogie à Paris en 1793*. But this is not conclusively proved. In 1803 Beaulieu published his history of the French Revolution in six volumes, entitled *Essais historiques sur les Causes et les Effets de la Révolution de France.* This is undoubtedly the best contemporary work on the subject, and is quoted by historians of every party. Although a Royalist, Beaulieu displays the greatest impartiality; he advances nothing without proof. Personally acquainted with most of the leading Revolutionaries, he speaks of what he himself saw and heard, and never allows himself, like Montjoie, to be carried away by his feelings. Beaulieu was arrested on the 29th of October 1793, and imprisoned first at the Conciergerie, then at the Luxembourg, from which he

---

[1] " Montjoie is a party man, but he dates and specifies, and his evidence, when elsewhere confirmed, deserves to be admitted " (Taine, *La Révolution*, iii. 37). M. Flammermont draws an interesting comparison between Montjoie and the *Deux Amis de la Liberté*, pointing out that the latter is in reality a patchwork of current rumours, the authors "have no settled system, they have not criticized each of the sources of which they have made use ; on every point they content themselves with choosing the version which seems to them most likely, thereby arriving at the strangest contradictions. . . . *En résumé*, this considerable work has no original value, at any rate for the narrative of the 14th of July. In Galart de Montjoye we meet at last a man who has the courage of his opinions, and who signs his work, which was not without danger at the period when he published it. Indeed, he loudly proclaims he is a Royalist, and takes up his stand as a declared adversary of the Revolution, but at the same time he is nearly always moderate in his language, and he takes pains to support his opinions and his judgements by the most authoritative testimony " (*La Journée du 14 Juillet*, p. cxxxvii). See also the opinion of the English contemporary, John Adolphus, *Biographical Memoirs of the French Revolution*, ii. 205.

was released after the fall of Robespierre. Between 1813 and 1827 he collaborated with Michaud in compiling the great *Biographie Universelle*, for which he wrote articles on several of the Revolutionaries he had known.

3. Ferrières.—The *Mémoires* of the Marquis de Ferrières, though more frequently quoted by English writers than the *Essais de Beaulieu*, are of far less original value, as they are largely composed of quotations from the writings of other contemporaries. Ferrières was a disaffected noble, and, although a Royalist, does not err on the side of over-indulgence for the Court, but as an ardent anti-Orléaniste throws an interesting light on the intrigue at work behind the earlier revolutionary movement.

The above are the authorities mainly consulted for the purpose of this book; the evidence of historians is only quoted in the case of those who had access to the archives of France or other contemporary documents not to be found in this country. In this respect Taine, Granier de Cassagnac, Mortimer Ternaux, Edmond Biré, Gustave Bord, Chassin, Dauban, Wallon, Campardon, and Adolphe Schmidt are particularly valuable. The opinion of M. Louis Madelin is also occasionally referred to as being founded on the most recent researches, and as representing the last word in modern French thought on the vexed questions of the Revolution.

CONTENTS

PLANS

PROLOGUE

PROLOGUE

BEFORE attempting to describe the outbreaks of the Revolution, it is necessary to indicate as briefly as possible the ills from which the people were suffering, the reforms that they demanded, and, on the other hand, the influences at work amongst them which diverted the movement for reform into the channel of revolution.

THE PEOPLE BEFORE THE REVOLUTION

Nearly every author in embarking on the story of the Revolution has considered it *de rigueur* to enlarge on the progress of philosophy that heralded the movement. The oppressions that had prevailed during the reigns of Louis XIV. and Louis XV. had, we are told, been endured in a spirit of dumb resignation until the teaching of Rousseau, Diderot, and other social reformers proclaimed to the nation that they need be endured no longer. If we regard the Revolution from the point of view of the people, this time-honoured preamble may, however, be dispensed with. Doubtless the philosophers played an important part in preparing the Revolution, but their direct influence was confined to the aristocracy and the educated bourgeoisie ; to the peasant tilling the soil, the *Encyclopédie* and the *Contrat Social* were of less pressing interest than the condition of his crop and the profit of his labour. How the abuses of the Old Régime affected him in this tangible respect we can read in Arthur Young's *Travels*, in Albert Babeau's *Le Village sous l'Ancien Régime*, or in the works of Taine, where all the injustices of tailles, capitaineries, corvées, gabelles, etc., are set forth categorically, and are too well known to be enumerated here. Suffice it to say, these oppressions were many and grievous, but they sprang less from intentional tyranny than from an obsolete system that demanded readjustment. Thus certain customs that originated in benevolence had, through the progress of civilization, become oppressive—the *liberty* to grind at the seigneur's mill had become the *obligation* to grind at the seigneur's mill, whilst many feudal exactions and personal services were merely relics of the days when rent was paid in

3

kind or in labour. It is evident, moreover, that many of these feudal oppressions that look so terrible on paper had fallen into disuse ; thus, although the parchments enumerating the seigneurial rights were still in existence, "the power of the seigneurs over the persons of their vassals only existed in romances " at the time of the Revolution.[1] In every ancient civilization strange archaic laws might be discovered—does not our own legal code enact that a man may beat his wife with any weapon no thicker than his thumb ? but so far the women of England have not found it necessary to rise in revolt against this extraordinary stipulation.

For the peasant of France the most real grievances were undoubtedly the inequality of taxation and the " capitaineries " or game-laws, monstrous injustices that crippled his energies and often made his labour vain.   Yet were the peasants of old France the wretched, down-trodden beings that certain historians have described them ?   The strange thing is that no contemporary evidence corroborates this theory ; in none of the letters or memoirs written before the Revolution, even by such advanced thinkers as Rousseau and Madame Roland, do we encounter the starving scarecrows of the villages or the ragged spectres of the Faubourg Saint-Antoine portrayed by Dickens ; on the contrary, gaiety seems to have been the distinguishing characteristic of the people.   The dancing peasants of Watteau and Lancret were no figments of an artist's brain, but very charming realities described by every traveller.   Arthur Young, who has been persistently represented as the great opponent of the Ancien Régime, records few actual instances of misery or oppression, and, as we shall see, Young was later on led to reconstruct his views on the old government of France in a pamphlet which has been carefully ignored by writers who quote his earlier work in support of their theories.

But the most remarkable evidence on peasant life before the Revolution is to be found in the letters of Dr. Rigby, who travelled in France during the summer of 1789. This curious book, published for the first time in 1880, aroused less attention in England than in France, where it was regarded as an important contribution to the history of the period.[2] The accounts it

[1] *Mémoires du Chancelier Pasquier*, p. 46.
[2] See, for example, the opinion of the pro-revolutionary writer M. Jules Flammermont in his *Journée du 14 Juillet* : " Another witness of this surprising revolution (the revolution of July 1789) is Dr. Rigby, whom the chances of travel brought to France and kept in Paris during these glorious days.   His letters to his wife form valuable evidence of which neither the authenticity nor the impartiality can be disputed. . . . He was a practical agriculturist and at the same time a man of science, and his letters, though perhaps rather optimistic, make the counterpart to the criticisms of Arthur Young, who saw the dark side of everything."

contains are so subversive of the accepted theories on peasant misery current in this country, and have been so little quoted, that a few extracts must be given here.

Between Calais and Lille "the most striking character of the country" through which Dr. Rigby passed was its extraordinary fertility : "We went through an extent of seventy miles, and I will venture to say there was not a single acre but what was in a state of the highest cultivation. The crops are beyond any conception I could have had of them—thousands and ten thousands of acres of wheat superior to any which can be produced in England. . . .

"The general appearance of the people is different to what I expected ; they are strong and well-made. We saw many agreeable scenes as we passed along in the evening before we came to Lisle : little parties sitting at their doors, some of the men smoking, some playing at cards in the open air, and others spinning cotton. Everything we see bears the marks of industry, and *all the people look happy*. We have indeed seen few signs of opulence in individuals, for we do not see so many gentlemen's seats as in England, but then *we have seen few of the lower classes in rags, idleness, and misery*. What strange prejudices we are apt to take regarding foreigners ! . . .

"What strikes me most in what I have seen is the wonderful difference between this country and England . . . the difference seems to be in favour of the former ; if they are not happy, they look at least very like it. . . ." Throughout the whole course of his journey across France Dr. Rigby continues in the same strain of admiration—an admiration that we might attribute to lack of discernment were it not that it ceases abruptly on his entry into Germany. Here he finds "a country to which Nature has been equally kind as to France, for it has a fertile soil, but as yet the inhabitants live under an oppressive government." At Cologne he finds that "tyranny and oppression have taken up their abode. . . . There was a gloom and an appearance of disease in almost every man's face we saw ; their persons also look filthy. The state of wretchedness in which they live seems to deprive them of every power of exertion . . . the whole country is divided between the Archbishop and the King of Prussia . . . the land is uncultivated and depopulated. *How every country and every people we have seen since we left France sink in comparison with that animated country !*" It is evident that, however rose-coloured was Dr. Rigby's view of France, the French people had certainly not reached that pitch of "exasperation" that according to certain historians would account for the excesses of the Revolution. Lady Eastlake, Dr. Rigby's daughter, who edited these letters from France, fearing apparently that her father will be accredited with telling travellers' tales, attempts in the preface to explain his remarks by quoting the observation of De Tocqueville : " One must not be deceived by the gaiety the Frenchman displays in his greatest troubles, it only proves that, believing his unhappy fate to be inevitable, he tries to distract himself by not thinking about it—it is not that he does not feel it." This might possibly describe the attitude of the French people towards their government during the centuries that preceded the Revolution, when, convinced of their impotence to revolt, they resigned themselves to oppression ; but at the period Dr. Rigby describes the work of reform had long since begun and they had therefore no cause for hopelessness or despair. Louis XVI. had not waited for the gathering of the revolutionary storm in order to redress the evils from which the people suffered ; in the very first year of his reign he had embarked on the work of reform with the co-operation of Turgot and Malesherbes. In 1775 he had attempted to introduce the free circulation of grain—thereby enraging the monopolizers who in revenge stirred up the " Guerre de Farines " ; in 1776 he had proposed the suppression of the corvée which the opposition of the Parlements prevented; [1] in 1779 he had abolished all forms of servitude in his domains, inviting " all seigneurs of fiefs and communities to follow his example " ; in 1780 he had abolished torture ; in 1784 he had accorded liberty of conscience to the Protestants ; in 1787 he had proposed the equality of territorial taxation, the suppression of the gabelle or salt tax, and again urged the abolition of the corvée and the free circulation of grain ; in 1787 and 1788 he had proposed reforms in the administration of justice, the equal admission of citizens of every rank to all forms of employment, the abolition of *lettres de cachet*, and greater liberty of the press. Meanwhile he had continued to reduce the expenses of his household and had reformed the prisons and hospitals. Finally on August 8, 1788, he had announced the assembling of the States-General, at which he accorded double representation to the Tiers États.

In this spring of 1789 the French people had therefore every reason to feel hopeful of the future and to believe that now at last all their wrongs would be redressed. Had not the King sent out a proclamation to the whole nation saying, " His Majesty has desired that in the extremities of his kingdom and in the

---

[1] The Parlements, which played an active part in the revolutionary movement, had proved continually obstructive to the King's schemes of reform, and it was they, as well as the monopolizers, who had opposed the free circulation of grain. " It must appear strange," wrote Arthur Young, " in a government so despotic in some respects as that of France, to see the parliaments in every part of the kingdom making laws without the King's consent, and even in defiance of his authority " (*Travels in France*, p. 321).

obscurest dwellings every man shall rest assured that his wishes and requests shall be heard " ?

" All over the country," says Taine, " the people are to meet together to discuss abuses. . . . These confabulations are authorized, provoked from above. In the early days of 1788 the provincial assemblies demand from the syndicate and from the inhabitants of each parish that a local enquiry shall be held ; they wish to know the details of their grievances, what part of the revenue each tax removes, what the cultivator pays and suffers. . . . All these figures are printed . . . artisans and countrymen discuss them on Sunday after mass or in the evening in the great room at the inn. . . ."

The King has been bitterly reproached by Royalists for thus taking the people into his confidence over schemes of reform ; such changes in the government as were needed, they remark, should have been effected by the royal authority unaided by popular opinion. But the King doubtless argued that no one knows better than the wearer where the shoe pinches ; and since his great desire was to alleviate the sufferings of his people, it seemed to his simple mind that the best way to do this was to ask them for a list of their grievances before attempting to redress them. Believers in despotism may deplore the error in judgement, but the people of France did not mistake the good intentions of the King, for in the *cahiers de doléances* or lists of grievances that arrived from all parts of the country in response to this appeal the people were unanimous in their respect and loyalty to Louis XVI.

What, then, did the cahiers demand ? What were the true desires of the people in the matter of government ? This all-important point has been too often overlooked in histories of the Revolution ; yet it must be clearly understood if we would realize how far the Revolution as it took place was the result of the people's will. Now the summarizing of the cahiers by the National Assembly [1] revealed that the following principles of government were laid down by the nation :

I. The French government is monarchic.
II. The person of the King is inviolable and sacred.
III. His crown is hereditary from male to male.

On these three points the cahiers were unanimous, and the great majority were agreed on the following :

IV. The King is the depositary of the executive power.
V. The agents of authority are responsible.
VI. The royal sanction is necessary for the promulgation of the laws.

[1] *Moniteur,* i. 215.

VII. The nation makes the laws with the royal sanction.
VIII. The consent of the nation is necessary for loans and taxes.
IX. Taxes can only be imposed from one meeting of the States-General to another.
X. Property is sacred.
XI. Individual liberty is sacred.

In the matter of reforms the cahiers asked first and foremost for the equality of taxation, for the abolition of that monstrous privilege by which the wealthier classes of the community were enabled to avoid contributing their rightful share towards the expenses of the State ; they asked for the free admission of citizens of all ranks to civil and military employment, for revision of the civil and criminal code, for the substitution of money payments in the place of feudal and seigneurial dues, for the abolition of gabelles, corvées, franc-fief, and arbitrary imprisonment.

In all these demands we shall find no element of sedition or of disaffection towards the monarchy, but the response of a loyal and spirited people to the King's proposals for reform. Such animosity as they displayed was directed against the " privileged orders," and, as we shall see, this sentiment was not wholly spontaneous. Hua, a member of the Legislative Assembly, has well described the attitude of the people in pages that may be summarized thus :

The Ancien Régime had very real abuses, there was every reason to attack it. The clergy and noblesse had lost their power and their *raison d'être* ; they were obliged to let the Third Estate come into its own by giving up their privileges. Nothing could have stopped this or ought to have stopped it. " It has been said that the Revolution was made in public opinion before it was realized by events ; this is true, but one must add that it was not the Revolution such as we saw it . . . *it was not by the people that the Revolution was made in France.*" And in confirmation of this statement, with which, as I shall show, contemporaries of all parties agree, Hua points out that " the voice of the nation cried out for reform, for changes in the government, but all proclaimed respect for religion, loyalty to the King, and desire for law and order."[1]

What, then, was needed to kindle the flame of revolution ?

To understand this we must examine the intrigues at work amongst the people ; these and these alone explain the gigantic misunderstanding that arose between the King and his subjects, and that plunged the country on the brink of regeneration into the black abyss of anarchy.

---

[1] *Mémoires de Hua, député à l'Assemblée Législative*, published by his grandson François Saint Maur in 1871.

At the beginning of the Revolution the principal intrigue, and the one that paved the way for all the rest, was undoubtedly

THE ORLÉANISTE CONSPIRACY

Louis Philippe Joseph, fifth Duc d'Orléans in direct descent from the brother of Louis XIV., and therefore fourth cousin once removed to Louis XVI., came into the world with a heredity tainted from various sources. His great-grandfather Philippe, Regent of France during the minority of Louis XV., had married the daughter of Louis XIV. and Madame de Montespan. More German than French—for his mother was the Princess Elizabeth of the Palatinate, whose memoirs are perhaps the most nauseous reading of the period—the Regent had introduced into the gay gallantry of France the bestial forms of vice that prevailed in those days at the courts of Germany. Amongst the most dissolute frequenters of the Palais Royal during the Regency was Louis Armand, Prince de Conti, a moral maniac of the Sadic variety, and it was his daughter who, married to the fourth Duc d'Orléans, became the mother of Louis Philippe Joseph, later to be known as Philippe Égalité. Of such elements was the man composed—if indeed he was the son of the duke and not—as the people of Paris believed, and as he himself afterwards declared to the Commune—of the duchess's coachman.

In appearance, certain contemporaries assure us, Philippe was not unattractive, since he had blue eyes, good teeth, and a fine white skin; but when they proceed to relate that his face was bloated and adorned with collections of red pimples, whilst his portraits show him to us with a large fleshy nose, thick lips, and a massive neck and chin, we find it difficult to understand the charm he exercised over his *intimes*. Yet so fervent was their admiration that when Philippe in time grew bald his boon companions loyally shaved off their front hair in compliment. The Anglomania which had increased his popularity amongst the young bloods of the day disgusted Louis XVI., since it consisted in no appreciation for the better qualities of the English, but in adopting all their worst habits—the betting, gambling, and heavy drinking that prevailed in England at that date. As the leader of this imported fashion, the Duc d'Orléans affected English dress of the sporting kind, appearing habitually in a cloth frock coat, buckskin breeches, and top boots; thus attired he rode to race-meetings, or drove about the town in his English " whisky." His two ruling passions, says the Duc de Cars, were money, and after money debauchery. Entirely indifferent to public opinion he flaunted his vices in the eyes of all Paris; arm-in-arm with the Marquis de Sillery he might be seen on the steps of the

Coliseum in the Champs Élysées, insolently accosting women who had the misfortune to meet his eye; at Longchamps he would gallop ostentatiously beside the carriage of some notorious *demi-mondaine*, whilst at the Palais Royal his entourage was composed of the most worthless men and women of the day. The evil reputation borne by society at the time of the Revolution is attributable more to the Duc d'Orléans and his set than to any other cause, whilst as a climax of hypocrisy the severest strictures on the morals of society emanated from the pens of the very men and women who outraged them—Laclos, Chamfort, and Madame de Genlis. By the side of the Duc d'Orléans and his boon companions the follies of the Comte d'Artois and the Polignacs fade into insignificance, and the games of " descamptivos," so luridly described by Orléaniste writers as the favourite diversion at Versailles, seem innocuous indeed compared with the ducal pastime of " collecting girls from the lowest quarters of Paris, and thrusting them nude and inebriated into the park of Monceaux."

Yet this was the prince who, we are asked to believe, became the idol of the Paris populace. It is only one of the many calumnies directed against the people by so-called democratic writers. The instincts of the people are not naturally perverse ; they do not admire a bad master, a faithless husband, a man of corrupt and vicious tastes. We have only to consult the records written before the Revolution to find that the people of Paris loathed and despised the Duc d'Orléans. The duke returned their aversion with contempt ; to the future bearer of the name " Égalité" the people were indeed less than the dust. In order to keep up the " aristocratic" character of his garden at the Palais Royal, he had issued an order that no admittance was to be granted to " soldiers, men in livery, people in caps and shirts, *to dogs or workmen*." [1]

" The Duc d'Orléans," a chronicler writes on April 5, 1787, " allowed himself to be so carried away by the ardour of the chase that he followed the quarry he was hunting, with his train, through the Faubourg Montmartre, the Place Vendôme, and the Rue Saint-Honoré, as far as the Place Louis XV., not without having overturned and wounded several people." Thereupon the Parisians composed satirical verses on the duke, ending with these lines :

> . . . au sein de Paris, un grand, noble de race,
> Sans respect pour les droits des gens,
> Écrase quelques habitants
> Pour goûter en plein jour le plaisir de la chasse.[2]

---

[1] *Journal d'un Étudiant*, edited by M. Gaston Maugras, p. 9.
[2] *Correspondance Secrète sur Louis XVI et Marie Antoinette*, edited by M. de Lescure, p. 126.

It was certainly no easy task for the party who wished to substitute the Duc d'Orléans for Louis XVI. on the throne of France to persuade the people that the man who treated them with so much insolence had now become the champion of their liberties. M. Émile Dard in his interesting book, *Le Général Choderlos de Laclos*, declares that the Orléaniste conspiracy originated with Brissot as early as 1787, and that in this year he sketched out, in a letter to Ducrest, the brother of Madame de Genlis, his plan for inaugurating a second Fronde with the Duc d'Orléans at its head. "His cause must be identified with that of the people." If in the beginning the duke were to distinguish himself by "striking acts of benevolence and patriotism," he would soon become "the idol of the people." "Let him then embrace the doctrines in vogue, disseminate them in writing, and gain the leaders to his side."

Whether this scheme was adopted on the advice of Brissot or not, it was precisely the one pursued by the duke and his supporters. From the moment the States-General met, says a democratic pamphlet of the day, "the seigneur who was the hardest towards his vassals, the most exacting and the most severe, especially in the matter of pecuniary rights, made a show of moderation, generosity, and even lavishness."[1] It is a common ruse of Orléaniste writers to represent the duke as an amiable, weak, and irresponsible puppet, incapable of serious designs. This was precisely the impression he intended to create ; an affectation of irresponsibility is a time-honoured ruse of conspirators. At the same time it is probable that, left to himself, the Duc d'Orléans would have had neither the wit nor the energy to form a conspiracy ; the genius of Laclos was needed to devise and organize a vast and formidable intrigue.

Choderlos de Laclos belonged to a poor and recently ennobled family of Spanish origin, and in 1788, at the age of forty-seven, after leaving the army, he was introduced to the Palais Royal by the Vicomte de Ségur, who obtained for him the post of *secrétaire des commandements* to the Duc d'Orléans. Laclos had already made a name for himself as the author of the scandalous *Liaisons Dangereuses*, a novel describing in the form of letters from country-houses the depraved morals of society. "A monster of immorality" himself, he revelled in depicting the baser sides of human nature—"according to him, good people, if any such existed, would be simply lambs amongst a herd of tigers, and he holds it better to be a tiger, since it is better to devour than to be devoured."[2]

[1] "Grand Triomphe de M. le Duc d'Orléans, ou Examen Impartial de Conduite," p. 5, August 23, 1790.
[2] Montjoie, *Conjuration de d'Orléans*, i. 213.

To the cynical mind of Laclos there was something infinitely diverting in the idea of placing the dissolute duke at the head of the kingdom, and the very weakness and want of energy that characterized his royal protégé offered all the wider a field to Laclos's own ambition.

In order to inspire the duke with the will to collaborate in this scheme Laclos well knew, moreover, the vulnerable side from which to approach him. Place and power had little attraction for Philippe d'Orléans ; as king he would have access to no more money and to less pleasure than fell to his share as " first prince of the blood." " The Duc d'Orléans," a wit had once remarked, " would always be afraid to belong to any party where he would not have the chorus-girls of the opera on his side." But if incapable of great ambitions, the duke possessed one characteristic that lent not merely energy but fire to his otherwise sluggish nature—this was the spirit of revenge. If he could not devise, if he could not scheme, if he could not strive to achieve some settled purpose, he could *hate*. He was immeasurably and unrelentingly vindictive. To revenge himself on any one who had piqued his vanity or thwarted his designs, he would stick at nothing, he would know no pity. And now for years all the bitter rancour of which he was capable had been growing in intensity towards one woman who had humiliated him—the Queen of France.

In a lesser degree he hated the King also : had not Louis XVI. refused to make him grand admiral of the fleet, in consequence of his conduct at the battle of Ouessant ? But it was Marie Antoinette who had withheld her consent to the marriage of his daughter with the Duc d'Angoulême, it was to her he owed his banishment from the Court, and it was her rejection of his infamous love-making that still rankled in his mind.

The Duc d'Orléans was not the only member of the Palais Royal set who had suffered a like rebuff. " The Queen," says M. Émile Dard, " was proud and *coquette* ; she held back with disdain those that her charm attracted. The spite of men was directed against her as cruelly as the jealousy of women. Under a chaste king many courtiers had hoped that the reign of lovers would succeed to that of mistresses. What a prospect for the ambitions of the Court ! What glory and profit for roués like Tilly, Biron, Bézénval, Ségur, to record amongst their successful ventures the Queen of France ! In how many calumnies did self-interest and vanity find their vent ! " Biron, we know from his insufferable memoirs, had actually made overtures to the Queen, and we may safely accept the version of this incident given by Madame Campan, who states that the interview ended after a few moments with the words pronounced in indignant tones by Marie Antoinette, " Sortez, monsieur ! " and the hasty exit of Biron from her presence.

The advances of the Vicomte de Noailles met with no better success,[1] and both these *séducteurs* became the bitterest enemies of the Queen.

On such resentments was the animosity of the Palais Royal roués for the Court founded. At the duke's country-house of Monceaux all these malcontents collected, and it was here, amidst the clinking of champagne glasses, that the foulest libels, the most obscene verses on the Queen, were uttered and afterwards circulated through the underworld of Paris.

The exile of the Duc d'Orléans in 1787 provided his party with a fresh *cause de guerre*. At the Séance Royale the King had announced two fresh taxes—the *timbre* and the *subvention territoriale*—to be imposed on the "privileged classes"; whereupon the duke at the instigation of Ducrest rose and declared the royal decree to be " illegal." " Do not imagine," he said afterwards to Brissot, " that if I made this stand against the King it was in order to serve *a people I despise,* or a body of which I make no account (the Parlement), but that I was indignant at a man treating me with so much insolence." [2] The insolence, however, seems to have been entirely on the side of the duke. Louis XVI. on his return to Versailles remarked that it was not the declaration of the Duc d'Orléans that had offended him, but the threatening tone in which the words were pronounced, and the way he had looked at him as he spoke.[3] On the advice of the Queen he accordingly exiled the duke, stipulating that he should not go as he wished—for reasons we shall see later—to England, but to his property at Villers-Cotterets.

This edict admirably served the interests of the Orléanistes, since the duke was now able to pose as the victim of despotism, and it did much to inflame his fury against the King and Queen. When two years later he was elected deputy in the States-General, he cynically declared : " I laugh at the States-General, but I wished to belong to them if only for the moment when individual liberty should be discussed in order to vote for a law that will enable me to go where I like, so that when I want to start for London, Rome, or Pekin, I shall not be sent to Villers-Cotterets. I laugh at all the rest." [4]

Such were the motives that inspired the " democracy " of the Palais Royal party. Directed by the genius of Laclos, and financed by the millions of the Duc d'Orléans, the vast organiza-

---

[1] *Mémoires du Comte de Tilly,* ii. 110.
[2] *Le Général Choderlos de Laclos,* by Émile Dard, p. 153.
[3] Montjoie, *Conjuration de d'Orléans,* i. 93.
[4] *Les Fils de Philippe Égalité pendant la Terreur,* by G. Lenôtre, p. 12.

tion of the Orléaniste conspiracy took form and grew, until by
the spring of 1789 the plan of campaign was complete. Orléaniste
propaganda were circulated all over France in preparation for
the States-General ; models of cahiers drafted by Sieyès and
Laclos were distributed to different constituencies, and it was
undoubtedly by this means that the people's animosity towards
the noblesse was largely engineered, for in the upholders of the
Old Régime the. Orléanistes saw the most serious obstacle to
their schemes.

But the crowning triumph of the Orléaniste conspiracy was
the acquisition of Mirabeau. This amazing man, whose striking
personality and thunderous oratory must have ensured the
success of any party to which he attached himself, was lost to
the royal cause mainly by the ineptness of the King's ministers.
It is almost certain that at this crisis Mirabeau needed only the
slightest encouragement to throw himself into the movement for
reform by peaceful methods, and in this he rightly saw that the
King was the real leader.   Such rancour as he entertained against
the Old Régime was directed against the noblesse who had shunned
him on account of his irregularities ; the royal authority he was
prepared to defend.   He alone of all the men who should have
advised the King on the assembling of the States-General foresaw the disasters impending from the unpreparedness of the
Government, and in a letter addressed to the King's minister
Montmorin in December 1788 he implored him to be advised
in time.

Alas, for the eternal weakness of Conservatism, the fatal
unresponsiveness that has driven many a would-be ally into the
enemy's camp ! To Montmorin, Mirabeau with his discreditable
past and his unscrupulous business transactions was a man to
distrust, and therefore to be rejected. He failed to realize the
truth of Gouverneur Morris's aphorism—a maxim that should
surely be laid to heart by every one concerned in government :
" *There are in the world men who are to be employed, not trusted.*"
Mirabeau was decidedly not to be trusted. " I was born to
be an adventurer ! " he once said gaily to Dumont and Duroverai.
But was that a reason not to employ him ?   Were not some of the
greatest men who ever lived adventurers ?   Was not France saved
ten years later by the great adventurer from Corsica ?   Yet with
this term Conservatism too often brands the man whose dynamic
force is needed to counteract its own inertia. The letter of
Mirabeau was ignored, his *mémoire* never reached the King, and all
the disasters he had foreseen came to pass. So the man who
might have saved the monarchy, smarting at this rebuff, threw
himself into the opposite camp, and devoted all his force, his
eloquence, and his vast energy to overthrowing the Government

that had repulsed him. At the very moment that Montmorin refused his services, the Orléanistes were making every effort to secure him. It is evident that from the first the Duc d'Orléans inspired him with no sympathy, but he needed a field for his talents, he needed a goal for his ambitions, and alas, he needed also the wherewithal to satisfy his taste for luxury and pleasure ! Convinced that for the present he could hope for nothing from the Court, Mirabeau therefore allowed himself against his inclination to be drawn into the Orléaniste conspiracy.[1]

With the annexation of Mirabeau the success of the conspiracy seemed assured. The duke and a number of his supporters— the Duc de Biron, the Marquis de Sillery (husband of the famous Madame de Genlis), the Baron de Menou, the Vicomte de Noailles, and the De Lameths—had succeeded in securing election to the States-General, and with Mirabeau at their head consti- tuted a formidable faction. At Montrouge, a little house near Paris belonging to the Duc de Biron, the conspirators met by night and discussed their schemes, but " of those nocturnal confabulations," remarks M. Dard, " nothing transpired either for contemporaries or for posterity."

The amazing thoroughness with which the intrigue was carried out has never been surpassed except by the pan-German plot of our day. At the Palais Royal, Laclos, " like a spider in his web," wove the almost invisible network of intrigue that soon covered France, and stretched out into other countries—England, Holland,

---

[1] That Mirabeau was definitely working in the interests of the Duc d'Orléans throughout the summer of 1789 is perfectly obvious from the evidence of all contemporaries, even those who were his friends, such as Dumont and La Marck, the latter only attempting—very unconvincingly— to prove that Mirabeau was not *paid* by the duke. Weber, however, declares that Mirabeau and the Duc d'Orléans " troubled so little to conceal their connection that notes signed by the Duc d'Orléans in favour of Mira- beau were seen publicly negotiated on the Paris Bourse " (*Mémoires de Weber*, ii. 17). Perhaps the best summary of Mirabeau's policy at this date is that given by Mounier : " I have seen him pass from the nocturnal committees held by the friends of the Duc d'Orléans to those of the enthusi- astic republicans, and from these secret conferences to the cabinets of the King's ministers ; but if from the first months (of the Revolution) the ministers had consented to work with him he would have preferred to uphold the royal authority rather than to ally himself with men he de- spised. His principles must not be judged by the numerous contradictions in his speeches and writings, where he said less what he thought than what happened to suit his interests under such and such circumstances. He often communicated his real opinions to me, and I have never known a man of more enlightened intellect, of more judicious political doctrines, of more venal character, and of a more corrupt heart " (*De l'Influence attribué aux Philosophes, Franc Maçons et Illuminés*, p. 100). This passage gives the key to the whole of Mirabeau's conduct during the early stages of the Revolution. On the nocturnal meetings between Mirabeau and the Duc d'Orléans see also Garat's *Conspiration de d'Orléans.* '

Germany. In Paris he had enlisted the services of various unscrupulous agitators who stirred up the Faubourgs of Saint-Antoine and Saint-Marceau ; pamphleteers in the pay of the duke loaded the bookstalls with seditious pamphlets ; at the street corners and in the garden of the Palais Royal mob orators inflamed the minds of the people, and in the palace of Versailles the spies of Orléans hovered round the Queen, gained access to her correspondence, and sent copies of her letters to the councils of Montrouge.[1]

It is probable, however, that all these schemes would have proved unavailing to produce a revolution had not the country at this crisis been faced with famine. Hua, looking back on the beginnings of the Revolution, was convinced that but for the threatened famine the people would have remained indefinitely submissive to the Old Régime. "Everywhere they know how to endure, to expect from time improvements that often do not come, but for which they continue to hope. They know only present evils, and of these famine alone is intolerable to them. Struck by this terrible scourge, it is not a change in the State that they demand, *it is bread*. So the French people would long have endured their accustomed burdens, they would have continued to pay taxes, tithes, to carry out feudal duties, to bend beneath the corvée and the other miseries of vassaldom. I find the proof of their patience in the means employed to make them lose it."[2] It was here the conspirators saw their greatest opportunity. "Bread," says Hua, "was the potent lever by which the people were roused to action. What lies, what fables were thrown to public credulity ! " It is evident from all accounts that the famine was more fabulous than real. The people were not starving, but haunted by the fear of starvation. And to this fear was added exasperation, owing to the conviction that no real scarcity of grain existed. It was true that a fearful hailstorm in July of the previous year had destroyed many of the crops round Paris, but had not the minister Necker declared that, in spite of this disaster, " the stores of grain in the country were more than sufficient to supply the needs of the nation until the next harvest " ? The want of bread in itself is bad enough, but to believe that bread is being wilfully withheld from one is enough to stir the meekest to revolt. This was the " lever " employed by the conspirators. When the peasants of France creeping to their doors saw wagons laden with wheat winding their way through the village street, voices were not lacking to whisper, " There is corn in plenty, but it is not for you ; it is to be stored for the Court, the aristocrats, the rich, who will feast in plenty

[1] *Histoire de la Révolution*, by Louis Blanc, ii. 331 ; *Essais de Beaulieu*, i. 302.   [2] *Mémoires de Hua*, p. 53.

while you go hungry." And forthwith the maddened people
would hurl themselves on to the sacks of corn and fling them
into the nearest river.[1] The fact that in many cases the corn
was destroyed and not appropriated by the people proves that
hunger was less the incentive to revolt than rage at the monopolizers; and if the name of a supposed monopolizer were but
whispered likewise, the unfortunate man fell a victim to the same
fate as the sacks of corn. It is, of course, impossible to defend
such excesses, yet if during a time of scarcity there were really
profiteers enriching themselves at the expense of the people, the
fury of the peasants is certainly justified. Their guilt must
therefore be measured by the facts on which their suspicions
were founded.

Was the scarcity of grain, then, imaginary or real? Undoubtedly it was not to be entirely accounted for by the failure
of the crops. On this point contemporaries of all parties agree.
But the question of monopolizers is one on which pro-revolutionary historians are strangely silent, since for their purpose—
the glorification of the revolutionary leaders—it does not bear
examination. The truth is probably that the monopolizers
were in league with the very men who were stirring up popular
fury against monopoly—the leaders of the Orléaniste conspiracy.
Montjoie asserts that agents employed by the Duc d'Orléans
deliberately bought up the grain, and either sent it out of the
country or concealed it in order to drive the people to revolt, and
in this accusation he is supported by innumerable contemporaries,
including the democrat Fantin - Désodoards, Mounier, whose
integrity is not to be doubted, the Liberal Malouet, Ferrières,
and Madame de la Tour du Pin.

Beaulieu, however, one of the most reliable of contemporaries,
considers that the Orléanistes would have been unable to create
a famine by these means, but that they accomplished their
purpose by stirring up public feeling on the subject of monopolizers, thereby inducing the people to pillage the grain. The
farmers and corn merchants, therefore, fearing that their supplies
would be destroyed in transit, were afraid to release them. By
this means a fictitious famine was created.[2]

M. Gustave Bord, whose researches into the question of the
famine are perhaps the most complete of any French historian's,
believes that the farmers and bakers were not altogether guiltless, but that many had an interest in producing a scarcity in

---

[1] Letter of Lord Dorset, March 19, 1789, in *Dispatches from Paris*,
ii. 175.
[2] This was also the opinion of Arthur Young, who likewise believed that
the revolutionary leaders had an interest in keeping up the price of corn.
See *Travels in France* (edited by Miss Betham Edwards), p. 154.

order to raise the price of bread : " It is they who were the real
authors of the scarcity, and the Old Régime hunted them down
without mercy. In their rôle of *exploiters of the people* they were
the natural allies of the revolutionaries, who upheld them in
their calumnies. It was they who triumphed in 1789, and who
succeeded in deluding history by throwing the responsibility on
their enemies."

Yet against these enemies, that is to say " the Court," the
noblesse, the clergy, and the King's ministers, not a shred of
evidence was ever produced. The ridiculous legend of the
" Pacte de Famine," by which certain revolutionary writers have
sought to prove that Louis XV. speculated in grain,[1] has no
bearing on the question, since at this date Louis XV. had been
dead for fifteen years, and against Louis XVI. not even the most
rabid of revolutionary writers has ventured to raise such an
accusation. On the contrary, the King, the noblesse, and the
clergy [2] contributed immense sums towards the relief of the famine,
and the King's ministers, headed by Necker, were incessantly
occupied with the problem of ensuring corn supplies, and in
thwarting the designs of speculators.

All through the terrible winter of 1788-1789 the *intendant*
of Paris, Berthier de Sauvigny, travelled about the country
interviewing farmers to find out how much grain they had in
reserve, how much they required, and what surplus they could put
on the market ; when, however, in the spring, a shortage occurred,
and Berthier applied to these men for the grain they had promised
him, they immediately put up the price to a prohibitive figure,
and Montjoie declares that this price was paid by agents of the

---

[1] On this point see the articles on the " Pacte de Famine " by M.
Gustave Bord, M. Léon Biollay, and M. Edmond Biré, which all demonstrate
that even Louis XV. was innocent of this crime, and that the " bleds du
roi " consisted in a benevolent scheme for keeping down the price of grain
by storing supplies, and releasing them in a time of scarcity at a lower
price than that demanded by the corn merchants and farmers.

[2] On the immense liberality of the noblesse and clergy see Montjoie,
Conjuration de d'Orléans, i. 202 ; Taine, *La Révolution*, i. 5. " The poor and
needy," says the English contemporary Playfair, " whom shame prevented
from seeking aid, were themselves sought after, and relief was forced upon
the poor starving family in their cold and hungry retreat by those same
clergymen and nobility who soon after were driven from their own abodes.
. . . These acts of charity were not the acts of a few, they were general,
and were done without ostentation or show, as such actions always ought
to be." The Duc d'Orléans loudly proclaimed his charities in the press, but
these, says Montjoie, existed principally on paper, at any rate they did not
prevent him from investing, at this crisis, in a gorgeous new set of plate
which his friends—and presumably not the hungry multitude—were
invited to the Palais Royal to admire (*Mémoires of Madame de la Tour
du Pin*, i. 164). The Archbishop of Paris at the same moment sold all *his*
plate to feed the poor.

Duc d'Orléans : " They did not bargain, they gave what was asked. The farmers and monopolizers alone profited by this manœuvre ; the artisan, the labourer, the poor man could not afford the price that the monopolizers offered, and it was only by outbidding them that the Government succeeded in wresting from these vampires a portion of their spoil."

Whether, then, the Orléanistes achieved their purpose by actually cornering supplies, or by terrorizing the farmers into holding them up, there can be no doubt that *the famine of 1789 was deliberately engineered by the agents of the duke, and that by this means the people were driven to the pitch of desperation necessary to produce the Revolution.*

The Orléanistes, however, did not constitute the only revolutionary element in the country ; a second intrigue was at work amongst the people, that of

THE SUBVERSIVES

These men desired no change of dynasty or in the government ; their aim was purely destructive. Three years later, when the monarchy was abolished, many of the revolutionary leaders declared that they had all along been Republicans at heart, but if we examine their earlier writings we shall find that at the beginning of the Revolution none of them had formulated any such political creed. ." There were not ten of us Republicans in 1789," Camille Desmoulins wrote afterwards, and since Camille at this date was one of the Duc d'Orléans' most enthusiastic admirers, the number may be reduced at least by one. With the exception perhaps of Lafayette, whose experiences in the American War of Independence inspired him with Republican sympathies, those of the earlier revolutionaries who were not Orléanistes had no definite theories of reconstruction—their aim was merely to clear the ground of all existing conditions. " All memories of history," said Barrère, " all prejudices resulting from community of interest and of origin, all must be renewed in France ; we wish only to date from to-day." " To make the people happy," said Rabaud de Saint-Étienne, " their ideas must be reconstructed, laws must be changed, morals must be changed, men must be changed, things must be changed, *everything, yes, everything must be destroyed*, since everything must be re-made." [1]

---

[1] Rabaud lived to see these theories carried into effect and to realize too late their disastrous folly. " France," he wrote only a short time later, " might have been likened to an immense chaos ; power was suspended, authority disowned, and the wrecks of the feudal system were added to the vast ruins." He repented still more bitterly when, in the reign of

These subversive theories emanated from certain secret societies of which an English writer calling himself John Robison described the aims in the title of his book, *Proofs of a Conspiracy against all the Religions and Governments of Europe carried on in the Secret Meetings of the Free-Masons, Illuminati, and Reading Societies.* Robison, who was himself a genuine Freemason, made a tour of the Continental lodges, where he found that a new and spurious form of masonry had sprung into existence. Both in France and Germany " the lodges had become the haunts of many projectors and fanatics, both in science, in religion, and in politics, who had availed themselves of the secrecy and freedom of speech maintained in these meetings. . . . In their hands Freemasonry became a thing totally unlike, and almost in direct opposition to, the system imported from England, where the rule was observed that nothing touching religion or government shall ever be spoken of in the lodges. . . ." The Association, in fact, was " all a cheat, and the leaders . . . disbelieved every word that they uttered and every doctrine that they taught . . . their real intention was to abolish all religion, overturn every government, and *make the world a general plunder and wreck.*"

A further development of German Freemasonry was the Order of the Illuminati founded in 1776 by Dr. Adam Weishaupt, a professor of the University of Ingoldstadt in Bavaria. Weishaupt, who had been educated by the Jesuits, succeeded in persuading two other ex-Jesuits to join him in organizing the new Order, and it was no doubt this circumstance that gave rise to the belief entertained by certain contemporaries that the Jesuits were the secret directors of the sect. The truth is more probably that, as both Mirabeau and the Marquis de Luchet, in their pamphlets on the Illuminati, asserted, Illuminism was founded on the régime of the Jesuits, although their religious doctrines were diametrically opposed.[1] Weishaupt, whom M. Louis Blanc described as "one of the deepest conspirators that ever existed," had adopted the name of Spartacus—the leader of an insurrection of slaves in ancient Rome—and he aimed at nothing less than *world revolution.*[2] Thus the Order of the Illuminati "abjured Christianity, advocated sensual pleasures, believed in annihilation, and called patriotism and loyalty narrow-minded prejudices incompatible with universal benevolence"; further, "they accounted all princes usurpers and tyrants, and all privileged orders

---

anarchy that followed, he was led to the scaffold. His wife killed herself in despair.

[1] Confirmed by the Abbé Barruel, *Mémoires sur le Jacobinisme,* iii. 11.

[2] *Ibid.* p. 25; *Histoire de la Révolution,* by Louis Blanc, ii. 84, 85.

as their abettors; they meant to abolish the laws which protected property accumulated by long-continued and successful industry; and to prevent for the future any such accumulation, they intended to establish universal liberty and equality, the imprescriptible rights of man, and as preparation for all this they intended to root out all religion and ordinary morality, and even to break the bonds of domestic life, by destroying the veneration for marriage-vows, and by taking the education of children out of the hands of the parents." [1]

These were precisely the principles followed by the Subversives of France in 1793 and 1794, and the method by which this project was carried out is directly traceable to Weishaupt's influence. Amongst the Illuminati, says Robison, " nothing was so frequently discoursed of as the propriety of employing, for a good purpose, the means which the wicked employed for evil purposes ; and it was taught that the preponderancy of good in the ultimate result consecrated every means employed, and that wisdom and virtue consisted in properly determining this balance. This appeared big with danger, because it seemed evident that nothing would be scrupled at, if it could be made appear that the Order would derive advantage from it, because the great object of the Order was held superior to every consideration." [2]

It is this doctrine that provides the key to the whole policy of the leading revolutionaries of France, and that, as we shall see later, brought about the Reign of Terror.

Quintin Craufurd, the friend of Marie Antoinette, writing to Pitt in 1794, remarked : " There is a great resemblance between the maxims, as far as they are known, of the Illuminés and the early Jacobins, and I am persuaded that the seeds of many of those extravagant but diabolical doctrines that spread with such unparalleled luxuriance in the hotbeds of France were carried from Germany." [3] The lodges of the German Freemasons and Illuminati were thus the source whence emanated all those anarchic schemes that culminated in the Terror, and it was at a great meeting of the Freemasons in Frankfurt-am-Main, three years before the French Revolution began, that the deaths of Louis XVI. and Gustavus III. of Sweden were first planned.[4]

The Orléanist leaders, quick to see the opportunity for ad-

---

[1] Robison's *Proofs of a Conspiracy*, pp. 107 and 375.

[2] *Ibid.* p. 107.

[3] Craufurd here uses the word " Germany " as it was employed at that date, *i.e.* as a name covering Austria as well as Prussia and the other independent German states. Yet it was not in Austria, but in such towns as Berlin, Frankfurt, Mainz, Göttingen, Brunswick, Gotha, Breslau, etc., that Illuminism flourished most vigorously.

See the evidence of two French Freemasons present at this meeting published by Charles d'Héricault, *La Révolution*, p. 104.

vancing their own interests, joined the Freemasons, and the Duc
d'Orléans succeeded in getting himself elected Grand Master of
the Order in France.   A little later Mirabeau went to Berlin, and
whilst in Prussia attracted the attention of " Spartacus " and
his colleague " Philo," alias the Baron Knigge of Frankfurt-am-
Main, who through the influence of Mauvillon, a disciple of
Philo's, persuaded him to become an Illuminatus.   On his return
to Paris Mirabeau, together with Talleyrand and the Duc de
Lauzun, inaugurated a lodge of the Order, but none of the three
being as yet adepts they were obliged to apply to headquarters
for aid.   Accordingly two Germans were sent to initiate them
further in the doctrines of the sect.   Before long the Club Breton,
the first revolutionary club, later to be known as the Club des
Jacobins, became the centre of Illuminism and Freemasonry, for
all its members were also members of the two secret societies.
But though the leading Orléanistes were all Freemasons, all Freemasons were not Orléanistes ; some were pure Subversives, and M.
Gustave Bord is no doubt right in stating that the duke was only
the visible head of the sect whose members used him as a cover
to their designs, whilst he and his supporters used them with
the same object.   Thus Chamfort, though a member of the
Orléaniste conspiracy, was at heart a Subversive, as an illuminating conversation he once held with Marmontel at the beginning
of the Revolution testifies.   Chamfort having remarked that it
would not be a bad thing to level all ranks and abolish the
existing order of things, Marmontel replied :

"Equality has always been the chimera of republics
and the bait that ambition offers to vanity.   But this
levelling down is all the more impossible in a vast monarchy,
and in attempting to abolish everything it seems to me that
we should go further than the nation expects, and further
than it wishes."

" True," said Chamfort, " but does the nation know what it
wishes ?   One can make it wish, and one can make it say what it
has never thought . . . the nation is a great herd that only
thinks of browsing, and with good sheepdogs the shepherds can
lead it as they please."   He went on to explain that one must
help the people according to one's own lights, not according to
theirs, and spoke cheerfully of a Revolution that would make
a clean sweep of the Old Régime, a scheme he thought by no
means impossible to carry out, for though it might be difficult
to move the industrious citizens, there was always the class
that has nothing to lose and everything to gain which could
be stirred up by rumours of massacre, famine, and so forth.
The Duc d'Orléans, he ended by remarking, must be made use of
for this purpose.   When to this Marmontel suggested that the

duke had hardly the makings of a leader, Chamfort replied imperturbably :

"You are right, and Mirabeau, who knows him well, says it would be building on mud to count on him, but he has identified himself with the popular cause, he bears an imposing name, he has millions to distribute, he hates the King, he hates the Queen still more."

Such, then, were the "democratic" principles of the Subversives, and the methods described by Chamfort were, as we shall see, precisely those employed to work up the people. The first item on their programme was the systematic dissemination of class hatred and the promise of unlimited booty.

"Name me as your representative at the States-General," said Robespierre in his electioneering speeches, "and you will be for ever exempt from those burdens which have so far been required of you on the pretext of the needs of the State. . . . This will not be the only benefit you will enjoy if I succeed in becoming one of your representatives ; too long have the rich been the sole possessors of happiness. It is time that their possessions should pass into other hands. The castles will be overthrown and all the lands belonging to them will be distributed amongst you in equal portions." To the agricultural labourers he promised the fields they cultivated, to the retainers of the nobles he offered freedom from all duties. "Everything will be changed, for masters will become servants, and you will be served in your turn." [1]

It will be seen, therefore, that from the outset "equality," the great watchword of the Revolution, had no place in the minds of the Subversives ; conditions were simply to be reversed, wealth was to change hands, a process that was to be never-ending, since that which was at the top was to be perpetually thrust to the bottom, and that which was at the bottom raised to the top.

Towards religion the Subversives displayed the same attitude as towards government ; their animosity was not directed against the Church of Rome more than against Protestantism ; it was religion in itself they detested, and that they set out to destroy. When we study the manner in which they carried out their design, when we read of the frightful profanity that was inaugurated during the Terror, the desecration of the churches, the blasphemies against Christ and the Holy Virgin, and the worship of Marat, it is almost impossible to disbelieve in demoniacal possession, to doubt that these men, inflamed with hatred against all spiritual influences working for good in the world, became indeed the

[1] Montjoie, *Histoire de la Conjuration de Maximilien Robespierre*, pp. 36, 37.

vehicles for those other spirits, the powers of darkness, whose cause they had made their own. And in their hideous deaths, for nearly every one perished on the scaffold, were they not, perhaps, like the Gadarene swine, victims of the demons that drove them to destruction ?

PRUSSIA

Whilst the Illuminati of Germany strove to plunge France and all the rest of the world into anarchy, the Government of Prussia was engaged on another intrigue against the French monarchy. Optimists who believe that the desire of modern Germany to dominate the world was a form of temporary insanity which originated with Nietzsche and Bernhardi, and may terminate in a return to the " peaceful philosophy " of what they fondly describe as " old Germany," would do well to study the policy of that idol of the German people—Frederick the Great.

No event had so seriously disturbed the serenity of Frederick as the marriage of the Dauphin to Marie Antoinette in 1770, since by this union of the royal families of France and Austria the alliance between the two countries—both the hated rivals of Prussia—was definitely sealed. It must be remembered that in the eighteenth century France was the richest and most thickly populated country on the Continent, whilst the Court of Versailles far eclipsed in splendour that of any other kingdom, and in the mind of Frederick the memory of the " Roi Soleil " lingered as a constant source of irritation. Austria, on the other hand, as the head of the German Empire, enjoyed a power and prestige that reduced the little kingdom of Prussia to comparatively small importance. Meanwhile the Rhine provinces, more French than German in their sympathies, showed no anxiety to unite with Prussia, thereby forming the Germanic Confederation that was the dream of Frederick. To break the alliance between France and Austria became therefore the great ambition of his life, and the one on which he concentrated all his energies.

In Von der Goltz, his ambassador, who arrived at the Court of Louis XV. in 1772, Frederick hoped to find an instrument to carry out his design, which was not to consist in open warfare but in a system of political mischief-making that would sow discord between the Courts of Versailles and Vienna. At the same time Von der Goltz was to act as a spy by getting information out of Maurepas and sending it to the King of Prussia. In this the ambassador at first proved successful, for the frivolous Maurepas loved to be amused and Von der Goltz possessed a merry wit, but the reports he forwarded to Berlin were far from satisfying to his Prussian Majesty. The correspondence that took place between Frederick and the luckless ambassador, whom he treated with brutal sarcasm, is a revelation in Prussian diplomacy.[1] Frederick, it appears, was in the habit of confiding sums of money to his representatives at the various courts of Europe which were to be employed in bribery and corruption. Meanwhile their own personal expenses were but meagrely defrayed. Accordingly Von der Goltz on arriving in France was obliged to borrow money from Necker to pay the rent of his house, which he eventually opened as a gambling-saloon in order to meet his creditors. Appeals to Frederick for financial assistance met only with indignant replies : " You are a spendthrift ! . . . Did you not fritter away at the Court of Petersbourg thousands of écus which I entrusted to you for corruptions ? " In France Frederick is convinced that Von der Goltz is simply amusing himself instead of obtaining information on affairs of state. " You drive my patience to its limit," he writes on December 21, 1780, " by the clumsy way in which you fill your post. . . . One might excuse it in a student who had just left the University, but it is unpardonable in a man of your age who has been so long employed in affairs of state. So if you do not bestir yourself and bring more reflection to bear on them, I shall be obliged to find you a successor in whatever corner of Europe I have to look for him."

To these reproaches Von der Goltz replies with the utmost meekness, even when Frederick goes so far as to accuse him of being occupied with some " grosse Margot " instead of attending to his affairs—this suspicion, he makes answer, is unfounded, since neither his health nor his finances permit of such diversions.

The point on which this extraordinary correspondence turns is of course the Queen. As long as Marie Antoinette retains her popularity Frederick realizes that there is little hope for the success of Prussian intrigue. This point needs emphasizing, owing to the curious confusion of thought that exists on the Queen's policy. No reproach has been more often repeated against Marie Antoinette than that of sympathizing with Austria ; undoubtedly she sympathized with Austria and wished to cement the alliance between the country of her birth and that of her adoption. This was only natural, but the point so continually overlooked is that sympathy with Austria at this date was precisely the opposite of sympathy with Prussia, and this alliance that the Queen was so anxious to maintain was the greatest safeguard France possessed

[1] The correspondence from which all the following extracts are taken is to be found in a work entitled *Rapport sur les Correspondances des Agents Diplomatiques étrangers en France avant la Révolution conservées dans les Archives de Berlin, Dresde, Genève, Turin . . . Gênes . . . Londres*, etc., by Jules Flammermont (Paris, Imprimerie Nationale, 1896).

against Prussian aggression. *The cry of "l'Autrichienne!" raised against Marie Antoinette throughout the Revolution probably originated therefore in Prussia*, and was foolishly taken up by the French people with fatal blindness to their real interests.

No one rejoiced more heartily than Frederick the Great at the estrangement that existed between Louis XVI. and Marie Antoinette during the first seven years of their marriage, and in 1776 we find him writing to confide to Von der Goltz his fears that the impending visit of the Emperor Joseph II. to the Court of France may bring about a closer relationship between the husband and wife. In a letter dated December 26, 1776, Frederick points out to his ambassador that the best way to counteract the Emperor's influence will be for Von der Goltz to repeat to the royal family of France remarks the Emperor is supposed to have made about them : " It will be a good thing if you can manage *by means of subterranean insinuations* to increase the dissension between the two Courts. With this object the ambitious views of his Imperial Majesty on Italy, Bavaria, Silesia, Alsace, and even Moldavia will open a vast field to your political career, and if to these you add the sarcasms that prince permitted himself on the subject of his brothers-in-law when he said: 'I have three brothers-in-law ; the one at Versailles is an imbecile, the one at Naples is a lunatic, and the one at Parma is a fool,' it cannot fail to make an impression and to prejudice the Court at which you are against him in such a way that all further understanding will be extremely difficult if not impossible. But this," Frederick adds, " must be done cleverly "—a feat of which Von der Goltz was apparently incapable, for the Emperor's visit resulted in the reconciliation Frederick was so anxious to avoid, and the birth of a princess to the royal family of France destroyed his hopes for the future.

A further check to Prussian intrigue occurred in the dismissal of Maurepas, for his successor Vergennes had no confidence in Von der Goltz, and refused to discuss anything with him. Accordingly in 1784 another ambassador was sent to France in the person of Frederick's brother, Prince Henry of Prussia, who was instructed to effect an alliance between the Courts of Versailles and Berlin. " The Prince," remarks M. de Croze Lemercier, " came amongst us as a good Prussian . . . he was charged by his brother Frederick the Great to embroil us with Austria—which he nearly succeeded in doing—and he only flattered our national vanity in order the better to exploit it. . . . Hatred of Austria was then the fashion (in France), and public opinion was so blind as not to see that *we had enemies still more dangerous*. The Prince became popular for the same reason that made the unfortunate Marie Antoinette hated."

Prince Henry certainly succeeded in exciting some degree of

sympathy with Prussia at the Court of France, but the Queen, as before, remained the insuperable obstacle. When, three years later, yet another envoy, the Baron von Alvensleben, was despatched by Frederick to report on the state of feeling at Versailles he found the Queen still irreconcilable.

· " *The hatred of the Queen for everything that bears the name of Prussian,*" he wrote to Frederick, " is so indisputable, that I have, so to speak, the proofs under my hand."

This, then, was one of the great crimes of the unhappy Queen—that she was anti-Prussian. Those amongst the French who still revile her memory would do well to remember that she was the first and greatest obstacle to those dreams of European domination that, originating with Frederick the Great, culminated in the aggression of 1870 and 1914.

Marie Antoinette paid heavily for her aversion to Prussia. There can be no doubt whatever that certain of the libels and seditious pamphlets published against her before and during the Revolution were circulated by Von der Goltz at the instigation of the King of Prussia. In the course of this book we shall see the further methods employed by Prussia to undermine the monarchy of France and to overthrow the balance of power in Europe by breaking the alliance between the two rivals to her supremacy.

There was thus a double strain of German influence at work behind the French Revolution—the political and the philosophical. The first, inspired by Frederick the Great and carried out by Von der Goltz; the second, inspired by Weishaupt and conducted by Anacharsis Clootz, the Prussian sent to France for the purpose.

ENGLAND

In the minds of certain contemporaries no doubt exists that yet another intrigue at work behind the revolutionary movement was that sinister influence—" the gold of Pitt." England, they declare, resentful of the help given by France to the American insurgents, took advantage of the disturbed state of the country to wreak her vengeance on the French Government by encouraging and actually financing sedition. Montmorin told Gouverneur Morris that he " had indisputable evidence of the intrigues of Britain and Prussia that they gave money to the Prince de Condé and the Duc d'Orléans." Bézenval, describing the riots of July 1789, speaks of the brigands employed by the Duc d'Orléans and by England. According to Madame Campan, Marie Antoinette herself shared the conviction of England's complicity, and regarded Pitt as the leader of the intrigue. " Do not go to Paris to-day," she is said to have remarked, " the English have been distributing money there ! " or again : " I cannot hear the name of Pitt without feeling cold shivers down my back ! "

What was the explanation of these rumours ? Was the Government of England really animated by a spirit of revenge ? It is certainly probable that the intervention of France on behalf of America appeared to Pitt as hostile an act as the sending of the Kruger telegram appeared to our Government of 1896, yet it must be remembered that Louis XVI. had entered reluctantly into the war, whilst the leaders of the expedition to America— Lafayette, Lauzun, De Ségur, and others—were later on partisans of the Revolution. If, therefore, Pitt desired revenge is it likely that he would have sought to obtain it by joining forces with the very men who had taken part against him ?

At the same time it is undeniable that a serious rivalry existed between France and England. As the two principal monarchies of Europe this was inevitable, nor in the past had it proved wholly disastrous. The perpetually recurring wars between the two rival powers had been conducted with gallantry and generosity on both sides, and had left little bitterness in the mind of either nation. But the reign of Louis XVI. introduced a more formidable menace to the power of England. For the first time in her history she saw her most cherished possession, the dominion of the seas, seriously threatened. Louis XVI. was an enthusiast for the navy ; on the subject of shipbuilding he displayed surprising knowledge, and his visit to the port of Cherbourg—the construction of which was the greatest triumph of his reign—brought him a popularity he had never before enjoyed. Across the sea England watched and wondered. As a seafaring nation it was perhaps the most anxious moment in her existence. In the correspondence of English diplomatists at this date we find a vague fear piercing, and with the outbreak of the Revolution an undeniable breath of relief. " It is certainly possible," writes Lord Dorset from Paris in September 1789, " that from this chaos some creation may result, but I am satisfied that it must be long before France returns to any state of existence which can make her a subject of uneasiness to other nations." Earlier in the year Hailes had expressed the same conviction.

Yet to show a certain degree of complacency at the spectacle of a foreign power that had threatened aggression weakening itself with internal dissensions is surely not to imply that one has deliberately set out to organize these dissensions. George III. throughout showed himself resolutely opposed to the Revolution, and Pitt, who consistently supported the King, could have had no conceivable object in furthering a movement that shook all the thrones of Europe. Far from sympathizing with the revolutionary leaders Pitt invariably displayed a marked aversion to the Orléanistes, whilst the Jacobins who were avowedly "the natural enemies of England" were the last people with whom he would be likely to ally himself. The hatred expressed for Pitt by both these parties of revolutionaries is again surely proof of his non-complicity—if Pitt was helping to finance them, why should they regard him as their enemy? Why should "l'or de Pitt" be mentioned by Jacobin writers with the same indignation as by Royalists? When, therefore, we find Pitt suspected by Royalists of abetting the Revolution and accused by Revolutionaries of aiding the Royalists,[1] we may surely conclude that his attitude was, as he professed, one of strict neutrality. Moreover, as Madame de Staël points out, how could Pitt dispose of the vast sums of money he was said to have scattered among the rioters without accounting for them to Parliament? Necker, she says, made minute investigations during his ministry, but "was never able to discover the faintest trace of complicity between the popular party and the English Government,"[2] and M. Granier de Cassagnac adds that "historical documents have since then confirmed this conviction of Necker's, for the official accounts of the finances of the emigration at the Bibliothèque Nationale prove that of all governments of Europe the English Government is the only one that never contributed any sum of money towards the divers enterprises of different parties during the French Revolution."[3]

Even Sorel, who misses no opportunity of denouncing the aggressive policy of England, is obliged to admit the integrity of Pitt :

"The ministry, that is to say William Pitt, was perfectly pacific. The Revolution ridded him for a time of a formidable rival ; it assured him of the peace he needed for his financial reforms, and surrendered to England all the benefits of which the crisis in public affairs deprived French industry and commerce. In every market, as in every chancellery, England was free to substitute herself for France. Pitt would have been careful not to obstruct the development of a revolution so advantageous to his designs. He also held that a king of France deprived of his prestige, with his rights limited and his power contested, would marvellously answer the convenience of England. But he was not one of those greedy politicians blinded by jealousy, whose covetousness leads them to take a brutal advantage of fortune.

---

[1] See, for example, the 5th number of the *Vieux Cordelier*, in which Camille Desmoulins accuses Pitt of being in league with Calonne, Malouet, and Luchesini to create a "counter-revolution."

[2] *Considérations sur la Révolution Française*, i. 329, 331.

[3] *Histoire des Causes de la Révolution Française*, i. 59.

Certain of these, and *notably his allies in Berlin,* marvelled at his not seizing this occasion to throw himself on France, to crush her and take over her colonies. He was careful to refrain from this. The natural elevation of his soul restrained him as much as the foresight of his mind. Such perfidy was repugnant to him, and he held it to be dangerous." [1]

This testimony of a hostile critic, and at the same time of the historian most versed in the politics of the eighteenth century, is surely convincing. If, in the opinion of Sorel, Pitt was above taking advantage of the Revolution to declare open war on France, is it conceivable that he would have descended to the ignoble policy of financing sedition, to the brutal expedient of scattering gold amongst an enraged mob? The thing is unthinkable, and it is time that this gross calumny on our Government should be finally demolished. Suleau, the Royalist pamphleteer, knew better than many of his contemporaries when he wrote these noble words :

" The English people have not degenerated from the magnanimity of their ancestors, and here wise policy is allied to generosity, for it would not be difficult to prove that the splendour of France will always be the surest guarantee for the prosperity of Great Britain."

England, then, far from abetting the Revolution, regarded it with undisguised aversion. Such liberal-minded men as Wordsworth and Arthur Young, who at first hailed it as the dawn of liberty, lived to recognize their error. " In England," says Cardonne, " the majority of the people, including almost all those who belonged to the Government, the rich and noble owners of property, had conceived such a horror for the principles and acts of the French revolutionaries, and such a dread of seeing them adopted in their country, that they were anxious to break off all commerce between the two nations." As we shall see in the course of this book, the " people " of England shared the opinion of their rulers.

What, then, is the explanation of the belief in English cooperation with the revolutionary movement? Of the English guineas found on the rioters? Of Englishmen mingling in the mobs of Paris during popular agitations? Of the seditious pamphlets printed in London? Of the traffic in letters, messages, and money maintained between England and the revolutionary leaders? Many of these leaders, moreover, were constantly in England, both before and during the Revolution ; Marat lived for years in Soho, whilst Danton, Brissot, Pétion, St. Huruge, Theroigne de Méricourt, and the ruffian Rotondo were all habitués of London. These facts admit of no denial ; to suppose, how-

[1] *L'Europe et la Révolution Française,* ii. 29.

ever, any complicity on the part of the English Government is illogical and absurd. The explanation seems to me to lie in a perfectly different direction.

I have already referred to the Duc d'Orléans' predilection for visits to London—a predilection that is not to be altogether accounted for by the "anglomanie" he professed. "M. d'Orléans," a contemporary shrewdly remarks, "often went to England. . . . M. d'Orléans was very fond of England, though not of the English. The wisdom of their laws mattered very little to him, but the liberty of London mattered to him a great deal. This apparent love of the Duc d'Orléans for the English was in the end the cause of all the calumnies against England with which the leaders of the different factions influenced public credulity, so as to throw on the policy of that nation the excesses of which they alone were guilty." [1]

Here, then, is the key to a great part of the mystery; the theory of " l'or de Pitt " was a fable circulated by the duke himself to shield his own manœuvres, and such was the skill with which it was disseminated that it was believed even by the Queen, who, as we know, never fully realized the complicity of the duke with the revolutionary outbreaks.

For ten years before his death, that is to say from 1783 onwards, the Duc d'Orléans continually deposited sums of money in London banks, and these sums, estimated at between ten to twelve millions of francs, were not exhausted in 1794.[2] Now since countless witnesses testify that the revolutionary mobs were financed by the duke, it is surely more than probable that many of the guineas found on rioters were the Duc d'Orléans' money,[3] which with diabolical cunning he drew out in English coin, and had sent over to France in order to throw suspicion on the English. This may to a large extent account for the sums distributed, but it does not entirely dispose of the belief in English co-operation. A further light is thrown on the matter by the following passage of Montjoie :

" During his visits to London the Duc d'Orléans personally, and by means of his agents in Holland, *made fresh loans of money in England*. . . . He attached to his interests . . . Milord Stanhope and Dr. Price. These two men were the most important members of a society calling itself ' The Revolution Society.' . . . D'Orléans also knew how to interest all that party known as the ' Opposition ' in his cause. Fox, one of the oracles of

---

[1] *Histoire des Factions de la Révolution Française*, by Joseph Lavallée, i. 25 (1816).
[2] See letters from General Montesquiou and the Duc de Chartres published at the end of the *Mémoires de Mallet du Pan*, edited by A. Sayous, p. 455.   [3] Fantin Désodoards, *Histoire Philosophique*, ii. 436.

this party, was throughout attached to d'Orléans, and still is to his family (1797) ; he is the declared protector of all the Frenchmen who belong to the faction of this prince."

Is it not possible, then, that the duke, fearing that even his vast fortune might prove inadequate to the demands made on it during the course of nearly five years, for financing insurrection, may have supplemented it by sums raised amongst his friends in England ? In this case English gold *did* play a part in the revolutionary movement, but *it was provided not by the Government, but by its opponents.* The Opposition party in London formed an exact counterpart to the duke's party in Paris ; headed by the Prince of Wales, the roués of Carlton House formed a Fronde against George III., such as the roués of the Palais Royal formed against Louis XVI. In the House of Commons Fox, the so-called " friend of the people," demanded that the enormous debts of the Prince of Wales should be defrayed by the nation. Thus in both countries it was the " democratic " party, the revolutionaries of France and the Whigs of England, who supported the follies and extravagances of these two dissolute princes, whilst in both countries the cause of order and morality was represented by the sovereign whom the democrats wished to dethrone. George III., like Louis XVI., was intensely respectable ; the Duc d'Orléans was therefore even less to his taste than his own prodigal son, and he rightly discerned the de-moralizing influence that the duke exercised over him. " George, the Prince of Wales," says Ducoin, " had done the honours of the brothels and gambling-houses of the old city, and in Paris the Duc d'Orléans had returned the hospitality shown him by the Prince of Wales in the suppers and orgies of London. Like Philippe, the Prince of Wales had adopted the Revolution, and hailed the dawn of a new era." This era was apparently to consist in placing George III. under restraint and proclaiming the Prince of Wales Regent, a scheme in which the Prince's boon companions, Fox, Sheridan, and others, heartily concurred. Meanwhile the same process was to take place in France, the regency in both countries being merely the preliminary to a change of sovereigns. With these two merry monarchs, George IV. and Philippe VII., on the thrones of England and France, an era of liberty seemed assured for the *bons vivants* of Carlton House and the Palais Royal, who found themselves perpetually hampered by the exercise of the royal authority.

Under these circumstances it is not surprising that Louis XVI. found it necessary to prohibit the Duc d'Orléans from visiting England too frequently. In the *Correspondance Secrète* we find on April 9, 1788, the following significant entry :

" It is confirmed that one of the conditions that the Duc

d'Orléans' exile should be cancelled is that this prince should make a long journey to anywhere except England. To the well-founded reasons the King may have for preventing him from breathing British air there is, they say, to be added the entreaty of George III., who, wishing to maintain the footsteps of the Prince of Wales on the paths of order and morality, has begged his most Christian Majesty not to allow his friends from Paris to approach him."

This, then, was the reason why Louis XVI. stipulated that the duke should not spend the term of his exile in England, a stipulation that, as we have seen, contributed more than any other cause to the duke's animosity towards the Court of France.

The prohibition to visit England was, of course, a serious obstacle to the designs of the Duc d'Orléans and Choderlos de Laclos. These journeys, made ostensibly for pleasure, held a deeper purpose. Whilst the wine flowed freely, and George and Philippe basked in the smiles of their various enchantresses, who could suppose that plots of a serious nature were in progress, and that anything more important than the pleasure of the hour occupied the brains of the revellers ?

In England, as in France, however, the conspirators were divided in their aims. Not all the English revolutionaries belonged to the Prince of Wales's party ; many, like their French counterparts, desired no change of sovereign but simple anarchy. Throughout the history of our country subversive spirits have from time to time arisen to advocate " equality " and the levelling of all ranks to an indifferent public. " Pride," said the Prince de Ligne, " disdains revolutions ; vanity produces them." The British people, far more proud than vain, have always responded with lukewarm interest to the instigators of class hatred ; perfectly satisfied with their own position in the social scheme they care not who considers himself their superior. Liberty they demand as a right ; equality they wisely recognize as impossible, and dismiss from their calculations. But in England, as in France, a minority has always existed, totally distinct from the people, whose vanity is greater than its pride. To them obscurity is far more intolerable than oppression. Usually members of the middle class employed in sedentary occupations and deprived of the mental balance that manual labour brings, or occasionally of an aristocracy that has failed to show them the appreciation they desire, they seek to avenge their own wrongs rather than to redress those of the people. Like the Subversives of France they have seldom any definite plans of reconstruction—their aim is only to destroy. Of such elements were the " Revolution Societies " of England in 1789 composed. Dr. Robinet, who has described them admiringly in his *Danton Émigré*, under the title of " The English Jacobins," has given us illuminating details of their conduct during the course of the Revolution. Like nearly every French revolutionary, Dr. Robinet detests England, and his comments on the attitude of the British people towards the Revolution are very bitter—there were in England, he says, " only a respectable minority, a numerous *élite*," who sympathized with the movement. This " respectable minority " consisted of the Prince of Wales and his boon companions, and of the Revolutionary Societies headed by the renegade Lord Stanhope, by Dr. Price, Dr. Priestley, and the drunkard Thomas Paine. The natural allies of their country's bitterest enemies, the Jacobins of France, we shall find them throughout the Revolution, not merely abetting the excesses committed abroad, but seeking to create a kindred movement at home. It was they, as I shall show, who subscribed towards the Revolution ; it was they who fraternized with the revolutionary agitators on their visits to London ; it was they who committed the crimes that certain writers have falsely attributed to our Government.

The complicity of these English Subversives with the revolutionaries of France is a fact we should do well to realize, both in justice to the French nation and also with a view to understanding the potentialities of our own. The smug belief that none amongst our fellow-countrymen would have been capable of the atrocities committed in France is shattered at a blow when we read the comments of English revolutionaries on these deeds of horror— deeds not to be attributed as we are accustomed to attribute them to the excitability of the Latin temperament, but to political passions, of all passions the most terrible and relentless which men of our own race displayed at the same period without the same provocation. In the course of this book we shall see that the crimes committed by the lowest of the Paris rabble, and execrated by the honest democrats of France, were applauded by educated men and women in our country, and if England was not plunged in the horrors of anarchy it was not because she did not hold within her forces capable of producing them.

These, then, were the four great intrigues of the French Revolution. Their aims may be briefly recapitulated thus :

I. The intrigue of the Orléanistes to change the dynasty of France.
II. The intrigue of the Subversives to destroy all religion and all government.
III. The intrigue of Prussia to break the Franco-Austrian alliance.
IV. The intrigue of the English revolutionaries to overthrow the governments both of France and England.

To these four organized intrigues must be added the innumerable people of all classes, belonging to no particular party,
but with private grievances of their own, and all ready to throw
themselves into any subversive movement—Madame de la
Motte, who raged at her punishment in the affair of the necklace,
and to whom many of the libellous pamphlets against the Queen
are due ; courtiers who had failed to secure the favours they
solicited ; women who had been refused admittance to the Court,
or like Madame Roland, felt humiliated by its magnificence
—all those people who, either by the misfortune of their circumstances or by a natural biliousness of temperament, resented
prosperity in others, and below them all that underworld of vice
and misery that in every old civilization sinks to the bottom
like the dregs in an old wine, and that any violent convulsion
brings to the surface with terrible effect. All through the Revolution we shall see these heterogeneous rebels, inflamed with
their own burning thirst for vengeance, mingling with the great
conspiracies, and the great conspiracies in their turn joining
forces with each other ; we shall see the agitators of the Palais
Royal fraternizing with the emissaries of Prussia, Madame de la
Motte circulating libels through the agents of the Duc d'Orléans,
and English revolutionaries corresponding with the cut-throats of
September. All this confused and turbulent movement, formed
of such conflicting units, running concurrently with the genuine
movement for reform, succeeded so skilfully in blending with it
as to deceive not only contemporaries, but the greater part of
posterity. " They had," says Malouet, " the art and the wisdom to
appear in a mass, marching under one banner, the banner of
liberty, which floated over the heads of men whose secret aims
were widely divergent, thus presenting a united front to the
world." So, though all the revolutionary elements put together
formed but a small minority in the State, they were able, by means
of this union, to hold their own against the immense but disunited
majority that composed the Old Régime—a king at variance with
his Court, a noblesse divided against itself, and a people who
for want of leaders in their own ranks allowed themselves to
be swayed by every breath of opinion. Before this rising tide
of insurrection the Government erected no barriers, to the
superb organization of the Orléaniste conspiracy provided no
counter-organization, and to seditious doctrines replied with no
corrective propaganda. " Will posterity believe," cried Arthur
Young, as he watched the engineering of the Revolution, " that
while the press has swarmed with inflammatory productions,
that tend to prove the blessings of theoretical confusion and
speculative licentiousness, not one writer of talent has been
employed to refute and confound the fashionable doctrines,

nor the least care taken to disseminate works of another complexion ? "

Playfair, another English contemporary, was amazed by the incredible inertia of the ruling classes : " In this state of things, did the proprietors pay a single man of merit to plead their cause ? No. If by chance a man of merit refuted their enemies, did they make a small sacrifice to give publicity to his work ? No. He who pleaded the cause of murder and plunder saw his work distributed by thousands and hundreds of thousands, and himself enriched ; while he who endeavoured to support the cause of law, of order, and of the proprietor, had his bookseller to pay and saw his labours converted into waste paper." [1]

So at the outbreak of the Revolution all dynamic force, all fire and energy, were to be found on the side of demolition, whilst the Old Régime, resolutely blind to the coming danger, allowed itself to be destroyed without striking a blow in self-defence.

[1] Playfair's *History of Jacobinism*, p. 108.

THE SIEGE OF THE BASTILLE

THE SIEGE OF THE BASTILLE

THE AFFAIRE RÉVEILLON

THE spring of 1789 found the citizens of Paris divided between two great emotions, hope and fear—hope verging on ecstasy at the prospect of the States-General that were to regenerate the kingdom, fear amounting to panic at the threatened famine and the presence of mysterious strangers in their midst.

The immense charities of the King, noblesse, and clergy had had the effect of attracting crowds of hungry peasants to Paris, where they were employed at the King's expense in working at the Butte Montmartre, and soon fell a prey to the Orléaniste leaders, who enlisted many of them in their service for the purposes of insurrection. But even this formidable addition to the underworld of Paris formed but a small minority amongst the law-abiding of the population, and a further measure was devised by the leaders. Towards the end of April the peaceful citizens saw with bewilderment bands of ragged men of horrible appearance, armed with thick knotted sticks, flocking through the barriers into the city. This sinister contingent is not, as certain historians would have us believe, to be confounded with the former crowds of peasants—" they were neither workmen nor peasants," says Madame Vigée le Brun, " they seemed to belong to no class unless that of bandits, so terrifying were their faces," and Montjoie adds that this aspect was intentional—" they had been instructed to disfigure their faces in a manner so hideous that they were objects of horror to all the Parisians." Other contemporaries, whose accounts exactly coincide with the foregoing, add that these men were " foreigners "—" they spoke a strange tongue " ; Bouillé states that " they were bandits from the South of France and Italy," whilst Marmontel describes them as " Marseillais . . . men of rapine and carnage, thirsting for blood and booty, who, mingling with the people, inspired them with their own ferocity."

The Marseillais were therefore not called in for the first time in 1792, as is generally supposed, and their aid was evidently evoked at the later date in consequence of their successes at the beginning of the Revolution. That brigands from the South were deliberately enticed to Paris in 1789, employed and paid by the revolutionary leaders, is a fact confirmed by authorities too numerous to quote at length; and the further fact that the conspirators felt such a measure to be necessary is of immense significance, for it shows that in their eyes *the people of Paris were not to be depended on to carry out a revolution.* In other words, the importation of the contingent of hired brigands conclusively refutes the theory that the Revolution was an irrepressible rising of the people; it proves that, on the contrary, the movement was deliberately and laboriously engineered. No one understood human nature better than such men as Laclos, Chamfort, and the other leaders of the Orléaniste conspiracy, and they doubtless realized that in the past the irresponsible, pleasure-loving people of Paris had shown little initiative in the matter of bloodshed, but had needed always to be given the lead before they entered into the spirit of the thing and played at killing. Thus at the Massacre of Saint-Bartholomew had not the lead been given by the German Behme and the Italian Catherine de Medicis before the people of the city joined in the hue and cry after the flying Huguenots? ⟨ Pitiless as they could be at moments, they were prone to sudden revulsions of feeling that in an instant transformed their victims into objects of admiration; they lacked the hot blood of the South that revels in cruelty and does not tire of the spectacle. Just as the Anarchists of our own day have always realized that it is amongst the descendants of the Roman populace who gathered in the Coliseum to watch the brutal sports of the arena that they must seek the assassin they needed to track down their royal victim, so the conspirators of 1789 knew that it was to the South that they must look for that sombre ferocity which the light-hearted Parisians lacked, and in the sun-baked regions of Italy and Provence, where a dagger-thrust is still but the everyday ending to a quarrel, they found the terrible instruments that they required.

Thus side by side the work of reformation and the work of revolution had gone forward, and whilst the deputies of the people were assembling the leaders of insurrection were likewise mustering their forces. It was a race between the two—who was to be first in the field? those who desired to build up or those who sought only to destroy? Revolution won the day, and on the 27th of April the first outbreak occurred in Paris.

The victim of this extraordinary riot was a certain wall-paper manufacturer of the Faubourg Saint-Antoine named Réveillon, who had recently been chosen elector for the Tiers État in opposition to the Orléaniste candidate. According to certain historians " the rumour went round " that Réveillon had spoken slightingly of working-men at the electoral assembly, but Montjoie states that this accusation was definitely proclaimed through the streets by a horde of the brigands dragging with them an effigy of Réveillon, and calling out to the people that he had said a workman could live quite well on fifteen sous a day.

This device of inventing a phrase and placing it in the mouth of any one they wished to offer up to popular fury was regularly adopted by the agitators in all the earlier riots of the Revolution, and often succeeded in completely deceiving the people. In the case of Réveillon, however, the calumny was palpably absurd ; the paper-maker was well known and respected in the Faubourg ; he himself had started life as a working-man, and when he had made his fortune resolved that his *employés* should never know the hardships he had endured. Not one of his workmen was paid less than twenty-five sous a day, and during the recent severe winter he had kept them all on at full pay although unable to give them work. The inhabitants of the Faubourg knew better, therefore, than to believe the calumny against their benefactor, and refused to riot. The agitators and their allies the brigands were consequently obliged to resort to force in order to raise a mob. Montjoie, who was an eye-witness of the whole affair, and whose account is confirmed in nearly every point by other reliable contemporaries, states that " these ruffians went into the factories and workshops and compelled the workmen to follow them. This method of swelling a mob of insurrection . . . was adopted throughout the whole revolution. To begin with, about fifty rioters, men or women, surround the first person they meet on their way, two of the rioters hold him tightly under the arms and carry him off against his will . . . by this means, when the troop has arrived on the battle-field, its numbers alarm those against whom it is directed. On this occasion the horde of brigands was increased by all the workmen they had enrolled against their wills." [1]

By this laborious method a disorderly mob was collected who marched to Réveillon's house in the Rue de Montreuil, which, on arrival, they found to be surrounded by a cordon of troops. The street being thus rendered impassable the crowd was held up, but at this opportune moment the Duc d'Orléans *happened* to drive past on his way to the race-meeting at Vincennes, where his horses were running against those of the Comte d'Artois.

---

[1] Bézenval, who was in command of the Swiss Guards, exactly corroborates this statement : " All the spies of the police agreed in saying that the insurrection was caused by strange men who, in order to increase their numbers, *took by force* those they met on their way ; they had even sent three times to the Faubourg Saint-Marceau to raise recruits without being able to persuade any one to join them. These spies added that they saw men inciting the tumult and even distributing money."

He stopped his carriage, got down, spoke a few words to the rioters, and then drove on again. The duke afterwards admitted his appearance on the scene, but explained it by saying that his intention was merely to soothe the people, and that the words he had spoken were " Allons, mes enfants, de la paix : nous touchons au bonheur." The exhortation did not, however, have the effect of dispersing the mob, which continued to besiege the house of Réveillon until the evening, when the Duchesse d'Orléans in returning from Vincennes passed by the Rue de Montreuil, which was still barricaded by the troops. Out of respect for the duchess—whom no one associated with her husband's intrigues— the soldiers immediately opened a way for her, and thereupon the mob, seeing their opportunity, burst through the same passage and fell upon the house of Réveillon, which they proceeded to pillage and destroy.

Three more regiments were now sent to the scene of action, and the officers called upon the invaders to retire. The order was repeated three times without effect, the rioters replying only with a hail of stones and tiles that they hurled from the housetop on the soldiers, killing several. Then by way of warning a few shots were fired into the air by the troops, and this time the mob retaliated with still more formidable missiles in the shape of roof-beams and immense blocks of stone torn from the invaded building. So at last the soldiers, finding pacific methods of no avail, opened fire on the housetop, carrying death and destruction into the ranks of the rioters—" the unhappy creatures fell from the roofs, the walls dripped with blood, the pavement was covered with mutilated limbs." The survivors took refuge inside the house and prepared to carry on the siege, but the troops entered with fixed bayonets, and by dint of hand-to-hand fighting succeeded finally in clearing the premises and ending the riot.

Montjoie afterwards visited the wounded and questioned them on the motives that had inspired their actions : " Unhappy one, what were you doing there ? " And one and all made the same reply, " What was I doing there ? I went, like you, like every one else, just to see." But one poor wretch dying in agony exclaimed, " Mon Dieu, mon Dieu, must one be treated in this way for twelve miserable francs ? " He had, in fact, exactly twelve francs in his pocket, and the same sum was found on many of the other rioters.[1]

Meanwhile Réveillon himself had succeeded in escaping during the tumult and fled for refuge to the Bastille, where he remained under the protection of the governor, De Launay, until he could venture out again in safety. Compensation was made him by the King for his ruined industry.

[1] Montjoie, *Conjuration de d'Orléans*, i. 275.

Such was the Affaire Réveillon which historians are fond of describing as mysterious and inexplicable. Yet contemporaries of all parties admit that it was engineered by agitators; the only question on which they differ is, " By whom were these agitators employed ? " The revolutionaries according to their usual custom reply, "The Court." The Court and aristocracy, they solemnly assure us, deliberately provoked the riot *in order to find an excuse for firing on the people*! Later on we shall find the aristocrats accused of burning down their châteaux for the same purpose. The suggestion is too ludicrous to be taken seriously. Why should the Court wish to provoke a riot against itself ? Why should a mob raised by aristocrats reproach Réveillon with being a friend of aristocrats ? Why should the Court incite popular fury against a law-abiding citizen and a loyal subject of the King ? Above all, if the Court wished for an excuse to use force against the people, why did they not hasten to use it ? Why was every conciliatory method resorted to before force was employed?

That the Affaire Réveillon was the work of the Orléaniste conspiracy no one who brings an impartial mind to bear on contemporary evidence can possibly doubt ; the presence of the duke, and it is said also of Laclos, amongst the crowd, the fact that the riot was carried on to the cry of "Vive le duc d'Orléans!" and even " Vive notre roi d'Orléans ! " [1] is surely proof enough of the influences at work. Talleyrand—who well knew the intricacies of the Orléaniste intrigue—definitely stated that it was organized by Laclos, whilst Chamfort, himself a member of the conspiracy, admitted to Marmontel that the movement was financed by the duke. " Money," he said, " and the hope of plunder are all-powerful with the people. We have just made the experiment in the Faubourg Saint-Antoine, and you would not believe how little it cost the Duc d'Orléans to get them to sack the manufactory of the honest Réveillon, who amidst these same people was the means of livelihood for a hundred families. Mirabeau cheerfully asserts that with 100 louis one can make quite a good riot." [2]

What was the Orléanistes' object in singling out Réveillon

[1] See, for example, the letter from the English ambassador in Paris, the Duke of Dorset, to the Duke of Leeds, April 30, 1789 : " The Duc d'Orléans has experienced repeated marks of popular favour lately, and particularly on Tuesday last. As he was returning through the Faubourg Saint-Antoine the people frequently called out ' Vive la maison d'Orléans ! ' " Madame de la Tour du Pin, who drove through the Faubourg during the riot with some of the Palais Royal party, relates that " the sight of the livery of Orléans . . . stirred the enthusiasm of this riff-raff. They stopped us a moment calling out, ' Long live our father, long live our King Orléans ! ' " (*Journal d'une Femme de Cinquante Ans*, i. 177).
[2] *Mémoires de Marmontel*, iv. 82.

as a victim ? The defeat of their own candidate at the elections was certainly disconcerting to their projects, but it is evident that there was a still more definite reason for their animosity. The Faubourg Saint-Antoine, where Réveillon's manufactory was situated, had an entirely working-class population, whilst the Faubourg Saint-Marceau was the centre of destitution. These two poor and populous quarters of the city were the strongholds of the agitators ; popular movements never originated there, but were devised at Montrouge or the Club Breton, worked up at the Palais Royal, whence they spread to the Faubourgs and produced the desired explosion. By this means the Faubourg Saint-Antoine became simply the echo of the Palais Royal. But an influential agent was needed in the district, and Montjoie asserts that Réveillon was therefore approached by the Orléanistes with the view of enticing him into the conspiracy. These overtures were met, however, with an indignant refusal by the honest paper-maker, and the post was offered to the rough and brutal brewer Santerre, who accepted it with alacrity. From this moment " Général Mousseux "—as Santerre was nicknamed by the people on account of the frothy beer he manufactured—became an *intime* of the Duc d'Orléans, driving about Paris with him in his cabriolet, dining with him at cabarets,[1] and whilst referring to the people as " vile brigands and rascally rabble," [2] scattering amongst them the gold with which the duke provided him. It is easy, therefore, to understand that Réveillon with his three to four hundred well-paid and contented workmen, in the very quarter where the agitators were exerting every effort to sow discontent, proved highly obnoxious to the conspirators, and the destruction of the paper factory was hardly less necessary to their designs than the destruction of that other building in the same district—the château of the Bastille. The factory and the fortress must therefore both be destroyed before the agitators could depend on the Faubourg to carry out their designs unchecked.

The Affaire Réveillon thus served a double purpose, for it had not only cleared the ground of one obstacle, but it had prepared the way for the removal of the other ; it was, in fact, an admirable rehearsal for the attack on the Bastille, it had enabled the conspirators to test the efficacy of their methods for assembling a mob, and if it had ended in defeat they realized that they had but to overcome the loyalty of the troops in order to ensure the success of the further venture. As this book will show, every one of the great popular tumults of the Revolution was preceded by

---

[1] Montjoie, *Conjuration de d'Orléans*, i. 210, 211, confirmed by Maton de la Varenne, *Histoire Particulière*, etc.

[2] *Mémoires de Sénart*, edit. de Lescure, p. 27.

some such abortive rising—the 14th of July by the 27th of April, the 6th of October by the 30th of August, and the 10th of August 1792 by the 20th of June. On each of these occasions the agitators, finding it impossible to rouse the people to the required pitch of violence, were obliged to cast about for fresh methods to achieve their ends.

It will be seen, therefore, that any account of the Siege of the Bastille must begin with its prelude in the Affaire Réveillon. From this moment the conspirators never relaxed their efforts to corrupt the troops and to undermine the royal authority. In order to understand how they accomplished their purpose we must follow their movements not only in the city of Paris but in the States-General that met at Versailles on the 5th of May, a week after the Affaire Réveillon.

THE WORK OF REFORM

It is a common device of pro-revolutionary writers to represent the National Assembly (into which the States-General were transformed on June 17) as divided into two opposing camps formed by revolutionary leaders who desired reforms and by reactionaries who opposed them. According to this theory the delay in framing the Constitution was caused merely by the recalcitrance of the noblesse and clergy in relinquishing their privileges. But if we study the reports of the debates that took place in the Assembly we shall find that the real obstructionists were the revolutionary deputies. For in the Assembly, as in the city of Paris, two of the great conspiracies had their representatives—the *Orléanistes* led by Mirabeau and including Barnave and the two Lameths, also the duke himself and his boon companions the Duc de Biron and the Marquis de Sillery, and the *Subversives* who consisted in a herd of quarrelsome nonentities, of which Robespierre was the typical representative.[1] These two revolutionary factions, far from representing democracy, were concerned solely in furthering their own designs. For since not a single cahier had expressed dissatisfaction either with the reigning dynasty or with the monarchy, the faction that wished to replace Louis XVI. by the Duc d'Orléans and the faction that wished to destroy the monarchy were both equally opposed to the people's wishes. The election of these members as repre-

---

[1] Gouverneur Morris well described this faction under the name of the " Enragés " : " These are the most numerous, and are of that class which in America is known by the name of pettifogging lawyers, together with a host of curates and many of those who, in all revolutions, throng to the standard of change because they are not well" [sic] (*Diary and Letters of Gouverneur Morris*, i. 277).

sentatives of the people had therefore been secured on false pretences, and their attitude from the outset was necessarily one of duplicity and imposture. Unable to avow their real policy lest they should be disowned by their constituents, they adopted a method which effectually delayed the work of reform—that of diverting attention from the real issues at stake by perpetual quibbles over matters of no importance.

It was against these revolutionary obstructionists far more than against the reactionary portion of the noblesse that the true reformers had to contend. Now the party which advocated true reform was represented by several very able and enlightened men—Jean Joseph Mounier, a magistrate from Dauphiné, noted for his integrity and love of justice, Pierre Victor Malouet, the Comte de Virieu, the Comte de Lally Tollendal, and the Comte de Clermont Tonnerre. This party, known as that of the "Royalist democrats " and later as the " Constitutionals," represented in reality the cause of true democracy, and their royalism resulted solely from the fact that in the person of Louis XVI. they saw, as did the people, the surest guarantee of liberty and justice. " The majority of the people," says Bouillé, " were attached to this party, as also all the municipalities of the kingdom and the Gardes Nationales. The plan of the leaders was to establish a democratic monarchy that they called ' a royal democracy.' " If we refer again to the cahiers we shall find that this policy was exactly in accord with the unanimous desires of the nation, and we shall then recognize the fundamental error of regarding the Revolution as the movement for reform carried to excess. *Reform and revolution were two totally distinct movements*, and not only distinct but *directly opposed to each other.*

Since, in all assemblies, those who make the most noise are those that most readily obtain a hearing, the Tiers État allowed itself to be dominated by the two contentious factions, and the voice of reform was drowned by floods of futile verbiage. So, although revolutionary writers depict the people of France at this crisis as on the verge of starvation and " groaning under oppressions," we have only to consult the *Moniteur* to find that *during the first four weeks after the opening of the States-General not one word was spoken in the hall of the Tiers État on the subject of the famine or the sufferings of the people.* When at last after a month it was suggested, *not by the Tiers État but by the clergy,* that the Assembly should turn its attention to the question of the people's bread, the proposal was received with a howl of execration by the revolutionary factions. " It was just like the clergy ! " to try by these means to divert attention from the union of the orders ! " The clergy should be denounced as seditious ! " Robespierre in a violent diatribe demanded why the clergy, if they were so concerned for the people's welfare, did not sell all they possessed to supply their needs.[1] The speech was as senseless as it was unjust ; the liberality of the clergy in the matter of relieving distress had been unbounded, and, as everybody knew, the famine was not caused by lack of funds but by the difficulty of obtaining and circulating grain. But this was the point of all others on which the revolutionary factions were the most anxious to avoid inquiry, and their complicity with the monopolizers is evident from the debates that took place on the subject of monopoly. Now, if ever, was their opportunity for publicly denouncing the " aristocrats " they accused of cornering the grain, but far from substantiating these charges their policy was invariably to suppress all discussion of the question. Thus, as M. Louis Blanc in a rare fit of candour admits, " the sacred question of feeding the people was lost to sight," and " the Assembly in a way passed over social misery and the hunger of the people to other subjects." These subjects were, of course, inevitably party quarrels in general, and the " Union of the Orders " in particular.

This is not the place to discuss the vexed question of a single chamber ; much was to be said for it, much against it. The true democrats of the Assembly undoubtedly desired it on the ground that no reforms could be effected if the noblesse and clergy were enabled to obstruct them. Arthur Young considered this unreasonable. " Among such men, the common idea is that anything tending towards a separate order, like our House of Lords, is absolutely inconsistent with liberty ; all which seems perfectly wild and unfounded."

Whether the union of the three orders was advisable or not, one thing is certain—that the revolutionary factions did everything in their power to prevent it taking place by their aggressive attitude towards the nobility and clergy. But the great objection to the union of the three orders lay in the fact that the Tiers État insisted on admitting strangers indiscriminately to their debates, with the result that the most frightful confusion prevailed, and that the deputies, instead of expressing their real convictions, were tempted to talk to the galleries in order to win popularity. " Learn, sir," said the deputy Bouche to Malouet in a speech on May 28, " that we are debating here in the presence of our masters ! "

The revolutionary leaders took care to ensure support from the galleries, and a great part of the audience was their own *claque*, composed of Paris idlers and ruffians in their pay, whom they sent for to intimidate their adversaries, and who, before long, not content with applauding sedition, expressed

---

[1] *Souvenirs sur Mirabeau*, by Étienne Dumont, p. 44.

their disapproval by boos and hisses. What assembly, however democratic, could continue to debate under such conditions ? [1]

So great was the confusion into which the revolutionary factions succeeded in throwing the Assembly that Louis XVI. finally resolved to intervene, and announced his intention of holding a Séance Royale. For this purpose it was necessary to make use of the hall of the Tiers État, the " Salle des Menus Plaisirs," which, being the largest of the three, was the only one capable of containing the deputies of all three orders, and had therefore been used for the meeting of the States-General. Accordingly the Tiers were informed that the hall must be closed to debates *for two days only*,[2] and in order to avert ill-feeling the halls of the noblesse and clergy were closed likewise. The announcement was received without a murmur by the " privileged orders," but the Tiers, furious at the royal edict, repaired to the " tennis court " close by and held an indignation meeting, where, at the instigation of Mounier—who afterwards bitterly repented his action—they swore not to separate until they had framed the Constitution.

Regardless of this act of open insubordination Louis XVI. appeared at the Séance Royale on June 23 [3] and announced his intentions to the Assembly. In dignified yet touching words he besought the representatives of the people to carry on the work of reform he had inaugurated ; he reminded them that the

---

[1] See the evidence of Arthur Young, an eye-witness of these scenes : " The spectators in the galleries are allowed to interfere in the debates by clapping their hands, and other noisy expressions of approbation : this is grossly indecent ; for if they are permitted to express approbation, they are, by parity of reason, allowed expressions of dissent, and they may hiss as well as clap, which it is said they have sometimes done : this would be to overrule the debate and influence the deliberations. Another circumstance is the want of order among themselves ; more than once to-day there were more than a hundred members on their legs at a time," etc. (*Travels in France*, p. 165). Lord Dorset in a letter to the Duke of Leeds on June 4, 1789, confirms this description : " I am told that the most extravagant and disrespectful language against Government has been held, and that upon all such occasions the greatest approbation is expressed by the audience, by clapping of hands and other demonstrations of satisfaction : in short, the encouragement is such as to have led some of the speakers on to say things little short of treason. The Nobility, as may be supposed, are roughly treated in these debates, and their conduct does not escape being represented in the most odious light possible. The Clergy and Nobility hold their meetings in separate chambers, and neither of them admit strangers to be present at their deliberations " (*Dispatches from Paris*, ii. 207).

[2] The Séance Royale was announced for Monday, June 22, and the hall was closed on Saturday the 20th. As the Assembly did not sit on Sundays, this meant the Séance of Saturday only would be missed.

[3] At the request of Necker the Séance Royale was afterwards postponed till Tuesday the 23rd.

States-General had been assembled for nearly two months, yet had not been able to agree on the preliminaries of their work ; he appealed to their love for their country, to their traditions as Frenchmen, to cease from dissensions and work together for the common good. " I owe it to myself to put an end to these disastrous differences ; it is with this resolution that I have gathered you around me as the father of all my subjects, as the defender of the laws of my kingdom."

Since it was essential, without further delay, to meet the demands of the people, the King proceeded to enumerate the reforms that, acting on the royal prerogative, he proposed to introduce. These were, above all, the equality of taxation and abolition of the pecuniary privileges of the noblesse and clergy ; further, the total abolition of the taille, of corvées, francs-fiefs, lettres de cachet, mainmorte, and personal charges, greater liberty of the press, the mitigation or even the abolition of the gabelle, and the restriction of capitaineries or game-laws.

Thus of his own accord the King had redressed the principal grievances of the Old Régime ; he refused, however, to abolish all the feudal rights of the noblesse and clergy, which he held not to be his to do away with. This sacrifice was therefore left to the two orders to make themselves, and they made it voluntarily six weeks later. The King's speech ended with these significant words :

" You have heard, messieurs, the result of my inclinations and my views . . . and if by a fatality far from my thoughts you abandon me in so great an enterprise, alone I will accomplish the welfare of my people, alone I shall consider myself as their true representative ; and knowing your cahiers, knowing the perfect accord that exists between the general wishes of the nation and my benevolent intentions . . . I shall walk towards the goal with all the courage and firmness that it inspires in me."

What could this mean ? One thing only. Those two ominous phrases had made the King's intentions clear—" *alone* I will accomplish the welfare of my people, *alone* I shall consider myself as their true representative." In other words, the King intimated that *if the Tiers Etat did not cease its quarrels and " get to business," he would dissolve the States-General and carry out the work of reform himself.*

What wonder that the King's discourse was received in gloomy silence by the Tiers ? What wonder that the factions trembled in their seats ? What wonder that Orléanistes and Subversives alike feared for those fortunes they had hoped to build on public confusion ? What wonder that Mirabeau, seeing the ministry he coveted vanishing into space, rose in wrath to utter his famous " apostrophe " ? The King had left the hall, and De Brézé, the master of ceremonies, declared the sitting ended, when Mirabeau, who exactly a week before in supporting the royal veto had stated, " I could imagine nothing more terrible than the sovereign aristocracy of 600 persons who to-morrow might declare themselves immovable," now insolently defied the King's order with the words, " We will only leave our places by the force of the bayonet ! "

So ended this sitting that might have laid the foundations of French liberty for ever. The thing that the revolutionary factions dreaded more than any other threatened to occur—the regeneration of the kingdom was to be accomplished peacefully and the monarchy established on a free and constitutional basis. If any further proof were needed that the work of the revolutionary factions was actively opposed to the work of reform, it is to be found in this one undeniable fact that, throughout the whole Revolution until the fall of the monarchy, *every concession made by the King to the desires of the people, every step in the work of the reform, was the signal for a fresh outbreak of revolutionary fury.*

Accordingly the immense reforms of the Séance Royale, far from bringing a peaceful settlement of the crisis, were followed by renewed scenes of violence. Two days later the Archbishop of Paris, beloved by all the true people for his benevolence and the uprightness of his life, was attacked by a band of hired rioters as he was leaving the Assembly, and only escaped with his life owing to the speed of his horses and the courage and presence of mind of his coachman.

The fact that four days after the Séance Royale the noblesse and clergy, in obedience to the King's command, settled the burning question of a single chamber by joining the Tiers État, did nothing to allay the fermentation the revolutionaries had succeeded in creating. If, as the Tiers État had declared, the refusal of the noblesse to concede this point had been the only obstacle to the work of reform, why did this work not proceed now that the obstacle had been removed? On the contrary, the Tiers, once they had the noblesse and clergy at their mercy, showed themselves more aggressive than ever and in no way disposed to discuss peaceably the regeneration of the kingdom. True, a " committee of subsistences " was formed for dealing with the question of the famine, but as it consisted almost entirely of Orléanistes, including the Duc d'Orléans himself, nothing was done to relieve the distress of the people, and the famine continued its ravages.

THE HOTBED OF REVOLUTION

Whilst these scenes were taking place at Versailles the agitators of Paris, in close touch with the revolutionary factions of the Assembly, had been busy stirring up insurrection. Night and day the dusty garden of the Palais Royal was filled to overflowing ; no longer merely a haunt of vice, it had now become a political arena—a sort of Trafalgar Square and Burlington Arcade combined—where every device was employed to play upon the passions of men—women, wine, the lust of gold, envy, hatred, and revenge. At the little tables outside the cafés idlers gathered in heated debate ; under the long arcades, where the *marchands de frivolités* displayed their wares, painted women of the town walked arm-in-arm attracting with bold glances the soldiers who passed by ; in the gambling hells the rattle of the dice and the clink of coin continued far into the night, and under the trees cheap-jack politicians with rolling eyes and furious gestures stirred the people to violence. With these mob orators noise was of the first importance, and working themselves up into convulsions of revolutionary frenzy they shrieked invectives against the aristocrats and the Court, or yelled foul blasphemies on God and religion.

Most violent of all was the Marquis de St. Huruge, an ex-convict, whose stentorian voice seemed indefatigable ; above the heads of the crowd his white hat could be seen afar, a rallying point for disorder, whilst with an immense cudgel, manipulated like a conductor's baton, he roused or soothed the passions of his auditors. Philippe d'Orléans, looking down on this scene from his windows at the end of the long square, had reason to congratulate himself on the vast machinery that the genius of Choderlos de Laclos had set in motion. Recently a number of new recruits had been added to the conspiracy, of which the most important was a young journalist from Guise, Camille Desmoulins—discovered by Mirabeau—who tempted the greed of the populace with promises of booty to be wrested from the nobility and clergy :

" The brute is in the trap, then kill it ! . . . Never was richer prey offered to the conqueror ! Forty thousand palaces, hotels, and châteaux, two-fifths of the wealth of France, will be the price of valour ! "[1]

The services of several new agitators had also been enlisted —the comedian Grammont, a man of extraordinary ferocity, with, as we shall see later, a *literal* " taste for blood " ; a convict from San Domingo known as Fournier l'Américain,, Stanislas

[1] *La France Libre.*

Maillard, a future director of the September massacres, and one woman whose wit and daring was to prove an immense acquisition to the cause.[1]

Anne Terwagne of Marcourt was a Belgian *demi-mondaine* and an old friend of the Duc d'Orléans when the Revolution broke out. Several years before she had been introduced to him in London by the Prince of Wales, and it was to the duke she owed her rise to fortune, for on her return to Paris she became a brilliant courtesan with jewels, carriages, and horses, and under the name of " Comtesse de Campinados " travelled about the Continent with various rich protectors.[2] The " Comtesse " was in Rome when the States-General met, but the gathering of the revolutionary storm brought her hurriedly back to Paris, where, adopting " Théroigne de Méricourt " as her *nom de guerre*, she threw herself into the cause of her old benefactor, the Duc d'Orléans. Théroigne was far from resembling the " unfortunate female " burning to avenge her wrongs on a corrupt society, who masqueraded under her name through the pages of Carlyle, for it was with the most corrupt portion of society that she now identified herself. Small and fragile, with brilliant black eyes, an impertinent retroussé nose, and " a waist that a man could encircle with his ten fingers," Théroigne at her salon in the Rue de Bouloi reigned as a queen of the demi-monde, assembling around her the leaders of the Orléaniste conspiracy, of which the Abbé Sieyès was her particular idol.

The rôle played by courtesans in the earlier stages of the Revolution has never been properly estimated by historians ; but for the co-operation of these women, from Théroigne de Méricourt down to the humblest *fille de joie*, it is doubtful whether the great scheme of the Orléanistes—the defection of the army—could ever have been realized. The French Guards, the gayest and most essentially Parisian regiment in the army, were habitual frequenters of the Palais Royal, and thus became the allies of the courtesans who lodged in the surrounding houses and haunted the arcades ; in some cases the soldiers played the part of *souteneurs*, sharing the incomes of the *filles de joie*, and these incomes being now largely increased by the bounty of the duke, both reaped the golden harvest sown by the conspirators. By this means the French Guards, who had stood firm at the Affaire Réveillon, were gradually turned from their allegiance. Towards the end of June, the regiment having been confined to barracks for insubordination, three hundred broke loose and paraded the streets of Paris, finally presenting

[1] Montjoie, *Conjuration de d'Orléans*, i. 221 ; *Philippe d'Orléans Égalité*, by Auguste Ducoin, p. 50.
[2] *Théroigne de Méricourt*, by Marcellin Pellet, p. 10.

themselves at the Palais Royal, where they received a rapturous reception from the courtesans and were regaled with wine and good cheer.

This open revolt at last spurred the authorities to action and eleven of the ringleaders were imprisoned in the Abbaye. Immediately a yell of indignation went up from the Palais Royal, and an army of brigands, led by Jourdan, with Maillard as his aide-de-camp and Théroigne de Méricourt as Amazon, set forth to deliver the " victims of despotism." With clubs and hatchets the doors of the Abbaye were broken down, and all the prisoners— not only the deserters but a number of criminals—were let loose in the streets. Once more the Palais Royal received the rebels, a magnificent supper was spread, whilst bonfires and fireworks turned night into day. Yet even after this outbreak the King was persuaded to pardon the insurgents. It is the custom of historians, whether Royalist or Revolutionary, to accuse Louis XVI. of weakness. This charge, brought by those who believe that a king should be the ruler and not the servant of his people, is certainly consistent, but for believers in the sovereignty of the people to accuse Louis XVI. of weakness is both unjust and illogical. Louis XVI. carried out the principles of democracy to their utmost conclusion ; he believed that he existed for his people, not his people for him. " Despotism," says the demo-cratic Bailly, " had no place in the King's character ; he never desired anything but the happiness of his people ; this was the only means that could be employed to influence him—a less kind-hearted king, cleverer ministers, and there would have been no revolution." As long, therefore, as the mob orators inveighed against the Court, and the agitators incited the people to rise against his own authority, the King refused to put down sedition by force ; only when the people turned on each other he held it his duty to save them from themselves. When at last the scenes of violence taking place at the Palais Royal had reached such a pitch that no law-abiding citizen could venture inside the garden, the King was placed in the frightful dilemma of having to decide whether to bring out troops to restore order, and, as at every crisis in the Revolution, he found himself torn between conflicting counsels. On the one hand the so-called demo-crats of the Assembly represented the iniquity of opposing the " sovereign will of the people," on the other hand the noblesse and clergy protested that it was " a cruel derision thus to con-found the people it was necessary to restrain with those it was necessary to protect," and therefore urged the King to order out troops for the defence of the town. So great, indeed, was the alarm of the citizens that by the end of June the commons of Paris began to inaugurate a *garde bourgeoise* for protection against

the brigands. Since the assembling of the troops round Paris
has been habitually accepted as the principal reason for the
Revolution of July, this point is important to remember.

The King finally decided to employ the army for the defence
of the town ; and as it was essential to guard against further
defection, two regiments of Swiss and German auxiliaries were
included, partly because these men were especially amenable
to discipline, but mainly because their ignorance of the French
language rendered them less liable to corruption by the agents
of the Palais Royal.[1] The circumstance of their nationality,
however, afforded a fresh pretext for stirring up the crowd—
" foreign legions to be employed against the nation ! "   Yet
the revolutionaries did not hesitate to welcome these foreigners
into their own ranks when by their usual methods of women,
wine, and money they succeeded in seducing them from their
allegiance to the King. A German hussar mounted in the
ranks for the defence of French citizens was a " foreign mercenary " ; the same hussar drinking with the courtesans of
the Palais Royal to the downfall of the French monarchy was
a man and a brother. This throughout the Revolution, as we
shall see, was the " patriotism " of the leaders.

The presence of any loyal troops, whether foreign or otherwise, was naturally calculated to thwart the designs of the
conspirators, for, apart from the opposition they offered to insurrection, the troops acted as a guard to the convoys of grain
intended for the capital. The Maréchal de Broglie, the Baron
de Bézenval, and the Prince de Lambesc had proved untiring
in their efforts to protect the wagons of corn from the onslaughts of the brigands that lay in wait round Paris, and for
this reason had become odious to the agitators.[2]

The mob orators of the Palais Royal therefore set to work to
stir up a fresh panic. " Vast hordes of foreign soldiers were to
be marched against the capital to massacre the citizens—the
Palais Royal would be given over to pillage—the city was to be
bombarded with red-hot cannon-balls and everything put to
fire and sword. Meanwhile at Versailles the National Assembly
was to be blown up by mines laid beneath the floor." This
wild farrago of nonsense was believed not only by the ignorant
populace of Paris, but was seriously repeated by the deputies
themselves. Mirabeau at the Assembly, working on their alarms,
exerted all his energy to fan the flame of insurrection :

" When troops advance from all sides, when camps are formed

---

[1] Marmontel, iv. 137; *Dispatches from Paris*, letter from Lord Dorset,
dated July 9, 1789.

[2] Montjoie, *Conjuration de d'Orléans*, ii. 19; *Mémoires de Bézenval*,
ii. 396.

around us, when the capital is besieged, we ask ourselves with astonishment, ' Does the King doubt the fidelity of his people ? What means this threatening display ? Where are the enemies of the King and State that must be subdued ? Where are the plotters that must be restrained ? ' "

This whilst the Palais Royal was a hotbed of sedition, when " almost every day produced some act of violence," [1] when the citizens of Paris themselves were arming for purposes of self-protection !

The tirade was a masterpiece of hypocrisy and cunning ; no one knew better than Mirabeau the necessity for maintaining order, no one realized more keenly the horrors of anarchy, and no one was less truly democratic.

The King's reply to the demands of the deputies for the withdrawal of the troops was brief and to the point :

" No one is ignorant of the disorders and scandalous scenes that have taken place repeatedly in Paris and Versailles under my eyes and those of the States-General. It is necessary that I should employ all the means within my power to restore and maintain order in the capital and its surroundings. It is one of my principal duties to guard public safety. These are the motives that led me to assemble troops round Paris, and you can assure the States-General that they are intended only to repress or rather to avert such-like disorders, to enforce the law, even to assure and protect the liberty that should reign in your deliberations. . . . Only evilly-disposed persons could mislead my people as to the true motives for the precautionary measures I have taken. I have invariably sought to do all that I could to contribute to their happiness, and I have always had reason to believe in their love and loyalty."

That the King was absolutely sincere in making these assurances was afterwards proved by the trial of Bézenval, the commander of the Swiss Guard. In January 1790 the Commune of Paris, at the instigation of the Orléanistes, arraigned Bézenval before the tribunal of the Châtelet for " having entered into a conspiracy formed against the liberty of the French people, of the National Assembly, and particularly of the city of Paris " in the preceding July. No proof whatever of a conspiracy was forthcoming ; on the contrary, it was proved by documentary evidence that the intentions of the Ministry and of M. de Bézenval " were the most pacific and paternal " ; the letters produced " manifested the plan of this officer for guarding the provisionment of Paris, *for which purpose the troops were assembled,* and that, far from any design to destroy the citizens, they had been assembled to protect them." They were necessary also " to

---

[1] *Dispatches from Paris,* ii. 237, letter from Lord Dorset.

repress the brigands who had already caused disorders in Paris and who might be plotting further disorders." These facts having been proved Bézenval was acquitted, and, in spite of the protests of Marat, the *Moniteur* itself recognized the justice of the decision : " The information taken was immense, but nothing criminal was discovered against the defendant and he was acquitted. It would be necessary to have very strong proofs to suspect a perfidious collusion between a respected municipality and an esteemed tribunal only for the purpose of deceiving the populace concerning *pretended offences of which the most minute investigation has been unable to prove the reality.*" [1] That the troops were therefore intended for no aggressive purpose is certain, and the necessity for assembling them is now recognized by enlightened French historians. [2]

The King's speech had the effect of allaying public anxiety, and Mirabeau thereupon set immediately to work on a new address that would stir up fresh discontent. [3]

To Louis XVI. the situation now became completely bewildering. Content to do his duty according to his lights, he could not understand why his actions were perpetually misconstrued by the people, he could not guess the existence of the influences brought to bear on their minds by the agitators who made it their business to avert popular satisfaction at every concession to the people's desires.

Why did none of the Royalist democrats in the Assembly enlighten the King on the true state of affairs ? That they knew of the Orléaniste conspiracy is certain, for they afterwards described the efforts made by the duke's supporters to secure their co-operation—overtures that were all indignantly repulsed. Mounier and Bergasse were approached by Mirabeau, [4] Virieu by Sillery, [5] and both conspirators met with almost identically the same reply : " Understand, monsieur, that if any one here were to dare to call M. le duc d'Orléans to the throne in the place of the King, I would stab him with my own hand ! " Lafayette, whose first enthusiasm for the Revolution had raised hopes in the minds of the conspirators, proved no less intractable, for if he cared little for the King he detested Orléans, and to the suggestion that a price having been set on his head and on that of the duke by the Court he would do well to join forces with him,

[1] *Moniteur* for Jan. 4, Feb. 4, and March 3, 1790.
[2] For example, *La Révolution*, by M. Louis Madelin, p. 62, " It will be understood that under these circumstances the ministry advanced troops on Paris. The least reactionary government would have been forced to do this."
[3] *Appel au Tribunal de l'Opinion Publique*, par Mounier, 1790.
[4] *Ibid.*
[5] *Le Roman d'un Royaliste*, par Costa de Beauregard.

Lafayette coldly replied that "the Duc d'Orléans was nothing to him, and that it was needless to form a party when one was with the whole nation." [1]

But instead of merely rejecting these advances, why did not these men use their immense influence to quell the intrigue? We cannot believe that they lacked courage, since later on they faced the full tide of revolution to support the tottering monarchy; why then did they wait until it was too late? The only explanation seems to be that at this crisis they believed the Orléaniste conspiracy to be incidental to the Revolution; they recognized its existence but failed to realize its extent, and feared that in crushing it they might arrest the whole revolutionary movement which they still held to be necessary to the regeneration of the kingdom. In a word, they were visionaries, and at times of national crisis visionaries are of all men the most dangerous; intent on the pursuit of unattainable ideals they shut their eyes to realities, and instead of facing danger prefer to ignore it.

Most culpable of all was Necker—Necker whom both the King and Queen had trusted to steer the ship of state to safety. From the beginning his only consideration had been popularity, his only policy to temporize. His method of dealing with the financial crisis had consisted in raising perpetual loans; in the matter of the famine Arthur Young declared that "his edicts had operated more to raise the price of corn than all other causes together," and though having made this initial mistake he apparently did his best to repair it by untiring efforts to feed the people, he shrank from taking the most effectual step towards this end—that of exposing the monopolizers.

The attitude of Necker admits only of two explanations—either he was in league with the Orléanistes or he was afraid of them. In either case his conduct was contemptible, as contemporaries of all parties agree. It is a strange fact that, although Necker is the only demagogue of the period who has never found a panegyrist—except in his own daughter, Mme. de Staël—it was the King's discovery of his incapacity, which all the world now acknowledges, that has been accepted as an adequate pretext for the Revolution of July.

By the beginning of this month Louis XVI. finally realized that Necker must go and a strong ministry be formed if the impending crisis was to be averted. Accordingly he dismissed his ministers and nominated in their place De Breteuil, De Broglie, La Galaizière, and Foullon.

Joseph François Foullon was an old commissary of '74 who had grown grey in the service of the army. His large fortune, attributed by the revolutionary leaders to speculation or monopoly

---

[1] *Mémoires de Lafayette*, ii. 53.

in grain, resulted from the emoluments of his office and from his marriage with a Dutch heiress.[1] It is evident that Foullon was unpopular with the people, yet no proof is forthcoming that he had ever treated them with harshness ; on the contrary, during the preceding winter he had spent no less than 60,000 francs in providing work for the peasants of his province, " not wishing to humiliate them by charity." [2] A stern man, however, and a believer in discipline, Foullon came forward at this juncture to offer the King his advice on the situation in the form of two alternative schemes by which he believed the Revolution might be averted. In the first he expressed himself plainly on the Orléaniste conspiracy ; he advised that the duke and his accomplices amongst the deputies of the Assembly should be arrested, and that the King should not be parted from his army till order was re-established ; in the second he suggested that the King should identify himself with the Revolution before its final explosion, that he should go to the Assembly, demand the cahiers himself, and then make the greatest sacrifices in order to satisfy the true desires of the people before the sedition-mongers could turn them to the advantage of their criminal designs.[3]

This proposal of the new minister throws an important light on the Revolution of July, for according to Madame Campan it reached the ears of the Orléanistes by means of the Comte Louis de Narbonne and Madame de Staël, and naturally explains their fury at the change of ministry and also their animosity to Foullon. Whichever of the two schemes were followed their doom was equally certain, since a peaceful settlement of the crisis would have proved no less fatal to their designs than the more rigorous measure of their own arrest.

[1] *Biographie Michaud*, article on Foullon ; *Histoire de la Révolution Française*, by Poujoulat, p. 121, quoting contemporary documents.
[2] *Ibid.*
[3] *Mémoires de Mme. Campan*, p. 242 ; *Histoire du Règne de Louis XVI*, by Joseph Droz, p. 311. This story of Mme. Campan's is confirmed by a contemporary manuscript in the possession of Berthier's descendants. See *La Conspiration Révolutionnaire de 1789*, by Gustave Bord, p. 195. D'Espremesnil had already given the King the same advice a few weeks earlier, for just after the " Serment du Jeu de Paume " he had requested an audience with the King, and urged him not only to arrest but to hang the Duc d'Orléans and his accomplices, to dissolve the Assembly, and to follow out his plan of himself granting to the people the reforms they asked for in the cahiers (*Mémoires Secrets d'Allonville*, ii. 155). Strangely enough the Duke's mistress, Mrs. Elliott, was of the same opinion with regard to the treatment that should have been meted out to the royal conspirator : " Had he (the King), when the nobles went over to the Tiers État, caused the unfortunate Duke of Orleans, and about twenty others, to be arrested and executed, Europe would have been saved from the calamities it has since suffered ; and I should now dare to regret my poor friend the Duke " (*Journal of Mrs. Elliott*, p. 57).

It is evident that they were aware of Necker's impending dismissal several days before it actually took place, and immediately in the midnight council of Montrouge a scheme of insurrection was planned. The advance of the troops and the departure of Necker were to be made the pretexts for stirring up the people ; with that superb capacity for eating their own words which is the true art of demagogy, Necker, whom they had hitherto overwhelmed with their sarcasms and openly accused of monopolizing the grain, was to be represented to the people as their one hope of salvation, and in the panic that would follow on his dismissal the people—" that foolish herd " that, as Chamfort said, " good shepherds could drive as they pleased "—were to be worked up to revolt. Then the Duc d'Orléans, profiting by the general confusion, was to be made lieutenant-general of the kingdom, if not raised at once to the throne. " It only depended on himself," said Mirabeau, who admitted the whole scheme later to Virieu ; " his part had been arranged for him (*on lui avait fait son thème*) ; the words he had to use had been prepared." [1]

Mirabeau rose triumphantly to the occasion. Hitherto he had frankly disparaged Necker, referring to him as " the Genevese penny-snatcher " [2] (*le grippe-sou genevois*) or " the clock that always loses," and on the eve of his dismissal had already prepared a speech for the Assembly accusing him of complicity with the famine. But now that Necker's dismissal was to be made a pretext for insurrection, Mirabeau, like the gigantic humbug that he was, declared that " we can only regard with terror the abyss of misfortune into which the country will be dragged now that the exile of M. Necker, so long desired by our enemies, has been accomplished." [3]

Already on the 9th of July the agitators of the Palais Royal had begun to alarm the people concerning the fate destined for their idol. " Listen to me, citizens ! " cried a mob orator who had succeeded in collecting a crowd around him ; " we have assembled here in order to declare to you that we shall regard as a traitor to the country any one who shall make an attempt not only on the life but on the ministerial office of M. Necker, whom we intend to make permanent minister of the nation, and since our King, though good and confiding, is incapable of governing his kingdom, we nominate M. le duc d'Orléans lieutenant-general of the kingdom ! " [4]

---

[1] *Procédure du Châtelet*, déposition du comte de Virieu.
[2] *Souvenirs sur Mirabeau*, by Étienne Dumont, p. 208.
[3] " Courrier de Provence, lettre 19," *Mémoires de Bailly*, i. 332.
[4] Montjoie, *Histoire de la Révolution de France*, chap. xli.; evidence of M. Périn, *Procédure du Châtelet*, ii. 113.

The proposition does not seem to have been received with great enthusiasm, and the agitators merely succeeded in producing in the people a state of mind aptly described by M. Louis Madelin as a *crise de nerfs*. Already they had sufficient causes for alarm—the growing fear of famine, the brigands that surrounded them, the assurances of the Palais Royal orators that the King's troops were closing in on them for the purpose of massacre, and now, following on all these terrors, came the fresh alarm that Necker was to be dismissed, and the country involved in bankruptcy and ruin. What wonder that the unhappy people were thrown into a condition bordering on hysteria?

THE 12TH OF JULY

The state of the weather further added to the excitement of the Parisians, for the cold spring had been followed in July by a burst of almost tropical heat, a circumstance that seems always to have reacted on the minds of the populace, since nearly every great day of tumult during the Revolution in Paris was unusually hot. Sunday morning, the 12th of July, the day after Necker's departure, was torrid; the sun poured down from a cloudless sky on to the crowds that from an early hour had filled the garden of the Palais Royal. Already at nine o'clock a vague rumour had reached the city that the worst had happened, that Necker was dismissed, and as the panic news passed from mouth to mouth the terrified citizens hurried to the Palais Royal to ascertain the truth. By midday the garden was so packed from end to end that no more standing room was available, and people climbed on to the trees until the branches bowed beneath their weight; even the mob orators, after vainly attempting to pile up chairs and tables for their platforms, were reduced to hanging from the boughs of the lime-trees whilst they harangued the crowd. "This agitation," says Montjoie, who looked on at the scene, "was terrifying. One must have seen it to be able to form any idea of it." At every moment a fresh rumour was circulated, adding to the general consternation; now a messenger, wild-eyed, rushing into the square and crying out that he had just arrived from Versailles where the deputies were being massacred; now a panic-monger announcing that the Duc d'Orléans was exiled—thrown into the Bastille—condemned to death; now warnings shrieked to the terrified people that the troops were marching on the city to put everything to fire and sword. The seething multitude that filled the garden and arcades was like a sea lashed by a hurricane; at each new alarm a long deep moan arose from thousands of throats, a moan that now grew into a muffled roar of fury, now died away into the silence of consternation. Then suddenly rumour gave way to certainty. A fresh messenger from Versailles announced the terrible news — Necker was dismissed, had already taken his departure, the country's doom was sealed ; and at this confirmation of their fears the maddened people turned on the bearer of ill-tidings and were with difficulty prevented from drowning him in one of the fountains of the garden.

It was now twelve o'clock and the sun had reached the meridian, beating down on the dense mass of heads and on the burning glass of the Palais Royal. Suddenly a strange thing happened. The glass mirror reflected the sun's rays on to the cannon of the palace and, setting light to the charge, fired it with a terrifying report, and so " the sun himself gave the first signal for the Revolution." [1]

The effect of this circumstance on the minds of the people was indescribable. The wildest scene of confusion began. Men haggard with fear, women pale and tearful rushed hither and thither ; the streets were filled with bands of citizens, silent and distraught, hurrying like frightened sheep they knew not whither. Unhappy people driven desperately to and fro by the men who had made themselves their shepherds !

Yet the shepherds did not find their work too easy ; even sheep refuse at moments to be driven in the right direction, and still the people, for all their panic, showed no inclination to carry out the designs of the agitators and begin the revolution in earnest. Camille Desmoulins afterwards described his desperate efforts that afternoon to stir the people up to violence ; some, indeed, were so misguided as to cry, " Vive le Roi ! " " In vain I tried to inflame their minds," says Camille ; " no one would take up arms ! "

It was three o'clock in the afternoon when at last Camille, coming out of the Café de Foy where the Orléaniste leaders forgathered, encountered several young men walking arm-in-arm and shouting, " Aux armes ! Aux armes ! " Immediately he saw his opportunity and joined them ; in an instant he was hoisted up on to a table in front of the café, from which position he afterwards related that he delivered an eloquent harangue :

" Citizens, you know that the nation had asked for Necker to be retained, for a monument to be raised to him, and he has been driven away ! Could you be more insolently defied ? After this stroke they will dare anything, and for to-night they are meditating, have perhaps arranged, a Saint-Barthélemy of patriots ! To arms ! To arms ! Let us take green cockades the colour of hope ! " He waved a green ribbon, fastened it in

---

[1] Montjoie, *Histoire de la Révolution de France*, chap. xl.

his hat, and instantly the crowd, tearing down leaves from the trees above their heads, adorned themselves with the same emblem. Then, striking an attitude, Camille pointed a quivering finger at the crowd, pretending to see amongst them the agents of the police. " The infamous police are here ! Let them look at me ! Let them observe me ! Yes, it is I who call my brothers to liberty ! " He raised a pistol in the air. " At least they shall not take·me alive, and I shall know how to die gloriously ; only one misfortune can befall me—that of seeing France become again enslaved ! "

Such is Camille's version of his tirade, but it seems probable that much of it was inspired by *esprit d'escalier* and never found utterance, for none of his auditors record it in these words. Montjoie, in fact, declares that Camille's performance consisted merely in standing on the table waving a pistol and calling out " Aux armes ! " making horrible grimaces the while to overcome his stutter.

At any rate his efforts were rewarded, for he was hauled down from the table and carried in triumph on the shoulders of the crowd, who now at last responded to the cry of insurrection, and arming themselves with sticks, hatchets, and pistols poured into the streets thirsting to do battle with the menacing legions —the legions that meanwhile remained peacefully encamped in the Champ de Mars.

This was undoubtedly the great moment to which the Orléaniste conspiracy had been leading up. The people's minds had been prepared by the alarms concerning the fate of the duke, and were therefore more than usually disposed in his favour as the victim of despotism. If he had now come forward and shown himself to the frenzied crowd it seems probable that he could have placed himself at the head of the movement. But at this crucial moment the duke was not forthcoming, for he had gone off at eleven o'clock that morning with his mistress, Mrs. Elliott, to spend the day at his château of Raincy, and did not reappear until the evening. Was his absence arranged by the conspirators to give colour to their stories of his exile or imprisonment ? Or did he disappoint his supporters by refusing to be present ? We know that the pusillanimity of the duke at every crisis made him the despair of his party, and that this fear, moreover, was founded on a very real danger—that of assassination. When he fainted in the Assembly that summer day only a few weeks earlier, and his coat was unfastened to give him air, had it not been discovered that he wore beneath it no less than four waistcoats, including one of leather, to protect him from a dagger-thrust ? [1]   It is possible, therefore, that at

[1] Montjoie, *Conjuration de d'Orléans*, i. 296 ; *Mémoires de Ferrières*, i. 52.

the last moment his courage failed him ; but at any rate his absence was foreseen by the conspirators, for the duke himself being unavailable they led the crowd to the waxwork show of M. Curtius in the Boulevard du Temple, where—*by mere coincidence*, Orléaniste historians would have us believe—the busts of the Duc d'Orléans and Necker lay ready to hand.

Camille Desmoulins' subsequent remarks on this incident show that he certainly did not believe in the theory of coincidence, but recognized very clearly the design of the faction—from which, like every other Orléaniste, he became anxious to disassociate himself. " Will any one make me believe," he wrote four years later, " that when I mounted a table on the 12th of July and called the people to liberty, it was my eloquence that produced that great movement half an hour later, and that made the two busts of Orléans and Necker spring from the ground ? " [1] The procession with the two effigies had therefore been premeditated, and Mirabeau, hardly less an *enfant terrible* than Camille in giving away the secrets of his party, confirms this statement. Referring to the 12th of July in his answer to the *Procédure du Châtelet,* he attempted to prove the duke's innocence on this day by remarking, " When his bust was paraded he hid himself." [2] Then the duke *knew* that his bust was to be paraded ? Otherwise where was the virtue of his disappearance from the scene *four hours earlier* ? Again, why should he *hide* himself ? Why not, if he was innocent, have come forward boldly and denied all complicity with the movement ? Thus from Orléaniste evidence alone it is obvious that the incident of the two busts was a ruse devised by the conspirators, with the idea of putting popular feeling to the test ; it had been resolved to try the people with the duke's effigy, and if, as seemed not unlikely, it met with a hostile reception, nothing but wax would suffer ; if, on the other hand, it was received with acclamations, the duke was to be recalled from his retreat and placed at the head of the movement. The effigy of Necker was, of course, merely a cover to the real design—" to parade only one," remarks Prudhomme shrewdly, " would have been clumsy." [3] Accordingly the two busts, wreathed in black crêpe and *crowned*, were carried in procession through the streets whilst Orléaniste agents, posted in the crowd, cried out, " Hats off ! The country is in danger ; here are its restorers. Vive D'Orléans ! " Then, as the people failed to take up the cry, the agitators went amongst them repeating, " Call out ' Vive

---

[1] *Fragment de l'Histoire Secrète,* p. 8, April 1793.
[2] *Moniteur,* ii. 33.
[3] *Crimes de la Révolution,* by Prudhomme, iii. 111.

D'Orléans!'" For answer some asked wonderingly, "What does all this mean?" and the agitators replied, "Why, don't you understand that Monsieur le duc d'Orléans is to be proclaimed king and M. Necker his prime minister? Come, cry with us 'Vive D'Orléans!'"[1] Even at the Palais Royal the busts met with a no more enthusiastic reception. On arrival in the garden one of the men bearing the effigies, pointing them out to the people, called aloud, " Is it not true that you want this prince for your king, and this good man for his minister? " But only a few voices answered, " We wish it ! "[2]

After this discouraging response the procession made its way by the Boulevards to the Place Louis XV., where it encountered a regiment of the Royal Allemands under the Prince de Lambesc, who rode up with drawn sword and scattered the rioters. During the fray the bust of Orléans fell into the gutter ; a linen-draper's assistant, Pépin by name, rushed to its rescue, and in his attempt to pick up the mutilated effigy was wounded in the leg and fell bleeding to the ground.[3] Raised in the arms of sympathizers, Pépin was carried off to the Palais Royal to exhibit his wounds ; he was not, however, too seriously wounded to harangue the multitude. Dr. Rigby, an eyewitness of the scene, describes " the whole mass agitated afresh by the appearance of a man with a green coat whose countenance and manner bespoke the utmost consternation. ' To arms, citizens,' he cried, ' the Dragoons have fired on the people, and I myself have received a wound,' pointing to his leg. This acted like an electric shock."

Meanwhile the Prince de Lambesc and his troops made their way towards the Tuileries across the great Place Louis XV, which at this hour was filled with holiday-makers returning from their Sunday afternoon festivities in the Bois de Boulogne and the neighbouring villages ; through this crowd the troops advanced at foot pace, gently pushing aside those who obstructed their passage, but the people, infuriated by the sight of the soldiers, greeted them with a hail of stones. Gouverneur Morris, who at this moment arrived upon the scene, thus describes the incident : " The people take post among the stones which lie scattered about the whole place, being then hewn for the bridge now building. The officer at the head of the party (a body of cavalry with their sabres drawn) is saluted by a stone, and

[1] *Crimes de la Révolution*, by Prudhomme, iii. 112.
[2] *Mém. de Ferrières*, and statement by Clermont Tonnerre at the *Procédure du Châtelet*. See also *Souvenirs de Mme. Vigée le Brun*, p. 129.
[3] Montjoie, ii. 48, confirmed by Pépin himself, witness cxxiv. at the *Procédure du Châtelet*. According to these two witnesses this encounter took place in the Place Louis XV. ; according to Bailly (i. 327) and to Flammermont, *La Journée du 14 Juillet* (CLXXVII.), in the Place Vendôme.

immediately turns his horse in a menacing manner towards the assailant. But his adversaries are posted in ground where the cavalry cannot act. He pursues his route, and the pace is soon increased to a gallop, amid a shower of stones. One of the soldiers is either knocked from his horse, or the horse falls under him. He is taken prisoner and at first ill-treated. They fired several pistols, but without effect ; probably they were not even charged with ball. A party of the Swiss Guard are posted in the Champs Élysées with cannon."

The Prince de Lambesc, having thus reached the entrance of the Tuileries, crossed the swing bridge into the garden with his troops, but was again immediately assailed by a hail of stones, chairs, and bottles that the crowd, assembled on the terraces at each side of the bridge, flung down on the regiment.[1] In spite of these outrages the soldiers still refrained from retaliating, and in order to avoid bloodshed the prince ordered the troops to evacuate the garden, whereupon the crowd rushed forward and attempted to cut off their retreat by closing the swing bridge. One old man, a schoolmaster named Chauvet, in the act of performing this manœuvre, was slightly injured by the Prince de Lambesc, who struck him with the flat of his sword, causing a wound that was speedily healed by means of a brandy compress.[2]

Such was " the brutal charge " of the " ferocious Prince de Lambesc," retailed with so much virtuous indignation by revolutionary writers. It is interesting to compare the evidence of eye-witnesses, of Gouverneur Morris, of Montjoie, and of those who appeared later at the trial of the Prince, with the version circulated that night in Paris by the leaders of the agitation. Dr. Rigby, who unfortunately was not present, thus records the account given him by Jefferson :

" About seven in the evening Prince de Lambesc, who commanded a regiment of German Dragoons, entered the Tuileries . . . and made its gay crowds of citizens the objects of his attack, enforced his commands by a sudden discharge of musketry. The terrified multitude fled in all directions, and the middle of the square was suddenly cleared of all but a feeble old man, whose infirmities denied him the power of running. Against this single defenceless individual the cowardly Prince lifted up his arm, and either desperately wounded or killed him with one stroke of his sabre."

This story—every word of which was afterwards disproved, and is now believed by no responsible historian [3]—was loudly

---

[1] *Deux Amis*, i. 276. Even this authority admits that the people were the aggressors.

[2] Taine, *La Révolution*, i. 62.

[3] " The sanguinary Lambesc and his blindly ferocious troop were singularly debonair; ten accounts testify to it. Although they were

proclaimed at the Palais Royal, and the alarm was followed by messengers rushing into the square frantically declaring that citizens were being massacred in the garden of the Tuileries, and dragoons with drawn swords were crushing women and children beneath their horses' feet. These fearful tidings had the effect that for seven hours the mob orators had striven in vain to produce, of arming the mob.

"From this moment," says Dr. Rigby, "nothing could restrain the fury of the people ; they burst forth into the streets calling ' Aux armes ! Aux armes ! ' Every house likely to afford any was immediately entered. The gunsmiths' shops were ransacked, and in a very short time the principal streets were filled with a tumultuous populace, armed variously with guns, swords, pikes, spits, and every instrument of offence and defence." This disorderly band, joined by numbers of deserters from the Gardes Françaises, now marched on the King's troops in the neighbourhood of the Place Louis XV. Let us consult the revolutionary account of the day to discover the manner in which these bloodthirsty soldiers received the onslaught.

"Assembled in force near the depot on the old boulevard," say the Two Friends of Liberty, " they (the armed mob) advance in good order, attack a detachment of the Royal Allemand, and at the first discharge cause three horsemen to bite the dust. *These, although assailed, endure the fire of their adversaries without replying*, and double back on the Place Louis XV, where was the main body of their regiment." [1]

This, then, was the conduct of the troops accused by the revolutionary leaders of carrying out a "massacre of Saint-Barthélemy" amongst the citizens ! What further proof is needed of the King's sincerity in assuring the people that these forces had been summoned merely to protect them ? Nothing could exceed the heroic forbearance of these much-tried men, and those historians who would have us believe that their attitude was owing to the fact that they sympathized with the people and therefore could not be induced to use their arms against them, calumniate not only the officers in command, but the people themselves. Is it conceivable that the people could be so

---

stoned by the people in ambush behind the stone-heaps they contented themselves with advancing without charging. . . . That only one old man was knocked over and that so much was made of this in the popular camp indicates better than all the contemporary accounts how mild was the ' repression ' " (Madelin, p. 63). " It was the crowd that began the attack ; the troops fired into the air. . . . All the details of the affair prove that the patience and the humanity of the officers was extreme " (Taine, *La Révolution*, i. 62). See also *La Journée du 14 Juillet*, by Jules Flammermont, p. clxxviii.

[1] *Deux Amis de la Liberté*, i. 117.

cowardly as to insult and attack men they knew to be their friends ? All contemporary evidence points to the one conclusion—the men were acting under orders from their officers, and the officers, in their turn, were obeying the King's command —at all costs to avoid bloodshed. The order given to Bézenval, and produced later at his trial, is proof positive of this assertion : " Give the most precise and moderate orders to the officers in command of the detachment you employ that they shall act only as protectors, and shall have the greatest care to avoid compromising themselves or engaging in any combat with the people unless they show themselves inclined to cause fires or commit excesses or pillage that would endanger the safety of citizens." [1]

It was a frightful position for the men in command, and Bézenval, in deciding to withdraw the troops to the Champ de Mars, was evidently only doing what he conceived to be his duty. Royalists who reproached him for not adopting stronger measures, and revolutionaries who laughed at his retreat, were alike incapable of appreciating his dilemma. " If I had marched the troops into Paris," he wrote afterwards, " I should have started civil war on one side or the other ; precious blood would have been shed without any useful result. . . ." True, but how much innocent blood might have been spared that flowed hereafter ? Civil war with all its horrors cannot equal the horror of leaving the mob to execute its own vengeances unrestrained, for a rioting mob, like a woman in hysterics, needs firmness to bring it to its senses ; too great solicitude but weakens its power of self-control, and leaves it a prey to frightful convulsions even more dangerous to itself than to those against whom its fury is directed. Paris, which through that feverish Sunday had worked itself up into a nervous crisis that nothing but iron discipline could have allayed, was now, through the mistaken humanity of those in command, left unprotected, and at the withdrawal of all lawful authority rapidly passed into a state of frenzied panic. To all law-abiding citizens, the night that followed was a night of terror, for, at the signal of insurrection, the hordes of brigands, that since the Affaire Réveillon had been kept in reserve by the leaders to create fresh scenes of violence,[2] came forth armed with sticks and pikes and paraded the streets, pillaging the armourers' shops, and threatening to burn down the houses of the aristocrats. The *Quinzaine Mémorable* puts the number of these professional bandits at 20,000, Droz at no less than 40,000, and when we remember the terror created in the provinces of France only a few years ago by half-a-dozen motor bandits—Bonnard and his gang—it is easy to imagine the horror and confusion

---

[1] Order given to Bézenval on July 12, 1789. See the *Moniteur*, iii. 33.

[2] Bailly, i. 337.

inspired by thousands of such ruffians suddenly let loose and armed in the streets of an undefended city.[1]

To these hired bands were added all the dregs of the Faubourgs —drunkards, wastrels, degenerates, prototypes of the modern *Apache*, whose native love of violence needed no incentive; prostitutes who tore the ear-rings from the ears of passers-by, " and if the rings resisted, tore the ears " ; smugglers who saw their chance of booty and led the crowd to burn down the barriers and defraud the customs.[2] Where in all this pandemonium were " the people " to be found ? No good citizens were abroad that hot and terrible night, the true " people," the peaceful bourgeois, the quiet and laborious working men and women of Paris, hid themselves in their humble dwellings no less fearfully than the aristocrats in their hotels of the Faubourg Saint-Honoré, whilst all the while the tocsin sounded drearily and the cry of the rioters, " Des armes et du pain ! " rang out in the darkness. " During that disastrous night," say the Two Friends of Liberty, " sleep descended only on the eyes of children ; they alone reposed in peace whilst their distracted parents watched over their cots."

THE 13TH OF JULY

Morning dawned on a demented city ; wild bands still paraded the streets, and were only prevented by good citizens, who mingled with them, from committing horrible excesses. One horde, however, succeeded in breaking into the convent of Saint-Lazare, " the asylum of religion and humanity," where, disregarding the entreaties of a white-haired priest who threw himself on his knees and begged them to spare the sacred precincts, they proceeded to pillage and destroy the library, laboratory, and pictures, and finally descending to the cellars broke open the casks of wine, gorging themselves with the contents. Next day no less than thirty unfortunate wretches, both men and women, were carried dead or dying from the scene.

The news of this senseless outrage burst on Paris " like a clap of thunder " ; terrified tradesmen shut their shops, and good citizens once more barricaded themselves behind closed shutters. " To the cries of fear," say the Two Friends of Liberty, " are added the tumultuous cries of several lawless bands, bold-eyed, and ready to dare and do anything, who rove through the streets and public places, and in whose hands the weapons they carry

---

[1] Note that even the Two Friends of Liberty admit these to have been " hired brigands " (*Deux Amis*, i. 283), though they carefully refrain from mentioning who hired them.   Are we to believe again this time that it was the Court ?

[2] *Histoire du Règne de Louis XVI*, by Joseph Droz, p. 292.

seem even more dangerous than those of the enemies (*i.e.* the King's troops!). The moment was the more perilous since all the springs of public administration were broken, and Paris seemed abandoned to the mercy of whoever chose to make himself master."[1] On the 13th of July the worst fears of the people were thus not caused by the King's troops but by the brigands, and further, the removal of all lawful authority added immensely to the panic.

When at ten o'clock of this dreadful morning the tocsin of the Hôtel de Ville rang out again it was, therefore, in no sense a signal of revolution, but a summons to all good citizens to take up arms in defence of their lives, their wives and children, and their property.[2] In this moment of real and immediate peril the imaginary menace of the King's troops was forgotten, and men of all classes, rich men, nobles, bourgeois and working-men alike, hastened to the Hôtel de Ville to demand arms for their defence. Inevitably, however, a number of brigands and emissaries of the Palais Royal, who already that morning had burst into the Hôtel de Ville and carried off by force 360 guns, now mingled with the law-abiding citizens, and threw the authorities into a frightful predicament. They wished to arm the *milice bourgeoise*, yet not to reinforce the brigands. Bézenval, appealed to later in the day, flatly refused, declaring he could give up no arms without an order from the King;[3] Flesselles, the provost-marshal, adopted less courageous tactics and attempted to put the people off with fair words, temporizing as a father

---

[1] *Deux Amis de la Liberté*, i. 284.

[2] M. Louis Madelin has emphatically refuted the error perpetuated by historians on this point. The *milice bourgeoise*, he explains, had been formed " not at all—as a hundred years ago so many historians and a crowd of their readers believed—against the Court but against the brigands. . . ." Thus since the 25th of June the Hôtel de Ville had been preparing for the coming danger, and the message carried by its bell must not be misinterpreted. " This bell of the Hôtel de Ville had until the last few years a very definite significance for the historians of the Revolution—it called the great city against the Government of Versailles. The more recent researches, and those least to be suspected of retrospective anti-revolutionism, convey to us a different sound. The city called for help, desperately, because in the night the bandits, that for three weeks had been dreaded, were invading it, pillaging the shops, robbing the passers-by. Far from wishing to destroy the Bastille, the bourgeois of the Hôtel de Ville—Liberals of yesterday— would rather have built twenty more to enclose the beasts of prey that infested the disorganized city " (Madelin, pp. 62, 64). Yet even " recent researches " were not needed to prove this fact, since the oldest authority of all, the *Deux Amis*, had clearly stated it.

[3] Bézenval suspected the good faith of certain of these deputies: " Although the orators of these deputies had prepared their speeches skilfully, it was easy to see they had been prompted, and that they were asking for arms for the purpose of attacking us rather than to defend themselves " (*Mémoires de Bézenval*, ii. 369).

might do with a sick and fretful child that asked for a razor as a plaything : " My friends, I am your father, you will be satisfied," he told the frenzied multitude, and sent them in all directions to seek arms where none were to be found. For this he has been bitterly condemned by historians, yet what was the unfortunate Flesselles to do ? An officer in charge of an arsenal suddenly confronted with a heterogeneous crowd of civilians clamouring for firearms, and threatened with death if he gives a direct refusal, must possess a very ready wit if he can hold his own diplomatically. Yet so far was Flesselles from wishing to thwart the good citizens of the *milice bourgeoise*, that he sent to Versailles for an order authorizing their equipment.

Versailles meanwhile was ill - informed of the progress of events in Paris. The Assembly, persisting in its assertion that the tumult was caused solely by the presence of the troops, continued to send deputations to the King demanding their removal from the environs of Paris, whilst the King, seeing in the troubles of the capital only the work of the brigands,[1] held this to be no moment for the withdrawal of armed force, and repeated his former statement that the troops were necessary for the defence of the citizens. Whilst heartily approving the formation of the *milice bourgeoise*,[2] he did not consider this body of armed civilians sufficient to cope with the situation unsupported by regular troops, and therefore insisted on keeping the troops within reach of the city ready to come to the rescue if required. At the same time he replied to Flesselles' message with an order authorizing the organization and equipment of 12,000 men for the *milice bourgeoise*, and naming the officers he desired to command these patriotic legions. " What amazes us," remarks M. Louis Madelin, " is that this correspondence between Flesselles and the Court should have appeared next day, even to calm minds, as ' an unfortunate connivance sufficient to justify the massacre of the magistrate by the people.' "[3]

Before the King's reply to Flesselles had reached the capital, however, the citizens had already formed the *milice bourgeoise*, and instead of 12,000 men enrolled 40,000, which they later increased to 48,000. These patriotic civilians at first showed themselves perfectly capable of maintaining order. All contemporaries, whether Royalist or revolutionary, speak of the admirable way in which the *milice bourgeoise* dealt with the situation. " The magistrates assembled at the Hôtel de Ville, and the inhabitants of the several districts," writes Dr. Rigby, " were called together in the churches to deliberate upon the measures proper to be taken. . . . It was resolved that a certain

[1] Bailly, i. 340.   [2] *Ibid.* 367 ; Rivarol, p. 45.
[3] Madelin, p. 65.

number of the more respectable inhabitants should be enrolled and immediately take arms, that the magistrates should sit permanently at the Hôtel de Ville, and that committees, also permanent, should be formed in every district of Paris to convey intelligence to the magistrates and receive instructions from them. This important and most necessary resolution was executed with wonderful promptitude and unexampled good management."

By the evening of the 13th order was, therefore, once more restored throughout the greater part of the city, but unfortunately the ringleaders were as usual left unimpeded to continue the work of insurrection. A few obscure wretches, mere tools of the conspirators, were hanged, having been handed over to justice by the men who had set them in motion, and who now proceeded to work up a fresh agitation at the Palais Royal and other revolutionary centres of the city. Once more the menace of the troops served as a pretext for inflaming the minds of the people, and the fact that throughout the day these same troops had remained completely inactive, had allowed the citizens to arm without resistance and were even now preparing to withdraw from the neighbourhood of Paris, did not prevent this absurd alarm from gaining ground.

Amongst the most energetic of the panic-mongers on this day was a new recruit to the Orléaniste conspiracy, a young lawyer of peculiarly frightful appearance named Georges Jacques Danton, whose eloquence consisted in a form of noisy badinage that rendered him immensely popular at street corners. His massive head and somewhat Kalmuck features lent themselves singularly well to the violence of his oratory, as, now chaffing, now thundering, he kept his audience in good humour—that pleasure-loving Parisian audience that he, essentially the man of pleasure, understood so well.

Another lawyer, Lavaux, entering the convent of the Cordeliers, the centre of one of the new districts of Paris, found a mob orator in frenzied tones calling the citizens to arms in order to resist an army of 30,000 men who were preparing to march on Paris and massacre the inhabitants. Lavaux was surprised to recognize in this panic-monger his old colleague, Danton, and, never doubting his sincerity, took advantage of the orator pausing for breath to assure him that these fears were unfounded—he himself, Lavaux, had just returned from Versailles, where all was quiet. "You do not understand," Danton answered; "the sovereign people have risen against despotism. Be one of us. The throne is overturned and your employment is gone. Think it well over." [1]

[1] *Danton*, by Louis Madelin, p. 19.

There was in Danton a certain frankness that disarmed criticism ; he made no secret of the fact that in the Revolution he saw less the fulfilment of any political aspirations than the opportunity for pleasure and profit.[1] " Young man," he said later on at the Cordeliers to Royer Collard, " come and bellow with us ; when you have made your fortune you can then follow whichever party suits you best." [2]

That Danton was definitely financed by the Duc d'Orléans was not only the belief of his political adversaries but the general opinion of Paris. When in August 1790 he sought election as a " notable " of the Constitutional Commune of Paris, he was reported to be " a paid and perfidious agent of the Duc d'Orléans," and rejected for his venality by forty-two out of forty-eight sections of Paris.[3] Even M. Louis Madelin, who admires Danton, is unable to clear him from this charge : " The most generally received opinion was that the Duc d'Orléans supported Danton. If we admit that he was paid, it is there, I think, that we must seek the principal payer." And he adds this sentence that in a word sums up Danton's political creed : " *Danton was all his life an Orléaniste.*" [4] After such an admission it is idle to accredit Danton with either patriotism or disinterestedness ; that any man who loved his country could sincerely believe he was working for its good in attempting to replace the honest and benevolent Louis XVI. by the corrupt and despotic Duc d'Orléans is inconceivable. The popular conception of Danton as a patriot burning with zeal for liberty and the Republic is therefore based on a fallacy ; Danton was neither a democrat nor a Republican, but a paid agitator of the party who would have instituted a far worse despotism than France had ever before endured.

Already on this 13th of July a triumph had been secured by the conspirators ; the green cockade was discarded as representing the colours of the Comte d'Artois, and red, white, and blue, the livery of the Duc d'Orléans, substituted as the emblem of liberty. The fact that these were also the colours of the town of Paris was a fortunate coincidence that served to veil the manœuvre.[5]

[1] See, amongst many contemporary testimonies, the article on Danton by Beaulieu in the *Biographie Michaud* : " This man had not, like many others, embraced the Revolution as a philosophical speculation ; his views were less elevated. More attached to sensual pleasures, he belonged to that class of intriguers who lend themselves to great upheavals in order to make their fortunes ; sometimes indeed he made no mystery of his projects in this respect."   [2] *Essais de Beaulieu,* iii. 192.

[3] *Études et Leçons sur la Révolution Française,* by Aulard, iv. 134.
[4] *Danton,* by Louis Madelin, p. 48.
[5] Historians of all parties have endeavoured to deny this Orléaniste

Throughout the night that followed the leaders of the conspiracy were at work organizing the insurrection of the morrow. A plan of attack on the Bastille had already been drawn up,[1] it only remained now to set the people in motion. This was to be effected by circulating the news early in the morning that the troops were advancing on the city and that the citizens were to be bombarded from within by the cannons of the Bastille. The members of the " committee of electors " at the Hôtel de Ville were now denounced as traitors to the country,[2] and the death of Flesselles was ordained.[3] A further list of proscriptions included the Comte d'Artois, the Prince de Condé, the Maréchal de Broglie, the Prince de Lambesc, the Baron de Bézenval, Foullon and Berthier,[4] and the people were to be made to carry out these vengeances of the demagogues by the same means that had been employed in the case of Réveillon, that is to say, by affixing to each victim a calumny calculated to rouse the fury of the mob. Thus Broglie, Bézenval, and Lambesc, whose real crime in the eyes of the demagogues was to have ensured the safe transit of supplies into Paris, were to be accused of plotting with " the Court " to massacre the citizens ; Foullon, for whose condemnation we have already seen the reason, was

---

origin of the *tricolore*, but contemporary evidence is strongly in favour of these colours being chosen as those of the duke. Thus Ferrières (*Mem.* i. 119) : " The revolutionaries adopted the cockade made of white, blue and red, it was the livery of the duc d'Orléans." Beaulieu (*Essais*, i. 522) : " Blue, red and white, which are said to be the colours of the town of Paris, but belong just as much to the duc d'Orléans." Lord Dorset (*Dispatches from Paris*, ii. 243) : " Red and white in honour of the duc d'Orléans." Lafayette (*Mem.* iii. 66) speaks of " the strange coincidence that the colours of the town should happen also to be those of the duke." Most convincing of all is the statement of Mrs. Elliott, the duke's mistress, whose sole aim was to exonerate the duke of all complicity in the revolutionary movement (*Journal*, p. 33) : " The mob obliged everybody to wear a green cockade for two days, but afterwards they took red, white and blue, the Orléans livery." Moreover, Camille Desmoulins later on admitted the same : " When patriots needed a rallying sign, could they have done better than to choose the colours of the one who first called us to liberty ? " (*Révolutions de France et de Brabant*, iv. 439).

[1] This important point, which entirely refutes the idea of the march on the Bastille as a spontaneous movement of the people, is admitted even by revolutionary authorities, by *Deux Amis*, i. 313, note : " It is certain that the taking of the Bastille was planned, and that the day before plans of attack had been drawn up." Also Dussaulx, *De l'Insurrection parisienne et de la Prise de la Bastille*, p. 44 : " The taking of the Bastille had been planned. M. le Marquis de la Salle certified to me that the day before he had received for this purpose a plan of attack."

[2] Marmontel, iv. 180; Dussaulx, p. 206 (edition Monin).

[3] Marmontel, iv. 199 ; Bailly, i. 381, 382

[4] *Histoire du Règne de Louis XVI*, by Joseph Droz, p. 293 ; *Histoire de la Révolution*, by Montjoie.

to be declared to have said that " if the people had no bread, they could eat hay " ; his son-in-law, Berthier, whose untiring energy in combating the famine had seriously obstructed the designs of the conspirators, was to be denounced to the people as " a monopolizer of grain," and in the case of Flesselles, whose sole crime was loyalty to the King, a forged note was prepared in order to inflame the minds of the populace.　For the murder of the Comte d'Artois no pretext was needed ; the principal, perhaps the only truly reactionary member of the Royal family, he was already too unpopular to require calumniating, and a placard offering a reward for his head was boldly affixed at the street corners.[1]

It will be seen, therefore, that the motives that inspired the demagogues were totally different from those acted on by the people, and this fact explains the confused and frequently abortive nature of the succeeding revolutionary tumults.　The leaders had planned that the mob should do one thing, and *the mob, not being in the secret*, did another, hence the apparently inexplicable and pointless crimes that took place.　Amongst these, we shall see, was the massacre of the garrison at the Bastille, which had *not* been ordained by the Palais Royal.

THE 14TH OF JULY

Whilst the panic concerning the approach of the troops was thus being prepared, how were these bloodthirsty legions engaged? Bézenval, having waited in vain for orders throughout the whole day of the 13th, decided at one o'clock in the morning of the 14th to retreat to the Champ de Mars and the École Militaire on the other side of the Seine ; and thus at the very moment that the alarm of their advance on the city was trumpeted to the terrified population, the troops were actually moving away to the distance.　This circumstance might have been expected to refute the false alarm in circulation, but the agitators were clever enough to turn it to their own advantage.　The troops were on the move, they told the people, and though they might *appear* to be retreating, this manœuvre was only a question of *reculer pour mieux sauter*—it was evident that De Broglie intended to unite these troops with superior forces in order to make an overwhelming advance on the capital, and reduce it to ashes. Such was the amazing credulity of the Parisians that this ludicrous story was universally believed and once more threw the city into a state of frenzied panic.　The citizens, who yesterday had flown to arms against the brigands, now prepared themselves to do battle with the bloodthirsty troops of the King.[2]

[1] *Essais de Beaulieu*, i. 522.
[2] Montjoie, *Histoire de la Révolution*, p. 87 ; Marmontel, iv. 182.　See

The terror and confusion that prevailed throughout the city was indescribable ; from seven o'clock in the morning of the 14th false alarms succeeded each other without intermission— the Royal Allemand had already encamped at the Barrière du Trône, other regiments had actually entered the Faubourg Saint-Antoine, cannons had been placed across the streets, whilst those on the ramparts of the Bastille were pointing at the city. "At the Palais Royal the most violent motions followed each other with terrifying rapidity ; the most vehement orators, mounted on tables, inflamed the imagination of the audience that crowded around them, and spread itself about the city like the burning lava of a volcano ; inside the houses were seen the distress of husbands and wives, the grief of mothers, the tears of children : and in the midst of this universal confusion the tocsin sounded without interruption at the cathedral, at the palace (the Palais de Justice) and in all the parishes, drums beat the 'générale' in every quarter, false alarms were repeated, and the cry of 'To arms ! To arms !' The machinery of war and desolation, convulsive movements, and the sombre courage of despair—such is the horrible picture that Paris presented on the 14th July."

One might suppose this lurid description to emanate from the pen of an incorrigible reactionary, unable to see in the tumult of the capital the sublime spectacle of a nation rising as one man to oppose tyranny, and representing as agitators those noble orators who called the citizens to arms. Not at all. This account is given by no other than the Two Friends of Liberty themselves, who thus ingenuously disclose the methods used by the revolutionaries to create a panic. For all this terror and confusion, these tears and cries and "movements of despair," *there was no cause whatever* ; the troops at the Champ de Mars remained completely inactive, the Bastille was utterly unprepared for defence, still less for aggression, and the only soldiers in the Faubourg Saint-Antoine were the increasing numbers of deserters from the army, whilst the one real danger—the brigands —had been disarmed and subdued by the *milice bourgeoise*. Thus the whole agitation was the work of the revolutionary leaders who, in order to accomplish their designs, did not scruple to strike terror and dismay into the hearts of the people. What,

---

also *Deux Amis de la Liberté*, ii. 297 : "The regiments encamped in the Champs Élysées *had retired during the darkness*, but their real motive and the place of their retreat was unknown. An attack was expected every moment ; nothing was talked of but the troops that were to come and make an assault on the capital." Historians have almost invariably misrepresented this point, confounding the panic caused by the brigands on the 13th with that caused by the troops on the 14th.

indeed, were the " tears of mothers " or the " cries of children "
to cynics such as Laclos and Chamfort, to the members of the
councils of Montrouge and of Passy, and the agitators of the
Palais Royal, to Danton, Camille Desmoulins, Santerre, and St.
Huruge ? The " people " existed to serve their purpose, not
to inspire their pity.

But how was an unarmed multitude to carry out the attack
on the Bastille ? The disarming of the brigands by the patriotic
citizens the day before had deprived the revolutionary leaders
of their most valuable instruments, and, in order to re-arm these
ragged legions, it was necessary to drive the population once
more to raid the armouries. This was speedily effected, and in
the course of the morning thirty to forty thousand people of all
sorts and conditions, with Théroigne de Méricourt in their midst,
invaded the arsenal of the Invalides and seized every weapon
they could find, whilst the troops in the neighbouring Champs
de Mars—obedient to the order not to shed the blood of the
citizens—offered no resistance. " Famished tigers," say the
Two Friends of Liberty, " fall less rapidly upon their prey."
In the struggle several were suffocated, others killed in their
furious endeavours to wrest the weapons from each other. Such
were the citizens to whom Flesselles was denounced as a traitor
for not delivering arms.

But now the moment had arrived to turn the attention of
the people in the direction of the Bastille, for so far the alarm
of the pointing cannons had created no popular determination
to attack the state prison. A further incentive must therefore
be provided in order to produce the effect desired by the leaders
of a spontaneous movement of the people to overthrow the
monument of despotism. For this purpose a fresh rumour was
circulated by a bandit posted in the crowd collected in the Place
de Grève around the Hôtel de Ville—the arms the people sought
had been conveyed to the Bastille, it was there that they must
go to find them. And at this news a roar arose from the excited
crowd, and from thousands of throats the cry went up, " Let us
go to the Bastille ! "

*   *   *   *   *   *

What was the Bastille, that monument of despotism, at
whose destruction lovers of liberty all over the world rejoiced ?
A grey stone fortress with eight pointed towers, surrounded by
a dry moat and separated by two drawbridges from a gateway
opening into the Rue Saint-Antoine. Over the poor and populous
Faubourg it loomed forbiddingly, a mysterious relic of the past,
holding within its wall many ancient secrets. Yet was it the

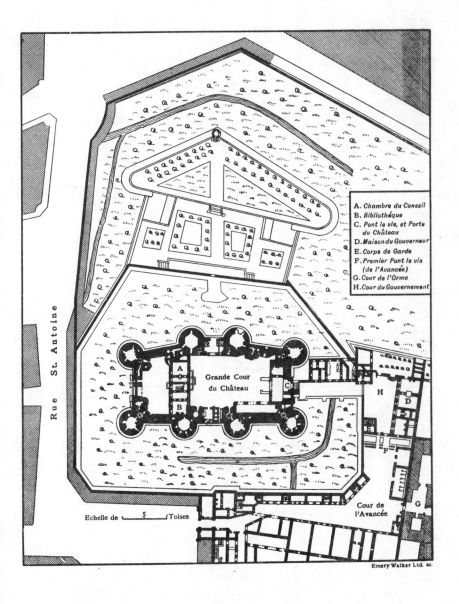

A. *Chambre du Conseil*
B. *Bibliothèque*
C. *Pont le vis, et Porte du Château*
D. *Maison du Gouverneur*
E. *Corps de Garde*
F. *Premier Pont le vis (de l'Avancée)*
G. *Cour de l'Orme*
H. *Cour du Gouvernement*

Rue St. Antoine

Grande Cour
du Château

H
D
F
G

Cour de l'Avancée

Echelle de 5 Toises

Emery Walker Ltd. sc.

place of horror it has been represented ? In order to realize how far its evil reputation was merited in its day we must compare it with other prisons of the period. Now if we consult the report of the philanthropic John Howard on the *State of the Prisons* all over Europe, published in 1792, we shall find that the prisons of France in the reign of Louis XVI. compared very favourably with those of other countries. In England, Howard tells us he saw prisoners during the years 1774, 1775, and 1776 " pining under diseases, expiring on the floors in loathsome cells, of pestilential fevers," half starved and in rags ; in some gaols they occupied " subterranean dungeons, of which the floor was very damp, with sometimes an inch or two of water." Even women were loaded with heavy irons. Many of these unhappy creatures were, moreover, innocent, being detained in prison a year before trial. When Elizabeth Fry visited Newgate over thirty years later, matters had not improved very appreciably. All this, however, was due less to deliberate cruelty than to the carelessness that characterized our forefathers, and is not to be compared with the deliberate brutality exercised in German prisons. Howard, on visiting Germany, was taken down into " a black torture chamber round which hung various instruments of torture, some stained with blood. When the criminals suffer the candles are lighted, for the windows are shut close, to prevent their cries being heard abroad."

In France, Howard found active reforms being carried out in the prison system. " The King's declaration . . . dated the 30th of August 1780, contains some of the most humane and enlightened sentiments respecting the conduct of prisons. It mentions the construction of airy and spacious infirmaries for the sick . . . a total abolition of underground dungeons." Howard had, unfortunately, not provided himself with a permit to visit the Bastille, and so was unable to gain admission,[1] yet in one sentence he sums up the feeling that the state prison inspired in the minds of contemporaries : " In this castle all is mystery, trick, artifice, snare, and treachery."

Imagine an old house where, at the end of a long passage, a black door was to be found, locked and bolted, through which one might not pass, leading into a room that held a secret of some strange and terrible kind, known only to the owner of the house ; then picture the wild imaginings to which the mystery would give rise, the children hurrying past with

---

[1] Visitors were admitted on a permit to the Bastille. " M. Howard could, therefore, have obtained admittance like any one else—he had taken no steps to obtain permission to enter and was sent away, so he was only able to speak of the facts he had collected on the subject " (*Bastille dévoilée,* 2ième Livraison (1789), p. 13).

bated breath, the servants whispering their suspicions to the village, conjuring up monstrous theories of what was to be found there.

Thus the Bastille at the end of the Rue Saint-Antoine, with its grim portals and its eight grey towers, provided a perpetual matter of speculation to imaginative minds; and if at times the preposterously thick doors with their gigantic locks opened to admit the curious, they suspected that much was still concealed from them. Down below those stone floors, hidden from the light of day, were there not subterranean dungeons, "the resort of toads, of lizards, of monstrous rats and spiders," where the victims of despotism "pined in darkness and solitude" until the mind gave way, so that when at last deliverance came, the prisoner had passed beyond all human aid? Worse still, were there not dreadful torture-chambers, iron cages eight feet long, in which unhappy captives were confined, and, beneath the masonry of those stone walls, the mouldering skeletons of men done to death secretly at dead of night? Most gruesome of all was the story of the *chambre des oubliettes*, a room of outwardly smiling aspect, scented with flowers, and lit by fifty candles. Here the unsuspecting prisoner was led before the governor and promised his liberty. But the human monster who presided over the destinies of the captives waited only to see the rapture of his victim before giving a signal at which the floor opened, and the wretched man fell upon a wheel of knives and was torn to pieces.[1]

Such is the legend of the Bastille, perpetuated by Louis Blanc and Michelet, and in our country by Carlyle and Dickens, but which rests on no shadow of a foundation. It should be noted that it was not amongst the people that the legend arose; "the people," says Mercier, "dread the Châtelet more than the Bastille; they are not afraid of the latter because it does not concern them, consequently they hardly pity those imprisoned there." Such awe as it inspired in them, such curiosity as it aroused in their minds, had therefore been instilled in them by the men whose wealth or talents or importance entitled them to *lettres de cachet*—the tickets of admission to the Bastille. The State Prison, known ironically to contemporaries as the "Hôtel des Gens de Lettres," was almost exclusively reserved for people suspected of designs against the State, for conspirators, forgers, writers of obscene books or seditious pamphlets whose lively imaginations threw a lurid light over their experiences. Of these, the most vehement in their denunciations were Latude and Linguet, both, as M. Funck Brentano and M. Edmond Biré have proved, unscrupulous liars whose testimony is refuted not

[1] *Deux Amis*, i. 375.

merely by the statements of other prisoners, but by the still existing archives of the Bastille.

Researches also made by M. Alfred Begis, M. Victorien Sardou, M. Victor Fournel, M. Ravaisson, and M. Gustave Bord have unanimously revealed the fact that under Louis XVI. the Bastille, though dreadful merely as a place of captivity, bore no resemblance to its legendary counterpart. The damp, dark dungeons had fallen into complete disuse ; since the first ministry of Necker in 1776, no one had ever been imprisoned there. All the rooms were provided with windows, and either stoves or fireplaces, good beds, and furniture, whilst the prisoners were allowed to occupy themselves in various ways—with books, music, drawing, and so on—and in certain cases to meet in each other's rooms for games. The food was excellent and plentiful ; many of the menus recorded by prisoners would tantalize the palate of an epicure, and this was so even under Louis XV., when De Renneville, in a pamphlet written after his release with the object of denouncing the Bastille, admitted that " certain people had themselves imprisoned there in order to enjoy good cheer without expense." [1]

Yet, for all these amenities, the abolition of the Bastille as a place of *arbitrary imprisonment* was undoubtedly desired by the nation, and had been demanded by the cahiers of the noblesse as well as of the Tiers États. The request was made, moreover, in no spirit of sedition ; the King was confidently appealed to, in virtue of his well-known humanity, to demolish this relic of bygone tyranny.

As early as 1784 the architect Corbet had published the *Plan of a Public Square to the Glory of Louis XVI. on the Site of the Bastille*, and this scheme was being openly discussed in 1789. Moreover, in the Séance Royale on June 23, Louis XVI. had again proposed the abolition of *lettres de cachet*, thereby, as M. Biré points out, sounding the knell of the Bastille.

The destruction of the Bastille by force was therefore needless from the point of view of the nation as a whole, but necessary to the designs of the revolutionary leaders, firstly, because it deprived the King of the glory of destroying it ; secondly, because it served as a pretext for an insurrection ; thirdly, because it exercised a restraining influence over the Faubourg Saint-Antoine ; and fourthly, because its continued existence was a menace to their personal security. The State Prison must be demolished instantly if they were to make sure of not expiating their crimes within its precincts.

This was the task the people were to be worked up to by terror to perform. It is evident, however, that no intention of this

[1] *De l'Inquisition Française ou Histoire de la Bastille*, 1724.

kind existed in their minds when the march on the Bastille began.[1]
On this point all reliable contemporaries are agreed—*the idea of
" the people" rising as one man to overthrow the " monument of
despotism" is a fiction; the greater proportion of the crowd that
marched on the Bastille were animated by one motive only—that of
procuring arms for their protection.*[2]   " It was not," says M.
Funck Brentano, " a question of liberty or of tyranny, of delivering prisoners or of protesting against authority. The taking of the
Bastille was carried on to the cries of ' Vive le Roi ! ' ' March,'
said the women to their men, ' it is for the King and country ! ' "[3]

*   *   *   *   *   *

Whilst the honest citizens, animated by no sanguinary intentions, thus prepared to march on the Bastille, what was the
disposition of the Governor, De Launay ? It is amusing to
compare the fiction circulated amongst the populace with the
reality recorded by the colleagues of De Launay.   " Despotism,"
say the Two Friends of Liberty, " threatened us from the ramparts of the Bastille.   De Launay, worthy minister of its vengeance, was entrusted with the care of its fearful dungeons,
shuddering at the very name of liberty, trembling lest, with the
tears of his victims, the gold that was the object of his desires,
the price of their torments and of his brutality, should cease :
the cowardly and avaricious satellite of tyranny had long been
surrounding himself with arms and cannons.   Since the insurrection of the Faubourg Saint-Antoine (the Affaire Réveillon) he
had been unceasingly engaged in preparations for defence. . . ."[4]
The truth was that De Launay had reduced the other officers
to desperation by his unpreparedness.   In vain Bézenval had
warned him that the castle was unfit to resist the attack ; in vain
De Flue, the captain of the Swiss contingent, sent to reinforce
the garrison on July 7, urged him to take measures of defence.
" From the day of my arrival," says De Flue, " I learnt to know
this man ; by the meaningless preparations he made for the
defence of his post, and by his continual anxiety and irresolution,
I saw clearly that we should be ill commanded if we were attacked.
He was so overcome with terror that at night he took for enemies

---

[1] " This resolution (to attack the Bastille) appeared sudden and un-
expected amongst the people, but it was premeditated in the councils of
the Revolutionary leaders " (Marmontel, iv. 187).
" There is every reason to conclude, by the false reports and alarms
that were circulated everywhere, that it was desired to keep up, to increase
the agitation, and lead to the siege of the Bastille " (Bailly, i. 375).
[2] " They went to the Bastille, but only to get arms and munitions "
(Dussaulx, p. 211, edition Monin).
[3] *Précis exacte du Cousin Jacques.*
[4] *Deux Amis,* i. 306.

the shadows of trees and other surrounding objects. . . ." [1]   Even
M. Flammermont is obliged to admit the pacific intentions of the
Governor : " One sees that De Flue cannot understand the
weakness of poor De Launay. For him, a soldier by profession
and a foreigner, the besiegers are simply enemies—' Feinde '—
this is the word he constantly applies to them ; *whilst the Governor
no doubt saw in them citizens whose blood he feared to shed* even in
the defence of the fortress confided to his care." [2]

This tribute from a writer whose sole object is to glorify the
besiegers of the Bastille effectually disposes of the theory of De
Launay as the instrument of despotism. In fact, as all evidence
proves, he did everything in his power to settle matters by peaceful arbitration. When at ten o'clock in the morning of the 14th
a deputation of three citizens arrived at the Bastille to complain
that "the cannons on the ramparts were pointing in the direction of
the Faubourg Saint-Antoine "—a position they had always occupied [3]—De Launay received them with his customary urbanity
and invited them to breakfast with him. The cannons, he assured
them, should be drawn back in their embrasures ; the embrasures
themselves should be boarded over to soothe the alarms of the
people. No injury whatever should be done to the Faubourg
Saint-Antoine, and in return he hoped that the inhabitants would
refrain from aggression.

The deputies lingered so long at De Launay's hospitable board
that the crowd of citizens who had followed them, and were
waiting meanwhile in the outer court, began to grow impatient.
The sight of the cannons being drawn back in their embrasures
added further to their excitement, and it was immediately
concluded that this movement had been made for the purpose
of charging the guns with balls.

De Launay and the three deputies were still at breakfast
when a second deputation arrived from the district surrounding
the Bastille, headed by M. Thuriot de la Rozière, and again
followed by a crowd. De la Rozière was admitted to the
Governor's apartments opposite the entrance to the courtyard
of the prison, and as soon as the three former deputies had
departed he addressed De Launay in these words :

" I come, sir, in the name of the nation and of the country to
represent to you that the cannons placed on the towers of the
Bastille are a cause of great anxiety and spread alarm throughout

[1] *La Journée du 14 Juillet*, by Jules Flammermont, p. lxviii.
[2] *Ibid.* p. lxix.
[3] " If cannons were perceived on the battlements it was because they
were habitually used for firing salutes on fête-days : since the far-off Fronde
no balls had been fired from them. The Faubourg saw them every morning, but such was the popular excitement that this morning they seemed to
assume a threatening aspect " (Madelin, p. 66).

Paris. I beg you to have them taken down, and I hope you will acquiesce with the demand I have been ordered to make to you." De Launay may not have been lion-hearted, but to this proposition he had the courage to reply : " That is not in my power ; these cannons have been on the towers from time immemorial and I cannot take them down without an order from the King. Already informed of the alarm they cause in Paris but unable to be taken off their mountings, I have had them drawn back from their embrasures."

No governor of a fortress could possibly make a more pacific reply, but it did not satisfy De la Rozière, who now requested De Launay to admit him to the prison. To this the Governor at first demurred, but finally allowed himself to be over-persuaded by Major de Losme, the most humane and broad-minded of all the officers at the Bastille, known as the " Consoler of the Prisoners," and the very antithesis of the despotic De Flue.

The Governor having led De la Rozière over the smaller drawbridge into the courtyard of the Bastille, they found the Swiss Guard, some of the Invalides, and all the officers assembled there, whereupon De la Rozière proceeded to appeal to them " in the name of honour, of the nation, and of their country, to change the direction of the cannons and to surrender."

It is difficult here to recognize the " ferocious De Launay shuddering at the very name of liberty " : for at this open defiance of his authority he joined De la Rozière in making the soldiers swear that they would not fire or make use of their arms unless they were attacked.[1]

De la Rozière, however, not content with this assurance, insisted on wasting more time by going up to inspect the battlements, whilst the people outside grew more and more impatient and excited. De Launay, who had accompanied him, now looked forth from the heights of the Bastille and saw for the first time the large and threatening multitude that completely blocked the end of the Rue Saint-Antoine and was beginning to penetrate into the outer courtyard of the prison. At this sight, it is said, the Governor grew pale ; the thing he had long dreaded had come to pass : the people were marching on the Bastille. Was it cowardice that whitened the cheek of the unfortunate Governor ? It seems unlikely ; De Launay was provided with formidable measures of defence—" fifteen cannons bordered the towers, and three field-pieces were placed in the great courtyard opposite the entrance gate presenting a certain death to those bold enough to attack it. Ammunition, moreover, was not

---

[1] " On the provocation of the Governor himself the officers and soldiers swore that they would not fire and would not make use of their arms unless they were attacked " (*Bastille dévoilée*, ii. 91).

wanting. . . ." Why, then, should the Governor tremble ? Could he not, with a few volleys from his guns, sweep both street and courtyard clear of the encroaching multitude ? This was, however, precisely the course he feared to take, so he found himself in the dilemma that faced all upholders of the royal authority throughout the Revolution—the necessity for repressing violence, coupled with a dread of shedding the blood of the people. The power was all in their hands, but they feared to use it, and this fear—the outcome of the philosophy of the age, increased by a knowledge of the King's humanity—paralysed the arm of law and order, and gave to the revolutionaries an immense advantage. This, then, was the fear that caused De Launay to grow pale, and that, according to De Flue, would have made him surrender the castle had not De Flue and the other officers represented to him that he could not thus betray his trust to his royal master.[1]

When at last De la Rozière left the castle it was too late to stem the rising tide, and a short half-hour later the armed crowd arrived on the scene. This crowd that we have already seen setting forth for the purpose of obtaining arms had now, however, been reinforced by other elements, which it is important to distinguish if we would attempt to understand the chaotic movement that followed.

First of all, then, there were the honest citizens who desired arms for their defence ; secondly, the revolutionary leaders, the ferocious Maillard, Théroigne de Méricourt, and Jourdan, later to be known as " Coupe-tête," all determined to accept no pacific measures but to destroy the castle ; thirdly, the motley crew of " brigands " not in the secret of the leaders, thirsting for violence, consisting not only of the aforesaid Marseillais and Italians, but also, according to Marat, of large numbers of *Germans*,[2] presumably deserters from the royal troops ; fourthly and lastly, the crowds of merely curious who longed to explore the innermost recesses of the Bastille, to see for themselves the ghastly torture-chamber, the iron cages and the oubliettes, and bring to light the many nameless and unhappy prisoners lingering forgotten in dark dungeons down below.

This tumultuous and heterogeneous mob, armed with guns, sabres, and hatchets, now surged into the outer courtyard (the Cour de l'Avancée) shouting, " We want the Bastille ! Down with the troops ! "

---

[1] *La Journée du 14 Juillet*, p. cxcviii.

[2] " The Bastille, ill defended, was taken by a few soldiers and a troop of wretches, mostly Germans and also provincials. The Parisians—those eternal idlers (*ces éternels badauds*)—appeared at the fortress, but curiosity alone brought them there to visit the dark dungeons of which the mere idea froze them with terror " (Marat, *Ami du Peuple*, No. 530).

The besiegers were, however, confronted by the raised draw-bridge known as the Pont de l'Avancée opening into the Cour du Gouvernement, and beyond that by the second drawbridge leading into the castle itself. Two men, Tournay and Bonne-mère,[1] thereupon climbed to the roof of the shop of M. Riquet, a perfumer, and by this means reached the wall surrounding the moat of the Bastille. Sitting astride on the top they managed to work themselves along to the Corps des Gardes by the side of the drawbridge, and the amazing point is that the garrison allowed them to do this without firing a shot, contenting them-selves merely with shouting warnings from the battlements,[2] and this conciliatory attitude was maintained even when the two men proceeded to cut through the chains of the drawbridge " de l'Avancée," which fell with a terrific crash, killing one man in the crowd and wounding another. Instantly the whole mob rushed forward into the Cour du Gouvernement, and now for the first time the garrison, anxious to prevent their attacking the second drawbridge, opened a fire of musketry, scattering the people in all directions, and finally driving them back into the outer courtyard. This was the incident which gave rise to the legend that De Launay, having let down the drawbridge and enticed the people into the Cour du Gouvernement, treacher-ously opened fire on them.

Around this treachery—the first of the two with which De Launay was accused during the siege of the Bastille—contro-versy raged for over a century, but responsible French historians are now agreed that the incident occurred as it is here described.[3]

The most convincing proof in favour of De Launay lies perhaps in the inexpediency of such a manœuvre. If he would not make use of the legitimate means of defence at his disposal, why should he resort to treachery and thereby needlessly enrage the people ? Had he wished to carry death and destruction into their ranks he had only to fire any of his fifteen cannons from the ramparts. There was no necessity to entice them within range of musketry fire.

---

[1] *Bastille dévoilée*, ii. 92 ; *Deux Amis*, i. 317. The citizens of the Fau-bourg Saint-Antoine gave their names as Davanne and Demain, but M. Flammermont (p. ccv, *note*) and M. Victor Fournel, *Les Hommes du 14 Juillet*, p. 216, accept the former statement.

[2] Even the Two Friends of Liberty admit this : " Two men . . . get up on to the roof of the guard-house in spite of the cries and threats of the garrison of the fortress." See also *Bastille dévoilée*, ii. 93 ; Marmontel, iv. 191. M. Flammermont's assertion that they acted under the fire of the garrison is therefore contrary not only to evidence, but to probability, for, considering the slow rate at which they must have progressed, they would have proved an easy target had the garrison chosen to fire.

[3] " This pretended treachery of De Launay, which was immediately noised all over Paris . . . is disproved not only by the accounts of the

It is easy, however, to understand the misunderstanding that gave rise to the story of De Launay's treachery. The rear-guard of the crowd, seeing the fall of the drawbridge, the onrush of the people in the front, and then the fire directed on them from the battlements, could not know by what means the draw-bridge had been let down, and immediately concluded that the order had been given by De Launay so as to lure the people on to their destruction. The cry of treachery having once been uttered, the agitators, mingling in the crowd, saw their oppor-tunity to fan the flame of popular fury, and messengers were despatched all over Paris to circulate the news of De Launay's hideous perfidy. At the Hôtel de Ville it raised a storm of indignation, and a further deputation was sent to the Bastille to inquire of M. de Launay whether he " would be disposed to receive into the château the troops of the Parisian militia, who would guard it with the troops already stationed there and who would be under the orders of the town." But when the deputa-tion arrived, the fusillade going on between the garrison and the besiegers made it impossible to communicate with the Governor, and in the frightful uproar that now prevailed the white handkerchiefs waved by the deputies in sign of truce passed unperceived. A second deputation, armed this time with a flag and drum, succeeded, however, in attracting the attention of the Governor and officers on the battlements, who replied by inviting the deputies to come forward, but to persuade the crowd to keep back. At the same moment a subordinate officer on the ramparts, to prove the good faith of the garrison, reversed his gun in sign of peace, and this example was followed by his comrades, who called out loudly to the crowd, " Have no fear, we will not fire, stay where you are. Bring forward your flag and your deputies. The Governor will come down and speak to you."

But here another misunderstanding occurred which gave rise to the story of a second treachery on the part of De Launay,

---

besieged but of the besiegers themselves, and is rejected to-day by all historians " (Funck Brentano, *Légendes et Archives de la Bastille*, p. 256). M. Flammermont admits with regard to this accusation : " All that is false." Even M. Louis Blanc with a rare impulse of fairness absolves De Launay from this charge : " Such was the confusion that the greater number (of the crowd) were not aware under what intrepid effort the chains of the first bridge had been broken ; they believed that the Governor him-self had given the order to let it down in order to entice the multitude and more easily to make carnage amongst them. . . . De Launay was capable of having given the order to fire but not of having committed the perfidious atrocity imputed to him, and justice demands that his memory should be openly cleared of it " (*Histoire de la Révolution*, ii. 381). In spite of all this evidence the story of De Launay's treachery is persistently repeated by nearly every English writer.

for just as the deputies were about to advance, a man in the crowd—obviously an agitator posted there to prevent arbitration—started a fresh alarm that one of the cannons was pointing at the people, and immediately every one took up the cry and urged the deputies not to trust the " perfidious promises " of the garrison.[1] The deputies thereupon retreated into the Cour de l'Orme and remained standing there for a quarter of an hour, disregarding the shouts of the garrison urging them to advance. De Launay, now convinced that the signals of peace were merely a ruse to obtain admittance to the castle by treachery, remarked to his officers : " You must perceive, messieurs, that these deputies and this flag cannot belong to the town ; the flag is certainly one that the people have seized and which they are using to surprise us. If they were really deputies they would not have hesitated, considering the promise you made them, to come and declare to me the intentions of the Hôtel de Ville ! "[2]

Then, since the crowd continued to fire at the garrison, the garrison once more returned their fire, and the battle continued with redoubled violence. The story of this second treachery of De Launay was again circulated through Paris—the Governor, it was said, had replied to the flag of truce with signs of peace and, the deputies having confidingly advanced, the garrison had discharged a volley of musketry, killing several people at their side. Around this point again controversy has raged, but all reliable evidence proves that the second accusation of treachery was as unfounded as the first,[3] for on two points all accounts agree—the deputies did not advance and the crowd continued without interruption to fire on the garrison.

Moreover, to this second charge of treachery, as to the first,

---

[1] *Deux Amis*, i. 325.

[2] " Récit des Assiégés," *Deux Amis*, i. 321 ; *Bastille dévoilée*, ii. 97.

[3] The legend was repeated at the time by a great number of writers, including even Lord Dorset, who was not present at the siege, and whose account is inaccurate in nearly every point. It is refuted, however, not only by Montjoie, Beaulieu, and Marmontel, but by the principal revolutionary authorities—*Bastille dévoilée* (ii. 99) ; Dussaulx, p. 219 (edition Monin) : " In order to have the right on all these points, to accuse the Governor and his garrison of perfidy one would have to be very certain that they saw and recognized the signals of the deputies, and if they did indeed perceive them it must be admitted that it was impossible for them to cease action whilst the fire of the besiegers continued, and whilst they were being shot at not only from the foot of the fortress but from the tops of the neighbouring houses." Beaulieu explains the situation by stating that a part of the garrison—that is to say the Invalides—were on the side of the people, and that it was they who signed to them to advance, whilst the rest—the Swiss—were for holding out, and it was they who fired. This is the view taken by Louis Blanc (ii. 385), who also in this instance denies De Launay's treachery. " No historian any longer admits this legend," says M. Louis Madelin.

the same line of reasoning may be applied—what object could De Launay possibly have for needlessly infuriating the people, though still at this stage of the siege he refused to open fire on them from the cannons? Further, why should he fire on a deputation when we know from the evidence of his officers that he would have seized any opportunity to capitulate, and that it was mainly at the instance of the Swiss De Flue that he continued the siege? [1] Obviously, as Beaulieu remarks, " there was no treachery, but only a frightful confusion."

At the Hôtel de Ville the news of De Launay's latest perfidy roused a fresh storm of indignation, and the wildest rumours were circulated amongst the crowd assembled in the Place de Grève. Now, amongst the groups of citizens angrily discussing the situation, there moved a tall young man, who listened eagerly to all that was said, and at last entering into the conversation heard of the " massacre of citizens " that was taking place at the Bastille. This young man was Pierre Hulin, the manager of a laundry on the outskirts of Paris ; he had come into Paris early that morning on business, and, finding a crowd assembled in the Place de Grève, he joined it at the precise moment that the news of De Launay's second treachery had set all minds aflame. Hulin, who was a brave man, unconnected with any intrigue, shared the general indignation, and seeing that his handsome countenance and commanding appearance had evidently found favour with the multitude, he turned and addressed them in these spirited words :

" My friends, are you citizens ? Let us march on the Bastille ! Our friends, our brothers, are being massacred. I will expose you to no chances, but if there are risks to run, I will be the first to run them, and I swear to you on my honour that I will bring you back victorious or you will bring me back dead ! " [2]

The people, taking this courageous and eloquent young man to be at least an officer, immediately rallied around him, and the whole Place de Grève resounded with the cry, " You shall be our commander ! "

Hulin accepted and found himself at the head of an army by no means contemptible ; here were grenadiers of Ruffeville, fusiliers of the company of Lubersac, a host of bourgeois, and three cannons, and these on their way to the Bastille were reinforced by several Invalides and two more cannons.

In this second start for the Bastille there was undeniably a strong element of heroism ; these men setting forth, burning with indignation at a supposed outrage on their fellow-citizens,

---

[1] *Bastille dévoilée*, ii. 127, 128. See also account by De Flue in *Revue Retrospective*.
[2] Montjoie, *Hist. de la Révolution*, xlv. 110 ; *Deux Amis*, i. 327.

are in no way to be confounded with the brigands who had preceded them. To attack the fortress, which at this moment they honestly regarded as the stronghold of tyranny, belching forth fire and smoke on all those who attempted to approach it, was indeed a brave adventure that required no little personal courage and self-sacrifice. The fact that all the commotion was based on a misunderstanding does not detract from the gallantry of the enterprise. The incident is all the more remarkable in that *it was the one and only occasion in the history of the Revolution when a crowd was led by a true man of the people*, and not by the professional agitators or their tools. Hulin was a noble and disinterested man, and, as we shall see, proved himself worthy of the confidence the people had placed in him.

This formidable contingent with their five cannons, Hulin marching at the head of the bourgeois, sergeants leading the Gardes Françaises, arrived at the Bastille by way of the Arsenal to find a scene of indescribable confusion. The crowd, infuriated by De Launay's supposed treachery, had bethought themselves of a plan for burning down his house by wheeling wagon-loads of straw into the Cour du Gouvernement and setting light to them. The brigands in the crowd, not content with inanimate objects on which to vent their fury, seized on a pretty girl, Mlle. de Monsigny, the daughter of a captain of the Invalides, whom they took to be the daughter of De Launay, and by signs intimated to the garrison that they would burn her alive if the castle were not surrendered. The girl, who was little more than a child, fainted with terror, and was dragged unconscious on to a heap of straw. M. de Monsigny, seeing this from the towers of the castle, rushed to his daughter's rescue, but was knocked down by two shots from the besiegers, and the horrible crime was only averted by the bravery of Aubin Bonnemère—he who had cut the chains of the drawbridge—and who now succeeded in carrying the girl away to a place of safety.

It is difficult to reconstruct the exact order of events at this point of the siege, but it would seem that the arrival of Hulin and the army with cannons coincided with the setting light to the wagon-loads of straw, and that at this moment the first and only charge was fired from one of the cannons of the Bastille. According to Montjoie the discharge was made when the garrison perceived the cannons of the besiegers arriving on the scene; according to the Two Friends of Liberty it followed on the attempt to set fire to the Governor's house; but on one point all authorities are agreed—*the Bastille had fifteen cannons, and during the whole siege one was fired once.*[1] No further proof is needed of

[1] *Bastille dévoilée*, ii. 101 *note*, 121; *Deux Amis*, i. 326; Montjoie, *Histoire de la Révolution de France*, xlv. 112; Marmontel, iv. 193.

De Launay's humanity : had he chosen to make use of the means within his power, even the authors of the *Bastille dévoilée* are obliged to admit, he could have swept the courtyard clear of assailants : " If the platform of the great bridge had been lowered, and the three cannons charged with grape-shot in the courtyard had been fired, what carnage would not have been made ? " [1] But now the artillery of the besiegers being brought into play, the confusion reached its height : the roar of the cannons and the rattle of musketry mingled with the howls of the mob, whilst the smoke of the burning wagon-loads of straw blinded and neaily suffocated the besiegers. A brave soldier, Élie, of the Queen's Infantry, assisted by a " muscular and intrepid linen-draper, Réole," at the risk of their lives dashed into the flames and removed the wagons, thereby clearing the atmosphere, but in no way quieting the pandemonium. On all sides men were falling dead and dying to the ground, but most of these casualties were caused, not by the fire of the Bastille, but by the crowd itself who, not knowing how to load the cannon, were killed by the recoil or were fired on by each other. Hulin had succeeded, however, in destroying by gunfire the chains of the drawbridge de l'Avancée, whereupon the whole mob pressed forward once more into the Cour du Gouvernement, and two cannons were mounted opposite the second drawbridge leading into the Bastille itself.

This movement seems to have entirely deranged De Launay ; obliged to choose, and choose immediately, between the shame of surrender and the wholesale massacre of the people by cannon fire, he was indeed between the devil and the deep sea, and it is said that, unable to decide on either course, he now resolved on the desperate measure of setting light to the powder magazine and blowing up the castle. But two Invalides, Becquard and Ferrand, restrained his hand, thereby saving both besiegers and besieged from total destruction.

One thing is certain, the garrison made almost no defence. " I was present at the siege of the Bastille," says the Chancelier Pasquier, " and the so-cal ed combat was not serious ; the resistance shown was practically nil. . . . A few shots from guns were fired (by the besiegers) to which no reply was made, then four or five cannon shots. . . . What I did see perfectly was the action of the soldiers, Invalides and others, ranged on the platform of the high tower, raising the butts of their rifles in the air, and expressing by every means used under such circumstances the wish to surrender." [2]

---

[1] *Bastille dévoilée*, ii. 126 ; Montjoie, *ibid.* xlv. 112.

[2] See also *Bastille dévoilée*, ii. 121 : " The garrison, so to speak, made no resistance." Georget, one of the besieging gunners, expressed the same opinion

It is evident, as Beaulieu says, that the garrison were divided, the Swiss, with De Flue at their head, urging the Governor to continue the siege, and the Invalides, whose sympathies were with the people, begging him to capitulate.[1] At last De Launay, yielding to the entreaties of the latter, ordered two of his men to go up to the battlements with a drum and a white flag of truce. No flag was forthcoming, but the Governor's handkerchief was hoisted on a staff, and with this banner the men paraded the towers of the prison for a quarter of an hour. The people, however, continued to fire, and replied to the overtures of the garrison with cries of "Down with the bridges! No capitulation!"

De Launay then retired to the Salle de Conseil and wrote a desperate message to the besiegers : "We have twenty thousand weight of powder ; we shall blow up the garrison and the whole district if you do not accept the capitulation."

In vain De Flue represented to De Launay that this terrible expedient was wholly needless, that the gates of the fortress were still intact, that means of defence were not lacking, that the garrison had suffered the loss of only one man killed and two wounded—the note was handed to a Swiss, who passed it through a hole in the raised drawbridge to the crowd beyond. The besiegers gathered on the stone bridge at the other side of the moat were at first unable to reach it, but a plank was fetched, a man in the crowd came forward, walked along it, fell into the moat and was killed instantly. A second man followed—according to one report Élie, according to another Maillard—and this time the slip of paper was safely conveyed to the people. At the words, read aloud by Élie, a confused cry arose, "Down with the bridges!" but whilst some added, "No harm shall be done you," others continued to shout, "No capitulation!" But Élie answered loudly, "On the word of an officer no one shall be injured; we accept your capitulation; let down your bridges!"

On the strength of this promise De Launay gave up the key of the smaller drawbridge, the bridge was let down, and the leaders of the people—Élie, Hulin, Tournay, Maillard, Réole, Arné, and Humbert—entered the castle. The next moment an unknown hand inside the courtyard of the prison lowered the great drawbridge, and instantly the immense crowd poured on to it and with a mighty rush surged forward into the Bastille. Whose was the hand that did the deed? No one to this day knows for certain. De Launay had not intended

---

[1] "The Swiss exhorted the Governor to resist, but the staff and the non-commissioned officers strongly urged him to surrender the fortress" (*Deux Amis*, ii. 333).

admitting the crowd before parleying with the leaders, and it seems probable that the bridge was treacherously lowered by certain of the Invalides who were in collusion with the people.[1]

If so, they paid dearly for their cowardice ; for the mob, according to the habit of mobs, did not pause to discriminate, but fell upon the Invalides with fury, leaving the Swiss to escape unharmed.

Meanwhile Élie and his comrades approached the Governor, who was standing with his staff in the great courtyard dressed in a grey coat, with a poppy-coloured ribbon in his buttonhole, and holding in his hand a gold-headed sword-stick. According to certain accounts Maillard, or a man named Degain, thereupon seized him, crying out, " You are the Governor of the Bastille." Legris addressed him brutally.[2] Marmontel shows a nobler picture of this dramatic moment :

" Élie entered with his companions, all brave men and thoroughly determined to keep their word. Seeing this the Governor came up to him, embraced him, and presented him with his sword and the keys of the Bastille." " I refused his sword," Élie told Marmontel, " I only accepted the keys." Élie's companions greeted the staff and officers of the castle with the same cordiality, swearing to act as their guard and their defence.[3] Hulin, too, kissed the unfortunate Governor, promising to save his life, and De Launay returning the embrace, pressed the hand of Hulin, saying, " I trust to you, brave man, and I am your prisoner."

But though these pioneers showed themselves magnanimous, " those that followed them breathed only carnage and vengeance," for at the fall of the great drawbridge it was the brigands armed with forks and hatchets who first penetrated into the castle, leaving the soldiers who had carried on the siege at the other side of the moat. This horrible crowd gathered so threateningly around the Governor that Élie, Hulin, and Arné resolved to lead him out of the castle to the Hôtel de Ville. At the risk of their lives the little procession started out, Élie carrying the

---

[1] " An Invalide came to open the door situated behind the drawbridge and asked what they wanted. ' That the Bastille should be surrendered,' they replied. Then he let them in " (Deux Amis, i. 337). " I was very much surprised . . . to see four Invalides approach the door, open them, and let down the bridges " (Relation de de Flue, Flammermont, ccxxxv.).

[2] " Récit de Pitra," La Journée du 14 Juillet, p. 48 ; Montjoie, Hist. de la Révolution, xlv. 115.

[3] Marmontel, iv. 194. " The ones who entered first approach the vanquished with humanity, throw their arms round the necks of the staff officers as a sign of peace and reconciliation, and take possession of the fortress as surrendered by capitulation " (Deux Amis, i. 338).

capitulation on the point of his sword, Hulin and Arné following with De Launay held between them.

Thus began the terrible journey to the Place de Grève; fighting every inch of the way, the two heroic men led their prisoner, receiving on their heads and shoulders the blows of the multitude. All through the seething Rue Saint-Antoine Hulin never left the arm of De Launay; struck at, fired at, insulted, he struggled forward; once, fearing that the bare head of the Governor exposed him to danger, Hulin quickly covered it with his own hat, but the next instant nearly fell himself a victim to the fury of the populace. Three times the people tore De Launay from his arms, and three times Hulin wrenched him from their clutches with torn garments and blood streaming from his face. De Launay, wounded from head to foot, pale but resolute, " with head held high and a still proud eye," made no complaint, uttered not a single murmur, only when the crowd had again hurled themselves upon him, and Hulin once more dashing into the fray had caught him in his arms and borne him from their midst, the old man pressed him to his heart and cried, " You are my saviour. Only a little more strength and courage. . . . Stay with me as far as the Hôtel de Ville." And turning to Élie he exclaimed, " Is this the safety you promised me ? Ah, sir, do not leave me."

But Hulin's strength was now rapidly failing him. The interminable journey was almost ended; they had reached the Arcade de St. Jean—only forty steps onward to the Hôtel de Ville and safety. But even as they entered the Place de Grève a furious horde of brigands bore down on the procession, and once more De Launay was torn from the arms of his protectors, whilst this time Hulin, utterly exhausted, sank upon a heap of stones— or, according to another account, was dragged there by the hair and flung down senseless. When again he opened his eyes it was to see the head of De Launay raised on a pike amidst the savage cries of his murderers.

" I have seen the Sieur Hulin more than a year afterwards," writes Montjoie, " grow pale with horror and shed torrents of tears as he recalled that bloody sight. ' The last words of the Marquis de Launay will always echo in my heart,' he said; ' night and day I see him, overwhelmed with insults, covered with blood, and gently addressing his murderers with these words, " Ah, my friends, kill me, kill me on the spot ! For pity's sake do not let me linger ! " ' "

Ghastly as was the massacre of De Launay, it was followed by crimes even more glaringly unjust. The Swiss who, as we have seen, during the siege of the Bastille were the keenest to continue the defence, and to whom most of the firing was due, one and all escaped without injury, but to the Invalides, who had sympathized with the besiegers, the crowd showed no pity. Three were immediately put to death, and amongst these was Becquard, who had restrained De Launay from blowing up the castle. The hand that had thus saved the lives of countless citizens was cut off and paraded through the streets, then Becquard himself was hoisted to the fatal lantern. Three officers also perished, and to make the senseless violence of the day complete, De Flue, who throughout the siege had urged the Governor to greater severity, was allowed to escape, whilst the merciful De Losme was barbarously butchered.

Two former Bastille prisoners, the Marquis de Pelleport and the Chevalier de Jean,[1] entered the Place de Grève at the moment of De Launay's death. Pelleport, seeing that the same fate would befall De Losme, who during his captivity had always been his friend, rushed forward and threw his arms around him.

" Wait ! " he cried to the mob, " you are going to sacrifice the best man in the world ! I was five years in the Bastille, and he was my consoler, my friend, my father ! "

At this De Losme raised his eyes and said gently, " Young man, what are you doing ? Go back, you will only sacrifice yourself without saving me."

But Pelleport still clung to De Losme, and since he was unarmed, attempted with his hands to keep off the raging multitude.

" I will defend him against you all ! " he cried ; " yes, yes, against you all ! "

Thereupon a brigand in the crowd dealt Pelleport a blow with an axe that cut into his neck, and raising the weapon was about to strike again when De Jean flung himself upon him and threw him to the ground. But De Jean in his turn was assailed on all sides, struck with sabres, pierced with bayonets, until at last he fell fainting on the steps of the Hôtel de Ville. Then De Losme was massacred, and his head was raised on a pike and carried in procession with De Launay's.

The remaining Invalides were led through Paris amidst the execrations of the crowd : twenty-two of these unfortunate old men and several Swiss children in the service of the Bastille were brought to the Hôtel de Ville, where on their arrival a revolutionary elector [2] brutally addressed them with these words : " You fired on your fellow-citizens, you deserve to be hanged, and you will be on the spot." Instantly a chorus of voices took up the cry : " Give them up to us that we may hang them ! " But the Gardes Françaises, with Élie at their head, interposed, throwing themselves courageously between the Invalides and their assailants.

---

[1] Charles de Jean de Manville, half-brother to the Comtesse de Sabran, a *mauvais sujet* who had been imprisoned in the Bastille for forging a will.

[2] *Bastille dévoilée*, ii. 110 ; *Hist. de la Révolution*, par Montjoie.

" I shall never forget that terrible moment," wrote Pitra ; " the crowd hurling itself upon the prisoners, the Swiss on their knees, the Invalides clasping the feet of Élie, who, standing on a table crowned with laurels, vainly strove to make his voice heard above the tumult, whilst the Gardes Françaises surrounded them, making a rampart of their bodies and tearing them from the hands of those who would have dragged them away."

So, says Montjoie, " men of no education, soldiers and rebels, gave a lesson in justice and humanity to the barbarous elector."

But this mobile crowd, stirred by a word to violence, was also by a word moved to pity. Suddenly one of the Gardes Françaises cried aloud, " We ask for the lives of our old comrades as the price of the Bastille and of the services we have rendered ! " Élie in a broken voice, with trembling lips, joined his entreaties to theirs, " I ask for mercy to be shown to my companions as the prize of our deeds " ; and pointing to the silver plate belonging to De Launay which had been offered to him he added, " I want none of this silver ; I want no honours. Mercy, mercy for these children," he turned to the little Swiss standing by him ; " mercy, mercy for these old men," he added, taking the hands of the trembling Invalides, " for they have only done their duty."

" Élie," says Dussaulx, " reigned supreme, as he continued to calm the minds of the people. His disordered hair, his streaming brow, his dented sword held proudly, his torn and crumpled clothing, served to heighten and to sanctify the dignity of his appearance, and gave him a martial air that carried us back to heroic times. All eyes were fixed on him. . . . I seem still to hear him speaking : ' Citizens, above all, beware of staining with blood the laurels you have bound about my head—otherwise take back your palms and crowns ! ' "

At these noble words a sudden silence fell on the tumultuous crowd, then a few voices murmured " Mercy ! " and the next moment a mighty shout went up from every mouth. " Mercy, yes, mercy, mercy for all ! " and the great hall re-echoed the cry of pardon.

So at last the Invalides and little Swiss were led out by the same crowd that had clamoured for their blood, and fêted amidst general rejoicing.

" Thus ended this great scene of fury, of vengeance, of victory, of joy, of atrocities, but where there gleamed a few rays of humanity." [1]

More than a few rays ! On this terrible 14th of July great deeds were done, deeds of glorious valour and self-sacrifice. Against the murky background of brutality and horror the names of Élie, Hulin, Arné, Bonnemère stand out in shining letters, and

---

[1] Bailly, i. 385.

the fact that these men took no part in the subsequent excesses of the Revolution shows that they were not the tools of agitators but honest men acting on their own initiative and, as such, truly representative of the people.   For patriots like these the revolutionary leaders had no use ; the instruments they needed were of a different stamp.   Jourdan, Maillard, Théroigne, Desnot, the " cook out of place " who had cut off the head of De Launay, all these will reappear again and again in the great scenes of the Revolution, but of Élie we shall hear no more.

What share must we attribute to the people in the crimes of this day ?   Out of the 800,000 inhabitants of Paris only approximately 1000 took any part in the siege of the Bastille,[1] and we have already seen the elements of which this 1000 were composed.   That the mob by whom the atrocities were committed consisted mainly of the brigands, the evidence of Dussaulx further testifies :

" They were men," he says, " armed like savages.   And what sort of men ?   Of the sort that one could not remember ever having met in broad daylight.   Where did they come from ?   Who had drawn them from their gloomy lairs ? "   And again :   " They did not belong to the nation, these brigands that were seen filling the Hôtel de Ville, some nearly naked, others strangely clothed in garments of divers colours, beside themselves with rage, most of them not knowing what they wanted, demanding the death of the victims pointed out to them, and demanding it in tones that more than once it was impossible to resist."   Further, that they were actually *hired* for their task is evident.   Mme. Vigée le Brun records that on the morning of this day she overheard two men talking ; one said to the other, " Do you want to earn 10 francs ?   Come and make a row with us.   You have only got to cry, ' Down with this one ! down with that one.'   Ten francs are worth earning."   The other answered, " But shall we receive no blows ? "   " Go to ! " said the first man, " it is we who are to deal the blows ! "

Dussaulx confirms this statement in referring to the *lanterne*, " where butchers *paid* by real assassins committed atrocities worthy of cannibals."

But tools when they happen to be human are sometimes difficult to manipulate.   In massacring the garrison of the Bastille it is evident that the brigands exceeded their orders,

---

[1] So little commotion did the siege of the Bastille cause in Paris that Dr. Rigby, unaware that anything unusual was going on, went off early in the afternoon to visit the gardens of Monceaux.   " I doubt not that it (the attack on the Bastille) had begun a considerable time and even been completed before it was known to many thousands of the inhabitants as well as to ourselves."

for neither De Launay nor the Invalides had been proscribed in the councils of the revolutionary leaders.[1] The murder of Flesselles, the provost-marshal, had, however, as we have seen, been ordained during the preceding night. The forged note was prepared and handed round amongst the populace ; it purported to be a message from Flesselles to De Launay and contained these words : " I am keeping the Parisians amused with promises and cockades ; hold out till the evening and you will be reinforced." This note, of which only a copy was produced, and the original, though sought for during six months, could never be discovered, is admitted by Dussaulx, Bailly, and Pitra to have been merely the faked-up pretext given to the people by those who desired the death of Flesselles. But on this occasion " the people " proved recalcitrant, and Flesselles was allowed to pass unharmed out of the Hôtel de Ville. Then a hired assassin, " not a man of the people," says Montjoie, but a well-to-do jeweller named Moraire, approached him as he came down the steps and fired a revolver into his ear. Flesselles fell dead, and the crowd, once more carried away by the sight of blood, cut off his head and bore it on a pike with De Launay's to the Palais Royal. Thus perished the first victim on the list of proscriptions drawn up by the Palais Royal ; the only other in Paris at the time was the Prince de Lambesc, but though attacked by the mob, his carriage seized and burnt, he was able to make good his escape. At the King's command the Comte d'Artois, De Breteuil, and De Broglie left Versailles and succeeded in reaching the frontier unmolested, thus avoiding the fate designed for them by the conspirators, but the Prince de Condé on his journey from Chantilly encountered at Crépy-en-Valois— the constituency of the Duc d'Orléans—emissaries sent by the duke to stir up the peasants, and narrowly escaped drowning in the Oise.

Foullon, though warned of the conspirators' intentions regarding him, was at his château of Morangis and refused to fly. To the supplications of his daughter-in-law he only answered : " My daughter, you are aware of all the infamies circulated about me ; if I leave I shall seem to justify my condemnation. My life is pure, I wish it to be examined, and to leave my children an untarnished name." He consented, however, to go to the château of his friend M. de Sartines at Viry, and on the morning of the 22nd of July he started forth on foot. M. de Sartines was out when he arrived, and Foullon awaited his return in the garden, when suddenly a horde of ruffians, led by one Grappe,

[1] Malouet, i. 325 ; Montjoie, *Conjuration de d'Orléans*, ii. 87. On this point Montjoie shows great fairness, for he does not attribute to the Orléanistes crimes that were not of their devising. It is evident that he had definite grounds for his accusations.

burst in upon him.   His whereabouts had been discovered by
the treachery of a servant of Sartines'—not, as certain writers
have stated, his own servant, who remained with him and endeavoured to protect him from his murderers.

Then the unfortunate old man of seventy-four was led to
Paris, and in ghastly mockery the ruffians proceeded to mimic
the sufferings of our Lord, crowning Foullon with thorns and,
when on the long road to Paris he complained of thirst, giving
him vinegar to drink.

At the Hôtel de Ville Lafayette vainly attempted to save
him from the fury of the populace.   " But this agitation," says
Bailly, now the mayor of Paris, " was not natural and spontaneous.
In the square, and even in the hall, people of decent appearance
were seen mingling in the crowd and exciting them to severity.
One well-dressed man, addressing the bench, cried out angrily,
' What need is there to judge a man who has been judged for
thirty years ? ' "   The lying phrase attributed to Foullon, " If
the people have no bread let them eat hay," was successfully
circulated, and at last the infuriated mob stuffed his mouth with
hay and hung him to the lantern.[1]

Meanwhile Foullon's son-in-law, Berthier, was arrested at
Compiègne, in the midst of his efforts to assure the provisioning
of Paris.   It was said, to inflame the passions of the crowd, that
he had ordered the corn to be cut green so as to starve the people.
The truth was that letters had reached him from all sides describing the urgent demand for grain, and Necker himself had
written on the 14th of July ordering him to cut 20,000 septiers
of rye before the harvest in order to supply the present need,[2]
but Berthier had refused to comply, preferring to ensure the
circulation of grain already stored, and by means of untiring
activity he succeeded in providing the necessary supplies.   This,
of course, the revolutionaries could not forgive him, and Berthier
was driven to Paris amidst the execrations of the populace.   As
he entered the capital, followed by a mob of armed brigands, the
head of his father-in-law was thrust through his carriage-window
on the end of a pike.   Faint with hunger and sick with horror
he reached the Hôtel de Ville, but before the lantern could be
lowered a mutineer of the Royal Cravatte plunged his sabre into
his body.   Thereupon " a monster of ferocity, a cannibal," tore

---

[1] Von Sybel, in his *History of the French Revolution*, i. 81 (Eng. trans.),
says of the death of Foullon : " This crime was not the result of an outbreak of popular fury, it had cost the revolutionary leaders large sums of
money, for which thousands of assassins were to be had.   In Mirabeau's
correspondence the following statement occurs : ' Foullon's death cost
hundreds of thousands of francs, the murder of the baker François only a
few thousands.' "

[2] *La Prise de la Bastille*, by Gustave Bord, p. 33.

out his heart, and Desnot, the " cook out of place " who had cut off the head of De Launay and again " happened " to be on the spot, carried it to the Palais Royal.[1] This ghastly trophy, together with the victim's head, was placed in the middle of the supper-table around which the brigands feasted.

Such were the consequences of the siege of the Bastille so vaunted by panegyrists of the Revolution. Well may M. Madelin exclaim : " A new era was born of a prodigious lie. Liberty bore a stain from its birth, and the paradox once created can never be dispelled."

And what of the Bastille, that haunt of despotism, whose destruction was to atone for these atrocities ? Alas for the deception of the people, their investigation of the hated fortress revealed nothing remotely resembling the visions presented to their imaginations—no skeletons or corpses were to be found, no captives in chains, no oubliettes, no torture - chambers.[2] True, an " iron corselet " was discovered, " invented to restrict a man in all his joints and to fix him in perpetual immobility," but this was proved to be an ordinary suit of armour ; a destructive machine, " of which one could not guess the use," turned out to be a printing-press confiscated by the police ; whilst a collection of human bones that seemed to offer a sinister significance was traced to the anatomical collection of the surgery.

The prisoners proved equally disappointing. Seven only were found — four forgers, Béchade, Lacaurège, Pujade, and Laroche ; two lunatics, Tavernier and De Whyte, who were mad before they were imprisoned, and the Comte de Solages, incarcerated for "monstrous crimes " at the request of his family. The first four disappeared into Paris. The remaining three were paraded through the streets and exhibited daily as a show to an interested populace. Finally, the Comte de Solages was sent back to his inappreciative relations, whilst a kind-hearted wig-maker attempted keeping Tavernier as a pet, but was obliged to return him hastily to the Comité, who despatched him with De Whyte to the lunatic asylum at Charenton.

The Revolution showed itself less indulgent to Bastille prisoners than the Old Régime. The romantic conception of Dickens in the *Tale of Two Cities*, wherein a former victim of

---

[1] Note that even the Two Friends of Liberty admit that the death of Berthier was engineered : " It seems that the people, without knowing it, were the blind instruments of the vengeance of the intendant's private enemies or of the cruel prudence of his accomplices. Electors noticed from the windows of the Hôtel de Ville several people scattered about the square who seemed to be the leading spirits of the different groups and to direct their movements " (*Deux Amis*, ii. 73).

[2] *Bastille dévoilée*, ii. 21, 39, 82.

despotism is made to remark that "as a Bastille prisoner not a soul would harm a hair of his head," is entirely refuted by history. Two, as we have already seen, were nearly massacred in their attempts to save De Losme, and subsequently *no less than ten Bastille prisoners perished at the hands of the revolutionaries*—eight were guillotined and two were shot. Of these—greatest irony of all—was Linguet, the man whose revelations had contributed more than any other evidence to inflame public feeling on the subject of the Bastille. Linguet did his best to atone for the calumnies he had circulated, for in December 1792 he wrote to Louis XVI. begging to be allowed the honour of defending him. Eighteen months later, in one of the many horrible prisons of the Terror where he awaited his summons to the guillotine, Linguet had leisure to meditate on the amenities of the Bastille.

THE KING'S VISIT TO PARIS

It was through the medium of the Palais Royal that the news of the taking of the Bastille reached Versailles, for the King's messengers were waylaid by revolutionary emissaries, whilst the Vicomte de Noailles and other Orléanistes were deputed to announce the events of the day to the Assembly. Needless to say, these events were ingeniously distorted to suit the purpose of the intrigue—the Bastille had been taken by force, De Launay had fired on the deputation of citizens and met with the just reward of his treachery at the hands of "the people." The presence of the troops was, of course, still represented as the only reason for these disorders.

The King, informed of the desperate state of affairs, replied to the Assembly : " You rend my heart more and more by the account you give me of the troubles of Paris. It is not possible to believe that the orders given to the troops can be the cause." They were most certainly not the cause, and the removal of the troops was followed a week later, as we have seen, by disorders still more frightful in the massacres of Foullon and of Berthier. But the King, assured by succeeding deputations that no other measure would restore peace to the capital, torn between his own convictions and the entreaties of the deputies, finally resolved to appeal to the better feelings of the Assembly. Accompanied by his two brothers he appeared in the great hall, and in the simple human language peculiar to him, that contrasts so strangely with the redundant periods of the day, he implored their aid in dealing with the crisis :

" Messieurs, I have assembled you to consult on the most important affairs of state, of which none is more urgent, none touches my heart more deeply, than the frightful disorder that

reigns in the capital. The head of the nation comes with confidence into the midst of its representatives to tell them of his
grief, to ask them to find means for restoring calm and order."
Then, referring to the hideous calumnies circulated on his intentions—notably the monstrous fable that he had ordered the
hall of the Assembly to be mined in order to blow up the deputies
—he added, with a pathos and dignity that won for him the
sympathy of almost the whole Assembly :

" I know that people have aroused unjust suspicions in your
minds ; I know that they have dared to say that your persons
were not in safety. Is it necessary to reassure you concerning
such criminal rumours, refuted beforehand by your knowledge
of my character ?   Well, then, it is I, who am one with my nation,
it is I who trust in you ! Help me in these circumstances to
assure the salvation of the State ; I await this from the National
Assembly, from the zeal of the representatives of my people. . . ."

Then, since he was persuaded the *milice bourgeoise* were
competent to maintain " order " in the capital, he ended by
announcing that he had ordered the troops to retire from Paris
to Versailles.

In the wild enthusiasm that followed this speech of the
King the voice of the revolutionary factions was for once stifled,
and Louis XVI. was escorted back to the Palace amidst the
acclamations of deputies and people.   Cries of " Vive le Roi ! "
resounded on every side, and so immense a crowd assembled
that the King took an hour and a half to cover the short
distance between the Salle des Menus and the Château.   The
unfortunate monarch, pressed upon from every side, saluted
unresistingly on both cheeks by a woman of the people, grilled
by the rays of the July sun, suffered almost as much by the
warmth of his subjects' affection as two days later he was to
suffer by their coldness, and he reached at last the marble staircase nearly suffocated and streaming with perspiration.

Meanwhile the Queen, holding the Dauphin in her arms
and little Madame Royale by the hand, came out on to the
balcony—that same balcony from which less than three months
later she was to face a very different crowd.   The children of the
Comte d'Artois came to kiss her hand ; the Queen stooped to
embrace them, holding the Dauphin towards them.   The little
boys pressed him to their hearts, and Madame Royale, slipping
her head under her mother's arm, joined in the caresses.   The
King arrived at this moment and appeared on the balcony amidst
the cheers and benedictions of his people.

In Paris, likewise, the people longed for peace.   When on
the same day eighty-four deputies went to the capital to read
aloud the King's discourse, and to announce the dismissal of the

troops, they were received with acclamations, and from thousands of throats arose the cry, "Vive le Roi! Vive la Nation!" The whole city was in an ecstasy of happiness. Lally, the tender-hearted Lally, took advantage of the restored good-humour of the people to address them at ,the Hôtel de Ville and entreat them to put an end to disorder :

"Messieurs, we have come to bring you peace from the King and the National Assembly. (Cries of Peace! Peace!) You are generous ; you are Frenchmen ; you love your wives, your children, your country. (Yes! Yes!) There are no more bad citizens. Everything is calm, everything is peaceful . . . there will be no more proscriptions, will there ? " And with one voice the people answered, "Yes, yes, peace; no more proscriptions ! "

Then the Archbishop of Paris (Monseigneur de Juigné) spoke with fatherly compassion of the misfortunes of the capital, after which he led the people amidst thunderous applause to sing a Te Deum of thanksgiving at Notre Dame.

Alas, the people were not allowed to enjoy for long this restored harmony! Such was the amazing ingenuity of the agitators and the credulity of the Parisians that in the space of a few hours the city was thrown into a fresh panic—" The troops are not being sent away—flour intended for Paris is being held up—soldiers are tearing the national cockade off passers-by and stuffing their guns with them—the city has only three days' supplies." The workmen engaged in demolishing the Bastille were told that their bread and wine were poisoned.[1]

Then, when the fury of the populace was once more thoroughly aroused, deputations of fishwives were sent by the leaders of the conspiracy to demand that the King should come to Paris. *It was the first of the series of attempts made by the revolutionaries to have the King assassinated by the people.* They dared not do the deed themselves, for they knew the frightful punishment attaching to regicide ; they knew, moreover, the furious indignation so foul a crime would arouse in the minds of the people in general to whom the King was still almost a sacred being. But if the populace could be sufficiently inflamed, and at the psychological moment the King were brought amongst them, might not some brigand lurking in the crowd, some obscure fanatic, give way to a sudden impulse and pull the trigger of his rusty flint-lock ? The thing was not impossible.[2]

---

[1] " Paris again worked on by its perfidious agitators " (Marmontel, iv. 214). See also Ferrières, i. 154 ; Montjoie, *Conjuration de d'Orléans*, ii. 73 ; *Deux Amis*, ii. 32.

[2] Montjoie, *Conjuration de d'Orléans*, ii. 77 ; *Souvenirs d'un Page* (le Comte d'Hézecques), p. 300.

The Queen, who foresaw the same possibilities, threw herself in vain at the King's feet and implored him not to expose himself to the threatening populace. But the King, convinced "that if each citizen owes to his sovereign the sacrifice of his life, the sovereign equally owes to his country the sacrifice of his, turned a deaf ear to all forebodings, trusted to his people and the good genius of France, and in spite of the Queen's entreaties showed himself firm and unshakable. 'I have promised,' he said; 'my intentions are pure; I trust in this. The people must know that I love them, and, anyhow, they can do as they like with me.'"[1]

"Louis XVI.," says De Lescure, "was neither a superior intellect nor an energetic will, he was *an incorruptible conscience,*" and these words give the clue to all his oscillations, for conscience is necessarily a more uncertain guide than policy or self-interest. As long as he felt convinced a certain course was right he followed it without a thought for his personal safety or advantage—the trouble was that he could not always decide which course was right, and allowed himself to be swayed by conflicting counsels. On this occasion he did not hesitate—the people wished him to go to Paris; he would go, and his conscience being at rest he could meet any fate with tranquillity.

At ten o'clock in the morning of July 17 the King, escorted by the deputies of the Assembly and the *milice bourgeoise,* set forth for Paris. His guards were taken from him, and in their place marched 200,000 men armed with scythes and pickaxes, with guns and lances, dragging cannons behind them, and women dancing like Bacchantes, waving branches of leaves tied with ribbons. In order not to tire the people the King had ordered the procession to move at foot's-pace, and it was four o'clock by the time it reached Paris.[2] In the midst of this threatening escort Louis XVI. sat pale and anxious, and on entering the city he leant forward, casting his eyes wonderingly over the assembled multitude that received him in an ominous silence, for the people had been forbidden to cheer him. So potent was the spell exercised over the popular mind by the leaders of the Revolution that not a soul dared to utter the cry of "Vive le Roi!" and brigands posted in the crowd silenced the least murmur of applause.[3] Thus, dragged like a captive through the streets of the city, the King was obliged to endure this terrible humiliation for which no cause whatever existed; he had done absolutely nothing to forfeit the popularity which only two days earlier he had enjoyed. The good Archbishop of Paris fared still worse at the hands of the populace, for alone of all the procession he was hissed by those he had ruined

---

[1] *Deux Amis,* ii. 42 ; Montjoie, *Conjuration de d'Orléans,* ii. 77.
[2] Montjoie, *Conjuration de d'Orléans,* ii. 81.   [3] Marmontel, iv. 214.

himself to feed. Sitting in his carriage, his eyes downcast, striving to overcome the agitation of his mind, his thoughts must have indeed been bitter.

As the procession passed through the Place Louis XV the possibility that both the Queen and the revolutionary leaders had foreseen was realized—a hand in the crowd pulled the trigger of a gun, and the shot missing the King killed a poor woman at the back of the royal carriage.[1] The incident was hushed up, and even the King was unaware it had occurred. Thus, saved by the mysterious power which protected him every time that he was brought face to face with the people, the King reached the Hôtel de Ville.

Under an archway of pikes and naked swords he passed to the throne prepared for him. Bailly presented him with the tricolour cockade, and the King accepting it as that which it professed to be—the cockade of Paris—placed it in his hat. Then suddenly it seemed that the spell was broken, and cries of " Vive le Roi ! " broke out on all sides. Once more Lally passionately appealed to the people's loyalty :

" Well, citizens, are you satisfied ? Here is the King for whom you called aloud, and whose name alone excited your transports when two days ago we uttered it in your midst. Rejoice, then, in his presence and his benefits." After reminding the people of all the King had done for the cause of Liberty he turned to assure the King of the people's love : " There is not a man here who is not ready to shed for you the last drop of his blood. No, Sire, this generation of Frenchmen will not go back on fourteen centuries of fidelity. We will all perish, if necessary, to defend the throne that is as sacred to us as to yourself. Perish those enemies who would sow discord between the nation and its chief ! King, subjects, citizens, let us join our hearts, our wishes, our efforts, and display to the eyes of the universe the magnificent spectacle of one of its finest nations, free, happy, triumphant, under a just, cherished, and revered King, who, owing nothing to force, will owe everything to his virtues and his love."

Again and again Lally was interrupted by tumultuous applause, and the King, overwhelmed by this sudden revulsion of popular feeling, could only murmur brokenly in reply, " My people can always count on my love."

His departure for Versailles was as triumphant as his arrival had been humiliating. When he entered his carriage with the tricolour cockade in his hat an immense crowd gathered round him, crying, " Long live our good King, our friend, our father ! "

[1] Montjoie, *Conjuration de d'Orléans*, ii. 82 ; *Essais de Beaulieu*, i. ; Bailly, ii. 61.

It was eleven o'clock before he reached the Château. On the marble staircase the Queen, with the Dauphin in her arms, was waiting for him in an agony of suspense, and at the sight of the husband she had not dared to hope ever to see again Marie Antoinette fell weeping on his neck. But when she raised her eyes and saw that sinister badge—the enemy's colours in his hat —her heart sank ; from that moment she felt that all was lost.

But the King was happy, not because his life had been spared, but because he believed that he had regained the love of his people.

RESULTS OF THE JULY REVOLUTION

So ended the Revolution of July, and what had it brought to the people ? To the immense majority, unaffected as we have seen by *lettres de cachet*, the destruction of the Bastille meant no more than the destruction of the Tower of London would mean to-day to the inhabitants of Whitechapel. Indeed, certain amongst them shrewdly recognized that in attacking it they were fighting for a cause that was not their own. The Abbé Rudemare, walking amongst the ruins of the Bastille the day after the siege, came upon a workman engaged in the task of demolition who brusquely accosted him with the words : " Mon chevalier, vous ne direz pas que c'est pour nous que nous travaillons ; c'est bien pour vous, car nous autres, nous ne tâtions pas de la Bastille : on nous f . . . à Bicêtre. N'y a-t-il rien pour boire à votre santé ? " [1]

The people had indeed admirably served the design of the conspirators, taking on themselves all the risks and facing all the dangers of revolt, whilst the men who had worked them up to violence remained discreetly in the background. Now, in all the great outbreaks of the Revolution we shall find that the mechanism was threefold, consisting of, firstly, the Instigators ; secondly, the Agitators, and thirdly, the Instruments; and of these three classes only the last two incurred any danger. Thus at the siege of the Bastille the mob and its leaders alone took part in the battle, whilst the Instigators prudently effaced themselves. For the rôle of the Instigators was not to lead insurrection but only to provoke it, and having laid the mine to retreat into safety the moment it produced the desired explosion. So throughout the whole course of the Revolution we shall never find Danton figuring in the tumults he had helped to prepare ; he was, therefore, not present at the siege of the

---

[1] " Journal d'un prêtre parisien, 1789–1792," published in *Documents pour servir à l'histoire de la Révolution de France*, by Charles d'Héricault and Gustave Bord, i. 165.

Bastille, but he visited it next day when all danger was over ; [1]
St. Huruge also kept away, but he was at Versailles the day after
shaking his fist at the Queen's windows and uttering furious
invectives against the royal family ; [2] Santerre contented himself
with sending his dray-horses to represent him in the fray ; [3] whilst
Camille Desmoulins, the hero of the 12th of July, who first called
the people to arms, was careful to postpone his arrival on the
scene until after the capitulation.

The women of the Orléaniste conspiracy proved more courageous : Théroigne was in the thick of the fight and received a sword
of honour from the leaders ; Mme. de Genlis watched the siege
from the windows of Beaumarchais' house, opposite the gate of
the Bastille, with the Ducs de Chartres and Montpensier—the
sons of the Duc d'Orléans—at her side.

The duke himself behaved with his usual pusillanimity ;
instead of going to the King and boldly requesting to be made
lieutenant - general of the kingdom, as the conspirators had
planned, he presented himself timorously at Versailles and asked
permission to go to England " in the event of affairs becoming
more distressing than they were at present." The King looked
at him coldly, shrugged his shoulders, and made no reply.

But though the Orléanistes had failed to bring off their great
coup of putting the Duc d'Orléans at the head of affairs, they had
nevertheless accomplished a great deal. The destruction of the
Bastille by force and not by the King's decree had proved a
powerful blow to the royal authority, but the most important
result of the outbreak from the point of view of both the revolutionary factions was the effect produced on the public mind.
The people before the Revolution of July, says Marmontel, " were
not sufficiently accustomed to crime, and in order to inure them
to it they must be practised in it." The Parisians, always eager
for spectacles and enchanted by novelty of any kind, had now
been initiated into a new form of entertainment—the fashion of
carrying heads on pikes and of hoisting victims to the lantern ;
and though it would be unjust to accuse the mass of the true
people—the law-abiding and industrious citizens—of sympathy
with these atrocities, it is undeniable that from this date the
populace of Paris—the idlers, wastrels, and drunken inhabitants
of the city—acquired a taste for bloodshed that made them the
ready tools of their criminal leaders. So, although, as we shall
see, the crimes that followed were invariably instigated, if not
performed, by professional revolutionaries, we shall find henceforth a steady deterioration in the mind of the populace, and
even in the mass of the true people a growing indifference to

---

[1] *Danton*, by Louis Madelin.   [2] *Mémoires de Mme. Campan*, p. 235.
[3] *Le Marquis de Saint-Huruge*, par Henri Furgeot, p. 202.

bloodshed and submission to violence, that five years later made the Reign of Terror possible.   Thus the Revolution of July, whilst serving the cause of the Orléaniste conspiracy, had likewise paved the way for Anarchy.

In England the news of the siege of the Bastille was received with mingled feelings.   All true lovers of humanity rejoiced at an event that at the time they believed to herald the dawn of liberty, though many Englishmen, like Arthur Young [1] and Wordsworth, lived to realize their error.   Burke, more far-seeing, wondered whether to blame or applaud ; thrilled by the struggle for freedom he shuddered nevertheless at the outbreak of " Parisian ferocity," and dreaded its recurrence in the future. But to the Whigs and the revolutionaries of England this triumph of the Orléaniste conspiracy was a matter for the heartiest congratulation.   " How much the greatest event it is that ever happened in the world and how much the best ! " wrote Fox to Fitzpatrick.   To the Duc d'Orléans, whose despicable conduct had sickened even his supporters in France, Fox thought fit to send his warm compliments :   " Tell him and Lauzun (the Duc de Biron) that all my prepossessions against French connections for this country will be altered if this Revolution has the consequences I expect."   The anniversary of the " fall " of the Bastille was celebrated the following year by the Revolution Society at the tavern of " The Crown and Anchor," where more than 600 members, presided over by Lord Stanhope, drank to the liberty of the world, and Dr. Price demanded the inauguration of a " league of peace."

But whilst the Subversives of this country gave way to

---

[1] It is perhaps not generally known that Arthur Young, who has been falsely quoted as the panegyrist of the French Revolution on account of his earlier works, *Travels in France*, 1789, and *On the Revolution in France*, 1792, entirely recanted from his former opinions, and in 1793 wrote a denunciation of the Revolution no less vehement than that of Burke. This pamphlet, entitled *The Example of France, a Warning to Britain*, has been very carefully ignored by democratic writers in this country.   Lord Morley, in his essay on Burke (English Men of Letters, p. 162), accounts for it by describing Young as becoming " panic-stricken."   There is, however, I believe, a simple explanation of Young's complete *volte-face* on the subject of the Revolution.   His earlier work was written in France under the influence of the set in French society that he frequented, and this set we shall find on examination to have been entirely Orléaniste—hence his exaggerated strictures on the Old Régime.   With the best portion of the " noblesse," and even with the " royalist democrats," he was unacquainted, and the disgust he expresses at the cynical behaviour of certain nobles at a dinner-party he attended is readily explained by the fact that the party consisted of the Duc d'Orléans and his supporters (see entry for June 22, 1789).   It was from these sources, therefore, that Young gleaned his earlier opinions on the state of France, and which a fuller knowledge of facts and not " panic " led him to relinquish.

rejoicing, the Government of England resolutely refrained from any expressions of satisfaction at the blow to the monarchy of France ; out of respect to Louis XVI. the playhouses of London were prohibited from representing the siege of the Bastille on the stage.

The conduct of England provided, indeed, a marked contrast to that of Prussia. " All the symptoms of anarchy in France," writes Sorel, " all the signs of discredit in the French state, are seized upon abroad eagerly by the Prussian agents and commented on in Berlin with acrimonious satisfaction. Hertzberg, whilst priding himself on his ' enlightened views,' shows himself on this occasion as good a Prussian as the favourites of his master. This is because the crisis serves his intrigues and he hopes to profit by it. ' The prestige of royalty is annihilated in France,' he writes to the King on the 5th of July ; ' the troops have refused to serve. Louis has declared the Séance Royale null and void ;[1] this is a scene after the manner of Charles I. Here is a situation of which the governments should take advantage.' " That the English Government should not seize this opportunity to attack the rival to her naval supremacy is inconceivable to the mind of the good Prussian. " The 14th of July overwhelms him (Hertzberg) with joy. . . . He hails it after his fashion as a day of deliverance. ' *This is the good moment,*' declares Hertzberg ; ' the French monarchy is overthrown, the Austrian alliance is annihilated, *this* is the good moment, and also the last opportunity presented to your Majesty to give to his monarchy the highest degree of stability.' "[2]

Von der Goltz, still faithful to the precepts of his former master, showed himself as enthusiastic as Hertzberg ; he, too, sees in the 14th of July the final defeat of the Queen he had so long sought to defame in the eyes of the French nation, and is equally unable to understand the attitude of the British ambassador, Lord Dorset, who allows his personal feelings of gratitude and affection for the royal family of France to override the satisfaction he might be expected to experience at the unique opportunity offered to his country. The Comte de Salmour, minister for Saxony, had filled his post more ably. " The Saxon Minister," Von Goltz writes to the King of Prussia on July 24, " though principally frequenting the society of the Queen, on account of his uncle, the Baron de Bézenval, nevertheless, I must do him the justice to admit, continues to behave very well to me (*i.e.* assists Von der Goltz in his schemes against the Court ?). The ambassador for England, owing to his personal attachment to the Queen and the Comte d'Artois, is as distressed

---

[1] This was, of course, absolutely untrue.
[2] *L'Europe et la Révolution Française,* ii. 25.

by all that has happened as if the blow had fallen on the King, his master.   In truth it must go to his heart, but would it not be well if he distinguished better between his personal affections and the interests of his post ? " [1]   Frederick William, delighted at the zeal of his ambassador, thereupon wrote to order Von der Goltz to get into touch with the revolutionary leaders in the National Assembly and to continue his campaign against the Queen.   Von der Goltz, obedient to these commands, stirred up further hatred for Marie Antoinette, " intrigued against the Court of Vienna, and thanks to his equivocal relations with the revolutionaries paralysed the measures of the French ministry." [2] *By the Prussians, therefore, the fall of the Bastille is regarded as the triumph of Prussia over Austria.*   The Government of Berlin, says Sorel, " sees that which it dared not hope for by the happiest fortune, that which all the diplomacy of Frederick had so often vainly attempted to secure—the Austrian alliance dissolved, the credit of the Queen lost for ever ; influence acquired by the partisans of Prussia, and in consequence *all avenues opened to Prussian ambition.*" [3]

---

[1] Flammermont, *La Journée du 14 Juillet,* and *Rapport sur les Correspondances des Agents Diplomatiques, etc.,* p. 128.

[2] Sorel, *L'Europe et la Révolution Française,* ii. 69 ; Flammermont, *Rapport sur les Correspondances des Agents Diplomatiques, etc.,* p. 127.

[3] Sorel, *L'Europe et la Révolution Française,* ii. 25.

THE MARCH ON VERSAILLES

THE MARCH ON VERSAILLES

DISORDERS IN THE PROVINCES

THE desire of the people for peace and for a return to law and order after the King's visit to Paris on the 17th of July necessitated strenuous efforts on the part of the revolutionary leaders to fan up anew the flame of insurrection. Often the task seemed almost hopeless, and Camille Desmoulins—now embarking on his sanguinary *Discours de la Lanterne*, in which the Parisians were incited to hang further victims—afterwards described to the Assembly the immense difficulty the agitators encountered in overcoming the disinclination of the people to continue the Revolution. "I reduce to three," wrote Buzot later, "the methods employed by the masters of France to lead this nation to the point she has now reached—*calumny, corruption,* and *terror,*"[1] and though in these words Buzot alluded to the men who afterwards became his enemies, the Terrorists, they might still more aptly be applied to his former colleagues, the members of the Orléaniste conspiracy.[2]

Calumny directed against the victims, corruption of the instruments, and terror created in the minds of the people—such is the history of the three months that led up to the march on Versailles.

Of these three methods terror proved the most potent ; in order to rouse the people one must begin by frightening them. It was Adrien Duport,[3] one of the most inventive members of the Club Breton, who devised the project known to contemporaries as "the Great Fear," a scheme which consisted in sending messengers to all the towns and villages of France to announce the approach of imaginary brigands, Austrians or English, who were arriving to massacre the citizens.

On the same day, the 28th of July, and almost at the same hour, this diabolical manœuvre was repeated all over France ;

[1] *Memoirs of Buzot,* p. 61.
[2] It is probable that Buzot was never an Orléaniste but, like Robespierre, he worked with them at the beginning of the Revolution.
[3] *Essais de Beaulieu,* i. 506.

everywhere the panic-stricken peasants flew to arms, and thus the great aim of the revolutionary leaders was realized—the arming of the entire population against law and order.[1]

By this means anarchy was complete throughout the kingdom, and the crimes of July 14 and 22 in Paris were followed in the provinces by atrocities too revolting to describe. This Reign of Terror, organized by the Orléanistes, was, in fact, even more frightful than the Terror of Robespierre four years later ; the victims were arraigned before no Revolutionary Tribunal, received no warning of their fate, but suddenly found themselves the centre of a raging mob, accused of crimes they had never committed, reproached for words they had never uttered, and put finally to a death even more horrible than the guillotine.

In no case, however, do we find these outrages to be the spontaneous work of the people ; the conception of down-trodden peasants rising incontrollably to overthrow their oppressors, as in the earlier *jacqueries,* is entirely mythical, and exists in the minds of no contemporaries. Such violence as the people committed was invariably instigated by revolutionary emissaries who persuaded them to act under a misapprehension, and methods of diabolical ingenuity were employed to overcome their reluctance. Thus, for example, the agitators, taking advantage of the King's benevolent proclamations in favour of reform, succeeded in making the peasants believe that Louis XVI. wished to take part with them against the noblesse, and to invoke their aid in demolishing the Old Régime. Messengers were sent into the towns and villages bearing placards or proclaiming by word of mouth : " The King orders all châteaux to be burnt down ; he only wishes to keep his own ! " and such was the amazing credulity of the country people that they set forth to burn and destroy, believing in all good faith that they were carrying out the orders of " not' bon roi." [2]

When, however, the people proved recalcitrant, the revolutionaries were obliged to resort to force ; in Dauphiné in Burgundy, in Franche Comté, real bands of brigands were employed to stir up the villagers, who in some cases offered a spirited resistance. " This troop of maniacs went into all the villages, rang the bells to collect the inhabitants, and forced them with a pistol at their throats to join in their brigandage. . . . This

---

[1] *Moniteur,* i. 324 ; Beaulieu, i. 506 ; *Appel au Tribunal de l'Opinion Publique,* by Mounier ; *Mémoires de Frénilly,* p. 121. See the very curious account of the scene that took place at Forges in Normandy given by Mme. de la Tour du Pin, *Journal d'une Femme de Cinquante Ans,* i. 191. Note that the manœuvre was admitted and *approved* by Louis Blanc, *La Révolution,* i. 337.

[2] Montjoie, *Conjuration de d'Orleans,* ii. 105 ; *Deux Amis,* ii. 255 ; *Moniteur,* i. 324 ; *Essais de Beaulieu,* ii. 16.

army of bandits threw the whole of Burgundy into consternation, where the bravest inhabitants of the towns and country places united all their efforts and advanced against these common enemies of the human race, who breathed only murder and pillage."[1] At Cluny the peasants, led by the monks to whom they were devoted, received the brigands with guns and cannon-fire and with stones flung from the windows. "They did not allow a single brigand to escape, they were all killed or led away as prisoners to the royal prison. They were found in possession of printed forms : ' By order of the King.' This document gave instructions to burn down the abbeys and châteaux because the seigneurs and the abbots were monopolizers of grain and poisoners of the wells, and intended to reduce the people and the subjects of the King to the lowest pitch of misery."[2]

At St. Germain the brigands unfortunately won the day, and the inhabitants sent a deputation to the Assembly protesting against the murder of their mayor, Sauvage, guiltless of any offence, the victim of " a crowd of strangers who had thrown themselves upon the town " and torn the unhappy man from the hands of his fellow-citizens.[3] The mayor of St. Denis, Châtel, met with a still more terrible fate. Throughout the preceding winter he had been seen " always surrounded by the unfortunate, to whom he gave free orders for bread and meat and wood . . . so that the inhabitants of St. Denis called him ' the father and the saviour of the poor people.' " But suddenly Châtel found himself accused by messengers from Paris of monopolizing grain, and was put to a lingering death of which the details are so unspeakably revolting that it is impossible to describe them.[4] Huez, the mayor of Troyes, another " bene-factor of the poor," was also butchered in much the same manner.

It will be seen, therefore, that the aristocrats and clergy were not the only victims pointed out for vengeance to the people : the law-abiding bourgeois, the benevolent citizen, what-ever his rank, was equally abhorrent to the revolutionary leaders ; the houses of peasants who would not join in excesses were burnt likewise.[5] It was *not* a case of " misdirected popular fury," but of a definite system pursued by the agitators which

---

[1] *Deux Amis*, ii. 257.

[2] *Lettres d'Aristocrates*, published by Pierre de Vassière, p. 256 ; *Deux Amis*, ii. 258.

[3] *Deux Amis*, ii. 93 ; " Report of Deputation from St. Germain to the National Assembly," *Moniteur*, i. 184.

[4] Montjoie, *Conjuration*, ii. 91 ; *Deux Amis*, ii. 172.

[5] In Maçonnais, not far from Vesoul, banditti to the number of 6000, collected together, set fire to the houses of those peasants who would not join them, and cut down 230 of them (*Report to the National Assembly*, March 22, 1791).

consisted in exterminating every one who encouraged contentment with the Old Régime. Three years later the minister,
Roland, gave the clue to this design when he stated that " in
1789 the misguided people allowed themselves to be worked
up into fury and to immolate the men who were occupied in
feeding them." [1] The massacre of these good citizens is therefore to be explained in the same way as the attacks on Réveillon
and Berthier.

So obvious was it, indeed, to all contemporaries that these
outrages were contrary to the interests of the people, that revolutionary writers can only explain them by the theory that they
were instigated by the " enemies of the Revolution," that is
to say, by the aristocrats themselves, who, in order to bring the
cause of " liberty " into disrepute, stirred the people up to violence, and for this purpose *had their own châteaux burnt down* ! [2]
But if the object of the aristocrats in persuading the people
to burn down their châteaux appears incomprehensible, the
object of the revolutionary leaders in doing so is very obvious,
for by this means not only were the nobles driven out of the
country, but in the process of destruction the seigneurial granaries
were frequently burnt down likewise, fields of standing corn
were trampled under foot, and consequently the famine was
seriously aggravated. [3]

The manner in which the news of all such excesses was
received at the National Assembly proves only too clearly the
collusion between the revolutionary deputies and the agitators
of the provinces. No historian has revealed this more clearly
than Taine, and his strange inconsequence in heading his chapter
on the disorders in the provinces as " spontaneous anarchy "
has been commented on by several modern French historians. [4]

" Thus," writes Taine himself, " is rural ' jacquerie ' *prepared*,

[1] *Le Ministre de l'Intérieur aux Corps Administratifs*, September 1,
1792.

[2] See, for example, *Deux Amis de la Liberté*, ii. 90 and following pages,
where all the excesses described by Montjoie are related in almost identical
language, but the recital ends with the words : " Such was the march of
aristocracy ! " Let any one who can make sense out of the following
passage : " The enemies of the Revolution, profiting by the general disposition to credulity, strove to fatigue the people by alarms spread for the
purpose in order afterwards to lull them into a false security : their plan
was to drive them to excesses so as to bring them through licence under the
yoke of despotism." Since few reprisals were ever taken, however, it is
difficult to follow this line of reasoning.

[3] *Moniteur*, i. 324 ; Fantin Desodoards, p. 196 : " Hordes of brigands
paid by the Duc d'Orléans devastated rural property without distinguishing
to which party the proprietors belonged ; the granaries disappeared with
the grain they contained."

[4] *La Conspiration révolutionnaire de 1789*, by Gustave Bord, p. 62 ;
Chassin, i. 109 ; *La Révolution*, by Louis Madelin, p. 74.

and the fanatics who fanned up the flame in Paris fan it up likewise in the provinces. ' You wish to know the authors of the troubles,' writes a man of good sense to the Committee of Inquiry ; ' you will find them amongst the deputies of the Tiers, and particularly amongst those who are attorneys or lawyers. They write incendiary letters to their constituents, these letters are received by the municipalities which are likewise composed of attorneys and lawyers . . . they are read aloud in the principal square, and copies are sent into all the villages.' " [1]

" I will tell my century, I will tell posterity," cries Ferrières, " that the National Assembly authorized these murders and these burnings ! " [2]

In vain the true democrats in the Assembly—Mounier, Malouet, Lally Tollendal, Virieu, and Boufflers—rose to protest against outrages on humanity and civilization committed in the name of liberty ; the members of the revolutionary factions in every case defended these excesses.

On July 20 Lally, in harrowing terms, described the horrors that were taking place in Normandy, Brittany, and Burgundy, and ended with the words : " A citizen king forces us to accept our liberty, and I do not know why we should wrest it from him as from a tyrant. If I insist on the motion I have put forward, it is that love of my country impels me, it is that I accede to the impulse of my conscience ; and if blood must flow, at least I wash my hands of that which will be shed." [3]

The speech was received with cries of fury from all parts of the Assembly, though the side of the nobles ventured to applaud.

The murder of Foullon and Berthier had filled Lally with burning indignation. On the morning of the 22nd of July, he told the Assembly, the son of Berthier, pale and disfigured, had entered his room crying out, " Monsieur, you spent fifteen years defending the memory of your father ; save the life of mine and let him be given judges ! " But Lally appealed in vain to the humanity of the Assembly. Barnave, rising furiously, exclaimed with a violent gesture, " Is this blood then so pure that one need fear to shed it ? " [4]

[1] Arthur Young was present when one of these letters was received in the provinces. " The news at the table d'hôte at Colmar curious, that the Queen had a plot, nearly on the point of execution, to blow up the National Assembly by a mine, and to march the army instantly to massacre all Paris. . . . A *deputy had written it* ; they had seen the letter. . . . Thus it is in revolutions, one rascal writes and a hundred thousand fools believe " (*Travels*, date of July 24, 1789).

[2] Ferrières, i. 161.   [3] *Moniteur*, i. 183.

[4] Article on Lally Tollendal in *Biographie Michaud* ; also Second Letter of Lally Tollendal to his Constituents. This speech of Lally's and the exclamation of Barnave, though recorded by countless contemporaries, are suppressed in the *Moniteur's* account of the debate that took place on July 23.

Mirabeau went further. " The nation," he declared, " must have victims ! " In a letter to his constituents he had openly defended the crimes attending the siege of the Bastille :- " The people must be essentially kind-hearted since so little blood has been shed. . . . The anger of the people ! ah ! if the anger of the people is terrible, the cold-bloodedness of despotism is atrocious ; its systematic cruelties create more wretchedness in a day than popular insurrections create victims in the course of years." [1]

The unhappy people of France had yet to learn that demagogy can be systematic too ; that demagogy, moreover, can become more potent than despotism, because it does not merely bring external force to bear upon the people, but like a skilful jiu-jitsu wrestler turns the people's own power against themselves. This was the whole secret of the early revolutionary movement : the people, by calumny, corruption, and terror, were made to work out their own destruction, to kill their best friends, and to strike down the hands that fed them.

THE WORK OF REFORM

In Paris, as in the provinces, a great fear held all hearts in its grip. " The anarchy is most compleat," wrote Lord Auckland on August 27 ; " the people have renounced every idea and principle of subordination . . . even the industry of the labouring class is interrupted and suspended . . . in short, it is sufficient to walk into the streets and to look at the faces of those who pass to see that there is a general impression of Calamity and Terror." [2]

" The National Assembly," Fersen wrote a week later, " trembles before Paris, and Paris trembles before 40,000 to 50,000 bandits and vagabonds encamped at Montmartre and in the Palais Royal." [3]

In the midst of these alarms the Royalist Democrats of the Assembly struggled bravely on with the work of reform. Already the foundations of the Constitution had been laid at the Séance Royale of the 23rd of June ; it only remained for the nobility and clergy to complete the scheme the King had inaugurated by surrendering their seigneurial rights.

Now " the people " of France are by nature retentive of their possessions, and were therefore not disposed to believe that any class enjoying privileges would voluntarily renounce them.

[1] Eighteenth Letter of Mirabeau to his Constituents. See *Moniteur*, i. 191, note 2.
[2] Letter of Lord Auckland to Pitt, Auckland MSS.
[3] *Le Comte de Fersen et la Cour de France*, i. xlix.

The great scheme of the revolutionary leaders from the beginning of the Revolution had been to play on this conviction.[1] In the cahiers drafted by Laclos and Sieyès the " privileged classes " were persistently represented as opposed to reform, and later the disorders in the provinces were instigated by the same propaganda.

The moment had now come to bring off the great *coup* of the revolutionaries and show the nobility and the clergy to the people as their declared enemies. This was to consist in proposing to the Assembly to abolish at a sweep the entire feudal system. The privileged orders would be sure to protest, and a further triumph would thus be provided for the Orléaniste cause. What a signal for fresh insurrections in the provinces if it could be proclaimed to the people that the nobles and clergy had formally refused to relinquish their privileges ! On the other hand, if the " privileged orders " capitulated the Orléanistes would still score a victory, for, as I have shown, the weakening of the noblesse was an essential part of their scheme for making the Duc d'Orléans a monarch à la Louis XIV. " Thus," says Montjoie, " d'Orléans on coming to reign would find no longer those provincial states, those sovereign courts, that clergy, that *noblesse* . . . which formed a tribunate between the King and his subjects . . . there would be in France only one master and a people without protectors." [2]

Even the Republican Gouverneur Morris clearly recognized this danger when he urged Lafayette " to preserve if possible some constitutional authority to the body of the nobles as the only means of preserving any liberty for the people."

The Orléanistes, of course, had no intention of giving liberty to the people, and so the destruction of both nobility and clergy was necessary to their designs. Accordingly, at a meeting of the Club Breton,[3] it was decided that the Vicomte de Noailles, a penniless member of the nobility and an ardent supporter of the Duc d'Orléans, should propose to the Assembly the complete abolition of seigneurial rights.

The plan was carried out on the evening of the 4th of August, but to their eternal honour the nobility and clergy of France rose as one man to renounce all their ancient privileges—seigneurial

---

[1] *Mémoires de l'Abbé Morellet*, i. 335.

[2] On this point the opinion of Montjoie is confirmed by no other than Robespierre himself, for in his illuminating *Rapport* on the Orléaniste conspiracy, delivered four years later through the mouth of St. Just, we find this passage : " They (the Orléanistes) made war on the *noblesse*, the guilty friends of the Bourbons, *in order to pave the way for d'Orléans*. One sees at each step the efforts of this party to ruin the Court and to preserve the monarchy."

[3] Montjoie, *Conjuration*, ii. 120 ; *Histoire de l'Assemblée Constituante*, by Alexandre de Lameth, i. 96.

justice, dîmes, the rights of the chase, and all those feudal dues the loss of which reduced many landed proprietors to beggary.

At the end of the sitting Lally Tollendal rose to remind the Assembly that it was the King who had first set them the example of self-sacrifice by the surrender of his rights, and to propose that "Louis XVI. should now be proclaimed the Restorer of French liberty." [1] This time the eloquence of Lally carried all before him ; the proposal was instantly taken up by both deputies and people ; for a quarter of an hour the hall of the Assembly rang with shouts of "Vive le Roi ! Vive Louis XVI, restaurateur de la liberté française ! "

The decision was conveyed to the King in an address from the Assembly, and Louis XVI., in accepting the title of honour conferred on him, declared his sympathy with the new reforms : " Your wisdom and your intentions inspire me with the greatest confidence in the result of your deliberations. Let us go and pray Heaven to guide us, and render thanks to Him for the generous feelings that prevail in the Assembly." [2] The last obstacle to the work of reform had now been removed, and nothing remained but to frame the Constitution in accordance with the wishes of the King, nobles, clergy, and *people*.

On July 27 the Royalist Democrat, Clermont Tonnerre, had presented to the Assembly the " Declaration of the Rights of Man," [3] and by this charter and the *résumés* of the cahiers the wording of the Constitution was to be framed. Now, on August 27, Mounier, in the name of the Committee of the Constitution, came forward with an improved plan by the Archbishop of Bordeaux.[4] It will be seen, therefore, that the Royalist Democrats were again the leaders of reform and rightly earned the name they bore later of " the Constitutionals," whilst on the other hand we have only to consult the *Moniteur* to find that in the debates that took place on the subject of the Constitution the revolutionary leaders in the Assembly were conspicuous by their silence. The thunderous eloquence of Mirabeau, the biting irony of Robespierre, so potent to destroy, ceased directly the work of reconstruction began. True, the Abbé Sieyès, that " dark horse " of the Assembly—now Royalist, now Republican, and all the while the *intime* of the Orléanistes—had taken part in framing the Constitution, but when it came to renouncing his own privileges Sieyès showed the worth of his Liberalism and openly opposed the abolition of the dîmes,[5] whilst the Arch-

---

[1] *Moniteur*, i. 287 ; Bailly, ii. 217 ; article on Lally Tollendal in *Biographie Michaud*.

[2] *Moniteur*, i. 335.   [3] *Ibid*. i. 216.   [4] *Ibid*. i. 390.

[5] *Ibid*. i. 328 ; *Mémoires de Rivarol*, p. 147.

bishop of Paris, hissed by the mob as an aristocrat, came forward at the head of the clergy to renounce them.[1] The history of the Revolution is full of these little ironies.

It now became evident to the revolutionary leaders that the tide was turning irresistibly against them ; during the discussion on the Constitution the existence neither of the monarchy nor of the reigning dynasty had been brought into dispute—for, so far, no one dared to differ from the unanimous demands of the cahiers—and it was plain that not only the monarchists but Louis Seizistes were leading the House. " Louis XVI.," a deputy had declared, " is no longer on the throne by accident of birth ; he is there by the choice of the nation." [2]

To both Orléanistes and Subversives the future, therefore, looked very black indeed ; at this rate France would be re-generated without further convulsions, and both monarchy and reigning dynasty established more firmly than ever. From the Orléaniste point of view the Constitution would inevitably prove disastrous, for either it would stop the Revolution altogether, or, if they were able to continue it and bring about the desired change of dynasty, the Duc d'Orléans would have to content himself with becoming a Constitutional monarch—a position it would not amuse him in the least to occupy. Some pretext must therefore be found immediately for creating fresh dissensions. This was provided by the debate on the " royal sanction " which began on August 29 and turned on the questions : " Should the King be allowed to retain the right of the ' Veto ' ? If so, should the ' Veto ' be ' absolute ' or ' suspensive '—in other words, should the King be able absolutely to 'veto' the promulgation of a law or merely to suspend its promulgation until a later date ? "

Undoubtedly the Royal Veto was a relic of autocracy, and as such might reasonably be condemned by independent democratic thinkers, but, as several deputies immediately pointed out, the question was one on which the Assembly had no power to deliberate, since " the royal sanction had been demanded by the people in the cahiers." [3]

" The law was made by the nation," said D'Espréménil, " we have only to declare it." [4]

Thus spoke the spirit of pure democracy.

The Royalist Democrats, true to their cahiers as to their King, therefore unanimously supported the royal sanction. " I regard the royal sanction," declared Lally Tollendal, " as one of the first ramparts of national liberty." [5] " I would defend

[1] *Moniteur*, i. 331 ; Rivarol, p. 146.   [2] *Moniteur*, i. 391.
[3] See Articles VI. and VII. quoted on pp. 7 and 8.
[4] *Moniteur*, i. 397.   [5] *Ibid.* i. 419.

it," he said again, " to my last breath, less for the King than for the people." [1]

Here, then, was the pretext needed by the revolutionary leaders for once more stirring up insurrection, and agitators were sent into the clubs and cafés of Paris to tell the citizens that " traitors in the Assembly had voted for the absolute Veto of the King, who would now revoke all the decrees of August the 4th and France would be again enslaved." [2]

They were careful, however, not to mention to the people that several of the Orléaniste deputies, including Mirabeau himself—acting presumably in the interests of the duke—had voted for the *absolute* Veto.[3] The Royalist Democrats alone, and *not* the Royalists who opposed reform, were represented to the people as their enemies. Playfair is one of the few English contemporaries who have commented on this significant fact : " Perhaps the thing that may the most convince impartial men of the existence of a criminal plot is, that the moderate party of the reformers in the Assembly, that is those who were royalists, but had obtained popular favour by their eloquence and *love of liberty*, were those whom the party in power, the Lameths, Barnave, Mirabeau, etc., turned against with the greatest fury. Mounier, the Count de Lally Tollendal, and upwards of forty more of the moderate party, received anonymous letters threatening their lives. . . . This would seem to be proof that the reigning party were more afraid of the men who were attached to liberty than of the pure royalists, as the personal characters of the former left no hopes of leading them over to the violent measures in view." [4]

So again we find *the revolutionary movement diametrically opposed to the work of reform.* Let any one who challenges this statement explain the following circumstance : the plan of the Constitution founded on the Declaration of the Rights of Man— universally agreed to be the purest expression of democracy—was given to the Assembly by the Royalist Democrats on August 28, and two days later a price was set on the heads of all these men by the revolutionaries at the Palais Royal.[5] Mounier, who

---

[1] *Moniteur*, i. 399.

[2] *Deux Amis*, ii. 361 ; *Mémoires de Bailly*, ii. 327 ; Ferrières, i. 222.

[3] According to the *Mémoires de La Fayette*, Mirabeau had voted for the absolute Veto on the advice of Clavière, the future Girondin : " ' You see that bald head,' he said, pointing out Clavière to several deputies who spoke to him in favour of the Suspensive Veto, ' I do nothing without consulting it.' And the bald head, Republican in Geneva on the 10th of August (1792), had declared for the absolute Veto " (*Mémoires de La Fayette*, iii. 311).

[4] Playfair's *History of Jacobinism*, p. 244.

[5] Article on Mounier in *Biographie Michaud* by Lally Tollendal.

from the first had shown himself the most intrepid champion of liberty—Mounier who in an excess of democratic zeal had proposed the Oath of the Tennis Court, and to whom more than to any one the principles of the Constitution were due—was now held up to popular execration, and from this moment his life was perpetually threatened.[1] Could there be any explanation but the one offered by Mounier himself—that the whole agitation was a plot to prevent the framing of the Constitution ?[2]

FIRST ATTEMPT TO MARCH ON VERSAILLES

By the usual methods of calumny and terror the mind of the populace was once more stirred up, and a panic on the subject of the Veto spread through Paris. The fact that to many of the people the Latin word conveyed no meaning whatever greatly facilitated the work of the agitators. " Do you know what the Veto is ? " they cried out at the street corners. " Listen, then. You go home and your wife has prepared your dinner, then the King says ' Veto ! ' and you get nothing to eat ! "[3]

The " suspensive Veto," a peasant told Bertrand de Molleville, was the right of the King to suspend, *i.e.* to *hang*, any one he pleased. Some people, indeed, believed the Veto to be alive : " What is he, this Veto ? What has he done, this brigand Veto ? "[4]

By the evening of Sunday, August 30, the garden of the Palais Royal had become once more a raging sea ; so immense was the crowd that it overflowed into the surrounding houses ; the windows and the very roofs were packed with people. Suddenly from a window of the Café de Foy there shot forth the shoulders and shaggy black head of Camille Desmoulins, who shouted excitedly to the assembled multitude :

" Messieurs, I have just received a letter from Versailles telling me that the life of the Comte de Mirabeau is no longer safe, and it is for the defence of our liberty that he is exposed to danger ! "[5]

The panic news was passed from mouth to mouth—" Mirabeau has paid with his life-blood his attachment to the cause of the

---

[1] " M. Mounier, one of the principal authors of the Revolution and one of the first leaders of the patriotic party, became suddenly the object of the people's hatred and of the favour of aristocracy ! " (*Deux Amis*, iii. 166). For " people " as usual read " revolutionaries " !

[2] Mounier to the Assembly, August 31 : " It is evident that perverse men desire to build up their fortunes on the ruins of the country. You see the plan to prevent the Constitution from being formed and developed " (*Moniteur*, i. 400).

[3] *La Révolution*, by Louis Madelin, p. 87.

[4] Article on St. Huruge in the *Revue de la Révolution*, published by Gustave Bord, vol. vi. p. 251.

[5] *Procédure du Châtelet*, evidence of Dwall, witness cccxvii.

people "—"Mirabeau has been stabbed to the heart—no, poisoned "—a letter from Mirabeau himself warned the people that the country was in danger, that fourteen men had betrayed their cause.[1]

These tidings drove the crowd into a frenzy of alarm, and thus the ridiculous situation was created of a vast multitude inveighing against the Veto and at the same time stricken with panic for the safety of its chief supporter—Mirabeau ! " The people," remarks Bailly, " did not as yet know their lesson." [2]

It was now that the Orléanistes saw their opportunity for launching their great scheme of *a march on Versailles*. If the King persisted in retaining his popularity with the people by giving into their demands and continuing to favour reforms, it was idle to hope that the people would rise against him. The remoteness of Versailles from the centre of agitation added greatly to the glamour that surrounded the person of the King ; shut in behind the gilded barriers and the dim red walls of the great château of the Roi Soleil, Louis XVI. still retained to some degree the character of a sacred being, whose infrequent appearance in public inspired the great mass of the people with wondering awe. But if Louis XVI. could be brought to Paris to become the object of everyday contemplation by the multitude, the halo might be expected to fall from his head. At the palace of the Tuileries, close to the Palais Royal, the revolutionary leaders would have him in their power,[3] and the populace they held at their command could be trained to degrade the Royal Family in the eyes of the still loyal people.

Accordingly it was announced at the Palais Royal that in order to save the country from the horrors of the Veto, and to ensure the safety of Mirabeau, a deputation must be sent to the Assembly to insist that the King and the Dauphin should be brought to Paris. Camille Desmoulins shrieked that the Queen must be imprisoned at St. Cyr and that the deputation should consist of 15,000 armed men. At the same time threatening messages were despatched to the President of the Assembly, the bishop of Langres ; one signed by St. Huruge ran thus : " The Patriotic Assembly of the Palais Royal have the honour to inform you that if that portion of the aristocracy, composed of a party in the clergy, a party in the noblesse, and 120 members of the Commons, ignorant and corrupt, continue to disturb harmony and to demand the ' absolute sanction,' 15,000 men are ready to light up their houses and châteaux, and yours in

[1] Ferrières, i. 220 ; *Deux Amis*, ii. 360.
[2] *Mémoires de Bailly*, ii. 327.
[3] *Appel au Tribunal de l'Opinion publique*, by Mounier, p. 65.

particular, Monsieur, and to inflict on the deputies who betray their country the fate of Foullon and of Berthier."[1]

The authorship of these two murders was thus clearly revealed. But the number of insurgents promised by the leaders was not forthcoming, and at ten o'clock in the evening St. Huruge, armed with the petition, set forth at the head of only 1500 unarmed men for Versailles. The aspect of their leader was terrible enough to inspire his followers with courage—a massive figure surmounted by a huge red face, eyes of extraordinary audacity flaming forth from under a thick black wig, St. Huruge appeared the very incarnation of the revolutionary spirit.[2]

But the daring of St. Huruge, like the daring of Danton, was more apparent than real ; the first sight of danger reduced him to the utmost meekness.[3] On this occasion danger of a very formidable kind confronted him—Lafayette, the great opponent of the Orléaniste conspiracy, was ready for him. The procession having marched boldly down the Rue Saint-Honoré found their passage blocked by the National Guard, of which Lafayette was the commander, and being turned back they proceeded to march to the Hôtel de Ville, where Bailly and Lafayette himself were waiting to receive them. The popular general had little difficulty in reducing St. Huruge to submission ; perfectly docile and even " contented " he consented to retire from the scene, but for greater safety Lafayette imprisoned him in the Châtelet.

So ended this first attempt to march on Versailles. But the project was not abandoned. On the contrary, from this moment it was perpetually discussed, and a fresh pretext was sought for stirring up the people.

EVENTS AT VERSAILLES

When on the 18th of September the King made his reply to the demands of the Assembly requesting him to sanction the reforms of the 4th of August, it became evident that no opposition could be hoped for from the royal authority. The King's reply was both reasonable and sympathetic ; in a long and detailed analysis he discussed each reform in turn, pointing out that certain articles were only the text for laws that the Assembly must frame. He ended with the words : " Therefore I approve

---

[1] *Mémoires de Bailly*, iii. 392.
[2] *Esquisses historiques de la Révolution Française*, by Dulaure, p. 286.
[3] A contemporary records that St. Huruge having been once reproached for allowing himself to be flogged without retaliating, he replied, " I never interfere with what goes on behind my back " (*L'Ami des Lois*, 17 pluviose, An VIII). See article on St. Huruge in the *Revue de la Révolution* edited by Gustave Bord, vol. vi.

the greater number of these articles, and I will sanction them
when they have been drawn up into laws."

This conciliatory reply left the revolutionary leaders no
further ground for agitation, and they contented themselves
with insolently remarking that the King had not been asked to
"sanction" the decrees of the Assembly but only to "promulgate"
them. Floods of rhetoric were then expended on the precise
significance of the two words. But as the King sensibly observed,
how was it possible to " promulgate " laws that had not yet
been framed ? However, in order to pacify the contentious
deputies, he finally yielded to their demands, and two days later,
on August 28, accorded his " acceptation pure and simple " to the
decrees of August 4.[1]

The Assembly then proceeded to discuss the embarrassment
in the finances. But here again the King showed his desire to
relieve the situation by coming forward to offer all his silver
plate to the nation, whilst at the same time the Queen sent 60,000
livres' worth to the Mint. The proposition met with immediate
remonstrance from the Assembly, but the King persisted in his
resolution.[2]

This was the moment chosen by Mirabeau for a tirade against
" the rich "—" the frightful gulf of bankruptcy must be filled,"
he declared to the Assembly. " Well, then, here is the list of
French proprietors. Choose amongst the richest so as to sacrifice the fewest citizens. . . . Strike ! Immolate without pity
those wretched victims ; precipitate them into the abyss ; it will
close again ! . . . You shrink with horror ? Inconsistent men !
Pusillanimous men ! "[3]

The speech was received with " almost convulsive applause "
by the Assembly.

Yet how was Mirabeau himself carrying out the principle of
austere self-sacrifice ? Camille Desmoulins will tell us. On the
29th of September—exactly three days after Mirabeau's tirade—
Camille wrote these words : " I have been for a week at Versailles
with Mirabeau. We have become great friends ; at least he
calls me his dear friend. At every moment he takes me by the
hands, he thumps me, then he goes off to the Assembly, resumes

[1] The King is frequently stated to have refused this sanction until
October 5, but contemporaries of all parties are explicit on this point.
See *Deux Amis*, iii. 29 ; *Mémoires de Bailly*, ii. 379 ; Marmontel, iv. 238 ;
Histoire de l'Assemblée Constituante, by Alexandre de Lameth, i. 142.

[2] *Moniteur*, i. 496 ; Bailly, ii. 389. On the question of the King's
" rigid economy " with regard to his personal expenses see the address from
the National Assembly on January 5, 1790 (*Moniteur*, iii. 52).

[3] *Moniteur*, i. 519. Molé, the actor, who was present on this occasion,
delighted Mirabeau by telling him he had missed his vocation—he should
have gone on the stage ! (*Souvenirs d'Étienne Dumont*, p. 133).

his dignity as he enters the hall and works wonders, after which he comes back to dine with excellent company and sometimes with his mistress, and we drink excellent wine. I feel that his too delicate fare and overloaded table corrupt me. His claret and his maraschino have a virtue that I vainly seek to ignore, and I have all the difficulty in the world in resuming my republican [1] austerity and in detesting the aristocrats whose crime is to give these excellent dinners. I prepare motions, and Mirabeau calls that initiating me into great affairs. It seems to me that I ought to think myself happy when I remember my position at Guise. . . ." Oh, people, these are your defenders !

It is said that only a few weeks before, Mirabeau, looking out of the window and seeing a crowd of poor people fighting at a baker's shop for bread, uttered the cynical remark, " That *canaille* there well deserves to have us for legislators ! " Like Danton he at least was frank, and no one would have been more amused than Mirabeau himself at the efforts of his biographers to represent him as a lofty idealist and lover of the people.

What was the truth about Mirabeau at this juncture when the march on Versailles was being planned in the councils of the Orléaniste leaders ? Was he amongst them ? His panegyrists have vainly endeavoured to absolve him from complicity, but contemporaries, even those who were his friends, are obliged to admit that he knew what was to take place even if he did not help to prepare the movement.

" I am inclined to think," says Dumont, " that Mirabeau was in the secret of the events of the 5th and 6th of October. . . . What I believe is, taking everything into consideration, supposing that the insurrection of Versailles was led by the agents of the Duc d'Orléans, that Laclos was too clever to confide everything to the indiscretion of Mirabeau, but that he had made sure of him conditionally. . . . It is impossible not to believe in some *liaison* between them." [2] This from the *intime* of Mirabeau is conclusive. Camille Desmoulins, who at this date " idolized " Mirabeau, also gave away his friend later on : " Will any one make me believe that when I stayed at Versailles with Mirabeau immediately before the 6th of October . . . I saw nothing of

---

[1] The use of the word " republican " by Desmoulins at this date may seem to contradict the statement that he was an Orléaniste, but the word was frequently used during the earlier stages of the Revolution to signify simply " public-spirited " (see, for example, the remark of Mounier to Mirabeau on p. 140). On the other hand, Montjoie may be right in saying that at this moment Camille Desmoulins had temporarily gone over to Lafayette and Republicanism (*Conjuration de d'Orléans*, ii. 153). This would explain the disagreement that seems to have taken place between Desmoulins and Mirabeau at the end of this visit to Versailles.

[2] *Souvenirs sur Mirabeau*, p. 121.

the precursory movements of the 5th and 6th ? Will any one make me believe that when I went to Mirabeau at the moment that he heard the Duc d'Orléans had started for London, his anger at seeing himself abandoned, his imprecations . . . made me conjecture nothing ? " [1]

The plan of the conspirators was undoubtedly either to persuade the mob to march on Versailles and murder the King and Queen, or more probably to murder the Queen only and bring the King to Paris. Of all this Mirabeau was evidently well aware—even if he was not one of the authors of the scheme —and it would seem that at moments the dreadful secret preyed on his mind. Perhaps amidst the mire of his life some hereditary traditions of honour, some instincts of chivalry, had survived which made him shrink from the brutal crime of which a noble and beautiful woman was to be the chief victim, and at these moments he was almost tempted to abandon the sordid intrigue into which he had been drawn and throw himself into the worthier cause of defending his King against the designs of a usurper. Yet if he did so, what reception would he meet with from the Court ? The King and Queen, he well knew, regarded him with aversion. Was it not possible, therefore, that by deserting the conspiracy he might simply become the enemy of Orléans and gain no favour with the King ? Thus haunted with the horror of the thing he wished the King would find out for himself the tragedy that was impending. Often at this time Mirabeau, in speaking of the Court to his friend La Marck, would ask uncontrollably, " What are these people thinking of? Do they not see the abyss that is opening under their feet ? " Once in a violent outbreak of exasperation he cried out, " All is lost ; the King and Queen will perish—you will see it—and the populace will batter their corpses." And then, seeing the horror on the face of La Marck, he repeated, " Yes, yes, their corpses will be battered—you do not understand sufficiently the danger of their position ; it ought to be made known to them."

But it *had* been made known to them, and by Lafayette himself in a letter to the Comte de St. Priest dated September 17. On the 23rd, therefore, the King warned the Assembly of " the threats of ill-disposed persons to march out of Paris with arms," and of the measures he had taken for the protection of the deputies. The Assembly, however, was already aware of the intention. "I repeat without fear of contradiction," says Mounier, " that every day the ministers received the most alarming information on this subject, and the King's Guards were several times obliged to spend the night in readiness to mount their horses." [2]

[1] *Fragment de l'Histoire secrète de la Révolution*, 1793.
[2] *Appel au Tribunal de l'Opinion publique*, p. 67.

What law obliged one at Versailles to wear the cockade ? Why should one not have been allowed to prefer the hat from all time had been that of our flag ? Why, on that the Royal Family was threatened, should not all ous men have rallied round this sign of fidelity ? "[1]

range incident followed the banquet. A chasseur of the vêchés was found by Miomandre, an officer of the Royal e, sunk in despair, with his forehead resting on the hilt word. When asked what was his trouble he broke out s and disjointed sentences in which the following words ere audible : " That fine household of the King . . . I am fool . . . The monsters, what do they demand ? . . . those of a commander and D'Orléans ! " Then falling on his e attempted to take his life. At this moment several omrades appeared on the scene, and hearing what had l one of them exclaimed, " He is a good-for-nothing— t get rid of him ! " Thereupon they kicked the wretched death " as one would crush an insect."[2]

ill be seen, then, how frightful were the consequences to who attempted to betray the designs of the conspirators, tent was the Orléaniste " terror " that during the first f the Revolution held sway over the minds of men and he lips of those who would have revealed the truth con- the preparations for the insurrection of October 5.

IMINARIES OF THE MARCH ON VERSAILLES

story of the Guards' " orgy " had served the purpose of g this loyal regiment odious to the people, but a further must be removed from their path if the conspirators succeed in their scheme of bringing the King to Paris. s necessary," says Mounier, " in order to execute their get rid of the King's guards and of all those who would fended his liberty. *They feared the courage of the Queen,* he must be given over to the fury of the people."[3] Louis urrounded by his feeble and purblind ministers, was not ared ; they had but to assure him that the people wished go to Paris and to Paris he would go. But the Queen ee the plot and offer resistance. " The King," said u a year later, " has only one man with him—that is ."[4]

y every species of calumny, by the circulation of the

[1] *Appel au Tribunal*, by Mounier, p. 91.
[2] *Deux Amis*, iii. 134 ; Ferrières, i. 279.
[3] *Appel au Tribunal*, p. 65.
[4] *Correspondance entre Mirabeau et La Marck*, p. 107.

If under these circumstances a plan was formed by certain Royalists to convey the Royal Family to Metz or to some other place of safety, is it altogether surprising ? That any such project existed has never yet been proved—the only evidence brought forward by the revolutionary writers being the rough copy of a letter from the Comte d'Estaing to the Queen[1] which fell into the hands of the conspirators—but even if the supposi- tion were correct, what perfidy would this imply on the part of the Royalists ? Why, if the lives of the King and Queen were daily threatened, should not their loyal supporters attempt to rescue them from their assassins ? The scheme involved no design on the liberties of the nation, and the flight of the Royal Family to Metz would have been undertaken, like the flight to Varennes two years later, simply in self-defence. At any rate, one undeniable fact remains—the plan was not attempted, the King and Queen of their own free will decided to stay at Versailles and face the danger.

THE BANQUET OF THE BODYGUARD

The municipality of Versailles, alarmed no less for the safety of the town than of the Royal Family, now decided, on the advice of the Comte d'Estaing, commander of the National Guard of Versailles, to request the King to summon another regiment as a reinforcement of the bodyguard, the Swiss dragoons and *milice bourgeoise* that at present constituted the garrison, and were held to be inadequate " to resist the attack of 2000 armed men."[2] Accordingly the " Régiment de Flandre " was ordered to Versailles and arrived on September 23. Immediately the conspirators set to work to corrupt the newly arrived troops, and women of the town were sent to distribute money, food, and wine amongst the soldiers,[3] and to exact from them the promise not to defend the King in case of insurrection. " One would not have supposed," writes a revolutionary chronicler of the day, " that it is to the vilest class of our prostitutes that we owe the happy event that brought the King to Paris and the consolation that the day of October the 5th was not more murderous. . . . The leaders of the people . . . sent to Versailles . . . in bands and by different routes three hundred of the prettiest street-walkers of the Palais Royal with money, instructions, and the promise of being disembowelled by the people if they did not carry out

[1] *Deux Amis*, iii. 101 ; Montjoie, *Conjuration de d'Orléans*, ii. 167.
[2] *Deux Amis*, iii. 112 ; Bailly, ii. 281 ; Rivarol, p. 256.
[3] Montjoie, *Conjuration de d'Orléans*, ii. 172 ; Ferrières, ii. 273 ; evidence of Elizabeth Pannier, wife of a restaurant keeper at Versailles, witness xx. in *Procédure du Châtelet*.

their mission faithfully. It was these female deputies who, amidst the pleasures of love, obtained from the soldiers the patriotic oath which rendered their arms powerless before their fellow-citizens." [1]

By the same means which had been employed to seduce the Gardes Françaises before the siege of the Bastille, the men of the Regiment de Flandre were now turned from their allegiance to the King, and *as a sign of defection* adopted the tricolour cockade.[2]

The loyal troops of the King saw all this with growing alarm, and resolved to bring the Flemish regiment back to its allegiance. Now it was a time-honoured custom for the King's bodyguard to entertain at supper any newly arrived regiment; accordingly the officers of the Regiment de Flandre were invited to a banquet at which a number of the Swiss Guards, the *milice bourgeoise*, and others were also present. The theatre of the Château, lent by the King for the occasion, was brilliantly decorated, and lit by hundreds of candles; around a huge horse-shoe table the officers of the bodyguard and the officers of the Flemish regiment were seated alternately, and the bands of the two regiments played throughout the feast. Were the faithful soldiers of the King to blame if they took this opportunity to revive the waning loyalty of their comrades? Were they to be reproached with treachery to the nation if under their influence the men of the Flemish regiment broke out into cries of " Vive le Roi ! "

When at this juncture the Royal Family entered the hall, the Queen leading Madame Royale by the hand, an officer of the bodyguard carrying the Dauphin in his arms, enthusiasm knew no bounds, and a storm of acclamation burst forth unrestrained.

To the minds of Frenchmen there was something intensely tragic in the sudden apparition of the little group over whose heads so terrible a storm was gathering, and at the sight of the Queen—a beautiful woman, a wife, a mother, whose life they knew was daily threatened—all the ancient chivalry of France awoke in them, and to a man they resolved to defend her. The last touch of pathos was given by the band of the Regiment de Flandre with the air from " Richard Cœur de Lion " :

O ! Richard ! o mon Roi ! l'univers t'abandonne !

The selection was painfully apt ; all the world was deserting the unhappy King, and with the passionate loyalty of their race the gallant bodyguard at this supreme moment mustered around him. Men of both regiments sprang on to their chairs, waved

[1] *Correspondance secrète*, i. 414.
[2] *Faits relatifs à la dernière insurrection*, by Mounier.

their glasses aloft, and shouted them [...]
" Vive le Roi ! Vive la Reine ! Vive [...]

The scene was afterwards descri[...] as a " drunken orgy " ; it is possible [...] had gone to the heads of the revell[...] unprecedented in the annals of regi[...] fact implies no criminal intention tow[...]

The occasion provided, however, [...] conspirators were waiting, and the st[...] lated in Versailles and carried to the [...] the Duc d'Orléans himself [1]—that th[...] had refused to drink the health of th[...] under foot the " national cockade." [...] ally denied by eye-witnesses of the sc[...] of one man alone, a certain Laurent [...] officer in the *milice bourgeoise* of Ver[...] rancour against the bodyguard becau[...] to the banquet,[3] and who was therefo[...]

The exact truth about the " toast [...] to discover, but from the evidence of [...] it appears that the health of the nat[...] the toast was not a customary one, a[...] this or any former occasion.[4] It was [...]

As to the incidents of the cockade[...] guard could not have torn off the nati[...] on them, for the simple reason that t[...] but were still wearing the white cock[...] seems that white cockades were distr[...] Court to the Régiment de Flandre, a[...] to exclaim, " Long live the white coc[...]

But when we remember that th[...] colours of the Duc d'Orléans, that it h[...] " national " but the " revolutionary c[...] amongst soldiers as the badge of d[...] that those who desired the King's [...] designs of a usurper should have atte[...] royal emblem ? If so, as Mounier p[...]

[1] Evidence of De Pelletier and of De [...] *Châtelet*.
[2] *Mémoires de Mme. Campan*, p. 248 ; s[...] to the Assembly on October 1, 1790, in *Mo[...] La Brousse de Belleville, witness XXII. in [...]
[3] Montjoie, *Conjuration de d'Orléans*, i[...] Mounier, p. 111.
[4] Ferrières, i. 275.
[5] *Ibid.* i. 260 ; *Deux Amis*, iii. 128.
[6] *Faits relatifs à la dernière Insurrectio[...]

crime [...]
of Pa[...]
colour[...]
a day[...]
coura[...]

A [...]
Trois [...]
Ture[...]
of his[...]
into s[...]
alone [...]
a grea[...]
rascal[...]
sword [...]
of his[...]
occur[...]
we m[...]
man t[...]

It [...]
any o[...]
how [...]
stages[...]
sealed[...]
cernin[...]

PR[...]

Th[...]
rende[...]
obsta[...]
were [...]
" It [...]
plan, [...]
have [...]
and s[...]
XVI.[...]
to be [...]
him t[...]
would[...]
Mira[...]
his w[...]
So[...]

foulest libels, by every method the "infernal genius" of Laclos could devise,[1] popular rage was stirred up against the Queen at the Palais Royal and in the Faubourgs of Paris. "The Queen was at the head of a counter-revolution—the Queen was the sole cause of the disorder in the finances—the Queen had said that the happiest day of her life would be when she could wash her hands in the blood of the French," that she "would not mind being shut up in Paris, provided the walls of her prison were made of the bones of Frenchmen."[2] But the accusation that stirred most deeply the passions of the people was that the Queen was responsible for the scarcity of bread. For, in spite of a magnificent harvest only six weeks earlier, the supplies of grain were again declared to be insufficient, the bakers' shops were besieged, working-men waited all day to obtain a 4 lb. loaf and returned empty-handed to their starving families.

Hunger is apt to render one light-headed; under its dizzying spell many things seem possible that with a well-nourished brain one would recognize as absurd, and so the half-famished dwellers in the Faubourgs readily accepted the assurance that the King, the Queen, and the "aristocrats" were at the bottom of the trouble. Gouverneur Morris thus describes an orator haranguing the people : "The substance of his discourse was : ' Messieurs, we are in want of bread, and this is the reason—it is only three days since the King has had the suspensive Veto, and already the aristocrats have bought suspensions and sent the grain out of the kingdom.' To this sensible and profound discourse his audience gave a hearty assent. ' Ma foi ! he is right. It is only that ! ' Oh, rare ! These are the modern Athenians ! "

But were these poor people altogether to blame for their credulity ? Many of them could neither read nor write. How were they to know that neither Court nor aristocrats had anything whatever to do with the circulation of grain at this crisis, since the whole question had been placed under the control of the "Committee of Subsistences," headed by the popular mayor, Bailly, who, helpless as ever before the manœuvres of the Orléanistes, vainly endeavoured to thwart the monopolizers ?[3]

The truth is that this famine, like the one that had threatened earlier in the year, was *fictitious* ; the want of bread, as con-temporaries of all parties agree, did not really exist, but was artificially produced in order to inflame the minds of the people

[1] "I know that several of the libels published then (before the 5th of October) were paid for by the agents of the Duc d'Orléans" (*Mémoires de Malouet*, i. 344). Others were undoubtedly paid for by Von der Goltz.

[2] *Lettre d'un Français sur les moyens qui ont opéré la Révolution*, pp. 11, 12, and 31.

[3] *La Conspiration révolutionnaire de 1789*, by Gustave Bord, p. 211.

against the Court and Government.[1] This point, habitually over-looked by historians, gives the key to the whole movement of October 5.

Moreover, that this artificial famine was again the work of the Orléaniste conspiracy there can be no doubt whatever, for apart from the statements of Montjoie, Rivarol, the Comte d'Hézecques, and Mounier, which all exactly agree, we have that of Bailly himself, and no one was in a better position than the mayor to judge of the real state of affairs, nor was any man less likely to defend the Court against the accusation of a plot if any such had existed. Who were the authors of the plot Bailly, however, indicates very clearly : " The parties who sought to bring about an insurrection, well realizing that there was no finer opportunity than the want of supplies, made every effort to make an unequal division either by pillaging our convoys without (the city) or taking them by force from the bakers within, or else by cornering the bread so that one should have too much and the other go without, or in purposely placing amongst the crowd assembled at the bakers' doors strong men who could ill-treat and injure the weak so as to make the people complain. When I passed in front of one of these shops and saw this crowd, my heart was torn, and I can still hardly see a baker's shop without emotion." [2] A further method employed by the agitators was to tell the people that the flour was bad, and as much of that which was now on the markets came from abroad, and differed in colour and flavour from the home - grown variety, this story was readily believed, and the people were persuaded to rip up the sacks, dispersing the contents.   No less than 2000 sackfuls were thrown into the Seine.[3] These diabolical methods had the desired effect of denuding the markets and driving the poor of Paris to desperation.

[1] See, amongst the assertions of innumerable contemporaries, that of Mounier, *Appel au Tribunal*, p. 74 : " At the time of October the 5th, means were adopted that had been tried several times before, that of creating a famine and then accusing those who were called aristocrats so as to give the impression that abundance was at the disposal of a prince without power, and thus to associate the feeling of vengeance with the feeling of want." Mounier goes on to point out that Brissot himself was obliged to admit that before the insurrection of October 5 " there had existed for some days that apparent famine of which we spoke before. *This famine did not really exist.*"   Brissot then proceeded to accuse " the aristocrats," but as Mounier observed : " We will not seek to show how absurd it was to accuse of these manœuvres those who were to be the victims of them, whilst it would have been much more correct to conclude that since the aristocrats of Versailles were the objects of the people's hatred, that hatred was excited by the partisans of the democracy. It is at any rate true that M. Brissot admitted the famine was *fictitious* and consequently that a plot existed."

[2] Bailly, ii. 406.   [3] *Ibid*. ii. 359.

Meanwhile the agitators were hard at work.   In the Faubourg Saint-Antoine, Santerre and the orator Gonchon, whose red and blotchy countenance rivalled in hideosity that of Danton or of St. Huruge, stirred up insurrection.[1] At the Palais Royal, on Sunday, October 4, " Danton roared his denunciations," and " Marat made as much noise as the four trumpets on the Day of Judgment." It was now that the morrow's march on Versailles was publicly announced on the pretext of " the scarcity of bread, the desire of avenging the national cockade, and of bringing the King to Paris."[2]

By these means the movement, like the one that had preceded the siege of the Bastille, was made to appear spontaneous — an uncontrollable rising of the people that the leaders were powerless to subdue. But at the Duc d'Orléans' house in Passy[3] the march had already been planned, and the elements of which the mob was to be composed arranged by the conspirators.

" If an insurrection were possible," Mirabeau had said, " it would only be in the event of women mingling in the movement and taking the lead."[4] Did the idea of a " hunger march of women " originate with Mirabeau ? Or had he merely in one of his frequent moments of indiscretion given away the secret of his party ? The truth will never be known, yet one thing is certain — the plan did not originate with the women, but was adopted for an excellent reason by the organizers of the expedition.

Now, the leaders of the revolutionary mobs were never fond of facing artillery or troops of whose defection they had not previously assured themselves, and at Versailles they well knew that not only the King's faithful bodyguard awaited them, but also certain cannons which pointed threateningly at the Avenue de Paris, by which the procession must approach the Château. If, however, a contingent of women could be induced to march first and form a screen between them and the troops, the rest of the army could safely advance with their artillery.[5] The plan was well thought out, and the conspirators entertained no doubt that the women of Paris could be incited by the pangs of hunger to co-operate. Accordingly supplies were now entirely cut off,

---

[1] Gonchon received the sum of 30,000 to 40,000 francs for each insurrection he succeeded in exciting (*Memoirs of the Comtesse de Bohm*, p. 196, edited by De Lescure).

[2] *Appel au Tribunal*, by Mounier, p. 123.

[3] *Histoire de la Révolution de France*, by Fantin Désodoards, i. 340.

[4] *Crimes de la Révolution*, by Prudhomme, iii. 161.

[5] *Appel au Tribunal*, p. 123 : " Those who directed it (the insurrection) had judged it expedient to make it begin with women, so that the soldiers would be less likely to use force."

and when the wet and windy morning of Monday the 5th of October dawned, the Faubourgs of Saint-Antoine and Saint-Marceau found themselves absolutely without bread.

THE 5TH OF OCTOBER

This was the signal for the insurrection to begin, and as early as six o'clock bands of rioters, led by harridans of ferocious aspect, started out to collect recruits. Now, according to the history books that enlightened our youth, the women thus assembled and induced to march on Versailles were principally fishwives, ragged and dishevelled furies, endowed, like their counterparts in our own old Billingsgate, with a peculiar talent for invective. Rivarol, however, in a passage which we shall find later on confirmed by unquestionable evidence, shatters this time-honoured legend. " The women who went from Paris to Versailles are always designated by the name of *poissardes*. This is unfortunate for those who sell fish and fruit in the streets and markets; truth compels one to say that, far from joining forces with the *sham poissardes* who came to recruit them, they asked at the guard-house at the point of Saint-Eustache for help in driving them back." [1] Why, indeed, should the *poissardes* wish to march on Versailles ? In the past the King and Queen had no more loyal subjects than the women whom the Old Régime courteously designated " the Ladies of the Market." Was it not their privilege to present themselves before their Majesties and express in prose or verse their congratulations or condolences on every event of importance ? Moreover, the gala dress of black silk and diamonds they wore on these occasions [2] proclaimed them to be no wretched victims of want and misery, such as we have seen depicted riding on the cannons to Versailles, but prosperous " citizenesses " who took a truly Parisian pride in their appearance. What wonder, then, that the " Ladies of the Market " indignantly refused to join the motley crowd that had collected on the Place de Grève for the purposes of insurrection ?

Indeed, it was obvious to all onlookers that this crowd was not what it pretended to be—a gathering of hungry women driven by desperation to revolt. " The first women who presented themselves at the Hôtel de Ville were powdered, *coiffées*, and dressed in white, with an air of gaiety, and gave evidence of no evil intentions ; gradually their numbers increased ; some rang the tocsin, others laughed, sang, and danced in the court-

---

[1] *Mémoires de Rivarol*, p. 263.
[2] *Mémoires de Mme. Campan*, p. 167.

yard," [1] which proves, as Mounier says, "that amongst these women a large number were not suffering from want, but were only sent to stir up the others." [2]

Moreover, the aspect of certain of the harridans and so-called *poissardes* who led the movement struck observers as peculiar, for it was noticed that beneath ragged skirts there peeped forth trousers, that shaven chins appeared above muslin fichus, and that large heavily-shod feet presented an odd contrast to rouged and powdered faces. In a word, it became apparent that a number of these " hungry women " were not women at all but *men in women's clothes*,[3] and it was said that amongst them were recognized several of the Orléaniste leaders—Laclos, Chamfort, Latouche, Sillery, Barnave, and one of the Lameths [4]—whilst one " monstrously fat " *poissarde* was declared by the people to be the Duc d'Aiguillon.[5] According to certain contemporaries these gentlemen—notably Laclos and Chamfort—were accompanied by their mistresses, and Taine adds that their number was swelled by a quantity of deserters from the Gardes Françaises with the women of the Palais Royal, to whom they acted as *souteneurs*, and from whom they may have borrowed their disguises.[6]

These, then, were the elements that formed the nucleus of the expedition, and it will therefore be understood why the first contingent of women presented so gay and prosperous an appearance. But in order to give a popular air to the rising it was necessary to secure the co-operation of as many " women of the people " as could be induced to join the procession, accordingly shops, workrooms, and private houses were entered, and cooks, seamstresses, mothers of families were bribed or forced to follow —threatened with violence if they refused. A washerwoman on the Seine described to the Chevalier d'Estrées the efforts made to enlist working-women in the movement. " What ! " the Chevalier had said ironically to this woman on the 5th of October, " you are not at Versailles ? " to which the washer-woman indignantly replied, " Monsieur le Chevalier, you are mistaken, like every one else, in imagining that it is laundresses

---

[1] Evidence of M. de Blois, member of the Commune, witness xxxv. in the *Procédure du Châtelet*.

[2] *Appel au Tribunal*, p. 124.

[3] On the men in women's clothes see *Appel au Tribunal*, by Mounier, p. 124, and the testimony of eye-witnesses VII., IX., X., XXXIII., XXXIV., XXXV., XLIV., LIX., XCVIII., CX., CXLVI., CLXV., CCXXXVII., CCCXVI., and many others in the *Procédure du Châtelet*.

[4] *Mémoires concernant Marie Antoinette*, by Joseph Weber, ii. 210; Montjoie, *Conjuration de d'Orléans*, ii. 245; evidence of the Chevalier de La Serre, witness CCXXVI. in *Procédure du Châtelet*.

[5] Evidence of La Serre and St. Martin (officer in the Régiment de Flandre), witness XCVIII. in *Procédure du Châtelet*.

[6] Taine, *La Révolution*, i. 153.

and other women of the same kind who have gone to Versailles. Some one certainly came to my boat and made the proposal to myself and my companions, and it was a woman who offered us six and twelve francs, but that woman is no more a woman than you are; I recognized her distinctly as a seigneur living at the Palais Royal or near it, whose valet I wash for." [1]

But if the honest and industrious women of the people showed themselves unwilling, there lurked nevertheless a terrible element of violence in the underworld of Paris that even another century of civilization has never robbed of its ferocity, and that once its passions are aroused knows neither reason nor pity. From this underworld there now poured forth bands of wastrels and degenerates, drink-sodden women clutching broomsticks, above all, street-walkers inflamed with the easily-roused passions of their kind, reckless, abandoned, shrieking foul invectives—all these assembled on the Place de Grève and proceeded to attack the Hôtel de Ville. With a hail of stones they drove back the mounted guards defending the entrance, and battering down the doors swarmed into the building, pillaged the armoury, carried off two cannons, eight hundred guns, as well as munitions and silver, attempted to hang a luckless priest they discovered in the belfry, shouting the while, " The men have no courage, they dare not take revenge! We will act for them! The representatives of the Commune are traitors and bad citizens, they deserve death, M. Bailly and Lafayette first of all—they must be hanged to the lantern."

These imprecations again show very clearly the influences at work amongst the crowd, for both Bailly and Lafayette were the idols of the people, but had rendered themselves odious to the agitators—Bailly by his indefatigable efforts to provide the capital with bread, and Lafayette by his steady opposition to the Orléaniste conspiracy. So once again we see the power of the mob turned against the people.

Meanwhile the men who had carried out the attack on the Bastille—known as the *volontaires de la Bastille*—were summoned and now arrived on the Place de Grève led by Maillard, who seized a drum, beat a roll-call, and invited the women to follow him to Versailles. This heterogeneous army of women, of men in women's clothes, and brigands from the Faubourgs, armed with pistols, scythes, pikes, and muskets, mustered in the Champs Élysées, and at one o'clock set forth for Versailles with Maillard at their head. As usual, the organizers of the movement had been careful to expose themselves to no danger, those who joined in the procession prudently sheltering themselves behind

---

[1] Evidence of St. Firmin, bourgeois de Paris, witness XLV. in *Procédure du Châtelet*.

petticoats from the possible fire of the King's troops, whilst the men whose eloquence had stirred up popular agitation—Danton, Marat, Santerre, Camille Desmoulins, Gonchon—took no part in the day's proceedings, but kept away altogether from the scene of action.[1] The only prominent Orléanistes who ventured forth on this occasion without the safeguard of an *incognito* were Maillard, the " Generalissimo of the Brigands," and Théroigne de Méricourt, who now appeared on a black horse, dressed in a scarlet riding-habit and black hat, and escorted by a jockey in the same colours, which were the racing colours of the Duc d'Orléans.[2]

Again, as at the siege of the Bastille, it was mainly on a few obscure ruffians that the conspirators depended for the execution of their designs—Desnot, the " cook out of place," who had joined in the murder of De Launay and of Foullon, and Mathieu Jourdan, *alias* Jouve, in turn butcher, blacksmith, smuggler, and artist's model—" the man with the long beard " of whom eye-witnesses speak shudderingly, and who on this famous day was to earn the name of " Coupe-Tête."

So in the wind and rain the ten-mile march to Versailles began, and if in this setting out we can detect no element of heroism as in the start for the Bastille, there is yet a poignant note of pathos to be found amongst the working-women dragged from their peaceful labours and forced to embark on the hazardous enterprise of which they could not dimly understand the purpose. Several of these women—poor patient tools of the conspirators—afterwards described the methods employed to goad them onwards as, shivering in the cold drizzle, they started on the weary journey. The imprecations of the *sham poissardes* against the Royal Family increased their disenchantment. " Yes, yes ! " cried one of the furies, a notorious *demi-mondaine*, armed with a sword, " we are going to Versailles to bring back the Queen's head on the point of a sword." *But the other women silenced her.*[3]

Many of the crowd were bribed ; barefooted women drew from their pockets six-écu pieces wrapped in paper, ragged men tossed gold and silver coins in the air, and the hope of further gain still drove them onwards.[4] Others trudged patiently, lured

---

[1] St. Huruge was still safely lodged in the Châtelet, so his courage could not be put to the test.

[2] Evidence of Jeanne Martin, a sick-nurse forced to march " with threats of violence," witness LXXXII., and De Villelongue, witness LXXIX. in *Procédure du Châtelet.*

[3] Evidence of Jeanne Martin and of Madeleine Glain, charwoman, witness LXXXIII. in *Procédure du Châtelet.*

[4] Evidence of witnesses X., LVI., LXXXII., CXCIX., CCLXXII., and CCCLXXXVII. in *Procédure du Châtelet.*

by the promise of bread which the good King was to give them, and, indeed, amongst the marching multitude food was sorely needed. By the time they reached Sèvres the pangs of hunger had become acute,· and the terrified inhabitants having closed their shops and barricaded themselves behind doors and windows, the women flung themselves upon the restaurants, battered down the shutters, and after feasting on all the food and wine that lay at hand proceeded to Versailles, which they entered about four o'clock in the afternoon, shouting " Vive le Roi ! " tumultuously as they marched.[1]

Whilst these scenes had been taking place in Paris the calm of Versailles continued undisturbed. Every one knows that the King went hunting, for no historian has forgotten to mention the fact, but few, if any, have remembered to add that he knew nothing whatever about the tumult in Paris.[2] It was certainly known to many deputies of the Assembly, but no one seems to have thought it necessary to inform the King, and he was allowed to start for Meudon serenely unconscious of the coming danger. Moreover, such was the detachment of " the representatives of the people " from the troubles of the capital that, whilst the revolutionary mob was mustering, they continued tranquilly discussing the new criminal code.

Mirabeau afterwards admitted that he was warned in the morning of " the increasing agitation of the people," and " the nature of things " told him that Paris was marching on Versailles, yet he had spent the afternoon with La Marck studying maps of Brabant.[3] This confession, intended to prove his non-complicity with the movement, certainly testified to the amount of sympathy he entertained for the people. The King's apparent unconcern is therefore less singular than it has been made to appear. But though the Assembly had omitted to tell the King of the disturbances in Paris, they had not forgotten to reiterate their demand for his sanction to the first principles of the Constitution and the Declaration of the Rights of Man. Before starting for the hunt Louis XVI. sent his reply to this request.[4]

The principles of the Constitution he frankly admitted did not " present indiscriminately to his mind the idea of perfection," and could only be judged on their completion. " If, however," he added, " they will fulfil the wishes of my people and assure the tranquillity of the kingdom, I accord, in conformity to your wishes, my consent to these articles, but on the express condition,

---

[1] Evidence of Maillard, witness LXXXI. in *Procédure du Châtelet ; Deux Amis,* iii. 178.

[2] No messengers were able to reach the King, as they were all stopped by the mob of women on the road from Paris (*Deux Amis,* iii. 177).

[3] *Moniteur,* vi. 31.　　　　　　　　　　[4] *Ibid.* ii. 8.

from which I shall never depart, that *in accordance with the result of your deliberations* the executive power shall reside wholly with the monarch (*ait son entier effet entre les mains du monarque*)." In other words, the King stipulated *that he should not be called upon to renounce the power accorded him by the Constitution itself.*[1]

The Declaration of the Rights of Man he confessed that he found difficult to understand—doubtless it contained excellent maxims, but could only be "justly appreciated when its real meaning had been defined by the laws to which it must serve as the basis."

Louis XVI. was a disciple not of Rousseau but of Fénelon; the tangible needs of the people he could comprehend, but vague theorizing on equality and universal happiness simply bewildered him.

The King's reply provoked a fresh outburst of fury from the revolutionary factions in the Assembly. Robespierre declared it to be destructive of the Constitution, " contrary to the rights of the nation "; Pétion, taking advantage of the ensuing tumult, arose to denounce the banquet of the bodyguard. Cries broke out on all sides—" Orgies—threats—the patriotic cockade trampled underfoot." [2] The Orléanistes, Sillery, Mirabeau, the Lameths, called out in furious tones, " The nation must have victims ! " [3] The Comte de Barbantane, seated in a tribune with Madame de Genlis and the two sons of the Duc d'Orléans—the Duc de Chartres and the Duc de Montpensier—cried threateningly, " It is evident that these gentlemen want more lanterns ; well, they shall have them ! " and the voice of the Duc de Chartres was heard to add, " Yes, yes, messieurs, we must have more lanterns ! "

At this the Marquis de Raigecourt and the Marquis de Beauharnais rose indignantly exclaiming, " It is abominable that any one should dare to express such sentiments here ! " [4]

Monsieur de Monspey demanded that Pétion should substantiate his charges against the bodyguard, but Mirabeau interposed. " Let the Assembly declare that in France every one except the King is inviolable, and I will make the denunciation myself ! " and turning to the deputies around him he added

---

[1] Principles of the Constitution, article iii. : " The supreme executive power resides exclusively with the King (*réside exclusivement dans les mains du roi* " (*Moniteur*, i. 390).

[2] Ferrières, i. 295.

[3] Montjoie, *Conjuration de d'Orléans*, ii. 204.

[4] This scene is, of course, not recorded in the *Moniteur*. It was related by the Marquis de Digoine du Palais, witness CLXVIII., and the Marquis de Raigecourt, witness CCIV., in the *Procédure du Châtelet*, and confirmed by other witnesses present, including Mounier, president of the Assembly, in his *Appel au Tribunal*, p. 233.

these terrible words : " I will denounce the Queen and the Duc de Guiche ! "

Again a voice was heard from the tribune occupied by Madame de Genlis and the sons of the Duc d'Orléans : " What ! the Queen ? " And another voice in the same tribune replied, " The Queen as much as any one else if she is guilty ! " [1]

Whether Mounier heard these words or not it is evident that, like all other witnesses of the scene, he realized that Mirabeau's declaration to the Assembly was directed against the Queen,[2] and might prove the signal for her assassination by the occupants of the gallery if the denunciation were proceeded with ; accordingly he closed the discussion.

Mounier at this crisis had no further doubts as to Mirabeau's complicity with the criminal plot against the Royal Family. During the scene that had just taken place Mirabeau had left his seat, and going round to the President's chair had whispered to Mounier under cover of the tumult :

" Monsieur le Président, 40,000 men are arriving from Paris ; hurry the discussion, close the sitting—be taken ill—say you are going to the King ! "

" And why, Monsieur ? "

" Here is a letter, M. le Président, announcing the arrival of 40,000 men from Paris." [3]

" All the more reason," answered Mounier, " for the Assembly to remain at its post."

" But, Monsieur le Président, you will be killed ! "

" So much the better," Mounier said with bitter irony, " if they kill us all, but *all*, you understand, without exception ; public affairs will go the better (*les affaires de la république en iront mieux*)." [4]

" Monsieur le Président, the phrase is neat (*le mot est joli*) ! "

But whilst this dialogue was taking place the advance guard of " women " from Paris had marched down the Avenue de Paris that faces the Château of Versailles, and were now collected at the door of the Assembly clamouring for admittance. Maillard,

[1] Evidence of the Marquis de Digoine du Palais in *Procédure du Châtelet* ; Ferrières, i. 299.

[2] *Faits relatifs à la dernière Insurrection*, by Mounier.

[3] Note that Mirabeau afterwards stated that he only guessed " by the nature of things " that Paris was marching on Versailles. See *Moniteur*.

[4] *Appel au Tribunal*, p. 302. Mirabeau, in recounting this scene (*Moniteur*, vi. 31), described Mounier as saying, " So much the better, we shall be all the sooner a republic ! " This was probably intended to discredit Mounier in the eyes of the Royalists, but it is obvious that Mounier, who never concealed his allegiance to the monarchy, could not have said this, and that he used the word *république* in the sense of *res-publica* —the public good—in which it was frequently employed at this period by Royalists as well as revolutionaries.

in a shabby black coat with a naked sword in his hand, at the head of twenty women, was permitted to enter, and at once began in furious tones to denounce the " monopolizers of grain " : " The aristocrats wish to make us die of hunger ; to-day they have sent a miller a note of two hundred livres telling him not to grind."

" Name them ! Name them ! " cried the Royalists of the Assembly.

But before this direct appeal both revolutionary deputies and delegates of the people were dumb. At last Maillard, or according to other accounts the women, answered, " It is the Archbishop of Paris ! " [1]

At this monstrous calumny even the Assembly rose indignantly, and with one voice declared, " The Archbishop of Paris is incapable of such an atrocity ! " [2]

Maillard, once more urged by Mounier to substantiate his charges, could only murmur with an air of embarrassment that " a lady he had met in a carriage on the road to Versailles " had assured him of the fact.

To this, then, were the accusations of the revolutionary leaders against the " aristocrats " of monopolizing grain reduced !

In order to satisfy the demands of the women, the Assembly finally decided to send several of their number as a deputation to the King, who had now returned from the hunt.

Not until several bands of women and brigands (who had marched ahead of the revolutionary mob) were actually in Versailles had Louis XVI. been informed of the insurrection. De Cubières, an equerry, rode out to Meudon with a note from the Comte de St. Priest ; the King read it, and turning to his gentlemen said, " Messieurs, Monsieur de St. Priest writes that the women of Paris are coming to ask me for bread." His eyes filled with tears. " Alas ! if I had any I should not wait for them to come and ask me for it. Let us go and speak to them."

Nothing was further from his mind than the idea of a hostile demonstration ; it was to him, the father of his people, these " hungry women " had turned in their distress, and his only concern was to help them.

A stranger present, M. de la Devèze, seeing his emotion, mistook it for fear. " Sire, I beg your Majesty not to be afraid."

" Afraid, Monsieur ? " the King answered proudly. " I have never been afraid in my life ! " and mounting his horse he rode off to the Château at a gallop. The Comte de Luxembourg

---

[1] De Juigné, to whose benevolence I have already referred.[1]
[2] *Deux Amis*, iii. 183.

was waiting for him and asked for orders to be given to the bodyguard.

" Orders ? " said the King with a laugh.   " Orders of war against women ?   You must be joking, Monsieur de Luxembourg ! "

The ruse of the Orléanistes had succeeded, and by the advance guard of so-called women the King's defenders were disarmed.

From the windows of the Chambre de Conseil Louis XVI. looked out on the armed mob advancing through the wind and rain along the Avenue de Paris towards the Château ; before long the Place des Armes had become a sea of pikes and muskets. Amidst this raging multitude Mounier, at the head of his deputation, was advancing on foot through the mud, and during the quarter of an hour of waiting for admittance at the grille of the Château was obliged to endure the insults of the mob, who cried out that " the deputies of the Assembly with their 18 francs a day enjoyed good cheer, whilst they allowed the poor to die of hunger " ; that " when they had only one King they had bread, but since they had 1200 they perished in misery." [1]

The deputation, consisting of six deputies with six women clinging to their arms, was increased by six more women before their admission to the Salle de Conseil.   Louis XVI. received them with his customary benevolence.

" Sire," said Louison Chabry, a pretty flower-seller of seventeen from the Palais Royal, " we want bread."

" You know my heart," answered the King ; " I will order all the bread in Versailles to be collected and given to you."

Whereat Louison, overcome by the King's goodness, fell fainting to the ground.   Smelling salts were brought ; Louison revived and begged to be allowed to kiss the King's hand.

" She deserves better than that ! " said Louis XVI., embracing her.

Louison departed with the other women, enchanted by their visit, crying out, " Long live the King ! Long live our good King ! Now we shall have bread ! "

But one of their number still displayed resentment.   The Chevalier de la Serre attempted to reason with her, pointing

---

[1] These words, uttered by the people themselves and heard by a member of the deputation, Alexandre de Lameth (see his *Histoire de l'Assemblée Constituante*, i. 150), were afterwards attributed by Mirabeau to St. Priest in the Assembly (*Moniteur*, ii. 36), evidently as a revenge on St. Priest for having explained to the women that the Commune of Paris and not the King was responsible for the provisioning of the capital (see St. Priest's letter to the National Assembly in *Mémoires de Bailly*, iii. 422).   But if, as several contemporaries state, Mirabeau himself was amongst the crowd outside the *grille* of the Château when these words were uttered, it is evident where he really heard them.

out that they had to do with a good King, a good father, that
their condition greatly distressed him ; but the woman replied,
" Our father is the Duc d'Orléans ! "

Her companions interrupted her by repeating, " Vive le
Roi ! "

" Non, f. . . .," she retorted, " it is ' Vive le Duc d'Orléans ! ' "[1]

It is evident, therefore, that certain of the women had been
primed by the Orléanistes, but the greater proportion were, as
Ferrières says, " acting in all good faith : they did not know
the plans of the conspirators. Dragged by force to Versailles,
hearing it incessantly repeated that the people were dying of
hunger, and that the only way to stop the famine was by appealing to the King and the National Assembly, they thought they
had achieved the object of their journey by obtaining a decree
of the Assembly and getting it sanctioned by the King." [2]
What, then, was their dismay when they returned triumphantly
to the waiting multitude with the King's promise to find themselves received by howls of execration : " They are cheats, they
have been given money ! They have received no written order,
they must be hanged ! " A fury in the crowd, tearing off her
garter, dragged one of the women towards a lamp-post, and
would have hanged her there had not an officer of the bodyguard rushed to her rescue and brought her with the rest of the
deputation into safety, inside the Cour Royale. These women
then begged to be allowed to return to the King and ask for his
order in writing, and the request having been granted they
reappeared once more waving the royal signature aloft. Their
accounts of the King's goodness had the effect of temporarily
calming the excitement of the crowd ; cries of " Vive le Roi ! "
went up on all sides ; for the moment the King's defenders thought
the situation saved.

The women who had formed the deputation, now realizing
that they had been the dupes of the conspirators, insisted on
returning to Paris in order to tell the Commune of their reception
at Versailles, and Louis XVI., informed of their intention, ordered
royal carriages to be provided for the journey. Lest, however,
too glowing an account of the King's benevolence should be
conveyed to Paris, Maillard was deputed by the leaders of the
insurrection to accompany the women and counteract their
influence.

In all probability, if the tumult had been, as it is habitually
represented, the spontaneous rising of a hungry multitude
driven by want to beg the King for bread, the matter would

---

[1] Evidence of the Chevalier de la Serre, witness CCXXVI. in *Procédure
du Châtelet.*

[2] Ferrières, i. 308.

have ended there, and the people having accomplished their purpose would have returned peacefully to their homes. But the conspirators had determined otherwise.

Immediately on the arrival of the armed mob every effort had been made to provoke a quarrel with the bodyguard, but these gallant men, true to their orders not to use force against the people, endured insults and threats without replying. When at last a man of the Paris militia attempted, sword in hand, to break through the regiment, the Marquis de Savonnières, followed by three other officers, pursued the insurgent and struck him with the flat of his sword, but a shot fired by Charpentier of the Versailles militia broke the arm of Savonnières and inflicted injuries from which he died some weeks later.

This affray provided the signal for battle; on all sides the cry went up that the Guards were charging the people; the militia hastily advanced their cannons in the Avenue de Paris towards the grille of the Château, and the mob, closing around the bodyguard, attacked them with pikes and stones and fired into their ranks, fortunately with so little certainty of aim that the men escaped with slight injuries. Still the bodyguard refrained from retaliation, and Lecointre—he who had denounced their "orgy" four days earlier—seeing this, and fearing that no pretext would be provided for further violence, rushed forward and overwhelmed them with reproaches.[1] It was at this crisis that the King, informed of the cries of "Vive le Roi!" and the momentary cessation of hostilities produced by the deputation of women, and concluding that peace was now restored, sent his fatal message to the bodyguard to retire. The militia of Versailles, taking advantage of the movement, immediately opened a volley of musketry fire on the retreating troops, whilst brigands armed with guns and pikes pursued them with shots and blows. It was said afterwards by the Orléanistes that the bodyguard now returned the fire of the insurgents and treated the people with harshness, thrusting them aside with their sabres, but of these acts only two eye-witnesses could be produced, the Orléaniste, De Liancourt,[2] and again Lecointre,[3] the inveterate enemy of the bodyguard who was brought forward at every turn by the conspirators to prove their charges against the King's defenders. On the other hand, reliable contemporaries speak only of the patience and forbearance of these gallant men who, in obedience to orders, refrained from using the weapons at their

---

[1] *Appel au Tribunal*, by Mounier, p. 145. Evidence of La Brosse de Belville, witness XXII. in *Procédure du Châtelet*. Miomandre de Sainte Marie, garde du corps, witness XVIII., also stated that it was Lecointre who stirred up the crowd against the bodyguard.

[2] *Appel au Tribunal*, by Mounier, p. 155.   [3] *Ibid.* p. 148.

command.[1] So once again the arm of law and order was paralysed, and the people who should have been protected were left to become the victims of the conspirators.

Whilst these scenes were taking place in the Place d'Armes, Mounier, imagining that reforms in the government would satisfy the multitude who were calling out for bread, continued to importune the King for his sanction to the principles of the Constitution and the Declaration of the Rights of Man. Louis XVI., whose sound common sense showed him the absurdity of according the royal sanction to philosophical axioms, repeated his opinion that at this stage his acceptance would be premature, but, on the assurance of Mounier that nothing else would allay the tumult, finally appended his signature to the words : " I accept purely and simply the articles of the Constitution and the Declaration of the Rights of Man." Then, confident that he had done all that lay within his power to restore public tranquillity, he awaited events with calmness. In response to the entreaties of the Comte d'Estaing that measures should be taken for the defence of the Château, he wrote at seven o'clock on this terrible evening, after the departure of Mounier and his fellow-deputies, these astounding words :

" You wish, my cousin, that I should express my opinion on the critical circumstances in which I find myself, and that I should take a violent course, that I should make use of legitimate means of defence, or that I should leave Versailles. Whatever may be the audacity of my enemies they will not succeed ; the Frenchman is incapable of regicide. . . . I dare to believe that this danger is not as urgent as my friends are persuaded. Flight would be my total undoing and civil war the disastrous result. . . . Let us act with prudence. . . . If I succumb at least I shall have no cause to reproach myself. I have just seen several members of the Assembly and I am satisfied. . . . God grant that public tranquillity may be restored—but no aggression, no action that could let it be believed that I think of avenging or even of defending myself."

Meanwhile Mounier, returning triumphantly to the Assembly with the royal sanction, found the wildest scene of confusion taking place. A mob of women,[2] of brigands, and of men in

---

[1] *Appel au Tribunal*, p. 148. Alexis Chauchard, captain of infantry, witness CI. in *Procédure du Châtelet*, stated that "the King's guards behaved in this affair with the greatest circumspection ; that he saw the people throw mud and stones at them and vomit imprecations against them without their making any attempt to repulse this attack."

[2] It should be noted that eye-witnesses, unlike historians, do not describe the women who created this uproar in the Assembly as *poissardes* but as "light women," some even of a class too superior to be regarded as "kept women" (see evidence of the Vicomte de Mirabeau,

women's clothes, had invaded the hall and taken possession of the seats of the deputies, where they regaled themselves with ham sandwiches, pies, and wine brought in from a neighbouring restaurant. The brigands, ragged and of ferocious aspect, adopted a threatening attitude, but the *filles de joie* were enjoying themselves immensely. It was a situation that appealed irresistibly to their mocking humour ; true *gamines* of Paris, they found it exquisitely funny to chaff these solemn legislators and dance on the platform of the President, to overwhelm the unhappy bishop of Langres—occupying the President's chair in the absence of Mounier—with obscene pleasantries. " Now you must kiss us, *calotin* ! " And the bishop, amidst screams of laughter, was obliged, sighing deeply, to submit to their vinous embraces.

Mounier, arriving in the midst of this pandemonium with his precious document, fondly imagined that the announcement of the " royal sanction " would act as oil upon the troubled waters, and profiting by a lull in the tumult read the King's message aloud. But to the women of Paris, as to the King himself, these vague formulas conveyed but little meaning, and Mounier's announcement was greeted by the hungry elements amongst them with the cry, " Will that give bread to the poor people of Paris ? "

The President, realizing the impossibility of continuing the debate—most of the deputies indeed had already left the hall—broke up the Assembly. But the women had no intention of being done out of their evening's entertainment, and imperiously demanded the return of the deputies. The President's bell was rung, members were fetched from their beds, the Assembly resumed its sitting. Once again the message containing the royal sanction was read aloud, only to be met with the same cry of " Bread ! Give us bread ! "

Nothing is more amazing in the history of the Revolution than the total inability of the " representatives of the people " to understand the people's mind. The King, appealed to by the hungry women, could readily enter into their sufferings, but the Assembly, in response to their cries for bread, offered them— the foundation-stone of the Constitution. For at this supreme moment these so-called democrats, actually surrounded by the

witness CXLVI. in *Procédure du Châtelet*), whilst nearly all state that a great many men disguised as women were seen amongst them. No doubt there were a certain number of " women of the people " who had been forced to march to Versailles amongst those calling out for bread, but the " indecent scenes " described were evidently produced by the Orléaniste conspirators and the women they had brought with them. It was mainly the leaders of the expedition who crowded into the Assembly ; most of the poor creatures from the Faubourgs were left outside in the rain.

clamouring multitude, calmly resumed their discussion on the criminal code.

It is hardly surprising that at this the indignation of the women broke out afresh, and the Assembly was peremptorily ordered to discuss the question of food-supply. The voice of a deputy addressing the House was drowned by shouts of " Bread ! bread ! not so many long speeches ! " and " Shut up that babbler. It doesn't matter about all that—it is bread that matters ! " Some of the women clamoured for Mirabeau, whose grotesque appearance amused them : " Where is our Comte de Mirabeau —our little mother Mirabeau ? " A man in the tribune next to the President exclaimed loudly that the deputies should concern themselves with the people.

At this Mirabeau, who had no intention of allowing the *canaille* to command, arose and thundered, " I should like to know by what right any one should dictate to us the course of our debates ? Let the tribunes remember the respect they owe to the National Assembly ! "

The women, enchanted at this display of authority, noisily clapped their hands and cried " Bravo ! "

Whilst this tumult raged in the Assembly scenes far more terrible were taking place outside on the Place d'Armes. The wild autumn day had faded into a wet and cheerless night, and the immense multitude, unable to find shelter, gathered round huge fires they had lit at intervals about the square, and at one of which a horse of the bodyguard, massacred in the fray, was being cooked and eaten. On such a scene of misery and squalor did the great Château of the Roi Soleil look down that dreadful evening ! The women, wet to the skin, caked with mud after the long march from Paris, wandered round the courtyards sobbing pitifully, crying out that " they had been forced to march and did not know what they had come for " ;[1] others, savage with hunger and fatigue, danced round the bonfires shrieking furious imprecations against the Queen, Lafayette, Mounier, the Abbé Maury, the Archbishop of Paris. " Marie Antoinette has danced for her pleasure, now she shall dance for ours ! " " Yes, let the jade skip, we will throw her head from the windows ! We will have the drunkard for our king no longer, it is the Duc d'Orléans that we must have for king ! "

Thus the furies of the under-world, revolting enough in truth, but surely less revolting than the Duc d'Orléans, skulking through the crowd in the Avenue de Paris, " endeavouring to escape detection but unable to flee from his conscience," [2] less revolting

---

[1] *Mémoires de Madame de la Tour du Pin*, i. 222.
[2] Ferrières, i. 313 ; evidence of De Boisse of the King's bodyguard, witness ccxiv. in *Procédure du Châtelet*.

far than the petticoated roués of the Palais Royal, stirring up a poor and hungry populace to commit crimes they dared not undertake themselves. It was said by many witnesses, and never disproved by any conclusive alibi, that all through that fearful night, and again the following morning, the members of the conspiracy were at work distributing money and inciting the people to violence ; that Mirabeau, brandishing a naked sword, was seen in the ranks of the Régiment de Flandre exhorting them to defection ;[1] that Théroigne in her scarlet habit went from group to group giving the names of deputies to be massacred, and distributing money done up in paper packets ;[2] that fine gentlemen in embroidered waistcoats " slipped coins concealed in cockades into the hands of the women " ;[3] that Laclos, Sillery, Barnave, the Duc d'Aiguillon, dressed as women, were again recognized mingling with the crowd, fanning up the flame of popular fury in preparation for the massacres of the morrow.[4]

Suddenly at midnight, when the frenzy of the populace had reached its height, the roll of drums and the red glare of torches announced the arrival of Lafayette at the head of the Gardes Françaises in the Avenue de Paris.

How did Lafayette come to be leading this second army of insurgents to Versailles ? The fact has provided Orléaniste writers with the pretext for shifting the blame of the insurrection on to their opponent, and it was precisely in order to be able to do this that they had contrived to implicate Lafayette in the movement. As a matter of fact Lafayette had held out for hours against the entreaties of his men, who, prompted by the

---

[1] Montjoie, Conjuration de d'Orléans, iii. 90 ; Weber, ii. 207 ; Fantin Désodoards, i. 213 ; Procédure du Châtelet, witnesses XXXVI., CLVII., CLXI., CCXXVI. ; Ferrières, i. 307.

[2] Procédure du Châtelet, witnesses XCI. and CLVI.

[3] Evidence of an eye-witness, Anne Marguerite Andelle, CCXXXVI. in Procédure du Châtelet, a linen-worker dragged by force to Versailles. On the money distributed amongst the soldiers of the Régiment de Flandre and amongst the people see also witnesses XLIX., LVI., LXXI., LXXXII., CX. and CXXVI.

[4] " All the roués of the Palais Royal, the accomplices, or rather the instigators of the Duc d'Orléans, Laclos, Sillery, Latouche, d'Aiguillon, d'Oraison, Mirabeau, and several other minor personages, were on foot all night in the midst of this rabble, whom they intoxicated in every manner. Public evidence subsequently showed some of them as having adopted the most ignoble disguises so as not to be recognized " (Weber, ii. 210). See also Montjoie, Conjuration de d'Orléans, ii. 245, and evidence of the Chevalier de Lasserre, witness CCXXVI. in Procédure du Châtelet. Jean Diot, curé and deputy of the National Assembly, witness CX., described a conversation he heard during this night in which a man dressed as a woman, " tall and of great corpulence," offered two of the people fifty louis on behalf of the Duc d'Orléans to murder the Queen on the following morning.

Orléanistes, insisted on his leading them to Versailles. At the Hôtel de Ville that morning, whilst Lafayette was occupied in sending off despatches to warn Versailles of the approaching invasion, six grenadiers had entered and accosted him with these words : " General, we are deputed by six companies of grenadiers: we do not think you are a traitor, but we think that the Government is betraying us. It is time all this ended. . . . The people are wretched ; the source of the evil is at Versailles ; we must go to fetch the King and bring him to Paris ; we must exterminate the Régiment de Flandre and the bodyguard who dare to trample on the national cockade. If the King is too weak to wear his crown, let him renounce it. We will crown his son, a council of regency will be nominated, and all will go well."

As this was precisely the plan of the Orléaniste conspiracy Lafayette immediately realized that the men were merely repeating their lesson, and, recognizing the trap laid for him, he attempted to dissuade them from marching on Versailles.

" What ! " he said, " you mean then to make war on the King and force him to abandon us ? " The use of the final pronoun is significant ; even the Republican Lafayette was obliged in his more honest moments to admit that Louis XVI. was on the side of the people, and the soldiers, thus appealed to, momentarily forgot their lesson and readily concurred :

" General, indeed we should be very sorry, for we love him well, but if he left us we have Monsieur le Dauphin."

In vain Lafayette continued to remonstrate ; the men once more took up the refrain : " The source of the evil is at Versailles ; we must go and fetch the King and bring him to Paris ; all the people wish it." Finally Lafayette went out on to the Place de Grève and, with Bailly, attempted to address the crowd collected there. But the people, he had begun to discover, were easier to rouse than to pacify, and the spirit of insubordination he had openly encouraged at the beginning of the Revolution was now turning against himself. In vain he strove to make himself heard ; an angry uproar arose ; one voice was heard above the others crying, " It is strange that M. de Lafayette should wish to command the people when it is for the people to command him ! "

Then Lafayette, reluctantly mounting his white charger, placed himself at the head of the troops, whose numbers were now being rapidly increased by the lowest rabble of the Faubourgs, which, armed with pikes and pitchforks, with cutlasses and hatchets, poured into the Place de Grève crying out, " Bread ! bread ! To Versailles ! "

At the sight of this terrible army Lafayette once again

hesitated, and, seeing this, the crowd broke into fury; howls of
rage, threats of death rose from a thousand throats ; for the first
time Lafayette, idol of the people, heard the voice of the people
raised against himself. At that he grew first red, then pale, made
a movement as if he would dismount, but a dozen hands gripped
his bridle: " No, General, you shall not escape us ! " While
he temporized a message from the Commune was slipped into his
hand ordering him to march. Lafayette glanced at the paper,
grew paler still, then gathered up his reins, and with a set countenance gave the word of command to march. " He rode at the
head of his troops," says Montjoie, " like a criminal led to
execution " ; and that in all probability he was going to his death
Lafayette well knew, but, bitterer thought still, this was to be
death with dishonour !

So it came to pass that at midnight, after an eight hours'
march, Lafayette entered Versailles. Calling a halt at the turning of the road leading to the National Assembly he demanded
of his army to take the oath of fidelity to the nation, the law,
and the King ; then entering the Assembly filled with the drunken
crowd he made his way through the turmoil to the President's
chair and assured Mounier that he could answer for the loyalty
of his troops.

Although so exhausted that he was hardly able to drag himself
up the staircase, Lafayette afterwards presented himself at the
Château and administered the same soothing assurances. " I
was without apprehension," he wrote later ; " the people had
promised me to remain quiet."

But the Queen, who had no confidence in the benevolence of
revolutionary mobs or in generals who marched at their heads,
received Lafayette coldly. She realized, as he with his foolish
optimism could not, the frightful danger that confronted them
that night. " I know," she said, " that they have come to
demand my head, but I learnt from my mother not to fear death,
and I can await it with calmness."

All around her in the Château terror and confusion prevailed ;
women ran hither and thither, peeping forth fearfully from the
windows at the dull glare beyond the railings, where by fire and
torchlight that raging sea of humanity tossed tumultuously,
listening with beating hearts to the hoarse murmurs, broken now
and again with savage howls and fiendish laughter ; others,
helpless and distracted, paced the great Galerie des Glaces, the
scene of so much splendour, and in all minds one question arose
—was this night to be their last ?

Amidst these scenes Marie Antoinette alone was calm, and
with undisturbed serenity continued to rouse the fainting spirits
of those around her. When a number of her gentlemen came to

her door to beg for permission to order out the horses from the royal stables and mount them in defence of the Royal Family, the Queen returned only this reply : " I consent to give you the order for which you wish on the condition that if the life of the King is in danger you should make immediate use of it, but if I alone am imperilled you will not use it."

Her women, realizing that she was the chief victim designated by the conspirators, threw themselves at her feet and begged her to escape. " No," she answered, " never, never will I abandon the King or my children ; whatever fate awaits them, I will share it."

Then dismissing her attendants she remained alone, waiting for death. At this moment a note was brought to her ; she opened it, and read these terrible words : " I warn her Majesty that she will be murdered to-morrow morning at six o'clock." She knew then that she had still six hours of life, and, placing the note in her pocket, quietly announced her intention of retiring to bed. In vain her gentlemen begged to be allowed to remain and protect her. " No, Messieurs," she answered without a trace of emotion, " take your leave, I beg you ; to-morrow will prove to you that you had need of rest to-night."

With these words she left them and slept an untroubled sleep until the frightful dawn of the morrow.

THE 6TH OF OCTOBER

Lafayette, according to current report at this crisis, retired and slept also. " Il dormit contre son roi," wrote Rivarol bitterly. But did he really sleep ? The truth will probably never be known. Montjoie says no ; Lafayette himself said that, worn out with fatigue, he went to the Hôtel de Noailles and was about to snatch a few hours of slumber when the tumult of the morrow recalled him to the Château. But if he did sleep the fact must surely be attributed not to treachery but uncontrollable physical exhaustion, combined with the conviction that the Gardes Françaises were completely under his control and that further disturbance was impossible.

But the bodyguard, more alive to the danger, had refused on the assurances of Lafayette to leave the Château unprotected, and remained therefore throughout the night as sentries before the doors of the Royal Family. For greater safety the Queen's waiting-women, Madame Thibault and Madame Augué, seated themselves against the doors of her bedchamber, and by this devotion saved her life.

For nearly three hours all was calm : the Queen slept in her great bedroom looking out on to the quiet Orangerie ; the King

slept in his facing the courtyards and the now deserted Place
d'Armes ; the crowd slept likewise, anywhere and everywhere—
in sheds and stables, on the floors of outhouses and kitchens ;
eight or nine hundred spent the night on the benches of the
Assembly.

But all night Luillier of the bodyguard, commander of the
Scotch company, kept his watch, wandering around the Château
and assuring himself that if the tumult began again the great
gilded barriers would avail to keep out the raging populace.
Then towards dawn an unseen hand unlocked a gate in the
railing, and immediately a band of women and armed men
streamed through to the courtyards and the garden that lay
beneath the Queen's windows on the other side of the Château.

Luillier in consternation sought the Marquis d'Aguesseau,
major of the bodyguard, and, encountering him at the foot of
the great marble staircase leading to the Queen's apartments,
said, "Monsieur, the King and Royal Family are lost if the
brigands now passing through the courtyards to the terrace
penetrate into the Château. I implore you to give positive
orders."

"Place two sentinels at each of the gates," answered
D'Aguesseau ; and turning to the bodyguard he said, "Messieurs,
the King orders and begs you not to fire, to hit no one—in a
word, not to defend yourselves."

"Monsieur," said Luillier, "assure our unhappy master that
his orders will be carried out, but we shall all be assassinated."

For sublime devotion to duty, for heroic obedience to insane
commands, the conduct of the King's bodyguard on this 6th of
October can show no parallel in history except, perhaps, in the
charge of Balaclava. Of all historians Montjoie alone has paid
these gallant men their due, and it is from his pages that we must
borrow the glorious story of their stand against odds so terrible
and overwhelming. Do not their very names bring with them
a breath of chivalry ? Guéroult de Berville, Guéroult de Valmet,
Miomandre de Sainte Marie, De Charmand, and De Varicourt—
we seem to be reading in some gold-emblazoned scroll that tells
of knightly deeds done by followers of Saint Louis around the
walls of Antioch. It has been said that the Old Order was
effete, and this might well be so if it were judged by the faithless
courtiers who at the first hint of danger deserted King and
country ; but amongst these soldiers of the King there was yet
stern stuff that, had it been allowed full play, must have saved
the monarchy. For the last time we see them, these warriors
of old France, rallying in a final expiring effort around the
tottering throne. Henceforth the King must look elsewhere for
his defenders—Swiss Guards will bleed and die for him, super-

annuated gentlemen will draw ineffectual swords in his service, women will throw their fragile bodies between the King and his assassins, but the heroic bodyguard will appear no more on the scene—the long romance of French chivalry is ended.

It was a quarter to six in the grey dawn of the autumn morning when the raging mob burst through the side gate into the Cour Royale. The sentinels of the Paris militia, vouched for by Lafayette, offered no resistance, and seeing this the brigands, who at first had trembled at finding themselves within the royal precincts, realized that they incurred no danger, and " flung themselves like tigers on all the members of the body-guard that they encountered." [1] The brave Deshuttes fell pierced with a hundred wounds; his body was dragged into the Cour des Ministres, where Jourdan " Coupe-Tête " cut off his head, and in a sudden access of homicidal fury smeared his face, his arms, his long and ragged beard with the blood of his victim. And at this horrible spectacle the mob went mad likewise and, bespattering themselves in the same manner, danced around the mutilated corpse. Then the cry went up, " We must have the heart of the Queen ! " But already a large portion of the mob had poured through the archway by the Chapel and the Cour des Princes and burst into the Château.

The scene that followed was horrible ; even at this distance of time one's heart stands still as one reads the descriptions of contemporaries who, with awful realism, bring before one's eyes the mad rush of the crowd up the great marble staircase of the Roi Soleil towards the Queen's apartments ; we can see, hear, even smell them, those tattered brigands of the Faubourgs, those dishevelled harridans and blaspheming women of the town, mud-stained and haggard with fatigue after the long march from Paris and the few brief hours of sleep snatched on floors and benches, and all mad for blood, all clutching cruel weapons of their own devising—knives tied to broomsticks, scythes and pikes and billhooks—and howling as they tear upwards like a pack of wild beasts rushing on their prey. " Where is that *f*. . . . *coquine* ? We will cut off her head ; we will tear out her heart ; we will make cockades of her entrails, and it will not end there ! " And amidst these hideous imprecations again the same refrain : " Long live Orléans ! Long live our father, our king Orléans !"

Was the Duc d'Orléans himself amongst the cannibal horde on the marble staircase ? Did his hand point the way to the door of the Queen's apartments ? Many contemporaries believed it, but to this point we shall return later and leave it to the

---

[1] Evidence of M. de Sainte-Aulaire, lieutenant-commander in the body-guard, witness CLVIII. in *Procédure du Châtelet*.

reader to form his own opinion of the evidence brought forward. One thing is certain, the crowd never paused, never hesitated for a moment, as people unfamiliar with the interior of the Château might be expected to do, but made straight for the hall of the Queen's bodyguard " *as if led by some one who knew the way.*" [1]

There on the threshold twelve of the guards were waiting to receive them. Miomandre de Sainte-Marie stepped boldly forward and attempted to check the wild onrush of the mob by one despairing appeal to their vanished loyalty :

" My friends, you love your King, yet you come to disquiet him in his very palace ! "

For answer the crowd rushed upon Miomandre and nearly felled him to the ground, and the guards, forbidden to defend themselves, were driven back into the hall where, with a quick movement, they succeeded in closing the doors in the face of their assailants. Only three rooms now between the Queen and her assassins—four folding doors to be beaten down before the savage horde could close around her bed and thrust their terrible weapons into her heart ! The guards, to gain time, barricaded the doors of their hall, but the fragile panels quickly yielded to the blows of pikes and muskets ; the crowd rushed forward into the hall. Already De Varicourt was killed and his head gone to join Deshuttes' on a pike outside in the courtyard. The guards were driven back step by step over the parquet into the Grande Salle ; Du Repaire was left alone to guard the door of the Queen's bodyguard. The next moment Du Repaire was overthrown and dragged to the head of the staircase ; a man with a pike and another in woman's clothes [2] seized him— Miomandre rushed to the rescue and saved the life of Du Repaire who, wresting a pike from his assailants, continued to defend himself. Then Miomandre, his face streaming with blood, realizing that nothing now could keep back the raging mob, dashed to the door of the Queen's antechamber, opened it, and cried out to Madame Augué, one of the Queen's women, "Madame, save the Queen, they have come to kill her ! I am here alone against two thousand tigers ; my comrades have been forced to leave their hall ! "

There was nothing for it but to leave the brave Miomandre to his fate. Madame Augué quickly shut the door, pushed in the great bolt, and flew to the Queen's bedside : " Madame, get out of bed ! Do not dress ; escape to the King ! "

The Queen sprang out of bed ; her ladies threw a mantle

---

[1] *Mémoires de Madame de la Tour du Pin*, i. 227.

[2] " At the moment that he was thrown down he saw a coloured trouser beneath the skirt of one of those who attacked him " (evidence of Du Repaire, witness ix. in *Procédure du Châtelet*).

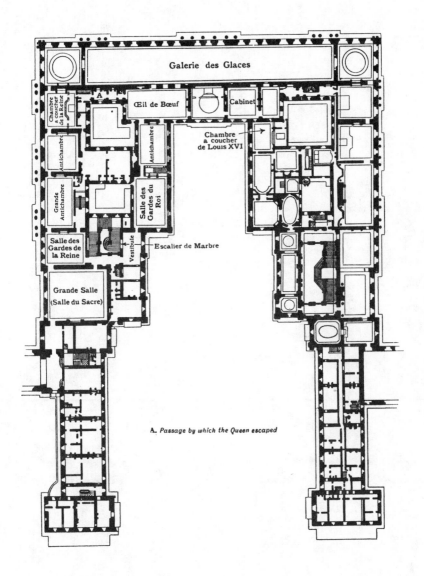

Galerie des Glaces

Œil de Bœuf

Cabinet

Chambre à coucher de la Reine

Antichambre

Grande Antichambre

Salle des Gardes de la Reine

Grande Salle (Salle du Sacre)

Antichambre

Salle des Gardes du Roi

Vestibule

Chambre à coucher de Louis XVI

Escalier de Marbre

A. *Passage by which the Queen escaped*

around her shoulders, a petticoat over her head, and hurried her through a side door leading to the Œil de Bœuf by a narrow passage. At the end of this the door, invariably open, was, on this day of all others, *locked*. She beat on the panels ; after five agonizing minutes a servant opened to her, and she reached the King's rooms in safety, crying out, " My friends, my dear friends, save me and my children ! "

So, owing to the courage of the two heroic guards, the Queen still lived—the great *coup* of the conspirators had failed.

Meanwhile around the door of the Queen's guards the fight continued ; now at last the guards made use of weapons—Du Repaire with the pike he had captured, Luillier and Miomandre with their swords, defended their lives against the horde of assassins. Miomandre by a blow from a pike was thrown to the ground, and an assassin standing over him raised the butt-end of his gun, bringing it crashing down on his victim's skull. Miomandre, bathed in his blood, was left for dead, but the crowd having swept onwards through the doorway into the Queen's apartments, he raised himself, staggered to his feet, and escaped.

The next moment the door of the Queen's bedchamber was beaten down, and the furious horde, amongst them two of the men disguised as women, rushed forward to the bed to find it empty. It is said by Montjoie and Rivarol that in their rage they plunged their pikes into the mattress, slashed at the bed-clothes with their sabres, and then by way of the great Galerie des Glaces proceeded to attack the Œil de Bœuf ; according to Madame Campan they did not enter the Queen's room, but reached the Œil de Bœuf through the hall of the King's guards. In either case their intention was to break down the doors of the Œil de Bœuf, where a few remaining members of the bodyguard were entrenched, and having massacred the King's last defenders to fall upon the Royal Family, who had taken refuge in the King's bedroom beyond. But this plan was frustrated by an un-expected check—a detachment of grenadiers belonging to the old Gardes Françaises drawn up before the doors of the Œil de Bœuf. What had happened to bring about this sudden return to loyalty in the mutineers who, at the siege of the Bastille, had rallied to the standard of revolt ? One thing only—Lafayette, at last aroused from his optimistic lethargy, had risen to the occasion. From the moment the attack on the Château began—that attack which he had persisted in believing would never take place—his conduct was admirable, and it is unquestionably to Lafayette that must be accorded the eternal honour of saving the lives of the Royal Family on this 6th of October. At the first sound of the tumult he had sprung up, mounted his horse, and summoned his grenadiers to the rescue of the King and the bodyguard. "Grenadiers," he cried, "will you suffer brave men to be basely assassinated? . . . Swear to me on your honour as grenadiers that no harm shall be done to them!"

The grenadiers took the oath, and rallying around their still adored commander hastened to rescue the guards who had fallen into the clutches of the assassins. They were joined immediately by the men of the Parisian militia, and these, clasping in their arms the white-haired brigadiers of the bodyguard, cried out, "No, we will not murder brave men like you!"

So again, as after the siege of the Bastille, the mutinous soldiers were turned by a word from revolutionary fury to sentiments of humanity, and it was these men who but yesterday had marched against their King that were drawn up in his defence outside the Œil de Bœuf.

Inside the room the officers of the bodyguard, who had been driven back from the door of the Queen's apartments, were waiting to prevent the insurgents from reaching the Royal Family collected in the King's bedroom beyond, and the grenadiers, wishing now to effect a coalition with their former enemies, rattled at the door-handle to attract their attention, whilst at the same time keeping the mob at bay.

Chevannes, Vaulabelle, and Mondollot of the bodyguard cried through the door, "Who knocks?"

"Grenadiers!"

Then Chevannes, opening the door, courageously confronted the men he took to be his enemies. "Messieurs," he said, "is it a victim you seek? Here is one. I offer myself. I am one of the commanders of the post; it is to me that belongs the honour of dying the first in defence of my King, but, by God, learn to respect that good King!"

But Gondran, commander of the grenadiers, held out his hand: "Far from wishing to take your life, we have come to defend you against your assassins."

In an instant grenadiers and guards fell into one another's arms, mingling tears of joy, calling each other friends and comrades; the guards consented to wear the tricolour cockade, and finally the men of the two regiments joining forces drove the rabble from the Château.

The tide had now turned irresistibly against the conspirators. Down below in the Cour de Marbre the grenadiers were still fighting bravely for the lives of the guards, and the King, seeing the fray from the windows, rushed out on to the balcony of the great bedroom of Louis XIV. and cried out to the people for mercy to be shown to his faithful defenders. Several of the guards in attendance followed after him, and waving their hats, adorned with the tricolour cockade, cried out, "Vive la nation!"

The situation was saved ; in a moment that strange Parisian crowd had forgotten their fury, and to the shouts of " Vive la nation ! " responded with cries of " Vive le Roi ! "

Then the conspirators determined on one final effort to achieve their purpose, and voices were raised calling for the Queen to appear likewise on the balcony.

All this time Marie Antoinette had remained in the King's bedroom with her children, surrounded by her weeping women and distracted courtiers ; the ministers Luzerne and Montmorin appeared incapable of action, whilst in a corner Necker, the people's idol, sat sobbing helplessly. Marie Antoinette alone was calm, rousing the courage of those around her, quieting the little Dauphin who repeated plaintively, " Maman, I am hungry." Only at one moment her serenity failed her, as, looking down from the windows, she perceived suddenly amongst the raging multitude the figure of Philippe d'Orléans walking gaily arm-in-arm with Adrien Duport,[1] and at the sinister vision the Queen caught the Dauphin to her heart and, half rising from her seat, cried out in an agony of terror, " They are coming to kill my son ! " Marie Antoinette well knew that it was not " the people " who were most to be feared.

The cries of " Vive le Roi ! " that had broken out when the King appeared on the balcony showed that he at least had not lost his place in their hearts, and when at this moment word was brought that the Queen too must show herself to the crowd, she advanced confidently towards the balcony holding the Dauphin and Madame Royale by the hand.

" She took her children with her for safety," says a revolutionary writer—she who would have died a hundred deaths to save them ! No more cruel calumny has ever been uttered against Marie Antoinette. It is easy to understand the idea that inspired her action. What mother worthy of the name does not believe that the sight of her offspring must melt the fiercest heart ? And surely no stronger appeal could be made to the women she believed to be the same *poissardes* who, but a few short years earlier, had presented themselves at this very spot to hail the birth of the Dauphin than to show his younger brother to them now ! Were not the *poissardes* mothers too ? Undoubtedly, if the *poissardes* had composed the crowd, the result would have been just as the Queen anticipated, but the conspirators shrewdly

---

[1] Ferrières, i. 327. See also the evidence of the Marquis de Digoine du Palais, witness CLXVIII. in *Procédure du Châtelet* : " In the same place (the Cour de Marbre) was M. le Duc d'Orléans walking with M. Duport whom he held under the arm, and with whom he was talking in a very gay and easy manner." The duke was also seen at this hour by witnesses CXXVII., CXXXII., CXXXIII., CXXXVI., CXCV., who described him playing with a light switch he carried in his hand and " laughing incessantly."

foresaw this also, and a man's voice in the crowd cried out threateningly, " No children ! " At that Marie Antoinette, comprehending that the rage of the multitude had not abated, handed the children to Madame de Tourzel and came forward alone.

As she stood there on the balcony in the pale light of the October morning, her hair disordered, a little yellow-striped wrapper hastily thrown over her night attire,[1] her face, of which the dazzling tints had once defied the painter's art, now changed to a stricken pallor, Marie Antoinette had never seemed so much a Queen. Folding her hands on her breast she raised her eyes above the angry sea of pikes and muskets, filling the courtyards of the Château and stretching right away across the Place d'Armes to the Avenue de Versailles, and looked to heaven, " like a victim offering herself up to death."

And at this sight a hush fell over the tumultuous crowd, a breathless and tremendous silence during which the Queen's life hung in the balance. But amongst all that vast multitude only one man was found ready to carry out the design of the conspirators. This brigand raised his gun to his shoulder, took aim at the Queen, but, according to Ferrières, dared not pull the trigger ; according to Weber, the weapon was angrily dashed from his hand by his companions. The next moment the silence was broken by a wild outburst of applause ; cries of " Vive la Reine ! " resounded on every side. Lafayette, coming forward into the balcony, raised the Queen's hand to his lips and kissed it. The storm of acclamation redoubled ; the situation was saved.

So once again the designs of the Orléanistes were frustrated ; only one hope remained to them—if the King and Queen were to be brought to Paris the people might yet be worked up to the pitch of fury necessary to their assassination. Accordingly a voice in the crowd [2] was heard calling out, " The King to Paris ! The King to Paris ! " and instantly the cry was taken up by the multitude. Hearing this the King decided to consult the Assembly, and a message was sent to the hall requesting that the deputies should come to the Château to discuss the situation. " We must not hesitate," replied Mounier ; " let us fly to the King." But Mirabeau had no mind to expose his person to the tender mercies of the revolutionary crowds whose benevolence he was never tired of praising,[3] and immediately opposed the

---

[1] Evidence of the Comte de Saint-Aulaire, witness CLVIII. in *Procédure du Châtelet.*

[2] Ferrières says " a few voices " ; Bertrand de Molleville, " one voice only."

[3] " M. le Comte de Mirabeau represents *the danger* of leaving the accustomed place for sittings " (*Moniteur,* ii. 12).

suggestion. " It is inconsistent with the dignity of the Assembly to go to the King ; we cannot deliberate in a King's palace."

" Our dignity," retorted Mounier, " consists in doing our duty, and at this moment of danger our sacred duty is to be with the King ; we shall reproach ourselves eternally if we neglect it."

Then the King, with the courage which the deputies lacked, announced his intention of going to the Assembly since the Assembly would not go to him, and thereupon the Assembly, " with the sound of musketry fire all around," settled down to a long discussion on the manner of receiving him.[1]

Whilst these inconceivable delays were taking place the crowd was becoming more and more excited, and at last the King, despairing of the Assembly's co-operation, resolved to take the matter into his own hands and accede to the demands of the people. Going out once more on to the balcony he accordingly addressed them in these words :

" My children, you wish that I should follow you to Paris. I consent, but on the understanding that I shall not be separated from my wife and children, and I ask for the safety of my body-guard."

The crowd replied with cries of " Vive le Roi ! Vive les gardes du corps ! " Guns were fired as a sign of rejoicing. But once again the agitators succeeded in turning the tide of popular feeling, and it was in the midst of a raging herd that the Royal Family set forth on the terrible seven hours' drive to Paris. Around the carriage the vilest of the rabble had collected, pressing against it so closely that it seemed to be borne upon their shoulders ; sitting astride on cannons were the sham fishwives, carrying branches of poplar adorned with ribbons, and women of the streets, still drunk with blood and wine, singing foul songs of the gutter, and insulting the Queen by their gestures and grimaces.

In order to give colour to the story that the Court had been monopolizing the grain, the Orléanistes now released supplies and brought up wagon-loads of grain to join in the procession.[2] The people, completely duped by this manœuvre, surrounded the wagons, crying out repeatedly, " We are bringing you the baker, the baker's wife, and the baker's boy (*Nous vous amenons le boulanger, la boulangère et le petit mitron*)."

In the rear were the tragic remnants of the bodyguard—forty to fifty shattered men, disarmed, bareheaded, worn with hunger and fatigue, their garments torn and blood-stained, led prisoner by brigands armed with pikes and sabres, to meet, for all they knew, with a fate as hideous as their comrades Deshuttes and

Varicourt, whose heads had been carried two hours earlier to Paris, and brought in triumph to the Palais Royal.[1]

As the procession passed through Passy the Duc d'Orléans, who had hurried on ahead, was seen on the terrace of his house surrounded by his children, and with them Madame de Genlis, frantically impatient to witness the humiliation of the Queen, to whose Court she had never been able to gain admittance. At the sight of their vanquished rivals joy unrestrained broke out on the countenances of this ignoble family. Mademoiselle d'Orléans gave way to hysterical laughter. Some of the brigands in the crowd, recognizing the duke, in spite of his efforts to conceal himself behind the rest of the group, cried out, " Vive le Duc d'Orléans ! Vive notre père d'Orléans ! " nor could ducal frowns and gestures silence these incriminating acclamations.[2]

It was seven o'clock in the evening when the Royal Family reached the Hôtel de Ville to be complimented by Bailly on " the beautiful day " that had brought the King to Paris. Louis XVI., in a voice faint with hunger and exhaustion, replied that he came " with joy and with confidence into the good city of Paris." Bailly, in repeating the King's words to the people, omitted to say " with confidence," but the Queen, whose presence of mind even at this crisis had not deserted her, interposed in clear tones : " You forget, Monsieur, that the King said ' and with confidence.' " Whereat Bailly, turning to the people, added, " You hear, Messieurs ? You are more fortunate than if I had said it myself." At half-past nine, by the glare of torches, the Royal Family entered the palace of the Tuileries that for nearly three years was to be their prison. It is said that the King was radiant, his confidence in his people once more restored, for at this, as at every other crisis of the Revolution, he never lost sight of the fact that the people were misled and to be pitied rather than blamed.

" There are evil men," he said next day to the little Dauphin, " who have stirred up the people, and the excesses committed are their work ; *we must not bear a grudge against the people.*" In this conviction, which to the last day of his life Louis XVI. never relinquished, is to be found the secret of that amazing spirit of forbearance which has been attributed to his weakness.

---

[1] Many contemporaries, including Madame de Campan, say that these heads were carried in the procession, but Weber, the *Deux Amis*, Bertrand de Molleville, and Gouverneur Morris distinctly state that they were carried on ahead and arrived in Paris at twelve o'clock, before the procession had started from Versailles. The Chancelier Pasquier saw them carried into the Palais Royal (*Mémoires*, p. 72).

[2] Montjoie, ii. 273 ; *Histoire de la Révolution de France*, by the Vicomte F. de Conny ; evidence of the Vicomte de Mirabeau, witness CXLVI. in *Procédure du Châtelet.*

THE RÔLE OF THE PEOPLE

The point that Louis XVI. failed to realize was that the revolutionary mob which marched on Versailles was not the people at all, but an assemblage composed of impostors both male and female, and of hired rabble from the Faubourgs ; the only element that could be described as representing the people being those poor women forced against their will to march.

So indignant were the true women of the people at the masquerade conducted in their name that, on the morning after the arrival of the Royal Family in Paris, a deputation of the " Ladies of the Market " presented themselves at the Commune of Paris to repudiate all complicity with the movement by means of the following petition :

" Messieurs, we come to represent to you that we at the corn market took no part in what happened yesterday ; we disapprove of it . . . ; we devote to public justice women who have no other qualification than that of light women (*femmes du monde*) and prostituted to those who, like themselves, only wish to disturb the peace and tranquillity of good citizens." [1]

The deputation proceeded to declare that " they disapproved of the indecent way in which the women had presented themselves to the King and Queen, and that, far from having spoken against Messieurs Bailly and Lafayette, they would defend them to the last drop of their blood." They requested that the National Guard should be ordered to bring these women back to order. This little petition was deposited on the table and signed by the members of the deputation, but amongst these only three were able to write their names.[2]

According to Rivarol the *poissardes* also went to the Tuileries on the same morning and " presented a petition to the King and Queen to demand justice for the horrible calumny which rendered them accomplices of the violence committed the day before towards their Majesties." [3]

---

[1] A confirmation of the statement made by certain contemporaries that Laclos, Chamfort, and other leading Orléanistes took their mistresses with them.

[2] " Extrait du procès verbal des représentants de la Commune de Paris," published in the *Histoire Parlementaire* of Buchez et Roux, iii. 137.

[3] *Mémoires de Rivarol*, p. 263. Madame Campan in her *Mémoires* also refers to this visit of the *poissardes* to the Tuileries, but, contrary to Rivarol, describes them as identical with the women who marched on Versailles, and declares that they opened the interview with reproaches against the Queen, though they ended by crying " Vive Marie Antoinette ! Vive notre bonne reine ! " But Madame Campan's account of the 6th of October is incorrect in several points ; moreover, we know that her loyalty to the Queen

In the light of the deputation to the Commune this statement of Rivarol's seems credible enough ; if the women protested to the electors of Paris, why should they not have protested to the King and Queen ? It may be suggested that it was the women of the *corn* market only who went to the Commune, but if so, why did they not say that it was from the women of the *fish* market that they wished to disassociate themselves, instead of stating distinctly that the women who marched on Versailles were of a totally different class—the class of " light women " that the " respectable poor " usually hold in abhorrence ?

The whole of this incident has been very carefully kept dark by the conspiracy of history, for, of course, it effectually disposes of the cherished revolutionary legend that the march on Versailles was conducted by women of the people. Even if we doubt the veracity of Rivarol, the petition to the Commune is an absolutely unanswerable refutation of this theory, and therefore no mention has been made of it by any revolutionary writer, either amongst contemporaries or amongst posterity.

From the point of view of the people the march on Versailles proved naturally disastrous ; the cause of liberty had been disgraced in the eyes of the world and the work of reform arrested in full swing. Several of the democratic deputies realizing this left the country in despair, and amongst this number were two of the most ardent defenders of the people—Mounier [1] and

---

is more than doubtful, and since she refrained from any reference to the deputation to the Commune which testified so strongly in the Queen's favour, she is quite as likely to have misrepresented the truth about the deputation to the Tuileries. On the loyalty of the " Dames de la Halle " at this moment see also *Lettres d'un Attaché de Légation,* date of October 16 ; *Documents pour servir à l'Histoire de la Révolution Française,* by Charles d'Héricault and Gustave Bord, 2nd series, p. 260.

[1] Mounier's denunciation of the 6th of October in his *Appel au Tribunal de l'Opinion publique* contains one of the most eloquent testimonies to the democracy of Louis XVI. : " Without doubt the nation had been long oppressed by a crowd of abuses ; the rights of citizens were not sufficiently protected against arbitrary power. But had these abuses begun under the reign of Louis XVI. ? Had he done nothing to merit our gratitude ? What prince ever lent a more attentive ear to all those who spoke to him in favour of his people ? . . . Did he dishonour his reign by sanguinary orders, by proscriptions ? Did he steal property ? And what an atrocious exaggeration to describe the mistakes of his Ministers as excesses which wore out the patience of the people, and to consider them as sufficient reasons for dethroning the King ! I will not speak here of all the advantages we owe to his benevolence—the abolition of servitude in his domains, the abolition of *corvées* and of torture, the establishment of provincial administration, the civil state of the Protestants recognized, the liberty of the seas. *Would he have lost all his authority if he had had less confidence in the love of his people ?* " Note that all these reforms mentioned by Mounier dated from *before* the Revolution.

Lally Tollendal. Clermont Tonnerre remained to be massacred at his post, Virieu to perish on the scaffold; Malouet alone of the Royalist Democrats survived the succeeding storms of the Revolution.

THE RÔLE OF THE ORLÉANISTES

Even the eyes of Lafayette were now at last opened to the truth about the Orléaniste conspiracy. Hitherto his Republican fervour had prevented him from offering a too determined opposition to the revolutionary movement, but if the 14th of July had moderated his revolutionary ardour, the 6th of October, he declared to the Comte d'Estaing, had made him a Royalist.[1] It was all over with liberty, he now saw, if the Orléanistes were to prevail, and with a courage he too seldom displayed he resolved to tell the King the whole truth, and to insist on the exile or conviction of the duke. At the same time Lafayette sought an interview with the duke himself, of which the following account is given in the *Correspondence of Lord Auckland* :

" The duke was at the head of a formidable party, the purpose of which was to send the King away, if not worse, and to make himself to be named Regent, etc. M. de Lafayette has worked out this plot in wonderful silence, and once master of every proof he waited on the duke last Saturday (Oct. 10) for the first time, and told him these words on which you may depend :

" ' Monseigneur, I fear there will soon be on the scaffold the head of some one of your name.'

" The duke looked surprised.

" ' You intend, Monseigneur, to have me assassinated, but be sure that you will be yourself an hour later.'

" The duke swore on his word of honour that he was not guilty.

" The other continued, saying :

" ' Monseigneur, I must accept your word of honour, but as I have under my hand the strongest proof of your whole conduct, your Highness must leave France or else I shall bring you before a tribunal within twenty-four hours. The King has descended several steps of his throne, but I have placed myself on the last ; he will descend no further, and in order to reach him you will have to pass over my body. You have cause for complaint against the Queen, and so have I, but this is the moment to forget all grievances.'

[1] " M. de Lafayette swore to me on the road (from Versailles to Paris on Oct. 6) that the atrocities had made a Royalist of him " (Letter from the Comte d'Estaing to the Queen, October 7, 1789).

" The duke consented to depart. The day after they were with the King, before whom 'the marquis repeated to the duke all he had said." [1]

But Louis XVI., always magnanimous, refrained from humiliating his cousin by a public exposure of his conduct, and contented himself with sending him on a pretended mission to England. According to Montjoie he hoped by this indulgence to dissuade the duke from continuing to monopolize the grain. " In the situation where so many misfortunes and crimes have placed me," he said to Orléans, " I see only the needs of the people. My sole desire and likewise my first duty is to give them back their subsistence." Accordingly he agreed to forgive everything that had taken place on the condition that the duke would open his granaries, of which a number were in England, and restore the corn he had concealed. A mission to the English Court was to be the pretext for his departure.[2]

Whether Montjoie is right on the real object of the duke's journey—and his statement is confirmed by the revolutionary Désodoards [3]—it is certain that the mission of the Duc d'Orléans to England was not, as his supporters would have us believe, an official one, but a pretext either to cover his restoration of the grain or simply to get him out of the country. The correspondence of English contemporaries on this point is conclusive, and shows that in England likewise the Duc d'Orléans was universally regarded as the author of the atrocities committed on the 6th of October.[4]

The Royalist Democrats, amongst whom we may now count Lafayette, refused, however, to be satisfied with the mere exile

---

[1] Letter from Mr. Huber in Paris to Lord Auckland, dated October 15, 1789. The above conversation is given by Mr. Huber in French. His account of the incident is confirmed in the *Memoirs of Lafayette*.

[2] *Conjuration de d'Orléans*, ii. 318.

[3] *Histoire Philosophique*, by Fantin Désodoards, i. 222.

[4] See besides the foregoing letter to Lord Auckland those from Lord Henry Fitzgerald in Paris to the Duke of Leeds, published in *Dispatches from Paris*, edited by Oscar Browning. On October 29 Fitzgerald writes : " In short, my Lord, the general impression is that the Prince was chief promoter of all the disturbances here, of the expedition on Monday the 5th of this month to Versailles, that his designs against the King were of a very criminal nature, that he aimed at the Regency of the kingdom for himself and proposed to bring his own party into power. It is supposed also that M. de Lafayette is the person who discovered the conspiracy forming, and that, having made it known to the King, his Majesty in goodness of heart employed him on a pretended commission to England, as a pretext only, and to shield him by honourable exile from further pursuit."
Again on November 6 : " I must assure your Grace that I have every reason to believe that his commission to England was a pretended one," etc.
See also Playfair's *History of Jacobinism*, p. 220, note ; *Biographical Memoirs of the French Revolution*, by John Adolphus, ii. 249 and following.

of the duke, and resolved to expose the whole design of the Orléaniste conspiracy. Mounier was the chief instigator of this movement.[1]

Accordingly in November the Châtelet of Paris opened an immense inquiry into the events of October 5 and 6. In spite of the threats of the Orléanistes a great number of witnesses came forward to testify against the infamous manœuvres of the duke and his supporters, and these witnesses were not taken only from amongst aristocrats or Royalists, but from amongst men and women of all classes—soldiers, hairdressers, deputies of the Assembly, washerwomen, ladies-in-waiting, tradesmen, and domestic servants jostle each other in the 570 pages published by the Châtelet, and no one should attempt to write a line on October 5 and 6 without consulting the graphic descriptions given by these eye-witnesses of the manner in which the march on Versailles was engineered.[2]   In the light of this great mass of evidence no impartial mind can possibly doubt that the whole insurrection was the work of the Orléaniste conspiracy—the forcing of the women to march, the men in women's clothes, the money distributed amongst the crowd, the presence of the duke himself and of his supporters in the thick of the tumult always followed by cries of "Vive le bon duc d'Orléans! Vive notre *roi* d'Orléans!" All these facts were proved beyond dispute.

That the duke was indeed actually amongst the crowd on the marble staircase showing them the way to the Queen's apartments can hardly be doubted, but on this point the reader must be left to form his own opinion from the evidence given in the Appendix of this book.[3]

The Châtelet having thus accumulated information from every quarter, finally sought the testimony of the victim against

---

[1] Avant-propos to the *Tableau des Témoins . . . dans la Procédure du Châtelet,* 1790.

[2] The whole of the inquiry is to be found at the British Museum under the heading *Procédure criminelle instruite au Châtelet de Paris sur la dénonciation des faits arrivés à Versailles dans la journée du 6 octobre 1789. Imprimée par ordre de l'Assemblée Nationale.* Museum press mark, 491.1.2. Readers should beware of consulting the Orléaniste publication, *Abrégé de la Procédure criminelle instruite au Châtelet,* etc., in which the most important evidence is suppressed, but the brochure entitled *Tableau des Témoins et recueil des faits les plus intéressants,* etc., an answer to the aforesaid *Abrégé,* is a genuine résumé of the inquiry.

[3] Von Sybel, the German historian, considers that "the strongest evidence against the Duc d'Orléans was furnished several years later by the discovery of a letter bearing the date of October 6 in which he directs his banker not to pay the sums agreed upon : ' Run quickly, my friend, to the banker . . . and tell him not to deliver the sum ; the money has not been gained, the brat still lives !' (*le marmot vit encore*)." This would

whom all the worst outrages of October 6 had been directed—
the Queen of France. But to the inquiries of the commissioners
who presented themselves at the Tuileries for the purpose, Marie
Antoinette made only the reply : " I saw everything, I heard
everything, I have forgotten everything (*J'ai tout vu, j'ai tout
entendu, j'ai tout oublié*)." [1]

The supreme opportunity had been given her to bring her
arch-enemy to justice—a course that might have saved the lives
of the Royal Family and put an end to the whole Revolution,
but with sublime magnanimity she chose to reject it. Yet there
are still historians capable of saying that Marie Antoinette
" knew not to forgive " !

But the evidence collected by the Châtelet was already more
than sufficient to prove that the events of October 5 and 6 were
the work of a conspiracy. Even the " Comité des Recherches "
of the municipality of Paris, to whom the Châtelet applied for
information, though in collusion with the Orléanistes—Brissot
was, in fact, one of its leading members—admitted in its report
that " the execrable crime which defiled the Château of Versailles in the morning of Tuesday the 6th of October had for
instruments bandits set in motion by clandestine manœuvres
who mingled with the citizens," but in order to avert investigation as to the authors of these manœuvres the Comité refused
to extend its inquiries to anything that took place before the
morning of the 6th. By this means, as Mounier points out, all
the preparations that led up to the march on Versailles, and
even the organization of the march itself, were to be kept dark,
so as to throw the entire blame on a " few obscure ruffians "
whom the conspirators were quite ready to deliver over to justice.[2]

In spite of these obstacles the Châtelet had no difficulty,
however, in deciding who were the true authors of the insurrection, and on the 5th of August 1790 the magistrates unanimously
convicted the Duc d'Orléans and Mirabeau as deserving of arrest.

The following day a deputation from the Châtelet presented
themselves at the Assembly and placed all the documentary
evidence they had collected on the table.

---

seem to indicate that some one had been bribed to murder the Dauphin,
but the incident rests only on the authority of Réal, minister of police
under the Empire, who declared that he had held the note in his hands.
See *Philippe d'Orléans Égalité*, by Auguste Ducoin, p. 72.

[1] Montjoie, *Conjuration de d'Orléans*, ii. 71 ; *Dispatches from Paris*,
ii. 311.

[2] *Appel au Tribunal*, p. 76. See also Fantin Désodoards, p. 283 :
" The Orléanistes had no doubt that the Châtelet would regard this affair
from the point of view indicated by themselves, and would throw all the
odium on a few obscure ruffians who could easily be represented as secret
agents of the Royalists."

Boucher d'Argis then opened the debate with these dramatic words :

" At last we have torn aside the veil from the deplorable event now all too celebrated. They will be known—those secrets full of horror ; they will be revealed—those crimes that stained the palace of our kings in the morning of October the 6th ! "

But the Orléanistes had still far too much power over the Assembly to be brought to justice. Chabroud, the hireling of the duke,[1] was deputed to draw up a report exonerating both the delinquents, and this was followed by tirades from Mirabeau and the Duc de Biron, which had the usual effect of cowing the Assembly. To any impartial mind these speeches for the defence are hardly less convincing proof of the conspirators' guilt than the report of the Châtelet. Not a single charge against the defendants is effectually refuted ; the feebleness of the arguments employed is equalled only by their audacity. The "people" whom these demagogues did not hesitate to stigmatize as "ruffians" or as "tigers"[2] were alone to blame ; the only conspiracy was that of the "enemies of the Revolution"! In other words, it was the "aristocrats" who had organized the march on Versailles !

Mirabeau, adopting his usual device of drowning his lack of reason or logic in floods of meaningless verbiage, thundered against the Châtelet : "This history is profoundly odious. The annals of crime offer few examples of infamy at the same time so shameless and unskilful." Several of the most incriminating accusations he boldly admitted,[3] but endeavoured to explain them away by sophistries so futile that even the Assembly would have been forced to reject them had not Mirabeau, with superb cunning, hit on an argument that terrified the Assembly into acquiescence. "It is not the 6th of October," he cried, "that is being brought to trial—it is the Revolution ! " And at this

---

[1] Montjoie, *Conjuration de d'Orléans*, iii. 84. Fantin Désodoards (*Histoire Philosophique*, etc. i. 286) says Chabroud received 60,000 francs from the Duc d'Orléans for this report.

[2] " Perhaps ruffians had mingled with the multitude and it had become their mobile instrument. . . . A homicidal band advances, in its frenzy it respects nothing. Soon there is nothing between the tigers and Louis XVI." (Speech of Chabroud).

[3] For example, Dr. la Fisse, witness LV. in the *Procédure du Châtelet*, had stated that Mirabeau, on receiving a note from the Duc d'Orléans after the 6th of October saying that he was leaving for England, had exclaimed furiously to those around him, " See here—read ! He is as craven as a lackey, he is a blackguard (*jean foutre*) who does not deserve all the trouble taken for him ! " (Compare this with Camille Desmoulins' description of Mirabeau's " anger at seeing himself abandoned," quoted on p. 126 of this book.) Mirabeau admitted having made this remark, but explained he only meant it was " a mistake " for the duke to go to England !

the Assembly, dominated by the two revolutionary factions, who well knew that if the Revolution ended it was all over with them, hastily reversed the judgement of the Châtelet and declared both Orléans and Mirabeau innocent. At this monstrous decision of the Assembly a cry of indignation went up from all those who loved justice, and who from the beginning of the Revolution had striven for the cause of true liberty.[1]

Amongst these was Mounier, who wrote from Switzerland his *Appeal to the Tribunal of Public Opinion* denouncing the report of Chabroud : " I can conceive nothing so revolting as the efforts of M. Chabroud to justify the most frightful crimes, his indulgence towards the assassins, his hatred for the victims, his outrages against the witnesses and against the judges (of the Châtelet), the threatening tone of the Duc d'Orléans and the Comte de Mirabeau, the eagerness with which the conclusions of the reporter (Chabroud) were hastily admitted, without examination and without discussion. Nothing of all this should surprise me, yet it provoked in me indignation almost equal to that which I felt on October 5 and 6, 1789. Perhaps the apology of crime should inspire more horror than crime itself."

Yet it is this apology of the crimes of October 5 and 6 that for more than a hundred years has triumphed over truth and justice ; by nearly all historians the *Procédure du Châtelet* and the great denunciation of Mounier — whom up to this point they have quoted unceasingly in support of revolutionary doctrines—have been persistently ignored, and the character of the French people has been blackened for the better whitewashing of an ignoble prince and his boon companions. Such is the " democratic " method of writing history !

The truth is that the march on Versailles was nothing but an Orléaniste rising ; not only must the people be exonerated from blame, but so must also the other revolutionary intrigues. In all the preparations that took place beforehand, in all the sidelights thrown by the Châtelet on the crimes committed, we can find no trace of either Anarchist, English, or Prussian co-

---

[1] For the opinions of English contemporaries on the absolution of the Assembly at the instigation of " the whitewasher Chabroud," see, for example, Playfair's *History of Jacobinism*, p. 220 ; Robison's *Proofs of a Conspiracy*, p. 392 ; and the statement of Helen Maria Williams, a bitter enemy of the King, in her *Correspondence of Louis XVI.* i. 235. Even Dumont, the friend—and evidently, for a time, the accomplice—of Mirabeau, admitted the doubtful honesty of the Assembly in exonerating him. " The events of October 5 and 6," wrote Dumont, " have been imputed to the Duc d'Orléans, and the Châtelet implicated Mirabeau in the conspiracy. The National Assembly declared that there was no case for conviction against one or the other. *But the absolution of the Assembly is not the absolution of history*, and many veils yet remain to be raised before these events can be pronounced on " (*Souvenirs sur Mirabeau*, p. 117).

operation ; the leaders were men known to be devoted solely to the interests of the Duc d'Orléans, the instruments were in his pay.

But if these other intrigues took no actual part in the movement, they accorded it their heartiest sympathy. The outrages of the 6th of October had furthered the cause of anarchy. Robespierre could still afford to lie low, biding his time, whilst the Orléanistes proceeded with the work of demolition.

By the revolutionaries of England the events of October 5 and 6 were hailed with fresh rejoicings. At the meeting-house of the Old Jewry on November 4, Dr. Price delivered his famous political sermon in praise of the French Revolution. " What an eventful period is this ! I am thankful that I have lived to see it ; I could almost say ' Lord, now lettest thou thy servant depart in peace, for mine eyes have seen thy salvation '—I have lived to see a diffusion of knowledge which has undermined superstition and error. . . . I have lived to see thirty millions of people indignant and resolute, spurning at slavery and demanding liberty with an irresistible voice. Their king led in triumph, and an arbitrary monarch surrendering himself to his subjects."

After this discourse the members of the Revolutionary Society of Great Britain adjourned to the London Tavern and passed an address of congratulation on the " glorious example of France," which was transmitted by Lord Stanhope to the National Assembly.

But there was one man in England whose passionate love of liberty inspired him with the eloquence that alone could counteract these monstrous libels on a noble cause. Burning with indignation Edmund Burke arose and in his immortal *Reflections* opened the eyes of his fellow-countrymen to the true character of the French Revolution and the outrages of October 6. " Is this a triumph to be consecrated at altars ? to be commemorated with grateful thanksgiving ? to be offered to the divine humanity with fervent prayer and enthusiastic ejaculation ? . . . I shall never think that a prince, the acts of whose whole reign were a series of concessions to his subjects, who was willing to relax his authority, to remit his prerogatives, to call his people to a share of freedom not known, perhaps not desired, by their ancestors . . . I shall be led with great difficulty to think that he deserves the cruel and insulting triumph of Paris and of Dr. Price. *I tremble for the cause of liberty, from such an example to kings. I tremble for the cause of humanity in the unpunished outrages of the most wicked of mankind.*"

Burke's stirring appeal met with a prodigious success and carried all the sane portion of the people with him. Hitherto they had retained a certain sympathy with the Revolution ; the national " sporting " instinct had responded, as we have seen, to the enterprise of attacking the Bastille, but this same instinct recoiled at the cowardly attempt to massacre the defenceless Royal Family in their beds. " After the 6th of October," says the Republican Dumont, " many sensible men (in England) began to think that the French treated infamously a king who had done so much for them." [1]

The effect of Burke's speech was undoubtedly to save England from revolution ; Dumont even goes so far as to question whether he was not " the saviour of Europe." In vain the English revolutionaries retorted with a storm of seditious pamphlets ; their efforts were speedily transformed into waste paper, whilst Burke's denunciation will live as long as the English tongue is spoken.

" Its merit," wrote the contemporary John Adolphus, " can only be appreciated by the never-dying rancour it excited in the minds of his opponents, a rancour which age, affliction, sickness, and even death could not assuage." [2] It is not assuaged yet ! Still, after more than a hundred years, the Radical press does not weary of reviling the author of the great *Reflections*, and owing to its unremitting efforts England has never been allowed to know the debt she owes to Edmund Burke. [3]

But if England began henceforth to regard the French Revolution with aversion, Prussia continued to express unfeigned admiration for the principles of French liberty. The decrees of August 4, which deprived the German princes of their estates in Alsace and Lorraine, had already embittered feeling between Austria and France, and paved the way for the dissolution of the hated Franco-Austrian alliance ; and, although perhaps Prussia hardly realized it at the time, the first step had been taken towards the incorporation of these provinces with the future German Empire. Well might Hertzberg and Von der Goltz rejoice at each succeeding stage of the Revolution ! " A King without authority," wrote the Minister of Saxony to Berlin, whilst the march on Versailles was preparing, " a state without money or military power ; in a word, a vessel caught in a storm and of which Mirabeau is the only pilot—what importance can France have henceforth in Europe ? " [4]

---

[1] *Souvenirs sur Mirabeau*, p. 96.

[2] *History of the French Revolution*, by John Adolphus, ii. 298.

[3] So thoroughly has this propaganda been carried out that in the popular edition of the *Reflections*, which the good taste of the British public made it necessary to publish, a preface has been inserted explaining that Burke was ill-informed on the subject and urging the reader to consult Mr. Arthur Young's *Travels in France*. But the writer carefully refrains from mentioning Arthur Young's later work, *The Example of France*, which confirms every word uttered by Burke in rather stronger language !

[4] *L'Europe et la Révolution Française*, by A. Sorel, ii. 26.

Prussia had indeed every reason to be grateful to the Revolution. Was it a recognition of this debt that inspired the Prussians to enter Versailles eighty-two years later to the strains of the " Marseillaise " ? The 6th of October 1789 had proved but the prelude to the 8th of January 1871, and in the great gallery of the palace, stained with the blood of the King's bodyguard, William I. of Prussia was proclaimed German Emperor amidst the acclamations of his conquering hordes.

THE INVASION OF THE TUILERIES

THE INVASION OF THE TUILERIES

COURSE OF THE INTRIGUES IN 1790 AND 1791

A PERIOD of nearly three years elapsed between the second and third great outbreaks of the Revolution. During this interval changes so fundamental took place among the factions that the outbreaks of 1792 must be regarded as an entirely different movement—in fact as a new and distinct revolution.

In order to understand the causes that produced this second revolution it is necessary therefore to form some idea of the course taken by the revolutionary intrigues since the march on Versailles.

With the exile of the Duc d'Orléans and his mentor Choderlos de Laclos the Orléaniste conspiracy was temporarily arrested, and by the desertion of Mirabeau in the following spring lost its principal dynamic force. Mirabeau, it was said, had been "bought" by the Court; true, Mirabeau received payment, but this time only for the expression of his real opinions. He had always despised the Duc d'Orléans, and once the King's bounty had freed him from this ignoble servitude he devoted all his immense energy to building up the royal authority he had spent the previous years in overthrowing.

Louis XVI., who, as M. Sorel well expresses it, " saw only in the Revolution a misunderstanding between himself and his people, exploited and stirred up by a band of sedition-mongers," hoped by the capture of the chief agitator to put an end to hostilities.

On the 13th of July 1790, before taking his oath to maintain the Constitution on the following day at the Fête de la Fédération, Louis XVI. appeared at the Assembly, and delivered himself of this strangely human message to his people :

" Tell your fellow-citizens that I wish I could speak to them all as I speak to you here ; tell them again that their King is their father, their brother, their friend ; that he can be happy only in their happiness, great with their glory, mighty through their liberty, rich through their prosperity, that he can suffer only in their griefs. Make the words or rather the feelings of my heart to be heard in the humblest cottages and in the dwellings of the unfortunate; tell them that if I cannot go with you into their abodes, I desire to be there by my affection and by means of laws that will protect the weak, to watch with them, to live for them, to die if necessary for them. . . ."

But the return of the Duc d'Orléans two days earlier—which Lafayette was either too foolish or too cowardly to oppose—gave a fresh impetus to the conspirators, and insurrection broke out with redoubled fury at the Palais Royal. The professional agitators of 1789—St. Huruge, Grammont, Fournier l'Américain —were now reinforced by a gang of hired brigands, known as the company of the "Sabbat," raised by the De Lameths and consisting mainly of Italians—notably Rotondo, Malga, and Cavallanti—whom we now find mingling in all the revolutionary mobs, and committing every form of sanguinary violence.[1]   In the summer of 1790, soon after the Fête de la Fédération, Rotondo was despatched to St. Cloud to murder the Queen whilst she was walking in the garden, and failed only because the rain kept her indoors on the day appointed;[2] again in the following November Rotondo and Cavallanti led a mob to pillage the house of the Duc de Castries, who had wounded one of the De Lameths in a duel. At the same time the Duc d'Orléans entered into relations with another intriguer—Madame de la Motte, famous in the affair of the necklace, who now returned to Paris, and occupied a magnificent hotel in the Place Vendôme provided for her by the duke in return for fresh libels on the Queen.[3]

Meanwhile, in spite of the fact that he had sworn to maintain the Constitution and had placed no obstacles whatever in the way of the Assembly, the King was still kept a prisoner by Lafayette at the Tuileries in direct violation of the principles laid down by the people.[4]

It was under these circumstances that Louis XVI. decided in desperation to appeal for intervention by foreign powers.   At the end of October an envoy was despatched to the Marquis de Bouillé, in command on the frontier, to inform him that "the King's position under the gaolership of Lafayette had become so intolerable that he contemplated flight to the frontier to one

---

[1] La Conspiration révolutionnaire de 1789, by Gustave Bord, p. 20; Le Marquis de St. Huruge, by Henri Furgeot, pp. 192, 225; Crimes et Forfaits de L. P. J. d'Orléans découverts par un citoyen.

[2] Mémoires de Mme. Campan, p. 276.

[3] Mémoires de Lafayette, iii. 157; Correspondance secrète, p. 481.

[4] See the Résumé of the Cahiers, p. 7, Article II. "The person of the King is inviolable and sacred," Article XI. "Individual liberty is sacred." Therefore either as King or subject Louis XVI. could not legally be kept a prisoner, not only without the formality of a trial but without even any reason being given for his detention.

of the places under Bouillé's command, in order to muster around him all the troops and also those of his subjects who had remained faithful to him, to endeavour to win back the rest of his people who had been misled by sedition-mongers, and to seek support in the help of his allies if all other means to re-establish order and peace proved unavailing." [1]

Now since the suggestion contained in this letter of an appeal to the King's allies, the Austrians, has been made the chief ground of accusation against both Louis XVI. and Marie Antoinette, it is important to understand their real intentions on this question of the " Appel à l'Étranger." No one has explained the matter more clearly than M. Louis Madelin, the historian who best represents modern French opinion :

" Marie Antoinette . . . appears to have thought of this appeal to Europe towards the summer of 1790. The idea she entertained concerning it—a woman's idea, perfectly childish—is still little known in general. She dreamt in no way of a counter-revolution brought to Paris in the baggage-wagons of the foreigner, but of *a simple manifestation on the frontiers*, by means of which the Court would show that they ' disapproved of the way the King was treated.' The Emperor would mass his troops, make a feint of advancing, Louis XVI. would place himself at the head of the French army, and Leopold would then retire before his brother-in-law, who, aureoled by this victory, would re-enter Paris surrounded by the love of an expectant people."

The plan was futile, however, for the reason that the "friendly" sentiments of the European sovereigns to whom this appeal was made were outweighed by their political ambitions. " The cause of kings ! The cause of dynasties ! " cries M. Madelin ; " that will be said hypocritically in 1792, but the Revolution neither alarms nor scandalizes Europe in 1789 and 1790, it is rather a cause for rejoicing." All the splendour of old France that had evoked the envy and admiration of foreign monarchs was centred not only in the Court but in the Capetian dynasty, consequently the sight of France, their eternal rival, bleeding in the dust from self-inflicted wounds, seemed to these lesser powers no occasion for knight-errantry. As to the ties of blood which have been represented as binding together the royal families of Europe in a confraternity dangerous to the interests of their subjects, their feebleness was never better exemplified than in the French Revolution, for of all the European sovereigns Leopold II., Emperor of Austria, brother to the Queen of France, was perhaps the least eager to defend his sister's interests or even to ensure her safety, whilst Gustavus III. of Sweden, bound by no ties of kinship, alone displayed activity in responding to her appeal.

[1] *Mémoires de Bouillé*, p. 181.

In the case of Frederick William II. of Prussia, it was not merely a matter of passive acquiescence in the disorders of France, but, as we have already seen, of active co-operation. The intrigue of Von der Goltz—which we must follow in the pages of Sorel— had prospered marvellously since the march on Versailles, for he had succeeded in carrying out his Prussian Majesty's injunctions by forming a coalition with several of the most influential revolutionary leaders, notably the Orléaniste Pétion. In May of 1790 Frederick William had written to Von der Goltz ordering him " to keep this Pétion on the alert, to express the satisfaction he (the King) feels at his conduct, and to let them know in Berlin whether it would not be expedient to give him a pension." [1]

This letter was followed five months later by the despatch of a fresh emissary to France, a certain Jew agitator named Ephraïm, who arrived in Paris on September 14, 1790, armed with a letter from the King of Prussia to Von der Goltz instructing him to put Ephraïm in touch with the revolutionary leaders and pave his way for him :

" Goltz had been preparing it for a long time. He arranged for the admission of the royal go-between with Lafayette, with Barnave, with Lameth ; he put him in touch with Pétion, Brissot, Gensonné, and their friends (*i.e.* with the future Girondins). Ephraïm found them full of animosity against Austria and *full of cordiality towards Prussia.* He showed himself still more anti-Austrian than any one amongst them, and the cynicism of his language with regard to the Queen seemed a certain guarantee of the sincerity of his sympathy for France."

Ephraïm then tried to worm his way into the confidence of the King's minister, Montmorin, but without success. " ' The object he put forward,' said Montmorin, ' is a commercial treaty, but I have occasion to believe that his mission extends further and that he has been instructed to sound us on a political understanding.' . . . Montmorin had good reasons for distrusting all these Prussian manœuvres ; Ephraïm was playing a very perfidious part in Paris. He frequented the clubs and made himself noticed by his democratic violence. ' His object,' wrote Montmorin, ' is to embroil us with the Emperor of Austria, and he thinks that in stirring up the public against the Queen he will succeed in this more easily. He goes in for underhand dealings and tries to work upon the journalists. I am almost certain that he distributes money, and I know that he draws large sums from the banker.' " [2]

---

[1] All the following quotations are taken from *L'Europe et la Révolution Française,* by Albert Sorel, vol. ii. pp. 69, 157.

[2] It was his refusal to form an alliance with Prussia at this crisis that

Montmorin's suspicions were perfectly correct, for on this point we have the evidence of contemporaries belonging to absolutely opposite parties. Thus the Comte de Fersen, writing to Gustavus III. of Sweden on March 8, 1791, states that Ephraïm has been supplying money to the agents of revolutionary propaganda—" not long ago he again received 600,000 louis." [1] And Camille Desmoulins threw further light on the matter in 1793 by this significant phrase : " Is it not a fact aptly brought forward by Philippeaux that the treasurer of the King of Prussia, in giving him an account of the expenses for last year, produces an item of *six million écus for corruptions in France* ? " [2] In all the sordid annals of the Hohenzollerns no greater perfidy has ever been brought to light ; already they had embarked on the programme which in our own day they have pursued with unfailing success—the *engineering of revolution* in all those countries they wish to subdue. Well might the English Jacobin Miles exclaim : " Of all the sceptred miscreants who have dishonoured royalty since you and I have perambulated this earth, I know of none so base, so mean, so infamous as the present King of Prussia. He has authorized his agents throughout Europe to commit a kind of general pillage—to cajole and rob all nations."

For Miles, revolutionary though he was, displayed no small perspicacity in seeing through the intrigues of certain so-called democrats, and he was not deceived, as are our visionaries of to-day, by protestations of sympathy with the cause of liberty emanating from the willing slaves of Prussian despotism. " Some of the German courts," he wrote on March 12, 1791, " have emissaries here—all apostles of liberty—preaching equal

---

formed the principal charge against Montmorin when he was brought to trial by the Girondins two years later. The words in which this accusation is conveyed afford clear evidence that the Girondins were acting in the interests of Prussia, and throw a curious light on their political morality : " It had been assumed," runs the official report read aloud by the Girondin, Lasource, that M. de Montmorin " had not believed in the sincerity of the advances made by the Court of Berlin. It was not possible that this Court should not have been of good faith, since it (the Court of Berlin !) has been so from all time, and that it can only be the natural enemy of that of Vienna. . . . M. de Montmorin . . . knew that jealousy and rivalry was fomenting more than ever between these two Courts, since he knew and admitted himself that *it was the King of Prussia who had excited and fomented by his agents the insurrection of the Belgians and the Liégeois* (against Austria). He therefore knew perfectly the attitude of the King of Prussia, and if he refused to adopt his views it was not because he doubted his sincerity, but because he did not wish for an alliance with that Court. What reproaches, Messieurs, has not France to make against this ex-minister ? " (*Moniteur*, xiii. 591). Montmorin was therefore to be condemned as a traitor to France because he had refused to form an alliance with a Court that he knew to be fomenting sedition in a rival State !

[1] *Le Comte de Fersen et la Cour de France*, i. 87.

[2] *Fragment de l'Histoire secrète de la Révolution*, p. 44.

rights and *assuring the giddy multitude that their example will be followed by the whole world.* Prussia for intrigue takes the lead. She pays court to each party as appearances may seem to favour. The Tuileries she disregards. All her agents vociferate against the house of Austria as plotting with the Queen for the purpose of destroying the Revolution." [1]

The skill with which this intrigue was conducted shows that the teachings of Frederick the Great had been laid to heart by his disciples. Frederick had always believed in the dissemination of democratic doctrines abroad whilst remaining a past master in the art of counteracting their influence at home. The rulers of the various German states had now more than ever need to exercise this talent, for the people of Germany displayed alarming symptoms of revolutionary fever. The doctrines of the German Illuminés that had contributed so powerfully to the revolution in France were now making themselves felt in the country that gave them birth. Burke, writing in this very year of 1791, remarks : " A great revolution is preparing in Germany ; and a revolution, in my opinion, likely to be more decisive upon the general fate of nations than that of France itself. . . ."

This revolution, which might have proved the salvation of the civilized world by overthrowing the despotism of the Hohenzollerns, was averted by the revolution in France.

The death of Mirabeau in April 1791 removed a formidable obstacle from the path of Prussia. The author of *The Secret History of the Court of Berlin,* who had declared that " war is the national industry of Prussia," was not the man to be deceived by the pacific protestations of Frederick William's emissaries. Mirabeau knew far more than was convenient about the intrigues of the Hohenzollerns, and he detested Hertzberg. " That old fox," he declared exultingly to Dumouriez, " had only a short time to live." [2]

Four days later Mirabeau himself was dead. The truth of the verdict, " Death from natural causes," was never proved conclusively, and the Orléanistes were strongly suspected of avenging themselves by poison for the defection of their most valuable ally. But is it altogether impossible that Ephraïm may have been concerned in the matter ? The Jew agitator, at any rate, played an active part in the tumult that took place a fortnight later when the Orléanistes, once more hoping to achieve the King's death at the hands of the people,[3] drove a

---

[1] *The Correspondence of William Augustus Miles on the French Revolution,* i. 256.

[2] *Mémoires de Dumouriez.*

[3] " The object of the plot was the assassination of the King " (*Choderlos de Laclos,* by Émile Dard, p. 286).

mob to the Tuileries under the pretext of preventing the Royal Family from going to St. Cloud for Easter. The same thing had been attempted the year before when women were sent to incite the crowd to violence, but their efforts had proved unavailing, and the King had set forth upon his journey amidst the acclamations of the Parisians and cries of " Bon voyage au bon Papa ! " [1] The revolutionary leaders realized that more potent instruments must be employed if they were to bring off their coup. Danton, the principal organizer of the movement,[2] remained as usual in the background, but Laclos disguised as a jockey and Sillery as a lackey were recognized amongst the crowd. Again the professional agitators had been summoned—St. Huruge and the bloodthirsty members of the *Sabbat* ; " Malga gorged with gold and wine " mingled with the troops, inciting them to murder ; Rotondo led the rabble.[3] But it was said to be Ephraïm who had financed the movement with the funds confided to him by his royal master.[4]

This outrage finally decided Louis XVI. to carry out his plan of flight to the frontier, and on the 20th of June the Royal Family set forth on the fatal journey to Montmédy that ended in their arrest at Varennes. The Orléanistes immediately seized the opportunity to fan up popular fury against the King ; the gutter press in their pay poured forth pamphlets describing Louis XVI. as *le gros cochon,*[5] a besotted drunkard, " a monopolizer, a swindler, a false-coiner, a devourer of men." [6] At the Jacobin Club, Réal, amidst furious abuse of the King, proposed that the Duc d'Orléans should be urged to accept the regency.[7] The duke, who at the first news of the King's flight had driven round Paris with a smile on his lips congratulating himself on his victory, now became struck with panic, and exasperated his supporters by publishing a letter composed for him by Madame de Genlis declining the regency.[8] But Laclos, energetic as ever in the cause of his royal " protégé," drew up a petition in collaboration with Brissot, demanding the deposition of the King and, in spite of the protests of Brissot,[9] " his replacement by constitutional

---

[1] *Correspondance secrète,* p. 450.

[2] Danton boasted of this at his trial : " It was I who prevented the journey to St. Cloud." See *Notes de Topino Lebrun* ; also *Bulletin du Tribunal révolutionnaire,* No. 21822, "Défense de Danton."

[3] Émile Dard, *op. cit.* ; *Correspondance secrète,* 523 ; *Lettres d'Aristocrates,* by Pierre de Vaissière, p. 291.

[4] Émile Dard, *op. cit.*

[5] *Le Nouveau Paris,* by Mercier, i. 192.

[6] *Révolutions de France et de Brabant,* by Camille Desmoulins.

[7] *Séances des Jacobins* for July 3, 1791.

[8] *Mémoires de Mme. de Genlis,* iv. 92.

[9] *Mémoires de Mme. Roland,* ii. 285 ; *Mémoires de Brissot,* iv. 342.

means "—in other words, the substitution of the Duc d'Orléans for Louis XVI.

The Orléanistes, however, had over-reached themselves; in degrading the King they had succeeded in degrading the monarchy, and now *for the first time* the cry of " No more kings! " made itself heard, and the proposal was made that the phrase composed by Laclos should be replaced by one demanding the abolition of the monarchy.[1]

This suggestion of a Republic, emanating from the Club of the Cordeliers and a section of Paris entirely under their control known as the Théâtre Français,[2] met with the support of only a few isolated revolutionaries, including Brissot and Condorcet, whose Republican convictions were more than doubtful, and was violently opposed by the Jacobins, who were mainly Orléanistes. Already at a sitting of the Club, immediately after the flight to Varennes, a member who ventured to propose a Republic had been indignantly shouted down,[3] and the amendment suggested by the so-called " Republicans " was therefore rejected by the Jacobins, and the original proposal of Laclos retained in the petition which was to be presented at " the altar of the country " erected on the Champ de Mars.

By means of cajolery, threats, and the dissemination of panic news,[4] some thousands of signatures were obtained in the Faubourgs—principally those of women and children [5]—and early in the morning of the day appointed, July 17, 1791, a disorderly crowd assembled on the Champ de Mars, and after inaugurating the ceremony by the murder of two unoffending citizens—an old soldier and a wig-maker, who had taken refuge from the rays of the sun beneath the steps of the altar in order to enjoy a frugal breakfast [6]—proceeded to the usual revolutionary pastime of pelting the troops assembled by Lafayette with stones. Whereupon Lafayette and Bailly, the mayor, with unwonted firmness, hoisted the red flag and proclaimed martial law, but the soldiers, exasperated by the pistol shots that now succeeded to the hail of stones, without waiting for further orders fired on the rioters and killed a number of them.[7]

[1] Aulard's *Séances des Jacobins*, iii. 43.   [2] Buchez et Roux, x. 145.
[3] See *Journal des Débats de la Société des Amis de la Constitution*, etc., *Séance* of July 1, 1791. M. Varennes asks whether the throne shall be set up again, and whether a monarchic or republican government would be best: " Grand bruit, brouhahas "; the President calls the member to order. Also *Séance* of July 8, 1791, M. Goupil in a speech refers to " the opinions that prevail in this society in favour of Republicanism." The greatest tumult arises at this sentence, and a member reminds the speaker that " all this uproar is caused by your attributing to the society sentiments it has never entertained. (Universal applause.)"
[4] Beaulieu, ii. 540.   [5] *Ibid.* ii. 538.   [6] *Ibid.* ii. 541.
[7] Lafayette was ever after blamed for this so-called " massacre " by

As in all popular tumults, the display of force brought the mob to its senses; in an instant the whole Champ de Mars was swept clear of insurgents, but, what was more important, the fusillade had the effect of terrifying the revolutionary leaders. The Jacobins, assembled in their Club, hastily escaped by doors and windows, and ran for their lives amidst the jeers of the populace.[1] Brissot, Camille Desmoulins, and Fréron " disappeared " ; [2] Marat betook himself once more to a cellar ; [3] Robespierre, trembling in every limb, hurriedly changed his lodgings ; [4] Danton fled to the country, and thence to England ; [5] whilst Hébert, the terrible Père Duchesne, who for once had ventured out into a popular tumult and heard the bullets of the soldiery whistling past his ears, never recovered from his fright : " It seems," says his biographer, M. d'Estrée, " that every time his pamphlets mention this fusillade . . . they sweat anguish ; and this terror doubles his ferocity." [6] At the same time the Jew Ephraïm, openly accused by Royalist writers of financing seditious libels and plotting the death of the Queen, was arrested and imprisoned for two days in the Abbaye, after which he was sent back to Prussia and we hear of him no more.[7]

The tumult, described henceforth by revolutionary writers as " the massacre of the Champ de Mars," was, moreover,. not the only check received by the Orléaniste faction at this crisis ; a more serious reverse was the defection of several of the most influential Orléaniste leaders. Barnave, who with Pétion had been sent to escort the Royal Family on the terrible return journey from Varennes, had been won over by the sight of the Queen's

---

the revolutionary leaders ; Bailly paid for it with his life. Yet it is certain that Lafayette did everything in his power to restrain the indignation of the troops. See Beaulieu, ii. 543, and the evidence of Gouverneur Morris, who was an eye-witness of the scene : ".To be paraded through the streets through the scorching sun, and then stand like holiday turkeys to be knocked down by brickbats, was a little more than they (the troops) had the patience to bear ; so that *without waiting for orders* they fired and killed a dozen or two of the ragged regiment. The rest ran off like lusty fellows," etc. (*Diary and Letters of Gouverneur Morris*, i. 434).

[1] Beaulieu, ii. 545.

[2] *Histoire des Girondins*, by Granier de Cassagnac, i. 330 ; *La Tribune des Patriotes*, by Prudhomme ; *Révolutions de France*, by Camille Desmoulins, No. 86 ; *Camille Desmoulins*, by Édouard Fleury, i. 230.

[3] *Camille Desmoulins*, by Édouard Fleury, i. 227 : " The terror of Marat seems to have begun the day after the flight (to Varennes), when he was overcome by panic lest Louis XVI. should return at the head of an army and put him 'in a hot oven.' " See *L'Ami du Peuple*, No. 497.

[4] *Mémoires de Mme. Roland*, i. 65, 209, 210 and note. Robespierre's terror also began at the flight to Varennes (*ibid.* p. 204).

[5] *Danton Émigré*, by Dr. Robinet, p. 24.

[6] *Le Père Duchesne*, by Paul d'Estrée, p. 61.

[7] *Le Marquis de St. Huruge*, by Henry Furgeot, p. 233.

courage and suffering, and henceforth this most truculent of revolutionaries had no thought but to devote himself to the cause of the woman he admired and pitied so profoundly. On his arrival in Paris he succeeded in detaching a number of other members from the Orléaniste conspiracy ; amongst these were Le Chapelier, Adrien Duport, Alexandre de Lameth, the Vicomte de Noailles, Muguet de Nantou, and the Duc de Liancourt. This party now joined itself to Bailly and Lafayette in support of the King and the Constitution.[1]

The most dangerous agitators having thus been either intimidated or won over, the Revolution was once more brought to a standstill—most contemporaries indeed believed that it had finally ended.[2]

The truth is that by this time the people were heartily sick of the Revolution, which had not only brought them perpetual unrest and alarms, but had created the serious problem of unemployment. " The ill effects of the Revolution," wrote Arthur Young in 1792, " have been felt more severely by the manufacturers of the kingdom than by any other class of the people. . . . This effect, which was absolute death by starving many thousands of families, was a result that, in my opinion, might have been avoided. It flowed only from carrying things to extremities—from driving the nobility out of the kingdom and seizing, instead of regulating, the whole regal authority."

For the revolutionaries of 1789, like certain Socialists of to-day, whose one idea is to clear the ground of all existing conditions, had never paused to consider what manner of social edifice could be constructed on the ruins, and the result of destroying, impoverishing, or putting to flight the wealthy and leisured classes had been simply to dislocate the whole industrial system and to ruin agriculture. For this reason the democrats of 1789 had become the aristocrats of 1792, and it was no longer only the nobles who cursed the Revolution but the farmers, the manufacturers, and the industrious bourgeois who three years earlier had hailed " the dawn of liberty," and now found them-

---

[1] Montjoie, *Conjuration de d'Orléans*, iii. 139 ; Beaulieu, ii. 530 ; *Mémoires de Mme. de Campan*, p. 294. Fersen thought that this party only went over to the King out of self-interest, and neither he nor the Queen trusted them (*Le Comte de Fersen et la Cour de France*, ii. 7, 213). Marie Antoinette has been bitterly reproached for this, but when we remember their former record—Barnave's attitude to the murder of Foullon, the raising of the " Compagnie du Sabbat " by the De Lameths, and the infamous part they had all played in the former insurrections—it is not altogether surprising.

[2] It should be noticed that this reaction set in before the King's final acceptance of the Constitution on September 13, 1791. M. Louis Madelin (*La Révolution*, p. 187) says that from August 1 to October 1 it was the general opinion that the Revolution was over.

selves sharing the fate of the class they had been so eager to dethrone.[1]

With the employers of labour the workers suffered to an even greater degree. All the hands that had ministered to the needs or caprices of the rich were now idle—embroiderers, fan-makers, upholsterers, gilders, carriage-builders, bookbinders, engravers, wandered aimlessly through the streets of Paris ; 3000 tailors' apprentices, the same number of shoemakers and barbers, 4000 domestic servants collected in crowds to deliberate on the misery of their condition.[2]

To add to their hardships the insurrection, encouraged by the revolutionaries in San Domingo, had checked the import of colonial supplies, consequently " the carpenter, the locksmith, the mason, and the market porter no longer have their morning coffee and milk, and every morning they grumble at the thought that the reward of their patriotism is an increase of privations." [3]

But whilst in the great upheaval many of the people had been brought down to the depths of misery, a few had risen to the height of prosperity and had become the oppressors of the poor. When in June 1791 bands of working-men appealed to Marat for protection against their employers, it was against the masters who had been working-men themselves that their complaints were chiefly directed,[4] and against whom they could obtain no redress, for the Assembly with all its professed respect for the " sovereignty of the people " habitually displayed complete indifference to practical schemes of social reform.[5] In the

---

[1] " Doubtless there were French farmers who rejoiced at the spectacle of all the great properties of the kingdom being levelled by the nation ; they did not, however, foresee that it would be their own turn next ; that the principle of equality being once abroad, would infallibly level ALL property " (Arthur Young, *The Example of France*, p. 33).

[2] Taine, *La Révolution*, iii. 136.

[3] *Ibid.* v. 236.

[4] See this petition in Buchez et Roux, x. 196, where the worst offenders are specified by the workmen in such terms as " day-labourer now enriched with 50,000 livres of income," or " who arrived in Paris in sabots and now possess four fine houses."

[5] See, for example, the laws passed on June 14, 1791, suppressing " coalitions of workmen "—*i.e.* trades unions—in the following terms : " Article 1st. The annihilation of all kinds of corporations of citizens belonging to the same state or profession being one of the fundamental bases of the French constitution, it is forbidden to re-establish them on any pretext or under any form whatsoever." The workmen were further forbidden to " name presidents, keep registers, make resolutions, deliberate or draw up regulations on their pretended common interests," or to agree on any fixed scale of wages. These resolutions were passed almost without discussion and without a word of protest from Robespierre or any of the other so-called democrats of the Assembly (Buchez et Roux, x. 196) ; in fact, they were enforced with still greater severity later on under the reign of Robespierre. See the edicts passed by the Comité de Salut Public on

matter of the administration of justice throughout the country the revolutionary government had shown itself equally incapable, and the little lawyers now in power, " proud of finding themselves invested with the authority of the old police, exercised the most vexatious tyranny, pronounced arbitrary verdicts, and ordered citizens to be arrested and imprisoned on the feeblest pretext. Men and women were torn from their beds on the erratic order of a president of the district. . . ." [1]

In a word, the condition of the country had become perfectly chaotic ; no one could feel any security either for their persons or their property, and the universal desire was now for a return to law and order.   The revolutionary leaders were clever enough to turn this popular unrest to their own advantage ; all their troubles, they told the people, would end when the King had finally accepted the Constitution, which was now approaching completion, but they were careful to insinuate that the King was entirely opposed to the principles it contained.   This was, of course, absolutely untrue ; Louis XVI. had throughout concurred with every true reform, and had already accepted the principles of the Constitution *as expressed by the cahiers*, but he had made no secret of the fact that he did not approve of the superstructure erected by the Assembly, which not only deprived him of the authority accorded to him by the unanimous will of the people, but which he held to be directly opposed to the interests of the people themselves.   As a matter of fact the Constitution, in its finished form, was a mass of contradictions ; it was neither democratic nor autocratic, neither republican nor monarchic, and consequently satisfied neither Royalists nor revolutionaries.   " To tell the truth," Camille Desmoulins openly declared at the Jacobin Club, " there has been such a confusion of plans, and so many people have worked at it in contrary directions, that it is a veritable Tower of Babel." [2]

It was this Tower of Babel that Louis XVI. has been bitterly reproached for criticizing.   But by September 1791 the time had gone by for criticism ; every remonstrance, however reasonable, made by the King met only with insolence from the revolutionary factions in the Assembly, and Louis XVI. now realized that he must either accept the Constitution in its entirety or provoke another revolution.   He decided, therefore, to accept it unconditionally, leaving it to the people to find out its imperfections for themselves.   It is this that revolutionary historians

---

the 22nd of Frimaire, An II., quoted by Aulard, *Études et Leçons sur la Révolution Française*, iv. 51.

[1] *Mémoires de Ferrières*, iii. 204.

[2] " Discours sur la Situation politique de la Nation du 21 Octobre 1791," Aulard's *Séances des Jacobins*, iii. 208.

describe as the King's " duplicity in the matter of the Constitution "—" he was not sincere," they write, " in his acceptance." Now the precise attitude of the King towards the
Constitution, and also towards the question of the appeal to
foreign powers, is explained in a long and confidential letter that
he wrote to his brothers at this date, of which the most important
passages must be quoted verbatim :

" You have no doubt been informed," Louis XVI. wrote to
the Comte de Provence and the Comte d'Artois, " that I have
accepted the Constitution, and you know the reasons that I gave
to the Assembly, but these must not suffice for you ; I wish to
make known to you all my motives. The state of France is such
that she is on the verge of complete dissolution, which will only
be hastened if one wishes to bring violent remedies to bear on
the ills that overwhelm her. The party spirit that divides her
and the destruction of all authority are the causes of her trouble.
Divisions must be made to cease and authority re-established,
but for this purpose only two means are possible—union or force.
Force can only be employed by foreign armies, and this means
having recourse to war. Can a King allow himself to carry war
into his own States ? Is not the remedy worse than the disease ?
. . . I have therefore concluded that this idea must be abandoned,
and that I must try the only other means left me—the union of
my will with the principles of the Constitution. I feel all the
difficulties of governing so great a nation. I might say I feel
its impossibility, but any obstacle I had placed in the way would
have caused the war I was anxious to avoid, and would have
prevented the people from judging of the Constitution, because
they would have seen nothing but my constant opposition. By
adopting their ideas and following them in all good faith they
will learn the cause of their troubles ; public opinion will change ;
and since without this change one can hope for nothing but
fresh convulsions, I shall bring about a better order of things by
my acceptance than by my refusal. . . . I wished to let you know
the motives for my acceptance, so that your conduct should be
in accord with mine. Your attachment to me and your wisdom
should make you renounce dangerous ideas that I do not adopt.
. . . I was just finishing this letter when I received the one you
sent me . . . [the two princes had written refusing to recognize
the King's acceptance of the Constitution]. You cannot believe
how much this action has pained me. I was already much
grieved at the Comte d'Artois going to the Conference of Pilnitz
without my consent, but I will not reproach you, my heart
cannot bring itself to do so. I will only point out to you that
in acting independently of me, he thwarts my plans as I disconcert
his. . . . I have already told you that the people endured all their

privations because they have always been assured that these would end with the Constitution. It is only two days since it was finished, and you expect that already their mind is changed. I have the courage to accept it, so as to give the nation time to experience that happiness with which it has been deluded, and you wish me to renounce this useful experience ! Sedition-mongers have always prevented it from judging of their work by talking to it incessantly of the obstacles I placed in the way of its execution ; instead of taking from them this last resource, would you serve their fury by having me accused of carrying war into my kingdom ? You flatter yourselves to outwit them by declaring that you are marching in spite of me, but how can one persuade them of this when the declaration of the Emperor and the King of Prussia was occasioned at your request ? Will it ever be believed that my brothers do not carry out my orders ? Thus you will show me to the nation as accepting (the Constitu-tion) with the one hand and soliciting foreign powers with the other. What upright man could respect such conduct, and do you think to help me by depriving me of the esteem of all right-thinking people ? "

It is precisely this tortuous conduct, so strongly deprecated by the King, which has been attributed to him by the conspiracy of history, and represented to posterity as the cause of the second Revolution. "Louis XVI.," we are told, " accepted the Constitution without any intention of maintaining it, and whilst at the same time soliciting foreign intervention by force of arms." The truth—which no revolutionary writer has ever been able to disprove—is that, in the words of Bertrand de Molleville, from the moment of his acceptance of the Constitution " the King never varied a single instant from the resolution of faithfully executing the Constitution by every means in his power " ; that far from inviting foreign aggression he wrote at the same moment to the Emperor of Austria begging him to refrain from further intervention, and Leopold, only too thankful to abandon the campaign, formally undertook to interfere no further in the affairs of France.[1]

All was now peace, and the King's acceptance of the Con-stitution provoked a wild burst of popular enthusiasm.

Writers who represent the flight to Varennes as having finally lost the King the affection of his people entirely disregard the unanimous evidence of contemporaries that two or three

---

[1] " Leopold had no intention of entering upon hostiliti s, and found a loophole by which to escape from declaring war in the acceptance by Louis XVI. of the completed Constitution on 21st September 1791. He then solemnly withdrew his pretensions to interfere in the internal affairs of France " (*Revolutionary Europe*, by H. Morse-Stephens, p. 103).

months after that fateful journey not only the King but the Queen were more popular than ever.[1] When they appeared in public the people pursued them with " Bravos ! " At the opera the Queen was greeted, particularly by the women, with frantic enthusiasm and cries of " Vive la Reine ! " In the streets a new popular refrain was heard :

> Not' bon Roi
> A tout fait
> Et not' bonne Reine
> Qu'elle eut de la peine !
> Enfin les v'là
> Hors d'embarras !

The attempt of the deputies at the new Legislative Assembly to insult the King by keeping on their hats when he entered the hall, and by depriving him of his titles of honour, met with violent remonstrance from the people. " On Saturday at the comedy," writes a contemporary, " the people in the crowds around the door cried out, ' Long live the King and Queen ! Give us back our *noblesse* who provided us with a living, our clergy and our courts ! ' And in the theatre they cried, ' Vive Sire,' and ' Sa Majesté,' and a patriot who called out ' Vive la Nation ' was roughly handled, dragged outside, and ducked in the gutter. At the Assembly the deputies were grievously insulted and called ragamuffins (*va-nu-pieds*), and this because, by a decree which they were forced to revoke the next day, they had deprived the King of the name of Sire and the title of ' Majesté,' of the chair of honour at the Assembly, and finally of precedence to the President." [2]

The King, overjoyed at the renewed understanding between himself and his people, wrote thankfully : " The end of the Revolution has arrived ; may the nation resume its happy character ! "

What need was there for further agitations ? The fear of foreign aggression had been finally removed, all the demands of the nation had been satisfied, and the only cause for popular discontent was not that the Revolution had not gone far enough, but that it had gone too far.

---

[1] Prudhomme, *Révolutions de Paris*, ix. 570 ; *Journal d'un Étudiant*, by Gaston Maugras, p. 166 ; Madelin, p. 186 ; *The Journal of Mary Frampton*, letter from James Frampton dated October 2, 1791 : " You cannot conceive how ridiculous it is to hear the amazing popularity of the King at present." Also letter in same volume from C. B. Wollaston on October 12, 1791.

[2] Letter from M. Fougeret to M. Lecoy de la Marche, October 10, 1791, in *Lettres d'Aristocrates*, by Pierre de Vaissière, p. 413 ; *Diary and Letters of Gouverneur Morris*, i. 462.

Why, then, did a second Revolution occur? For one reason only—that the factions were resolved to overthrow the King and Constitution. Far more than at the beginning of the first Revolution were the aims of the revolutionaries opposed to those of the people. *Then* the nation had unanimously demanded a change in the government, and for a time the work of revolution and of reformation had run concurrently; *now* the two were diametrically opposed, for the people had no further grievance, the existing order of things had been framed according to their will, and therefore the attempt to overthrow it was a deliberate and criminal conspiracy against the will and the liberties of the nation.

In order to understand the manner in which this conspiracy was carried on, it is necessary to form some idea of the elements that composed the National Assembly at the beginning of 1792.

Now when, on the completion of the Constitution in September 1791, the Constituent Assembly was dissolved, all its members— that is to say all the men who had framed the great reforms in the government—were, on the proposal of Robespierre, precluded from sitting in the Legislative Assembly that followed. This measure, which excluded Robespierre himself, was less of a self-denying ordinance than might at first appear, for by 1791 it was no longer the Assembly that governed France but the Jacobin Club, of which Robespierre was a leading member. This association, which started as the Club Breton at Versailles in 1789, where, as we have seen, the partisans of the Duc d'Orléans forgathered, had moved to Paris after the 6th of October, and installed itself in the Dominican convent in the Rue Saint-Honoré, commonly known as the Jacobins, because the principal convent of the order was in the Rue Saint-Jacques. It was here that under the name of " Friends of the Constitution " a revolutionary centre was inaugurated, and before long the Jacobins, as they were popularly known, had started branches of the club in the towns and villages all over France. By this means, at a signal from headquarters, insurrections could be organized, or addresses purporting to come from the inhabitants of country districts could be drawn up and sent to Paris by the agents of the society.

Nothing in the history of the Rèvolution is more surprising than the skill with which this system was carried out. The French as a nation are notoriously unmethodical, and the fall of the Old Régime may be largely attributed to its lack of organization. Whence, then, this talent for organization displayed by the revolutionary leaders alone? Robison, in his *Proofs of a Conspiracy*, supplies the key to the problem. The earlier revolutionary leaders were, as we have seen, the disciples of the German Illuminés, and it was they who initiated them into the art of forming political committees " to carry through the great plan of a general overturning of religion and government. . . . These committees arose from the Illuminati in Bavaria . . . and these committees produced the Jacobin Club." " The chief lesson," Robison goes on to observe, that the revolutionary leaders took from Germany, " was the method of doing business, of managing their own correspondence, and of procuring and training pupils." These propaganda were very systematically carried out amongst the people, and in the confidential memoranda sent out from headquarters was an " earnest exhortation to establish in every quarter secret schools of political education, and schools for the public education of the children of the people, under the direction of well-principled masters," of masters, that is to say, who would inculcate in their pupils a contempt for all religion and all government.

The Germans, as we to-day have reason to know, are past masters in the art of disseminating lying propaganda and of duping the uneducated classes, and the fact that the Jacobins of France were their disciples explains the extraordinary resemblance between the methods of the French revolutionary leaders and those of the German leaders in the recent war. Thus the plan of committing atrocities and then attributing them to one's enemies, of justifying aggression by the plea that one was acting merely in self-defence, of announcing sinister designs on the part of one's own intended victim, is a form of Jesuitry peculiar to the German mind, and this was throughout the plan of the French revolutionaries. Whenever they contemplated an attack upon the King, an alarm was circulated that the King was meditating a massacre of the people ; the unarmed citizens, the unoffending priests, the women and children who perished, were invariably " conspirators " harbouring dark designs, and with such skill were these propaganda carried out as to deceive not only ignorant contemporaries but educated posterity.

By means of this German system of propaganda the Assembly ceased to be democratic—that is to say, it ceased to be the expression of the people's will. In 1789 the people had chosen their own representatives at the Constituent Assembly ; in 1791 the deputies of the Legislative Assembly were the choice of the Jacobin Club. " This society," says Dumouriez, " extending everywhere its numerous affiliations, made use of the provincial clubs to make itself master of the elections. All the cranks, all the seditious scribblers, all the agitators were chosen to go and represent the nation, ' to defend its interests,' it was said, ' against a perfidious court.' Very few wise or enlightened men, still fewer nobles, were chosen, and the National Assembly, thus composed, assembled armed with prejudices and hostile views against the unfortunate Louis and his court. It began by ' adoring ' the Constitution so as to establish itself securely. . . ."[1]

Prudhomme, a more consistent democrat than most revolutionary writers, endorses this description : " This new body did not include the three castes that existed in the Constituent Assembly, it was almost half composed of lawyers who had thrown themselves into the Revolution, as we shall see, rather for personal interests than for love of their country or of Liberty."[2] " These men showed very little attachment to the Constitution they had sworn to defend " ; amongst them all Prudhomme could only mention two " who having received powers from their constituents for the maintenance of the royal charter . . . had the courage "—and we might add the honesty— " to carry out their instructions."[3]

Under these circumstances the King's situation was hopeless from the outset. What could avail his resolution to maintain the Constitution when all the leaders of the new Assembly, with the Jacobins at their back, were secretly conspiring to overthrow both it and him ? A further complication lay in the fact that these leaders were all divided in their aims, and the Jacobin Club itself was rent by the disputes of opposing factions.

THE FACTIONS IN 1792

In order to understand the causes that led up to the Revolution of 1792, it is important to form some idea of the policy that inspired each of these factions, yet nothing is more difficult, since their avowed opinions not only varied perpetually, but in no way coincided with their secret aims. Afterwards, when the Republic had become an established fact, all the leading revolutionaries declared they had been Republicans from the beginning, but until that date they not only refrained from admitting to such opinions but indignantly disavowed them.

If these men were not Republicans, what, then, were they ? As far as it is possible to form any conclusion from their ambiguous and conflicting statements, the policy of these factions may be broadly indicated as follows :

I. The *Cordeliers*, who took their name from the church of the Cordelier monks where they first held their sittings, were led by Danton, and included Marat, Camille Desmoulins, Hébert—the Père Duchesne—and the Prussian Clootz. According to Beaulieu their sympathies were divided between Orléanism and anarchy.[4] Several of these men, as we have seen, had begun their revolu-

---

[1] *Mémoires de Dumouriez*, ii. 117.   [2] *Crimes de la Révolution*, iv. 1.
[3] *Ibid.* iv. 213.   [4] Beaulieu, iii. 192.

tionary career as minor instruments of the Orléaniste conspiracy, and now, owing to the defection of the duke's aristocratic allies, they had risen from the position of mere mob-orators to that of influential politicians. Yet their allegiance to the Duc d'Orléans was evidently spasmodic ; thus in 1791 we find Marat " blessing Heaven for the gift of Louis XVI.," a little later clamouring for a " military dictator," then in the following year publicly demanding 15,000 francs from the Duc d'Orléans for the printing of his pamphlets, and all the while crying out for " heads " and yet " more heads " with dreary reiteration. Desmoulins, after the temporary lapse, when, according to Bouillé, he was bought over to the Court by Lafayette,[1] had returned to the Orléanistes, and showed himself indefatigable in writing furious abuse now of Louis XVI., now of his enemies the Brissotins. Danton, less sanguinary than Marat and less vitriolic than Desmoulins, was, however, more venal than either. Essentially a man of pleasure, he displayed all the *bonhomie* of the spendthrift and voluptuary when his desires were satisfied, all the fury of thwarted passion when lack of funds necessitated self-denial. And at first the Revolution had proved disappointing. Reduced to living on a louis a week, allowed him by his father-in-law—a prosperous *limonadier*—at the beginning of 1789, his activities as an Orléaniste agitator had brought him only a comfortable competence by the end of the year.[2] But a comfortable competence was of no use to Danton, and 1791 found him once more deeply in debt.

At this juncture Louis XVI. allowed himself to be persuaded by his minister, Montmorin, to negotiate with Danton, in the hope of " moderating his anarchic fury and his guilty intrigues." [3] Danton accepted the King's money, invested part of it in a large property at Arcis-sur-Aube,[4] carried a few useless motions in the King's favour at the Cordeliers, and then returned to his true affinity, the Duc d'Orléans. Danton was probably the most sincere Orléaniste of all ; henceforth we shall find him constantly

---

[1] *Mémoires de Bouillé*, i. 185. See also Mirabeau's note (*Correspondance entre Mirabeau et le Comte de la March*, ii. 68), in which he says of Desmoulins, " this man is very accessible to money." Barbaroux declared that Desmoulins " received indiscriminately from aristocrats and patriots alike " for the opinions he expressed in his journal (*Mémoires de Barbaroux*, p. 9).

[2] *Mémoires de Mme. Roland*, i. 333.

[3] *Mémoires de Lafayette*, iii. 85. On the venality of Danton and his payment by the Court contemporary evidence is overwhelming. See, for example, Beaulieu, iii. 10 ; Bertrand de Molleville, i. 354 ; *Mémoires de Brissot*, iv. 193 ; *Correspondance entre Mirabeau et le Comte de la March*, iii. 82 ; also summing up by Taine, *La Révolution*, v. 317, and by Louis Blanc, *Histoire de la Révolution*, x. 409.

[4] Danton, aware that the acquisition of this property had excited suspicions of his integrity, explained to the Commune that it was only an obscure farmhouse bought with the sum paid him in compensation for his

attached to the interests of the duke, possibly for little or no remuneration; but since, in the influential posts he occupied successively, his hand was in every till, he could afford to dispense with this tangible recognition of his services.

As for the Republicanism professed by the Cordeliers on the one occasion of the petition at the Champ de Mars, we can discover no further trace of it in their speeches and writings during the year that followed. On the contrary, three months later we find Camille Desmoulins indignantly protesting against the imputation of Republicanism. " Let no one slander me again; let no one say that I preach the Republic, and that kings should be done away with. Those who recently called us Republicans and the enemies of kings, so as to defame us in the opinion of imbeciles, were not acting in good faith ; *they well knew that we are not ignorant enough to make out liberty to consist in having no King.*" [1]

Later we find Danton declaring to Lafayette : " General, I am more a monarchist than you are ! " and Marat, at the very moment that the Republic is inaugurated, passionately warning his fellow-countrymen of the disasters that must attend it : " Fifty years of anarchy await you, and you will only come out of it with a dictator ! "

II. The *Brissotins*, later to be known as the *Girondins*—by which name, to avoid confusion, it is simpler to refer to them— were, like the Cordeliers, led by a member of the Orléaniste conspiracy. It was with Brissot, as we have seen earlier in this book, that the idea of a " second Fronde," with the Duc d'Orléans at its head, had first originated, whilst Buzot, Pétion, Servan, and Clavière had all taken an active part in the Revolution of 1789. But with the advent of the deputies of the Gironde— Vergniaud, Guadet, Gensonné, Ducos, and Fonfrède—at the Legislative Assembly, a new element was introduced into the faction, and a variety of aims arose which all consisted not in a change of government but only in a change of king. Amongst the candidates proposed was still the Duc d'Orléans, but other members of the faction—notably Dumouriez—preferred his son

---

post as solicitor to the King's Council which was now abolished (Beaulieu, iii. 198). But M. Lenôtre reveals that the " farmhouse " was " almost a château " in a park of approximately 27 acres (see *Paris révolutionnaire*, p. 260), and the *Mémoires de Lafayette* explain the transaction to which Danton referred in these words : " Danton had sold himself on condition that he should be paid 100,000 livres for his post of solicitor to the council which since its suppression was worth only 10,000 livres. The King's present was therefore of 90,000 livres. . . . *Danton was ready to sell himself to all parties* " (*Mémoires de Lafayette*, iii. 85).

[1] " Discours sur la Situation politique de la Nation du 21 Octobre 1791," Aulard's *Séances des Jacobins*, iii. 206.

the Duc de Chartres; others, again, suggested deposing Louis XVI. and placing the Dauphin on the throne, with members of their own party to exercise the power of regency. But the most outrageous scheme of all was one on which the conspiracy of history has remained discreetly silent, for nothing is more discreditable to the Revolution. It will be remembered that amongst the revolutionary leaders approached by Frederick William's emissary, the Jew Ephraïm, were the principal members of this faction—Brissot, Pétion, Gensonné, and their friends—and so successful were the efforts of Ephraïm that a definitely pro - German party was formed amongst them, of which the policy was to consist not merely in breaking the alliance between France and Austria, but in *placing a prince of German origin on the throne of France.*

This prince was to be either the Duke of York, son of George III. of England, or the celebrated Duke of Brunswick, the future signatory of the famous *Manifesto*, who had long been revered by the exponents of " democracy " in France.

That this plan was seriously entertained by certain of the Girondins, and played an important part in the Revolution of 1792, cannot be doubted, from the evidence of authorities so divergent in their political bias as Montjoie, Prudhomme, Camille Desmoulins, and St. Just ; [1] we shall, in fact, find reference to it in the works of nearly all contemporaries—several of the Girondins actually admitted it themselves.[2]

The Duke of York seems to have been the candidate first entertained by this party, and, as it was further suggested to marry him to Mlle. d'Orléans, the scheme appealed particularly to those Girondins who had retained a sympathy for the Orléaniste cause. Brissot, who had married one of Mlle. d'Orléans' maids, was no doubt influenced by this connection in favour of the project. It was apparently for the purpose of effecting this change of dynasty that Pétion was sent to London in the autumn of 1791 with Mlle. d'Orléans and her governess, Madame de Sillery

[1] Montjoie, *Conjuration de d'Orléans*, iii. 204 ; Prudhomme, *Révolutions de Paris*, xiii. 526. See also *Deux Amis*, viii. 93 ; *Mémoires de Barère*, ii. 45. The statements of Camille Desmoulins and St. Just will be given later in this book.

[2] Beaulieu records that early in 1793, when the Brissotins began to find themselves falling under the power of Robespierre, General Wimpfen came upon Pétion and Buzot, who were engaged in conversation. " Well," he said to them, " so this Republic that you wish to establish in the Constituent Assembly is now putting you in a great fix." " I," replied Buzot, " never wished for a Republic in France ; its size and the character of its inhabitants are opposed to the establishment of such a form of government." " What do you want, then ? " " A change of dynasty." " But whom would you choose ? " " A prince of the royal house of England." (*Essais de Beaulieu*, v. 192.)

(*alias* Madame de Genlis), who had throughout played an insidious part in the Orléaniste conspiracy. In the *Correspondance secrète*, under the date of November 26, 1791, we find a significant reference to this journey :

"... a new plan hovers over Republicanism, and has taken birth in the midst of the Jacobins. It consists, in the event of the deposition of Louis XVI., in calling to the throne a son of the King of England, on the condition that he upholds the Revolution against those who wish to destroy it. It seems that this project was the reason for the journey that M. Pétion made to England, where he concerted with the ' Society of Friends of the Revolution of 1688.' [1] It has, we are assured, been warmly taken up by the Protestants and Republicans of our southern provinces."

It will be seen, therefore, that in England it was not, as in Prussia, with the Government that the revolutionary intrigues were conducted, but with the opponents of the Government—the English Jacobins. The Duke of York himself does not appear to have been consulted in the matter, and, as we shall see later, the plot was indignantly denounced by George III. when it came to his ears. By the beginning of 1792 this plan for a change of dynasty had matured sufficiently for a member of the conspiracy to propose it publicly at a Séance of the Jacobins. The member who acted as the mouthpiece of the party was a certain Jean Louis Carra, who had undergone two years' imprisonment for robbing a widow. One of the most furious enemies of Louis XVI., Carra had long been an ardent admirer of German royal personages, and in 1783 had received from Frederick the Great the present of a gold and enamelled snuff-box set with pearls, in recognition of " the reiterated proofs " he had given his Prussian Majesty " of his attachment." [2] The idea of a German King, even of the anglicized variety, was therefore naturally pleasing to Carra, and on the 4th of January he ascended the tribune of the Jacobin Club and definitely suggested dethroning Louis XVI. in favour of the Duke of York.[3] The speech met with a remon-

---

[1] See the description given by Pétion in his discourse to the Jacobin Club on November 18, 1791, of the " flattering reception " given him by the " Friends of the Revolution " in England. Several members of the Society wore the tricolour badge, a tricolour flag decorated the ceiling of the hall, and the band played the " Ça ira ! "

[2] *Précis de la Défense de Carra*, p. 17.

[3] This proposal is so discreditable to the Jacobins that it is suppressed in the report of their debates. The *Journal des Débats* records the incident in the following words : " M. Carra ascends the tribune where he delivers a discourse on the object of the war. . . . Certain propositions which do not seem in accord with the principles of the Constitution arouse the attention of M. Danton, and at his motion the orator is called to

strance from Danton, and Carra was called to order, but in a manner that did not deter him from repeating his proposal five days later in print.[1] Moreover, in Danton's rebuke we can distinguish none of that thunderous eloquence with which he is popularly supposed to have denounced the enemies of his country. " Audacity and yet more audacity " might be necessary in order to subdue the supporters of the French throne, but the mildest tones of remonstrance sufficed him when it was merely a matter of handing that throne over bodily to the foreigner. Possibly in Carra's suggestion Danton saw more an indiscretion than a flagrant betrayal of his country, for the truth is that Danton himself did not hesitate to make use of foreign intervention when it could serve his interests, and he was just now engaged in an intrigue with precisely the same party in England as that approached by Pétion and supported by Carra. " Danton," says his panegyrist, Dr. Robinet, " at first had hopes of Germany, where he counted on the influence of the adversaries of the Austro-Prussian alliance, but it was the English Opposition that formed his most serious support." [2]

When, after the riot of the Champ de Mars, Danton fled to England, he had taken the opportunity to carry out a political mission. The main object of this mission was to obtain the neutrality of England in the war that the French revolutionaries hoped to bring about with Austria, and Danton, who knew England well, was instructed to enlist the sympathies of the Whigs. With the help of his old friend Thomas Paine, and of Christie, another English revolutionary, Danton obtained interviews with Fox, Sheridan, and Lord Stanhope, with whom he succeeded in establishing cordial relations.[3] Danton having

---

order in the name of the Constitution and of the Society." M. Aulard supplies the missing clue in his *Séances des Jacobins*, iii. 311. Moreover Carra admitted it later at his trial. See *Précis de la Défense de Carra*, p. 13.

[1] *Annales Patriotiques* for January 9, 1792. This journal of Carra's, one of the most violent of all the revolutionary publications, exerted an immense influence over the provinces of France. Wordsworth, in Paris at this date, thus described the important part played by Carra in the Revolution of 1792 :

> The land all swarmed with passion, like a plain
> Devoured by locusts,—Carra, Gorsas,—add
> A hundred other names, forgotten now,
> Nor to be heard of more ; yet, they were powers,
> Like earthquakes, shocks repeated day by day,
> And felt through every nook of town and field.
>
> *The Prelude*, " Residence in France."

[2] *Danton Émigré*, by Dr. Robinet, p. 4.
[3] *Ibid*. pp. 5, 24.

thus paved the way, Talleyrand—who, according to Dr. Robinet, was Danton's political ally—went to London in the following spring and offered to hand over the Isles of France, of Bourbon, and of Tabago to England, and also to demolish the fortifications of Cherbourg—the triumph of the reign of Louis XVI.—if England would form an alliance with France and go to war with Austria.[1] Brissot went further, and suggested ceding Calais and Dunkirk to England.[2] And these were the men who accused Louis XVI. of intriguing with foreign powers to betray the interests of France !

The missions, both of Danton and of Talleyrand, met with very tangible success, for by the summer of 1792 a brisk correspondence had been started between the French and English Jacobins; a number of the latter came over to Paris —some, indeed, actually became members of the Club in the Rue Saint - Honoré — and, what is more important, English guineas were sent to finance sedition. On April 26 the author of the *Correspondance secrète* writes complacently : " A collection has been opened in England in aid of our Revolution; one private person alone has written himself down for 1500 louis."

What further proof is needed as to the origin of the " gold of Pitt " ? For again with superb cunning it was to Pitt these corruptions were attributed by the revolutionary factions—to Pitt, who had resolutely refused to associate with the Duc d'Orléans, who detested Danton,[3] and who received the revolutionary deputation under Talleyrand with such undisguised aversion that Chauvelin was reduced to the dignified expedient of stamping on Pitt's toe in revenge.[4]

The policy of both the Cordeliers and the Girondins was therefore to dethrone Louis XVI. in favour of an Orléaniste or a foreign monarch. There was no question of a Republic. This even the revolutionaries themselves admit; Brissot afterwards declared there were only three genuine Republicans at this date— Buzot, Pétion, and himself,[5] and we have already seen in what Pétion and Buzot's " Republicanism " consisted. Pétion put

---

[1] *Diary and Letters of Gouverneur Morris*, i. 510, 516. Talleyrand " received for answer that England could not take any engagement whatever respecting the affairs of France."

[2] *Ibid.* p. 511.

[3] *Danton Émigré*, p. 90.

[4] *Souvenirs d'Étienne Dumont*, p. 302. " As for Talleyrand," Mr. Burges writes from London to Lord Auckland on May 29, 1792, " he is intimate with Paine, Horne Tooke, Lord Lansdowne, and a few more of that stamp, and . generally scouted by every one else " (*Journal and Correspondence of Lord Auckland*, ii. 410).

[5] Pamphlet by Brissot, *A tous les Républicains.*

the number at five immediately before the 10th of August.[1]
Perhaps M. Biré is nearest the truth in saying there were exactly
two—the Englishman Thomas Paine and the Prussian Baron
Clootz.[2]

III. And what of *Robespierre* ? The rôle of Robespierre at
this moment is of so much importance that, although he had not
yet formed a definite party of his own, he must be regarded as a
party in himself. For it was Robespierre who from the end of
1791 proved the great opponent to all plans of usurpation.
Although at the beginning of the Revolution he had worked with
the Orléanistes, it is probable that he had never entered into
their design of placing the Duc d'Orléans on the throne; his plan
was simply to make use of the revolutionary machinery they had
constructed in order to annihilate the Old Régime.[3] The orgies
of Philippe and his boon companions held no attractions for the
austere Maximilien. " The wine of Champagne," he said, " is
the poison of liberty." It was not without reason that he earned
the title of " Incorruptible " ; for money he had no use; his
abnormal nervous system precluded him from all forms of
excess. No longer the aimless Subversive he had been in 1789,
he now above all things desired power—a power that was to
be accorded to him by the people. For this reason Orléanistes
and Girondins were alike abhorrent to him; with Philippe or
a German prince on the throne the people would have no voice
whatever—even the present monarch was preferable to such a
government. Since, therefore, he shrewdly realized that at this
stage of the Revolution any attempt to dethrone Louis XVI.
would inevitably lead to a government far less democratic than
that of the Old Régime, he loudly proclaimed himself in favour
of the existing monarchy. His speech at the Jacobins four days
before the riot of the Champ de Mars was really admirable in its
common sense and logic :

" I have been accused, in the midst of the Assembly, of being
a Republican ; they do me too much honour, I am not one. If
I had been accused of being a monarchist they would have dishonoured me ; I am not that either. I would first observe that

---

[1] *Discours de Jérôme Pétion sur l'accusation intentée contre Maximilien
Robespierre,* November 1792.

[2] *Journal d'un Bourgeois de Paris,* i. 95.

[3] On this point contemporaries are divided ; Montjoie and Pagès botl
represent Robespierre as an Orléaniste, whilst Beaulieu (*Essais,* ii. 159) and
the Marquis de Bouillé (*Mémoires,* p. 100) assert that he merely pretended
sympathy with the Orléanistes in order to further his own designs. I have
adopted the latter theory because it seems to me the most convincing and
alone explains Robespierre's conduct at certain crises of the Revolution.
For it will be noticed that whenever he could deal a blow at the Orléanistes
without injuring his own cause he never failed to do so.

for many people the words 'republic' and 'monarchy' are entirely void of meaning. The word republic signifies no form of government in particular ; it applies to every government of free men who own a country. Thus one can be just as free with a monarch as with a senate. What is the present French constitution ? It is a republic with a monarch. It is therefore neither a monarchy nor a republic—it is both." [1]

Eight months later, when the Jacobin Club had fallen under the dominion of the Girondins, Robespierre indicated his policy still more clearly, disassociating himself from their schemes of usurpation :

" As for me, I declare, and I do so in the name of the Society, which will not refute me, that I prefer the individual which chance, birth, and circumstances have given us for a king to *all the kings that they would give us*." [2]

This veiled reference was characteristic of Robespierre. It is not without reason that so many of those who knew him describe Robespierre as a " tiger-cat "—feline was his nature and feline were his methods. His plan was always to make use of one faction to destroy another, and he still had need of the Girondins and the Orléanistes to destroy Lafayette, whom he suspected, not without reason, of aspiring to the rôle of Cromwell. When, therefore, a courageous deputy of the Assembly, Raimond Ribes, denounced the attempts of the Orléanistes to effect a change of dynasty, and the intrigues of Talleyrand and Brissot to betray the interests of France by ceding ports and colonies to England,[3] Robespierre, who was later on, by the pen of Camille Desmoulins and the mouth of St. Just, to confirm all these accusations, joined with his fellow-Jacobins at the Club in declaring them to be founded on a fable. So with superb cunning the tiger-cat lay crouching, watching with cold green eyes the manœuvres of the rival factions. The time had not yet come to spring.

Such, then, was the complicated situation that faced the unfortunate Louis XVI. in the autumn of 1791. As with every other concession he had made to the cause of liberty his acceptance of the Constitution was followed by a fresh outbreak of revolutionary fury, and a month later the terrible affair of the Glacière d'Avignon took place. On this occasion it seems that the people of Avignon, hungry peasants, women, labourers out of work, indignant at the plundering of the churches by a horde of brigands—mostly foreigners, led by Jourdan Coupe-Tête—rose spontaneously against the revolutionary leaders and put one of them to death. In retaliation Jourdan and his troop, gorged

---

[1] Aulard's *Séances des Jacobins*, iii. 12, Séance du 13 Juillet 1791.
[2] *Ibid.* iii. 420, Séance du 2 Mars 1792.   [3] *Moniteur*, xii. 583.

with fiery liquors, turned on the people, and a three days' massacre began in which, amidst atrocities too horrible to record—rape and cannibalism and drunken fury [1]—the unhappy victims, old men, women, children, mothers with babies at their breasts, were flung, some dead and some alive, into a deep ditch known as the " Glacière " and covered over with quicklime.[2]

The Girondins secured an amnesty for the perpetrators of these deeds !

The massacre of Avignon was followed by further bloodshed in the provinces, and by the end of the year it was evident that no hope remained of restoring order to the kingdom unless by help from the outside.

Marie Antoinette at this juncture no doubt believed that nothing else than open warfare could save the situation, but Louis XVI. still shrank from violent measures and now reverted to his former idea of intervention by foreign powers. Accordingly he wrote to the principal sovereigns of Europe proposing that they should form " a congress supported by an armed force as the best method for arresting the factions and establishing a more desirable order of things in France." [3] There was no question of armed aggression, of hostile legions marching against the French people, but of invoking moral support to suppress disorders, and if this failed, of summoning friendly allies to the rescue not only of the monarchy but *of the people themselves.* If the King, then, appealed for support from abroad, it was not against the people but against their betrayers, the men by whom they were being starved, oppressed, imprisoned, and massacred. Could even hostile armies have produced worse horrors than those that were already taking place ? The King did not wish for war ; on the contrary, he did everything in his power to prevent it by providing a peaceful solution to the crisis.[4]

[1] *Crimes de la Révolution,* by Prudhomme, iv. 21.

[2] *Ibid.* iv. 2.

[3] It should be noted that the date of this letter is uncertain ; D'Allonville and Bertrand de Molleville state emphatically that it was written on December 3, 1790, before the King's final acceptance of the Constitution, but the *Correspondence of the Comte de Fersen* tends to prove that the date was December 3, 1791, that is to say, nearly two months after his final acceptance, during which interval the Glacière d'Avignon and other atrocities in the provinces had occurred. Beaulieu, who also takes this view, explains the King's motives in writing it (*Essais,* iii. 133).

[4] See the evidence of the King's minister, Bigot de Sainte-Croix : " From the spring of 1791 onwards the King prevented the execution of a secret plan framed at Mantua for two months later attacking France whose armies were incomplete and whose frontiers were undefended ; in the summer of the same year he hindered the effects of the Convention of Pilnitz ; the following autumn he concerted with the Emperor to restrain beyond the Rhine the designs and hostile preparations formed there. Let

When, in March 1792, the Brissotins succeeded in driving his ministers from office, the King, wishing to give his enemies no further *cause de guerre*, resolved on the desperate measure of forming a new ministry from among the Jacobins themselves. " I had chosen for my first agents," he wrote to the Assembly, " men known for their principles and invested with the confidence of the public ; they have left the ministry; I have therefore thought it my duty to replace them by men who have obtained credit for their *popular* opinions. You have often told me it was the only method to make the government work ; I thought it my duty to employ it so as to leave to malevolence no pretext for doubting my desire to co-operate with all my might in the welfare of our country."

Accordingly the King decided to nominate the six Girondin ministers designated for him by Brissot—the feeble and irascible Roland, the dour and atrabilious Servan, the stock-jobbing banker Clavière, Dumouriez, an Orléaniste adventurer, and—by an error of Brissot's—two honest men, Lacoste and Duranton.

Unfortunately the King's choice was not as " popular " as he imagined, for the Girondins were precisely the faction least in touch with " the people." It was the middle classes—not the law-abiding *bourgeoisie* but the visionaries of the literary world, the little lawyers, the adorers of Rousseau—amongst whom the Girondins found their following; for "the people " they had nothing but contempt.[1]

No more merciless light has ever been shed on the " democracy " of the Girondins than by an habituée of Madame Roland's salon, Sophie Grandchamp. After describing the political discussions that took place amongst the Rolands and their friends, Madame Grandchamp goes on to remark :

" I was an interested witness of these debates, yet amidst all this fine zeal I thought I perceived that very few would have shown it if public welfare had been the sole recompense. The

---

them give us back our correspondence that it may be published ; it will all testify to the efforts of the King to avert this war which was provoked and begun by those who to-day dare to impute it to him " (*Histoire de la Conspiration du 10 Août*, p. 152). See also Fantin Désodoards, *op. cit.* iv. 48.

[1] For example, Buzot (*Mémoires*, pp. 32, 35, 43, 195) : " One must have the vices of the people of Paris to please them. . . . The stupid people of France. . . . Souls of mud ! . . . What a people is that of Paris ! What frivolity, what inconstancy, how contemptible it is ! " . Barbaroux (*Mémoires*, p. 84) : " The people do not deserve that one should attach oneself to them, for they are essentially ungrateful ; the more one defends their rights the more they take advantage of one." Madame Roland (*Mémoires*, i. 300) : " Cowardice characterized by selfishness and corruption of a degraded people whom we hoped to be able to regenerate . . . but which was too brutalized by its vices."

austere dress that they adopted as the livery of their party seemed to me a petty ostentation for men truly enamoured of liberty, besides which it contrasted in a ridiculous way with the frivolous tone and morals they displayed. I asked Roland what good could be expected of a people who had no respect for the most sacred social ties. . . . ' They will help to overthrow despotism,' replied my friends ; ' their private actions do not affect the truths they spread.' It was, however, these private actions which propagated corruption and destroyed our hopes. Never was the love of pleasure, of the table, of women, and of gaming greater than at the moment when they wished to improve us. They left the precincts where the destinies of the Empire were being weighed in the balance to fly into the arms of lust and debauchery. A few pompous phrases on liberty and the sovereignty of the people sufficed to sanction or at least to excuse the most irregular conduct. . . ."

Phrases ! Always phrases ! " La phrase les enivre ! " remarks M. Louis Madelin, and nothing could better describe the much-vaunted eloquence of the Girondins. They belonged to that eternal class which proves disastrous to all sane government, " Political Intellectuals," adepts in *word - weaving*, who care nothing for the consequences to which their theories may lead, if only those theories sound plausible in speech and print. Thus Brissot had devoted his literary talents to writing philosophical treatises in which he justified theft [1] and advocated cannibalism,[2] whilst the virtuous Roland, famous for his systems on the subject of commerce and manufacture, had drawn up a scheme in 1787 which he presented to the Academy of Lyons for utilizing the bodies of the dead by converting the fat into lamp-oil and the bones into phosphoric acid [3]—a proposal which Lyons, unenlightened by " Kultur," rejected.

If, as Madame Roland indignantly records, Louis XVI. did not take his new ministers seriously, is it altogether surprising ? Their manners bewildered him no less than their mentalities. Men of the people he could have understood, but these philo-

[1] " Our social institutions," wrote Brissot, " punish theft—a virtuous action commanded by Nature herself " (*Recherches philosophiques sur le Droit de Propriété*, etc.). As Brissot himself had been imprisoned for theft this point of view is not surprising.

[2] " Should men nourish themselves on their kind ? A single word decides this question, and this word is dictated by Nature herself. All beings have the right to nourish themselves in any manner that will satisfy their needs " (*Bibliothèque philosophique*, by Brissot de Warville, vi. 313).

[3] *Histoire particulière des Évènements qui ont eu lieu en France pendant les Mois de Juin, Juillet, d'Août, et de Septembre 1792*, by Maton de la Varenne ; *Mémoires pour servir à l'Histoire de la Ville de Lyon pendant la Révolution*, by l'Abbé Guillon de Montléon, i. 58, 59.

sophers, " dressed like Quakers in their Sunday best," who talked him down, interrupted him in the middle of a sentence, quarrelled amongst themselves and nearly came to blows in his presence,[1] were like nothing he had ever come across before. But Louis XVI., for all his heaviness, was not without a certain slow sense of humour, and we detect a hint of this in Madame Roland's assertion that he treated his new ministers with the greatest good-nature (*la plus grande bonhomie*), and led the conversation away from all questions of political importance. " The council was soon nothing but a café where they amused themselves with chatting." [2]

During these interviews the new ministers discovered that the King was in no way the imbecile he had been represented by his enemies, that he " had a fine memory and showed much activity, that he was never idle and read often. He kept in mind the various treaties made by France with neighbouring powers ; he knew his history well ; he was the best geographer in his kingdom. . . . One could not present any subject to him on which he could not express an opinion founded on certain facts." [3]

By degrees in this genial atmosphere the ministers lost some of their austerity : Roland began to boast of the royal favour shown him ; Clavière, encouraged by the King's graciousness, presented a request for 95,000 livres to furnish his own apartments.[4] For a time it seemed that the King had succeeded in disarming his opponents. But he had counted without Madame Roland—and, except perhaps for the Duc d'Orléans, the King, and more particularly the Queen, had no bitterer enemy.

Madame Roland's malevolence was of long standing. Eighteen years earlier, as Manon Phlipon, the daughter of a Paris engraver, she had gone to Versailles with her mother on the invitation of an old lady in the service of the Court. During a whole week she had looked on at the dinners of the Royal Family, the Mass, the card-playing, the presentations. But Manon was unimpressed by these glittering functions, and when, after a few days, Madame Phlipon inquired whether her daughter was pleased with her visit, Manon bitterly replied, " Yes, provided that it soon comes to an end ; a few more days and I shall detest all these people so heartily that I shall not know what to do with my hatred."

She had never known what to do with her hatred ; all through the years that followed it had remained pent up in her heart, poisoning her youth, turning the joy of life to gall. The remembrance of those exalted beings, whose graciousness towards her-

[1] *Deux Amis*, vii. 235.   [2] *Mémoires de Mme. Roland*, i. 238.
[3] *Ibid.* p. 233.   [4] *Révolutions de Paris*, by Prudhomme, xii. 485.

self she had interpreted as patronage, became an obsession ; further encounters with their kind only increased her resentment. Yet she despised the *petite bourgeoisie* amongst which Fate had placed her as heartily as she hated the class above it ; the overtures of obscure lovers who presented themselves in crowds merely humiliated her. By her marriage to dull old Roland de la Platière she saw some hope of " rising to the rank that became her." Yet this too led to nothing ; her attempt to secure for him " a title of nobility " met with no success ; country life bored her to exasperation. When at last the revolutionary storm burst over France, Manon Roland hailed it with rapture, ostensibly as the dawn of liberty, in reality as a retribution on the social system which accorded her a place of no importance. In the terrible letter she wrote to Bosc immediately after the massacre of Foullon and Berthier all the old hatred flamed out, and under its influence this woman who had fed on the classics descended to the language of a bargee :

" You are occupying yourself," she wrote on July 26, 1789, " with a municipality, and you allow heads to escape that will plot fresh horrors. You are but children ; your enthusiasm is a blaze of straw ; and if the National Assembly does not formally bring to trial two illustrious heads, or some generous Decius does not strike them off, you are all f. . . ."[1] The sentence ends with the usual revolutionary obscenity.

When at last in March 1792 Roland was elected to the Ministry, Manon knew a moment of exaltation ; the transition to the gorgeous Hôtel de Calonne, which had been given over to the Ministry of the Interior, restored her from a state of " consuming languor " to sudden exuberant vitality. But once again disillusionment awaited her. Of what avail were gilded salons, painted ceilings, giant lackeys standing at each side of the great folding doors, to open one or both according to the rank of the arriving guest [2]—observe the equality practised by our austere exponents of democracy !—if the Tuileries ignored her ? Over there in that remote mysterious Château, standing aloof from the noisy Paris world amidst its stately gardens, there dwelt the woman on whom Manon had resolved to wreak her vengeance. She knew what to do with her hatred now, and from this moment she pursued her victim with a malevolence that even at the foot of the scaffold knew no relenting.

The failing of great historians is to overlook the existence of apparently unimportant details, yet many a world-shaking event can be traced to trifling causes. The 20th of June 1792 was largely the result of a woman's desire for revenge.

---

[1] *Lettres de Mme. Roland aux demoiselles Cannet*, ii. 573.
[2] *Souvenirs de Sophie Grandchamp.*

It was not that Madame Roland created the elements of revolution—these lay already to hand—but that she provided the pretexts for stirring up agitation. As Laclos had been "the soul of the Orléaniste conspiracy," galvanizing into activity the idle roués of the Palais Royal, Manon Roland, with untiring ingenuity, goaded on the vain and foolish Girondins, who, but for influence, might have rested content with their accession to the Ministry. When Roland and his colleagues returned from the councils at the Tuileries, and declared that the King was evidently sincere in his determination to maintain the Constitution, Manon Roland laughed them to scorn. "During three weeks," she writes, " I saw Roland and Clavière enchanted with the King's attitude, dreaming only of a better order of things, and flattering themselves that the Revolution was ended. ' Good God ! ' I said to them, ' every time I see you start for the council full of this fine confidence, it always seems to me that you are ready to commit some folly.' ' I assure you,' Clavière answered me, ' that the King feels perfectly that his interest is bound up with the maintenance of the laws which have just been established ; he reasons about them too pertinently for one not to be convinced of this truth.' ' Ma foi,' added Roland, ' if he is not an honest man he is the greatest rogue in the kingdom ; no one could dissemble in that way.' And as for me I replied that I could not believe in love of the Constitution on the part of a man nourished on the prejudices of despotism and accustomed to enjoy it, and whose conduct recently proved the absence of genius and of virtue. The flight to Varennes was my great argument." [1]

Because, therefore, *she*, Manon Roland, could not conceive it possible that any one possessing power or privileges should be willing to renounce them, the King was to be accused, *without any proof whatever*, of wishing to violate the Constitution. From this moment Mme. Roland devoted all her energies to the one purpose of shaking the people's confidence in the King.

But this, at the beginning of 1792, was no easy matter, for the public was still convinced of the King's sincerity, as the following significant passage from the journal of a young student then in Paris—an ardent admirer of the Girondins—reveals :

"Oh ! fatal error ! traitors have succeeded in persuading this too credulous and confiding people that a King who from his tenderest infancy has sucked the venomous juice of despotism has all of a sudden been converted to patriotism. . . . By degrees he is making numerous partisans, above all he is attaching public opinion to himself . . . he will succeed in invading national liberty. The Parisians themselves appear to wish to hasten this disastrous moment. Listen to them in the groups at the Palais Royal and

[1] *Mémoires de Mme. Roland*, i. 236

in the Tuileries; they are hurrying towards inevitable slavery.
. . . Who would have thought that this people would mistake
its true friends so far as to distrust the inestimable Pétion, and
would lavish its confidence and its applause on those perfidious
beings who, profiting by its blindness and its torpor, abuse the
sacred words of law and constitution in so execrable a way as
to lead it to the feet of a king, to the feet of a traitor, of a perjurer,
a true tiger disguised as a pig. The National Guards, above all,
have degenerated extraordinarily. . . . They are real *sbirri* animated by that *esprit de corps* so fatal to liberty. . . . This is the
sad state of affairs in Paris, and I see only two great ills capable
of saving liberty—war or the flight of the King. I will even say
that I ardently desire one of these terrible afflictions, because,
as Mirabeau foretold us, our liberty can only be ensured in so
far as she has for her bed mattresses of corpses, and because, in
order to ensure this liberty, I consent, if necessary, to become one
of these corpses." [1]

Madame Roland and her friends saw this pacific disposition
of the people with growing alarm, and thereupon devised a scheme
characteristic of their political morality. Large placards attacking the royal authority were to be posted up all over Paris, and
in order to defray the expenses necessary for this purpose they
applied to their ally, Pétion, the Mayor of Paris, for a sum of
money to be taken from the fund he held at the disposal of the
Paris police. Pétion proved only too willing to co-operate;
unfortunately the police fund happened at this moment to be
exhausted. Accordingly Dumouriez, as Minister of Foreign
Affairs, was deputed to ask the King to supply Pétion with a
large sum for the police, which was then to be handed over to
the Rolands. Louis XVI., approached on the matter, displayed
a certain perspicacity, but decided to give Pétion a chance of
proving his good faith.

" Pétion is my enemy," he said to Dumouriez; " you will see
that he will spend this money on writings against me, but if you
think it will be any use, give it to him." [2]

The sum was made over and, of course, employed as the King
suspected. " *The expedient*," remarks Madame Roland, " *was
simple*, and it was adopted." [3]

We marvel as we read these words, not so much at the base
treachery of securing money on false pretences and, as the King
himself expressed it, of " asking him to supply rods with which

---

[1] *Journal d'un Étudiant pendant la Révolution*, edited by M. Gaston
Maugras, p. 203.
[2] *Mémoires de Dumouriez*, ii. 152, 153; *Mémoires de Mme. Roland*,
i. 142.
[3] *Ibid.* i. 83.

to scourge himself," but at the complete lack of all sense of honour which made it possible for Madame Roland, quite unblushingly, to admit the scheme in her memoirs. She does not see that the manœuvre was in any way discreditable ; to her mind it was "quite simple."

But defamatory placards alone would not avail to bring about a revolution ; some definite *cause de guerre* must be provided. If only the King could be represented as violating the Constitution or of plotting with the enemies of France, it would be easier to arouse popular indignation. But the King displayed an irritating fidelity to the Constitution—indeed his habit of producing a copy of the charter from his pocket and quoting it on every possible occasion was beginning to get on the nerves of his ministers—whilst any correspondence he had been carrying on with Austria could not be described as treasonable, since Austria still remained the ally of France.

In order, therefore, to prove the King a traitor, not only must the alliance of 1756 be broken, but war must be brought about between France and Austria. It was necessary, in the words of Brissot himself, "to find an opportunity for *setting traps for the King*, in order to demonstrate his bad faith and his collusion with the princes who had emigrated."[1] It is well to remember this admission when reading the diatribes directed against Louis XVI. for inviting foreign invasion. The war, which for twenty-three years was to impoverish France and decimate her population, was not declared by Austria, but was brought about by the Girondins largely in the interests of Prussia at a moment when Austria appeared reluctant to enter France.[2] At the Jacobins both Danton and Robespierre opposed it, for they shrewdly perceived that if the foreign powers needed an incentive to march to the rescue of the Royal Family, the declaration of war was a direct invitation to them to advance. But the pro-Prussian party carried the day, and the scheme of Frederick the Great was finally realized.

If further evidence were needed of the manœuvres of Prussia it is to be found in the debates that took place in the Assembly, for we shall notice that, although on February 7 Prussia formed an alliance with Austria, and on March 7 the Duke of Brunswick was placed at the head of the allied armies, it was against Austria alone that the Girondins desired war to be declared ; in all their speeches it was against Austria, never against Prussia, that their invectives were directed ; it was the Hapsburgs, not the Hohenzollerns, who inspired their fury.

---

[1] *Mémoires de Lafayette*, iii. 299 ; Beaulieu, iv. 187.
[2] *Moniteur*, xii. 183, 184 ; *Deux Amis*, vii. 156.

The Girondins well knew they had nothing to fear from Prussia or from Brunswick.

" The Duke Ferdinand," writes Sorel, " had always loved France and professed to detest Austria. . . . The revolutionary party professed a singular esteem for his person. Far from seeing in him ' an abettor of tyrants ' many revolutionaries held him to be a friend of enlightened doctrines and a natural ally of France. The Girondins respected him, Dumouriez admired him. . . ." [1] So great was this admiration that at the very moment when the duke was given the supreme command the Girondins embarked on their further scheme of placing him on the throne of France.

" I read on March the 18th," writes Mallet du Pan, " a writing, supported by good authority, in which it is affirmed that the plan of the leaders of the Jacobins is not exactly a republic but a change of dynasty, because they consider that the King will always be attached to the *noblesse* and little to the Constitution. Consequently *they have offered the crown to the Duke of Brunswick.* . . . By making the duke and England adopt this project they flatter themselves to be able to detach Prussia from the House of Austria, *they even offer him other advantages.* The method devised for dethroning the King is to make the National Assembly declare that he has lost the confidence of the nation. Messieurs Condorcet, Brissot, and others are only the instruments, the agents of the enterprise, of which the principal chief and author is the Abbé Sieyès. . . ." [2] But Sorel is probably right in considering Mallet du Pan had been misinformed on this last point ; no other evidence convicts Sieyès of complicity with this plot, of which the chief author was undoubtedly Carra.

In all the debates that took place in the Assembly on the subject of the " Austrian Committee," which the King and Queen were accused of holding at the Tuileries, and of which the Girondins attempted in vain to prove the existence, it was always Carra who inveighed most loudly against the perfidy of Marie Antoinette and her Austrian allies. But it was not until Brunswick was actually marching against France that Carra showed his hand by publicly proposing to give him the crown.

All through the year of 1792 the French revolutionary leaders admirably served the cause of Prussia—whether as dupes or as accomplices it is impossible to say with certainty. Even the cause of the Orléanistes was now subordinated to the purpose of carrying out the great scheme of Frederick the Great—the rupture of that alliance which barred the way to Prussian

---

[1] *La Mission de Custine à Brunswick*, by Albert Sorel ; *Revue Historique*, i. 157.
[2] *Mémoires de Mallet du Pan*, i. 259.

aggrandizement. This, then, was the policy of the faction that
led all the attacks on Louis XVI. for intriguing with foreign
powers, and that later on had the audacity to accuse him of
precipitating France into war. Yet there were tears in his eyes
when on the 20th of April he formally announced the declaration
of war against Austria.[1]

The Queen, however, breathed a sigh of relief. Anything, she
felt, would be better than the present situation. The state of
Paris was growing daily more alarming. This spring of 1792 a
new and terrible element had made its appearance in the city—
the band of ruffians who, from the tattered garments they wore
that did duty as breeches, became known as the Sans-Culottes.
The members of this ragged legion, mostly young boys, were of a
class not peculiar to revolutionary France, but corresponded to
the "hooligans" of modern London, the Apaches of modern
Paris, or the Bowery toughs of New York, and it is easy to
imagine the terror they inspired amongst the peaceable citizens
when formed into a corps and protected, not restrained, by the
police. Montjoie relates that at the mere sight of two Sans-
Culottes armed with pikes, wearing the red caps of galley-slaves
that this spring of 1792 became the badge of revolution, the
inhabitants of a Paris street would fly trembling into their
houses and barricade their doors.[2]

Every day two to three hundred of these Sans-Culottes invaded the gardens of the Tuileries and stirred up popular feeling
against the Queen.[3]

" You see me in despair," she said one day to the King in the
presence of Dumouriez. " I dare not stand at the window on
the side of the gardens. Yesterday evening to breathe the air I
showed myself at the window on the side of the Court ; a canonnier
apostrophized me with a coarse insult, adding, ' How pleased I
shall be to see your head on the point of my bayonet.' . . . If I
cast my eyes on that dreadful garden there is a man standing
on a chair reading aloud horrors against us, there is a soldier
or an abbé being dragged to the fountain and overwhelmed with
blows and insults. . . . What an abode ! What people ! "

" The Queen," says Ferrières, " was not exaggerating : the
Orléanistes and Girondins never ceased exciting the populace
against the King and Queen. . . . A crowd of hired orators daily
declaimed the libels composed by the faction. . . . Louis XVI.
was represented as a Nero, a sanguinary monster breathing only
murder and carnage, wishing to bring foreign troops into France
and use them to support him in the execution of his plans. . . .

---

[1] *Deux Amis*, vii. 166 ; *Mémoires tirés des Papiers d'un Homme d'État*,
i. 333.   [2] Montjoie, *Conjuration de d'Orléans*, iii. 171.
   [3] *Correspondance secrète*, p. 600.

The Queen was painted either under the degrading colours of a Messalina given up to the most shameful licentiousness, or as a fury seeking only to bathe herself in the blood of the French. These slanderous horrors were cried aloud in all the streets, were repeated at the tribune of the Jacobins, at the bar of the Assembly."

What wonder that Marie Antoinette longed for her own people to come and deliver her ? What wonder if she despaired of the French nation when this was the portion of it daily presented to her sight ?

Louis XVI. was even more affected by the horror of the situation, and at last, Madame Campan relates, " fell into a state of depression which reached the point of physical collapse. He was ten days in succession without uttering a word even in the midst of his family . . . the Queen drew him out of this disastrous condition . . . by throwing herself at his feet, now conjuring up visions calculated to alarm him, now expressing her love for him." [1] It was a clear case of mental break-down, and must be taken into consideration in judging the King's conduct at this crisis. Undoubtedly he vacillated, at one moment lending an ear to the men who would persuade him that salvation lay in this or that revolutionary faction, the next convinced by Fersen or the Queen that nothing but foreign intervention could avail to restore law and order. So the months of spring went by and June arrived—the last June of the monarchy.

PRELIMINARIES OF THE 20TH OF JUNE

The plan of raising a mob to march on the Tuileries, one of the leaders afterwards admitted, was " conceived and planned in the salon of Madame Roland." It is certain at any rate that, as Mortimer Ternaux pointed out, " the day of June the 20th had been prepared long beforehand by the agitators of the Faubourgs ; the date had been settled—it was that of the Oath of the Tennis Court [2]—the rôles were distributed, complicity agreed on and

---

[1] *Mémoires de Mme. Campan*, p. 328. See also *Correspondance secrète*, p. 600, and the *Journal d'un Étudiant*, edited by M. Gaston Maugras, p. 248.

[2] Note the hypocrisy of this pretext, since the men who had proposed the Oath of the Tennis Court were now regarded by the revolutionary leaders as their bitterest enemies—Mounier had been driven from the country, and Bailly, the object of their perpetual execrations, was to perish at their hands under circumstances of revolting brutality. The truth is, as Bigot de Sainte-Croix points out, that the 20th of June was chosen as the anniversary of the flight to Varennes in the hope of reviving the unpopularity which the Orléanistes had succeeded in arousing against the King on this day.

accepted, the issue alone was uncertain ; it depended on the degree of excitement and exasperation to which the masses could be brought." The reasons given by revolutionary writers for the invasion of the Tuileries are, therefore, only the pretexts that were given to the people in order to induce them to carry out the designs of the leaders. But, as we have already seen, the people at this moment were in no mood to rise. Even the Faubourgs of Saint-Antoine and Saint-Marceau showed little tendency to revolt, although perpetually stirred up by Santerre and by Gonchon.

Théroigne de Méricourt, no longer the light-hearted *fille de joie* who had ridden with the mob to Versailles, but a haggard and embittered virago, was also hard at work in Saint-Antoine, where she had organized revolutionary clubs for women on the model of the Société Fraternelle that formed an annexe to the Jacobins and served as a training school for the future *tricoteuses*. But Théroigne's efforts met with violent remonstrance from the working-men of Saint-Antoine, who complained to Santerre that the sweetness of their wives' tempers was not increased by attendance at these assemblies, and the Jacobins were obliged to request Mlle. Théroigne "to moderate her activities." [1]

Nothing, indeed, is more surprising than the resistance shown by the inhabitants of the Faubourgs to the seductions of the Jacobins—a fact of which historians give no idea, but which is only revealed by a study of contemporary literature, especially of the ultra-revolutionary variety. It is in the pages of Prud-homme, in the reports of the Séances des Jacobins, that we discover the immense efforts made by the revolutionaries and their repeated failures to enlist the sympathies of the people. For when we consider the wretchedness of the people at this crisis, and realize that the arms of the Jacobins were always open to receive them ; when we remember that any deserter from the army who appealed to the Society for sympathy stood an excellent chance of receiving a civic crown, that any man or woman who entered the hall and uttered revolutionary sentiments received an ovation, and in many instances a sum of money, that any schoolboy who recited a revolutionary poem was invited to the honours of the Séance and overwhelmed with compliments, we can only wonder that the Faubourgs did not crowd *en masse*

---

[1] See Santerre's admission at a Séance of the Jacobins on April 13, 1792 : " The men of this Faubourg (Saint-Antoine) would like better, on coming in from their work, to find their homes in order than to see their wives return from an assembly where they do not always gain a spirit of sweetness, and therefore they have regarded with disfavour these assemblies that are repeated three times in the week."

to the club in the Rue Saint-Honoré. But no, only here and there does a stray dweller of the Faubourgs find his way there, and then with what triumph and at what length is the incident recorded in the journal of the Society !

True, we shall read often of deputations from the " sections of Paris " arriving, both at the Assembly and at the Jacobins, but we do not need the explanations of Montjoie, of Beaulieu, or the *Deux Amis de la Liberté* to realize that the speeches crammed with classical allusions delivered on these occasions were not the work of the poor and unlettered inhabitants of the Faubourgs, but of the revolutionary agents who distributed them to orators so unlearned that they were hardly able to read the words aloud.[1] As to any spontaneous expressions of the people's sentiments these were seldom accorded a hearing, and at any rate were not recorded in the press, which at this date was almost entirely in the pay of the revolutionary leaders. Thus we read of an imposing deputation from Saint-Marceau to the National Assembly consisting of 6000 men armed with pikes and forks, and women with their arms held threateningly aloft, and children carrying naked swords, led by " an orator in rags who spoke like Cicero " in praise of the Revolution, but a petition signed by 30,000 citizens which was presented a few days later to protest against the tyranny of the Jacobins is not even mentioned in the reports of the debates.[2]

Adolphe Schmidt, in his studies of revolutionary Paris, has worked out by statistics that out of all the 600,000 to 800,000 inhabitants of the capital there were, in 1792, not more than 5000 to 6000 real revolutionaries—a number that diminished in the following year to nearly half—and that during the whole

---

[1] *Deux Amis de la Liberté*, vii. 242, viii. 24. See also Montjoie, *Conjuration de d'Orléans*, iii. 189 ; *Essais de Beaulieu*, iii. 104. " Nothing was more usual than this kind of fraud," writes the contemporary Senac de Meillan ; " the sections and the Faubourgs were made to speak ; they were set in motion even without their knowledge. . . . We saw one day the Faubourg Saint-Antoine arriving, to the number of eight to nine thousand men. Well, this Faubourg Saint-Antoine was composed of about fifty bandits hardly known in the district, who had collected on their route every one they could see in the shops or workshops, so as to form an imposing mass. These good people were on the Place Vendôme, very much bored, not knowing what they had come for, and waiting impatiently for the leaders to give them permission to retire."

[2] This petition is recorded in the journal of Mme. Jullien, *Journal d'une Bourgeoise*, p. 89 : " There is a petition signed by 30,000 idlers (*badauds*) which is to appear on Sunday at the National Assembly against the Jacobins." We must not forget that in revolutionary language the terms " badauds," " brigands," or " canaille " signify the law-abiding members of the people. Thus Prudhomme, *Révolutions de Paris*, xii. 526 : " The horde of fanatics and counter-revolutionaries who, to the number of more than 60,000, have taken refuge . . . in the capital."

revolutionary period the anti-revolutionaries constituted nine-tenths of the population. In this June of 1792 the departmental administration placed in this category of " honest folk " and " young folk " " those useful and hard-working men attached to the State at every point of their existence and by all the objects of their affections—proprietors, cultivators, tradesmen, artisans, workmen, and all those estimable citizens whose activity and economy contribute to the public treasury, and animate all the resources of national prosperity. All these men profess a boundless devotion to the Constitution, and principally to the sovereignty of the nation, to political equality and to constitutional monarchy." " The Jacobin Club," the same report declares, " is alone responsible for any disturbances in the city."[1]

In order, therefore, to persuade the people of Paris to march on the Tuileries some very powerful incentive must be provided. For some months the Girondins, Brissot, Gensonné, and above all Carra, had endeavoured to inflame the popular mind by con-tinual declamations against the so-called "Austrian Committee," by means of which Marie Antoinette was declared to be betraying France to the Emperor of Austria, but their efforts to prove the existence of this committee had ended in ignominious failure. To the request for a written statement of their accusations they replied : " What do you wish us to prove ? Conspiracies can-not be written down (*Les conspirations ne s'écrivent pas*)." Later on at their trial, when they asked Fouquier Tinville for proofs of their guilt, Fouquier quoted these words to them and sent them to the guillotine.[2]

The scare of the " Austrian Committee " having failed to rouse the people, the Girondins set about devising further " traps " for the King. If only Louis XVI. were to refuse his sanction to any decrees passed by the Assembly the old cry against the " Veto " could be raised, and an insurrection might be expected to result. Accordingly three iniquitous decrees were placed before the Assembly. The first enacted that all the non-juring priests—that is to say, those who had not subscribed to the civil constitution of the clergy—should be deported; the second that the King should be deprived of his bodyguard of

---

[1] *Paris pendant la Révolution*, by Adolphe Schmidt, p. 21. This report of the Paris administration is quoted by Prudhomme, *Révolutions de Paris*, xii. 523, as an insulting " libel."

[2] *Mémoires de Hua*, p. 119. See Camille Desmoulins' reference to this incident in his *Fragment de l'Histoire secrète*, etc., p. 5 : ' Moreover I will establish against Brissot and Gensonné the existence of an Anglo-Prussian committee by means of a number of proofs a hundred times stronger than those by which they, Brissot and Gensonné, proved the existence of an Austrian committee."

1800 men accorded to him by the Constitution, but suspected by the revolutionaries of loyalty to his person, and the third that a camp of 20,000 men should be formed outside Paris. Louis gave his sanction to the second decree, but withheld it from the first and third. Now, since the first decree was mainly instigated by Roland, and the third was proposed by Servan—Madame Roland's particular ally in the ministry—it is impossible not to recognize the hand of Madame Roland in all this. The three decrees were, of course, directly unconstitutional, the last because, according to the terms of the Constitution, the King alone had the authority to propose any addition to the standing army, and the camp of 20,000 men was proposed by Servan entirely on his own authority, without reference to the King or even to the other ministers. Moreover, as the 20,000 men were to consist of " confederates " from the provinces, that is to say, they were to be chosen by the Jacobin Clubs all over France, the plan met with immediate remonstrance, not only from the King but from sane men of every party. Lafayette wrote to the King from his camp at Maubeuge urging him to persist in his refusal to sanction the decree ; even Robespierre expressed his disapproval.

The ministers themselves were violently divided on the subject, Roland, Servan, and Clavière supporting the plan, Dumouriez, Lacoste, and Duranton protesting—Dumouriez, indeed, nearly came to blows with Servan in the King's presence.[1]

But most of all was the proposal resented by the National Guard of Paris—a corps essentially representative of the people —who sent a deputation to the Assembly to protest against the imputation that they were incompetent to defend the capital. " Servan," said the orator of this deputation, " had violated the Constitution, had shown himself ' the vile instrument of a faction that rends the kingdom.' We citizens of Paris, we who were the first to conquer liberty, we shall know how to defend it at all times against every kind of tyrant ; we have still the force and courage of the men of the 14th of July." At this Vergniaud, rising in wrath, declared that the petitioners were guilty of " inconceivable audacity," and should be refused " the honours of the sitting "—in other words, that they should be driven from the hall. A further deputation of the National Guard, armed with a petition bearing 8000 signatures, met with a like reception, and the Assembly thereupon closed the debate.[2]

To this, then, had the " sovereignty of the people " been reduced. All through the Revolution we shall find the same method employed ; the only deputations recognized as representative of the people are those organized by the revolutionary leaders and marching to the word of command ; spontaneous

[1] Madelin, p. 219.   [2] Buchez et Roux, xv. 19-30.

demonstrations are invariably silenced and declared to be
" seditious."

The Jacobin Club, dominated by the Girondins, whose violence
during the early part of 1792 surpassed even that of the future
Terrorists, had succeeded in establishing a tyranny which roused
the indignation of all true lovers of liberty. At his camp in
Maubeuge, Lafayette received from the administrative and
municipal bodies all over the country further complaints of their
excesses, and now once again he resolved to come to the rescue
of the monarchy. His letter to the Assembly on June 16 is one
of the few admirable incidents in his vacillating career.

" Can you deny," he wrote indignantly, " that a faction
—and to avoid vague denominations, the Jacobin faction—has
caused all the disorders ? It is this faction that I loudly accuse.
Organized like an empire apart in its metropolis and its affiliations,
blindly directed by a few ambitious leaders, this sect forms a
distinct corporation in the midst of the French people, of which
it usurps the powers by subjugating its representatives and its
agents. It is there that at public meetings attachment to the
law is called ' aristocracy ' and its infringement ' patriotism ' ;
there the assassins of Desilles triumph, the crimes of Jourdan
find panegyrists. . . . It is I who denounce this sect to you . . .
and how should I delay any longer in fulfilling this duty when
each day weakens constituted authority, *substitutes the spirit of
party for the will of the people*, when the audacity of agitators
imposes silence on peaceful citizens and casts aside men who
could be useful. . . . May the royal power remain intact, for it is
guaranteed by the Constitution ; may it be independent, for that
independence is one of the mainsprings of our liberty ; may the
King be revered, for he is invested with the majesty of the nation ;
may he choose a ministry that wears the chains of no party, and
if there are conspirators may they perish beneath the power
of the sword.

" In a word, may the reign of the Clubs be destroyed by you
and give place to the reign of law . . . their disorganizing maxims
(give place) to the true principles of liberty, their delirious fury
to the calm and settled courage of a nation that knows its rights
and defends them, may party considerations yield to the real
interests of the country, which at this moment of danger should
unite all those to whom its subjugation and ruin are not a
matter of atrocious profit and infamous speculation."

These courageous words of Lafayette were received with
a howl of execration by the Girondins. Vergniaud rose angrily
to declare that " it was all over with liberty if a general were
allowed to dictate laws " to the Assembly.

No less than sixty-five departments of France and several

large towns hastened to endorse the sentiments of Lafayette.[1] But it was useless indeed for any one to oppose the Girondins at this crisis; the power was all in their hands, and Dumouriez, realizing this, dared not stand against them, so, although he had declared that " those who demanded the formation of a camp of 20,000 men near Paris were as much the enemies of the country as the enemies of the King," he ended by advising Louis XVI. to sanction the decree.

It was the crowning misfortune of the unhappy King at every crisis of the Revolution to lack disinterested advisers. Before the siege of the Bastille Necker had not dared to stand by him; at the march on Versailles all his ministers had distinguished themselves by their ineptitude; and now, before the invasion of the Tuileries, Dumouriez failed him ignominiously.

Long afterwards in his *Mémoires* Dumouriez completely justified the King's conduct in refusing his sanction to the two decrees, but his tribute to the integrity of Louis XVI. only places his own perfidy in a blacker light. One day, Dumouriez relates, the King, taking him by the hand, said, " in accents that neither art nor dissimulation could have imitated, ' God is my witness that I wish for nothing but the happiness of France,' and Dumouriez, with tears in his eyes, replied, ' Sire, I do not doubt it . . . if all France knew you as I do all our misfortunes would be ended ! ' " Yet, after this, Dumouriez betrayed him. For Louis XVI. having refused to sanction the two decrees, Dumouriez only waited for the inevitable explosion in order to resign his post in the ministry and return to the army—and the Duc de Chartres.

Meanwhile Madame Roland had seen her opportunity to bring about the crisis for which she had so long been waiting, and before the King could announce his final decision she had devised a further trap which this time was to prove effectual.

The dismissal of Necker had served as a pretext for the Revolution of July 1789; the dismissal of the three " patriot ministers," Roland, Servan, and Clavière, might be expected to bring about the Revolution of June 1792. Accordingly she composed a letter [2] which Roland was to hand to the King in the council as his own composition, but of which the authorship was only too plainly visible. Who but Madame Roland, with her insatiable greed for power, could have basely taunted Louis XVI. with the loss of those prerogatives that he had voluntarily renounced ? " Your Majesty has enjoyed the great prerogatives that he believed to belong to royalty. Brought up with the idea of retaining them he could not feel any pleasure at seeing them

---

[1] *Mémoires de Lafayette*, iii. 332.
[2] " Je fis la fameuse lettre," *Mémoires de Mme. Roland*, i. 241.

taken from him ; the desire to have them given back is as natural as the regret at seeing them done away with." Then, dropping the tone of contemptuous condolence, she proceeds to threaten him, and all the old ferocity flashes out anew : " Two important decrees have been drawn up, both of essential interest to the public tranquillity and the salvation of the State. The delay to sanction them inspires distrust ; if prolonged it will cause discontent ; and I am forced to say that in the present agitation of all minds, discontent may lead to anything. There is no time to draw back, it is no longer even possible to temporize—the revolution is made in the minds of the people, it will be finished at the price of blood, and will be cemented with blood, if wisdom does not prevent misfortune it is possible to avoid. . . .

" I know that the austere language of truth is rarely welcomed near the throne ; I know also that it is because it cannot make itself heard there that revolutions become necessary . . . and I know nothing that can prevent me from fulfilling my conscious duty," etc.

Not content with handing this precious document to the King, Roland, obedient to Manon's instructions, insisted on reading it aloud to him, after which he delivered himself of a violent tirade containing " the bitterest and most insulting details " on the conduct of the King, representing him as a " perjurer," reproaching him on the subject of his confessor and of his bodyguard, on the imprudences of the Queen, and the intrigues of the Court with Austria.[1] There was a limit to the patience even of Louis XVI. ; and this attack of Roland's had the effect of bringing things to a crisis. On the 12th of June the King dismissed Roland, Servan, and Clavière ; on the 19th he finally placed his " Veto " on the two decrees.

Nothing could have suited Madame Roland better. For once we may believe her to be sincere when she assures us that she was enchanted at the dismissal of the three ministers, for, if the King's action added fuel to her fury, it had provided the final pretext for insurrection.[2]

The plan concerted in Madame Roland's salon of collecting a mob to march on the Tuileries was matured in the councils of the Orléanistes. At Charenton, Danton, Marat, Santerre,

---

[1] *Mémoires de Dumouriez*, ii. 274.

[2] That the rising of the 20th of June had been planned long before the dismissal of the three ministers on the 12th and the King's final refusal to sanction the two decrees on the 19th, and that these circumstances were therefore only the pretexts given to the people for marching on the Tuileries, is further evident from the fact that the plan of insurrection was known in London at least ten days before it took place. On June 13 a member of the Jacobin Club read aloud a letter he had received from London announcing a movement that was to take place between the 13th and the

Camille Desmoulins[1] met by night, as the Orléanistes of 1789 had met at Montrouge or Passy, for it was they alone who could control the workings of the great revolutionary machine; it was they who chose and paid the mob leaders, they who distributed the rôles, prompted the orators, and lavished gold·and strong drink on the obedient multitude they held at their command. The Girondins could only suggest and perorate ; the Orléanistes knew how to lead from words to action. Then the conspirators set to work to inflame the minds of the people : Carra, Gorsas, Brissot, and Condorcet distributed seditious pamphlets, Pétion and Manuel placarded the walls of the city with fresh calumnies against the Royal Family.[2] A caricature was hawked on the quays representing Louis XVI. with his crown slipping from his head, seated at picquet with the Duc d'Orléans, and exclaiming, " J'ai écarté les cœurs, il a pour lui les *piques*, j'ai perdu la partie."[3] The pikes were literally those of Orléans, for Pétion had ordered 30,000 to be forged for arming the populace, and by a refinement of brutality the points were so constructed as not only to wound but to lacerate horribly the flesh of the victims.[4] These, together with 50,000 red caps of liberty, were distributed in the Faubourgs. Meanwhile Gorsas paraded the streets crying out, " My friends, we must go to-morrow to plant under the windows of fat Louis not the oak of liberty but an aspen ! "[5]

As usual, the people were not admitted to the secrets of the leaders, whose ingenious method was invariably to propose some apparently harmless demonstration, and then to stir the people up to commit excesses. By this means it was always possible to avoid responsibility, and to attribute the blame for any violence that took place to the uncontrollable passions of the populace.

20th, and in the *Correspondance secrète* for June 16 we find an entry to the same effect : " Letters from London announce a great movement in Paris for the 20th of this month. *It has been noticed that the great events of the Revolution have always been foretold us by the English.*" The co-operation of the English revolutionaries is here clearly evident.

[1] *Crimes de la Révolution*, by Prudhomme, iv. 43. Montjoie asserts that Robespierre was also present at the meetings, but this seems improbable, since the movement was conducted by his enemies the Brissotins and Orléanistes. Moreover, at the Jacobin Club he had strongly opposed the plan of insurrection. If he was present the fact is only to be explained by his natural timidity—he may have been afraid to stay away lest he should be accused of sympathy with the Court. But it seems unlikely that he took any active part in the proceedings.

[2] Montjoie, *Conjuration de d'Orléans*, iii. 174 ; Ferrières, iii. 105.

[3] A play on the word *pique*, which signifies both spades at cards and pikes.

[4] Montjoie, *Conjuration de d'Orléans*, iii 174 ; *Histoire particulière*, etc. by Maton de la Varenne.

[5] *Ibid.*

As on the 14th of July the people had only been told to march on the Bastille in order to procure arms for their defence, and on the 5th of October to go to Versailles and ask the King for bread, so before the 20th of June the programme officially put before the inhabitants of Saint-Antoine and Saint-Marceau was to form a procession in order to present a petition to the King and Legislative Assembly, asking for the sanction of the two decrees and the recall of the dismissed ministers.[1] After this they were to proceed to the terrace of the Tuileries and plant a " tree of liberty," to commemorate the anniversary of the Oath of the Tennis Court. Nothing more innocent could be imagined, and by way of inducement to the more peaceable amongst the people it was suggested how pleasant it would be to visit the inside of the Tuileries, and see Monsieur and Madame Veto at home.[2] But in order to ensure the co-operation of the populace more potent methods were employed, and amongst these, as in every outbreak of the Revolution, alcohol played the principal part. So in the Faubourgs throughout the 19th of June champagne, distributed by Santerre, flowed freely,[3] whilst the professional instigators of crime who had figured in all the former tumults— Gonchon, St. Huruge, Fournier l'Americain, and Rotondo—stirred up insurrection. In the Champs Élysées a feast was spread to which the inhabitants of Saint-Antoine and Saint-Marceau were bidden ; in the surrounding cabarets half - naked Sans-Culottes collected, incendiary speeches were made, the Prussian Clootz as toast-master proposed the deposition of Louis XVI. ; and although the more prudent of the leaders affected to support this proposition, the comedian Dugazon was permitted to sing verses provoking the people to murder the King.[4]

Louis XVI. well knew what was taking place in the city. That day he wrote to his confessor, asking him to come to him : " I have never had so great need of your consolations ; I have done with men, it is towards Heaven that I turn my eyes. Great disasters are announced for to-morrow ; I shall have courage." And as he looked out that summer evening across the great gardens of the Tuileries to the sun sinking behind the Champs Élysées, he said to good old Malesherbes standing by him, " Who knows whether I shall see the sun set to-morrow ? " Then with an untroubled conscience he went to rest, ready to welcome death that would deliver him from the hideous nightmare of life. And in hundreds of little French homes that night

[1] Roederer, *Chronique des Cinquante Jours* (edition de Lescure), p. 18.
[2] Mortimer Ternaux, *Histoire de la Terreur*, i. 141.
[3] *Deux Amis*, viii. 25.
[4] Maton de la Varenne, *op. cit.*; Ferrières, iii. 105 ; Montjoie, *Conjuration de d'Orléans*, iii. 175.

Other members rose to speak, when suddenly the waiting crowd, whose angry murmur had been growing louder, broke down the barriers and burst into the hall. A scene of indescribable confusion followed; cries of protest and alarm arose from all parts of the Assembly; members sprang on to the benches and vainly strove to make their voices heard above the tumult. The President hastily put on his hat to signify that the sitting was ended. Finally the advance-guard of the mob was driven out again, and after further discussion the Assembly decided to admit a deputation of " the people." The orator of the deputation, a man named Sylvestre Huguenin, formerly a deserter from the army, now an agent of brothels, was certainly not calculated to inspire confidence in the pacific disposition of his followers. Tall and gaunt, with a bald forehead, bloodshot eyes, a dry and withered skin, his aspect was no less frightful than the tirade he now delivered to the Assembly, of which every word was a veiled provocation to assassinate the King. " A single man shall not influence the will of 20,000 men. If out of consideration we maintain him in his post, it is on condition that he fills it constitutionally ; if he fails to do this he counts for nothing to the French nation *and deserves the extreme penalty*." [1] As an address supposed to have been framed by the inhabitants of Saint-Antoine the thing was the clumsiest of frauds, for in this, as in every other bogus petition presented to the Assembly, the phraseology of the Jacobin Club was clearly recognizable. Thus the working-men of Saint-Antoine were represented as saying : " Imitate Cicero and Demosthenes and unveil before the whole Senate the perfidious machinations of Catilina ! " or again in a wild medley of metaphor : " The people will it so, and their head is of as much value as that of crowned despots. That head is the genealogical tree of the nation, and beneath that sturdy oak the feeble reed must bend."

At each sanguinary threat the galleries broke out into tumultuous applause, and it was then decided to allow the Faubourgs to march through the Assembly. Immediately the wild horde, of which a great number were now reeling under the influence of drink, entered the hall led by Santerre and St. Huruge ; first came seven or eight musicians playing the " Ça ira ! " and behind them women armed with sabres singing and dancing to the strains, the men brandishing their ragged banners and ghastly trophies on the end of poles, and all shrieking incoherently, " Long live the Sans-Culottes ! Long live the nation ! Down with the Veto ! "

" The procession," says the deputy Hua, " lasted for three

[1] These words in italics given by Maton de la Varenne are suppressed by the *Moniteur* and Buchez et Roux.

hours ; hideous countenances were there ; I can still see that moving forest of pikes, those handkerchiefs, those rags that served as standards. . . ." Meanwhile outside the hall an immense congestion had taken place. In order to understand this we must realize the situation of the hall occupied by the Assembly. This hall was the royal Manège, that is to say, the riding-school of the Tuileries, and stood on the spot where at the present day the Rue Castiglione joins the Rue de Rivoli. At the time of the Revolution neither of these streets existed, for the great gardens of the convents and private houses of the Rue Saint-Honoré stretched right up to the line now occupied by the Rue de Rivoli, and were separated from the Tuileries only by a long and narrow courtyard known as the Cour du Manège, whilst a still narrower passage—the Passage des Feuillants—took the place of the Rue Castiglione leading from the Rue Saint-Honoré to the Porte des Feuillants opening into the Tuileries gardens. The hall of the Assembly was entered by two doors, one in the Cour du Manège, the other in the Passage des Feuillants, and it was at this latter entrance that the mob had drawn up demanding admittance. During the delay that ensued the rearguard of the procession continued to pour into the passage which, since the Porte des Feuillants was locked, formed a blind alley, and soon became packed to suffocation. Thereupon the crowd, stifling for want of air and wearied with inaction, began to seek an outlet, and whilst one party proceeded to break open the Porte des Feuillants and swarm into the gardens of the Tuileries, another bethought themselves of the poplar tree they had brought with them on a cart to represent the " tree of liberty."

Now the planting of this tree was to have formed the principal ceremony of the day, and the people, finding that their leaders had failed to carry out their programme, took the law into their own hands and, bursting into the garden of the Capucin convent next to the Assembly, amused themselves by planting there the tree of liberty. This diversion ended, the crowd began to grow bored, and were on the point of dispersing when the roll of drums and the strains of the " Ça ira! " sounding from the hall of the Assembly rallied them once more, and the whole mass moved forward through the doorway.

This long delay was undoubtedly an error on the part of the conspirators, for it had taken the first edge off the people's frenzy, who, if they had been marched straight on the Tuileries, might have shown themselves capable of greater violence. As it was, by the time they had finished parading through the hall, not only had they worked off a great part of their excitement, but also, no doubt, the effects of the wine that had inspired their hilarious entry to the Assembly.

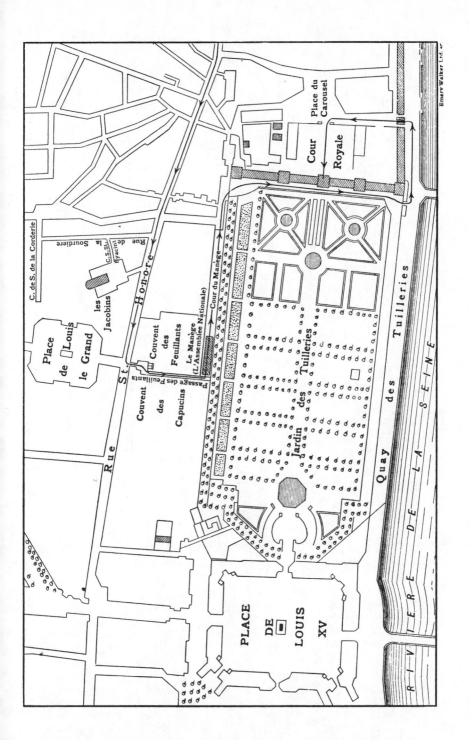

It was nearly four o'clock when at last Santerre, comprehending the necessity of getting to the real business of the day, began to herd his flock towards the exit, crying out in stentorian tones, " Forward ! March ! " The supreme moment had arrived. The terrible crowd of ragged men and women, victims of vice and misery, were now to consummate the crime that for three years the conspirators had vainly striven to effect. Three times already—on the 17th of July and the 6th of October 1789, and on the 18th of April 1791—this same rabble of Paris had been driven forward against their King, and on each occasion had refrained from violence ; now for the last time the great attempt was to be made, and, to judge by the ferocious aspect they presented, there seemed little doubt that amongst this savage horde a murderous hand would not be wanting.[1]

Santerre and St. Huruge, indeed, were evidently so confident that " the people " could be depended on to carry out the crime that, instead of marching at their head as they had done in the morning when leading them to the Assembly, they prudently remained behind in the hall. There was every reason to prefer this safe retreat, for to-day it appeared that the military authorities intended to oppose a very vigorous resistance to any invasion of the Château. Ten battalions of the National Guard were ranged along the west terrace, two more were stationed at the south end by the river, four other battalions as well as five or six hundred mounted police and twenty cannons guarded the Cour Royale.

So on this occasion it was not merely the prime authors of the movement—Brissot, Danton, Pétion, Manuel—who according to their invariable custom remained in the background, but even the mob leaders themselves who retreated into safety, leaving it to the wretched instruments they had collected to do the deed and face the consequences. It is remarkable that in all the accounts of the day we find no mention of any of the usual agitators—Rotondo, Grammont, Malga, or Fournier l'Américain —mingling with the crowd at this stage of the proceedings ; even Théroigne seems to have vanished, for we hear no more of her after her start for the Assembly at the head of her contingent.

The mob, left therefore entirely to its own devices, streamed along the Cour du Manège in the direction of the Château, and then paused as if uncertain whether to go on to the Place du

---

[1] Even Roederer is obliged to admit that this was the idea of the leaders : " The lack of concerted action between the people assembled seems to leave room for only one opinion—that the boldest and most subtle plotters of violence hoped that amongst so many disorderly people a fanatical hand would be raised against the monarch for whom it had not been thought necessary to designate or even to seek out an assassin." (*Chronique des Cinquante Jours* (edition de Lescure), p. 38).

Carrousel or whether to break into the garden of the Tuileries by the gate on their right known as the " Porte du Dauphin." It was, apparently, Mouchet, a little bandy-legged municipal officer stationed at this gateway, who persuaded them to adopt the latter course, and thereupon the whole crowd poured into the garden.[1]

But still the uncomprehending herd failed to enter into the designs of the conspirators, for they made no attempt to invade the Château—which was most accessible from this side—but proceeded along the terrace to the gate leading out on to the quay, and during this march past the troops their behaviour was so peaceable that the King with his family and *entourage* looking down on the procession from the windows, and watching it file through the gateway with immense relief, concluded the movement to have ended : for a moment it appeared that the 6th of October was not to be repeated.

Once outside the garden the crowd turned to the left, but instead of continuing its way along the quay drew up outside the gateway leading into the Carrousel, where they were met by the extraordinary notice, here posted up, that only " people armed, no matter in what way," were to be admitted. In response to this invitation—issued evidently by municipal officers in collusion with the leaders—the whole mob, armed and unarmed, poured into the square. Yet even now the people showed no intention of invading the Château, but streamed onwards to the Rue Saint-Niçaise, apparently with the intention of returning whence they came. The fact is that the day was very hot, and the people having been on their feet since dawn were growing tired of the whole performance. The tree of liberty had been planted, the petition read aloud to the Assembly, and now they were ready to go home.[2]

But Santerre and St. Huruge had been informed of the hitch in the proceedings, and, realizing that if the invasion of the Tuileries was to be accomplished they must place themselves once more at the head of the movement, they now appeared on the scene. Santerre, addressing his contingent from Saint-Antoine, shouted peremptorily, " Why have you not got into the Château ? We *must* get in ! it was for that we came here ! "[3] And turning to his gunners he ordered them to follow him with their cannons,

---

[1] It was at this moment that Napoleon Bonaparte, coming out of a restaurant near the Palais Royal with Bourrienne, made his memorable exclamation : "What imbeciles, how could they allow that rabble (*canaille*) to enter ? They should have swept away four or five hundred of them with cannons and the rest would still be running ! " (*Mémoires de Bourrienne*, i. 49).

[2] Mortimer Ternaux, i. 184 ; Buchez et Roux, xv. 118.

[3] Buchez et Roux, xv. 118.

declaring that if the doors were closed to them they must be broken down with cannon-balls. Then the mob, rallying at the word of command, surged *en masse* towards the gateway of the Cour Royale.

As we have already seen, the troops ranged round the gateway were far more than enough to resist the incursion of the crowd, and although the hundred mounted police in the Carrousel showed a disinclination to use force, the National Guard at the first onslaught offered a spirited resistance. " We will die rather than let them enter ! " cried some ; and others answered, " But we have no orders and no officers to command us ! " And this was true, for Ramainvilliers, their commander, remained absolutely inert, afterwards giving as his reason that having received no orders from the mayor he could not take upon himself to proclaim martial law ; but since the mayor was Pétion, the principal organizer of the movement, this omission is hardly surprising.

The truth is evidently that, as on the 12th and 14th of July and on the 5th of October 1789, the military leaders were paralysed by their knowledge of what Mr. Croker well describes as " the King's unfortunate monomania that no blow should ever be struck in his defence." This being so they dared not offer resistance, uncertain as to the consequences if any injury were done to the people. Maintaining, therefore, their attitude of strict neutrality, they allowed the mob to advance their cannons and point them against the great gateway of the Cour Royale.

By what perfidy was this gateway at last opened ? It is impossible to say with certainty, for just as at the siege of the Bastille an unseen hand had let down the last drawbridge, and at the invasion of Versailles another unseen hand unlocked the gate into the Cour de Marbre, so by the same mysterious agency the courtyard of the Tuileries was thrown open to the invaders. Santerre, says Roederer, had made sure beforehand of two municipal officers, and these men, rightly calculating on the authority inspired by their scarves of office, now came forward and in imperious tones demanded that the gates should be opened. Whoever then obeyed this order,[1] the fact remains that the great bar fastening the gates was raised from within and instantly the crowd poured into the Cour Royale.

Then at last four officers, more courageous than their comrades—Mandat, Pinon, Vanotte, and Acloque, a brewer of the Faubourg Saint - Antoine, rushed forward to close the doorway leading to the great staircase of the palace,

---

[1] Boucher Réné, a municipal officer, in his evidence to the police says " a gunner " ; La Reynie, who declared Boucher Réné to be one of the officers to give the order, says "men of the National Guard." Roederer and Mortimer Ternaux accept the latter statement.

summoning National Guards, gunners, and policemen to
their aid. But it was too late now to command obedience ;
the gunners, urged on by Santerre, were already in open rebellion
and thrust aside the officers in command.

Santerre was still reluctantly compelled to remain at the
head of the mob and conduct operations. For even at this crisis
the great mass of the people continued to display indifference,
and seemed, says Roederer, " to be only misled or carried away,
or brought there by curiosity, and not to understand that it was
an outrage on the King to violate his palace. Several were
yawning with fatigue and boredom. It would have been easy
to count the men led by violent passions and ferocious designs." [1]

Seeing this, a group of law-abiding citizens, who had collected
at the foot of the staircase, came forward and angrily apostrophized Santerre, threatening to make him responsible for all
the harm that might come from this fatal day, " because," they
said to him, " you alone are the author of this unconstitutional
assemblage, you alone have misled these good people, and amongst
them all you alone are a scoundrel ! "   At this Santerre turned
pale, and exchanging a glance with his ally, the butcher Legendre,
he turned to his troops and uttered these hypocritical words :
" Messieurs, draw up an official report of my refusal to march at
your head into the King's apartments ! " [2] Then the ruffians
that composed the cowardly brewer's following, understanding
his intention, threw the honest citizens to the ground, and like a
great tidal wave the mob, once more lashed to fury, burst into
the Château. So tremendous was the impetus of that mighty
onrush that a cannon, carried by the invaders, was borne upon
their shoulders right up the splendid staircase, wreathed with
the emblems of Louis XIV. and the arms of Colbert, into the
huge Salle des Cent Suisses, and there jammed in the doorway,
momentarily stemming the tide. But the obstacle was quickly
removed with hatchet blows upon the woodwork, and the crowd
swept onwards to the Œil de Bœuf.

Now at last they were on the threshold of that abode of
mystery—the King's apartments. Undoubtedly, amongst the
great proportion of the people, the predominating emotion at this
tremendous moment was curiosity, tinged with superstitious awe,
for, in the minds of many of the poor denizens of the Faubourgs,
royalty had not yet lost its glamour, in spite of all the agitators'
efforts to ridicule and degrade it. But that tumultuous sea
nevertheless held dangerous elements, brains that throbbed
wildly to the tune of the " Ça ira ! " hands that closed around
murderous weapons in feverish anticipation of coming violence,

---

[1] Roederer, p. 46.
[2] *Déposition de La Reynie*, Buchez et Roux, xv. 118.

and in these disordered imaginations superstition assumed a
terrible form—it was not Louis XVI., the descendant of St. Louis,
they were now to meet face to face, but that sinister personage
" Monsieur Veto "—Nero, Machiavelli, and Charles IX. in one
—the sanguinary monster, and his still more guilty consort, who
with diabolical cunning had lulled a confiding people into
security whilst planning a second massacre of St. Barthélemy
—perhaps on that same Quai du Louvre their feet had traversed
to the Château. Goaded to frenzy by these visions, the leaders
of the mob continued to beat on the closed doors, clamouring
loudly for admittance ; then, meeting with no response, they
proceeded to attack them with their weapons ; beneath their
savage blows the lower panels yielded and fell inwards—instantly
a cluster of pikes was thrust menacingly through the opening.
Suddenly from the inside a voice cried out, " Open ! I have
nothing to fear from Frenchmen ! " A Swiss guard threw wide
the doors. The crowd surged forward, then, like an angry wave
drawing back with a roar of foam, halted in confusion, for before
them stood—the King. The sensation produced on the crowd
by this sudden apparition, all contemporaries record, was one of
stupor—they were utterly disconcerted, for here they saw before
them no sanguinary monster but a homely personage, none the
more imposing for all his powdered hair and embroidered coat, who
stood regarding them with an expression of extreme benevolence
obviously unmixed with fear. Louis XVI. was not afraid at that
frightful moment. When the faithful Acloque had rushed into
his room, where all the Royal Family had collected, to announce
the incursion of the mob, the King had instantly decided to go
forward to meet them, only insisting that the Queen, against
whom the people's hatred had been principally directed, should
remain in safety ; and whilst Marie Antoinette, finally prevented
by force from following him, was hurried into the bedroom of
the Dauphin, the King passed calmly to the Œil de Bœuf, with
Madame Elizabeth clinging to his arm, and followed by those
of his loyal defenders who had remained at his side. Two hours
earlier the King, foreseeing the invasion of the Château, had sent
away nearly all his retainers lest their presence should serve to
irritate the populace, but several—amongst them the old Maréchal
de Mouchy, that bizarre personage the Chevalier de Rougeville,
and brave young Canolles, a boy of eighteen who had belonged
to the King's old bodyguard—had refused to leave him ; others,
borrowing pikes and ragged garments from some of the insurgents,
mingled with the mob, and thus disguised hovered around the
King for his protection.[1] Arrived in the Œil de Bœuf, Louis
XVI. called four grenadiers of the National Guard to his side,

[1] *Mémoires de Hua*, p. 136.

and one of these, De la Chesnaye, seeing that the doors were about
to be broken down, said to the King, " Sire, do not be afraid.'
" I am not afraid," answered the King; " put your hand on my
heart, it is calm and tranquil," and taking the hand of the
grenadier he pressed it to his heart, which in truth beat no
faster in the face of the appalling danger.

What was the secret of the King's intrepidity ? Revolutionaries, obliged to admit his amazing sangfroid at this crisis, have
tried to explain it by the natural phlegm of his character, but
in reality his courage throughout the Revolution can always be
traced to the same cause—the fact that, as Bertrand de Molleville
observed, *he was never afraid when he was face to face with the
people.* It was this conviction that from the people themselves
he had nothing to fear which had nerved him to take that perilous
journey to Paris on the 17th of July 1789, which had enabled
him to confront the raging mob on the 6th of October, and which
now again on the 20th of June inspired him with the serenity
that amazed all beholders. So, by the calm and undaunted aspect
of the King, the ragged horde was momentarily brought to bay
on the threshold of the Œil de Bœuf. But certain of the brigands,
having recovered from the first shock of surprise, thrust their way
into the room, brandishing pikes and sabres as they called aloud
for the death of the King. The Swiss Guards drew their swords,
but Louis XVI. interposed : " Put back your swords in their
scabbards, I command you." Then a man, armed with a
stick to which a spear had been affixed, sprang forward
crying out, " Where is Veto that I may kill him ? " Whereat
young Canolles threw himself on the assassin, and forcing him to
his knees at the King's feet obliged him to call out, " Vive
le Roi ! "[1]

This act of courage had the effect of once more stupefying
the crowd, and the King's defenders, profiting by the pause that
ensued, succeeded in leading him to a seat in the recess of a
window, forming there a rampart round him with their bodies.
The heroic band included the four grenadiers of the National
Guard, the Maréchal de Mouchy, aged seventy-seven, the intrepid
brewer Acloque, and Stéphanie de Bourbon-Conti, the natural
daughter of the Prince de Conti, who had armed herself with a
sword and sabre, and throughout the day never ceased defending
the King from the onslaughts of his assassins.[2]

Meanwhile Madame Elizabeth showed herself no less heroic ;
hearing the mob crying out for the head of the Queen she came
forward and, offering her breast to their daggers, said, " Here

---

[1] *Histoire particulière*, etc., by Maton de la Varenne. Canolles was
guillotined for this action on May 23, 1794.
[2] *Ibid.*

is the Queen ! " Several of her retainers cried out, " No, no, she is not the Queen, she is Madame Elizabeth ! "

" Ah, messieurs," she answered, " why undeceive them ? Were it not better that they shed my blood than that of my sister ? " The murderous weapons were lowered, and Madame Elizabeth was placed by her defenders in the embrasure of the window next to the one occupied by the King.

For four terrible hours Louis XVI. and Madame Elizabeth endured the threats and insults of the crowd. All through the hot June afternoon they breathed the fetid atmosphere exhaled by the densely packed mass of rags and nakedness that pressed around them ; they saw before their eyes all that was basest and most degraded in human nature, the dregs of foreign countries, above all brigands from the South, vomiting imprecations, dangling before their eyes those horrible emblems—the bleeding heart labelled "Cœur d'aristocrate," a miniature gallows to which a female figure was attached with the words " For Antoinette," a guillotine bearing the inscription " For the tyrant."

Close to the King's side a group of men had thrown themselves into the gilded armchairs of the palace, and gathered around a table covered with bottles of wine sat smoking and drinking amidst the tumult.[1] Some one passed a bottle to the King, ordering him to drink the health of the nation ; at the same time a cap of liberty was thrust upon his head.[2] Louis XVI. raised the bottle to his lips, exclaiming, " People of Paris, I drink to your health and to the health of the French nation ! " This courageous action, derided by the revolutionaries, went straight to the hearts of the people,[3] who broke out into applause, crying, " Vive la nation ! Vive la liberté ! " and even " Vive le Roi ! " If only Louis XVI. had known how to make the most of this moment, it is possible that the invasion of his palace would have turned into an ovation in his favour ; unhappily his slow-moving mind could never devise those happy phrases that exercised so great a power over the emotional Parisians. To this drama-loving people a King who on occasion could " strike an attitude," show himself commanding and heroic, must have proved irresistible. Louis XVI. was hopelessly undramatic ; his speech proceeded always directly from his heart, never from his imagination ; he

---

[1] *Mémoires de Hua.*

[2] According to Maton de la Varenne it was Santerre who thrust the cap of liberty on to the King's head ; according to Beaulieu it was Clément, but other contemporaries relate that the King put it on of his own accord. This seems improbable, and is contradicted by the King's statement to Bertrand de Molleville.

[3] " What saved Louis XVI. was his presence of mind in putting on the *bonnet rouge* and in drinking from a bottle offered him by a real Sans-Culotte " (*Crimes de la Révolution*, by Prudhomme, iv. 43).

could not calculate effects, declaim to order, play upon the emotions of the mobile crowd as the revolutionary leaders knew so well how to do, and thus at this supreme moment he remained inarticulate, leaving it to his enemies to wrest his victory from him. Legendre pressed forward and addressed him brutally :

" Monsieur, you are there to listen to us. You are a traitor, you have always deceived us, you are deceiving us still. But have a care, the measure is overflowing, and the people are tired of being your plaything." And he read aloud a petition filled with threats and insults, " expressing the wishes of the people, whose orator he declared himself to be." The King answered calmly :

" I shall do that which the law and the Constitution order me to do."

Whilst these scenes were taking place the mayor, Pétion, arrived, and making his way through the crowd addressed the King in these hypocritical words :

" Sire, I have only this instant heard of the situation in which you have been placed."

" That is very surprising," Louis XVI. interrupted brusquely, " since this has been going on for two hours."

" The zeal of the mayor of Paris," Condorcet afterwards had the effrontery to declare, " the ascendant that his virtues and his patriotism exercised over the people, prevented all disorders " ; as a matter of fact his presence served as a direct encouragement to disorder, for, since not a word of protest escaped him during the whole course of the afternoon, the brigands quickly recognized in him an ally and, protected by the support his official position afforded, proceeded to greater violence. Forcing their way to the front of the crowd they lunged at the King with their weapons, which were deflected only by the bayonets of the four courageous grenadiers. Two young men, Clément and Bourgoing, wearing long caps on which the words " La Mort " were inscribed in large letters, called out loudly for the death of the King and all the Royal Family. Clément, taking up his stand beside the mayor, continued to repeat incessantly the parrot phrases composed by the authors of the agitation : " Sire ! Sire ! I demand in the name of the 100,000 souls around me the recall of the patriot ministers you have dismissed ! I demand the sanction of the decree on the priests and on the 20,000 men and the fulfilment of the law, or you will perish ! " Throughout this tirade, accompanied by furious gestures, Pétion uttered no remonstrance, and, not content with complimenting the people on their behaviour, afterwards declared to the Assembly that " no one had been insulted, that no excess or offence had been committed, and the King himself had no cause of complaint."

On this day, at any rate, Louis XVI. showed himself not only heroic but capable of really amazing resolution. To the re-iterated demand for the sanction of the two decrees and the recall of the ministers he replied immovably, " This is neither the moment for you to ask nor for me to accord," and in the matter of the decree on the priests he added, " I would rather renounce my crown than submit to such a tyranny of consciences."

It was at this crisis that a deputation arrived from the Assembly. The scene that met their eyes was indescribable ; the splendid Salle de l'Œil de Bœuf presented the appearance of a tavern—through the suffocating atmosphere, thick with the fumes of foul tobacco, Louis XVI. was seen seated in the embrasure of the window, the red cap of liberty still perched upon his powdered head, contemplating his strange guests with perfect tranquillity.

When the deputies came forward to inform him that " the Assembly would neglect no means for ensuring his liberty," the King, indicating by a gesture the carousing brigands, the wine-bottles, the guns, the pikes, and sanguinary emblems by which he was surrounded, answered briefly, " So you see ! " Then turning to a member of the deputation he added with a sudden rare flash of humour, " You who have travelled much, what do you think they would say of us in foreign countries ? "[1]

Certain of the deputies venturing to repeat to the King that they had come to ensure his safety, Louis XVI. replied that he was in the midst of the French people and had nothing to fear.[2] Again turning to one of the grenadiers he placed the man's hand on his heart, saying, " See whether this is the movement of a heart agitated by fear ! "[3]

The intrepid attitude of the King was not without its effect on his assailants, and by eight o'clock in the evening it became evident that little hope remained of his assassination. Pétion, therefore realizing that nothing was now to be gained by further agitation, decided that the moment had come to pose as the restorer of law and order. Accordingly, mounting an armchair, he addressed the crowd of pikes and rags, the bearers of toy guillotines and gibbets, the drunken and half-naked brigands from the South, in the following words :

" People, you have shown yourselves worthy of yourselves ! You have preserved all your dignity amidst acute alarms. No excess has sullied your sublime movements. Hope and believe

---

[1] *Mémoires de Ferrières*, iii. 115.
[2] Evidence of the deputies Brunck and Lejosne, *Moniteur*, xii. 719.
[3] Evidence of the deputy Alos, *ibid.* The grenadier, a tailor by profession named Lalanne, was guillotined later " for having boasted that Capet had taken his hand and held it to his heart " (Granier de Cassagnac, *Causes de la Revolution*, iii. 217).

that your voice will at last be heard. But night approaches, and its shadows might favour the attempts of ill-disposed persons to glide into your bosom. People, withdraw yourselves ! " [1]

The mob, comprehending that this was really an order to disperse, showed themselves only too eager to comply and surged towards the doors. But the leaders had resolved to make a further venture and, instead of herding the people towards the staircase, led them to the Council Chamber where the Queen and her children had taken refuge. Santerre had already preceded them thither. On the arrival of the deputies, realizing the failure of the movement, he had been heard to mutter angrily, " Le coup est manqué ! " [2] But if the King had succeeded in overawing " that foolish herd, the people," the Queen might still serve to rouse their fury, so collecting a horde of brigands around him, and followed by a large portion of the mob, he had set forth in search of this further victim.

Now on the first incursion of the crowd into the Château, whilst the main army attacked the Œil de Bœuf, a band of furies had broken into the Queen's apartments on the ground floor and ransacked every corner in the hunt for their prey. Meanwhile Marie Antoinette, upstairs in the Dauphin's bedroom, vainly endeavoured to follow Louis XVI. into the Œil de Bœuf. " Let me pass," she cried to the gentlemen who barred her way, " my place is with the King. I will join him, or perish if necessary in defending him." But convinced at last that any attempt to penetrate the sea of pikes that separated her from Louis XVI, must prove the signal for bloodshed, she allowed herself to be drawn into the embrasure of the window in the Salle de Conseil. It was here that Santerre and his horde discovered her. Behind the great council-table Marie Antoinette sat surrounded by her ladies — Madame de Tourzel, Madame de la Roche - Aymon, Madame de Maillé, and the heroic Princesse de Tarente, ready to shed the last drop of her blood in defence of the Queen. By the side of Marie Antoinette stood little Madame Royale ; the Dauphin was seated on the table with his mother's arms around him. In front several rows of grenadiers belonging to the loyal battalion of the " Filles-Saint-Thomas " were drawn up. Santerre roughly ordered this bodyguard to stand aside : " Make way that the people may see the Queen ! " Instantly the crowd rushed forward pouring forth imprecations, but at the sight of the grenadiers paused uncertainly. One woman, bolder than the rest, flung a red cap of liberty down on the table, and in foul language ordered the Queen to place it on the head of the Dauphin.

[1] *Mémoires de Hua.* The *Moniteur* tones down this discourse.
[2] *Dernières années . . . de Louis XVI,* by François Hue, p. 239; Fantin Désodoards, *op. cit.* ii. 300.

The hideous badge of the galley-slave was drawn over the boy's fair curls.

The Queen and the brave women around her endured their terrible ordeal without a sign of weakness. When the main body of the ragged army, after evacuating the Œil de Bœuf, were driven through the Chambre de Conseil past the council-table, Marie Antoinette looked still unmoved at the ghastly emblems thrust before her eyes—the gibbet from which her effigy was suspended, the banners bearing obscene legends ; she heard without a tremor the furious imprecations mouthed at her by the dishevelled furies, and, as on the 6th of October, ended by disarming her assailants. The strange power that had touched even the corrupt heart of Mirabeau, that had changed Barnave from a sanguinary demagogue into a royalist ready to die in her defence, that later was to win reluctant admiration from her gaolers and wring pity from the *tricoteuses* at the Revolutionary Tribunal, gradually made itself felt amongst the women crazed with drink and revolutionary frenzy who gazed at her across the council-table at the Tuileries. Some of the furies in the crowd, melted to tenderness by the sight of the Queen—after all a woman and a mother like themselves, sheltering with her arm her little son who looked with wondering eyes at the strange spectacle before him—cried out that they would shed the last drop of their blood for the Queen and the Dauphin. Another, better remembering her lesson, began to pour forth fresh invectives, whereat the Queen asked gently, " Have I done you any injury ? " " No," said the woman, " but it is you who cause the unhappiness of the nation." " So they have told you," answered Marie Antoinette, " but you have been deceived. I am the wife of the King of France, the mother of the Dauphin. I am French ; never again shall I see my own country. I can only be happy or unhappy in France. I was happy when you loved me."

Then the fury, bursting into tears, besought the Queen's pardon, sobbing out, " It was that I did not know. I see now how good you are." [1]

At this Santerre, stupefied at the turn affairs had taken, exclaimed, " What is the matter with this woman that she weeps thus ? She must be drunk with wine." [2]

But a moment later Santerre, pushing his way through the crowd, found himself face to face with the Queen and suddenly fell likewise beneath her spell.[3] Planting his two fists on the table he roughly ordered the bystanders to take the red cap off the head of the Dauphin, who was stifling beneath its heat ; then turning to the Queen he said, " Ah, Madame, have no fear, I

---

[1] *Mémoires de Mme. Campan*, p. 331.
[2] *Vie de Marie Antoinette*, by Montjoie, p. 323.　　　[3] *Ibid.*

do not wish to harm you, I would rather defend you!" but quickly repenting of his weakness he added brutally, "Remember that it is dangerous to deceive the people!"

At these words Marie Antoinette raised her head and, looking Santerre imperiously in the eye, exclaimed with indignation, "It is not by *you*, monsieur, that I judge the people!"[1]

Santerre, utterly cowed by this reply, had no thought but to beat as hasty a retreat as possible. Turning to his brigand horde he gave the order to march, and pushing the rest of the crowd brutally before him he drove them like trembling sheep from the room.[2]

So in the growing twilight the mighty human tide ebbed from the Château of the Tuileries, leaving the great rooms "in solitude and stupor."

The Royal Family, once more united, fell weeping into one another's arms. The terrible ordeal was at last ended. A few moments later several deputies arrived from the Assembly; one turning to the Queen, standing amidst the wreckage left by the invaders—the broken furniture, the shattered panels, the doors torn from their hinges—observed with unconscious irony, "Without excusing everything, you must admit, Madame, that the people have shown themselves to be kind-hearted?"

"The King and I, monsieur," answered Marie Antoinette, "are persuaded of the natural kindness of the people; they are unkind only when they are misled."[3]

That the King could have been assassinated on this 20th of June if the people had felt any unanimous desire for his death, there can be no doubt whatever. What could his handful of defenders have availed against the determined onslaught of a mob numbering many thousand armed men? If "the people" had wished to kill him, he must have perished then. But on this point all contemporaries are agreed. The great majority of the crowd seemed throughout struck with stupor, and showed no inclination to join in the insults and bloodthirsty threats of the leaders.[4]

Santerre, driving his herd down the staircase of the Château,

---

[1] *Vie de Marie Antoinette*, by Montjoie, p. 323; Maton de la Varenne, *op. cit.*

[2] Ferrières, iii. 119; Maton de la Varenne, *op. cit.*; *Conjuration de d'Orléans*, by Montjoie, iii. 184.

[3] *Dernières années . . . de Louis XVI*, by François Hue, p. 244.

[4] "Nothing of all this could move the crowd. Divided between the King and his sister it remained motionless. One read in all eyes astonishment, stupidity, or apprehension" (Montjoie, *Conjuration de d'Orléans*, iii. 181).

"In truth, and we are glad to say it, amongst all the people who introduced themselves to the apartments very few shared this atrocious attitude. It appears, according to various reports, that the greater number only was heard to exclaim angrily, " The King was difficult to move to-day, but we will return to-morrow and make him evacuate ! " [1] But some poor creatures, all in rags, murmured to each other, " It would be a pity, somehow, he looks like a good sort of fellow ! " [2]

The day after the invasion of the Tuileries a witness, who appeared before a magistrate of Paris, related that he had traversed the whole Faubourg Saint-Antoine to discover the disposition of the people, that in an inn close to the Barrière du Trône he had listened to several men talking, and overheard these words : " Yes, we might have been able . . . but when we saw . . . it is so imposing . . . and then we are Frenchmen . . . Sacredieu ! if it had been any one else we could have wrung his neck like a child's . . . but he comes and he says, ' Here I am ! Here I am ! ' " The witness added that he had seen several of these men who had been led away by Santerre, and they assured him that the majority of the citizens of the Faubourg were distressed at the action taken towards the King, that it had not been their intention, and that one could be sure it would never happen again, and that there was something behind all this.[3]

The authors of the movement, however, knew no relenting. Madame Roland, hearing of the Queen's sufferings on that dreadful afternoon, cried out incontrollably, " Ah ! how I should have loved to look on at her long humiliation ! " [4]

But Manon's triumph was mingled with bitter disappointment. From the point of view of both Girondins and Orléanistes the day had proved a failure ; it was not merely to *humiliate* the Royal Family they had planned the invasion of the Tuileries, the great coup of the day, as Santerre said, had failed. The people, like Balaam's ass, had been driven forward for the fourth time against the King, and, seeing the angel with the flaming sword before them in the pathway, had refused to move in spite of blows and curses. So the crime from which the lowest rabble of the Faubourgs

showed the desire to see the King and Royal Family " (*Rapport fait au Conseil du Département par MM. Garnier, Leveillard et Demautort, Commissaires, au Sujet des Événements du 20 Juin*).

" The people, ashamed of finding themselves all at once in the presence of their King and in the midst of his apartments, seemed frightened by their own temerity, at the sight of the ancient majesty of the throne that fourteen centuries of respect had in some way rendered sacred " (Ferrières, iii. 113).

[1] Evidence of soldiers and commissioners, *Revue retrospective*, 2ième série, tome i. pp. 213, 254.

[2] *Crimes de la Révolution*, by Prudhomme, iv. 43.

[3] *Déclarations de la Reynie et Fayel reçues par le Juge de Paix de la Section du Roi de Sicile.*

[4] Lamartine, *Histoire des Girondins*, iii. 3.

had shrunk was left to men of education, to philosophers, and
" intellectuals " to execute.

EFFECTS OF THE 20TH OF JUNE

The " true people," the great mass of the citizens of Paris,
had, of course, taken no part in the 20th of June. " For the
honour of our country," cries Poujoulat, " and for the sake of
historical truth, it must be known that the crimes and ignominies
of the French Revolution were not the work of the French
nation. . . . The people of Paris were not beneath the filthy
banners of Santerre, St. Huruge, and Théroigne, they were around
the Tuileries on the 21st of June, raging against these criminal
attempts, pitying the King and Queen, cursing Pétion, the
Gironde, and the Jacobins, and signing their protestations."

All over France a great storm of indignation arose ; addresses
poured in from the provinces, denouncing in vehement language
the efforts of the factions to overthrow the King and Constitution.
The department of the Pas de Calais " has learnt with horror
what took place in the King's palace on the 20th of the month " ;
Rouen declares the country to be in danger, and demands justice
of the Assembly : " Punish the authors of the offences committed
on the 20th of this month at the Château of the Tuileries. It is
a public outrage, it is an attempt on the rights of the French
people who will not accept laws from a few brigands in the capital ;
we ask you for vengeance." The department of the Aisne urges
the Assembly to suppress the Jacobins and cease from dissensions :
" Put an end to the scandal of your divisions . . . put an end
to the intolerable oppression, the revolting tyranny of the
tribunes (the galleries occupied by the *claques* of the factions).
The factions of the capital have not the right to dictate public
opinion. The opinion of Paris is only the opinion of the 83rd
part of the Empire. We demand vengeance for the execrable
day of June the 20th, day of imperishable shame for Paris, of
mourning for all France." [1]

" The 20th of June," Hua records, " produced a salutary
commotion in all minds. . . . The National Guards, more than
ever roused, offered to the King their services and their entire
devotion. The inhabitants of Paris, who were particularly
answerable to France for the King's safety since he left Versailles
. . . ashamed of the excesses that had just been committed
in their name, demanded reparation and vengeance. A petition
addressed to the Assembly bore 20,000 signatures ; it was called
' the petition of the 20,000.' . . . Nearly all the departments of
France set themselves to deliberate, and forwarded unanimous

[1] *Moniteur*, xiii. 5.

demands for the punishment of the outrage. They offered to send all the forces that might be needed. It was a universal competition; it seemed as if all France had raised her arm to annihilate the factions." [1]

Needless to say, every effort was made by the Jacobins to suppress the reporting of these addresses, to silence the orators who were sent to read them aloud at the Assembly, to discredit the authors, to prove the signatures fraudulent, and also to provide counterblasts in the form of bogus addresses approving the events of June 20, and purporting to come from the provinces and from the sections of Paris. Thus, for example, on June 25, a deputation from Saint-Antoine, calling itself " the men of the 14th of July," presented itself at the Assembly, led by the professional orator, Gonchon, who proceeded to deliver a furious revolutionary harangue beginning with these words : " Legislators, it is we fathers of families, it is we, the conquerors of the Bastille, it is we who are persecuted, outraged, and calumniated," etc.

But where amongst this band of petitioners were the conquerors of the Bastille to be found ? Where were " the men of the 14th of July "—Élie, Hullin, Tournay, Bonnemère—the real heroes of that day ? We may look for them in vain amongst the ruffianly followers of Gonchon, but if we go into the gardens of the Tuileries we shall discover Hullin at that very moment otherwise employed. At half-past twelve of this same day, a *gendarme national* reported to the Jacobin Club, he had met the King in the Tuileries followed by a crowd of "brigands," at the head of which was M. Hullin following the King, and calling out with all his might, " Vive le Roi ! " A sub-lieutenant answered with the cry of "Vive la Nation," whereat " the brave Hullin " dealt him a heavy blow on the head, and but for the interposition of the gendarme would have marched him off to prison. [2]

This, then, was the attitude of the real " men of the 14th of July " to the second Revolution ; not *one* of their names occurs in the accounts of the outrages committed at the Tuileries or in the revolutionary deputations, and the only men of the first Revolution whose services the leaders were able to enlist were a couple of cut-throats, one of which named Soudin had distinguished himself by washing the heads of Foullon and Berthier and delivering them as trophies to the mob. [3]

As for Gonchon himself, who had now passed from the Orléanistes into the pay of the Girondins, Camille Desmoulins

[1] *Mémoires de Hua*, p. 138 ; *Deux Amis*, viii. 19 ; Dumont, *Souvenirs de Mirabeau* : " The whole mass of France was weary of the excesses of the Jacobins, and the outrage of June the 20th had excited a general indignation." See also Taine, *La Révolution*, v. 259.
[2] Aulard's *Séances des Jacobins*, iv. 48.
[3] Buchez et Roux, xv. 165, 237.

afterwards revealed that he had received over 2000 francs from Roland merely for reading the bogus petition to the Assembly.[1]

By methods such as these the voice of the true people was stifled, and the character of the French nation misrepresented to the whole civilized world. Nowhere were the outrages of June 20 more bitterly resented than in the armies on the frontier. Lafayette at last, overwhelmed with protests from his men, decided to leave Lückner in command and hastened to Paris. Presenting himself at the bar of the Assembly he denounced, in burning words, the efforts of the conspirators to overthrow the monarchy and Constitution: " The violence committed at the Château on the 20th of this month has excited the alarm of all good citizens ; I have received addresses from the different corps of my army. Officers, non-commissioned officers, and men are one, and herein express their patriotic hatred of the factions . . . already *many of them wonder whether it is really the cause of liberty they are defending.* . . . I implore, in my own name and in that of all honest men, that the Assembly should take efficacious measures to make constituted authority respected, and to give the army the assurance that no attacks will be made on the Constitution from the inside, whilst they are shedding their blood to protect it from outside enemies."

In spite of the insults with which the Girondins greeted these words, Lafayette succeeded in maintaining his popularity, and he was followed through the streets by crowds shouting, " Down with the Jacobins ! " But once again " the hero of the two worlds " showed his lamentable weakness. If at this crisis he had used his power and finally closed down the Jacobin Club, the whole situation might have been saved. The plan was proposed to him by a deputation of National Guards, who declared that if he would place himself at their head and march with two cannons to the Rue Saint-Honoré, they would undertake to clear the building. But Lafayette, always halting between two opinions—detestation of sedition-mongers on one hand and fear of the ultra-Royalists on the other—refused to accede to the proposal of his grenadiers.[2]

If, under these circumstances, the Queen declined to avail herself of his services, is it altogether surprising ? " It would be better to perish than to be saved by Lafayette," she cried, when at this juncture he came forward as champion of the monarchy. What reason, indeed, had she to trust him ? Lafayette, who before the siege of the Bastille had declared that " insurrection was the most sacred of duties," and had then

---

[1] *Fragment d'Histoire secrète de la Révolution*, by Camille Desmoulins, p. 55.
[2] *Essais de Beaulieu*, iii. 396.

denounced the tumults of July; who had convicted the Duc d'Orléans of conspiring to usurp the throne, and had then facilitated his return to France; who had subjected the King and Queen to the humiliations of his intolerable gaolership, and then talked of the respect due to the person of the monarch; who at one moment declared himself the opponent of disorders, and the next joined in singing " Ça ira ! "—what dependence was to be placed on such a weathercock ? Throughout the whole course of the Revolution it was rather as the enemy of the Duc d'Orléans than as the supporter of Louis XVI. that he had defended the throne; towards the Royal Family he had displayed neither sympathy nor allegiance, only when Orléanism raised its head Lafayette's hand went to his sword and he became the champion of Royalty. In this second Revolution he saw undoubtedly a revival of the hated conspiracy, but what guarantee was there that, once he had again succeeded in crushing it, he would not use his power to tyrannize over the King ?

So Lafayette, chilled by his reception at the Court, left Paris and returned to the frontier, whilst the Orléanistes triumphantly burnt his effigy in the Palais Royal.

Yet the 20th of June had disappointed the hopes of the conspirators, as indeed of all the revolutionary intrigues — Orléanistes, Girondins, Subversives, Prussians, English Jacobins alike had met with a severe reverse. For not only had the invasion of the Tuileries shown the King in his true character to the nation, but in arousing public indignation all over France had revealed the true desires of the nation to the world. So the day had ended not only in a victory for the King but for *the people.*

THE SIEGE OF THE TUILERIES

THE SIEGE OF THE TUILERIES

LA PATRIE EN DANGER

THE fiasco of June 20 and the energetic protests of the nation convinced the revolutionary leaders that such flimsy pretexts as "the dismissal of the three patriot ministers" and the King's Veto on the two decrees would not avail to bring about the deposition of Louis XVI., and that consequently some more potent means must be employed to rouse the people. Calumny and corruption had failed, but *terror* might yet prove effectual. The fear of foreign invasion was one that they well knew could always be depended on to rouse the patriotism of the nation, so when at the beginning of July Prussian troops arrived on the frontier, an admirable pretext was provided for creating a panic throughout the country by the proclamation of "La Patrie en danger."

The country certainly was now in danger of invasion, for the outrages endured by the Royal Family on the 20th of June had not only incensed the King's brothers and the *émigrés*, but had alarmed the Emperor of Austria and the King of Prussia. Frederick William at last realized that the revolutionary propaganda he had helped to disseminate had gone too far and was endangering the cause of monarchy, consequently some feint must be made of marching to the rescue of the Royal Family of France; but that he was never disinterested in this intention cannot be doubted in the light of after events.[1] True, the famous "Manifesto of

---

[1] Albert Sorel has thus admirably explained the policy of the King of Prussia in marching to the rescue of Louis XVI. "Conquests having escaped him," Frederick William "perceived that he had great duties to fulfil towards the world, towards kings, towards Germany. He forgot the Hungarians he had stirred up; the Belgians to whom he had promised independence; the Turks, the Swedes, and the Poles he had goaded into war. . . . Goltz provided the arguments necessary to convince . . . Frederick William. This perfect Prussian who had been employing himself in Paris . . . in shaking the throne, recognized that it would be at the same time more praiseworthy, more expedient, and more profitable to raise it up again." Goltz further calculated that France would have to compensate Austria by giving up to her Alsace or Flanders, and Austria should then, in order to maintain the balance of power, give up to Prussia equivalent territory in Bohemia and Moldavia (*L'Europe et la Révolution Française*, ii. 72).

Brunswick," which was proclaimed in Paris on the 3rd of August, expressed the deepest concern for the safety of the King and Queen of France, but merely had the effect of greatly aggravating the danger of their position. According to the terms of this proclamation, the Emperor of Austria and the King of Prussia announce that the great interest nearest to their hearts is " that of ending the domestic anarchy of France, of arresting the attacks which are directed against the altar and the throne, of re-establishing the legitimate power, of giving back to the King the freedom and safety of which he is deprived," etc.   At this point the Manifesto strikes a more diplomatic note, for it goes on to say : " Convinced as they are that the healthy portion of the French people abhors the excesses of a party that enslaves them, and that the majority of the inhabitants are impatiently awaiting the advent of a relief that will permit them to declare themselves openly against the odious schemes of their oppressors, his Majesty the Emperor, and his Majesty the King of Prussia summon them to return at once to the call of reason and justice, of order and of peace." The first part of this passage was undoubtedly true ; the vast majority of the nation was impatiently awaiting deliverance from the intolerable oppression of the Jacobins, but to follow up this conciliatory overture with commands and threats was to alienate even that loyal portion of the people who would have rallied around the standard of the King. Thus although their Majesties are represented as declaring that they have " no intention of interfering with the internal government of France," and that " their combined armies will protect all towns and villages which submit to the King of France," nevertheless those inhabitants who fire on the troops " will be punished with all the rigour of the laws of war " ; further, that if the Tuileries are again invaded, or the least assault perpetrated against the Royal Family, " their Imperial and Royal Majesties will take an exemplary and never-to-be-forgotten vengeance by giving up the town of Paris to military execution and to total subversion, and the guilty rebels to the death they have deserved."

This amazingly injudicious document, which is frequently regarded as a monument of Prussian or of royal arrogance, was in reality not the work of a foreigner or of a royal prince at all, but of a French *émigré*, the Marquis de Limon, formerly financial adviser to the Duc d'Orléans,[1] and though approved by the Emperor and the King of Prussia, it met with violent remonstrance from the democratic Duke of Brunswick, who at first refused to append his signature to it, and only complied at last in obedience to the commands of the aforesaid monarchs.

[1] *Le Comte de Fersen et la Cour de France*, ii. 25.

According to Beaulieu, De Limon consulted in the matter a certain Heymann, who had served in a regiment of the Duc d'Orléans ; both these men had formerly played an active part in the Orléaniste conspiracy.[1]

It is not, therefore, impossible that the famous Manifesto was inspired by Orléaniste influence, and that the misguided Comte de Fersen, and through his influence Marie Antoinette, in according it their approval played into the hands of their enemies. Fersen, always illusioned as to the good faith of the King of Prussia, undoubtedly imagined that the armies of Prussia could be counted on to save the Royal Family, and, realizing the cowardice of the revolutionary leaders, he believed that the threat of reprisals might be used with advantage to intimidate them. But the revolutionary leaders, better acquainted with the real policy of Frederick William, were not intimidated, and in their turn made use of the Manifesto to alarm the French people.

The people of France, though less alarmed than revolutionary writers would have us suppose, were, nevertheless, indignant at the truculent tone of the Manifesto. " No country," writes Dr. Moore, who arrived in Paris this August, " ever displayed a nobler or more patriotic enthusiasm than pervades France at this moment, and which glows with increasing ardour since the publication of the Duke of Brunswick's Manifesto and the entrance of the Prussians into the country."

The revolutionary leaders were clever enough to exploit this spirit of patriotism to the utmost, but, as we have seen, the attitude of certain men amongst them towards Brunswick was far from antagonistic. On the 21st of July, just a week before the publication of the Manifesto, the author of the *Correspondance secrète* writes : " It is said that it still enters into the plans of the Jacobins to come to an understanding with the Duke of Brunswick *by offering him the crown of France.*" Four days later this rumour was confirmed in the press, for on July 25, that is to say the *very day* that Brunswick signed the Manifesto prepared for him, Carra published the following passage in his *Annales Patriotiques* :

" Nothing is so foolish as to believe, or to wish to make us believe, that the Prussians desire to destroy the Jacobins. . . . These same Jacobins ever since the Revolution have never ceased to cry aloud for the rupture of the treaty of 1756, and for the formation of alliances with the House of Brandenbourg (*i.e.* Hohenzollern) and of Hanover, whilst the gazetteers, directed by the Austrian Committee of the Tuileries, have never ceased praising Austria and insulting the Courts of Berlin and La Haye. No, these courts are not so clumsy as to wish to destroy those

[1] Beaulieu, iv. 172.

Jacobins who have *such fortunate ideas for changes of dynasties,* and which, in case of need, can serve considerably the interests of the Houses of Brandenbourg and Hanover against Austria. Do you think the celebrated Duke of Brunswick does not know on what to rely in all this . . . ? He is the greatest warrior and the greatest politician in Europe, the Duke of Brunswick ; he is very well educated, and very amiable ; *he needs perhaps only a crown* to be, I will not say the greatest king in the world, but the true restorer of liberty in Europe. If he arrives in Paris, I wager that his first step will be to come to the Jacobins and put on the ' bonnet rouge.' "

It will be urged that these sentiments were those of only an individual, or of one faction in the Jacobin Club, but how are we to explain the fact that *no protest was raised* by any of the other revolutionary leaders, and that all these so-called patriots remained on the best of terms with the man who would have handed over the country to foreign despotism ? Moreover, when later on a delegate was needed to send to the frontier in order to parley with the Prussians, Carra was one of the emissaries chosen by the leaders. Not till long after were his treasonable pro-posals brought up against him by the Robespierristes, and then only as the means for destroying a rival faction. What con-clusion can we draw from all this but that the Jacobins had an understanding with Brunswick, and that although the plan of offering him the throne was not entertained by all of them, they were all nevertheless interested in remaining on good terms with him until they had overthrown the monarchy and finally usurped the reins of power ?

The Manifesto of Brunswick, which reached Paris three days after the publication of Carra's panegyric on its supposed author, merely served to moderate the ardour of the pro-German party for Brunswick and revive their enthusiasm for a Hanoverian monarch. On August 10 the author of the *Correspondance secrète* writes again :

" The Duke of Brunswick has fallen in the estimation of the Jacobins since his Manifesto ; *they think less of offering him the throne.* Their present system is for a Republic. However, they are waiting to see what form public opinion will take in this respect during the interregnum. They talk again of the Duke of York."

According to the *Mémoires de Barère,* the supporters of this change of dynasty were now Brissot, Pétion, Guadet, Gensonné, and Rabaud de St. Etienne. " On the 17th of July," a deputy of the Legislative Assembly wrote to Barère, " on the staircase of the Commission des Onze, at the Assembly, Brissot said to his associates of the moment : ' I will show you this evening, in my correspondence with the Cabinet of St. James's, that it depends on us to amalgamate our Constitution with that of England by making the Duke of York a constitutional monarch in the place of Louis XVI.' "[1]

As usual, of course, the English Government was used as a cover to the design concerted with the English revolutionaries. Brissot's lie is definitely refuted by the author of the *Correspondance secrète*, who records that the King of England, hearing of this intrigue, wrote to Louis XVI. " to warn him that the Duc d'Orléans was scheming to give the crown of France to the Duke of York with the hand of Mlle. d'Orléans." [2]

These, then, were the intrigues at work amongst the Jacobins, whilst the Prussians and Austrians were assembling on the frontier. Of all the revolutionary legends, the legend of the " patriotic fervour " displayed by the leaders is the most absurd of all ; the menace of foreign invasion served as a pretext for stirring up the people, not against the invaders, but against the King of France. Whilst on the 11th of July the citizens of Paris, in response to the proclamation of " La Patrie en danger," were pouring into the recruiting tents to offer themselves for the defence of the country, revolutionary orators, posted at the street corners, endeavoured to check their ardour. " Unhappy ones ! where are you flying to ? Think of the chiefs under which you must march against the enemy ! Your principal officers are nearly all nobles ; a Lafayette will lead you to butchery ! Ah ! do you not see that beneath the blinds at the Tuileries they are smiling ferociously at your generous but blind enthusiasm ? " [3]

" It is only necessary," says M. Mortimer Ternaux, " to glance through the *Journal de la Société des Amis de la Constitution* (*i.e.* of the Society of Jacobins) to see that at the moment when the National Assembly is devoting all its energies to national defence, the Jacobins only speak of our armies in order to denounce the treachery of the generals, and to excite the soldiers against their officers. *They are much less occupied with the means of defending the frontiers from invasion than in overwhelming the monarchy.*" [4]

THE ARRIVAL OF THE MARSEILLAIS

Amongst the mob orators the supporters of the Duc d'Orléans were the most active. " His creditors," writes Barbaroux, " his

---

[1] *Mémoires de Barère*, ii. 45.
[2] *Correspondance secrète*, p. 614, date of August 10, 1792.
[3] *Révolutions de Paris*, by Prudhomme, xiii. 139.
[4] *Histoire de la Terreur*, by Mortimer Ternaux, ii. 104.

hirelings, his boon companions, Marat and his Cordeliers, all the swindlers, all the men sunk in debt and dishonour, were seen at work in public places, urging the deposition (of the King), greedy of gold and honours, under a regent who would have been their accomplice and their tool." [1]

In order to give a popular air to this clamour for the over-throw of Louis XVI. the usual method of deputations was adopted, and, by way of swelling their numbers, men known as "confederates," from the camp at Soissons, were enlisted in the service of the Jacobins. "These petitions," says Beaulieu, "these incendiary addresses which demanded the head of La-fayette and the extermination of the King, were not the work of these confederates, all these were concocted at the private committee of the Jacobins; they (the confederates) only read them aloud so that the deluded people should believe that the overthrow of the throne was desired by the departments." [2]

At the same time a council, known as the "Committee of Insurrection," was formed, which held most of its sittings at a tavern in Charenton known as "Le Cadran Bleu," and included amongst its leading members Carra, Santerre, the German Westermann, Fournier l'Américain, and the Pole Lazowski.

On the evening of the 26th of July this committee met at the tavern of the "Soleil d'Or," at the entrance of the Faubourg Saint-Antoine, for the purpose of organizing a second march on the Tuileries. Every effort was made to excite the people; placards were displayed ordering them to join the march, and panic news was circulated to the effect that Chabot and Merlin had been assassinated by the *chevaliers du poignard*, and that the Château was arming itself against the citizens. But, although the agitators worked hard all night, the Faubourg on this occasion absolutely declined to rise. In vain, at four o'clock in the morning, the 400 or 500 confederates, whom the leaders had succeeded in collecting, sounded the tocsin and beat the *générale* in Saint-Antoine; only a few inhabitants armed with pikes and guns responded to the summons, whilst Carra, despatched to Saint-Marceau to find out what had happened to prevent the Faubourg arriving on the scene, found the whole quarter wrapped "in the most perfect tranquillity"—that is to say, in slumber.[3]

Throughout the whole of this month the people displayed the same apathy towards the revolutionary movement. "I am convinced," writes a contemporary on the 7th of July, "that our

---

[1] *Mémoires de Barbaroux*, p. 44.

[2] Beaulieu, iii. 409. Note the wording of one of these petitions where the *fédérés* describe themselves as Scaevolas! (Buchez et Roux, xvi. 205).

[3] *Pièces importantes pour l'Histoire*, quoted by Buchez et Roux, xvi. 189-192; Mortimer Ternaux, ii. 129.

sedition-mongers and *enragés* are beginning to be afraid, and all that they do denotes this. They would like to stir up the people to commit excesses, but I doubt whether they will succeed. They will work up the scoundrels under their orders whom they pay, but in general, what can be described as ' the people,' the workmen and *bourgeoisie*, do not think like these gentlemen. They are tired, wearied, and worn out with this wretched revolution, which produces nothing but evils, crimes, disorders, anarchy, and can do no good. . . . I walk about and observe impartially the groups that assemble, and I can assure you that, except for a few fanatics who preach murder and regicide, I can see no general inclination to insurrection." [1]

To the revolutionary leaders likewise it was now clearly evident that the people would never be persuaded to co-operate in the dethronement of Louis XVI. Marat, indeed, had long despaired of them altogether ; the Parisians, he said to Barbaroux, were but " pitiable revolutionaries (*de mesquins révolutionnaires*) "—" give me 200 Neapolitans armed with daggers, and with them I will overrun France and make a revolution." [2] It was a perception of the same truth that in the early days of the Revolution had led the Orléaniste conspirators to send for brigands from the South, and later to enlist Italians in the company of the *Sabbat*. Marat's advice was not lost on Barbaroux. This young lawyer from Marseilles had been discovered by Roland, and introduced to the deputies of the Gironde. It was thus that Barbaroux came to play an active part in the preparations for the 10th of August, and that, acting on the suggestion of Marat, he discussed with Monsieur and Madame Roland the advisability of appealing to the South for aid. The result of these deliberations, Barbaroux relates, was a message to Marseilles asking for " 600 men who knew how to die "—that is to say, 600 men who knew how to kill.

It is evident, however, that the celebrated contingent of 500 who arrived in Paris on the 30th of July, were only a small proportion of the number summoned by the Girondins, for thousands had already arrived in the course of the month. An honest deputy of Marseilles named Blanc-Gilli, seeing these bloodthirsty legions arriving in the capital, thereupon published a letter " to the good citizens of Paris" revealing the identity of the so-called Marseillais :

" The town of Marseilles, situated on the Mediterranean . . .," wrote Blanc-Gilli on the 5th of July, " must be considered on

---

[1] Letter from M. Lefebvre d'Arcy to M. Vanlerberghe in *Lettres d'Aristocrates*, by Pierre de Vaissière, p. 469. See also Ferrières, iii. 153 : " The people of Paris, tired of being continually tossed about, . . . remained in apathetic repose."

[2] *Mémoires de Barbaroux*, p. 57.

account of its port as the sink of vice for a great portion of the globe, where all the impurities of human nature forgather. It is there that we constantly see in fermentation the scum of crime, vomited by the prisons of Genoa, of Piedmont, of Sicily, in fact of all Italy, of Spain, of the Archipelago and of Barbary—deplorable fatality of our geographical position and of our commercial relations. This is the scourge of Marseilles, and the first cause of the frenzy attributed to all its citizens. . . . Every time that the National Guards of Marseilles have set forth on the march outside its walls, the horde of brigands without a country of their own has never failed to throw itself in their wake, and to carry devastation everywhere on their path. . . . Several thousands of these brigands have *for more than a month* been arriving in Paris ; a very large number is still on the road. I have sent numerous warnings to the administration." [1]

Such, then, were the foreign legions that the men who accused Louis XVI. of appealing for aid from abroad saw fit to summon to their own aid for the massacring of their fellow-citizens. The final contingent of 500 that arrived in Paris on the 30th of July, —romantically described by historians as " the brave band of Marseillais," " children of the South and liberty," " singing their national hymn, ' the Marseillaise,' "—included the same men who had carried out the horrible massacre of the Glacière d'Avignon,[2] and were to repeat like atrocities in Paris this September. As to the magnificent melody they had appropriated, it had nothing whatever to do with Marseilles, but had been composed three months earlier at Strasbourg, at the request of the mayor Dietrich, by Rouget de l'Isle, who little dreamt that his " trumpet call to arms against foreign cohorts " would become the war-cry of an alien cohort far more terrible than any gathered on the frontier.[3] It seems, indeed, that the Girondins themselves,

[1] See also *Crimes de la Révolution*, by Prudhomme, vi. 115, and *Mémoires de Hua*, p. 153, note : " This horde of bandits . . . was a collection of foreign adventurers : Genoese, Maltese, Piedmontais, Corsicans, Greeks, vagabonds, having for their principal leaders one named Fournier dit l'Américain and the Pole Lazowski." " Fifty Genoese," says Beaulieu, " were lodged together in the Rue Sainte-Marguerite, Faubourg Saint-Antoine. Many others could be cited ; the most furious revolutionaries, those who committed murders, were to a great extent foreigners, and the famous battalion from Marseilles included a great number of them ; I heard their accent, their bad jargon, and can certify this."

[2] Taine, *La Révolution*, v. 272 ; *Crimes de la Révolution*, by Prudhomme, iv. 96 ; Adolphus, ii. 346.

[3] The mother of Rouget de l'Isle wrote to him at this moment the following words : " What is this revolutionary hymn which is sung by a horde of brigands on their way across France and with which your name is associated ? " Rouget de l'Isle was imprisoned later under the Terror and the mayor Dietrich was guillotined. Thus did the Revolution reward the authors of the " Marseillaise."

seeing the instruments they had summoned to their aid, were overcome with panic, for it was not by Roland or his colleagues that the Marseillais were received, but by Santerre, Danton, and the other leaders of the Orléaniste faction.

" It was the 30th of July," writes Thiébault, " that these hideous confederates, vomited by Marseilles, arrived in Paris. . . . I do not think it would be possible to imagine anything more frightful than these 500 madmen, three-quarters of them drunk, nearly all of them in red caps with bare arms, followed by the dregs of the people, ceaselessly reinforced by the overflow of the Faubourgs Saint-Antoine and Saint-Marceau, and fraternizing in tavern after tavern with bands as fearful as the one they formed. It was in this manner that they processed in ' farandoles ' through the principal streets . . . and boulevards . . . to the Champs Élysées, where the orgy to which they had been bidden by Santerre was preceded by satanic dances." [1]

This orgy was held—evidently with intention—close to a restaurant where about 100 grenadiers of the Filles-Saint-Thomas—the most loyal of all the King's Guards—were holding a regimental dinner. The Marseillais, collecting a crowd of women and children, proceeded to pelt the soldiers with mud and stones, and ended by killing one and wounding several others. The Grenadiers thereupon took refuge in the Tuileries, where the Queen dressed their wounds, and this action was immediately interpreted by the revolutionaries as a plot concerted between the Court and the regiment.[2]

THE DEPOSITION OF THE KING PROPOSED

In vain Louis XVI. implored the factions to unite in face of the peril with which the Manifesto of Brunswick threatened France, to assure them that he was one with his people at this moment of national crisis. " Personal dangers," he wrote to the Assembly, " are nothing compared with public misfortunes. Ah ! what are personal dangers for a king from whom it is desired to take away the love of his people ? That is the sore that rankles in my heart. (*C'est là qu'est la véritable plaie de mon cœur*.) One day perhaps the people will know how dear their welfare is to me, how it has always been my only interest and my greatest need. What grief might be dispelled by the least sign of their returning to me ! "

The response to this appeal was a deputation, headed by Pétion, from the Commune de Paris reiterating the demand for

---

[1] *Mémoires de Thiébault*, i. 296.
[2] Beaulieu, iii. 428.

the dethronement of the King, in which, for want of any better grounds of accusation, Louis XVI. was denounced for " his sanguinary projects against the town of Paris," " the aversion he displayed towards the people," even for his action in the matter of closing the hall of the Assembly on the day of the " Oath of the Tennis Court " three years earlier! But Pétion showed his hand in one significant sentence : " As it is very doubtful that the nation can have confidence *in the existing dynasty*, a provisional government must be established." The words were universally interpreted to signify a change from the Bourbons to the House of Orléans, but they might equally well apply to the proposal for replacing Louis XVI. by a German monarch.

Pétion's speech was followed next day by a resolution forwarded from the revolutionary section of Paris, known as " Mauconseil," likewise demanding the deposition of the King. Forty-seven out of the forty-eight sections of Paris, revolutionary historians assure us, supported this resolution, and in confirmation of their statement they quote the journal of *Carra*![1] As a matter of fact, an examination of the registers of the sections made by M. Mortimer Ternaux reveals the fact that the proposition of Mauconseil was seconded by only fourteen sections of Paris, rejected by sixteen, passed over in silence by ten, whilst the reply of the remaining eight sections is unrecorded.[2] Several sections, indeed, entered very energetic protests at the Assembly, denouncing the efforts made " to divide the citizens of the Empire, to alight civil war, and to substitute the most horrible anarchy for the Constitution. . . ."[3] The astonishing fact is that the petition of Mauconseil was finally annulled as unconstitutional by the Assembly at the proposal of Vergniaud,[4] who only a month earlier had delivered himself of the most violent diatribe against the King.[5] Brissot likewise at this moment

[1] This statement was made by Carra in the *Annales Patriotiques* on the 28th of July before the appeal to the sections had been made, and was therefore a pure invention.

[2] Mortimer Ternaux, ii. 441.

[3] Address from the section of the Arsenal (Buchez et Roux, xvi. 330). See also the protests of the sections of the " Thermes de Jullien " and " Henri IV." (Buchez et Roux, xvi. 374).

Even the fourteen sections who nominally voted their support were far from representative of the wishes of the districts in question, for, as usual, every kind of trickery was employed. A citizen of the section of Mauconseil appeared at the Assembly and declared that " the address of this section for the dethronement of the King had been secured by intrigue and that many of the signatures were forged; he was able even to give names and addresses that had been fraudulently introduced into the petition." (Buchez et Roux, xvi. 344).

[4] Buchez et Roux, xvi. 323.

[5] Séance du 3 Juillet, *Moniteur*, xiii. 32.

displayed a sudden attachment to the monarchy and Constitution, for although on the 9th of July he had formally asked for the deposition of the King, declaring that " to strike down the court of Tuileries was to strike down all traitors at a blow," [1] he came forward on the 25th of July to denounce " that faction of regicides who would create a dictator and establish a Republic." " If that pact of regicides exists," he exclaimed, " if men exist who now seek to establish the Republic on the ruins of the Constitution, the sword of the law should strike at them . . . as at the counter-revolutionaries of Coblentz." [2]

Again, on the following day, Brissot represented to the Assembly that, as the King's collusion with the enemies of France had not been clearly proved, it would be premature to depose him. Moreover, might not the nation have something to say in the matter ?

Brissot only voiced the fear that lurked in the minds of all the revolutionary leaders when he described the possible consequences of overthrowing the monarchy and Constitution. " Do you not see from that moment the gates of the kingdom opened by the French themselves to foreigners ? Do you not see these Frenchmen shaking the hands of these foreigners, and inviting them to join with them in re-establishing their Constitution and maintaining the King on the throne in spite of the efforts of the factions ? " [3] Thus, in the opinion of one of the most prominent revolutionary leaders, *it was not only the Queen and her party who sighed for Brunswick, but many of the French people, who, before the arrival of the Manifesto, would have welcomed even foreign intervention in order to be saved from the intolerable tyranny of the Jacobins.*

What was the explanation of the Girondins' sudden change of front at this crisis ? Simply that they had perceived the revolutionary movement to be passing out of their hands into those of the Cordeliers and Robespierristes, and were ready to accept any measures that would bring their own party back to power.

It would, indeed, be idle to seek a more exalted policy amongst any of the revolutionary factions at this crisis, for none adhered consistently to any definite scheme of government.

" Amidst all this chaos, this general confusion," say the Two Friends of Liberty, " some wanted the deposition of the monarch, others his suspension ; these, that he should let himself be ruled by them, those, that he should give up the crown to his son ; that one of them should be regent, and that all the offices in the State should be reserved for them. A great number called

---

[1] *Moniteur*, xiii. 86. [2] *Ibid.* xiii. 242.
[3] *Ibid.* xiii. 279.

the Duc d'Orléans to the throne, some thought of a foreign prince, and seven or eight people of a republic." [1]

This wild medley of plans explains the fact that members of each faction in turn became alarmed, and at the last moment, before the monarchy was overthrown, secretly offered their services to the King. In the whirlpool that threatened to engulf them all none knew who would sink and who would swim, and so, struck with panic, they turned and clung to the ark of the Constitution that contained the King and that, as they all knew, was borne on that mighty tide—*the will of the people.*

It was thus that, at the eleventh hour, Brissot, Vergniaud, and Gensonné, through an intermediary, the painter Boze, warned the King of the impending insurrection, and undertook to quell it if the Girondin ministers were recalled and the decrees they had proposed sanctioned by the King.[2] Louis XVI. rejected this proposal, and so his "deposition was irrevocably decreed by those who had just declared that the salvation of France lay in the Constitution." [3]

Robespierre also at this juncture continued to defend the Constitution ; his colleague, the retired comedian, Collot d'Herbois, repeated incessantly : " Ah ! if the King were really a patriot he would choose his ministers and his agents among the Jacobins." But Louis XVI. distrusted this faction likewise, and so " these men obtaining nothing in one direction turned to the other and proclaimed themselves Republicans whilst becoming Anarchists."[4]

Meanwhile the Cordeliers, the principal instigators of the insurrection, were prepared to go to far greater extremities to save the King, provided they were sufficiently compensated for the enterprise. " Marat," says Barbaroux, " sent me, towards the end of July, a document of several pages, which he asked me to have printed and distributed to the Marseillais at the moment of their arrival. . . . The work seemed to me abominable, it was a provocation to the Marseillais to fall upon the Legislative Assembly. *The Royal Family*, it said, *must be safeguarded*, but the Assembly, evidently anti-revolutionary, exterminated."[5]

This statement of Barbaroux' is confirmed by Michaud, who relates that only a few days later—at the beginning of August—another Cordelier, Fabre d'Églantine, the friend and confidant of Danton, made precisely the same proposal to M. Dubouchage, the Minister of the Navy, with whom he had obtained an interview

---

[1] *Deux Amis*, viii. 94.

[2] *Crimes de la Révolution*, by Prudhomme, iv. 213 ; *Mémoires de Hua*, p. 141. Boze was arrested for this by order of Tallien on January 3, 1793 (*La Demagogie à Paris en 1793*, by C. A. Dauban, p. 8).

[3] Beaulieu, iii. 408.

[4] *Crimes de la Révolution*, by Prudhomme, iv. 212.

[5] *Mémoires de Barbaroux*, p. 60.

by writing several times to the King. Fabre d'Églantine presented himself at the rendezvous, and " after great protestations of interest and zeal for the King, of esteem and admiration for the true Royalists, entered into great details on the plots that were being formed against the Château of the Tuileries and on the dangers that surrounded the Royal Family. In consequence he proposed a plan which, he said, would be infallible, and would restore to Louis XVI. his former authority. This plan was to bribe the gunners and the leaders of sedition of whom he was sure, and then to fall on the Jacobins and the Assembly in force, and thus deliver France from its greatest enemies. For the execution of this plan he asked for the sum of three millions. M. Douchage rendered an account of this conference to the King, who was horrified by the violent measures proposed. . . ." Beaulieu adds : " Other propositions of this kind were made to Louis XVI. and the Queen, at the moment when they both knew for certain that the insurrection was about to break forth, and by people in whom they could have confidence ; they rejected them with horror, unable to endure the thought of seeing the innocent sacrificed with the guilty, and these men whom they had spared when they could have annihilated them described them as ' monsters, tigers, and cannibals.' " [1]

But, whilst unwilling to accede to the sanguinary suggestions of the Cordeliers, Louis XVI., realizing that greed for gold was at the bottom of most of their revolutionary frenzy, resolved once again to conciliate them with gifts of money. A week before the 10th of August Danton received the sum of 50,000 écus, and the Court, convinced that this time the great demagogue would be true to his bargain, felt no further apprehension. " Our minds are at rest," said Madame Elizabeth, " we can count on Danton." But the Court had miscalculated on the sum required. Danton pocketed the money and betrayed the King.[2]

The fact is that the Court was now too poor to buy partisans amongst the factions, who saw in the impending upheaval far greater opportunities of enrichment. " Alas ! " even the revolutionary Prudhomme is obliged to admit, " how many pretended Republicans would have been furious Royalists if the Court had been inclined to win them over, and had had enough money to pay them ! But it had not enough for all who asked, all who aspired. The Legislative Assembly was full of men of this kind, Royalists or Republicans, according to the way the wind blew, and it must be said, although to the shame of the Revolution, that these were the elements of the 10th of

[1] Beaulieu, iv. 17.
[2] *Mémoires de Lafayette*, iii. 85 ; *Mémoires de Hua*, p. 149.

August, during which *the people alone were disinterested and of good faith."* [1]

That Danton was the principal organizer of the 10th of August cannot be doubted. Towards the end of July Prudhomme relates that he received a visit from Danton, Camille Desmoulins, and Fabre d'Églantine. Danton said, "in the trivial language habitual to him " :

" We have come, *petit jean-foutre,* to consult you as an old patriot, although you are no longer up to the mark ; but as you have often foreseen events and their results, we want your opinion on a plan of insurrection."

Prudhomme inquired in what this plan consisted.

" We wish to overthrow the tyrant," answered Danton.

" Which one ? "

" The one at the Tuileries. This b—— of a Revolution has brought nothing to patriots."

" That is to say, messieurs, that you wish to make your fortunes in the name of liberty and equality. How do you think of overthrowing the monarchy ? "

" By assault."

Prudhomme urged the temerity of the proposal. " Your plan," he said, " is the work of a coterie of Jacobins and Cordeliers. You do not know the intentions of the inhabitants of Paris, or of the majority of those in the departments."

Fabre d'Églantine said, " We have the promise of a hundred deputies, Girondins and Brissotins and agents in all the popular societies of France."

" You wish to overthrow the monarch," Prudhomme answered. " Whom will you put in his place ? "

" The Duc d'Orléans," blurted out that *enfant terrible,* Camille Desmoulins.

But Danton hastily interposed :

" We will see afterwards what we will do. In revolutions as on the field of battle one must never look forward to the morrow. I undertake to stir up the *canaille* of the Faubourgs Saint-Antoine and Saint - Marceau. The Marseillais will be at their head—they have not come to Paris for plums." [2]

But even the *canaille* needed some incentive to rise, and just now none was forthcoming. It was in a mood of desperation inspired by these reflections that the deputy Chabot one day cried out incontrollably, " If only the Court would try to murder somebody ! " An attempt on the life of a " patriotic " deputy,

[1] *Crimes de la Révolution,* iv. 216.

[2] *Histoire des Causes de la Révolution Française,* by Granier de Cassagnac, iii. 456; *Journal d'un Bourgeois de Paris,* by Edmond Bire, i. 290.

he declared to Grangeneuve, would prove an invaluable pretext for stirring up the people. Unfortunately the Court displayed no intention of carrying out this scheme, but Chabot and Grangeneuve were not to be baffled by so trifling an obstacle. In a fit of " patriotic " fervour these two Tartarins thereupon decided *to have themselves murdered,* in order to provide an accusation against the Court. Chabot undertook to engage assassins who were to waylay and shoot them at the street corner. But on the night appointed Chabot seems to have thought better of the scheme, for neither he nor the assassins were forthcoming, and Grangeneuve, having made his will and waited about a long while to be murdered, returned home indignant to find himself alive.[1]

Thus deprived of any shadow of a pretext for marching a second time on the Tuileries, the leaders were obliged to invent one, and in order to persuade the people to attack the Château it was loudly proclaimed that the Château was about to attack the people—" 15,000 aristocrats are ready to massacre all the patriots." [2] But in spite of these alarms Paris remained sunk in lethargy. Still, on the evening of the 9th of August, all means had failed to rouse the great mass of the population. So the revolutionary leaders took the law into their own hands, and on this fateful night the terrible council of the " Commune," known as the " Conseil Général Révolutionnaire du 10 Août," came into being.

THE NIGHT OF THE 9TH OF AUGUST

The agitators of the Faubourg Saint-Antoine had at first met at the section of the Quinze Vingt in their own district, but finding their efforts to make this the centre of agitation abortive, they issued an appeal at eleven o'clock in the evening to the other forty-seven sections of Paris, asking them each to send their representatives to co-operate in the proposed insurrection with the Commune at the Town Hall.

A great number of sections failed to respond to this appeal ; some indeed protested energetically against the attempt to disturb the peace, whereupon the leaders had recourse to their usual methods of fraud and violence. " As soon as night draws on," says Beaulieu, " the revolutionaries, whose rôles had been prepared beforehand, go out into all the sections (*i.e.* the halls of the districts) which the peaceful bourgeois had abandoned, either in order to present themselves at the guard-house, or to return to their homes and give themselves up to rest. The revolutionaries, having thus made themselves masters of the debates, declare

[1] *Mémoires de Mme. Roland,* i. 157 ; *Mémoires du Chancelier Pasquier,* p. 81.

[2] Ferrières, iii. 204 ; Robespierre, *Défenseur de la Constitution,* No. 12.

themselves the sovereign people, usurp their rights, and decree that all constituted authority is in abeyance. This resolution being taken and communicated to each other, the revolutionary sections ring the tocsin in all the churches of Paris ; this alarm heard in the middle of the night strikes terror into all hearts. . . ." [1]

By methods such as these even sections that had protested against the plan of insurrection were represented as sending delegates to co-operate with the movement,[2] and so, although twenty sections still remained unrepresented,[3] it was possible to declare that the majority of the sections had responded to the appeal.

In this way the insurrectional Commune was formed. Prud-homme, at that date in the secret of the leaders, afterwards described the process in these illuminating words :

" On the eve of the famous day (the 10th of August) the confederates, towards ten o'clock in the evening, assemble to the number of twenty or thirty, and at once on their own initiative name new members without even collecting the wishes of the majority of the sections. This choice being made, the nominees, or rather the conspirators, arrange to meet at the Commune. They present themselves armed with the power to replace the magistrates then sitting. These hesitate a moment and are secretly threatened ; they give up their seats and all go out with the exception of Pétion and Manuel, who are retained. All this was arranged in the secret meetings (conciliabules) which had been held at the Palais Royal or the Rapée, where D'Orléans, Danton, Marat, Pétion, Robespierre, and others were to be found. . . . Paris changed magistrates without knowing it, and the insurrection took place . . . without any obstacle ; one would have supposed that every one was in accord." [4]

But with these secret confabulations the rôle of the leaders ended. As usual, when the hour of danger struck, those bold

---

[1] Beaulieu, iii. 448. This manœuvre is described in almost the same words by Montjoie, Conjuration de d'Orléans, iii. 189. See also the Histoire de la Conspiration du 10 Août, by Bigot de Sainte-Croix, p. 21, and the Révolution du 10 Août, by Peltier, i. 73 : " The fatal hour strikes, the tocsin makes itself heard, the générale is sounded, 300 rebels assemble the sham sections. All the citizens were with their battalions. At the section of the Lombards only eight people are to be found to name five commissioners." The researches of Mortimer Ternaux confirm these statements : " At the Arsenal six people who happen to be in the hall of the committee name three amongst them to represent 1400 ' active citizens ' (i.e. citizens who had the right to vote). Things happen much in the same way at the Louvre, the Observatoire, and the Roi de Sicile " (Histoire de la Terreur, ii. 234).

[2] For example, the sections of Montreuil, the Roi de Sicile, the Invalides and Sainte-Geneviève (Mortimer Ternaux, ii. 427, 431, 434, 437).

[3] Buchez et Roux, xvi. 423 ; Mortimer Ternaux, ii. 240, 444.

[4] Crimes de la Révolution, by Prudhomme, iv. 73.

patriots, Danton, Marat, Robespierre, and Camille Desmoulins, retired into hiding. On the eve of this second attack on the Tuileries, Marat, overcome with panic, had implored Barbaroux to smuggle him out of Paris disguised as a jockey,[1] and on Barbaroux's refusal betook himself once more to his cellar,[2] a course likewise adopted by Robespierre.[3] As to Camille Desmoulins and Danton, the journal of Madame Desmoulins reveals that they spent most of this night, whilst the insurrection was preparing, asleep at Danton's house. Just as the tocsin was about to ring, Danton, always prone to slumber, retreated into his bed, from which snug ambush the emissaries of the Commune had some difficulty in dislodging him, and even then he was soon back again, and still sleeping peacefully whilst the mob was marching on the Tuileries.

It was therefore again on this occasion the professional agitators who were left to carry out the plans of the leaders, and for a time it seemed that their efforts were to be rewarded with no success, for the Faubourgs still showed themselves recalcitrant, and as late as 2.30 in the morning of the 10th news was brought to Roederer at the Château that the insurrection would not take place. But at last, towards dawn, the revolutionary army began to muster. Santerre gathered round him the brigands of the Faubourg Saint-Antoine ; Lazowski and Alexandre enlisted a following in Saint-Marceau, and Barbaroux and Fournier led forth the Marseillais.

Meanwhile the Tuileries was preparing its plans of defence. The Marquis de Mandat, commander of the National Guard, warned of the impending insurrection, had sounded the call to arms, and all night his battalions streamed to the Château, where they took up their stand in the courtyards on the Carrousel and the terraces bordering the river and the garden. These battalions, sixteen in all, made up a total of 2400 men, whilst in the Château itself were 950 Swiss and 200 nobles armed with swords and pistols.

As on the 20th of June, the Château was therefore well defended ; moreover, the troops were this time commanded by no feeble Ramainvilliers, but by a leader who could be depended on to offer a vigorous resistance. Mandat, the revolutionary leaders well knew, was loyal to the King and, as Pétion, combining the rôle of spy with that of mayor of Paris, discovered on

---

[1] Marat wrote three times to Barbaroux on this subject. " On the evening of the 9th," says Barbaroux, " he informed me that nothing was more urgent, and again proposed to me that he should disguise himself as a jockey " (*Mémoires de Barbaroux*, pp. 61, 62).

[2] Mortimer Ternaux, ii. 241. See also Marat's placard issued from his " subterranean retreat " (*Marat*, by A. Bougeart, ii. 36).

[3] Ferrières, iii. 201 ; Barbaroux, p. 82 ; Maton de la Varenne, p. 228.

his wanderings round the Château, really had a plan of campaign. Therefore Mandat must be disposed of.

Accordingly, at seven o'clock in the morning, Mandat was summoned to the Hôtel de Ville, and ordered to give an account of his conduct in organizing the defences of the Château. Mandat replied that he had acted on the order of Pétion to resist attack by force. But all explanations were useless ; Mandat had been sent for to be murdered, not to be judged. Huguenin, the " orator " of June 20, now President of the Commune, with a horizontal gesture across his throat, said, " Let him be led away." Mandat was taken out, and half an hour later, on his way down the steps of the Hôtel de Ville to the prison of the Abbaye, a young man named Rossignol, employed by Danton,[1] approached and shot him through the head. Needless to say, this foul deed was ascribed by Pétion to the people.[2] Pétion himself had a personal reason for desiring the death of Mandat, and undoubtedly acted in collusion with Danton, for the order to resist attack by force had really been given by him to Mandat three days earlier in writing, and it was apparently in order to abstract this compromising document from his pocket that Mandat was assassinated.[3] Pétion's precise object in writing it is not clearly evident ; possibly, as Montjoie suggests, it was for the sake of giving a pretext to the Marseillais for firing at the troops, but it may also be accounted for by the fact that Pétion had received a large sum of money from the King just before the 10th of August to maintain order,[4] and for a moment he may have intended to earn his payment honestly. But when he saw that the insurrection was assuming formidable proportions, he was overcome with panic, and resolved to destroy the written evidence of his momentary defection from the revolutionary cause. At any rate, he now did everything in his power to assist the movement. So although, as head of the municipality, he refused during this night to supply the forces at the Tuileries with ammunition for the defence of the Château, he contrived that 5000 ball cartridges should be issued to the Marseillais. Pétion had also arranged with Carra that if the insurrection broke out he should be forcibly prevented from opposing it by a summons to the Town Hall, where he was to be detained during the attack on the Château. Carra omitted to do this, and Pétion

---

[1] Danton admitted this in his trial : " I drew up the death-warrant of Mandat who had been ordered to fire on the people." See *Notes de Topino Lebrun sur le procès de Danton.*

[2] *Récit du 10 Août par Pétion, maire de Paris.*

[3] Peltier, *Révolution du 10 Août*, i. 83, 84 ; Montjoie, *Conjuration de d'Orléans*, iii. 197 ; *Journal of Dr. John Moore*, i. 151.

[4] *Mémoires de Mme. Campan*, p. 342 ; *Mémoires de Malouet*, ii. 141.

spent a very uncomfortable hour or two waiting about in the garden of the Tuileries, shadowed by several loyal grenadiers who shrewdly suspected his perfidy. When the expected summons still failed to arrive he finally adopted the ingenious expedient of sending repeated orders to himself, and in response to these he left his post at 2.30, and after presenting himself at the Assembly placed himself under restraint in his own quarters at the Town Hall with a guard of 400 men to prevent him returning to duty.[1]

So through the basest treachery the Château was disarmed before its assailants. By the death of Mandat, as the conspirators had anticipated, all the plans for defence were disorganized, and the forces assembled at the Tuileries left without a leader.

THE 10TH OF AUGUST

The King and Queen well knew the fate that in all probability awaited them. Twice already since the 20th of June the Queen had narrowly escaped assassination—once at the Champ de Mars on the 14th of July, once at midnight when the murderer was arrested on the threshold of her apartment—and all through these weeks, says Montjoie, Louis XVI. had slept in his clothes ready to rise at the first alarm.

Now, as the sinister knell of the tocsin rang out over the city, the Queen sat weeping silently ; the King paced the great rooms of the Château striving to decide on the course of action to pursue. The troops, he knew, could offer a vigorous resistance to assault, but this meant bloodshed, and again the old question that at every crisis of the Revolution had tortured him arose in his mind : " Was a king justified in shedding the blood of his people in his own defence ? " Royalists said yes ; believers in the "sovereignty of the people" said no ; moreover the King's own conscience said no likewise.

This dilemma produced in Louis XVI. an agony of irresolution that could never have afflicted any of his predecessors. Henry IV., for all his benevolence, would have buckled on his sword, mounted his charger, and shown himself to his troops as their sovereign chief, and undoubtedly, if Louis XVI. had done

---

[1] See Pétion's own naïve account of this manœuvre in reply to Robespierre's accusation later on that he had not contributed to the 10th of August : " To reconcile my official position as mayor with my fixed resolution to forward the movement, it had been arranged that I should be arrested, so as not to be able to oppose any legal authority to it ; but in the hurry and agitation of the moment this was forgotten . . . Who do you think sent several times to urge the execution of this plan ? It was I, yes, I myself ; because as soon as I knew that the movement was general, far from thinking of arresting it I was resolved to facilitate it " (*Observations de J. Pétion sur la Lettre de Robespierre*).

this, even Barbaroux admits the day would have been won, for "the great majority of the battalions had declared themselves for him."

It seems that in the end the King, yielding to the entreaties of the Royalists, decided that the Château should be defended by force of arms, but this, to him a terrible decision, was reached only by hours of mental conflict. When at half-past five on the morning of the 10th he came forth from his apartments to inspect the troops, his defenders saw with dismay that the sang-froid which had saved him on the 20th of June was no longer at his command—*his nerve was gone.*

This was not the result of cowardice ; the hardest rider, the boldest airman, may find himself suddenly, as the result of continuous exposure to danger, the victim of nerve failure, and Louis XVI., as we know, was subject to such attacks under the influence of acute mental strain. From the accounts of all eye-witnesses it is evident that at this supreme moment the King was suffering from a return of the malady that had afflicted him three months earlier, and that now deprived him of all the energy he needed wherewith to meet the crisis. Above the violet of his coat his face showed white as death, his eyes were wet with tears, his powdered hair disordered—" he looked," says Madame Campan, " as if he had ceased to exist."

The effect on the troops was, of course, deplorable. Up to this moment their enthusiasm had remained at boiling-point, and as the King passed on his way " all the vaulted ceilings of the palace rang to the cries of ' Vive le Roi ! ' ' No, Sire,' cried the troops, ' do not fear a recurrence of the 20th of June, we will wipe out that stain ; the last drop of our blood belongs to your Majesty ! ' " [1] When the King came down into the courtyards loud cheers burst from every company of the National Guards : " Vive le Roi ! Vive Louis XVI. ! Long live the King of the Constitution ! We wish for him ! We wish for no other ! Let him put himself at our head and we will defend him to death ! " [2]

If only he had put himself at their head ! If only he could have found ringing tones in which to respond to these acclamations, have summoned smiles to his lips, and so won all hearts finally to his cause ! But it seems that Louis XVI., more than ever inarticulate under the stress of great emotion, cast a chill over the spirits of the men, and as the cries of " Vive le Roi ! " died down voices were heard to answer with " Vive la nation ! "

On the other side of the Château the situation assumed a more threatening aspect, for at the moment that the King entered the garden the advance-guard of the revolutionary army,

---

[1] *Histoire de la Conspiration du 10 Août*, by Bigot de Sainte-Croix, p. 40.
[2] *Procès verbal de J. J. Leroux, officier municipal.*

armed with pikes, arrived on the scene from the Faubourg Saint-Marceau, and as they filed past overwhelmed him with insults. By some strange mismanagement this revolutionary battalion was allowed to take up its stand amongst the other troops ; inevitably the spirit of insurrection spread, and when the King returned to the Château along the terrace bordering the river, angry cries were raised : " Down with the King ! Long live the Sans-Culottes ! " and other invectives of a grosser kind—only a dozen voices in all, yet loud enough to be heard in the Château.[1]

The sinister murmurs reached the ears of the Queen. M. Dubouchage rushing to the window cried out in horror, " Good God ! It is the King they are hooting ! What the devil is he doing there ? Let us go down and find him." The Queen burst into tears. " All is lost," she said, when a moment later the King returned pale and breathless, " this review has done more harm than good."

All indeed was lost. News had now arrived that Mandat had been either killed or arrested, that " all Paris " was on foot, and that the Faubourgs had assembled and were marching on the Château with their cannons. Then the Royalists who had collected in the palace knew that the moment had come to rally round the King, and M. d'Hervilly, a drawn sword in his hand, ordered the usher to open the doors to " the French nobility ! "

But where were the " 15,000 aristocrats " the revolutionaries declared to be concealed in the Château ? Where were the bloodthirsty *chevaliers du poignard* who were to execute a new massacre of St. Barthélemy at the bidding of Antoinette Médicis ? Nothing further from this description could be imagined than the strange procession that now streamed into the room led by the old Maréchal de Mailly, aged eighty-six, and composed of two to three hundred men and boys, many with no pretensions to " nobility," but " ennobled by their devotion " to a lost cause.[2] Few had been able to procure guns, and the greater number were armed only with swords or pistols, or with hastily improvised weapons they had seized on their passage—a squire and page had divided a pair of fire-tongs between them. Always, throughout the whole Revolution, the same unpreparedness, the same hopeless lack of design on the part of the Old Order, and on the other side foresight, method, superb organization ! Surely a warning to all ages that courage and devotion may prove unavailing before calculating cowardice and organized malevolence ? If bravery could have won the day on this 10th of August the Château must have triumphed. The Queen, now that the danger was actually at the gates, dried her tears, and resolved that,

---

[1] *Procès verbal de J. J. Leroux, officier municipal.*
[2] *Mémoires de Mme. Campan, p.* 348.

since the King could inspire no enthusiasm in his defenders, she herself would take up his rôle. When some of the National Guards murmured at the intrusion of the " nobility," which they regarded as a slur on their own ability to defend the Royal Family, Marie Antoinette begged them to be reconciled. " They are our best friends," she said; " they will share the dangers of the National Guards, they will obey you," and turning to some grenadiers standing near she added : " Messieurs, remember that all you hold most dear, your wives, your children, your property, depends on our existence; our interest is one; you must not have the least distrust of these brave people, who will defend you to their last breath."

According to Beaulieu, these words had the result of promoting a complete understanding between the two parties of the King's defenders, and all now stood together, resolved to resist attack by force of arms.

Meanwhile an order to the same effect was given by the attorney-general, Roederer,[1] and the municipal officer, Leroux, to the troops surrounding the Château, but in so half-hearted a manner as only to increase the audacity of the insurgents ; the gunners defiantly replied by unloading their cannons, and a deputation of seven or eight citizens came forward to demand the deposition of the King. The two magistrates thereupon decided that resistance was useless, and that the King must be persuaded to leave the Château with his family, and take refuge in the hall of the National Assembly. Leroux accordingly returned to the royal apartments and presented himself to the King, who was in his bedroom surrounded by his family and several ministers. The danger, said Leroux, was now at its height, the National Guards had been corrupted, and the King and Queen, with their children and entourage, would all be massacred if they remained at the Château.

Marie Antoinette had always held that " a king should die on his throne," and cried out indignantly that she would rather be nailed to the walls of the Château than leave it; but Louis XVI., ever anxious to avoid bloodshed, seemed not unwilling to consider the proposal. Seeing this the Queen seized his hand and, raising it to her eyes, covered it with tears.[2] Roederer, arriving a

[1] Roederer, whose *Chronique des Cinquante Jours* contains the most detailed account of June 20 and August 10, is a far from unbiassed witness, for his sympathies are all with the authors of these days. Croker during Roederer's lifetime frankly accused him of Orléanism : " M. Roederer—a courtier of the son of Égalité—will not *now* be offended at our saying that we have always considered him as of the Orléans party, to which Brissot and others of the Gironde originally belonged. . . ." (*Essays on the French Revolution*, p. 211).

[2] *Déclaration de Leroux.*

moment later, added his entreaties to those of Leroux, and to the repeated protests of the Queen replied, " You wish then, Madame, to make yourself responsible for the death of the King, of your own son, of your daughter, of yourself, and of all those who would defend you."

And at the mention of her children the Queen, touched in her most vulnerable spot, surrendered.

The King looked at her with tears in his eyes, rose from his seat, and said, " Allons, marchons."

His family gathered round him.

" Monsieur Roederer," said Madame Elizabeth, " will you answer for the King's life ? "

" Yes, madame, on my own."

But when, a moment later, the Queen repeated the question, " Will you answer for the King's life and for that of my son ? " Roederer responded gloomily, " Madame, we will answer for dying at your side, that is all that we can promise."

At Roederer's earnest request none of the Court was allowed to escort the Royal Family to the Assembly, and the King, obviously with the intention of signifying that they were now free to depart, turned to his nobles with the words, " Come, messieurs, there is nothing more to be done here either for you or me."

But at the foot of the staircase, overcome with misgivings for their safety, he paused, and looking back at his faithful defenders he said to Roederer, " But what will become of them all ? "

" Sire," answered Roederer, " it seemed to me that they were in coloured coats (*i.e.* not in uniform) ; those who have swords need only take them off and follow you, going out by the garden." Yet after this assurance, and although it was at Roederer's own request that the King left the Château and that the nobles did not escort him, Roederer allowed it to be said by his friend Pétion, without contradiction, that the King, " with complete sang-froid, left his satellites in the Château to be butchered." [1]

The Royalists, it is true, were indignant at his departure ; they were all prepared to fight for him, and believed that if he had held his ground and remorselessly ordered the Swiss to fire on the mob, the day would have been won. From the point

---

[1] This lie was repeated by Danton with additions a week later— " whilst his oldest courtiers shielded with their bodies the door of his room *where they believed him to be,* he (Louis XVI.) fled *by a back door* with his family to the National Assembly . . ." ("Lettre de Danton aux Tribunaux," August 18, 1792, published in Buchez et Roux, xvii. 294). Louis XVI. and his family, as everybody knew, left the Château publicly by the main staircase whilst all the courtiers looked on. See, besides the above account by Roederer, the *Mémoires de Mme. Campan,* p. 350.

of view of believers in despotism, the King was guilty therefore of criminal weakness, but for the advocates of democracy to blame him is monstrous. He left the Château solely to avoid bloodshed.

It must be remembered that the attack on the Château had not yet begun, and did not begin until about an hour after the King had left it, and he not unnaturally imagined that since it was against himself the movement was directed, his departure would remove all *cause de guerre* ; he could not possibly foresee that the revolutionary leaders would be guilty of such inconceivable cowardice as to wreak their vengeance on the unfortunate Swiss Guards—most of them men of the people who were only doing their duty by remaining at their posts. According to Montjoie, the King, on leaving the Château, gave strict orders to the Swiss not to fire on the insurgents, and to offer no resistance whatever happened, thereby depriving the Marseillais of any pretext for aggression, and, whether Montjoie is right or not, this, as we shall see, was precisely the course the Swiss pursued.

The King, satisfied therefore that no hostilities could now take place, led the way to the Assembly. The Queen followed with Madame de Tourzel, each holding a hand of the Dauphin ; Madame Elizabeth with Madame Royale, and the Princesse de Lamballe walked behind them with one of the ministers. An escort, formed of 150 Swiss and 300 National Guards, marched in line on either side of the Royal Family.

In the freshness of the glorious August morning the tragic procession made its way, first down the great central alley of the Tuileries garden, with its cool fountains and blazing flower-beds, then to the right under the shade of the ancient chestnut trees, from which, in the heat of this tropical summer, the leaves had already begun to flutter down on to the pathway, where the gardeners, unmoved by the fall of dynasties, were employed in sweeping them tidily into heaps. Perhaps it was the sudden recall to the normal facts of life produced by this circumstance that prompted the King's memorable remark, " The leaves are falling early this year."

But at the Porte des Feuillants grim realities reasserted themselves. Outside the gateway a crowd of men and women, evidently animated by hostile intentions, were waiting, and it was precisely at this moment, when the Royal Family most needed protection, that Roederer elected to deprive them of their military escort on the ridiculous pretext that the terrace of the Feuillants was the property of the National Assembly. Whether, therefore, by the official stupidity or the deliberate treachery of Roederer, the Royal Family was obliged to go forward into the midst of the crowd escorted only by a few deputies of the Assembly who now came to meet them. Instantly the horde of ruffians surged forward howling execrations. " No, no, they shall not enter the Assembly, they are the cause of all our troubles ! Down with them ! Down !" As usual, it was against the Queen that their fury was principally directed, and now, pressing closely around her, they snatched her watch and purse, overwhelming her the while with insults. A man of enormous height and " atrocious countenance " seized the Dauphin from his mother, but at the Queen's cry of terror said reassuringly, " Do not be afraid. I will do him no harm." And a passage through the crowd being at last cleared, he carried the boy in his arms to the Assembly.

The Royal Family entered the hall. " Messieurs," said Louis XVI., addressing the Assembly, " I have come here to prevent a great crime, and I think I cannot be more in safety than amongst you, messieurs."

Alas ! the King had not prevented crimes from taking place on that terrible day. The vengeance of the leaders was not directed only against the King and Royal Family ; other victims had been singled out, and nothing the unfortunate Louis XVI. could have done or said would have availed to slake their thirst for blood. Even as the King uttered these words three heads were carried on pikes past the door of the Assembly.

As usual in the revolutionary outbreaks, the mob collected at the Porte des Feuillants had not come forward spontaneously to insult the Royal Family. The emissaries of the Duc d'Orléans were behind the movement.[1] It was they who told the people that the Royal Family must not be allowed to take refuge with the Assembly, and it was they who drove the mob to carry out the first proscriptions on the list they had drawn up for the day.

Of all the enemies that the Duc d'Orléans had made for himself during his revolutionary career, none was so violent or so unrelenting as the journalist Suleau. François Louis Suleau was no aristocrat, but the son of a cloth-maker, and he had thrown himself into the counter-revolutionary movement with all the ardour usually to be found only in the opposing camp.

" A vigorous mind, always giving vent to witty sallies and bursts of boisterous laughter, with an unbridled but infectious gaiety . . . a Meridional of the North, loving danger for danger's sake . . . the joyous champion of lost causes . . . mocking at a revolution," [2] Suleau had all the makings of a rebel, and at the outbreak of the Revolution had marched in the vanguard of

[1] Ferrières, iii. 189.   [2] Article on Suleau by L. Meister.

insurrection.   But before long his fierce love of justice drew
him over to the cause of the King, in whom he recognized the
one hope of liberty for France, and in his far from respectful
Petit Mot à Louis XVI. 'he frankly declared his reason for
this allegiance : " If the good of humanity and the salvation of
my country did not happen to be identified with the interests of
your glory, you would find me amongst the most intrepid in
proving to you that I am a man and a citizen before I am your
subject." It was because he hated fraud and imposture, because
he dreaded the misfortunes which the usurpation of the throne
by the Duc d'Orléans would have brought on France, that from
August of 1789 he had devoted all his talents, all his wit and
untiring energy, to fighting the Orléaniste conspiracy.   Careless
of the consequences, perpetually menaced with assassination,
Suleau had continued with his pen to attack the duke—" he had
outraged him, threatened him, defied him in every way, before
the tribunals and the justice of men, and before the judgement
of God." [1]

Naturally, Suleau's name had long been on the list of proscriptions drawn up by the Orléanistes.   Two days before the
10th of August, Camille Desmoulins, his old college friend, who
had remained attached to him in spite of the fact that they were
now political antagonists, warned him that his head was one of
the first marked down by the leaders of the insurrection, and
offered him a refuge in his own house.   Suleau refused to com-
promise his friend, and went forward boldly to meet his fate—
the sacrifice of his life, he said, had long since been made.   At
eight o'clock in the morning of the 10th of August, Suleau, who
had spent the night in the Tuileries, came out on to the Terrasse
des Feuillants where the crowd, set in motion by the Orléanistes,
had assembled.   His handsome appearance, his fresh attire and
glittering sword attracted attention, and he was arrested on the
pretext that he formed part of a false patrol.   Suleau proved his
innocence and was liberated, but the Orléanistes had this time
made sure of their victim.   In the Cour des Feuillants Théroigne
de Méricourt was waiting for him—Théroigne at the very height
of revolutionary frenzy.   The little Belgian had a private vengeance to execute in attacking Suleau, for the witty journalist, in
his campaign against the Orléaniste conspiracy, had frequently
made Théroigne the butt of his pleasantries, and it was not only
as a partisan of the duke, but as a woman outraged in her vanity
and even in her prudery—for *fille de joie* though she was, Théroigne
could endure no imputations on her " virtue "—that she longed
to plunge her dagger into the heart of her persecutor.   Yet it
would be absurd to accept the view of M. Louis Blanc that

[1] *Philippe d'Orléans Égalité*, by Auguste Ducoin, p. 170.

Théroigne was acting independently on this occasion, for it was always as an agent of the Duc d'Orléans that she had figured in the revolutionary movement, it was as an Orléaniste that she had incurred the animosity of Robespierre and Collot d'Herbois,[1] and since, as we have seen, it was the Orléanistes who had planned the death of Suleau, it was obviously at their bidding that she carried out the design. Her personal rancour merely lent a sharper edge to her fury, which at this crisis reached a pitch bordering on the insanity that was later on to become chronic. Théroigne, on the morning of this 10th of August, was nearly as mad as the enraged hyena that afterwards bore her name in the Salpétrière, but this madness that was to rob her of all semblance to a human being gave her to-day a kind of diabolical beauty which amazed all beholders. Dressed in a blue riding-habit, wearing on her head a feathered hat *à la Henri IV.*, with a pair of pistols and a dagger in her belt, the little creature seemed suddenly to have recovered her lost youth, for her face, haggard in repose, was now lit by an inward fire that glowed in her dark skin, and flamed forth from her eyes obliterating the ravages of ill-spent years. Thiébault, meeting her at this moment, took her to be only twenty—no woman, he wrote long afterwards, had ever made such an impression on him : " I say, with a sort of horror, that she was pretty, very pretty, her excitement enhanced her beauty . . . for she was in the throes of revolutionary hysteria impossible to describe."

Forcing a passage through the crowd in the Cour des Feuillants with the cry of " Make way ! Make way ! " Théroigne sprang on to a cannon and shouted, " How long will you allow yourselves to be misled with vain words ? " Playing on the passions of the mob she urged them to violence. " Where is Suleau— the Abbé Suleau ? " she cried, for she had never seen her enemy and imagined him to be a priest.

Then Suleau saw his death had been resolved on, and, hoping by the sacrifice of his life to avoid further bloodshed, said to the National Guards around him, " I see that to-day the people wish for blood ; perhaps one victim will suffice, let me go towards them. I will pay for all." The Guards attempted to detain him, but Suleau rushed forward to face his assassins. For the first time these two sworn foes—the little virago mounted on the cannon, and the young man in all the beauty of his strength and fierce courage—looked each other in the eyes. The moment of

[1] See *Séances des Jacobins*, date of April 23, 1792, where " M. Collot rises to congratulate himself on the fact that Mlle. Théroigne has withdrawn her friendship from him as from M. Robespierre." At this Mlle. Théroigne flew at Collot with clenched fists and was removed from the hall amidst tumult.

reckoning had come at last.   Terrible in her rage, Théroigne
sprang upon her victim, seized him by the collar, and, with the
aid of the armed ruffians in her following, dragged him towards
the courtyard.   But if Suleau was prepared to die, he went not
as a lamb to the slaughter ; ever a fighter, he contrived to possess
himself of a sabre and fought his assailants like a lion.   Three
other victims fell beside him—the gigantic Abbé Bouyon and
two officers of the King's old bodyguard, M. de Solminiac and
M. du Vigier, known for his beauty as " le beau Vigier."   At last
Suleau, seeing that he too must now be overwhelmed, crossed his
arms and cried out defiantly, " Kill me, then, and see how a
Royalist can die ! "   Instantly Théroigne and her murderous
horde closed upon him—Suleau fell pierced with dagger thrusts.
His lifeless body was dragged to the Place Vendôme and hacked
to pieces.   Then that noble head was raised on a pike and carried
in triumph [1] past the door of the Assembly at the moment the
Royal Family entered the hall.

        Whilst these scenes were taking place around the Salle
du Manège, confusion reigned at the Château.   The troops,
left by the death of Mandat without a leader, could decide on
no plan of campaign ; some were for leaving their post and
retiring to barracks, declaring that now the Royal Family had
gone nothing but bricks and mortar remained to be defended.
The *gendarmerie* stationed on the Place du Louvre being of
this opinion calmly withdrew to the Palais Royal, leaving the
approach to the Château open to the enemy.
        But the nobles who remained in the royal apartments were
for standing their ground ;   only a few of their number had
followed the King, and the rest, rallying round the Maréchal de
Mailly, enthusiastically concurred in his plan for resisting invasion to the last.   " Here are the gallants !   Here are the last
of the nobility," cried the heroic old man as this pathetic legion
ranged itself in order of battle ; " the post of a general and of
his companions-in-arms is at the place where the throne is
attacked and in peril ! "   And as he went up and down the
ranks he continued to repeat, " Conquer or die, gentlemen,
conquer or die ! "
        The first detachment of the Marseillais had now arrived on
the Carrousel, but here a delay occurred in the attack on the
Château, for the Faubourgs failed to put in an appearance.
Once again Balaam's ass had refused to go forward.   Santerre
indeed, who was to lead Saint-Antoine, " the Faubourg of glory,"
to the assault, seemed at the last moment overcome with panic,

---

[1] Article on Suleau in the *Biographie Michaud*; Beaulieu, iii. 470 ;
Deux Amis, viii. 168 ; Peltier, i. 104.

and urged his battalions not to march on the Château, where he said the Royalists were assembled in force. Thereupon Westermann, holding his sword to Santerre's throat, ordered him to lead on his men, and Santerre obeyed; but at the Hôtel de Ville he contrived to have himself elected commander-in-chief, and, on the pretext that his post should now be at headquarters, absented himself from the army and was seen no more all day.

At last the Faubourgs, commanded by Westermann and Lazowski, arrived on the field of battle before the entrance to the Château. Such was the attacking army—a vanguard of Marseillais largely composed of Italians, a reluctant rearguard from the Faubourgs led by a German and a Pole.[1] And this was the French people rising as one man to overthrow the monarchy!

At the first onslaught the Marseillais and the confederates from Brest, in Brittany, alone displayed any resolution, and it was they who advanced towards the courtyards from which the Swiss and National Guards had retreated into the palace,[2] and beat on the great gates of the Château demanding admittance. The royal concierges withdrew the bolts and fled. A band of Marseillais rushed forward into the arms of the gunners of the National Guard, who, always the disloyal element in this body, immediately joined forces with the insurgents, and bringing out their cannons pointed them against the Château.

By this time the mob of Paris had at last begun to collect, for the impunity with which the revolutionary battalions had penetrated into the Carrousel and the courtyards reassured the most timorous, and streams of idlers, ever eager for a spectacle, hurried to the scene of action.

Only about 750 Swiss, a handful of National Guards, and 200 nobles now remained to defend the Château. If only the Swiss, therefore, could be suborned or vanquished, further resistance would be impossible; and the mob, seeing a number of these men looking down on them from the windows, shouted loudly, " Down with the Swiss ! Lay down your arms ! "

The Swiss, who entertained no hostile feelings towards the people, replied with conciliatory gestures by way of persuading them to desist from attack, and the better to prove their

---

[1] Beaulieu, iii. 471.

[2] This order was given directly the King left the Château; see account of August 10 given by M. Victor Constant de Rebecqui, officier aux gardes suisses du Roi, Auckland MSS. in British Museum : " The King and his family retire to the Assembly accompanied by a part of the regiment and our commanders; we are all made to retire into the interior of the apartments and to abandon the outer posts ; then the assailants break down the gate of the courtyard and enter at the same moment ; the gunners placed there for the defence of the Château abandon their cannons, which fall into the hands of those (*i.e.* the gunners) of the Faubourgs."

pacific intentions, threw down packets of cartridges amongst them.

But the group of Swiss sentinels drawn up at the foot of the staircase [1] presented a more formidable appearance, and for a quarter of an hour this gallant band held the immense mob at bay by their intrepid air and resolute countenances. At last a dozen Marseillais, led by Westermann, ventured forward and ordered the men to lay down their arms, adding, "We have come to fraternize with you."

The Swiss, who understood little French, remained immovable. Westermann repeated the demand in German, urging them not to sacrifice their lives at the bidding of their officers.

To this the Sergeant Blazer replied : " We are Swiss, and the Swiss only lay down their arms with their lives. We do not consider we have deserved such an insult. If the regiment is not needed let it be legally ordered to retire, but we will not leave our posts and we will not be disarmed." [2]

Thereupon Westermann and his troops retreated, for it was never the revolutionary way to advance upon armed men, however inferior in number, and none of the " brave Marseillais " felt inclined to engage the Swiss in open combat. Some of the insurgents happened, however, to be armed with long pikes hooked at the end, and these ruffians now ventured forward and, whilst remaining out of range of the sentinels' swords, contrived to harpoon five of the unfortunate men, dragging them at the same time towards them by means of the hooks affixed in their clothing.[3] This manœuvre delighted the mob, who gathered round with shrieks of laughter, whilst the five Swiss were disarmed, stripped, and finally massacred at the foot of the staircase.[4] Suddenly a shot was fired—by whom contemporaries are unable to agree in stating. The revolutionaries, of course, declared the Swiss were the aggressors, but D'Ossonville, an eyewitness, afterwards an agent of the Comité de Salut Public in the Terror, who as a revolutionary could have no object in whitewashing the Swiss, asserts that " several rebels having dressed up in Swiss uniform slipped amongst their ranks, fired on the insurgents, and directly the first report was heard, women, purposely stationed on the terrace, began to call out, ' Ah ! the rascals of Swiss are firing on our brothers the patriots ! ' At the same moment the fight began, and became general. . . . This is what has remained unknown but *what I saw and observed*. But

---

[1] Beaulieu, iii. 474 ; *Deux Amis*, viii. 180 ; Peltier, i. 111.

[2] Mortimer Ternaux, ii. 314.

[3] Montjoie, *Conjuration de d'Orléans*, iii. 195 ; Peltier, i. 111 ; Beaulieu, iii. 474.

[4] *Deux Amis*, viii. 180.

it was necessary to say that the King had ordered the attack when he had expressly forbidden it." [1]

The question of this discharge is, however, a matter of little importance, for the point is not who fired the first shot, but who shed the first blood. It was not the report of a gun that gave the signal for battle, but the cowardly murder of the five sentinels, and if the Swiss then fired they were in no way the aggressors. [2]

At any rate they did fire now, and they fired vigorously ; a perfect hail of musketry swept the front ranks of the assailants, whereupon the Swiss on the upper floors, with the nobles and the National Guards, joined in the fusillade, shooting down at the crowd from the balconies, roofs, and windows.

The effect of this was terrific, for the insurgents, after responding with a few cannon-balls, so uncertainly aimed as to do little damage, were suddenly overcome with panic, and all at once the vast mass of people that filled the courtyards and the Carrousel wavered, drew back, and finally stampeded. [3] The scene that followed was indescribable—hardy Bretons, brave Marseillais, red-capped Sans-Culottes armed with pikes, female " patriots " dragging terrified children by the hand, all running madly for their lives, and even springing over the parapet into the river ; mounted police tearing away at full gallop, crushing passers-by beneath their horses' feet, and all " pale as spectres," all screaming as they fled, " To arms, citizens, to arms ! they slaughter

[1] " Fragments des Mémoires de d'Ossonville," published in *Documents pour servir à l'Histoire de la Révolution Française*, by Charles d'Héricault and Gustave Bord, vol. ii. p. 2.

[2] On the supposed treachery of the Swiss see also the account given by the minister Bigot de Sainte-Croix, *Histoire de la Conspiration du 10 Août*, p. 58 : " When the troops posted in the courtyards had heard for certain of the departure of their Majesties they looked at each other, and whether the King's words had reached them or not, said to one another, ' There is nothing more to be done here ; why should we come to blows ? Why should we slaughter each other ? ' A deputation is sent to the confederates to bring the words of peace, and one of their detachments comes back with the deputation to ratify the agreement. The scoundrels ! They are no sooner in the middle of the courtyard than they make signs to their cohorts to follow them, they advance amidst insulting and ferocious laughter, and all at once dashing forward to the foot of the great staircase where the Swiss are standing, ' Where are the Swiss ? ' they cry in bloodthirsty tones, ' where are the Swiss ? ' And five of these sentinels have fallen beneath their blows. Then, yes, *then* the Swiss companies and the National Guards fell on the assassins ; *then* they opposed force with force, they fought for their lives and not for the defence of a palace in which the King was no longer ; but the rage of the maniacs saw in the palace men to massacre and walls to destroy. This, then, was the treachery of the defenders of the Court, these were the wishes of conciliation brought by the confederates ; this faith violated by signs of friendship and these fraternal embraces. . . ."

[3] Mortimer Ternaux, ii. 316 ; Beaulieu, iii. 475 ; Ferrières, iii. 195. " The Swiss and the National Guards drove back the insurgents beyond the Rue Niçaise " (D'Ossonville, *op. cit.*).

your parents, your brothers, your sons ! "[1]   Through every exit
from the Carrousel they rushed frantically, falling over each other
in the struggle ; on through the streets they ran, nor did some
stop running until they reached the Faubourg Saint-Antoine,
where they bolted themselves within their doors for safety.[2]

The Château had now scored a complete victory ; the only
insurgents who remained to carry on the siege took refuge behind
the buildings at the other side of the Carrousel, from which point
they continued to discharge their cannons spasmodically at the
palace, and, by way of variation, set fire to the buildings surrounding the courtyard.   The Swiss, seeing that the whole front of the
Château was now cleared of assailants, triumphantly descended
to the courtyards, and carried off some of the cannons left behind
by the Marseillais in their flight.

Why did no one tell the King the true state of affairs ?   Why
was no man of energy forthcoming to point the way back to his
palace and his throne reconquered for him by the gallant Swiss ?
But that malignant fate which ordained that at every crisis of
the Revolution the King should fall a victim to treacherous
counsels still pursued him, and a lying message was brought to the
Assembly that the Swiss were " massacring the people," and also
that the Château was about to be forced.   Panic-stricken deputies
gathered around him, entreating him to intervene on behalf of
his people.   Louis XVI., who knew nothing beyond what he was
told, which seemed to be confirmed by the roar of battle and the
crashing of cannon-balls on the roof of the Assembly, concluded
that his orders not to fire on the mob had been wantonly disobeyed, and therefore allowed himself to be persuaded to write
the fatal message to the Swiss, commanding them to cease fire
and join him at the hall of the Assembly.

" This order," says Beaulieu, " may be regarded as the last
blow dealt at the monarchy.   I have reason to believe, on
account of all I observed, that if the King's defenders had made
the most of their advantage the King would, in the course of the
day, have been on his throne again.   I know that several battalions were on the march to defend the Château, and amongst
them those of the Champs Élysées and the Pont Neuf.   If only
one of these had arrived in time it would have sufficed to ensure
victory and give courage to the Swiss, who till then had acted
alone, but when these battalions saw that all had been abandoned
they joined themselves to those they had wished to repulse
against those they intended to defend ; this is what has always
been seen and always will be seen to happen in all revolutions."

[1] *Révolutions de Paris*, by Prudhomme, xiii. 234 ; *Journal of Dr. John
Moore*, i. 41.
[2] Mortimer Ternaux, ii. 316 ; *Deux Amis*, viii. 182.

This disastrous act which sealed the fate of the monarchy was quickly noised abroad, and put fresh heart into the revolutionary legions. The Swiss had been forbidden by the King to fire on them—therefore they might with impunity return to the charge and massacre the Swiss ![1]

When, in obedience to the King's order, two columns of Swiss abandoned their posts and marched through the garden of the Tuileries, a hail of musketry fire was directed on them by insurgents concealed behind the trees. One column succeeded in reaching the Assembly in safety, and these men, together with their comrades who had accompanied the King to the Assembly, were deposited in the Church of the Feuillants and survived the massacre. But the other column, which had marched on towards the swing bridge leading to the Place Louis XV., were pitilessly butchered ; many fell beneath the chestnut trees of the garden ; the rest having reached the statue of Louis XV. in the centre of the great square, formed themselves into a phalanx and prepared for defence, but the mounted police charged them with their sabres and cut them down almost to a man. Napoleon, who passed through the garden at this moment, declared at the end of his life that none of his battlefields had given him the idea of so many corpses as the Tuileries on this August morning strewn with the bodies of the Swiss.

The entire garrison, however, had not evacuated the palace ; 300 to 400 Swiss, who had either not heard or not obeyed the order to retire,[2] still remained in the King's apartments, where a cannon-ball, bursting in amongst them, had killed or wounded a great number.[3] These soldiers, a few nobles and ladies of the Court, and about one hundred servants were, therefore, the sole occupants of the Château, which after the King's order to cease fire put up no further defence. The insurgents behind the Carrousel, finding that their fire now met with no reply, ventured at last timorously forward across the courtyards, and finally entered the hall of the palace, evacuated five minutes earlier by the two columns of Swiss. The impunity with which this manœuvre was executed reassured the crowd that lingered at a distance ; stragglers poured in from all sides, and before long an immense tumultuous mob burst into the hall of the Château.

---

[1] " The Swiss," said Napoleon, who was an eye-witness of the affray, " plied their artillery vigorously ; the Marseillais were driven back as far as the Rue de l'Échelle and *only came back when the Swiss had retired by order of the King.*" See also Mortimer Ternaux, ii. 325.

[2] Mortimer Ternaux, ii. 330.

[3] " I was then in the King's apartments with 300 to 400 of our men ; a cannon-ball had thrown us into disorder and killed a great number " (evidence of M. Victor Constant de Rebecqui).

So they had burst into this same hall seven weeks earlier ; so they had stormed up the great staircase breathing threatenings and slaughter, only to be brought to bay when they reached their goal ; now, with the ferocious Marseillais at their head, there was to be no pause, no relenting, and like a devastating torrent they swept onwards and spread themselves all over the palace.

A mad rage for destruction possessed them ; everything animate or inanimate fell beneath the blows of their pikes and muskets, furniture was flung from the windows, the great mirrors in which " Médicis-Antoinette had studied the hypocritical airs she showed in public " [1] flew into a thousand fragments ; treasures of art, clocks, pictures, porcelain, silver, jewels, were pillaged or destroyed. All the Swiss—the soldiers who had remained at their posts, even the wounded lying helpless on the floors and the doctors bending over them to dress their wounds—were barbarously butchered ; rivers of blood flowed over the shining parquet of the great apartments. Everywhere the savage horde pursued their victims, the grey-haired porters were dragged forth from their lodges, fugitives were tracked down to the deepest cellars, up to the remotest attics, and put to death. In the Queen's bedroom women of the town tore open the wardrobes and dressed themselves in the Queen's gowns; one throwing herself on the bed cried out that some one was concealed beneath the bedding, and the mattress being torn off amidst drunken laughter, a trembling Swiss was discovered and massacred. The scenes that took place were so unspeakably hideous that one would thankfully draw a veil over what followed, but if we are to understand the French Revolution as it really was, if we are to see this 10th of August, so vaunted by revolutionary writers, in its true colours, we must look facts in the face. And in full justice to the people one circumstance must not be forgotten—the mob that committed these atrocities was literally mad with drink. For in that first wild onrush a band of insurgents had found their way down to the cellars and gorged themselves with wine and liqueurs.[2] No less than two hundred, says Prudhomme, died of the effects. Then, whilst some remained lying in helpless stupor on the cellar floors, others bore supplies to their comrades up above—the contents of 10,000 bottles were distributed amongst the mob ;[3] the garden and courtyards around the Château became a sea of broken glass. The effect of this indiscriminate carousing on unaccustomed liquors wildly mingled was to produce in the people a condition of complete dementia, and it is as

[1] Prudhomme, *Révolutions de Paris.*
[2] Mercier, *Le Nouveau Paris,* i. 209.
[3] *Le Comte de Fersen et la Cour de France,* ii. 348.

creatures deprived of all reasoning faculty, of all semblance to humanity, no more responsible for their actions than Bedlam suddenly turned loose, that we must regard them.

For on this dreadful 10th of August, alone amongst all the great days of the Revolution in Paris, it *was* by " the people " that these atrocities were committed. The savage Marseillais showed themselves less ferocious. All the ladies of the Court were spared by order of their leaders, the word being given, " We do not kill women." [1]

Fifty or sixty of the flying Swiss were also saved by them ; [2] stranger still, the warlike old Maréchal de Mailly succeeded in disarming his assailants. " The face of the Maréchal," says Soulavie, " having arrested the hand of a confederate who had raised his arm to kill him, this man asks who he is, seizes him, pretends to ill-treat him, tells him to keep silence, pushes aside the crowd, and leads him back safe and sound to his house." [3]

The King's doctor, Lemonnier, was likewise led home in triumph. During the invasion of the Château he had remained quietly seated in his study ; suddenly " men with blood-stained arms " battered on the panels of the door. The old man opened to them. " What are you doing here ? " they said. " You are very quiet."

" I am at my post."

" What are you at the Château ? "

" Do you not see by my coat ?   I am the King's doctor."

" And are you not afraid ? "

" Of what ?   I am unarmed.   Does one injure a man who does no injury ? "

" You are a good fellow.   Listen ; it is not well for you here ; others less reasonable than us might confound you with the rest. You are not safe.   Where would you like to be taken ? "

" To the Palace of the Luxembourg."

" Come, follow us and fear nothing."

" I have already told you I have no fear of those to whom I have done no harm."

Then they led him through the serried ranks of bayonets and loaded guns, crying out before him as they went, " Comrades, let this man pass.   He is the King's doctor, but he is not afraid ; he is a good fellow." [4]

---

[1] Beaulieu, iii. 483 ; *Mémoires de Mme. Campan*, p. 351.

[2] *Journal of Dr. John Moore*, i. 60.

[3] Another contemporary, the Comte d'Aubarède (*Lettres d'Aristocrates*, by Pierre de Vaissière, p. 538), says it was by a poor artisan that the Maréchal was saved.   But the revolutionaries did not spare him ; he was guillotined under Joseph Lebon, at the age of eighty-seven.   His last words on the scaffold were " Vive le Roi !   I say it as did my ancestors ! "

[4] *Crimes de la Révolution*, by Prudhomme, iv. 70.

It is not, then, to the Marseillais that the greatest atrocities of the day must be attributed, but to the people, or rather to the populace of Paris—above all to the *women*, and, as in all the revolutionary outbreaks, it was " the people " themselves who fared worst at their hands.

To the servants in particular the mob showed no mercy. They, poor souls, had not thought of flying ; many, indeed, were imbued with revolutionary doctrines,[1] and, little dreaming that the rage of the populace would be turned against themselves, remained calmly at their work, in the midst of which the drunken mob surprised them. The kitchens, like the gilded apartments up above, became a shambles ; every man from the head chefs to the humblest scullions perished—" the cooks' heads fell into the saucepans, where they were preparing the viands." [2]

" Oh ! height of barbarism ! " cries Mercier, " a wretched undercook, who had not had time to escape, was seized by these tigers, thrust into a copper, and in this state exposed to the heat of the furnace. Then falling on the provisions every one seizes what he can lay hands on. One carries off chickens on a spit ; another a turbot ; that one a carp from the Rhine as large as himself . . . monsters with human faces collected in hundreds under the porch of the Escalier du Midi, and danced amidst torrents of blood and wine. A murderer played the violin beside the corpses, and thieves, with their pockets full of gold, hanged other thieves on the banisters." [3] Still worse horrors took place that cannot be written, nameless indecencies, hideous debaucheries, ghastly mutilations of the dead,[4] and again, as after the siege of the Bastille, cannibal orgies. Before great fires, hastily kindled in the apartments, " cutlets of Swiss " were grilled and eaten ; [5] the actor Grammont—one of the earliest hirelings of the Duc d'Orléans, and the last man to insult the Queen on her way to the scaffold—in a fit of revolutionary frenzy drank down a glass of blood.[6]

Outside, in the garden of the Château, ghastly scenes met the eye ; on the lifeless bodies of the Swiss women perched like vultures, gloating over their victims ; a young girl of eighteen was seen plunging a sabre into the corpses.[7]

[1] Beaulieu, iii. 482.

[2] Montjoie, *Conjuration de d'Orléans*, iii. 196 ; *Révolutions de Paris*, by Prudhomme, xiii. 236.

[3] Mercier, *Le Nouveau Paris*, i. 210.

[4] *Crimes de la Révolution*, by Prudhomme, iv. 69 ; Montjoie, *Conjuration de d'Orléans*, iii. 195 ; *Histoire particulière*, etc., by Maton de la Varenne, p. 139.

[5] *Crimes de la Révolution*, by Prudhomme, iv. 68.

[6] Beaulieu, iii. 482 ; *Révolution du 10 Août*, by Peltier.

[7] Montjoie, *Conjuration de d'Orléans*, iii. 196.

Needless to say, the mass of the true people took no part in these atrocities. " Peaceful citizens," says Mercier, " whom curiosity had attracted to the Tuileries to discover whether the Château still existed, wandered slowly, struck with gloomy stupor, along the terrace covered with broken bottles. They did not weep, they seemed petrified, dumbfounded ; they shrank with horror at each footstep at the odour and the aspect of these bleeding corpses. . . ."

THE RÔLE OF THE LEADERS

But whilst the true people shuddered, the authors of the day knew no pity. To them the 10th of August was a " glorious day," for which each one was now eager to claim the responsibility. Directly the Château had fallen and the mob had proved victorious, every patriot came bravely to the fore. " Danton," says Louvet, " who had concealed himself during the battle, appeared after the victory armed with a huge sabre, and marching at the head of a battalion of Marseillais as if he had been the hero of the day."

The other " great revolutionaries " had all remained likewise in their hiding-places until the danger was past. What, asks Prudhomme, were the leading Jacobins doing during the attack on the Château ? " They knew everything ; none of them appeared in arms at the siege of the Tuileries. Marat, Robespierre,[1] Danton, not one of them dared to show himself. All these people invariably displayed the greatest bravery, but only in the tribune ; the tongue was their favourite weapon. The few Jacobins who came out prudently placed themselves at the tail of the bands of Marseillais and Bretons. There is nothing more cowardly than a revolutionary from speculation ! "[2]

But if it was not to the efforts of these men that the 10th of August owed its triumph, the excesses of the day lie at their door alone. Is not the instigator of a crime infinitely more criminal than the wretched instrument who commits it ? And were not the orators and writers—Marat, Danton, Desmoulins, Brissot, Carra, Madame Roland—more truly the authors of these excesses than the crazed and drunken populace who put their precepts into practice ? For the cannibals of the Tuileries, the horrible women of the Paris Faubourgs plunging their knives into the bodies of their victims, had not evolved such deeds from

---

[1] Tallien, who took part in the siege, later, in the Electoral Assembly, accused Robespierre to his face of having " gone to earth for three days and three nights in his cellar and of having come out only in order to profit by the turn of events " (Notes d'Alexandre, published in the *Revue de la Révolution*, by Gustave Bord, viii. 175).

[2] *Crimes de la Révolution*, by Prudhomme, iv. 67.

their own inner consciousness; for months they had been trained for the part at the Sociétés Fraternelles of the Jacobins, where murder and violence were systematically preached, and every means employed to excite their passions. It will be urged that they themselves must have been inherently evil to respond in so atrocious a manner to the suggestions of their leaders ; the old theory of " Parisian ferocity " will be brought forward to explain the phenomenon. But we have only to study the memoirs of the period to discover that it was not the women of Paris alone on whom these doctrines produced the same dehumanizing effect.

Thus, for example, Thiébault, himself an ardent democrat, relates that soon after the 10th of August he dined with certain Prussian friends of his, Monsieur and Madame Bitaube, and amongst the guests were Chamfort, the Orléaniste, and an English authoress, Helen Maria Williams. Chamfort delighted Miss Williams with his revolutionary verses, and Thiébault adds : " The thing that struck me most was the political exaggeration of Miss Williams, who showed herself an enthusiast for our Revolution, *even for its excesses*, which in my opinion damned it." Still more amazing was the attitude of the two good Germans. " That M. and Mme. Bitaube," says Thiébault, " who were both over sixty, who were all that is best on this earth, who were distinguished, he for his merit, she for her fine and gentle wit, should have shown themselves more revolutionary than their two guests, that they should have become apologists of the 10th of August, that astounded me ! But it is not the only example I could quote of this kind of aberration." [1]

In order to appreciate the attitude of Miss Williams and her worthy German friends, we must refer to a description of the state of Paris at this moment given by Mr. Burges in a letter to Lord Auckland, dated September 4. " The English messenger, Morley," Burges writes, " has just returned from Paris, where he relates that pestilence is now expected. It was found easier to kill than to bury the victims of the 10th. Those who were amused by shedding blood soon grew tired of digging graves ; of course great numbers were put out of the way somewhat carelessly, and the cellars and other subterraneous places were found convenient receptacles for the dead bodies ; into these immense numbers were thrown, and when they were full they were shut up in the best way the hurry of the operation would permit. The natural consequences of interment now began to manifest themselves pretty strongly. Morley says that, being obliged, the last day or two he continued in Paris, to run about the town a good deal for his passports, he was saluted in several

[1] *Mémoires de Thiébault*, i. 313.

streets with such whiffs of putrefaction as to be obliged to cover his face and run off as fast as he could." [1]

Under these circumstances it was not possible for a moment to forget the recent massacres, whilst the chaotic state of the capital made it evident that the atrocities, which had just taken place, were but the prelude to others still more dreadful. " Ah ! how fortunate you are not to inhabit this town," writes a Parisian to a friend in the country on August 16. " People who think know no rest night or day. Every day, on rising, one hears of the death of neighbours or friends. So far these are only rose-leaves—the end of the month provides us with greater dangers." [2]

" You think," write two other contemporaries, " that one can see these horrors without shuddering ? One would be almost a barbarian ! " [3]

Yet it is no barbarian but an educated Englishwoman, an " intellectual " and a sentimentalist, that we find dining out amidst these ghastly scenes and enthusiastically applauding them. Let us have done, then, with the futile theory of " Parisian ferocity " by which panegyrists of the Revolution would explain its crimes ; these crimes were not accidental to the Revolution, they were *not* the outcome of the Latin temperament, but the direct result of those doctrines which produced in men and women of all nations, whether English, French, or German, a ferocity that knew no relenting.

THE RÔLE OF THE INTRIGUES

Helen Maria Williams was not unique amongst her race, for although the great mass of the English people shuddered at the atrocities of August 10, and the Court of St. James's withdrew its ambassador from Paris, the " English Jacobins " accorded their whole-hearted approval to their French allies. We shall reserve their congratulatory letters and addresses, however, till the end of the next chapter, for it was not until the massacres of September that their admiration was roused to its fullest pitch.

Prussia, needless to say, found likewise cause for rejoicing in the attack on the Tuileries and the subsequent imprisonment of the Royal Family in the Temple. " The most splendid dream a king can dream," Frederick the Great had been known to say, " is to dream that he is King of France." The 10th of August had removed all cause for envy from Frederick's successor.

As to the Girondins and Orléanistes who had engineered the

---

[1] *Correspondence of Lord Auckland*, ii. 438.
[2] M. Rochet à Mme. de Thomassin Mandat, *Lettres d'Aristocrates*, by Pierre de Vaissière, p. 533.
[3] MM. Simon et Pierre N. à M. Lhoste, *ibid.* p. 537.

movement, their triumph was destined to be short-lived. True, the throne was now vacant, and thus the first step had been taken towards a change of dynasty. But the laying of the mine had proved unskilful; too much dynamite had been employed, and the charge by which they had intended to blast their way to power had produced an explosion so terrific as to involve the whole existing order of things in chaos.

The effect of the 10th of August was to paralyse France. "The terror that it spread," says Hua, "was almost universal. In a few places there was an attempt at resistance, but nowhere could it be organized. All action to be powerful must emanate from a centre; the Revolution proved a thousand times that the fate of the departments is decided in Paris: those same authorities that had protested so energetically against the day of June the 20th were silent before that of August the 10th." [1]

Lafayette alone dared to raise his voice in remonstrance; and as soon as the news of the events in Paris reached him on the frontier, he issued a proclamation to the army asking them, "-as good citizens and brave soldiers, to rally around the Constitution that they had sworn to defend to the death." But although the troops immediately under his orders "showed by their cries of indignation that they shared the sentiments of their general," [2] and the district of Sedan where he was encamped, together with the department of the Ardennes, accorded him their vigorous support, Lafayette's efforts proved unavailing owing to the opposition of his fellow-generals—Lückner, hitherto loyal to the King, prudently went over to the stronger side, the Jacobins; Dumouriez resumed his Orléaniste intrigues; Dillon, who at first had seconded the protests of Lafayette, grew panic-stricken and recanted.

The power of the Jacobins carried all before it. The mayor of Sedan and the administrators of the Ardennes were arrested; and on the 19th of August the Assembly, trembling beneath the dictates of the Commune, issued a writ against " Motier Lafayette, heretofore general of the army of the North, convicted of the crime of rebellion against the law, of conspiracy against liberty, and of treachery to the nation."

Then Lafayette, once the gaoler of his King, himself tasted the pleasures of captivity. Reduced to the same expedient as the unfortunate Louis XVI.—flight to the frontier—he was arrested by the Austrians and imprisoned in the fortress of Magdeburg, where he had leisure to reconsider his earlier dictum that " insurrection is the most sacred of duties."

The insurrection of August 10 appeared, at any rate to La-fayette, an immeasurable disaster; it was not, however, the final

---

[1] *Mémoires de Hua*, p. 164.　　　　[2] *Ibid.* p. 165.

destruction of the Old Régime, but the destruction of new-found liberty he deplored.

" I know well," he wrote to the Duc de Rochefoucauld on the 25th of August, " that they will have talked about plots at the Château, collusion with the enemy, follies of all kinds committed by the Court ; I am not its confidant nor its apologist ; but the constitutional act is there, and it is not the King who has violated it ; the Château did not go to attack the Faubourgs, nor were the Marseillais summoned by him. The preparations that have been made during the last three weeks were denounced by the King. It was not he who had women and children massacred, who gave over to execution all those who were known for their attachment to the Constitution, who in one day destroyed the liberty of the press, of the posts, judgement by jury . . . in a word, everything that assures the liberty of men and of nations."

Lafayette had not overstated the case ; in the chaos that followed on the 10th of August the cause of liberty perished utterly, and the people, ostensibly the victors of the day, lost everything they had gained by the Revolution.

At first the rage for destruction that had held the mob under its sway during the attack on the Tuileries, and that continued throughout the weeks that followed, gave to the people some semblance of power. Whilst overthrowing the splendid statues of the kings in all the squares of Paris, the populace were able to imagine themselves indeed the " Sovereign people," but already their new masters were at work forging the chains that were to bind them in a servitude such as they had never known before.

On the 17th of August, at the instigation of Robespierre, the " Tribunal Criminel," precursor to the Revolutionary Tribunal of the Terror, was inaugurated by the Commune. Five days later Dr. Moore records that " a new kind of *lettres de cachet* are being issued by the Commune of Paris in great profusion," and " what makes this more dreadful is . . . that a man when arrested and sent to prison does not know how long he may be confined before he has an opportunity of proving his innocence." More sinister still was the appearance on the Place du Carrousel of that new instrument, the guillotine—symbol of the new era that was to dawn on France. For although revolutionary factions and populace alike rejoiced at their supposed victory, the 10th of August inaugurated the reign of neither Orléanistes, Girondins, nor " Sovereign people," but of one intrigue only, the intrigue that from the beginning of the Revolution had been slowly gaining force, and that in sweeping away king, nobles, and clergy was to destroy not only the throne itself, but all government, all religion, and establish in their place—the reign of Anarchy.

THE MASSACRES OF SEPTEMBER

THE MASSACRES OF SEPTEMBER

WITH the deposition of Louis XVI. and the rise to power of the Commune, the revolutionary movement entered on a new phase. The royal authority had been overthrown, but the " counter - revolutionaries " yet remained to be dealt with ; thus it is now less against the unhappy prisoners in the Temple than against the " gangrened portion of the nation " that the invectives of the revolutionary leaders are henceforth directed. What is the truth about this gangrene ? Did it exist ? In a sense, yes. But to understand how it came into being we must cast our eyes back over the history of the last twenty years.

When Louis XV., looking around him at the end of his reign, said, " Things will last my time, but after me the deluge ! " he diagnosed with remarkable accuracy the disease that afflicted the State. France, as she existed at this date, could not last, because no state in which one class is oppressed can maintain its vigour. Under Louis XV. the peasants, if less wretched than is popularly supposed—for feudal benevolence did more than history tells us to counteract the oppression of the Old Régime—were, nevertheless, *cyphers in the state* ; their wishes did not count, their voice was not heard, their needs were not officially recognized, and thus, by constriction, they became like a mortifying limb spreading germs of death throughout the body.

Louis XVI., as we have seen, from the first moment of his accession, resolved to remedy this state of affairs, to loose the bonds that bound the people down, to give the constricted limb free play. *It was not too late to do this*, as certain writers would have us believe ; the limb responded admirably to the treatment ; never had the people of France displayed greater vigour than on the eve of the Revolution. The body of the State, as M. Dauban points out, was at this moment " anything but inert and passive. Everywhere thought, passion, and blood circulate. The almost unanimous wish of the cahiers testifies to the force of cohesion in opinion and the power of the public mind. . . . Paris has no greater share in the spirit that animates it than Marseilles, Bordeaux, and the other parts of France. In the

289

three years that follow what enthusiasm, what ardour, what vitality in the provinces ! " [1]

But, at the very moment that the people were released from bondage, the Revolution intervened and reversed the process by seizing on two other limbs of the State, the nobility and clergy, and binding them down relentlessly. It was not even as if the revolutionaries had said to the " privileged orders " : " You have enjoyed too long exclusively the good things of life, now you shall share them with your fellow-men. Come, give up your châteaux and your rolling acres, and till the ground with the rest." Nothing of this kind was suggested, not the faintest glimmer of Socialist ideals seems to have illumined the minds of the earlier revolutionary extremists ; their only idea was to subject the hitherto privileged orders to a far worse oppression than that from which the people had been delivered. For if under the Old Régime the people had been neglected, ignored, crushed by taxation, under the revolutionary régime the nobles and clergy were actively ill-treated—insulted, spat upon, assaulted, robbed of all their goods, driven from the country, or massacred. The people had been left to struggle for existence ; the nobles and clergy were denied the very right to live.

They were also, as a class, denied any virtues. No distinction was drawn between the Liberal nobles who had marched in the vanguard of reform and the reactionaries who mustered around the Comte d'Artois, between the courtiers who for purely selfish reasons clung to the Old Régime and the provincial *seigneurs* who devoted themselves to the welfare of the peasants on their estates.[2] The generous enthusiasm with which, on the 4th of August, the nobles in a body had voluntarily relinquished their privileges was rewarded by the revolutionary leaders only with insults and abuse. " All Royalists," said Camille Desmoulins at the Jacobin Club, " live on the sweat of the people ; they have neither wits nor virtue but for intrigue and villainy." [3]

Under these circumstances what wonder that the nobles became irreconcilable, and that many who had sympathized with the Revolution turned against the whole movement, reviled the Constitution, and used all their efforts to restore the Old Order in its entirety ? " Damn liberty, I abhor its very name ! " an indignant Frenchman exclaimed to Dr. Moore, and the sentiment was doubtless echoed by thousands of his fellow-countrymen who, embittered by persecution, now desired a return to pre-revolutionary conditions. Nor was this resentment confined

---

[1] *La Demagogie en 1793*, by A. Dauban, p. ix.
[2] I have shown elsewhere how numerous these philanthropic nobles were. See *The Chevalier de Boufflers*, p. 256 and following.
[3] *Séances des Jacobins*, date of June 17, 1792.

only to the nobles and clergy, for since, as I have shown, the Revolution had resulted in the ruin and misery of great numbers of the bourgeois and the people, discontent prevailed in all classes. Thus, by a process precisely identical with that employed by Louis XV., but applied to a different portion of the nation, a fresh centre of mortification was set up, and the new order became as moribund as the old. Each revolutionary faction had worked only for momentary popularity, each demagogue in turn had proceeded on the principle, " Things will last my term of power, but after me the deluge," and, in order to prolong that spell of power, had striven not for the welfare of the nation as a whole, but to obtain the favour of one portion only—the mob of Paris.

MARAT

This, then, was the situation that, after the cataclysm of August 10, confronted the Commune, which now held the reins of power. On one side was a raging populace, intoxicated with the joy of new-found liberty to burn and to destroy, and, on the other, a great silent nation, amongst whom, as the protests following on the 20th of June had shown, a bitter hatred of the Revolution had arisen. For the silence that followed on the 10th of August was not, as the leaders well knew, the silence of assent but of momentary stupefaction, from which those of the nobles and clergy who remained in the country would make every effort to arouse the nation.

It was this that, in the opinion of the Commune, made the third Revolution necessary—the influence of the anti-revolutionaries could never be counteracted, therefore the anti-revolutionaries themselves must be destroyed.

Marat had all along understood this. Like Louis XV. he shrewdly diagnosed the disease from which the State was suffering. The other revolutionaries recognized the existence of the " gangrene," but overlooked the fact that it was of their own making. Marat alone traced it to its real cause. " If," he once said to Camille Desmoulins, " the faults of the Constituent Assembly had not created for us irreconcilable enemies in the old nobles, I persist in believing that this great movement might have advanced in the world by pacific methods ; but after the absurd edict which keeps these enemies by force amongst us (*i.e.* the decrees against emigration), after the clumsy blows struck at their pride by the abolition of titles, after violently extorting the goods of the clergy, I maintain there is now no way of rallying them to the Revolution . . . we must give up the Revolution or do away with these men. What I propose to you is not a vain rigour supported by laws. I want an armed expedition against foreigners, who have voluntarily placed themselves out-side our government. *We are in a state of war with intractable enemies ; we must destroy them.*" [1]

In a word, the only remedy for the disease was *amputation.* Isnard, the Girondin, in one terrible phrase, had ten months earlier proposed the operation : " Let us cut off the gangrened part, so as to save the rest of the body *!* " [2] But it was never the way of the Girondins to carry their sanguinary theories into practice ; they only suggested, and then recoiled in horror when their words were interpreted by bolder men into action. Isnard, who had condensed in his proposal the whole system of the Terror, was later on to devote all his eloquence to denouncing that same system, when it had passed from the region of ideas into a frightful reality. The scheme of the philosopher Isnard was left to the surgeon Marat to execute.

Jean Paul Marat, son of Jean Mara, a Spaniard, who had settled first in Sardinia, then in Switzerland, was born at Boudry, near Neuchâtel, and had spent many years in England, where he studied medicine, and practised for a time in Church Street, Soho. In 1777 Marat went to France, where he became brevet-surgeon to the Comte d'Artois' bodyguard, but the office appears to have proved unremunerative, for he was obliged to supplement his income by compounding quack medicines for a few confiding aristocratic patients.[3] During his stay in London he had, however, already embarked on his revolutionary career by the publication of a pamphlet entitled *The Chains of Slavery*, in which, posing as an Englishman, he endeavoured to stir up the nation against the Government.[4] Britain failed entirely to respond to this appeal and the pamphlet was a complete failure, but on the outbreak of the Revolution in France Danton, realizing Marat's value as an agitator, took him into his employ-ment.[5] Before long Marat's seditious writings attracted the attention of Lafayette, who marched a regiment against the wretched dwarf, and so terrified him that he was obliged to retire below ground into hiding. During the weeks that Marat spent in the cellars of Paris, he had leisure to evolve further political schemes, in which it would be impossible to discover any con-sistent plan of government. He certainly did not advocate a republic, but either a monarchy under Louis XVI. or the Duc d'Orléans, or a dictatorship under a man of the people or himself.

---

[1] *Histoire des Montagnards*, by Esquiros, p. 206.

[2] Isnard to the Legislative Assembly, November 14, 1791.

[3] *Histoire secrète de la Révolution*, by François Pagès (1797), ii. 19 ; Montjoie, *Conjuration de d'Orléans*, ii. 154 ; *Mémoires de Monseigneur de Salamon*, p. 15.

[4] *Marat en Angleterre*, by H. S. Ashbee.

[5] *Biographie Michaud*, article on Danton by Beaulieu.

The only continuous theme we can find running through all his writings is the abolition of all class distinctions, for which purpose every resisting element in the community must be destroyed. The petty persecutions of the Orléanistes and the Girondins had only served to irritate the " privileged classes " ; attacks on property had alienated the *bourgeoisie*, and nothing but wholesale massacre could now relieve the situation. This idea became an obsession ; by the end of his sojourn in the cellars Marat undoubtedly was mad. " Marat," said his admirer Panis, " remained six weeks on one buttock in a dungeon " ; hence Panis regarded Marat as a prophet—a second St. Simeon Stylites.[1] It would be nearer the truth to describe him as a " fakir." The banks of the Ganges teem with prophets of this variety, victims of an *idée fixe*, who have spent long years in precisely this attitude, gazing at the tips of their noses or repeating the sacred incantation, " Ram Sita Ram ! " Like the monotonous chant of the fakir, Marat's cry for " heads " was also a confession of faith, but it was none the less a symptom of insanity—the result of homicidal mania. The fact that at moments he could reason logically does not disprove this assertion ; lunatics are frequently sane to dulness on every point except their own particular mania.

In appearance Marat was not unlike the malignant dwarfs one encounters in the villages of his native Switzerland. Under five feet high, with a monstrous head, the broken nose of the degenerate, a skin of yellowed parchment, the aspect of " the Friend of the People " was more than hideous, it was supernatural. His portrait in the Carnavalet Museum is not the portrait of a human being but of an " elemental," a materialization of pure evil emanating from the realms of outer darkness. " Physically," says one who knew him, " Marat had a burning and haggard eye like a hyena ; like a hyena his glance was always anxious and in motion ; his movements were short, rapid, and jerky ; a continual mobility gave to his muscles and his features a convulsive contraction, which even affected his way of walking —he did not walk, he hopped. Such was the individual called Marat." [2] When to this outward appearance are added such

---

[1] *Révolutions de Paris*, by Prudhomme, xiii. 522.

[2] *Anecdotes*, by Harmand de la Meuse, member of the Convention. On the subject of Marat's appearance contemporaries are curiously in accord ; he seems to have inspired the same horror in all beholders. Thus, for example, Garat describes him as " a man whose face, covered with a bronzed yellow, gave him the appearance of having come out of the bloody cavern of cannibals or from the red-hot soil of hell ; that by his convulsive, brusque, and jerky walk one recognized as an assassin who had escaped from the executioner but not from the furies, and who wished to annihilate the human race." Dr. Moore exactly corroborates Garat : " Marat is a little

mental peculiarities as "furious exaltation, perpetual over-excitement, chronic insomnia, *folie des grandeurs*, the mania that one is the victim of persecution," [1] it is impossible to regard Marat as a responsible human being. "People feared to speak before Marat," says his panegyrist Esquiros ; "at the slightest contradiction he showed signs of fury, and if one persisted in one's opinion he flew into a rage and foamed at the mouth."

But, apart from all other evidence, Marat's writings are clear enough proof of his insanity ; we have only to turn over the pages of *L'Ami du Peuple* or the *Journal de la République Française* to realize that we are listening to the ravings of a mind in delirium. For example :

"Never go to the Assembly without having your pockets full of stones destined to throw at the rascals who have the impudence to preach maxims. . . ." [2] "Citizens, erect 800 gibbets in the gardens of the Tuileries, and hang there all the traitors to the country . . . at the same time that you construct a vast pile in the middle of the basin of the fountain to roast the ministers and their agents." [3] "Citizens, let the fire of patriotism be rekindled in your bosoms and your triumph is assured ; rush to arms ; you know to-day which are the real victims that must be immolated for your salvation ; let your first blows fall on the infamous general (Lafayette) ; immolate the whole staff . . . immolate the corrupt members of the National Assembly . . . cut the thumbs off the hands of the former nobles who have conspired against you ; split the tongues of all the priests who have preached servitude. . . ." [4] "It is not the retirement of the ministers, it is their heads we need. . . ." etc.

The number of heads demanded by Marat increased steadily as the Revolution proceeded ; in July of 1790 he asked only for 600 ; five months later no less than 10,000 would suffice him ; later the figures grew to 20,000, to 40,000, until by the summer of 1792 he explained to Barbaroux that it would be a really "humane expedient" to massacre 260,000 men in a day. "Undoubtedly," adds Barbaroux, "he had a predilection for this number, for since then he has always asked for exactly 260,000 heads ; only rarely he went to 300,000." [5]

It would be unnecessary to enlarge on the theories of so

man of a cadaverous complexion, and a countenance exceedingly expressive of his disposition ; to a painter of massacres Marat's head would be invaluable. Such heads are rare in this country (England), yet they are sometimes to be met with at the Old Bailey" (*Journal of a Residence in France*, i. 455).

[1] Taine, *La Révolution*, vii. 198. [2] *L'Ami du Peuple*, No. 258.
[3] *Ibid.* No. 198. [4] *Ibid.* No. 305.
[5] *Mémoires de Barbaroux*, p. 57 ; confirmed by Marat himself at Convention. See *Moniteur* for October 26, 1792.

obviously disordered a mind, were it not for the immensely important part played by Marat during the last year of his life. As Laclos had been " the soul of the Orléaniste conspiracy," and therefore of the first Revolution ; as Madame Roland was " the soul of the Gironde," and therefore of the second Revolution ; Marat was, as Bougeart truly says, " the soul of the Commune," and therefore of the third Revolution — of the Massacres of September and the Reign of Terror. For although Marat died before " the Great Terror " began, it was he who had inspired the system that produced it ; it was he who became the evil genius of Robespierre and of Danton, who stimulated the destructive fury of the Hébertistes, and let loose the horde of wild beasts that at the end of 1793 devastated the provinces of France.

MARAT PLANS THE MASSACRES

Directly after the 10th of August Marat began to incite the populace to massacre the Royalists and Swiss, who had been imprisoned after the siege of the Château. " What folly," he wrote, " to bring them to trial ! " And again he launched into the history of imaginary persecutions :

" How much longer will you slumber, friends of the country, whilst your ruin is being planned with more fury than ever ? Shudder at the fate that awaits you ! Thirty-seven amongst you, in which number the ' Friend of the People ' (Marat himself) had the honour to be included, were destined to be *fried in boiling oil* if the monsters of the Tuileries had been the victors, as certain valets of Antoinette have admitted, and 30,000 citizens would have been barbarously massacred. Let us hope for no other fate if we allow the victory to be taken from us. . . . Up, Frenchmen, you who wish to live freely ; up, up, and may the blood of traitors begin to flow. It is the only way to save the country ! " [1]

But already Marat had realized that the people were not to be depended on to carry out these schemes, and had consulted with Danton on the best method for " clearing out the prisons." Two days after Danton was made Minister of Justice, that is to say on the 14th of August, Prudhomme relates, Marat said to Danton, " *Foutre !* Would you like to have all the rascals who are in the prisons judicially punished ? "

" Why ? " Danton asked him.

" Because if you do not despatch them as in the Glacière d'Avignon, those ruffians will succeed in butchering us all ; there is a heap of nobles we must get rid of as well as priests."

Danton answered him, " I know quite well that a St.

[1] *L'Ami du Peuple*, No. 680, pp. 7 and 8, date of August 19, 1792.

Barthélemy is necessary, but the means for carrying it out seem to be difficult." Marat replied, " Leave it to me ; on your account prepare the deputies with whom you are acquainted : we have hairy ruffians (*bougres à poil*) in Paris who will give us a hand."

The next day they circulated the rumour of a great conspiracy on the part of the prisoners to massacre the patriots. Camille Desmoulins was in the secret, as also Fabre d'Églantine and Robert, all three secretaries of Danton.[1]

Danton was then deputed to confide the plan to Robespierre. But Robespierre, still at this period opposed to violent measures, demurred. " You must not trust absolutely to Marat," he said, " he is too hot-headed (*c'est une mauvaise tête*)." It was not the first time Robespierre had objected to the bloodthirsty schemes of Marat. Already a year earlier he had reproached Marat with having destroyed the immense influence of his journal by " dipping his pen in the blood of the enemies of liberty, in talking of ropes and daggers." To these remonstrances Marat replied by reiterating his demand for wholesale massacres.

" Robespierre," wrote Marat in his account of the incident, " listened to me with consternation ; he grew pale and was silent for some time. This interview confirmed me in the opinion I had always entertained of him, namely, that he combined the enlightened views of a wise senator with the integrity of a virtuous man and the zeal of a true patriot, but he lacked equally the views and the audacity of a statesman." [2]

To Robespierre the massacre in the prisons proposed by Marat seemed then too audacious, yet it is impossible to concur with his panegyrists in absolving him from all complicity. Robespierre knew of the projected crime, and never offered any serious opposition ; according to Prudhomme and Proussinalle he was even present at two meetings of the leaders ; afterwards he justified all that had taken place ; Robespierre must therefore be regarded as an accomplice, if not actually an author, of the massacres.[3]

[1] *Crimes de la Révolution*, by Prudhomme, iv. 155. This conversation is entirely ignored by the historians who have attempted to prove that Marat was not the author of the massacres of September. But Prudhomme as the *intime* of the Montagnards could have had no possible object in inventing it, he merely, like many other of their accomplices, ended by giving them away. Moreover, all Prudhomme's evidence on this period is exactly confirmed by other authorities. The dialogue is given in the same words by Proussinalle (*Histoire secrète du Tribunal révolutionnaire*, p. 39, published in 1815).

[2] Article by Marat, Buchez et Roux, xiv. 188.

[3] This is admitted even by M. Louis Blanc, *Révolution*, vii. 193 : " Between Danton concurring in the massacres because he approves them, and Robespierre not preventing them although he deplores them, I do not hesitate to declare that the most culpable is Robespierre."

ORGANIZATION OF THE MASSACRES

The manner in which the massacres in the prisons were organized differed entirely from that employed in the former revolutionary outbreaks. In these, as we have seen, the plan had consisted in stirring up the people to rise *en masse* and fall upon the victims designated by the leaders. This plan had failed, and the Commune, led by Marat, realized the futility of depending on Balaam's ass as a mode of progression ; on the 20th of June it had refused to go forward, on the 10th of August it had gone mad and terrified its riders. The murder of cooks and common soldiers, the hideous scenes of cannibalism and drunken fury that had taken place at the Tuileries, though applauded by the revolutionary leaders, served no real purpose, and if repeated might become dangerous to the leaders themselves. Marat, who had never trusted the people, voiced this fear later on when, in reply to the accusation of his enemies that he aspired to the supreme power, he declared that " if the whole nation at once were to place the crown on my head I should shake it off, for such is the levity, the frivolity, the changeableness of the people that I should not be sure that, after crowning me in the morning, they would not hang me in the evening." [1] The people of Paris—those " pitiable revolutionaries "—must therefore not be invited indiscriminately to co-operate, so on this occasion no army of pikes and rags was summoned from the Faubourgs, no mob leaders were called out, no *conciliabules* took place in the taverns of the Soleil d'Or or the Cadran Bleu. In a word, the old revolutionary machine was " scrapped " ; it had served its purpose, and must be superseded by a more effectual system.

According to Prudhomme the secret councils that preceded the massacres of September took place at the " Comité de Surveillance " of the Commune,[2] and were attended by Marat, Danton, Manuel, Billaud-Varenne, Collot d'Herbois, Panis, Sergent, Tallien, and, on the aforesaid two occasions, Maximilien Robespierre.[3] Here the whole scheme was mapped out with diabolical ingenuity. First of all a number of fresh prisoners were to be incarcerated, principally wealthy people, for the massacres were to be not merely a method of extermination, but a highway robbery on a large scale. The Commune wanted money—for what purpose we shall see later—and the systematic

---

[1] *Journal de la République*, No. 221.
[2] *Crimes de la Révolution*, by Prudhomme, iv. 156.
[3] *Ibid.*; Maton de la Varenne, *Histoire particulière*, p. 285 ; *Histoire secrète*, by Proussinalle, pp. 40, 41.

pillage it had inaugurated after the 10th of August, when not only the Tuileries and other royal châteaux but the houses of many private people had been looted by their agents,[1] had not yet brought in sufficient sums.

But, besides the men whose death was to be effected merely as the means of acquiring their possessions, a number of victims were designated for other reasons by different members of the Commune, and over this question heated discussions arose. Robespierre at one of these meetings, fearing indiscriminate slaughter, had said, " We must bring only the priests and nobles to justice." [2]   But when Marat proposed to add certain members of the rival faction—Brissot and Roland [3]—to the list, it seems that Robespierre's scruples vanished, and from after events it is evident that the hope of finally ridding himself of the hated Brissotins did more than anything else to reconcile Robespierre to the idea of the massacres.

Danton, however, showed himself magnanimous. He, too, would gladly have seen Roland removed from his path, for the Minister of the Interior had an inconvenient habit of asking the Minister of Justice to tender his accounts to the Assembly,[4] and Danton had recently drawn the sum of 100,000 écus from the public treasury for purposes he declined to reveal, contenting himself with the vague statement that he had given " 20,000 francs to such an one, 10,000 to another, and so on," " for the sake of the Revolution," " on account of their patriotism," etc.[5] Roland, who shrewdly suspected that it was his own patriotism Danton had seen fit to reward, persisted in his demands for the names of the persons to whom these sums had been paid, thereby profoundly irritating Danton. But whether he retained some sense of gratitude for Madame Roland's soup, of which he had recently partaken, or whether, through their common intrigue with the English Jacobins, he had some secret understanding with the Brissotins, Danton did not wish to have them murdered. So to the proposal that they should be included in the massacres he answered firmly, " You know that I do not hesitate at crime when it is necessary, but I disdain it when it is useless." [6]

Not content with this remonstrance, Danton went to Robespierre and interceded for Brissot and Roland. Robespierre said coldly, " Are not these two individuals counter-revolutionaries ? "

[1] Granier de Cassagnac, *Histoire des Girondins*, ii. 9 ; *Mémoires de Mme. Roland*, i. 112.
[2] *Crimes de la Révolution*, by Prudhomme, iv. 156.
[3] *Ibid.* iv. 158 ; Proussinalle, p. 43 ; *Mémoires de Hua*, p. 167.
[4] *Crimes de la Révolution*, by Prudhomme, iv. 161.
[5] *Mémoires de Mme. Roland*, ii. 94.
[6] *Mémoires de Hua*, p. 167.

Danton answered, " That is not yet proved ; besides, we can always find a good moment to judge them."

But Robespierre already had his plans for bringing them to justice, which he executed two days later.

Danton then hurried to Marat at the Commune.

" You are a blackguard," he said in the language habitual to them both, " you will spoil everything."

Marat replied, " I answer for success on my head ; if you were all ruffians (*des bougres*) like me there would be 10,000 butchered." [1]

The difficulty of achieving a massacre on a large scale became the subject of discussion at several meetings of the leaders. Even if only 2000 prisoners were incarcerated, how was so vast a number of human beings to be disposed of ? " Marat," says Prudhomme, " proposed to set fire to the prisons, but it was pointed out to him that the neighbouring houses would be endangered ; some one else advised flooding them. Billaud-Varenne proposed to kill the prisoners. . . . Another said, ' You propose to kill, but you will not find enough killers.' Billaud-Varenne replied with warmth, ' They will be found.' Tallien, who refused to take part in the discussion, showed disgust, but had not the courage to oppose the project." [2]

Billaud, who, according to most contemporaries, showed himself the most ferocious of all the men who organized the massacres, finally undertook to provide the necessary instruments, and in co-operation with Maillard—he who had led the women to Versailles on the 5th of October—succeeded in forming a band of assassins amongst the Marseillais and the revolutionary elements of Paris, but, contrary to his expectations, this contingent proved insufficient, and it was found necessary to swell its numbers by liberating a quantity of thieves and murderers now in the prisons. [3] Yet even to this criminal horde the leaders dared not avow their true intentions, and a lurid tale of conspiracies was invented by way of inducement to them to carry out the dreadful work. They described to the assassins, says Maton de la Varenne, " Paris given over to the enemy by rascals whose leaders were in the prisons, where they were still conspiring ; gibbets planted in all the streets on which to hang the friends of the Revolution, their wives and children massacred beneath their eyes ; Capet insolently re-ascending the throne and carrying out the most horrible vengeances. Wine flowed in torrents

---

[1] *Crimes de la Révolution*, by Prudhomme, iv. 159.

[2] *Ibid.* iv. 156 ; *Histoire particulière*, etc., by Maton de la Varenne, p. 285.

[3] *Histoire secrète du Tribunal révolutionnaire*, by Proussinalle, p. 42. (Proussinalle is the pseudonym of P. J. A. Roussel.)

throughout and after this infernal and slanderous harangue, and the lives of those whom they called the traitors were placed at thirty livres independently of the spoils." [1]

The same fabulous story of conspiracies, the same false alarms, were now spread abroad amongst the people in order to prepare their minds for the massacres and ensure their assent. For, though the people were not to be invited this time to co-operate, the whole movement was none the less to be attributed to them. In each prison a mock tribunal was to be set up at which judges provided by the Commune, and assassins hired by them, armed with lists of proscription drawn up at the secret councils of the leaders, were to carry out so-called " justice "—and this was to be described by the high-sounding title, " The Tribunal of the Sovereign People." [2]   The massacres were then to be represented as simply the result of "irrepressible popular effervescence," produced by sudden panic at the approach of Brunswick and the discovery of collusion between the invading armies and the " conspirators " in the prisons.   For this purpose a phrase was invented, which was afterwards to be said to have passed from mouth to mouth amongst the terrified Parisians, namely, that before marching on the enemy they must put all these conspirators to death. [3]

The pretext was palpably absurd.   Paris has never been wont to give way to panic in the face of danger from the outside, and it awaited the advancing legions of Brunswick with its habitual sang-froid.

" Whilst the Prussians were in Champagne," says Mercier, " who would not have thought that profound alarm existed in all minds ?   Not at all ; the theatres, the restaurants, both full, displayed only peaceful newsmongers.   All the vainglorious threats of our enemies—we did not hear ; of all their murderous expectations we were far from having the least idea.   The capital, whether by its size or by the feeling of its strength, always believed itself unassailable, sheltered from all reverses in battle, and calculated to overawe its enemies.   The plans of defence, regarded as absolutely unnecessary, were laughed at, since no one would ever dare to attack the great city.   This stoicism was one of the

---

[1] *Histoire particulière*, etc., by Maton de la Varenne, p. 285.   The rate of salary was fixed by Billaud-Varenne (see *Histoire des Girondins*, by Granier de Cassagnac, ii. 48, 49).

[2] *Histoire secrète du Tribunal révolutionnaire*, by Proussinalle, p. 41.

[3] " The Comité de Surveillance had undertaken to prepare the minds (of the people) for this frightful idea (the massacres of September) ; it circulated everywhere this *word of command* that it counted on exploiting later : ' Before flying to the frontiers we must make sure of leaving behind us no traitors, no conspirators'" (*Histoire de la Terreur*, by Mortimer Ternaux, iii. 194 ; cf. *Journal du Club des Jacobins*, No. CCLV.).

greatest ramparts of liberty . . . never were the people seriously intimidated, either by the banquets of the bodyguard, at which Antoinette was described under the name of tigress of Germany, holding the Dauphin in her arms and inciting the most blood-thirsty hostilities, or by the flight of the King, which seemed to dissolve all government, or by the taking of Verdun, or by the Manifestos of all the Kings of Europe. It was impossible to make them feel terror of the enemy. . . ." [1]

And these were the people who were to be represented as so craven-hearted that, in a fit of blind panic, they fell upon their fellow-countrymen and put them indiscriminately to death !

As to the fear of a "conspiracy" in the prisons, no such idea ever entered into the heads of the Parisians. How could people, shut up behind bolts and bars, cut off from all communication with the outside world, *conspire*? How could the priests, against whom the movement was principally directed, form an effectual reinforcement to the trained legions of Brunswick ? How could unarmed men, women, and children take part in a massacre ? The idea was preposterous, and originated in the minds not of the people but of the members of the Commune, who circulated it through Paris by means of agents placed in the crowd for the purpose. That a certain number of citizens believed it is undeniable, but to attribute to the intelligent Parisians the authorship of such a fable, or the cowardice of acting on it by falling on the prisoners, is a gross and hideous calumny which should be finally refuted.

DOMICILIARY VISITS

On the 29th of August the incarceration of wealthy prisoners began. At one o'clock in the night commissioners from the Commune were sent all over the city to carry out the inquisition known as "domiciliary visits," which consisted in arresting all citizens the Commune chose to regard as "suspect."

Peltier has vividly described the horror of this beautiful

---

[1] Mercier, *Le Nouveau Paris*, i. 154. The English doctor, John Moore, noticed exactly the same thing. On the 19th of August, after driving through the Champs Élysées, he writes : " All those extensive fields were crowded with company of one sort or another ; an immense number of small booths was erected, where refreshments were sold, and which resounded with music and singing. Pantomimes and puppet-shows of various kinds are here exhibited, and in some parts they were dancing in the open fields. ' Are these people as happy as they seem ? ' said I to a Frenchman who was with me. ' Ils sont heureux comme des dieux, Monsieur,' replied he. ' Do you think the Duke of Brunswick never enters their thoughts ? ' said I. ' Soyez sûr, Monsieur,' resumed he, ' que Brunswick est précisément l'homme du monde auquel ils pensent le moins ' " (*Journal of a Residence in France*, i. 122).

summer night, whilst the silence of death reigned over the once brilliant city. " All the shops are shut ; every one withdraws into his home and trembles for his life and property. . . . Everywhere people and possessions are being hidden, everywhere is heard the intermittent sound of the padded hammer striking slow muffled blows to complete a hiding-place. Roofs, attics, sewers, chimneys—all are the same to fear that takes no risks into calculation. This man withdrawn behind the panelling that has been nailed over him seems to be part of the wall, and is almost deprived of breath and life ; that one stretched along a strong wide beam in a closet covers himself with all the dust the place contains . . . another suffocates with fear and heat between two mattresses, another rolled up in a barrel loses all sensation of life by the tension of his nerves. Fear is greater than pain ; they tremble but they do not weep, their hearts are withered up, their eyes are dull, their breasts contracted. Women surpassed themselves on this occasion ; it was intrepid women who hid the greater number of the men." [1]

During the three nights of August 29 to 31 that the domiciliary visits lasted an enormous number of people were arrested —according to some accounts 3000, according to others 8000. A certain proportion were released, the rest were collected at the Hôtel de Ville to await incarceration in the different prisons.

Pillage on a large scale took place during these visits, and, in order to make sure of sufficient booty, the priests—whose houses no doubt offered small opportunity for looting—were told that they would shortly be sent on a long journey, and must, therefore, provide themselves with money ; they were advised, in fact, to carry all their valuables on their persons.[2] By this means the victims of the massacres were found in possession of all the gold watches, snuff-boxes, money and jewels that afterwards found their way into the hands of the Commune.[3]

The greater number of priests thus arrested were accused of no crime but that of refusing to violate their consciences by taking the oath of fidelity to the civil constitution of the clergy. Some, however, seem to have been the objects of private vengeances on the part of members of the Commune. Amongst these was a certain Abbé Sicard, who had devoted his life to the teaching of deaf-mutes.[4] On the 26th of August the Abbé was accordingly

---

[1] *Révolution du 10 Août*, ii. 219.

[2] *Histoire particulière*, by Maton de la Varenne, p. 287 ; *Histoire secrète du Tribunal révolutionnaire*, by Proussinalle, i. 45 ; *Mémoires de Monseigneur de Salamon*, p. 33 ; *Récit de l'Abbé Berthelet*, quoted by M. de Granier de Cassagnac, *Histoire des Girondins*, ii. 285.

[3] *La Demagogie à Paris*, by C. A. Dauban, p. 64.

[4] " Procès verbaux de la Commune," in *Mémoires sur les Journées de Septembre*, p. 272, note.

arrested. A few days later a deputation of his pupils presented themselves at the Assembly with a touching petition for his release ; the Assembly harshly replied that no exception could be made in favour of the Abbé, and the deaf-mutes were sent away with the empty consolation that " they had been accorded the honours of the sitting." [1]

The members of the Commune, however, were well able to make exceptions in the case of people in whom they were interested ; thus Danton secured the release of a friend of his who was a thief, Camille Desmoulins that of a priest to whom he was attached, and Fabre d'Églantine that of his cook, whom he had had arrested for stealing from him.[2] At the same time money played its part, and many aristocrats obtained their liberty by means of *largesse* judiciously distributed amongst the demagogues.

ALARM IN PARIS

All was now ready ; it only remained to give a popular air to the movement by starting the proposed panic on the subject of the " conspiracy in the prisons."

On the 1st of September a wretched wagoner named Jean Jullien, who had been condemned to ten years' hard labour, was, according to the barbarous custom still preserved under the Reign of Liberty, publicly exhibited on a pillory in the Place de Grève. Thus exposed to the jeers of the mob the man grew frantic, and broke out into furious cries of " Vive le Roi ! Vive la Reine ! Down with the nation ! " By the order of the Commune he was thereupon removed to the Conciergerie to await further trial, and the people were then informed that during his detention he had confessed his complicity in an immense Royalist plot which had ramifications in all the prisons.[3] As a matter of fact Jullien stated nothing of the kind, as the register of the Criminal Tribunal afterwards revealed,[4] but he was condemned to death as a conspirator, and guillotined on the Place du Carrousel.

" It is not possible," wrote Dr. Moore indignantly, " that the Court could have believed that this wagoner intended to excite any sedition ; what he said was a mere rash retort on the mob, who insulted him in his misery. If *their* cry had been ' Vive le Roi et la Reine ! ' *his* would have been ' Vive la nation ! '

---

[1] *Moniteur*, xiii. 587.
[2] *Le véritable Ami du Peuple*, by Roch Marcandier (secretary of Camille Desmoulins) ; *Histoire secrète du Tribunal révolutionnaire*, by Proussinalle, p. 43.
[3] Mortimer Ternaux, iii. 200.
[4] *Ibid.* iii. 472.

It is plain, therefore, that he was condemned to die to please the people." [1]

Dr. Moore, unacquainted with the undercurrent of events, misinterpreted the incident ; the unfortunate Jean Jullien was sacrificed not to please the people, but to whet their appetite for blood in preparation for the events of the morrow, and also to give colour to the story of the conspiracy in the prisons.

The same day pamphlets were distributed announcing— "Great treachery of Louis Capet. Plot discovered for assassinating all good citizens during the night of the 2nd and 3rd of this month." [2]

Meanwhile the lying rumour of the fall of Verdun was purposely circulated throughout Paris, and "nothing," remarks Madame Roland, " was forgotten that could inflame the imagination, magnify facts, and make the dangers seem greater." [3]

But it was not until twelve o'clock on the following day— Sunday, the 2nd of September—that the imminent arrival of the Prussians was officially proclaimed. " The enemy is at the gates of Paris ; Verdun, which arrests his march, can only hold out for a week. . . . Citizens, this very day, immediately, let all friends of liberty rally around its banner, let an army of 60,000 men be found without delay, let us march on the enemy. . . ." [4]

At the same time the tocsin rang, cannons were fired, the générale was sounded, and from all sides citizens flew to arms. Dr. Moore, coming out of church, " found people hurrying up and down with anxious faces ; groups . . . formed at every corner : one told that a courier had arrived with very bad news ; another asserted that Verdun had been betrayed like Longwy, and that the enemy were advancing ; others shook their heads and said it was the traitors within Paris and not the declared enemies on the frontiers that were to be feared." [5]

But it was not amongst the people this last alarm arose ; the panic-mongers were emissaries of the Commune sent out to circulate the parrot phrase composed by the leaders.[6] " Directly after the proclamation had been issued," says Beaulieu, " the men who have the orders to begin the massacres cry out that, whilst the friends of liberty are grappling with the soldiers of despots, their wives and children will be at the mercy of the aristocrats, and that before starting they must exterminate these scoundrels more eager for the blood of the patriots than the Prussians and Austrians themselves." [7]

[1] *Journal of a Residence in France*, i. 294.
[2] Madelin, p. 255.   [3] *Mémoires de Mme. Roland*, i. 100
[4] *Procès verbaux de la Commune*, Séance du 2 Septembre 1792.
[5] *Journal of a Residence in France*, i. 300.
[6] Fantin Désodoards, ii. 240.   [7] Beaulieu, iv. 96,

A great number of citizens listened with astonishment to these suggestions, asking themselves " why at the least danger people should find pleasure in throwing Paris into a state of alarm, in striking all its inhabitants with terror, instead of maintaining in their hearts that masculine energy which befits warriors and ensures victory in battle. Was this not, indeed, an effectual method for undermining their courage ? But those who did not know the secrets of the conspirators were soon enlightened by their own experience." [1]

Meanwhile at the Assembly Danton was delivering his famous speech. " It is very gratifying, Messieurs, for the Minister of Justice of a free people to have the task of announcing to it that the country will be saved. . . . You know that Verdun is not yet in the power of our enemies. One part of the people will march to the frontiers ; another will dig trenches, and the third will defend the interior of our towns with pikes. . . . The tocsin, which is about to sound, is not a signal of alarm, it is the charge against the enemies of the country. In order to overcome them, Messieurs, we need *audacity, more audacity, always audacity, and France is saved* ! "

These words, which have sounded down the years as the trumpet-call of patriotism, must be studied in their context in order to understand their true significance. Posterity that at a moment of national danger sighs, " Oh for a Danton ! " takes it for granted that the audacity to which the great demagogue referred was to be displayed towards the advancing Austrians and Prussians. In this case, why employ the word *audacity* ? In referring to soldiers marching against their country's enemies, we may speak of them as bold or courageous, we may describe them as " daring " for undertaking some novel or hazardous method of attack, but we do not call them " audacious." Audacity does not merely signify bravery, it implies a certain degree of effrontery, of insolent contempt for public opinion, the mental resolution to bring off a coup and brazen out the consequences. It was precisely in this sense that it was applied by Danton, for the tocsin to which he referred was not a summons to Frenchmen to march against Prussians, but the call to Frenchmen to fall upon Frenchmen ; *it was a signal for the massacres of September.* [2]

Danton, having uttered his famous apostrophe, returned home, and said to his colleagues who awaited him, " *Foutre !* I electrified them ! Now we can go forward ! " which, says Proussinalle, meant " we can begin the massacres." " It was then

[1] Mercier, *Le Nouveau Paris*, i. 98 ; *Histoire des Hommes de Proie*, by Roch Marcandier.

[2] " Every one knows to-day that the cannon of alarm was on that day of blood to be the signal of the massacre " (" Relation de l'Abbé Sicard," *Mémoires sur les Journées de Septembre*, p. 100).

twelve o'clock. The men of blood who were waiting this signal
went out hurriedly from the ministers ; soon the tocsin and the
cannon of alarm were heard, the assassins started for the prisons,
and the massacres began." [1]

A certain lawyer named Grandpré, relates Madame Roland,
was employed by Roland at this time to visit the prisons, and,
finding that great alarm prevailed there concerning the rumour
of a projected massacre, waylaid Danton the same morning
as he came out of a meeting of council at the Ministry of the
Interior, and begged him to ensure the safety of the prisoners.
" He was interrupted by an exclamation from Danton, shouting
in his bull's voice, with his eyes starting out of his head, and
with a furious gesture : ' What do I care about the prisoners !
Let them take care of themselves ! ' (*Je me f. . . . , bien des
prisonniers ! qu'ils deviennent ce qu'ils pourront !*) " [2]

Grandpré was not the only man to approach Danton on this
fatal morning. Prudhomme the journalist, seated in his office,
hearing the sound of the tocsin and the cannon, hurried to the
Ministry of Justice, where he found Danton, and said to him,
" What means this cannon of alarm, this tocsin, and the rumour
of the arrival of the Prussians in Paris ? "

" Keep calm, old friend of liberty," answered Danton, " it
is the tocsin of victory."

"But," persisted Prudhomme, "they speak of massacring——"

" Yes," said Danton, " we were all to have been massacred
to-night, beginning with the purest patriots. These rascals of
aristocrats who are in the prisons had procured firearms and
daggers. At a certain hour indicated to-night the doors were to be
opened to them. They would have scattered into all the different
quarters to butcher the wives and children of patriots who march
against the Prussians." Prudhomme, bewildered by this monstrous fable, inquired what means had been taken to prevent
the execution of the plot. " What means ? " cried Danton ; " the
irritated people, who were told in time, mean to administer justice
themselves to all the scoundrels who are in the prisons."

At this Prudhomme declares he was stupefied with horror ;
we may question whether he ventured, however, to remonstrate
at the time with quite the courage he afterwards attributed to
himself. When, a moment later, Camille Desmoulins entered,
Prudhomme goes on to relate, Danton turned to him with the
words, " Prudhomme has come to ask what is going to be done."

" Yes," said Prudhomme, " my heart is rent by what I have
just heard."

[1] *Histoire secrète du Tribunal révolutionnaire*, by Proussinalle, i. 48 ;
Crimes de la Révolution, by Prudhomme, iv. 141.
[2] *Mémoires de Mme. Roland*, i. 31.

" Then you have not told him," Camille said, turning to
Danton, " that the innocent will not be confounded with the
guilty ? " Prudhomme continued to remonstrate, but Danton
answered firmly, " Every kind of moderate measure is useless ;
the anger of the people is at its height, it would be actually
dangerous to arrest it. When their first anger is assuaged we
shall be able to make them listen to reason."

" But if," Prudhomme suggested, " the legislative body and
the constituted authorities were to go all over Paris and harangue
the people ? "

" No, no," answered Camille, " that would be too dangerous,
for the people in their first anger might find victims in the
persons of their dearest friends." [1]

Prudhomme went out sadly, and on his way through the
dining-room perceived a pleasant dinner - party in progress—
Madame Desmoulins, Madame Danton, and Fabre d'Églantine
were amongst the guests.[2] Word being brought at this moment
to Danton that " all was going well," the Minister of Justice
complacently took his seat at the table.[3]

So at the very moment that the assassins started forth on
their terrible work, the authors of the crime sat down to feast.

THE FIRST MASSACRE AT THE ABBAYE [4]

Punctually at twelve o'clock a troop of Marseillais and
Avignonnais confederates—amongst whom were a number of

---

[1] *Crimes de la Révolution*, by Prudhomme, iv. 91. Prudhomme, now
convinced by the reasoning of Danton that the massacres were really
a case of irrepressible popular fury at the discovery of a gigantic plot
against the lives of the citizens, published a justification of the movement in his *Révolutions de Paris*, No. 165. It was not till much later
that he realized he had been duped. "When in the *Révolutions de
Paris*," he wrote afterwards, " we described this day (the 2nd of September)
as ' The Justice of the People,' we were not only authorized by the ideas
we then entertained but also by the criminal silence of the legislative body
and of the ministers. It is, above all, the crafty and atrocious behaviour of
the Commune of Paris which caused us to commit many involuntary
errors " (*Crimes de la Révolution*, iv. 87). Revolutionary historians freely
quote the former work, but are of course perfectly silent about the latter.

[2] *Ibid.*; also *Histoire secrète du Tribunal révolutionnaire*, by Proussinalle,
i. 48.   [3] *Ibid.*

[4] Authorities consulted on the first massacre at the Abbaye : *Mémoires
de l'Abbé Sicard* ; *La Verité toute entière sur les vrais Acteurs de la Journée du
2 Septembre 1792*, by Felhémési. Felhémési is an anagram of Méhée fils.
The author of this pamphlet, a bystander, not a prisoner, was the son of the
recorder Méhée and a friend of Danton and Desmoulins ; his object, therefore, is not to tell the truth on the real authors of the massacres, for he
attributes all the blame to Billaud-Varenne, but as an eye-witness his
account of events is valuable.

men who had taken part in the Glacière d'Avignon [1]—arrived, obedient to orders and singing the " Marseillaise," at the Hôtel de Ville, to transfer the first batch of prisoners to the Abbaye. Twenty-four priests, among which, in spite of the appeal of the deaf-mutes, the Abbé Sicard was included, were thrust into several cabs, and the drivers received the order to proceed slowly through the streets under pain of being massacred on their seats if they disobeyed. The confederates, who formed the escort, loudly informed the prisoners that they would never reach the Abbaye, as " the people " to whom they were to be delivered intended to massacre them on the way. In order to facilitate this operation the doors of the cabs were left open, and all efforts on the part of the priests to close them were overcome by the soldiers, who, pointing at the prisoners with their sabres, cried out to the disorderly crowd following in the wake of the procession, " These are your enemies, the accomplices of those who delivered up Verdun, those who only awaited your departure to murder your wives and children. Here are our pikes and sabres ; put these monsters to death ! "

But if the leaders had hoped to give a popular air to the proceedings by inducing the mob to begin the massacres, they were disappointed, for the people around the cabs contented themselves with shouting insults, and the Marseillais were obliged to make use of their weapons themselves. After cutting at the defenceless priests with their sabres, one of the soldiers finally mounted on the steps of a carriage and plunged his sabre into the heart of the first victim.[2] His comrades quickly followed his example, thrusting at the prisoners through the open doorways, but the blows being ill-directed only a few were mortally wounded, and it was not until the procession stopped at the doors of the Abbaye, where Maillard and his hired assassins were waiting, that the massacres began in earnest. Out of the twenty-four prisoners, twenty-one perished ; two, including the Abbé Sicard, succeeded in escaping to the neighbouring " Committee of the Section," and, throwing themselves into the arms of the commissioners there assembled, cried out, " Save us ! Save us ! " Several of these men, terrified for their own lives, roughly repulsed the unhappy priests, answering, " Go away ! would you have us massacred ? " but one, recognizing the Abbé Sicard, led them into the inner hall, and closed the door on the mob. Here they might have remained in safety had not a " fury " in the crowd, who happened to be an accomplice of the Abbé Sicard's enemies, rushed to inform them of his escape. The next

[1] *Crimes de la Révolution*, by Prudhomme, iv. 96.
[2] Mortimer Ternaux, iii. 225.

moment heavy blows sounded on the doors and voices called aloud for the two prisoners.

The Abbé Sicard felt that his last hour had come. Handing his watch to one of the commissioners he said, " Give this to the first deaf-mute who asks for news of me."

The blows on the door redoubled. The Abbé Sicard fell on his knees, offered his last prayer, then, rising, embraced his comrade and said, " Let us hold each other close and die together ; the door is about to open, the murderers are there, we have not five minutes to live."

The next moment the assassins burst into the room and rushed upon the prisoners. The Abbé Sicard's companion fell dead at his side ; Sicard himself saw a pike levelled at his breast, when suddenly one of the commissioners of the section, a clock-maker named Monnot, thrust his way through the crowd, and, throwing himself between the assassins and their victim, bared his breast to their blows, crying out, " Here is the breast through which you must pass to reach that one. He is the Abbé Sicard, one of the men who have rendered the greatest service to his country, the father of the deaf-mutes. You must cross my body to get to him ! "

At these words the murderous pike was lowered, and for a moment it seemed that the brave clockmaker had succeeded in disarming the assassins. But outside the hall the rest of the ferocious band waited, howling like wolves for their prey. Then the good Abbé, showing himself at the window, obtained a moment of silence, and spoke in these words to the raving herd :

" My friends, here is an innocent man, would you have him die without giving him a hearing ? "

Voices answered, " You were with the others we have just killed. You are guilty as they were ! "

" Listen to me a moment, and if after hearing me you decree my death I shall not complain. My life is in your hands. Learn, then, what I do, who I am, and then you will decide my fate. I am the Abbé Sicard."

A murmur went round, " He is the Abbé Sicard, the father of the deaf-mutes, we must listen to him."

The Abbé continued : " I teach the deaf-mutes from their birth, and, as the number of these unfortunate ones is greater amongst the poor than amongst the rich, I belong more to you than to the rich." Then a voice cried, " The Abbé Sicard must be saved. He is too valuable a man to perish. His whole life is employed in doing a great work ; no, he has not time to be a conspirator."

Immediately a chorus took up the last words, adding, " We must save him ! We must save him ! "

Whereupon the assassins, standing behind the Abbé at the window, seized him in their arms, and led him out through the ranks of their blood-stained comrades, who fell on his neck, embraced him, and begged to be allowed to lead him home in triumph.

Nothing is stranger in all the strange history of the Revolution than the evidence of latent idealism that seems to have lingered in many ferocious hearts : how did it come to pass that, amongst this fearful horde, men could be found to applaud a noble life and perceive its value to the world, whilst themselves employed only in crime and destruction ?

But, although the Abbé Sicard had succeeded in disarming his terrible assassins by a direct appeal to their better feelings, he was quite unable to touch the hearts of the men who had ordained the crime, for, having refused to leave the prison until legally released by the Commune, he waited in vain for this order to arrive ; two days later we find him still writing plaintive appeals to the Assembly to rescue him from the place of horror in which he is confined, and where he is perpetually threatened with a hideous death. The Assembly contented itself with passing on the letter to the Commune. But since it was there his death had been decreed, the unfortunate Abbé was left to his fate, and it was not until seven o'clock in the evening of the 4th of September, by the intercession of the deputy Pastoret with Hérault de Sechelles, that the Abbé Sicard obtained his release.[1]

At five o'clock in the evening of the 2nd, when the carnage was temporarily suspended, Billaud - Varenne arrived in his puce-coloured coat and black wig, wearing his municipal scarf as delegate of the Commune.[2] Stepping over the bodies of the dead priests, he thus addressed the assassins : " Respectable citizens, you have killed scoundrels ; you have done your duty, and you will each have twenty-four livres." [3]

This discourse aroused afresh the fury of the assassins, and they began to call aloud for further victims. Then Maillard, known as Tape-Dur, answered loudly, " There is nothing more to be done here ; let us go to the Carmes ! " [4]

---

[1] "Relation de l'Abbé Sicard," also "Procès verbaux de la Commune de Paris," in *Mémoires sur les Journées de Septembre*, p. 272

[2] Felhémési ; Beaulieu, iv. 119.

[3] *Les Crimes de Marat*, by Maton de la Varenne.

[4] Felhémési.

THE MASSACRE AT THE CARMES [1]

At the Couvent des Carmes, in the Rue de Vaugirard, between 150 and 200 priests had been incarcerated after the 10th of August. For a time they had believed themselves to be threatened merely with deportation, but during the two days preceding the massacres a number of sinister indications showed them that they had only a little while to live. The patriarch of this band, the venerable Archbishop of Arles, who, in spite of his age and infirmities, insisted on sharing every hardship and privation with his companions, succeeded in inspiring them all with his own heroic spirit, and it was thus that in perfect calm and resignation they awaited their end. When on this terrible Sunday afternoon, the 2nd of September, Joachim Ceyrat, the principal organizer of this massacre, whose inveterate hatred of religion filled him with unrelenting fury towards its ministers, ordered them all to leave the church which served as their prison and assemble in the garden, they well knew that their last moment had come. Yet it was still with undisturbed serenity that for half-an-hour they paced the shady alleys, whilst the terrible band of Maillard came steadily nearer.

Then suddenly, at the entrance to the convent, cries of rage were heard; through the bars was seen the flash of sabres, and at this the priests, retreating into a small oratory at the far end of the garden, fell on their knees and gave each other the last blessing.

The Abbé de Pannonie, standing in the doorway of this chapel with the Archbishop of Arles, said, " Monseigneur, I think they have come to assassinate us."

" Then," said the Archbishop, " this is the moment of our sacrifice; let us resign ourselves and thank God we can offer Him our blood in so splendid a cause." And with these words he entered the oratory, and knelt in prayer before the altar.

Even as he spoke the garden gates were broken down, and a drunken band of assassins, armed with pistols and sabres, threw themselves with savage howls upon their victims. The first to perish was Père Gérault, who, absorbed in his breviary, walked up and down beside the fountain in the middle of the garden; the second was the Abbé Salins, who had hurried to the side of his fallen comrade.

Meanwhile another group of murderers made their way

---

[1] Authorities consulted on the massacre at the Carmes : *Le Couvent des Carmes*, by Alexandre Sorel ; *Histoire du Clergé*, by the Abbé Barruel (1794) ; *La Révolution du 10 Août*, vol. ii., by Peltier ; also Granier de Cassagnac and Mortimer Ternaux, *op. cit.* ; article on " Les Carmes " in *Paris révolutionnaire*, by G. Lenôtre.

towards the oratory, calling out furiously, " Where is the Archbishop of Arles ? Where is the Archbishop of Arles ? "

The Archbishop, hearing his name, rose from his knees and came towards the doorway. In vain his companions attempted to hold him back. " Let me pass," he said; " may my blood appease them ! "

Then, standing on the steps of the chapel, he fearlessly confronted his assassins.

" It is you, old scoundrel, who are the Archbishop of Arles ? " cried the leader of the band.

" Yes, messieurs, it is I."

" It was you who had the blood of patriots shed at Arles ? "

" Messieurs, I have never had the blood of any one shed ; nor have I ever injured any one in my life."

" Well, then, I will injure you ! " answered the murderer, striking the Archbishop across the forehead with a sabre. A second assassin dealt him a fearful blow with a scimitar, cleaving his face almost in two.

The heroic old man uttered never a murmur, but, still erect on the steps of the chapel, raised his hands to the streaming wound, then, at a third blow, fell forward at the feet of his murderers, and a pike was thrust through his heart.

At this sight a savage howl of triumph rose from all the assassins, and, levelling their pistols at the kneeling priests inside the chapel, they began a murderous fusillade ; in a few moments the floor was strewn with the dead and dying.

Amongst the priests who had not taken refuge in the oratory were a certain number of young men less resigned than their superiors, and these, seeing the massacre in progress, attempted to elude their murderers.

Then in the old garden a terrible man-hunt began ; around the trunks of trees, in and out amongst the bushes, the raging horde pursued their victims, uttering foul blasphemies against religion and singing the bloodthirsty refrain :

> Dansons la Carmagnole,
> Vive le son ! vive le son !
> Dansons la Carmagnole,
> Vive le son du canon !

A few of the young priests, with extraordinary agility, succeeded in scaling the ten-foot wall of the garden into the neighbouring Rue Cassette, helping themselves upward by means of the stone figure of a monk that stood close against it ; but some of these, after reaching safety, were stricken with remorse lest their escape should make the fate of those they had left behind more terrible, and with sublime courage they climbed back again into the garden and met their death.

Suddenly in the midst of the butchery a voice cried, " Halt !
This is not the way to go to work ! "

It was Maillard who, interposing between the assassins and their
victims, ordered those of the priests who still survived to be driven
into the church, whilst a tribunal was set up for their judgement.

At the Carmes this so - called " Tribunal of the Sovereign
People " was even more a mockery than at the other prisons,
for here none of the populace were even admitted to watch the
massacre ; [1] indeed, the " ladies of the quarter," that is to say,
the poor women from the surrounding streets, who had collected
outside the gate where they could catch a glimpse of the scene
taking place in the garden, loudly protested against the shooting
of the priests,[2] and it seems to have been mainly for this reason
that it was decided to finish the massacre in a more orderly
manner out of view of the street, whilst at the same time a
cordon of Gendarmes Nationaux, stationed at the gates, prevented the people from breaking in and interfering with the
assassins.[3] A table was then arranged in a gloomy cloister of
the convent, and here either Maillard or a commissioner named
Violette [4] seated himself with the list of the prisoners, drawn up
by Joachim Ceyrat, spread out before him. Needless to say, no
trial of any kind took place, for Ceyrat that morning had pronounced the verdict, " All who are in the Carmes are guilty ! " [5]
A few managed to find hiding-places and survived the massacre ;
a few others succeeded in melting the hearts of the assassins ;
the rest, summoned two by two from the church to appear before
the tribunal, rose from their knees blessing God for the privilege
of shedding their blood in His cause, and clasping the Scriptures
in their hands, with eyes raised to Heaven, went out into the
corridor to meet their death. In less than two hours one hundred
and nineteen victims had perished.

THE SECOND MASSACRE AT THE ABBAYE [6]

At seven o'clock in the evening, after the massacre at the
Carmes, Maillard and his band returned to the Abbaye, where

[1] " The principal door of the church opening into the Rue de Vaugirard
remained closed during the whole execution. The people did not take the
least part in it " (Peltier, *La Révolution du 10 Août*, ii. 245).

[2] Granier de Cassagnac, *Histoire des Girondins*, ii. 292.

[3] *Histoire du Clergé*, by l'Abbé Barruel, p. 251.

[4] Granier de Cassagnac says it was Violette ; Sorel (*Le Couvent des
Carmes*, p. 132) says it was more probably Maillard.

[5] Mortimer Ternaux, iii. 231.

[6] Authorities consulted on the massacres at the Abbaye (accounts of
prisoners) : *Mon Agonie de trente-huit Heures*, by Jourgniac de St. Méard ;
Mémoires de l'Abbé Sicard ; *Mémoires inédits de l'Internonce à Paris
pendant la Révolution, Monseigneur de Salamon* (Plon Nourrit, 1890) ;
Felhémési, *op. cit.*

a number of prisoners still remained incarcerated, for the murder of the contingent in cabs at the entrance had been only the prelude to a general massacre.

The Abbé de Salamon, a young papal nuncio, whose account of these September days is perhaps the most thrilling of all existing records, has described, with frightful minuteness, the agony of mind in which he and a company of fellow-priests passed that interminable Sunday afternoon. At half-past two, when they had just finished dining in the long dark hall assigned them as a prison, the gaoler noisily drew the bolts, and threw open the door with the words, " Be quick, the people are marching on the prisons, and have already begun to massacre all the prisoners." It was, in fact, at this very moment that the procession of cabs arrived at the Abbaye and the carnage began.

At this news, says the Abbé Salamon, " there was great agitation amongst us. Some cried, ' What will happen to us ? ' Others, ' Then we must die ! ' Many went to the door to look through the key-hole—a hole that did not exist, for prison locks only open from outside and show no opening on the interior. Others sprang up on their heels as if to look out of the windows, which were fourteen feet high; finally, others walking up and down without knowing where they were going knocked their legs violently against the seats and tables. . . . We began to hear the cries of the people ; it was like a great distant murmur."

Standing apart were two young Minim brothers—"the youngest one had an angelic face." The Abbé Salamon, going up to them, spoke words of comfort. " Ah, mon Dieu, monsieur," answered the younger, " I do not regard it as a disgrace to die for religion ; on the contrary, I am afraid they may not kill me because I am only a sub-deacon." The Abbé Salamon, none too devout himself, admits that he blushed at these words, " worthy of the earliest martyrs of the Church."

But the hour for martyrdom had not yet arrived ; the band of assassins, after murdering the priests at the entrance of the convent, had gone on to the Carmes, and for some hours all was quiet. The priests spent the rest of the afternoon in prayer and confession. Then suddenly the door was thrown open again, and the voice of the gaoler called out roughly, " The people are more and more irritated ; there are perhaps 2000 men in the Abbaye." And, indeed, the tumult and the howling of the mob could now be heard distinctly by the prisoners. The gaoler added brutally, " It is just announced that all the priests in the Carmes have been massacred." At these words the assembled company threw themselves with one accord at the feet of the Curé de St. Jean en Grève—a saintly old man of eighty, " who retained all the serenity of a noble soul "—and begged him to give them absolution *in articulo mortis*.

After this had been given all remained kneeling, whilst the old curé said, " We may regard ourselves as sick men about to die. . . . I will recite the prayers of the dying ; join with me that God may have pity on us."

But at the opening words, uttered with so great dignity by the aged priest, " Depart, Christian souls, from this world in the name of God the Father Almighty . . .," almost all burst into tears. " Some lay brothers loudly lamented at dying so young, and gave way to imprecations against their assassins. The good curé interrupted them, representing to them with great gentleness that they must generously pardon, and that perhaps if God were pleased with their resignation He might create means to save them."

Such were the men who were represented as planning to massacre the wives and children of the citizens !

Meanwhile, outside the gate of the prison in the Rue Sainte-Marguerite, the massacre of the prisoners had begun. A band of assassins, preceding that of Maillard, which was still occupied at the Carmes, had besieged the gate clamouring for victims, and the concierge, fearing to resist them, had handed out several prisoners committed to his care. It was thus that, when Maillard and his band returned from the Carmes, they found the hideous work already begun. This " band of massacrers," says Felhémési, " comes back covered with blood and dust ; these monsters are tired of carnage but not sated with blood. They are out of breath, they ask for wine, for wine, or death. What reply can be made to this irresistible desire ? The civil committee of the section gives them orders for 24 pints to be drawn at a neighbouring wine-merchant. Soon they have drunk, they are intoxicated, and contemplate with satisfaction the corpses strewn in the courtyard of the Abbaye."

It was then decided, in order to give an air of justice to their proceedings, that again a so-called " popular tribunal," under Maillard, should be set up.

Maillard, who was himself a thief,[1] had brought with him twelve swindlers to act as his accomplices, and these men, mingling in the crowd " as if by accident," came forward " in the name of the Sovereign People " and seized the registers of the prison. At this " the turnkeys tremble, the gaoler and the gaoler's wife faint, the prison is surrounded by furious men, cries and tumult increase." [2] Suddenly one of the commissioners of the section appeared on the scene, and standing on a footstool

[1] *Mémoires de Sénart* (edition de Lescure), p. 28.
[2] Felhémési.

attempted to soothe the mob, whom he took to be the cause of
the uproar : " My comrades, my friends, you are good patriots
. . . but you must love justice. There is not one of you who
does not shudder at the frightful idea of soaking his hands in
innocent blood ! " Even this vile mob, collected by the leaders
to abet them in their crimes, showed itself amenable to sentiments
of humanity and justice, and cried out loudly, " Yes ! Yes ! "

But those who had ordained the massacres had prepared
against any eventualities of this kind, and a man in the crowd
was ready with the prescribed phrase. Springing forward,
with blazing eyes and brandishing a blood - stained sword, he
interrupted the orator in these words : " Say, then, monsieur le
citoyen, . . . do you wish to lull us to sleep ? . . . I am not an
orator, I delude no one, and I tell you that I am the father of a
family, that I have a wife and five children whom I am willing
to leave here under the protection of my section in order to go
and fight the enemy, but meanwhile I do not mean that the
rascals who are in this prison, or the others who will open the
doors to them, shall go and murder my wife and children . . .
so by me, or by others, the prison shall be purged of all these
cursed scoundrels ! "

Instantly the mob, rallying to the word of command, shouted,
" He is right ; no mercy ! " and Maillard's accomplices called out
for a tribunal to be formed by their leader : " Monsieur Maillard !
Citizen Maillard as president ! He is a good man, Citizen
Maillard ! " [1]

In a hall opening on the garden of the convent the terrible
tribunal was then set up. At a table covered with a green cloth,
on which ink, pens, and paper were arranged, Maillard, in his
black coat and powdered hair, took his place, with the register
of the prison spread before him. This register, preserved by
the " Prefecture of Police," long remained one of the ghastliest
relics of the revolutionary era ; on the greasy pages great marks
of wine and blood might be seen, and all down the list of names
blood-stained finger-prints left by the assassins, as they indicated
the prisoner concerning whom they asked for orders.[2]

Needless to say, the verdicts had been arranged beforehand,
and it was then agreed that instead of pronouncing sentence of
death the words " To La Force ! " should be employed. By this
means the victims, imagining themselves to be acquitted and
about to be transferred to this other prison, would go forward
without a struggle into the arms of their assassins. The ruse,

[1] Felhémési, op. cit.
[2] Histoire des Girondins, by Granier de Cassagnac, ii. 165. M. de
Cassagnac made use of these documents for his work, but they were
destroyed later by the Commune in 1871.

no doubt, served a double purpose, for in cases where no evidence was forthcoming against the prisoner the so - called "judges" could absolve themselves of the injustice of condemning him, and attribute his death to the uncontrollable passions of " the people."

The first victims of this mock tribunal were the Swiss, who had been imprisoned after the siege of the Tuileries on the 10th of August. These, to the number of forty-three, were all common soldiers, for their officers, with the exception of M. de Reding, who lay wounded in the chapel of the Abbaye, had been taken to the Conciergerie. A voice, speaking through the window of the hall occupied by the " tribunal," and declaring itself to be " entrusted with the wish of the people," now exclaimed loudly, " There are Swiss in the prison, lose no time in examining them ; they are all guilty, not one must escape ! " And the rabble obediently echoed, " That is just, that is just, let us begin with them ! " The tribunal thereupon pronounced the words, " To La Force ! "

Maillard then went to the Swiss and ordered them to come forth. " You assassinated the people on the 10th of August ; to-day they demand justice, you. must go to La Force." The unhappy Swiss, instantly understanding the significance of these words, for the howls of the mob had reached them in their prison, fell on their knees, crying out, " Mercy ! Mercy ! " But Maillard was inexorable. Two of the assassins followed, saying harshly to the prisoners, " Come, come, make up your minds ! Let us go ! " Then " lamentations and horrible groans " arose ; the unhappy Swiss, all huddling together at the back of the room, clung to each other, embraced, gave way to pitiful despair at the sight of so hideous a death. A few white-haired old men, " whose looks resembled those of Coligny," almost succeeded in disarming their murderers. But a relentless voice cried, " Well, which of you is to go out the first ? " At this a tall young man in a blue overcoat, with a noble countenance and martial air, came forward fearlessly : " I pass the first ! " he cried, " I will give the example ! " Throwing off his hat he advanced proudly, " with the apparent calm of concentrated fury," and faced the raging crowd. For a moment the horde, stupefied by his intrepidity, fell back ; a circle formed around him ; with folded arms he stood defiant, then, realizing that death was inevitable, suddenly rushed forward upon the pikes and bayonets, and the next moment fell pierced with a hundred wounds.

All but one of his unhappy comrades shared the same fate ; this sole survivor, a boy " of ingenuous countenance," succeeded in enlisting the sympathy of a Marseillais, who bore him forth triumphantly amidst the applause of the crowd.

Four other victims followed, accused of forging assignats ;

then Montmorin, the former Minister of Foreign Affairs, and arch-enemy of Brissot and the pro-Prussian party. Montmorin had been summoned before the bar of the Assembly on the 22nd of August and accused by the Girondins of having opposed an alliance between France and Prussia, and of wishing to maintain the Franco-Austrian alliance, but the Assembly, not entirely dominated by this faction, had acquitted Montmorin, and so his death by violent means was decreed. Can we doubt that Peltier was right in saying that this foul crime lay at the door of Brissot,[1] and may not the hand of Prussia also be detected here ? Yet this too was attributed to the fury of "the people"! The register of Maillard bears these words, beside the name of Montmorin : "On the 4th of September[2] 1792, the Sieur Montmorin has been judged by the people and executed on the spot."

Other victims followed quickly—Thierry de Ville d'Avray, *valet de chambre* to the King, and guardian of the Garde Meuble where the Crown jewels were kept, was condemned with the words, "Like master, like man !" Two magistrates, Buob and Bosquillon, who had started an inquiry on the events of the 20th of June, the Comte de St. Marc, the Comte de Wittgenstein, the solicitor Séron—accused of calumniating the nation because he had complained of being rudely awakened from his sleep on the night of his arrest—were all put to death with indescribable barbarity.

Jourgniac de St. Méard has vividly described the agony of mind in which he and his fellow-prisoners passed this terrible night and the no less terrible day that followed, for the piercing screams of the victims penetrated to them in their prison, and none doubted that before long their own turn must come.

"The principal thing with which we occupied ourselves," says St. Méard, "was to know what position we should assume in order to receive death the least painfully when we entered the place of massacre. From time to time we sent one of our comrades to the window of the tower, to tell us what position those unfortunate people took up who were then being immolated, so as to calculate from their report that which it would be best for us to assume. They reported that those who held out their hands suffered much longer, because the sabre-cuts were stopped before reaching their heads—there were even some whose hands and arms fell before their bodies—and that those who held them behind their backs seemed to suffer much the least. . . . Well, it was on these horrible details we deliberated. . . . We calculated

---

[1] Peltier, *La Révolution du 10 Août*, ii. 193, 194, 389.
[2] This was an error. Montmorin was massacred on the 2nd of September.

the advantages of this last position, and we advised each other to assume it when our turn came to be massacred ! . . ."

It was not until nearly midnight that the company of priests, which included the Abbé Salamon, was led before the terrible tribunal.

" We walked," says the nuncio, who certainly had not acquired the resignation of his more devout companions, " escorted by a crowd in arms, in the midst of a great number of torches, and under the rays of a beautiful moon that lit up all those vile scoundrels." Arraigned before the green-covered table they awaited their sentence, whilst a quarrel took place amongst the judges. At last Maillard, by loudly ringing his bell, obtained silence, and one of his assistants addressed the crowd : " Here are a lot of rascals who are waiting for the just punishment of their crimes. All these people are priests ; they are the sworn enemies of the nation, who would not take the oath . . .; they are all aristocrats, we must begin with them, certainly they are the most guilty."

The form of interrogatory was confined to the one question, " Have you taken the oath ? " The first to answer it was the old Curé de St. Jean en Grève, who, owning courageously that he had not taken it because he regarded it as contrary to the principles of his religion, asked only to be spared a lingering death in consideration of his great age and infirmity. Instantly a storm of blows descended on the venerable head, and a moment later the lifeless body was dragged out to the cries of " Vive la nation ! " Nearly all his companions shared the same fate ; amongst the last to fall were the two Minim brothers, over whom a furious struggle took place, some of the assassins wishing to take them out and kill them, others to detain them in the hall. " I noticed," says Salamon, " that the under-deacon who so desired to die opposed less resistance to those who wished to drag him out than to those who wished to save him. In the end the scoundrels triumphed, and they were massacred."

Such was the nature of the " gangrene " which the re-generators of France held it necessary to destroy ! Of such stuff was made the clergy of the Old Régime, described to us as " vicious " and " effete," whose fate was but the just retribution of their deeds ! Amongst the priests who perished on these September days was not a single one who had been distinguished for profligacy or extravagance ; the great majority were humble, saintly men, many white-haired and venerable, whose lives had been passed in doing good, and who in death displayed a heroic resignation never surpassed in the earliest days of Christendom. No, the Old Order was not effete that produced such men as these !

The lay prisoners, however, were not all of the stuff of which martyrs are made. Some defended themselves vigorously. Two quite young men, who had been recognized as members of the King's new bodyguard, were dragged forward and denounced to the mob as *chevaliers du poignard*, who must be punished on the spot, whereat the mob replied with savage howls of " Death ! death ! "

" They were," says the Abbé Salamon, " two young men of superb figures and handsome countenances . . ."; the crowd " began to overwhelm them with insults ; then one man, more cowardly than the rest, gave the tallest one a violent blow with a sabre, to which he replied only with a shrug of the shoulders. Then began a horrible struggle between these vile drinkers of blood and these two young men, who, although unarmed, defended themselves like lions. They threw many (of their assailants) to the ground, and I think if only they had had a knife they would have been victorious. At last they fell on the floor of the hall all pierced with blows. They seemed in despair at dying, and I heard one crying out, ' Must one die at this age, and in this manner ? ' "

All through this dreadful night the massacres continued in the courtyards of the prison. The Abbé Sicard, still detained in the hall of the section, could hear the cries of the victims, the howls of the murderers, the savage songs and dances taking place around the bodies of the dead. At intervals an assassin, with sleeves rolled up, clutching a blood-stained sabre, would come to the section clamouring for more drink : " Our good brothers have been long at work in the courtyard ; they are tired, their lips are dry ; I come to ask for wine for them ! " And finally the committee tremblingly ordered them four more flagons. Then, crazed with the fumes of alcohol, the massacrers returned to their hideous task. " One," says the Abbé Sicard, " complained that these aristocrats died too quickly, that only the first ones had the pleasure of striking, and it was decided to hit them only with the flat of the sword, and then make them run between two rows of massacrers, as was formerly the practice with soldiers condemned to be scourged. It was also arranged that there should be seats around this place for the ' ladies ' and ' gentlemen.' . . . One can imagine," Sicard adds significantly, " what *ladies* these were ! "

The council of the Commune had taken care to provide not only the actors but the audience. The women of the district, trained at the Société Fraternelle, were reinforced during the massacres of September by a terrible brigade of female malefactors released from the prisons, whose rôle was to applaud the assassinations and incite the murderers to further violence. It was this legion that afterwards peopled the tribunes of the

Terror, and became known as the *tricoteuses* or " furies " of the guillotine.[1]

Nothing had been left to chance by the organizers of the massacres. In the middle of the night members of the Commune, alarmed lest under the influence of fiery drinks and excitement some of the spoils they counted on might elude them, deputed Billaud-Varenne again to harangue the massacrers.

" My friends, my good friends," cried Billaud, standing on a platform in their midst, " the Commune sends me to you to represent to you that you are dishonouring this *beautiful day*. They have been told that you are robbing these rascals of aristocrats after executing justice on them. Leave, leave all the jewels, all the money and goods they have on them for the expenses of the great act of justice you are exercising. *They will have a care to pay you as was arranged with you.* Be noble, great, and generous like the profession you follow. May everything in this great day be worthy of the people whose sovereignty is entrusted to you ! " [2]

And these were the massacres that the Commune afterwards declared itself powerless to *prevent* !

Even to the most ingenuous observer it was evident that the atrocities taking place were not a matter of misdirected popular fury, but the result of a deep-laid scheme. Honest Dr. John Moore, a stranger to all intrigues, had been told earlier in the day that " the people " had broken into the Abbaye and were massacring the prisoners. But at midnight, as he sits writing in his hotel, close by the prison, a sudden flash of revelation comes to him : all at once he understands, and with a thrill of realization writes these illuminating words : " *Is* this the work of a furious and deluded mob ? How come the citizens of this populous metropolis to remain passive spectators of so dreadful

---

[1] *Histoire secrète du Tribunal révolutionnaire*, by Proussinalle, p. 42 ; *Crimes de la Révolution*, by Prudhomme, iii. 272, 273.

[2] *Mémoires de l'Abbé Sicard* ; Felhémési, *op. cit.* It seems, however, that Billaud did not pay them as arranged, for Felhémési relates that a terrible uproar arose next day when he reappeared at the prison, and he was surrounded by a horde of the assassins clamouring for higher salaries. " Do you think I have earned only 24 francs ? " a butcher's apprentice, armed with a club, said loudly. " I have killed more than forty on my own account." This seems to confirm the statement of Maton de la Varenne that on engagement they were promised 30 livres, but some were only paid 24 livres, as the registers of the Commune reveal. The Abbé de Salamon, who saw them being paid on the Wednesday morning, September 5, by a member of the Commune wearing his municipal scarf, says : " The salary given to those who had, as they said, ' worked well '—that is to say, massacred well—was from 30 to 35 francs. A certain number obtained less. I even saw one who only obtained 6 francs. His work was not considered sufficient " (*Mémoires de Monseigneur de Salamon*, p. 122).

an outrage ? Is it possible that this is the accomplishment of a plan concerted two or three weeks ago ; that those arbitrary arrests were ordered with this view ; that false rumours of treasons and intended insurrections and massacres were spread to exasperate the people ; and that, taking advantage of the rumours of bad news from the frontiers, orders have been issued for firing the cannon and sounding the tocsin, to increase the alarm, and terrify the public into acquiescence ; *while a band of chosen ruffians were hired* to massacre those whom hatred, revenge, or fear had destined to destruction, but whom law and justice could not destroy ?

"It is now past twelve at midnight, and the bloody work still goes on ! Almighty God ! "

MASSACRE AT LA FORCE [1]

Not only at the Abbaye was the bloody work in progress ; during the same night the Châtelet and the Conciergerie had been invaded by other bands of massacrers. At one o'clock in the morning, the 3rd of September, the massacre began at La Force. It was here that a number of aristocrats had been incarcerated after the 10th of August ; these included M. de Rulhières, ex-commander of the mounted guard of Paris ; MM. de Baudin and de la Chesnaye, who had remained in command at the Tuileries after the murder of Mandat ; several of the Queen's ladies, Madame and Mademoiselle de Tourzel, Madame de Sainte-Brice, the Princesse de Lamballe, Madame de Mackau, Madame Bazire, and Madame de Navarre ; also a foster-brother of the Queen's named Weber, and Maton de la Varenne, the author of the memoirs already quoted. There were also ten or twelve priests ; the rest of the prisoners were common malefactors. Very few of the aristocrats perished, only about six in all ; these included De Rulhières and De la Chesnaye. Weber and Maton de la Varenne, though both ardent Royalists, were acquitted, amidst the frantic applause of the populace.[2] All the Queen's ladies, with one tragic exception, were likewise set at liberty by the Commune through the influence of Manuel. But there was one victim whom even Manuel was powerless to save. This was the Queen's friend, the ill-fated Princesse de Lamballe.

"The condemnation of the Princesse de Lamballe," MM. Buchez et Roux have the infamy to write, " is it not quite simply explained by the particular hatred the people bore her ? "[3]

[1] Authorities consulted on massacre at La Force : *Mémoires de Weber*, ii. 265 ; *Ma Résurrection*, by Maton de la Varenne ; *Les Crimes de Marat*, by Maton de la Varenne.
[2] *Moniteur*, xiii. 603.   [3] Buchez et Roux, xvii. 418

No blacker calumny was ever uttered against either the princess or the people. "Amidst all our agitations," even the revolutionary Mercier admits, "she had played no rôle ; *nothing could render her suspect in the eyes of the people*, by whom she was only known for innumerable acts of benevolence."[1] On the estates of her father-in-law, the Duc de Penthièvre, with whom she had lived since the early death of her husband, she was known as "the good angel"; in the whole world she had but one implacable enemy, her husband's brother-in-law, Philippe d'Orléans. It has been said that the princess's dowry had excited the cupidity of the duke, and that by her death he hoped to add it to his waning fortune; whether this was so or not the duke had a further reason for resentment, namely, that the princess, recognizing his complicity in the march on Versailles on the 5th of October 1789, had refused from that time onward to associate with him.[2] This was enough to arouse all the bitter hatred of which Philippe showed himself peculiarly capable, and under the influence of wounded vanity he planned a terrible revenge.

Manuel, who had hitherto been a partisan of the Duc d'Orléans, had, however, been paid the sum of 50,000 écus to save the princess, and, unlike Danton, Manuel displayed a certain degree of integrity with regard to compacts of this kind. Accordingly he carried out his promise to rescue Madame and Mademoiselle de Tourzel, for whom he had received a large ransom, and also gave orders that the Princesse de Lamballe should be set at liberty.[3] But the accomplices of the duke were too strong for him. Once again the services of the bloodthirsty Rotondo had been enlisted—Rotondo who, after the disbanding of the "Compagnie du Sabbat," still remained in the pay of the Orléaniste conspiracy, and now placed himself at the head of a band of ferocious assassins specially hired to carry out the vengeance of the duke. The men that composed this gang were Gonor, a wheelwright, Renier, known as "le grand Nicolas," an agitator of the Palais Royal called Petit Mamain, Grison, and Charlat.[4]

At eight o'clock in the morning of September 3 the Princesse de Lamballe was brought before the so-called "tribunal" presided over by Hébert,[5] hereafter to become for ever infamous

---

[1] Mercier, *Le Nouveau Paris*, i. 110.

[2] Montjoie, *Conjuration de d'Orléans*, iii. 210 ; *Histoire particulière*, by Maton de la Varenne, p. 395 ; Peltier, *Révolution du 10 Août*, ii. 313.

[3] Montjoie, *Conjuration de d'Orléans*, iii. 210 ; *Histoire particulière*, by Maton de la Varenne, p. 395.

[4] *Ibid.*; also Beaulieu, iv. 110 ; *Histoire des Girondins*, by Granier de Cassagnac, ii. 510, 515 ; Mortimer Ternaux, iii. 498.

[5] *Histoire particulière*, by Maton de la Varenne ; *Révolution du 10 Août*, by Peltier, ii. 305.

as the author of the atrocious accusation against the Queen at her trial. The verdict was, of course, a foregone conclusion.

" When the princess had arrived before this frightful tribunal," says Peltier, " the sight of the blood-stained weapons, of the murderers, whose faces and clothing were marked with blood, caused her so great a shock that she fell into one fainting fit after another." Then, as soon as she had sufficiently recovered consciousness, her cross-examination began.

" Who are you ? "

" Marie Louise, Princess of Savoy."

" Your position ? "

" Superintendent of the Queen's household."

" Have you any knowledge of the plots on the 10th of August ? "

" I do not know whether there were any plots on the 10th of August, but I know that I had no knowledge of them."

" Take the oath of liberty, of equality, of hatred for the King, the Queen, and royalty."

" I will willingly swear to the first, but not to the last. It is not in my heart."

Some one whispered to her, " Swear—if you do not, you are dead."

But this heroic woman, whose excessive nervousness had excited even the kindly derision of her friends, now that the supreme moment had come, never faltered in her resolution ; over the quivering flesh the indomitable spirit rose triumphantly. Without a word she walked towards the wicket, well knowing the fate that there awaited her.

The Judge then said, " Set Madame free."

These words were the signal of death.[1]

Instantly the hired band of assassins closed around her. The gate was opened. It is said that at the sight of the corpses piled around her she cried out faintly, " Fi ! l'horreur ! " and that two of her murderers, of whom one was Gonor, holding her beneath the arms, forced her to walk forward, fainting at each footstep, over the bodies of the dead.

But the hideous story of her end is already known to every one, and need not be related here. For the purpose of this book it is necessary only to follow the intrigue that ordained the crime, and to prove the non-complicity of the people.

The chief murderer of the Princesse de Lamballe was thus an Italian—Rotondo. Of this there can be no doubt whatever, for, besides the assertions of Montjoie, we have the evidence of Maton de la Varenne, who was in the prison of La Force at the

---

[1] Peltier, *Histoire de la Révolution du 10 Août*, ii. 306.

time,[1] and of Peltier, who was in London when Rotondo at a tavern in that city openly boasted of his share in the crime.[2] Moreover, when Rotondo later fled to Switzerland he was arrested by the Government as " one of the assassins of the Princesse de Lamballe," and imprisoned by the King of Sardinia.[3]

A further light is thrown upon the incident by a curious document that has been preserved amongst the Chatham papers at the Record Office in London. Apparently Pitt was in the habit of employing secret agents to give him information concerning the revolutionary intrigues, and from one of these he inquired about Rotondo, whose boast in the tavern had possibly reached his ears. To this inquiry his correspondent makes the astonishing reply that Rotondo was the husband of one of the Princesse de Lamballe's kitchen-maids, who helped to dismember the body of her mistress.[4]

Now it was said in Paris that several of the princess's footmen, disguised as massacrers, had attempted to save her,[5] but they were recognized amongst the crowd and overpowered. Who so likely to recognize them as their fellow-servant ? And since Rotondo had been for more than two years in the pay of the Duc d'Orléans, is it not possible that his wife—also perhaps an Italian—had been introduced to the Hôtel de Penthièvre as an accomplice of the Orléaniste conspiracy ?

It is evident, moreover, that the gang had been hired for this crime alone, since none of them were paid by the Commune,[6] nor do they appear to have taken any further part in the massacres, but as soon as they had carried out their sanguinary mission they marched off with their trophy, the head of the princess, to show to their employer. By a refinement of brutality they halted first at a hairdresser's for the long fair curls to be washed of blood-stains and freshly powdered, then, led by Charlat carrying the head on a pike, they went on to display it to the two best friends of the dead princess—Gabrielle de Beauvau, Abbess of the Abbaye de Saint-Antoine, and Marie Antoinette at the Temple. After this the procession marched on amidst the roll of drums and the sound of " Ça ira ! " to the Palais Royal.

The Duc d'Orléans was just sitting down to dinner with his mistress, Madame Buffon, and several Englishmen, when the savage howls of triumph that heralded this arrival attracted his attention. Walking to the window he looked out calmly on the

---

[1] Maton de la Varenne, *Histoire particulière*, etc., p. 395.
[2] Peltier, *Révolution du 10 Août*, ii. 313.
[3] *Vieilles Maisons vieux Papiers*, by G. Lenôtre, ii. 153.
[4] See Appendix, p. 504.
[5] *La Révolution du 10 Août*, by Peltier, ii. 380.
[6] See list of assassins published by Granier de Cassagnac, *Histoire des Girondins*, ii. 502.

scene, contemplated with a perfectly unmoved countenance the dead, white face, the fair curls fluttering round the pike-head, and without a word returned to his place at the table. One of the Englishmen present, overcome with horror, rose and left the room; the others remained to feast with the murderer.[1] Who these men were we shall see later.

But once again Philippe d'Orléans had overreached himself; the effect of this atrocious crime was to alienate the sympathies of at least two of his supporters. "Manuel," says Montjoie, "outraged by the assassination of the Princesse de Lamballe, from this moment declared war to the death against D'Orléans. Impulsive in his passions, knowing moderation neither in good nor evil, he was no longer either a Republican, or a Royalist, or a Constitutional, or a Monarchist; he was nothing but anti-Orléaniste. . . . It was not hatred, it was rage. The Abbé Fauchet was taken with the same fury. . . . He began to compose a newspaper which was nothing but a long tissue of insults and imprecations against the party he had finally abandoned. Often when re-reading his pages he would say, 'Ah, but my God! what must one do to have the honour of being butchered by these people?'"

Several members of the Convention later on ranged themselves on the side of Manuel and Fauchet.

Most of the assassins of the Princesse de Lamballe ended as miserably as their chief; after the 9th of Thermidor an inquiry was made into the massacres of September, and Renier, le grand Nicolas, was condemned to twenty years in irons, Petit Mamain to deportation, Charlat, bearer of the princess's head, and guilty of further outrages that cannot be described, was put to death by the soldiers of the regiment in which he enlisted, to whom he had boasted of his crime, whilst Rotondo, leader of the gang, lived a hunted life execrated by all his fellow-men, and died either in prison or on the gallows.[2]

THE VICTIMS OF THE MASSACRES

It is mercifully unnecessary to the purpose of this book to describe the rest of the massacres, which lasted for five days and nights in succession;[3] enough has already been told to give

[1] Montjoie, *Conjuration de d'Orléans*, iii. 211; Beaulieu, iv. 114; Peltier, ii. 312.

[2] Mortimer Ternaux, iii. 498; article on Rotondo in *Vieilles Maisons vieux Papiers*, by G. Lenôtre.

[3] That is to say, from Sunday the 2nd until Thursday the 6th, or possibly till Friday the 7th. Granier de Cassagnac, ii. 419; Beaulieu, iv. 115; *Mémoires de Monseigneur de Salamon*, p. 121; see also Pétion's Letter to the Assembly on September 7, *Moniteur*, xiii. 644

some faint idea of the horrors that took place throughout that week of infamous memory—the whole truth would be unbearable to read, still more to write. It only now remains to show who were the principal victims.

The number of aristocrats who perished was, as we have seen, comparatively infinitesimal ; several of the most ardent Royalists succeeded in disarming their assassins. At the Abbaye, where the massacre continued for two days and nights almost without intermission, the heroic Princesse de Tarente, having refused, in almost the same words as the Princesse de Lamballe, to betray the Queen, was carried home in triumph by the crowd.[1] Mademoiselle de Cazotte, with her arms around her white-haired father, touched the hearts of the spectators, and the old man was set at liberty by the populace,[2] only to fall a victim to the revolutionary tribunal three weeks later. Mademoiselle de Sombreuil, who really did drink the glass of blood to save her father's life, also secured for him a temporary reprieve.[3] Jourgniac de St. Méard was acquitted after boldly admitting himself to be " a frank Royalist." The Abbé de Salamon was saved by his housekeeper, Madame Blanchet, a heroic old peasant woman who had followed him weeping to the door of the Abbaye, and waited about there patiently for five days without touching solid food. Hearing at one moment that her master had been massacred, Blanchet and a friend, a woman of the people as robust and courageous as herself, made their way into the courtyard of the Abbaye, resolved to know the worst. Then, weeping bitterly the while, the two poor women turned over the naked corpses one by one, fearing each time to find the face they sought. When they had thus examined about a hundred of the dead, Madame Blanchet cried out with tears of joy, " He is not there ! " and from that moment she importuned every one she met to obtain his release. These efforts meeting with no success, Madame Blanchet at last seized a deputy of the Assembly by the collar of his coat as he made his way through the Tuileries garden, and forced him to intercede for the Abbé de Salamon. By this means the faithful Blanchet achieved her purpose, and her master was given back to her alive.

Whilst a number of aristocrats were thus saved from the massacres, to " the people," as on the 10th of August, the revolutionaries showed no mercy. For although the object of the massacres was, as we have seen, to rid the State of that gangrened

---

[1] *Révolution du 10 Août*, ii. 285, by Peltier.

[2] " The people, touched by this spectacle, asked mercy for him and obtained it " (*Mon Agonie de Trente-huit Heures*, by Jourgniac de St. Méard).

[3] This story has been declared to be a legend, but Granier de Cassagnac confirms it by documentary evidence ; see *Histoire des Girondins*, ii. 223, 226.

limb, the nobility and clergy, the operation was very imperfectly carried out, whilst on the other hand drastic amputation was exercised on " the people."

Thus at the Conciergerie, where the massacre began on the night of September 2-3, the prisoners were, with the exception of M. de Montmorin, governor of Fontainebleau, and seven or eight Swiss officers, all ordinary criminals of the poorer classes,[1] and of these at least 320 were massacred without even the formality of a trial.[2]   Thirty-six who survived were set at liberty on the condition they should join themselves to the assassins, and seventy-five women, mostly thieves, were enrolled with the rest of the liberated female delinquents to swell the ranks of the future *tricoteuses*.[3]   Only one woman—a flower-seller of the Palais Royal—perished here after the most inhuman tortures.[4]

The Châtelet, attacked on the same night, contained nothing but men of the people—all were thieves; 223 perished also without a trial.[5]

Of these poor victims of the cause of " liberty " we have no record ; in the great whirlpool of the Revolution they went down in one indistinguishable mass ; no chronicler was there to describe their last moments, no survivor wrote his memoirs ; of several hundred, indeed, it is unrecorded whether they lived or died— they simply disappeared.[6]   One trait of heroism stands out from the darkness of oblivion : a poor criminal, who had been offered his life on condition he should enrol himself amongst the massacrers, set himself to the ghastly work, struck one or two ill-aimed blows, then, overcome with horror at himself, flung down the hatchet, crying out, " No, no, I cannot !   Better be a victim than a murderer !   I would rather be given my death by scoundrels like you than give it to disarmed innocents. Strike me ! "   And instantly he fell beneath the blows of his assassins.

On the following day, the 3rd of September, the Tour Saint-Bernard was attacked ; here seventy-five men condemned to the galleys were put to death, and their bodies robbed of their poor savings.[7]   But of all the brutalities that took place on these September days, the massacre at Bicêtre was the most atrocious. Bicêtre had always been the prison of " the people," and, as we have seen earlier in this book, far more dreaded by them than the Bastille.   We might then have expected the breaking open

---

[1] Granier de Cassagnac, *Histoire des Girondins*, ii. 343
[2] *Ibid.* pp. 351-367.
[3] *Crimes de la Révolution*, by Prudhomme, iv. 112.   [4] *Ibid.* iv. 113.
[5] Granier de Cassagnac, *op. cit.* pp. 372, 377-389.
[6] *Ibid.* p. 352.
[7] Mortimer Ternaux, iii. 272 ; Granier de Cassagnac, *op. cit.* ii. 83, 468.

of this stronghold of despotism to end, as did the "taking" of
the Bastille, with the triumphant liberation of its victims. If
the Revolution had been made by the people this no doubt is
what would have happened, but it was by the revolutionary
sections of Paris, under the control of the Commune, that the
attack on Bicêtre was organized, and by them cannons were
provided for the purpose.[1] "They went to Bicêtre with seven
cannons," says the lying report of the Assembly; "the people
in exercising their vengeance thus showed their justice."[2] What
form did this justice take? The massacre of 170 poor people,
amongst whom were a number of young boys of *twelve* years old
and upwards—unfortunate little "street urchins" detained, in
many cases, at the request of their relations, as a punishment
for minor offences.[3] In all the annals of the Revolution there
is no passage more heart-rending than the account of this foul
deed given more than forty years later by one of the gaolers :

"They killed thirty-three of them, the unhappy ones! The
assassins said to us—and indeed we could see it for ourselves—
that these poor children were far more difficult to finish off than
grown-up men. You understand at that age life holds hard.
They killed thirty-three of them! They made a mountain of
them, over there in the corner . . . at your right. . . . The
next day, when we had to bury them, it was a sight to rend one's
soul! There was one who looked as if he were asleep, like an
angel of the good God ; but the others were horribly mutilated."[4]

At the Salpetrière, a house of correction for women, as Bicêtre
was for men, unspeakable barbarities took place ; thirty-five
victims in all perished, and these were not the most unfortunate.
The abominations committed towards little girls of ten to fifteen
years cannot be described.[5]

"If you knew the frightful details!" Madame Roland wrote
later of the massacre at the Salpetrière, "women brutally
violated before being torn to pieces by these tigers! . . . You
know my enthusiasm for the Revolution ; well, I am ashamed
of it ; it is dishonoured by villains, it has become hideous!"[6]

That the "people" were therefore the principal sufferers
in the massacres of September is not a matter of opinion but of
fact. The following table gives the precise statistics concerning
the class of victims sacrificed :—

---

[1] Granier de Cassagnac, *op. cit.* ii. 432.
[2] *Procès verbaux de l'Assemblée Nationale*, xiv. 219.
[3] Mortimer Ternaux, iii. 294 ; Granier de Cassagnac, ii. 434.
[4] Barthélemy Maurice, *Histoire politique et anecdotique des Prisons de
la Seine*, p. 329.
[5] *Crimes de la Révolution*, by Prudhomme, iv. 118, 119.
[6] Madame Roland, *Lettres à Bancal des Issarts*, pp. 348, 349.

ANALYSIS OF VICTIMS IN THE MASSACRES OF SEPTEMBER [1]

Name of Prison.	Aristocrats and Officials.	Priests.	People.	Total.
The Abbaye . .	circ. 28 (including 11 officers)	44	circ. 99 (including 69 soldiers)	circ. 171
The Carmes . .	1	119	..	120
St. Firmin . .	..	79	..	79
Châtelet . .	..	..	223	223
Conciergerie . .	8 (including 7 Swiss officers)	..	320	328
La Force . .	6 (including 2 officers)	3	160	169
Bernardins . .	..	..	73	73
Bicêtre . . .	..	..	170	170
Salpetrière . .	..	..	35	35
	43	245	1080	1368

If, therefore, we except the sixty-nine soldiers who perished as the last defenders of Royalty, we arrive at the enormous total of *1011 victims from amongst " the people " who had no connection whatever with the political situation.* Yet it was this senseless and wholesale butchery that the revolutionary leaders described as " just " and " necessary," but that, when they realized the universal horror it inspired, they basely attributed to the people.

" It was a popular movement," Robespierre afterwards declared, " and not, as has been ridiculously supposed, the partial sedition of a few scoundrels paid to assassinate their fellows." And with revolting hypocrisy he added, " We are assured that *one innocent* perished—they have been pleased to exaggerate the number—but even *one* is far too many without doubt. Citizens, weep for the cruel error, we have long wept for it . . . but let your grief have its term like all human things! Let us keep a few tears for more touching calamities! " [2]

---

[1] The totals of these lists are taken from M. Mortimer Ternaux (*Histoire de la Terreur*, iii. 548) ; the details from M. Granier de Cassagnac (*Histoire des Girondins*, vol. ii.). The numbers given are the lowest possible ; according to M. Granier de Cassagnac, 370 of the people perished at the Conciergerie ; according to Prudhomme, 380. See *Crimes de la Révolution*, iv. 86.

[2] Robespierre, *Lettres à ses Commettants*, No. 4, pp. 170, 172, 173. This " one innocent " was not, needless to say, the guiltless Princesse de Lamballe, nor was he to be found amongst the martyred priests or the poor little boys at Bicêtre. The victim in question was simply a good citizen, named an elector the day before by his section (Granier de Cassagnac, *Histoire des Girondins*, ii. 66).

Marat likewise heaped all the blame on to the people : " The disastrous events of the 2nd and 3rd of September were entirely provoked by the indignation of the people at seeing themselves the slaves of all the traitors who had caused their disasters and misfortunes." It was a " perfidious insinuation to attribute these popular executions " to the Commune—executions that, in the same breath, Marat, with his usual wild inconsequence, describes as " unfortunately too necessary." [1] If necessary, why was it perfidious to attribute them to the Commune ?

The historians who have made it their business to whitewash Marat, Danton, and Robespierre, effect their purpose by the same process of blackening the people.

" We believe that the massacre at the prison of the Abbaye," writes Bougeart, the adorer of Marat, " was executed by the people, *by the true people*. . . . Marat cannot be accused of it, for he did everything before and during the event to prevent such horrible atrocities." [2] Of all calumnies on the people uttered by the men who called themselves their friends, this accusation of having committed the massacres of September is the most infamous and the most unfounded. Apart from the revelations of Prudhomme, to whom the authors of the massacres confided their designs in the dialogues already quoted,[3] apart from the evidence of eye-witnesses who saw the assassins being paid by the emissaries of the Commune, we have documentary proof of these facts—the registers of the Commune recording the sums paid were preserved ; [4] a number of receipts signed by the murderers were still in existence until 1871.[5] The immense researches of M. Granier de Cassagnac and M. Mortimer Ternaux long ago laid bare the whole plot, and no revolutionary writer has ever succeeded in disproving their assertions. Yet, in spite of all this overwhelming evidence, we still read in English books —not merely the books of fanatics, but dry histories and manuals for schools—that the people of Paris, overcome by panic, marched on the prisons and massacred the prisoners !

[1] *Journal de la République*, No. 12.

[2] *Jean Paul Marat*, by Alfred Bougeart, ii. 93. Hamel, the panegyrist of Robespierre, also heaps all the blame on the people (*Vie de Robespierre*, i. 410).

[3] See also Prudhomme's definite statement : " The people did not kill ; the massacrers were men paid to do it " (*Crimes de la Révolution*, iv. 107).

[4] " Procès verbaux de la Commune de Paris," published in *Mémoires sur les Journées de Septembre*, pp. 286, 314 ; Mortimer Ternaux, iii. 525-528 ; Beaulieu, iv. 120-123.

[5] A bundle of twenty-four of. these receipts was preserved at the Prefecture de Police in Paris (Mortimer Ternaux, iii. 525, 527). M. Granier de Cassagnac has reproduced two in facsimile (*Histoire des Girondins*, ii. 514). These also were destroyed by the Commune of 1871.

THE ASSASSINS

Who were the men that the leaders succeeded in enlisting for the hideous task ? Very great pains have been taken, Dr. John Moore wrote on the 10th of September, to urge the notion " that the assassins were no other than a *promiscuous* crowd of the citizens of Paris." [1] This was absolutely untrue. The assassins formed an organized band of not more than 300 men—a point on which all contemporaries not in collusion with the leaders agree.[2] Nor is there any mystery concerning their identity, for the names and professions of the greater number are known, and have been published by M. Granier de Cassagnac.[3] There were then, in addition to the Marseillais and released convicts who formed the nucleus of the gang, a certain number of men who might be described as citizens of Paris, and, strangely enough, these were not mostly rough brutes from the barges on the Seine or the hovels of Saint-Marceau, but *boutiquiers* or small trades-men, bootmakers, jewellers, tailors—two of these were Germans—some, indeed, appear to have been men of education.[4]   It is this latter class that seems to have lent itself most willingly to the hideous work ; the rest were persuaded by various methods to co-operate.   The greater number undoubtedly yielded merely to the lust for gold, to the promise of wine and booty in addition to their salary ; others, the more ignorant no doubt, believed the story told them of the plot hatched by the prisoners to massacre their wives and children, and went forth in all good faith to destroy the supposed enemies of their country.   As to the ferocity they displayed once they had set themselves to the task, it is to be explained in the same way as the outrages com-mitted at the Tuileries on the 10th of August, by the effect of fiery liquor working on overwrought brains.   Moreover, this time it was not merely alcohol that had been given to them, but something more insidious that had been purposely introduced into the drink with which they were plied incessantly.   Maton

---

[1] *Journal of a Residence in France*, i. 374.

[2] " The number of assassins did not exceed 300 " (Roch Marcandier (an eye-witness), *Histoire des Hommes de Proie*) ; Louvet said about 200 (*Accusation contre Maximilien Robespierre*, Séance de la Convention du 29 Octobre 1792) ; " 300," says Mercier (*Le Nouveau Paris*, i. 94) ; M. Granier de Cassagnac gives 235 as the approximate number (*Histoire des Girondins* ii. 30).

[3] *Histoire des Girondins*, ii. 502-516.

[4] " They were not all of the dregs of the people," the Abbé Barruel says of the massacrers at the Carmes ; " their accent, their speeches be-trayed amongst them adepts whom the philosophy of the Clubs and the schools of the day, far more than boorish ignorance, had inflamed against the priests " (*Histoire du Clergé*, p. 248).

de la Varenne says that Manuel had ordered gunpowder to be mixed with their brandy, so as to keep them in a state of frenzy ; but the Two Friends of Liberty declare that they were *drugged* :

" It is incontestable that the drink that had been distributed to the assassins was mingled with a particular drug that inspired terrible fury, and left to those who took it no possibility of a return to reason. We knew a porter who for twenty years had carried out errands . . . in the Rue des Noyers. He had always enjoyed the highest reputation, and every inhabitant of the district blindly confided the most valuable parcels to him. . . . He was dragged off on the 3rd of September to the Convent of Saint-Firmin, where he was forced to do the work of executioner. We saw him six days later when we were ourselves proscribed, and, needing a man who could be trusted to help us move secretly, we addressed ourselves to him. He had returned to his post ; he was trembling in every limb, foaming at the mouth, asking incessantly for wine, without ever slaking his thirst and without falling a victim to ordinary drunkenness. ' They gave me plenty to drink,' he said, ' but I worked well ; I killed more than twenty priests on my own account.' A thousand other speeches of this kind escaped him, and each sentence was interrupted by these words, ' I am thirsty.' In order that he might not feel inclined to slake his thirst with our blood, we gave him as much wine as he wished. He died a month later without ever having slept in the interval." [1]

This circumstance explains the fact that at moments the assassins showed themselves capable of humanity—evidently, when the first effects of the drug had begun to wear off, they returned more or less to a normal frame of mind. Thus the two cut-throats, who conducted the Chevalier de Bertrand safely home, insisted on going upstairs with him to contemplate the joy of his family. The rescuers of Jourgniac de St. Méard—a Marseillais, a mason, and a wig-maker—refused the reward offered them with the words, " We do not do this for money." [2] Later on Beaulieu met these men at the house of St. Méard. " What struck me," he says, " was that through all their ferocious remarks I perceived generous sentiments, men determined to undertake anything to protect those whose cause they had embraced. The greater number of these maniacs, *dupes of the Machiavellian beings who set them in motion*, are dead or dying in misery." [3]

[1] *Deux Amis*, viii. 296.
[2] *Mon Agonie de trente-huit Heures*, by Jourgniac de St. Méard.
[3] Beaulieu, iv. 109.

THE RÔLE OF THE PEOPLE

From the point of view of the leaders, the populace proved disappointing during the massacres of September, for although it had not been thought advisable to march the Faubourgs *en masse* on the prisons, it was hoped that when the moment came a certain proportion of the Paris mob would join in the killing as they had done at the massacre of St. Barthélemy. " In spite of all the activity displayed," says Prudhomme, " the 30,000 victims, designated by Danton himself, did not find enough executioners. They (the leaders) counted on the people ; they accredited them with more ferocity. They hoped that they would not remain idle spectators of *five to six thousand* [1] massacres executed before their eyes ; they supposed that they would themselves strike *en masse*, and that, after having emptied the prisons, they would go into the houses and repeat the same scenes, but they could never succeed in exasperating the multitude to this extent." [2]

On the contrary, even by the mob assembled around the prisons, every single acquittal recorded was hailed with acclamations, often with rapturous applause—a prisoner who made a dash for liberty was certain to find the crowd opening out to let him through. The Royalist, Weber, could hardly extricate himself from the embraces of the bystanders, amongst whom savage-looking harridans, concerned for his white silk stockings, cried out reprovingly to the guards who led him, " Take care there ! You are making Monsieur walk in the gutter ! " Yet that the mob, obedient to the suggestions of the leaders, excited with drink and attacked by that strange insanity familiar to all who have studied " crowd psychology," did at other moments allow itself to be carried away into applauding the massacres, did indeed throughout stand idly by and utter only occasional words of protest, is undeniable. But were these " the people " ? A thousand times no ! We have already seen whence they were recruited ; the true men and women of the people remained far from such scenes as these.

" I will testify to Europe," cries Bigot de Sainte-Croix, " that the People of my country, that those of the capital, did not ordain, did not desire these massacres, that *the People did not even see them committed*. The People closed their windows, their workrooms, their shops ; they took refuge in the furthest corners of their dwellings so as to shut their ears and eyes to the uproar, and to the sight of those beings, strangers to the People and to human nature, who, armed with knives, sabres, and clubs, their

---

[1] Prudhomme, like Peltier, over-estimated the number of victims.
[2] *Crimes de la Révolution*, by Prudhomme, iv. 107.

faces and their arms stained with blood, carried through the streets heads and fragments of mutilated bodies, and deafened themselves with the ferocious hymn (the 'Carmagnole'?) that had been dictated to them. Ah! Why should the People again be calumniated ? . . ." [1]

And Mortimer Ternaux adds : " Yes, it is lying to history, it is betraying the sacred cause of humanity, *it is deserting the most obvious interests of democracy*, to calumniate the people, to take for them a few hundred wretches . . . going basely to seek their victims one by one in the cells of the Abbaye or of La Force. . . . The people, the true people, composed of honest and industrious workmen, warm-hearted and patriotic, of young bourgeois with generous aspirations and indomitable courage, did not mingle for a moment with the scoundrels recruited by Maillard . . . the people, the true people, were all at the Champ de Mars or in front of the recruiting platforms, offering their best blood for the defence of the country ; they would have been ashamed to shed that of defenceless victims." [2]

But, it will be urged, why did the people of Paris not interfere ? Why, instead of retiring into their houses and shutting their ears and eyes, did they not rush out into the streets and arrest the murderers ? instead of mustering at the Champ de Mars, march on the prisons and deliver the victims ?

" All Paris let it happen (*laissa faire*)," Madame Roland writes indignantly ; " all Paris is accursed in my eyes, and I hope no longer that liberty may be established amongst cowards insensible to the worst outrages that could be committed against Nature and humanity, cold spectators of crimes that the courage of fifty armed men could easily have prevented." [3]

Madame Roland well knew the true explanation of the people's conduct—her own behaviour during the massacres we shall refer to later ; she was perfectly aware that it was the cowardice of the authorities, of her friend Pétion, of " the virtuous Roland " himself that made it possible for the Commune to carry out its designs unhindered, that prevented the people from interfering.

" If the people," says Prudhomme, " did not put a stop to the murders committed in their presence, it was that, on seeing that their representatives, their magistrates, and the staff of their armed force made no attempt to prevent this butchery, they could only believe that these were acts of justice of a new kind." [4]

Here, then, is the explanation. In the first place, the people of Paris were told—and in some cases made to believe—that the

---

[1] *Histoire de la Conspiration du 10 Août*, by Bigot de Sainte-Croix, p. 104.　　[2] Mortimer Ternaux, iii. 185.

[3] *Mémoires de Mme. Roland*, i. 110.

[4] *Crimes de la Révolution*, by Prudhomme, iv. 130.

massacres were a necessary act of precaution in view of the conspiracy amongst the prisoners to massacre the citizens; secondly, the massacres were carried out officially under the eyes of the authorities, presided over by officials wearing their municipal scarves,[1] and executed in some instances by assassins masquerading in the uniform of the National Guards;[2] and thirdly, *the people were prevented by armed force from interfering.* We know from the researches of M. Mortimer Ternaux and M. Granier de Cassagnac that Santerre, the commander-general, was authorized to surround the prisons with troops during the massacres, " in order to prevent accidents,"[3] and the nature of these accidents is elsewhere very clearly revealed.   Thus, as we have already seen at the Carmes, a cordon of police was provided to protect the assassins from the crowd, and Sénart relates that the same precaution was demanded at La Force : " The butcher Legendre went to find one of the commanders of the Arsenal, and asked him for two hundred armed men to go to La Force in order to second the murderers and *protect them*, because the number of prisoners was very great and there were not enough massacrers "—a request with which the honest commander indignantly refused to comply.[4]   But the fact that the massacrers *were* given armed protection during their hideous task received additional confirmation just a hundred years later.   In the *Intermédiaire des Chercheurs et Curieux* for April 20, 1892, M. Alfred Bégis related that he had recently acquired a copy of a pamphlet, by Garat, that had belonged to Sergent, who, with Panis, the brother-in-law of Santerre, had been entrusted with the police and the prisons as members of the Comité de Surveillance of the Commune.   Now in this pamphlet, which was annotated throughout by the hand of Sergent, Garat asked the question why the people allowed the massacres of September : " How is it that so much blood flowed under other blades than that of justice without the legislators, without the magistrates of the people, *without the whole people themselves* summoning all the public forces to the place of these sanguinary scenes ? "

To this question Sergent made reply in the margin : " *The massacrers of the Abbaye asked to be protected during their dreadful work by a guard which was granted to them.*" The mob of Paris collected round the prisons had then attempted to interfere,

---

[1] Beaulieu, iv. 119 ; *Deux Amis*, viii. 308.

[2] Evidence of eye-witness, M. de la Roserie, who was present at the massacre at the Carmes, and stated that " half the assassins employed there were, by an infamous prostitution, in the uniform of the National Guards " (*Mémoires de Thiébault*, i. 319).

[3] Extract from the registers of the sections of Paris published by M. Mortimer Ternaux, *Histoire de la Terreur*, iii. 480.

[4] *Mémoires de Sénart* (edition de Lescure), p. 29.

since the murderers were obliged to ask for protection, and this was the kind of " accident " the armed forces were sent out to prevent !

Undoubtedly we must blame the soldiers for obeying this monstrous order, but it should be remembered that all the normal elements in the army were collected on the frontier, and that the only forces remaining in Paris were those of which the revolutionary leaders had made sure—the confederates from Marseilles, or Brest, or the camp at Soissons. The call to arms had thus admirably served their purpose by ridding them of all those loyal and patriotic citizens who might have been expected to prevent bloodshed.

THE AUTHORS OF THE MASSACRES

The truth is, then, that the only men who attributed the massacres of September to the people of Paris were the men who themselves had devised and ordered them. With consummate hypocrisy the Commune declared that it had sent emissaries to the prisons to oppose disorders, but that they could not succeed in calming the people. Apart, however, from the evidence of eye-witnesses, who unanimously asserted that the emissaries of the Commune incited the assassins to greater violence, we have further documentary proof of the Commune's guilt in the atrocious proclamation publicly sent out by it on the 3rd of September to the provinces, urging them to carry out the same butchery all over France, and passing on to them the same word of command that had served in Paris as a pretext for the massacres.

." The Commune of Paris hastens to inform its brothers in all the departments that a portion of the ferocious conspirators detained in the prisons have been put to death by the people : acts of justice which seemed to it indispensable in order to restrain by terror the legions of traitors concealed within its walls at the moment when it was about to march on the enemy ; and without doubt the whole nation, after the long series of treacheries which have led it to the edge of the abyss, will hasten to adopt this measure so necessary to public safety, and all the French will cry like the Parisians, ' We will march on the enemy, but we will not leave behind us brigands to murder our wives and children.'

" Signed—DUPLAIN, PANIS, SERGENT, LENFANT,
JOURDEUIL, MARAT, *l'ami du peuple*,
DEFORGUES, DUFFORT, CALLY."

That Marat was the principal author of the proclamation cannot be doubted, but it was sent forth under the countersign of Danton, the Minister of Justice. To Danton, then, attaches the greater blame, for Marat cannot be regarded as a responsible human being, whilst Danton throughout the Revolution retained full possession of his faculties. " That Marat," says Mortimer Ternaux, " the most shameless liar and the most daring forger who ever existed (we make use of the exact expressions that MM. Michelet and Louis Blanc employ with regard to this man), that Marat, we say, should have drawn up this frightful circular, and on his own authority should have appended to it the signatures of his colleagues, is strictly possible. But the two men who can never clear themselves of having co-operated in the propagation of this bloody work are Danton and Fabre d'Églantine, the Minister of Justice and his secretary." [1]

It is doubtful, indeed, whether Danton wished to clear himself of the responsibility of the massacres of September, or of the proposal to repeat them in the provinces. Now that the monarchy was overthrown, Danton knew that he had nothing to fear in avowing his share in the crimes of the Revolution ; securely encamped on the strongest side he was able to win that reputation for audacity which has aureoled him in the eyes of posterity.[2]

The massacres of September were, therefore, primarily the work of the Anarchists, but they were condoned, if not actually assisted, by the other intrigues, as we shall now see.

RÔLE OF THE ORLÉANISTES

On this point little remains to be said, for by September of 1792 the Orléanistes had ceased to be a distinct party, and had become indistinguishable from the Anarchists. According to many contemporaries, Danton and Marat, in promoting anarchy, were working solely in the interests of the Duc d'Orléans ; Montjoie believes that it was in order to effect the change of dynasty the massacres were devised.

But apart from these vague charges, there can be no doubt that the Duc d'Orléans had some secret connection with the leaders ; of this the murder of the Princesse de Lamballe by his agents is sufficient proof. Moreover, it was precisely at this moment—on the 2nd of September—that Marat publicly demanded 15,000 francs from the duke for the printing of several

---

[1] Mortimer Ternaux, iii. 309.

[2] According to Louis Philippe, Danton frankly admitted his responsibility for the September days. The future King, then the Duc de Chartres, related that when on a visit to Paris from the frontier he met Danton and ventured to blame the authors of the massacres. To this remonstrance Danton replied : " *It was I who did it.* All the Parisians are *jean foutres*. It was necessary to put a river of blood between them and the *émigrés* " (*Récit du Duc d'Aumale*, quoted by Taine, *La Révolution*, vi. 30).

of his pamphlets,[1] and apparently obtained it, for henceforth we shall find him always favourably disposed to " the citizen Égalité "[2]—the name the Duc d'Orléans soon after assumed when seeking election as deputy to the Convention.

But whatever were the ultimate intentions of these men who devised the massacres—and on this point no one can speak with certainty—their immediate purpose can be expressed in one word only—anarchy.

RÔLE OF THE GIRONDINS

The part played by the Girondins in the massacres of September was merely one of criminal connivance. With the exception of Pétion, whose sympathies were undoubtedly Orléaniste, no member of this faction seems to have taken an active part in the movement. Vergniaud, indeed, loudly denounced the arbitrary arrests that preceded the massacres, but since by this time the walls of Paris were already placarded by Marat with invectives against the deputies of the Gironde,[3] this was perhaps less an act of courage than a measure of self-defence. At any rate, from the moment the massacres began, not one member of this faction attempted to interfere.

On the 5th of September, whilst the third day of the massacre at La Force was in progress, Duhem afterwards related, he dined at Pétion's house with Brissot, Gensonné, and several other deputies. " Towards the end of dinner the folding doors opened, and I was surprised to see two cut-throats enter, their hands dripping with blood. They came to ask the orders of the mayor concerning the eighty prisoners who still remained to be massacred at La Force ; Pétion gave them drinks and sent them away, telling them to do everything for the best."[4]

As to Madame Roland, who afterwards cursed the people of Paris for their non-intervention, how was she employed ? On the evening of September 2, she relates, when the butchery had begun, " a crowd of about 200 men, violently agitated," came to the Ministry of the Interior to ask for arms ; we know from other sources that they were the massacrers,[5] who, imagining Roland to be one of their employers, asked also for the payment of their salary, and, according to Felhémési, they received it. But Felhémési as a Dantoniste need not be believed. At any rate, after this frightful scene, whilst the massacres were in full swing

---

[1] Prudhomme, *Révolutions de Paris*, xiii. 522.

[2] Beaulieu, iv. 145.

[3] Dr. Moore, *Journal of a Residence in France*, i. 256.

[4] *Procès des Vingt-Deux*, evidence of Duhem. According to the *Deux Amis de la Liberté*, viii. 304, the assassins entered with heads in their hands.

[5] *Mémoires de Sénart* (edition de Lescure), p. 34.

next day at La Force, the Abbaye, and the Tour Saint-Bernard, Madame Roland saw fit to give a luncheon-party—or, as the two o'clock meal in those days was called, a " dinner "—to a number of her friends and acquaintances, amongst whom " the events of the day formed the topic of conversation." One of the guests (afterwards disowned by Madame Roland) was the Prussian Baron Clootz, whom we shall meet later on as the apostle of " universal brotherhood," and who distinguished himself during the massacres of September by inventing the word " to *septemberize* "—it was a matter of regret, he afterwards declared, that they had not " septemberized " enough.[1]

The same day, however, the virtuous Roland ventured to utter a feeble protest against the continuance of the massacres. Beginning with a lengthy dissertation on the necessity for controlling the irrepressible indignation of the people—who, according to Madame Roland's later writings, he well knew were not the authors of these crimes,—amidst redundant eulogies of his own courage and disinterestedness, Roland thus described the massacres of September 2 : " Yesterday was a day over the events of which we should perhaps draw a veil ; I know that the people, terrible in their vengeance, yet bring to it a sort of justice," but now the moment had come for " the legislators to speak, for the people to listen, and for the reign of law to be re-established." [2]

The fact is that something had happened the evening before which made it highly desirable, from the Girondins' point of view, that the activities of the Commune should be restrained. Robespierre had been thwarted by Danton in his plan of including Roland and Brissot in the lists of proscriptions made out for the massacrers, but he had not abandoned all hope of his prey. Under cover of the general confusion that reigned in Paris on the 2nd of September the tiger-cat had seized the opportunity to spring. Supported by his ally Billaud-Varenne, Robespierre presented himself at the evening meeting held by the Council-General of the Commune, and openly accused Brissot and *a powerful party* of conspiring to place the Duke of Brunswick on the throne of France.[3] This accusation has been represented by the antagonists of Robespierre as a mere fable invented by him to bring about the downfall of Brissot, but, as we have

---

[1] *J. P. Brissot à ses Commettants*, p. 52 ; Beaulieu, v. 247.

[2] Buchez et Roux, xvii. 382.

[3] *Procès verbaux de la Commune de Paris*, date of September 2. The precise words employed by Robespierre are not given in this report, but are recorded in part by Peltier (*Révolution du 10 Août*, ii. 234) ; it is Hamel (*Vie de Robespierre*, i. 415) who states that Robespierre used the expression " a powerful party." On this accusation see also Beaulieu, iv. 147 ; *Moniteur*, xiii. 617, 620-622 ; Mortimer Ternaux, iii. 205.

already seen, the intrigue in favour of Brunswick was by no means fabulous—on the contrary, it was a matter of common knowledge. Had not Carra publicly proclaimed it six weeks earlier in his journal ? And was not Carra still the trusted confidant of Brissot and the Rolands ? Robespierre, then, was perfectly just in accusing Brissot ; two days later, in private conversation with Pétion—whose own intrigues he was apparently far from suspecting—he repeated his conviction that Brissot was on the side of Brunswick.[1] That by his timely denunciation he hoped to envelop the Brissotins in the massacres we cannot doubt, yet we must admit that in this he showed himself more logical than the other members of the Commune. For if any people were to be put to death on the suspicion of collusion with the Prussians, should they not be the members of the party still at liberty who had definitely proposed to hand the country over to the head of the invading armies, rather than a defenceless crowd of priests, unarmed men, women, and children safely imprisoned behind bolts and bars ?-

Brissot's reply to this accusation of Robespierre was characteristic of the ostrich policy displayed by the Girondins.

" Yesterday, Sunday," he wrote to his fellow-citizens, " I was denounced at the Commune of Paris, as also a part of the deputies of the Gironde, and other men equally virtuous. We were accused of wishing to give France over to the Duke of Brunswick, and to have received millions from him, and to have planned to escape to England. I, the eternal enemy of kings, who did not wait till 1789 to manifest my hatred towards them ; I the partisan of a duke ! Better perish a thousand times than acknowledge such a despot ! " etc.[2]

But considering that before 1789 Brissot had violently denounced in print " the abominable crime of attacking monarchy," that he had described Ravaillac and Damiens as " monsters vomited by hell," [3] and that only six weeks before the massacres of September—on July 25, 1792—he had declared that the blade of the law should strike any one who attempted to establish a Republic ; considering, moreover, that he had never disassociated himself from Carra, the avowed partisan of Brunswick, Brissot's defence was far from convincing.

The Brissotins, then, constituted a very real danger to the country at the moment when it was threatened by foreign invasion, but we should admire Robespierre's courage and patriotism in attacking them more if he had not waited so long to shoot

---

[1] *Discours de Pétion sur l'Accusation intentée contre Maximilien Robespierre*, p. 16.

[2] *Moniteur*, xiii. 623.

[3] *Les Moyens d'adoucir la Rigueur des Lois pénales en France*, 1781.

his bolt. The intrigue with Prussia had been going on for at least eighteen months—why had he not exposed it earlier ? Why, on the publication of Carra's preposterous plea for Brunswick, did not Robespierre arise and denounce him as a traitor, or at least demand his expulsion from the ranks of " patriots " at the Jacobin Club ? But no, Robespierre had hitherto maintained complete silence with regard to all three intrigues—the Orléanistes, English Jacobins, and Prussians—and had even, as we have seen, joined in ridiculing Ribes for denouncing them. The explanation lies undoubtedly in Robespierre's natural timidity ; it was never his way to fight his opponents, but always to remain quiescent until an opportunity offered for killing them outright—the tiger-cat knew better than to show his claws before the moment came to spring. The massacres of September had appeared to be the propitious moment, but Danton barred the way ; next time he was to say with tears, " I cannot save them ! "

The Girondins well realized the danger that had threatened them, and therefore, after condoning the massacres, ended by denouncing them. But if they now deprecated the reign of anarchy, it was principally because they saw the movement they had helped to produce turning against themselves, and the abyss into which they had precipitated the monarchy yawning beneath their own feet.

THE ENGLISH JACOBINS

The news of the massacres of September filled the sane portion of the English people with indignation, and alienated even those who, misled by the propaganda of the Whigs and the revolutionary societies in England, still retained a lingering sympathy with the supposed " struggle for liberty " taking place across the Channel. " The late horrors in France," Mr. Burges writes to Lord Auckland on the 21st of September, " have at least been attended with one good consequence, for they have turned the tide of general opinion here very suddenly. French principles, and even Frenchmen, are daily becoming more unpopular, and I think it not impossible that in a short time the impudence of some of these levellers will work so much on the tempers of our people as to make England neither a pleasant nor a secure residence for them."

A messenger from Paris reported to Lord Auckland on the 10th of September that the details passed all conception. " It is impossible for me to express the horror that I still feel ; I could not have believed till now that human nature was capable of such abominations." Lord Auckland himself is " so affected " that he " can hardly write of it "—all Gibbon's history, though the bloodiest book he ever read, " does not contain a story of such unprovoked and wanton cruelty."

Lord Stanhope, however, had nothing but pitying contempt for squeamishness that could recoil at such scenes as these. " The French Revolution," he wrote on September 18, " *has frightened some weak minds*, Mr. Paine's works others. And the late events in France have intimidated many. *However despicable such feelings may be*, abstractly considered, when they are pretty general, they must be treated with some respect." [1]

Amongst weak minds we must certainly include those of almost the entire population, for these " despicable feelings " were more than " pretty general " ; they were shared by all classes of the community. The sympathies of the nation were with the victims, not with the authors of the Revolution, and the unhappy *émigrés*, flying from the horrors of Paris to the shores of England, met with an enthusiastic welcome. One must have lived through three years of revolution, says one of these *émigrés*, amidst Girondins, Jacobins, and others, to understand what the first glimpse of the English conveyed, the ecstasy of arriving in this " isle of serenity " from the regions of terror : " it was the gentle awakening of the soul that, long tormented by the vision of monsters and furies, comes out of this frightful dream." [2] Once again humanity and compassion became a reality. Every boatload of priests was awaited by a sympathetic crowd ; even the sailors, seeing in these men the martyrs of religion, fell on their knees before them on the beach to ask their blessing. [3] " I was a witness," says Peltier, " of the zeal and eagerness with which all classes of society welcomed these unhappy pastors. From the throne to the simplest cabin, everywhere was their asylum, everywhere was consolation." In London a subscription raised by Burke, Wilmot, Stanley, and others met with an immense response ; the poor like the rich brought their contributions, and those who could not give money gave the work of their hands ; potato-sellers insisted on providing the priests with their wares for no remuneration, seamstresses offered their services for nothing, artisans worked overtime to earn money for them ; a day labourer, touched to tears by their appearance, cried out, " I am very poor but I can work for two ; give me one of these priests and I will feed him ! " [4] It was, then, only amongst an infinitesimal minority, composed of such men as Lord Stanhope and the middle-class malcontents who formed the

[1] *Life of Charles, third Earl of Stanhope*, by Ghita Stanhope and G. P. Gooch, p. 120.
[2] *Histoire du Clergé*, by L'Abbé Barruel, p. 349.
[3] *Histoire de la Révolution du 10 Août*, by Peltier, ii. 391.
[4] Barruel, *op. cit.* pp. 353, 354.

revolutionary societies of London and of the manufacturing towns of the north, that the Revolution found sympathizers. By these associations the massacres of September were greeted with frenzied approbation. On the 27th of September a long address of congratulation was forwarded to the Jacobin Club of Paris by the members of the Constitutional Society and the Reformation Society of Manchester, the Revolution Society of Norwich, the " Constitutional Whigs," the " Independents and Friends of the People." A few passages of this precious effusion must be quoted : [1]

" Frenchmen, our numbers may seem small compared to the rest of the nation, but know that they are steadily increasing . . . we can tell you with certainty, free men and friends, that education is making rapid progress amongst us . . . that men ask to-day, ' What is liberty ? What are our rights ? ' Frenchmen, you are free already, but Britons are preparing to become so ! Divested at last of these cruel prejudices industriously inculcated in our hearts by vile courtiers, instead of our natural enemies, we see in the French our fellow-citizens of the world, the children of that universal Father who created us to love and help each other, not to hate and murder one another at the command of feeble or ambitious kings or corrupt ministers. In seeking our real enemies we find them in the partisans of that aristocracy which rends our bosoms, aristocracy hitherto the poison of all countries on earth ; you acted wisely in banishing it from France. . . . Dear friends, you are fighting for the happiness of all humanity. Can there be any loss to you, however bitter, compared to the glorious and unprecedented privilege of being able to say, ' The universe is free ; tyrants and tyrannies are no more, peace reigns on earth, and it is to the French we owe it.' "

To these advocates of universal brotherhood it was a matter of poignant regret and bitter shame that the British Government refused to throw in its lot with the organizers of the late massacres in the prisons by taking up arms in defence of the French Revolution. To their profuse apologies on this subject the French Jacobins, under Hérault de Séchelles, replied : " Believe, generous Englishmen, that in preserving this demeanour (of neutrality) you are none the less joining with us in the work of universal liberty. Leave us to make a few more steps along the course where you were our precursors, and let us rejoice beforehand in a common hope for the epoch, not far distant, when the interests

---

[1] I have been unable to find this correspondence in English. These passages are taken from the *Histoire Socialiste de la Révolution*, volume *La Convention*, by Jean Jaurès, p. 196 and following, and from *Danton Émigré*, by Dr. Robinet.

of Europe and of the human race will invite both nations to hold out the hand of friendship to each other."[1] The hope was echoed by the Society for Constitutional Reform of London, which now wrote expressing the belief that, after the example given by the French, "revolutions would become easy," and that "before long the French would be writing to congratulate the National Convention of England."[2]

The Jacobins of Paris were ready to promise more than this ; they intended, they declared, "to seal an eternal alliance" with their English brothers, who had only to let them know that their liberty was being attacked for the "victorious phalanxes" of their French allies to "cross the Straits of Dover and fly to their defence."[3]

Thus was the suggestion calmly entertained by our exponents of universal brotherhood in 1792, that the revolutionary horde of cut-throats and assassins, who had just carried out the massacres of September, should land on our shores and produce the same horrors in England as had taken place in France.

The anti-patriotism of a section of so-called "democracy" in England has never been better exemplified. To men of this mentality it matters not whether it is with democracy or autocracy abroad that they strike a league of friendship ; the enemies of their country can always make sure of their support. Until the Germans of to-day England never had bitterer enemies than the Jacobins of France. Hatred of England, of the English character, of English ideas of liberty, was one of the first tenets of their political creed. In this they differed fundamentally from the earlier revolutionaries, the men who had framed the Constitution of 1791, and also from the Girondins, who no doubt entertained a sincere admiration for England ; the Jacobins, into whose hands the power was now passing, were, with the exception of Danton, the sworn foes not only of the English Government but of English "democracy"; they repeatedly declared that they despised Mr. Fox as much as they hated Mr. Pitt.[4]

The leading spirit of the anti-English campaign was undoubtedly Robespierre ; always the opponent of Internationalism—hence his ground of accusation later on against the Prussian Clootz—he never concealed his distrust of foreign sympathizers with the French Revolution ; four months earlier, supported by Collot d'Herbois, he had deprecated the correspondence of the Jacobins with their brothers in Manchester,[5]

---

[1] Date of November 7, 1792.   [2] Date of November 10, 1792.
[3] Date of November 28, 1792.
[4] Playfair's *History of Jacobinism*, p. 384.
[5] *Séances des Jacobins*, date of June 4, 1792.

and again in September it was he who opposed the election of Dr. Priestly to the Convention.[1]

For the present, however, the French Jacobins were quite ready to make use of their English allies ; hypocritical professions of friendship cost nothing, and met with very substantial rewards. Already in April, as we have seen, a subscription had been raised in aid of the French Revolution, and it seems probable that further sums were forthcoming during the course of the summer. In August Dr. Moore heard with incredulity of " the great number of English guineas now in circulation in Paris," which, as usual, were attributed to " the Court of Great Britain," whose object was to excite sedition in France.[2] If these mysterious guineas were not, as Dr. Moore believed, mythical, they were obviously those of Orléans or of the English Jacobins. At any rate, it is to the latter source that the " English gold " which arrived in Paris three weeks later can, with certainty, be traced, for the address of congratulation on the massacres of September, forwarded by Lord Sempill and three other members in the name of the London Constitutional Society, was accompanied by a present of 1000 pairs of shoes for the army and *£1000 in money*.[3] Besides this an immense quantity of arms was provided by the English Jacobins from the manufactories of Birmingham and Sheffield, for which a further public subscription was raised by means of an appeal in the newspapers to " all those who favoured the cause of liberty in France against the infamous conspiracy of crowned brigands." [4]

It is, moreover, in the late summer of 1792 that, for the first time, we find Englishmen personally co-operating in the revolutionary movement in Paris. Amongst these was Thomas Paine, who left the shores of England amidst the jeers and hisses of the crowd: " I believe had we remained much longer," a fellow - traveller remarks, " they would have pelted him with stones from the beach." [5] In spite of the fact that his face reminded Madame Roland of " a blackberry powdered with flour "—for Paine was constantly inebriated—the exponent of " The Rights of Man " was received with enthusiasm by the Girondins, and through their influence succeeded in becoming a member of the Convention.

Besides Paine a band of English Jacobins arrived in Paris at the same time. " Dr. Priestley," Mr. Burges writes to Lord

---

[1] *Mémoires de Mme. Roland*, ii. 300.
[2] *Journal of a Residence in France*, i. 134.
[3] Arthur Young, *The Example of France*, Appendix, p. 3.
[4] Oswald's Speech at the Jacobin Club, September 30, 1792.
[5] J. Mason to J. B. Burges, letter dated September 13, 1792 (*Fortescue Historical MSS.* ii. 316).

Auckland on September 4, " is also there, and is looked upon as the great adviser of the present ministers, being consulted by them on all occasions. There are also eight or ten other English and Scotch who work with the Jacobins, and in great measure conduct their present manœuvres. I understand these gentlemen at present are employed in writing a justification of democracy and an invective against monarchy in the abstract, which is to be printed at Paris, and distributed through England and Ireland. The names of some of them are Watts and Wilson of Manchester, Oswald a Scotsman, Stone an Englishman, and Mackintosh who wrote against Burke." [1]

All these men, then, were in Paris during the massacres of September, and not one uttered a word of protest. Oswald, indeed, in his tirades to the Jacobins, with whom he sought to ingratiate himself by insulting his king and country, showed himself more violent than them all, vied with Marat in his invectives against " royal tigers," and rivalled Hébert in his foul accusations against the imprisoned Queen of France.[2]

This being so, are we to regard it as impossible that Englishmen were present at the massacres in the prisons ? One would willingly remove this stain from our national character, but if we are to know the exact truth about the intrigues of the French Revolution, one cannot pass over the accusation in silence. The evidence on which it rests is, firstly, that of Jourdan, president of the Section des Quatre Nations, who was sent to the Abbaye during the massacre and stated that he saw two Englishmen plying the assassins with drink ; [3] and secondly, Prudhomme, who says that Englishmen were seen at La Force amongst the commanders of the butchery, and that " these Englishmen were the guests of the Duc d'Orléans ; they dined with him immediately after the death of the Princesse de Lamballe." [4]

These, then, were the Englishmen dining at the Palais Royal when the princess's head was carried under the windows. The only one of the number whose name is known was a certain Mr. Lindsay, who described the scene with horror to Mr. Burges after his return to England two days later, and whom it is impossible to suspect of collusion with such atrocities. But the contemporary Playfair distinctly states that the guests of the Duc d'Orléans at this particular dinner were " English democrats." [5] This supplies the key to the whole mystery. Since

[1] *Correspondence of Lord Auckland*, ii. 438.
[2] Oswald's Speech to the Jacobins on September 30, 1792 (Aulard's *Séances des Jacobins*, iv. 346).
[3] " Déclaration d'Antoine Gabriel Aimé Jourdan," in *Mémoires sur les Journées de Septembre*, p. 154.
[4] *Crimes de la Révolution*, iv. 123.
[5] Playfair's *History of Jacobinism*, p. 501.

we know that the English democrats then in Paris were ardently in sympathy with all the excesses of the Revolution, that their colleagues in England wrote letters of congratulation, and that Lord Stanhope, one of their most influential members, applauded the massacres, why should they not have personally encouraged the assassins ? From applauding at a distance to assisting on the spot is surely but a step.

Moreover, their presence at the Duc d'Orléans' dinner coincides exactly with Montjoie's assertion that certain English revolutionaries, notably Lord Stanhope, were in league with the Orléanistes. We know that precisely at this moment Lord Stanhope was in correspondence with Richard Sayre, or Sayer, the English agent in Paris, who had been deputed by the revolutionary societies of England to supply arms to the Jacobins of France ; [1] and the exceedingly compromising letters addressed by Sayre to Lord Stanhope—ingenuously published by the latter's admiring biographers [2]—show clearly that the English revolutionaries in Paris, of whom Lord Stanhope was the leading spirit, were engaged in some guilty intrigue with the enemies of their country.

The massacres of September cannot, therefore, be regarded as solely the work of the French ; they were devised and organized by the Spaniard, Marat, in co-operation with Frenchmen, executed by Frenchmen, Italians, and Germans, applauded by the Prussian Clootz, applauded and actively assisted by Englishmen. Again, as on the 10th of August, it is therefore to the doctrines that inspired them, not to the temperament of the nation amongst which they occurred, that the horrors which took place must be attributed.

PRUSSIA

Whilst Anarchists, Orléanistes, Girondins, and English Jacobins were fighting for the mastery in Paris, Prussia played her part in the final ruin of the French monarchy. The cannonade of Valmy—it cannot be described as a battle—that on the 20th of September checked the advance of the allied armies on the capital, is one of the enigmas of history which will never perhaps be entirely solved. Pro-revolutionary historians have endeavoured to explain the retreat of the best-trained troops of Europe before the undisciplined revolutionary army by the state of the weather, the muddy condition of the ground, by the fact that dysentery had broken out amongst the Prussians, or merely by the irresistible valour inspired by democratic doctrines.

[1] The arms referred to by Oswald in his speech (Aulard's *Séances des Jacobins*, iv. 346).

[2] *Life of Charles, third Earl of Stanhope*, by Ghita Stanhope and G. P. Gooch, p. 120.

These legends have now been almost universally accepted as fact, but in the minds of well-informed contemporaries no doubt exists that some further explanation must be sought for the check to the allied armies at Valmy and their subsequent retreat.

Thus Lord Auckland, writing to Sir Morton Eden from the Hague on October 19, 1792, hazards the opinion that "a complete victory (for the allies) might have been on the 20th (at Valmy), if the royal personage who was present had not prevented the engagement for unknown reasons." A note adds that this royal personage was the King of Prussia, but Fersen declares that the King of Prussia wished to attack, and that it was only the cowardice and indecision of the Duke of Brunswick that prevented the engagement. Thiébault, then with the army on the frontier, takes the same view. Matilda Hawkins, whose *Memoirs* were published in 1824, relates that her friend, the Comte de Jarnac, who "was with the army at the time of the Duke of Brunswick's unaccountable retreat from Paris," told her that the Duke himself said, "Why I retreated will never be known to my death."

According to prevailing opinion at the time the retreat after Valmy was effected *by negotiation*, and three different theories were advanced as to the authors of these negotiations. Firstly, then, Beaulieu and Pagès assert that Louis XVI., assured by Manuel, Pétion, and Kersaint that the presence of the allied armies was the main cause of irritation against him, allowed himself to be persuaded to write and ask the King of Prussia to withdraw, in return for which the three deputies promised him his life.[1] Secondly, the Mountain, represented by Camille Desmoulins, declared that the retreat was brought about by an understanding between the Girondins and the Prussians, and when we remember the eulogies lavished by Carra on the Duke of Brunswick in July, and find that Carra was the man chosen by Pétion to go with Sillery on the 24th of September to Dumouriez's camp at La Lune and confer with Manstein, the representative of the King of Prussia, this seems not improbable.[2] Thirdly, D'Allonville, the author of the *Mémoires secrets*, states that it was Danton who negotiated the "defeat" of the Prussians at Valmy and their subsequent retreat by the simple method of bribery. This was effected through the agency of Dumouriez, at this moment Danton's ally, to whom he wrote immediately after Valmy, instructing him to drive back the Prussians without attempting to destroy them, since the Prussians "*were not the*

---

[1] Beaulieu, iv. 169 ; Pagès, ii. 45.

[2] Carra had also been sent by Servan and Danton to "harangue the soldiers at the camp of ' La Maulde ' in August" (see *Précis de la Défense de Carra*, p. 29).

natural enemies of France." [1] The manner in which Danton procured the necessary sums is thus described by D'Allonville :

" Billaud - Varenne, who left Paris after the massacres of September, had reached the army on the 11th and had opened negotiations, of which the sums promised, but not yet paid, alone delayed the conclusion. Two or three millions, the fruit of the pillage of the 10th of August, were all that the Commune of Paris possessed, and it was not enough. ' Why do you not rob the Garde-Meuble (*i.e.* the depository where the Crown jewels were kept) ? ' cries Panis, and this thing was done on the 16th of September by the orders of Tallien and Danton, which produced, in different species, a sum of thirty millions. The first overtures had facilitated the escape of Dumouriez from the position in which he would have been irrevocably lost, others prevented him from being driven from his position during the cannonade of Valmy, and from the 22nd to the 23rd negotiations were, as we have said, actively carried out." [2]

This evidence is exactly confirmed by General Michaud, who was with the armies at the time. The deputies of the Gironde, Michaud declares, were not in the secret of the negotiations with the Prussians, and it is to the Orléaniste schemes of Danton that these are to be attributed. " It is only with audacity and yet more audacity that we can save ourselves," said the Minister of Justice. " Danton was, no doubt, a very audacious man, but when he pronounced these words it is certain that he knew of the secret negotiation, since he himself was directing it with his colleague Lebrun. . . . Already he was assured that the Prussians would not get to Paris, he knew that it was only a matter of satisfying them, and fulfilling the engagements entered into by Dumouriez. . . . Hence this resolution to remain in the capital, to pillage the Garde-Meuble, to massacre the prisoners and plunder the victims. . . . So it might be said, without exaggeration, that the horrible system of blood and terror . . . was a consequence of what had taken place in Champagne between the Prussians and the leaders of the Revolution, who were no other than the leaders of the Orléaniste faction." [3]

The theft of the Crown jewels was not attributed to Danton by Royalists alone. When on the night of the 16th to the 17th of September the Garde-Meuble was broken into and the Crown jewels were removed, no one seriously believed that the coup could be attributed to ordinary burglars, and by Girondins as well

---

[1] D'Allonville, *Mémoires d'un Homme d'État*, i. 401.

[2] D'Allonville, *Mémoires secrets*, iii. 95.

[3] *Biographie de Louis Philippe d'Orléans*, by L. G. Michaud, Appendix, pp. 16, 17.

as Royalists it was declared to be the work of the Commune. Why, indeed, should it not be so ? The Commune, as every one knew, had ordered the pillage that took place after the 10th of August, and it was again the Commune that had taken possession of the greater part of the spoils wrested from the victims of the massacres. When several large burglaries have been effected by the same gang in the same district, it is only reasonable to attribute a further one to the same agency. Madame Roland had no hesitation in designating Danton as the chief burglar of the Crown jewels and Fabre d'Églantine as his assistant, although, as usual in the case of crimes ordained by the revolutionary leaders, the obscure instruments who carried out the deed were arrested and put to death.[1]

At any rate, whatever were the means employed, it is clear that some pressure was brought to bear upon the Prussians in order to ensure their retreat. The unaccountable part of the affair lies not so much in the fact that their triumphant advance was checked by a reverse at Valmy, but that this one reverse should have turned the tide of the whole war, yet should not have resulted in the rout of the allied armies. For if the revolutionary troops were strong enough to arrest finally the enemy's advance, why did they not follow up their victory at Valmy with greater vigour ? This problem was so apparent to every one at the time that it was admitted even by Desmoulins, the ally of Danton, though, at the instigation of Robespierre, he cleverly turned it into an accusation against the Girondins.

" Is it not inconceivable to every one and unheard of in history," wrote Camille Desmoulins in his *Histoire des Brissotins,* " as I said to Dumouriez himself when he appeared at the Convention, that a general who with 17,000 men had held back an army of 92,000 men—after Dumouriez, Ajax Beurnonville, and Kellermann had announced that the plains of Champagne would be the tomb of the King of Prussia's army, like that of Attila, and that not one man would escape—should not have cut off the retreat of this army when it was reduced to nearly half by dysentery, when its march was impeded by nearly 20,000 sick, and that, on the other hand, the victorious army had increased to more than 100,000 men ! All the soldiers of the vanguard of our army will tell you that when the rearguard of the Prussians called a halt, we called a halt ; when they went to the right, we marched to the left ; in a word, Dumouriez led back the King of Prussia rather than he pursued him, and *there was not a soldier in the army who was not convinced that there had been an arrangement between the Prussians and the Convention by the medium of Dumouriez.*"

[1] *Mémoires de Mme. Roland,* i. 113.

Such, then, in the words of the revolutionary leaders themselves, was the "irresistible *élan* of the victorious revolutionary army"! Whether, therefore, the retreat of the Prussians was due to the Girondins or Orléanistes, whether Carra was acting in the interests of the Duke of Brunswick or the Duc d'Orléans, whether Danton had an understanding with the Girondins and afterwards disowned them, or whether he was carrying on an intrigue with Dumouriez as the agent of the Commune and later on betrayed him, representing him through Desmoulins as the accomplice of the Gironde, it is evident that *something happened at Valmy* which has never been explained to this day. Valmy and its sequel remain an insoluble mystery. Only, in the light of our present knowledge of Prussian diplomacy, it seems not impossible that some profounder policy may have underlain the action of both Frederick William and the Duke of Brunswick than has yet been attributed to them. At any rate, whether they realized it at the time or not, the "defeat" of Valmy was a superb victory for Prussia. For to march on to Paris at this crisis must have been to re-establish the Bourbons on the throne, and to leave the way open to a renewal of the Franco-Austrian alliance ; by leaving France to tear herself to pieces Frederick William worthily carried out the traditions of the great Frederick, and assured the future supremacy of Prussia. Valmy had but paved the way for Sadowa and Sedan.

Goethe, looking on at the famous fusillade, is said to have uttered these prophetic words : " From this place and from this day forth begins a new era in the world's history, and you can all say that you were present at its birth."

A new era in truth, an era wherein the civilization of old France should be utterly destroyed and the great barbaric German Empire should rise upon the ruins. The Golden Age had ended ; the Age of Blood and Iron was to begin.

THE REIGN OF TERROR

THE REIGN OF TERROR

" THE 2nd of September," said Collot d'Herbois, " is the great article of the Credo of our liberty." In other words, the massacres in the prisons were the prelude to the Reign of Terror, the first manifestation of that organized system of destruction which for ten months held sway over France. This is why, in relating the history of the Terror, it is necessary to begin at September 1792, in order to show the progressive stages which led up to the final climax.

For, before this system could be pursued with impunity, the demagogues were obliged to remove three principal obstacles from their path; these were, firstly, the monarchy, and consequently the Constitution of 1791 ; secondly, the King ; and thirdly, the Girondins. It was the struggle to effect this threefold purpose that for a year arrested the course of the Terror, which otherwise must have followed directly on the September massacres. We shall now see how one by one these obstacles were overthrown, and how, in each case, the schemes of the demagogues triumphed over the will of the people.

THE PROCLAMATION OF THE REPUBLIC

The idea no doubt prevails in this country that France became a Republic because the French nation was finally convinced of the advantages offered by a Republican form of government. Nothing is further from the truth. France, as the cahiers had shown, was solidly monarchical, and the protests following on the 20th of June gave evidence that this sentiment still prevailed throughout the country. " The Republicans," said Danton in September 1792, " are an infinitesimal minority . . . the rest of France is attached to the monarchy." [1]

If, however, any doubt existed on this point, if the demagogues had any reason to suppose that the opinion of the people had changed since the formation of the cahiers, the only course in accordance with the principles of democracy would have been to

---

[1] Danton to the Comité de Défense Générale (see Robinet, *Procès des Dantonistes*).

make a fresh appeal to the nation. For, however impossible it may be to consult the people on the details of legislation, it is obviously a farce to describe a State as democratic in which the form of government is not the choice of the nation as a whole. The only legitimate method by which the form of government can be changed is, therefore, a referendum to the people.

Nothing of this kind was done in France. When, on the 21st of September, the Convention that now superseded the Legislative Assembly held its first sitting, none of the deputies—amongst whom all the leading revolutionaries, Girondins, Dantonistes, and Robespierristes alike, were included—had made any attempt to discover the real wishes of their constituents on the question of abolishing the monarchy, whilst in the provinces the idea of a Republic had not even been considered.[1]

At one moment it seemed as if the new Assembly were endowed with some appreciation of the principles of democracy, for it began by passing this admirable resolution : " The National Convention declares that there can be no Constitution unless it is accepted by the people."

Yet after this, at the very same sitting, it proceeded with ludicrous inconsequence to discuss the fundamental point of the Constitution, the question of a Republic, without any reference whatever to the wishes of the people !

It was Couthon, the ally of Robespierre, who had first proposed the abolition of the monarchy, and the proposal was now seconded by Collot d'Herbois amidst " universal applause." True, one obscure member named Quinette rose to observe : " It is not we who are the judges of the monarchy, it is the people. We have only the mission to form a definite government, and the people will choose between the old one which included the monarchy, and the new one which we shall present to them." But the protest of Quinette was overruled by Grégoire, who declared that " no one could ever propose to preserve in France the disastrous race of kings. . . . We know too well that all dynasties have only been devouring races living on human flesh. . . . I ask that by a solemn law you should ordain the abolition of monarchy."

In vain Bazire interposed with the remonstrance that the Assembly should not allow itself to be carried away by a " moment of enthusiasm," that " the question of abolishing the monarchy should at least be discussed by the Assembly."

" What need is there for discussion," answered Grégoire,

---

[1] " It was only in Paris that the question of the Republic was considered. . . . In 1792 there are no principles (of Republicanism). They can only abolish the monarchy by advocating the deposition (of the King). They dare not proclaim the Republic " (Madelin, p. 266).

" when every one is agreed ? Kings are in the moral order of
things what monsters are in the physical order . . . the history
of kings is the martyrology of nations. Since we are all equally
penetrated by this truth, what need is there for discussion ? "

And, in response to this dignified discourse, the Assembly,
without further debate, passed the resolution : " The National
Convention decrees that monarchy is abolished in France." [1]

Thus, in flagrant violation of the first principle of democracy,
rule by the will of the people,[2] in direct contradiction to the
resolution passed by the Convention itself at that same sitting,
the Republic was proclaimed by an infinitesimal minority of
political adventurers. For if these men who took upon themselves to overthrow the ancient government of France had been
honest in their intentions, if they had themselves been convinced
of the advantages of a Republic over a monarchy, their action
might, to a certain extent, be condoned by their enthusiasm.
But it was not so. These men were *not* Republican by conviction,
for, as we have already seen, they were actuated by various
policies far removed from Republicanism. Still, at the inauguration of the Convention, it seems that the same schemes
for a change of dynasty survived ; the factions had merely undergone some slight modifications. Now, although at most stages
of the Revolution we find contemporaries disagreed on the aims
of the factions, it is curious to notice the extraordinary resemblance between the explanations given by writers belonging to
completely different parties of the motives that inspired the
proclamation of the Republic.

According to such divergent authorities as Montjoie, Pagès,
Prudhomme, and " The Two Friends of Liberty," Carra and his
party still inclined to the Duke of Brunswick ; Brissot and his
party to the Duke of York ; Sillery, Sieyès, and Laclos to the
Duc d'Orléans ; Dumouriez, Biron, and Valence to the Duc de
Chartres ; whilst Marat and Danton, now less disposed to support
the Duc d'Orléans, began to think of their own elevation and
joined forces with Robespierre, in order to establish either a

---

[1] *Moniteur*, xiv. 8.

[2] A working-man, a tiler of Saint-Leu, named Gillequint, himself a
convinced Republican, thus admirably summed up the matter in an
address to his fellow-citizens some months later : " The Sovereign (*i.e.*
the people) must be free in his opinion. Are we free to manifest ours ?
At the opening of the sittings of the Convention . . . a member proposed
the abolition of the monarchy. Without examination, without discussion,
the monarchy was abolished by a decree. . . . This decree was not sanctioned by the people, and since it is recognized that no decree can be made
law without the sanction of the people, it should only have been carried
out provisionally." For this expression of opinion Gillequint was guillotined on the 5th of Messidor, An II. (Wallon, *Tribunal révolutionnaire*,
iv. 386-388).

Dictatorship under one of their number or a Triumvirate composed of all three. Owing to these conflicting policies, none of which could be openly avowed, every one was obliged to profess Republicanism—" some voted for the Republic for fear Orléans should be King, others in order not to appear Orléanistes ; all wished to acquire or maintain their popularity." This was what Robespierre meant when he said later on, " *The Republic slipped in furtively between the factions.*" [1]

But once the Republic had been proclaimed and the monarchy declared to be finally abolished, it became necessary for the factions to reconstruct their policies, and so three main parties were formed in the Convention. These became known as the Gironde, the Plain, and the Mountain.

The first of these parties consisted of the deputies of the *Gironde* who had sat in the Legislative Assembly—Vergniaud, Guadet, Gensonné, Ducos, and Fonfrède—and also Brissot with his following, which included Buzot, Valazé, Isnard, and Condorcet. All these were henceforth described collectively as Girondistes or Girondins, and it was they who, as time went on, came to represent the truly Republican party in the Convention.

The *Plain* or *Marais* was composed of several hundred nondescript deputies, non-committal in their views, and afraid to move boldly in any direction.

But the real force of the Assembly lay in the *Mountain*, that fierce and subversive minority dominated by Danton, Marat, and Robespierre, and including the most violent members of the Jacobin and Cordelier Clubs—Camille Desmoulins, Billaud-Varenne, Collot d'Herbois, Fabre d'Églantine, Panis, Sergent, Legendre, and also the Duc d'Orléans, who, by the usual methods of bribes and cajolery, by dinners lavished on the new members of the Commune, and, in the opinion of many contemporaries, by the payment of 15,000 livres to Marat, succeeded in securing election as a deputy for Paris.[2]

Inevitably the Montagnards carried all before them ; it was they and not the pedantic Girondins who understood the art of

[1] Montjoie, *Conjuration de d'Orléans*, iii. 216; Pagès, ii. 10-14; *Deux Amis*, viii. 326; Prudhomme, *Crimes de la Révolution*, v. 24-27. These passages, written at about the same date, 1796 and 1797, should be carefully compared, and will be found to be almost identical; it is evident that each expressed the current opinion of the day.

[2] Prudhomme, *Révolutions de Paris*, xiii. 522. It was at this moment that the Duc d'Orléans was said to have declared to the Commune that he was not the son of the last Duc d'Orléans but of the duchess's coachman. Montjoie, *Conjuration de d'Orléans*, iii. 251 ; Peltier, *La Révolution du 10 Août*, ii. 9; Playfair's *History of Jacobinism*, p. 604; posthumous works of Lord Orford, *Historic Doubts*, ii. 250; *Les Fils de Philippe Égalité*, by G. Lenôtre, p. 2.

rousing popular passions. Hitherto, as we have seen, even the mob of Paris had needed to be systematically stirred up in order to take part in the revolutionary movement, and this is not surprising, for the issues at stake were outside their comprehension. What matter to them whether the " patriot ministers " were recalled or not, whether the King had the right of Veto, whether the non-juring priests were deported, and so forth ? As to the leaders of the Legislative Assembly, none had appealed to their mentalities; the eloquence of Vergniaud left them cold; the speeches repeated parrot-like by the so-called deputations from the Faubourgs were unintelligible alike to orators and audience.

But when Marat, Danton, and Robespierre assumed the reins of power everything was changed. Marat spoke a language the populace could understand ; instead of bewildering their minds with political subtleties he simply ordered them to go out and burn and pillage and destroy. By this means he appealed irresistibly to the craving for excitement which distinguishes the populace in every city, particularly in Paris, whilst his ostentation of poverty imposed for a while on some of the more credulous amongst the people themselves. It has been said that " Marat loved the poor," that from the beginning of the Revolution he had lived on the barest necessaries of life. This we now know to be untrue ; Marat, though of filthy and neglected appearance, lived in the greatest comfort, and was never known to make any personal sacrifices for the poor of Paris.[1] The vicious, the wastrel, the degraded alone inspired his sympathy ; honest and law-abiding men of the people, especially those who by their industry had achieved some degree of prosperity, became the objects of his contempt and hatred. " Give me 300,000 heads," he said, " and I will answer for the country being saved. . . . Begin by hanging at their doors the bakers, the grocers, and all the tradesmen.". When the people failed to respond to these

[1] " From the day the Revolution began," says Kropotkin, " Marat took to bread and water, not figuratively speaking, but in reality." No authority is given for this astonishing assertion. The researches of M. Lenôtre reveal, however, that at his flat in the Rue des Cordeliers, Marat was waited on by four women—his mistress, his sister, the portress, and the *cook*. Why a cook for bread and water ? Moreover, on the evening of his death, when during the visit of Charlotte Corday, his mistress, Simonne Evrard, entered the bathroom, she removed from the window-sill two dishes containing sweetbreads and brains for the evening meal—by no means a meagre menu for the Friend of the People at a moment when hungry crowds were drawn up outside his door waiting for crusts of bread (*Paris révolutionnaire*, by G. Lenôtre, p. 219). This confirms the story current amongst the people later that, although Marat's frugality had been vaunted, his table " was every day splendidly served and never consisted of less than eight dishes, and that she who called herself his wife was seen to buy objects of great luxury, either for his table or for other purposes. . . ." (Schmidt, *Tableaux de Paris*, ii. 167).

suggestions, Marat turned and rent them : " Oh ! babbling people, if you but knew how to act ! " [1] or again : " Eternal idlers, with what epithets would I not overwhelm you if, in the transports of my despair, I knew of any more humiliating than that of Parisians ! " [2] In this lay the difference between the policies of Robespierre and Marat. Robespierre aimed at *democracy*, not in the sense of government by the people, but of a State solely composed of " the people " ; [3] he would have liked to turn the whole world into a vast working-man's settlement, of which he would be the presiding genius ; whilst Marat wanted *ochlocracy*, a State dominated by that small portion of the people known as the " mob," making of the world a huge thieves' kitchen, in which he would play the part of brigand chief. Robespierre, now falling more and more under the influence of Marat, began to realize the superiority of Marat's method ; he perceived that in times of revolution it is to the subversive minority that a demagogue must look for support, and that to appeal to the reason of the people must ever prove less effectual than to rouse the passions of the mob. Hitherto he had sought to establish his popularity by fulsome adulation of the people's virtues,[4] but from this time onward we find him gradually abandoning the attitude of moderation he had maintained during the preceding year, and reverting to the subversive methods he had employed at the outset of the Revolution. Inveighing against the rich and great, appealing always to cupidity and envy, it was principally amongst the women of the Société Fraternelle and the female convicts released during the massacres of September that he found his following, and this dishevelled band that Danton derisively described as the *jupons gras* of Robespierre [5] filled the tribunes of the Convention and the Jacobin Club, drowning the debates in their clamour.

Danton, on the other hand, never theorized about democracy. Too lazy to put pen to paper, he is almost the only revolutionary leader who owned no journal and wrote no pamphlets ; his speeches, admirably suited to a recruiting platform with their sounding refrains of " Let us beat the enemy ! " " Let us save

---

[1] *L'Ami du Peuple*, No. 681.

[2] *Ibid.* No. 539.

[3] That Robespierre did not believe in government by the people has been admirably explained by M. Louis Blanc—who does not believe in it himself (see his *Histoire de la Révolution*, viii. 269).

[4] Thus : " In the matter of genius and civism the people are infallible, whilst every one else is subject to great errors " (Article de Robespierre, Buchez et Roux, xiv. 268). " The motives of the people are always pure ; they cannot do otherwise than love the public good," etc. (*Robespierre à ses Commettants*, ii. 285).

[5] Prudhomme, *Crimes de la Révolution*, v. 124.

the country ! " served merely to electrify the Assembly, especially the tribunes, and afford evidence of no definite or coherent political creed. It is, therefore, by his sayings that we know Danton best—words flung out at impetuous moments, recorded by innumerable contemporaries, and bearing so strong a family resemblance that it is impossible not to believe that some at least are authentic. It was thus that, like Mirabeau, he frankly admitted his own corruptibility. "Danton," says Prudhomme, " was known as a man who displayed little delicacy in revolution ; that is why he was always surrounded by bad characters and swindlers. Here is a remark habitual to him : ' The Revolution should profit those who make it, and if the Kings enriched nobles the Revolution should enrich patriots.' " [1] We shall find Danton giving vent to the same sentiments up to the very foot of the scaffold. Danton's own greed for gold led him to believe that the people were to be won by the same means ; money he held to be the great lever by which the revolutionary mobs could be moved to action.[2]

The fact is, Danton was not a politician, but simply a great agitator ; the "people" to whom he openly referred as the *canaille* must be made to serve the purpose of the demagogues, and he moved amongst them with no show of "fraternity" like Robespierre or Marat, but, as Garat expressed it, like "a grand seigneur of the Sans-Culotterie," scattering largesse and thundering words of command. Robespierre's scheme of a Socialist State held, therefore, little attraction for Danton, who had no desire to exchange his comfortable flat in Paris and his château at Arcis-sur-Aube for a cottage in a working-man's settlement.

But, although divided in their ultimate aims—and also secretly hostile to each other—the members of the Triumvirate that headed the Mountain were agreed in regarding a period of anarchy as necessary to the realization of their schemes, and were therefore content to work together in order to destroy existing conditions. For this purpose it was necessary to enlist the aid of the mob—that portion of the people, mainly women, who, having nothing to lose by general confusion, were ready in return for adequate remuneration to stamp and shout for each party in turn.[3]

---

[1] Prudhomme, *Crimes de la Révolution*, iv. 162.

[2] "Danton during his brief apparition at the ' Comité de Salut Public ' instituted that odious power of gold, that frightful system of corruption that bought speech or silence. . . . ' Get money given you,' said Danton to Garat, ' and do not spare it ; the Republic will always have enough.' . . . *To corrupt and to be corrupted* was for him the whole science of our morals, all the probity of the century. . . ." (*ibid.* v. 78-80).

[3] "Applauders and murmurers are to be had at all prices ; and as

Buzot has thus described the aspect of the deputations and audiences collected by Marat and Robespierre at the Convention :

" It seemed as if they had sought in all the slums of Paris and of the large cities for everything that was filthiest, most hideous, and polluted. Dreadful earthen faces, black or copper-coloured, surmounted by a thick tuft of greasy hair, with eyes half sunken in their heads, they gave vent with their fetid breath to the coarsest insults and shrill screams of hungry animals. The tribunes were worthy of such legislators : men whose frightful appearance gave evidence of crime and wretchedness, women whose shameless air expressed the foulest debauchery. When all these, with hands, feet, and voices, made their horrible din, one would have imagined oneself in an assembly of devils."

Such were the elements that now usurped the power, taking as their watchword the cry that Taine truly calls " the *résumé* of the revolutionary spirit": " The will of the people makes the law, *and we are the people.*" Henceforth the Revolution enters on a new phase, monarchy and aristocracy have both retired from the lists, and the struggle has begun between democracy and ochlocracy, between the people and the populace. And since the demagogues are on the side of the populace, inevitably ochlocracy triumphs, and everywhere, in the tribunes of the Convention and of the Jacobin Club, in the streets and public places, Marat's rabble, though an infinitesimal minority, holds sway over the great mass of the people.

THE DEATH OF THE KING

It is significant that even at this crisis, when the revolutionary leaders had at last succeeded in obtaining a following amongst the populace, the attempt was not renewed to achieve the death of the King at the hands of the mob. But the new demagogues were too expert crowd exponents not to realize the futility of such a project. Madame Roland might imagine that the Faubourgs of Paris could be incited to regicide ; Marat, Danton, and Robespierre well knew that if the King were to die they themselves must perform the deed. For in this matter even the populace they had enlisted in their service was not to be depended on.

" The people," writes a contemporary during the King's trial, " even that portion of the people who have so often steeped themselves in blood during the Revolution, does not wish to

females are more noisy and to be had cheaper than males, you will observe there are generally more women than men in the tribunes " (Dr. Moore's *Journal*, i. 211 ; see also Pagès, ii. 29).

shed that of the King; but there is a party to which it is necessary, and at this moment it dominates Paris, and even the Convention." [1]

Dr. Moore, mingling at this date with the people of Paris, likewise realized that the ferocity attributed to them was confined to their so-called representatives. New fears, he writes, have been expressed in the Convention of massacres taking place in the streets. " If there is really any danger of such an event, the inhabitants of Paris must be the worst of savages, but the only people I see of a savage disposition are certain members of the Convention and of the Jacobin Club, and a great majority of those who fill the tribunes at both those assemblies; but the shopkeepers and tradespeople (and I take some pains to be acquainted with their way of thinking) seem to be much the same as I have always known them; I am persuaded that there is no risk of massacres or assassinations but from a set of wretches who are neither shopkeepers nor tradesmen, but *idle vagabonds, hired and excited for the purpose.* When I hear it asserted from the tribune of the Convention, or of the Jacobin Society, that *the people are impatient for the death of the King,* or inclined to murder unfortunate men while they are conducted to prison, and *yet can perceive no disposition of that nature among the citizens,* I cannot help suspecting that those orators themselves are the people who are impatient for those atrocities, and that they spread the notion that this desire is general among the people on purpose to render it easier to commit them, and to make them more quietly submitted to after they have been committed." [2]

In vain the Commune marshalled deputations from the revolutionary " sections " to the bar of the Assembly to demand " the death of the tyrant "; the people in the streets and cafés gave the lie to all such demonstrations. Thereupon Prudhomme, still the King's implacable enemy, angrily apostrophized them : " Frenchmen, where will all this lead you ? . . . every hour of the day takes away millions of partisans from the Republic to give them to Royalism. . . . Already in your restaurants hired singers screech inane but touching laments on the fate of the tyrant. (This lament to the tune of ' Pauvre Jacques ' begins thus : ' O mon peuple, que t'ai-je fait ? ' It is being sold in thousands. The hymn of the Marseillais is forgotten for it.) I have seen, yes, I have seen the toper let fall a tear into his wine in favour of Louis Capet. . . . The French Republic is already three-quarters royalized." [3]

[1] M. de Bernard à sa Femme, date of December 27, 1792, in *Lettres d'Aristocrates,* by Pierre de Vaissière, p. 582.

[2] Moore's *Journal,* ii. 249.

[3] Prudhomme, *Révolutions de Paris,* xiv. 52.

On the 2nd of January 1793 a Royalist play entitled *L'Ami des Lois* was produced amidst a wild outburst of popular enthusiasm. The piece in itself was dull, but the opportunity it offered for applauding allusions to royalty and the person of the King, and for jeering at the leading demagogues travestied on the stage, drew an immense audience—the crowd struggling to obtain admittance was numbered at 30,000 people. In vain the Père Duchesne proclaimed his *Grande Colère* against " the mountebanks, heretofore actors of the King " ; in vain the younger Robespierre denounced this " infamous piece " in which they had the audacity to introduce his brother and " the excellent citizen Marat " ; in vain Santerre, surrounded by his staff and later 150 Jacobins, sword and pistol in hand, attempted to put a stop to the performance. The people responded with deafening cries of " L'Ami des Lois ! The piece ! The piece ! Raise the curtain ! " The voice of Santerre was drowned in shouts of " Down with the General Mousseux ! Down with the 2nd of September ! We want the piece ! The piece or death ! " The demagogues were obliged to submit ; the piece was played not once but again, four times in all, amidst scenes of indescribable enthusiasm.[1]

A still stranger scene took place at Bordeaux, where it was not simply a promiscuous crowd of citizens who protested against the designs of the Convention, but the chosen flock on whom the leaders depended for their following. By way of propaganda the Jacobin Society of Bordeaux had invited its members to a " patriotic play " called *The Republic of Syracuse, or Monarchy Abolished.* The sentiments this piece contained having been heartily approved by the leading members of the Club, it was hoped that the public would receive it with equal favour. This is, however, what occurred—the description must be given in the inimitable words of the patriot of Bordeaux, whose letter was read aloud at the Jacobin Club in Paris :

" On the day of the performance all the seats were filled at a very early hour. The curtain rises and the theatre represents the palace of M. Veto ; he is told of the complaints that his people make against him, and of the depredations of Mme. Veto. He gets angry ; an insurrection makes him gentler. The people wish to become free and give themselves a constitution ; a patriot general is placed at the head of the armed forces ; Mme. Veto tries to seduce him, but in the piece she does not succeed as in our Revolution.[2] The Constitution made, the

---

[1] *Journal d'un Bourgeois*, by Edmond Biré, i. 383.
[2] Lafayette seduced by Marie Antoinette !—Marie Antoinette who had cried out, " Better perish than be saved by Lafayette ! " There is no limit to the absurdities circulated by the Jacobins.

Constitutional Monarch swears and swears again everything they wish, but keeps nothing; at last the people open their eyes a second time, they see that this monarch is deceiving them; they attack the Château, take M. and Mme. Veto prisoners, and shut them up in a tower. They are brought to trial and the Senate of Syracuse sends them both to the guillotine. Here begins the fifth act. The guillotine on the stage excites a movement of stupor throughout the hall. Some said, ' How can they represent such things ? ' Women fainted. At last, in the midst of the most absolute silence, M. and Mme. Veto arrive at the foot of the fatal instrument. At the moment they mount the ladder a cry from the people demands mercy for them, and condemns them to perpetual imprisonment. At the cry of ' Mercy ! ' the hall resounded with applause, *so much has public opinion deteriorated in that city.* So no longer there does one hear the *générale* beaten or the cry to arms ; flat calm reigns. The patriot Terrasson tried to speak at the Society in favour of Marat, Robespierre, Danton, and others, who are regarded as sedition-mongers ; they would not listen to him . . . the Society passed the resolution that it would suspend all correspondence with the Jacobins of Paris, so long as these members remained amongst them." [1]

The Convention took a terrible revenge on Bordeaux ten months later.

It will be asked, " If the people did not wish for the death of the King, why did they not save him ? " Perhaps if they had known their power they might have done so, but, terrorized as they still were by the September massacres, they no doubt imagined the Commune to be far more powerful than it really was. They could not know, as we know now, that the following on which the leaders depended for support constituted approximately $\frac{1}{100}$ part of the population of Paris,[2] and that, had the remaining $\frac{99}{100}$ been able to coalesce, they could have swept away the demagogues almost without an effort. Convinced of their own helplessness, they showed the same submission to the decrees of the Convention concerning the King as they displayed when their own lives were at stake eighteen months later. But, above all, they lacked leaders, men of their own class to defend their interests against those of the middle-class men who composed the Convention. A few energetic working-men, placing themselves at the head of the Faubourgs, must have carried the day, for at this stage of the Revolution the demagogues would

[1] Aulard's *Séances des Jacobins*, iv. 619.
[2] Statement of a government reporter in June 1793 : " There are not 3000 decided revolutionaries in Paris" (*Paris pendant la Révolution*, by Adolphe Schmidt, p. 21).

not have dared to fire on them—the people so far were not crushed, they were only paralysed.

Meanwhile, had they only realized it, the Convention lived in terror of the people. All through the discussions that took place on the fate of the King there runs a haunting fear lest a popular movement should be made in his favour.[1] It was for this reason that Chabot urged the necessity for avoiding a Sunday or Monday for bringing the King to trial, since on those days the people were not at work and would be free to assemble.[2] Robespierre, the better to expedite matters, proposed that the Convention should pass sentence of death without according Louis XVI. the formality of a trial, whilst St. Just advocated simple murder. " Caesar," he said, " was immolated in the open Senate without any further formality than twenty-two dagger thrusts."

But the Girondins, either from a desire to maintain a reputation for justice, or because they really wished to save the King, insisted on a trial, and the 11th of December was the day fixed for Louis XVI. to appear at the bar of the Convention.

The debates that took place in the Convention must be read in order to realize the utter futility of the charges brought against the King, from Valazé's accusation of " monopolizing wheat, coffee, and sugar," [3] to the diatribes of Robert—convicted later of cornering large quantities of rum [4]—who declared Louis XVI. to be " guilty of more cruelties than Nero," of having " butchered more human beings than his life counted hours or moments," of " aspiring to the absurd privilege of bathing in the blood of his fellow-men." [5] For want of fresh pretexts all the old threadbare grievances were revived—the closing of the Assembly on the day of the Oath of the Tennis Court, the " orgy of the Guards " at Versailles on the 1st of October 1789, the flight to Varennes, the " massacre of the Champ de Mars " on July 17, 1791 (when the King was a prisoner at the Tuileries), the refusal to sanction the camp of 20,000 men, and so on. The charge of conspiring with foreign powers, that looms so large in the pages of revolutionary historians, played a comparatively small part in the trial, for no proofs whatever were forthcoming. Great hopes had been entertained of finding incriminating documents in the iron cupboard that Roland had

---

[1] " Those who wished his death were in constant dread of a return of humanity and affection in the hearts of the people towards him, and therefore were at great pains to fill the tribunes with persons hired to make an outcry against him : and they were so apprehensive on this subject as to suspect those very agents of relenting " (Moore's *Journal*, ii. 528).

[2] Buchez et Roux, xxi. 202.

[3] " Premier Rapport de Valazé," November 6, *Moniteur*, xiv. 401.

[4] *Essais de Beaulieu*, iv. 228.

[5] *Ibid.*

discovered at the Tuileries after the 10th of August, where the King had concealed his private papers, but this find proved disappointing, for though it offered to Roland the opportunity for abstracting documents that could have served to establish the innocence of Louis XVI.[1]—and also certain other documents that might have convicted Roland and his party of offering to sell themselves to the Court [2]—it provided not a shred of evidence that the King had been guilty of traitorous intrigues with the enemies of France.[3]

When, finally, Louis XVI. appeared at the bar of the Convention, and the long list of paltry charges, drawn up in the form of an indictment, was read aloud to him, he contented himself with brief and dignified denials ; only when they touched on his most vulnerable point, his conduct towards the people, his serenity momentarily deserted him.   Thus at the accusation of Barère that he had attempted to conspire by going to the Faubourg Saint-Antoine and distributing alms amongst the poor workmen of the district, his eyes filled with tears as he answered, " Ah ! monsieur, I have never known greater happiness than in giving to those who were in need." [4]   At this, one of the wretched women amongst Marat's following in the tribunes burst into loud sobs, exclaiming, " Ah ! mon Dieu, how he makes me weep ! " [5]   When, again, he was accused of shedding the people's blood—the one reproach of all that cut him to the heart—his voice vibrated with emotion as he replied, " No, monsieur, no, it was not *I* who shed their blood." [6]

" The King's appearance in the Convention," says Dr. Moore, " the dignified resignation of his manner, the admirable promptitude and candour of his answers, made such an evident impression on some of the audience in the galleries that a determined enemy of Royalty, who had his eye upon them, declared that he was afraid of hearing the cry of ' Vive le Roi ! ' issue from the tribunes, and added that if the King had remained ten minutes longer in their sight he was convinced it would have happened : for which reason he was vehemently against his being brought to the bar a second time." [7]

On the proposal of Pétion the King was allowed to appoint advocates for his defence.   No less than a hundred at once

---

[1] Moore's *Journal*, ii. 614.

[2] *Mémoires de Lafayette*, iii. 381.

[3] Beaulieu, iv. 267 ; Moore's *Journal*, ii. 468 ; see also the selections from these papers published by Buchez et Roux, xvii. 259.

[4] Montjoie, *Conjuration de d'Orléans*, iii. 224 ; Moore's *Journal*, ii. 512.

[5] *Éloge historique et funèbre de Louis XVI.*, by Montjoie, p. 247.

[6] Beaulieu, iv. 274 ; *Lettres d'Aristocrates*, by Pierre de Vaissière, p. 584.

[7] Moore's *Journal*, ii. 529.

offered their services.[1] The King's choice fell on his old friend Malesherbes, who at the beginning of his reign had co-operated with him in the work of reform, on Désèze, Tronchet, and Target. Target, it seems, had not volunteered, and had the cowardice to refuse the task. At this the *poissardes* were so indignant that they presented themselves at his door with birch-rods to scourge him, and the wretched Target, warned of their intention, was obliged to fly ; but to Tronchet who accepted they brought flowers and laurels.[2] They would have crowned, too, the head of brave old Malesherbes, that venerable white head that, as the penalty of his devotion, was to fall later upon the scaffold, but Malesherbes declined the honour, and the fishwives had to content themselves with hanging their garlands on his gate.[3]

All these symptoms seriously alarmed the revolutionary leaders, and when on the 26th of December the King appeared at the Convention to hear his defence read aloud by Désèze, immense precautions were taken to prevent the people from coming to his rescue. The whole route from the Temple to the Manège was lined with troops ; a mounted bodyguard as well as one on foot surrounded his carriage, six cannons preceded him and six followed behind, whilst strong patrols paraded the streets.[4]

The assembling of this guard had been no easy matter, for the men of the people had absolutely declined to take part in the proceedings. " It is said," writes a contemporary that evening, " that the Faubourgs Saint-Antoine and Saint-Marceau, which are the most thickly populated districts of Paris, refused to-day to form the King's Guard whilst he was at the Convention, saying that if any harm is to be done to him they will not be accomplices." [5] It was thus found necessary to form a sort of press-gang, and officers were sent to tear peaceful citizens from their beds and force them to join the escort.[6]

From the outset it was evident that the King's trial was to be a mere travesty of justice. " I look for judges ! " cried his advocate Désèze, " and I see only accusers ! " Even the revolutionary leaders themselves secretly recognized the truth of this indictment. The Convention, Prudhomme pointed out to Danton, had not the right to try Louis XVI. : " If the Parliament of England tried Charles I., it is because it was not a Convention ; the members of the Conventional Assembly cannot be

---

[1] Letter from M. Bernard to his wife in *Lettres d'Aristocrates,* by Pierre de Vaissière, p. 578.

[2] Moore's *Journal,* ii. 526 ; *Lettres d'Aristocrates,* pp. 571, 581.

[3] *Lettres d'Aristocrates,* by Pierre de Vaissière, p. 581.

[4] *Ibid.* p. 577.

[5] *Ibid.* p. 580.

[6] Prudhomme, *Révolutions de Paris,* xiv. 3, 4.

at the same time accusers, jury, and judges." "You are right," answered Danton, "nor shall we judge Louis XVI.; we shall kill him." [1]

This was the plan they now proposed to put into practice, and as soon as the King had retired Duhem rose to demand that his condemnation should be discussed without further delay. The evidence brought forward in his defence was thus not even to be considered.

At so monstrous an outrage on humanity and justice one man was found brave enough to protest—Lanjuinais, a Breton, member for Ile et Vilaine, whose courage and eloquence from this moment until the fall of the Gironde provide a striking contrast to the cowardice and treachery of both Girondins and Montagnards. "You cannot," Lanjuinais cried boldly, "remain judges, appliers of the law, accusers, juries for the accusation, juries for the judgement, having all expressed your opinions, having done so, some of you, with a scandalous ferocity!" [2]

The voice of Lanjuinais was drowned in howls of indignation. At last, after scenes of indescribable confusion, the Convention decided that the judgement of the King should be discussed. It seems that the Girondins now really wished to save the King, if only to arrest the increasing despotism of the Mountain; but, too cowardly to protest against his condemnation, they bethought themselves of a way out of the dilemma by proposing an appeal to the people through the primary assemblies. The Montagnards, who knew as well as the Girondins that the verdict of the people would be in favour of the King, naturally offered a furious resistance to the plan. The question was first put to the Convention by the Girondin Salles on the 27th of December in an admirable speech. "Either," he said, "the nation wishes that Louis should die or it does not; if it wishes it, you all who wish it also, your expectations will not be disappointed; but if it does not wish it, what right have you to send him to execution contrary to the wish of the nation?"

This was, of course, absolutely unanswerable from the point of view of true democracy, but presented no difficulty to the deputies of the Mountain. Every tortuous argument the heart of sophist could devise was brought forward during the seven days that the discussion lasted, to prove that an appeal to the nation would be in reality *un*democratic—a betrayal of the people's trust. "Virtue," Robespierre remarked sententiously, "was always in a minority on earth." He seemed to have forgotten he had once said that the people were infallible; on this occasion he evidently feared they might prove "subject to

[1] Prudhomme, *Crimes de la Révolution*, v. 120.
[2] Buchez et Roux, xxii. 63; *Moniteur*, xiv. 849.

error." St. Just, paying an unconscious tribute to the liberty
accorded to public opinion by the Old Régime, asked : " The
appeal to the people . . . would that not be bringing back the
monarchy ? " Nothing could be truer. Under the monarchy
the poorest of the King's subjects had enjoyed the right of
bringing him petitions ; from St. Louis seated beneath his oak
to Louis XVI. receiving the *poissardes* at Versailles, access had
always been granted to " the people." But when deputations
of poor women gathered around the doors of the Convention to
plead for the life of Louis XVI. they were turned away, after
waiting long hours, without a hearing,[1] whilst deputies who
persisted in demanding an appeal to the people were shouted
down with angry cries of " Death to the traitor ! "[2] In the
streets hawkers shouted, " Here is the list of the Royalists and
aristocrats who voted for the appeal to the people ! "[3]

For, as usual at a moment of crisis, the revolutionary leaders
had recourse to their great expedient—*terror.*

When the King—against whom nothing had been proved—
was finally pronounced " guilty," and the appeal to the people
was defeated by a majority of 424 to 283 votes, the Mountain
put all the machinery of revolution in motion to secure a final
verdict of death. Amongst the men employed for this purpose
the agents of the Duc d'Orléans were the most active. " The
Orléanistes," says Montjoie, " clearly understood that the people
were not for them ; they kept the blade unceasingly raised over
the heads of the voters ; they surrounded them with assassins."
The deputies of the Gironde, says Madame Roland, were obliged
to go about " armed to the teeth " in self-defence ;[4] brigands
brandishing sticks and sabres pursued them as they left the
Convention, crying out, " His life or yours ! "[5]

At eight o'clock on the evening of the 16th of January the
debate began that was to decide the great question : " What
penalty shall be inflicted on Louis ? " " It is impossible," says
Mercier, " to describe the agitation of that long and convulsive
sitting."

Lehardy opened the proceedings by asking what majority
would be necessary for the death sentence to be pronounced.
Thereupon Lanjuinais demanded that it should consist in two-
thirds of the votes, in accordance with the penal code framed by
the Constituent Assembly. But Danton, shrewdly foreseeing

---

[1] *Journal d'un Bourgeois*, by Edmond Biré, i. 409.
[2] *Ibid.* p. 407.
[3] Buchez et Roux, xxiii. 154.
[4] Madelin, p. 284.
[5] Lacretelle, *Histoire de la Convention* ; see also *Mémoires de Carnot*,
i. 293 : " Louis XVI. would have been saved if the Convention had not
debated beneath daggers."

that this majority would not be forthcoming, proposed that the Convention should pass a decree ordaining that a majority of *one* voice should be sufficient—in other words, *the law was to be altered to fit the case.*

At this Lanjuinais rose again in wrath : " You say all the time that we are a jury ; well, it is the penal code I invoke, it is the form of trial by jury for which I ask. . . . You have rejected all the forms that perhaps justice and certainly humanity demand, the right of challenging the jury and voting in silence. We seem to be deliberating in a free Convention, but it is beneath the daggers and the cannons of the factions." And he ended by demanding that three-fourths of the votes should be necessary for condemnation to death.

But the Convention without further discussion decreed that a majority of *one vote* should suffice.

Then the voting began and continued for twenty-four hours without intermission. One by one the deputies arose, and through the tense silence of the hall the fatal word rang out again and again : " Death ! " Some of the more violent—Marat, Frèron, Billaud - Varenne — added vindictively, " within twenty - four hours " ; several even amongst the Girondins now allowed themselves to be terrorized into voting for immediate death, others pleaded tremblingly for respite. It was reserved for Philippe d'Orléans to give the last touch of infamy to this terrible night. When in the semi-darkness of the hall, illumined only by a few feebly-burning candles, the bloated face of Égalité appeared in the tribune, the Assembly waited breathlessly for the words that were to fall from his lips : " Solely occupied by my duty, convinced that all those who have violated the sovereignty of the people deserve death, *I vote for death.*"

At this cowardly betrayal of his kinsman even the Convention shuddered ; a low murmur of indignation ran through the hall ; men rose from their seats with gestures of disgust, crying out incontrollably, " Oh ! horror ! Oh ! the monster ! " [1]

The miserable prince had shown his hand at last, had given the lie once and for all to his apologists, who declared him to be the weak and amiable puppet of a faction ; even in the eyes of the regicides he now became a thing of loathing, a pariah to be repudiated by each faction in turn.

The vote of the Duc d'Orléans was of paramount importance in the final decision, for, according to the official report, when the votes came to be counted up there were found to be 360 for imprisonment, banishment, for death with respite or conditional death, and exactly 361 for immediate and unconditional death ;

[1] Buchez et Roux, xxiii. 180 ; Montjoie, *Conjuration de d'Orléans,* iii. 237 ; Moore, ii. 577, 580 ; *Deux Amis,* xii. 16.

if this were so, then Philippe's had been the casting vote, and by throwing it into the scale of instant death he murdered the King as surely as if he had stabbed him to the heart with his own hand. But so much jugglery went on behind the scenes, and the votes of many deputies were so vaguely worded, that it is impossible to discover the exact figures.[1] According to a prevailing opinion at the time, there was a real majority of five votes for immediate and unconditional death. "They murdered him," Arthur Young wrote indignantly, "by a majority of five voices, though their law required three-fourths at least for declaring guilt or for pronouncing death—and the majority obtained by the menaces of the assassins paid by Égalité. The consummation of political infamy!"

The Convention itself recoiled in shame before the crime it was about to perpetrate. "The silence of terror," says Beaulieu, "reigned during the deliverance of this disastrous judgement, and even long after the President had ceased speaking. It seemed as if the revolutionaries were already plumbing the abyss they had created without being able to discover its depth."

The same evening the news was brought to the King's counsels that a majority of five votes had been obtained in favour of death. Thereupon Louis XVI. instantly demanded that an appeal should be made to the people, and Désèze, Tronchet, and Malesherbes

---

[1] The figures published by the official *Procès-Verbal* (see Buchez et Roux, xxiii. 206, and Mortimer Ternaux, v. 462, *not* the *Moniteur* which is incorrect) are as follows :

Total number of deputies, 749. Absent, 28 ; refused to vote, 5. Total number of voters, therefore, = 721.

For imprisonment or banishment 286	
For irons 2	
For death, with sentence postponed 46	
For death, but also, on the proposal of Mailhe, for discussion on postponement . 26	For immediate death, without discussion on postponement . 361
360	

The conclusion of the President that the majority was of 387 to 334 was arrived at by adding the 26 votes for death with discussion on postponement to those for immediate death. This is obviously incorrect, and M. Mortimer Ternaux and Mr. Croker (*Essays on the French Revolution*, p. 362) are, therefore, right in stating that there was a majority of one. Both Ferrières and Dr. Moore, however, say that there were 319 votes for imprisonment or banishment. Fockedey, a member of the Convention, says 334. (See *Documents pour servir à l'Histoire de la Révolution Française*, published by Charles d'Héricault, ii. 143.) These figures would reduce the votes for death still further, and result in a majority against death. Indeed the secretary Manuel afterwards declared this was the case (*Mémoires Secrets de D'Allonville*, iii. 139).

came to lay the request before the Convention. Malesherbes, overwhelmed with grief, was unable to utter more than a few broken sentences, but his colleagues forcibly portrayed the iniquity of pronouncing the death sentence contrary to the penal code by means of a decree passed at this same sitting. Robespierre replied that the King's defenders had no right to attack " great measures taken for public safety," and demanded that their appeal should be rejected. This proposal was adopted by the Convention.

The Girondins, now more than ever alarmed at the tyranny of the Mountain, ventured to remonstrate ; Guadet asked that the objections of the King's defenders should be considered. Buzot two days later protested against condemnation on so diminutive a majority, and even went so far as to declare that the party which desired the immediate death of the King wished to place the Duc d'Orléans on the throne. Thomas Paine represented the " universal affliction " the execution of Louis XVI. would create in America, where he was regarded by the people as " their best friend, the one who had procured them their liberty."

In the end the Girondins succeeded in carrying the motion that the question of postponing the sentence should be put to the vote. But by this time the whole Assembly was so cowed by the menaces of Orléans and the Mountain that the sentence of immediate death was carried by a majority of 380 to 310. The President then pronounced sentence of death to be executed within twenty-four hours.

Malesherbes has related that when he went to the Temple to break the news to Louis XVI. he found him seated in the semi-darkness, his back turned to the lamp, his elbows resting on a little table, and his face buried in his hands. As the old man entered the King rose and, looking him in the eyes, said solemnly : " Monsieur de Malesherbes, for two hours I have been trying to discover whether in the course of my reign I have deserved the least reproach from my subjects. Well, I swear to you in all truth as a man about to appear before God that I have always wished for the happiness of my people, that I have never formed a wish opposed to them."

" Ah, Sire," answered Malesherbes with tears, " I still have hope ; the people know the purity of your intentions, they love you and they feel for you. I found myself, on going out from the debate, surrounded by a number of people who assured me that you would not perish, or at least not until they and their friends had perished themselves. . . ."

" Do you know these people ? " Louis XVI. interposed hastily ; " go back to the Assembly, try to find some of them, tell them that I should never forgive them if a drop of blood were shed for me; I refused to shed it when it might have saved me my throne and my life . . . and I do not repent, no, Monsieur, I do not repent."

The cause of this unrepentance is not far to seek. Louis XVI. realized that his trust in the people had not been misplaced, for it was not by the people he had been condemned—an appeal to the people must inevitably have saved him. He knew, no doubt, the intrigues that had brought about the fatal sentence.

To numberless contemporaries it was evident that the influence of the Duc d'Orléans had contributed even more than that of Robespierre towards this end. According to rumours current at the time a certain Marquis de Lepeletier St. Fargeau had intended to vote against the King's death, and to induce twenty-five of his fellow deputies to do the same, but at the last moment he and his companions were persuaded by Orléans to throw their weight into the opposite scale.[1] Whether this was so or not, it provides the only explanation to a mysterious incident that occurred the evening before the King's execution. Lepeletier was dining in a restaurant of the Palais Royal when a man with black hair, dressed in a long grey overcoat, entered. This man was Paris, a member of the King's old bodyguard; all day he had wandered about the city, sabre in hand, seeking the Duc d'Orléans in vain.[2] Now he had found Lepeletier, and, going up to him, he accosted him thus : " You voted for the death of the King ? " " Yes, Monsieur, I voted according to my conscience. What matters it to you ? " But Paris, drawing out his sabre from beneath his cloak, cried, " Wretch, then you shall vote no more ! " and he plunged his weapon into the body of Lepeletier.

So little did the citizens who filled the dining-room resent the crime that not a murmur arose, and Paris was allowed to leave the restaurant unmolested.[3]

Such manifestations of public feeling were naturally disquieting to the regicides, and now more than ever they dreaded that a popular movement might be made in favour of the King. On the following day a formidable guard was again summoned to surround him on his way to the Place de la Révolution. "According to two Marseillais very hostile to the King," says M. Madelin, " Paris had been literally placed in a state of siege." Meanwhile Philippe Égalité, foreseeing that Louis XVI. might succeed in bringing the crowd to his rescue by words spoken from the scaffold, took elaborate precautions against such an

---

[1] Montjoie, *Conjuration de d'Orléans*, iii. 232 ; Pagès, ii. 69.

[2] Mercier, *Le Nouveau Paris*, i. 175 ; Dauban, *La Demagogie en 1793*, p. 27.

[3] *Journal d'un Bourgeois*, by Edmond Biré, ii. 5.

eventuality. "D'Orléans," says Sénart, " fears that he may speak to the people ; he fears that the people may deliver him, for the head of Capet was necessary to him at any price. There were various rendezvous for the Orléans faction. It was at one of these rendezvous that Santerre swore to D'Orléans, glass in hand, that he would make use of a sure method to prevent Capet from speaking, and thus was formed the plot of the famous roll of drums which occurred at the death of Capet." [1]

When the wet and dreary morning of January 21 dawned, the city was wrapped in the silence of consternation. " All the shops were shut ; silent patrols, composed of ill-clad men, moved slowly about the streets, where one met only pale, sad, and gloomy faces ; executioners and victims alike seemed aghast at the cruel sacrifice that was to be consummated ; stupor alone seemed to inhabit Paris. Such was the situation of that famous city, once so brilliant and the rendezvous for all pleasures." [2]

Mercier, who invariably endeavours to throw on the people the blame for all the crimes of the Revolution, has represented Paris as presenting a normal, even a gay appearance on this dreadful day—a testimony eagerly seized on by revolutionary historians, but which is contradicted by innumerable contemporaries, even by Prudhomme. Fockedey, a member of the Convention, has thus confirmed the evidence of Beaulieu :

" This day was for France, and above all for Paris, a day of bitterness and grief, of fear and mourning : the capital was in anguish. Almost all the shops and houses were closed, whole families were in tears. Consternation was seen on all the faces one met ; a great number of the National Guards, on foot since the morning, appeared themselves to be going to execution. No, never will the scenes I witnessed on that day be effaced from my memory. How many were the tears I saw flow ! What imprecations I heard against the authors of such a crime. . . . The Assembly that day was silent and gloomy, the voters for regicide were pale and shattered, they seemed to have a horror of themselves." [3]

As to the poor people of Paris, they could hardly bring

[1] Certain contemporaries declared that it was not Santerre who finally ordered the roll of drums (see Montjoie, *Conjuration de d'Orléans*, iii. 240), but the Comte d'Aya, a natural son of Louis XV. Beaulieu, however (*Essais*, iv. 353), and most reliable authorities state that it was Santerre; moreover, Santerre admitted it himself. See " Relation du Municipal Goret," in *La Captivité et la Mort de Marie Antoinette*, by G. Lenôtre, p. 146.

[2] Beaulieu, iv. 349.

[3] " Souvenirs du Conventionnel Fockedey," published in *Documents pour servir à l'Histoire de la Révolution Française*, by Charles d'Héricault, vol. ii. p. 142. On this point see also the contemporary evidence quoted by Edmond Biré, *Journal d'un Bourgeois*, i. 451.

themselves to believe that so dreadful a deed could really be accomplished. " On the 21st of January," writes the Comtesse de Bohm, " I saw upon the ramparts people of the lowest classes weeping, showing openly their grief at the outrage that was to take place. ' There are too many of them in Paris,' they said, ' they will prevent it.' The sun pierced through the clouds, shining on this crime. That national sense of shame that will be transmitted from age to age, of which the remorse will become for every Frenchman a personal offence, weighed heavily upon me."

But the Parisians made no effort to prevent the crime. The little band of Royalists, under the Baron de Batz, that dashed towards the King's carriage, crying, " Join with us, you who would save the King ! " met with neither resentment nor response; the immense multitude stood by stupefied and mute, hypnotized, it would seem, by the horror of the whole proceeding, for not a cry broke from them as the dark green coach passed between their ranks towards the great Place de la Révolution. Through the windows the outline of the King's face could be dimly seen beneath the shadow of his large hat, bent downwards to his breviary open at the prayers for the dying. He was, perhaps, the most tranquil man in Paris on that grey January morning. " God is my comforter," he had said to his confessor, the Abbé Edgeworth; " my enemies cannot take His peace from me."

Every effort was made by the revolutionary journalists to minimize the King's courage at the supreme moment. " Louis," Le Thermomètre du Jour declared, " had shown courage and assurance only because he did not believe the sentence would really be carried out, that to the very moment of his death he had reckoned on being saved." When he realized, however, his delusion, his serenity deserted him, and he " struggled with the executioner's assistants, by whom at last he was forcibly tied to the plank of the guillotine." It was Sanson, the executioner himself who refuted this lie, by coming forward boldly to testify not only to the King's courage but to the cause that inspired it.

" Citizen," he wrote to the editor of the Thermomètre, " a short absence has prevented me from replying sooner to your article concerning Louis Capet, but here . . . is the exact truth concerning what passed. On alighting from the carriage for the execution he was told that he must take off his coat ; he made some difficulty, saying that he could be executed as he was. On being assured that this was impossible he himself helped to take off his coat. He then made the same difficulty when it came to tying his hands, but he offered them himself when the person who was with him (the Abbé Edgeworth) had said to him that it was a last sacrifice. He inquired whether the drums would go on beating; we answered that we did not know, which was the truth. He ascended the scaffold, and tried to advance to the front as if he wished to speak, but it was represented to him that the thing was again impossible; then he allowed himself to be led to the place where he was tied, and where he cried out loudly, ' People, I die innocent ! ' Then turning towards us he said to us, ' I am innocent of all that is imputed to me. I desire that my blood may seal the happiness of the French people.' Those, citizen, were his last and exact words. The kind of little debate which occurred at the foot of the scaffold turned on his not thinking it necessary that his coat should be taken off and his hands tied. He also made the proposal to cut off his own hair.

" And in order to render homage to truth, he bore all this with a sang-froid and firmness which astonished us all, and I remain convinced that *he had derived this firmness from the principles of religion,* of which no one could seem more persuaded and imbued than he. You can be sure, citizen, that here is the truth in its fullest light.—I have the honour to be your fellow-citizen,

" Sanson."

Not content with maligning the King, the revolutionaries as usual maligned the people. " After the execution," says Mercier again, " they laughed and chattered, they walked home arm-in-arm as if returning from a feast, the theatres remained open as usual throughout the evening." True, hideous scenes of mirth took place on the Place de la Révolution ; joy shone out exultingly from the face of Orléans, watching the execution from his cabriolet ; around the scaffold brigands danced together, shouting " Vive la République ! " A citizen ascending the guillotine plunged his arm into the blood of the King and dashed it in the faces of the crowd. Then once again, like a tiger that has tasted blood, the mob went mad and broke out likewise into dancing ; wild, blood-bespattered figures whirled round in each other's arms ; all over the great Place de la Révolution the hoarse roar arose, " Vive la République ! Vive la Liberté ! Vive l'Égalité ! " [1]

But after this one moment of " crowd hysteria " it seems that even the mob came to its senses, and Paris once more relapsed into stupor. The people did not go home rejoicing ; on the contrary, says Lacretelle, they " returned gloomy and absorbed ; the multitude itself, whether from pity or from resentment at its curiosity being disappointed, loaded Santerre with imprecations for having drowned the last words of the King. All through the day that followed "—for the execution took place at half-past ten in the morning—" Paris was silent, almost

[1] *Diurnal de Beaulieu* ; Prudhomme, *Révolutions de Paris,* xiv. 205.

deserted ; people shut themselves up with their families to weep."
The women, Prudhomme reluctantly admits, were sad, " which
contributed not a little to that gloomy air which Paris presented
throughout this day." As to the theatres, it is true that they
were open that evening, but also they were empty, and the
managers found themselves obliged to return the money paid
for seats.[1] In the streets, say the Two Friends of Liberty,
" people dared not look each other in the face . . . the day
after the execution they had not recovered from this overwhelming
dejection."

Had France indeed, like Louis XVI. himself, some premonition
of the immense misfortunes this day was to bring her ? " I see
the people," he had said to Cléry on the night of his condemnation,
" given over to anarchy, becoming the victim of all the factions ;
I see crimes following one upon another and long dissensions
rending France."

For the people he grieved, knowing well in what hands he
was leaving them. Here, in the white light of eternity, we see
him at his best, his blunders atoned for by his great sincerity.
To the cause of despots he had proved a traitor, to " aristocracy "
he had shown scant sympathy, but to the people he had been
true. In him they lost not their best but their only friend.
Carlyle has written of " the great heart of Danton "—Danton,
whose last words, like those of nearly every one of the demagogues,
were to revile the people—for the great heart of Louis XVI. he
has nothing but contempt. Yet, of all the men who played their
part in the Revolution, there was only one who, realizing that
no hope for his life remained, could say from the depths of his
heart, as he stood on the threshold of the other world—the
platform of the guillotine—" I desire that my blood may seal the
happiness of the French." That one true patriot, that one man
ready to die for France and for the people, was the King.

ENGLAND AND THE DEATH OF THE KING

In England the news of the King's death was received by all
classes with horror. " I cannot describe to you," Lord Grenville
wrote to Lord Auckland on the 24th of January, " the universal
indignation it has excited here . . . the audience at one of the
play-houses stopping the play, and ordering the curtain to be
dropped as soon as the news was announced to them."

The Prince of Wales, hearing of the vote for death given by
his former boon-companion Philippe d'Orléans, pulled down the
portrait of the duke—a masterpiece by Sir Joshua Reynolds—

---

[1] Gorsas in the *Courier des Departements* for January 28, 1793. See
Journal d'un Bourgeois, by Edmond Biré, i. 453.

from the wall in Carlton House, and tore it into shreds with his own hands.[1]

But the lovers of true liberty mourned the most profoundly. It was because *the murder of Louis XVI. was the greatest crime ever committed against democracy* that Arthur Young, that ardent democrat, denounced it in unmeasured terms :

" This great abomination . . . ought to generate (for the real felicity of the human race) a tighter rein in the jaws of that monster . . . the metaphysical, philosophical, atheistical Jacobin Republican, abhorred for ever for holding out to all the sovereigns of the earth that the only prince who ever voluntarily placed bounds to his own power DIED FOR IT ON THE SCAFFOLD, and ruined his people while he destroyed himself. He gave ear to those who told him of abuses ; he wished to ease his people ; he fought popularity . . . he would not shed the blood of traitors, conspirators, and rebels. . . . This damned event, deep written in the characters of hell, has thrown a stupor over mankind." [2]

In Parliament Pitt spoke of " the murder of the King " as " that dreadful outrage against every principle of religion, of justice, and of humanity, which has created one general sentiment of indignation and abhorrence in every part of this island, and most undoubtedly has produced the same effect in every civilized country . . . it is the foulest and most atrocious deed which the history of the world has yet had occasion to attest."

And here, for the honour of our country, it is impossible to pass over in silence the accusation brought against Pitt in this connection by an English historian. " Information," wrote the late Lord Acton, " was brought to Pitt from a source that could be trusted, that Danton would save him (the King) for £40,000. When he made up his mind to give the money, Danton replied that it was too late. Pitt explained to the French diplomatist, Maret, afterwards Prime Minister, his motive for hesitation. The execution of the King of France would raise such a storm in England that the Whigs would be submerged." [3]

In other words, Pitt was willing for the sake of party interests to act as murderer to Louis XVI. And on what does Lord Acton found this monstrous charge ? On the assertion of Maret—a revolutionary emissary to England ! Now, even if Pitt had entertained so dastardly a plan, is it conceivable that he would have confided it to such a man as Maret ? The only

---

[1] *Moniteur* for February 6, 1793.

[2] *The Example of France*, Appendix, p. 10.

[3] *Essays on the French Revolution*, p. 254. Note here the value of Lord Acton's judgement as a historian, for, after admitting that Danton was actuated solely by mercenary motives in the matter of the King's death, he afterwards observes : " There was not in France a more thorough patriot than Danton," *ibid*. p. 282.

grain of truth in the whole story seems to be that Pitt did refuse to bribe Danton, but as he was very well aware of Danton's true character—was not Bertrand de Molleville in London at the time and able to enlighten him on the financial transactions he had conducted on behalf of the King with that " thorough patriot " ?—it is hardly surprising that Pitt should have hesitated to put £40,000 into the pocket of a man who would in all probability make. no return. The Revolutionary Tribunal was probably much nearer the mark when it declared that Pitt had assisted Malesherbes financially in defending the King [1]—a course the great statesman may well have held to be more reputable and at the same time more expedient than bribing Danton.

If any members of the British Parliament are to be accused of complicity in the murder of Louis XVI., it is certainly the Whigs ; Pitt, whom the revolutionaries regarded as their arch-enemy, would only have increased their animosity towards the King by interceding for him, but Fox, Sheridan, Lord Lansdowne, Lord Lauderdale, and Lord Stanhope were all on the best of terms with the members of the Convention, and might surely have exerted their influence to avert the crime. With the exception of Lord Stanhope—who, we know, definitely refused to intercede for Louis XVI., giving as his reason that " new discoveries of his treachery, perfidy, and duplicity " had just been made [2]—we may do these men the justice to believe that if they refrained from intervention it was because, like Pitt, they knew it would be hopeless.

A rupture between France and England had now become inevitable, for it was evident that the Anarchists of Paris, not content with devastating their own country, proposed to carry out the same process in every other country which they could succeed in entering. On the 19th of November they had issued the following proclamation :

" The National Convention declares in the name of the French nation that she will accord fraternity and assistance to all peoples who wish to recover their liberty, and charges the Executive Power to give the necessary orders to the generals in order to render assistance to these peoples, and to defend the citizens who have been vexed or who might be so for the cause of liberty." [3]

This decree, which the Convention ordered to be translated into " all languages," was therefore not an appeal merely to the

---

[1] Trial of Malesherbes, in *Bulletin de Tribunal révolutionnaire*.
[2] *The Life of Charles, third Earl of Stanhope*, by Ghita Stanhope and G. P. Gooch, p. 119.
[3] *Moniteur*, xiv. 517.

peoples of the countries with which France was then at war, but a call to universal insurrection. A few weeks later the revolutionary leaders explained their intentions towards the countries they had already entered in a further proclamation. On the 15th of December, Cambon, " in the name of the financial, military, and diplomatic committees," rose to define the line of conduct the generals of the revolutionary armies were to pursue :

" It is necessary that we should declare ourselves a revolutionary power in the countries that we enter. . . . Your committees consider that, after expelling the tyrants and their satellites, the generals on entering every ' Commune ' must publish a proclamation, showing the people that we bring them happiness, that they must immediately suppress tithes and feudal rights, and all forms of servitude.

" But you will have accomplished nothing if you confine yourselves only to these destructions. Aristocracy governs everywhere ; therefore *all existing authorities must be destroyed.* Nothing of the Old Régime must survive when revolutionary power shows itself." [1]

This, however, was not to be effected by the will of the people in the invaded countries, who indeed displayed no great enthusiasm for the benefits of French liberty. As in France, deputations and declarations, purporting to express the wishes of the people, were engineered by Jacobin agents,[2] and in no way represented public opinion. So, although it was announced that Belgium desired to embrace revolutionary doctrines and to be united to the French Republic, " the immense majority of the Belgian population remained attached to its old beliefs," and regarded the anarchic schemes of the invaders with horror.[3] In Germany the apostles of " democracy " met with a like resistance. Mayence boldly protested ; at Frankfort the citizens refused to plant a tree of liberty at the command of Custine.[4]

---

[1] *Moniteur,* xiv. 762.

[2] Immediately on Dumouriez's arrival in the towns of Belgium Jacobin Clubs were inaugurated under his auspices (Mortimer Ternaux, *Histoire de la Terreur,* v. 14, 61). It seems that large sums of money were also lavished on the inhabitants, for later on, when Danton was asked to account for the sum of 100,000 écus he had spent on his mission to Belgium—and which the Girondins suspected him of appropriating—Danton replied that the money had been spent in " executing the decree of December 15 "— that is to say, in bribing the Belgians to vote for union with the French Republic (Séance of April 1, 1793 ; Mortimer Ternaux, *op. cit.* v. 20).

[3] *Ibid.* p. 61. See also letter of Lord Auckland written from the Hague to Lord Loughborough on January 6, 1793 : " The spirit of Jacobinism makes no progress. In Italy and Germany it is the abhorrence even of the lowest ranks. In Brabant and Flanders the French are now infinitely more hated than the Austrians " (*Correspondence of Lord Auckland,* ii. 485).

[4] Mortimer Ternaux, v. 19.

But the revolutionary leaders were not to be baffled by these obstacles ; if the people did not accept " liberty, equality, and fraternity " when offered them with honeyed words, these inestimable blessings must be forced on them at the point of the sword.

It was in consequence of this recalcitrance that Cambon in the same speech went on to say : " But you will have accomplished nothing if you do not loudly declare the severity of your principles against whosoever desires only a half-liberty. You wish that the people against whom you carry arms should be free. If they reconcile themselves with the privileged castes you must not suffer this traffic with tyrants. You must therefore say to the people who wish to preserve the privileged castes, ' *You are our enemies,*' and then treat them as such, since they desire neither liberty nor equality."

At the end of this speech, delivered amidst unanimous applause, the Convention issued a further decree to each country entered by their armies, declaring that " from this moment the French Republic proclaims the suppression of all your magistrates, civil and military, of all the authorities that have governed you, and proclaims in this country the abolition of all the taxes you endure, under whatsoever form they exist," etc. In a word, every country entered by the French was to be thrown into chaos.[1]

Beside this proclamation it must be admitted that the Manifesto of Brunswick appears almost benign. The Emperor of Austria and the King of Prussia had definitely declared therein that they had " no intention of meddling with the domestic government of France " ; the revolutionaries announced their determination to destroy the existing form of government whether the people desired it or not. The Manifesto of Brunswick, moreover, had repudiated all ideas of annexation ; the revolutionaries made no attempt to conceal the fact that the conversion of the invaded countries to " democratic " doctrines was to be but the prelude to incorporation with the French Republic.

The moment the retreat of the foreign armies began, after Valmy, the pretext of carrying on war for the defence of France was abandoned, and the Republic embarked on its career of aggrandizement. Belgium, the Rhine provinces, Savoy, and Nice were all successively annexed without any pretext being offered for these acts of brigandage. Writers who enthuse over the glorious successes of French arms from the battle of Jemmapes onwards would do well to ask themselves by what right the French Republic pursued the invading armies beyond the

[1] *Moniteur*, xiv. 762.

frontier for the purpose of annexing territory? It will be answered Louis XIV. had done the same. True, but was not the spirit of the Revolution until 1792 diametrically opposed to the policy of Louis XIV.? Had not the French democracy itself declared that war was never justified except in self-defence? Only two and a half years earlier—in May 1790—at the Constituent Assembly, a league of perpetual peace had been decreed amidst immense enthusiasm. " Let all nations be free like ourselves," a deputy had cried, " and there will be no more wars!" And on the proposal of Robespierre the Assembly formally declared: " The French nation renounces the idea of undertaking any war with a view of conquest, and will never employ its forces against the liberty of any people." Yet it was the very men who framed it, Robespierre and his allies, who now repudiated this resolution and advocated pure aggression, and thus *the League of Peace proved but the prelude to the greatest war of conquest the civilized world had ever seen.* Had not Mirabeau foretold this when, in response to the enthusiasts of 1790, he had declared " free people to be more eager for war, and democracies more the slaves of their passions than the most absolute autocracies "? [1]

It was not, then, as is frequently and falsely stated, that Pitt " sought a pretext " for joining " the coalition of Kings " against the French Republic ; it was the wanton aggression of the Republic culminating in the seizure of the mouth of the Scheldt and of Antwerp—that in the hands of a dangerous enemy must inevitably prove, as Napoleon perceived, " a pistol held at the head of England "; it was the example of inhumanity and injustice offered to Europe by the murder of Louis XVI. ; above all it was *the declaration of world anarchy* published by the Convention, threatening not only England but the whole of civilization, that led Pitt to conclude his speech on the death of Louis XVI. by proposing preparations for war : " There can be no consideration more deserving the attention of this House than to crush and destroy principles which are so dangerous and destructive of every blessing this country enjoys under its free and excellent constitution. We owe our present happiness and prosperity, which has never been equalled in the annals of mankind, to a mixture of monarchical government. We feel and know we are happy under that form of government. We consider it as our first duty to maintain and reverence the British Constitution." He went on to present the contrast between England and " that country (France) exposed to all the tremendous consequences of that ungovernable, that intolerable and destroying spirit, which carries ruin and desolation wherever it

---

[1] Albert Sorel, *L'Europe et la Révolution Française*, ii. 86-89.

goes ! Sirs, this infection can have no existence in this happy land, unless it is imported, unless it is studiously and industriously brought into this country."

Pitt well knew the efforts that were being made to spread this infection, the insidious influences that emanated from Parliament itself. England has always had her " Illuminati," who, holding loyalty and patriotism to be " narrow-minded prejudices incompatible with universal benevolence," have ever been ready to plead the cause of their country's enemies —whether these enemies masqueraded under the name of democracy as in 1793, or rallied round the standard of autocracy as in 1800. Now at this most critical moment this band of anti-patriots came forward in defence of the French Jacobins ; Fox, Sheridan, Lord Lansdowne, Lord Lauderdale, Lord Stanhope poured forth floods of oratory to prove that public opinion on the revolutionary leaders had been influenced by " the absurdities of madmen, the monstrous propositions of the heated imaginations of individuals " ; [1] to show by tortuous sophistries that black was really white ; that if, indeed, crimes had been committed, the best way to express disapproval would be by shaking hands with the criminals. They themselves, honoured by the friendship of such men as Brissot—whom to their indignation Burke at this same sitting described as " the most virtuous of all pickpockets " —could answer for the pacific disposition of the French revolutionaries, their ardent desire to retain the good opinion of England. Yet less than three weeks earlier Brissot himself had referred at the Convention to " the comedy played in the House of Commons by the party of the Opposition " ! [2] and it was likewise Brissot who, in the following May, justified Pitt for refusing to form an alliance with the French Republic.[3]

[1] Speech of Lord Lauderdale (*Parl. Hist.* xxx. 326). These words of Lord Lauderdale were a deliberate misrepresentation of the truth, for Lord Lauderdale was himself in Paris with Dr. Moore during the September massacres, and Dr. Moore's evidence on the atrocities of which they were witnesses has been already quoted in this book. See also speech of Lord Lansdowne (*Parl. Hist.* xxx. 329), and Lord Stanhope's " Protest against a War with France " (*ibid.* p. 336).

[2] " Rapport fait par Brissot sur les Dispositions du Gouvernement britannique," Bouchez et Roux, xxiii. 81. See also speech of Kersaint on January 1, 1793, referring to the intrigues of Fox in " trying to profit by circumstances in order to seize the government," etc. (Buchez et Roux, xxiii. 366).

[3] " What has occasioned this last war ? There are three causes for it : 1st, The absurd and impolitic decree of the 19th of November, *which very justly excited uneasiness in foreign cabinets.* . . . 2nd, The massacres of September. . . . 3rd, The death of Louis. . . . It is madness or imbecility itself to reckon upon a peace, or upon allies, while we are without a constitution. *There is no making an alliance, there is no treating with anarchy* " (*J. P. Brissot à ses Commettants*).

But any illusions concerning the conciliatory sentiments of the French revolutionary leaders were abruptly dispelled by a declaration of war on England issued by the Convention two days after this debate took place. As long as possible Pitt had striven to bring the Jacobins of France to reason ; even at the last moment he had made a further attempt at conciliation by agreeing to a conference between Lord Auckland, the British ambassador at the Hague, and Dumouriez, commander-in-chief of the French armies in the Netherlands,[1] but on the very day arranged for the conference to take place the Convention precipitated matters by declaring war and thus incurred the full responsibility for the twenty-two years' conflict that followed. Yet even now the English admirers of the Jacobins were for conciliation ; even when the overture of Pitt had been thus insolently rejected they pleaded that England should humiliate herself and sue for peace — a peace, Pitt declared, that would be " precarious and disgraceful. . . . What sort of a peace must that be in which there is no security ? Peace is desirable only in so far as it is secure." War with the French Republic was finally voted by 270 votes to 44.

These, then, were the causes that led up to the inevitable rupture between France and England. To accuse Pitt of wishing to " destroy French liberty " is, therefore, a monstrous calumny ; for in France liberty had completely ceased to exist. Already the blade was suspended over the heads of the Whigs' supposed allies, the Girondins, and the country was rapidly passing under the most frightful tyranny the civilized world has ever seen—the reign of Robespierre. It was against this atrocious system, it was against anarchy and bloodshed, against cruelty and oppression, that England took up arms. So, by the master hand of Pitt, the ship of State was steered to safety, and England, true to her traditions, entered the lists in the cause of liberty and justice.

THE FALL OF THE GIRONDE

The Girondins had little realized that in voting for the death of the King they had signed their own death-warrant ; that by lending themselves to this monstrous injustice they had helped to frame the system that was to bring about their downfall. If they had only had the courage of their convictions, and persisted in their resolution that an appeal should be made to the people, they would have had public opinion almost unanimously on their side, and could have defied the threats of the Mountain. Their contemptible weakness not only lowered

---

[1] Speeches of Pitt and Lord Grenville (*Parl. Hist.* xxx. 351, 399).

them in the eyes of the multitude, but increased the audacity of their adversaries.

Ever since the beginning of the Convention angry murmurs against the Gironde had emanated continually from the Mountain, and as the months went by grew in volume ; the hall of the Assembly, always tumultuous, became at moments a pandemonium. Of this historians give no idea, but it must be realized in order to follow the true course of the revolutionary movement. For if we picture the Convention as it is habitually represented to us under the guise of a serious Senate sitting in debate on great political questions, and led by statesmen of commanding personalities inspired with pure zeal for the country's welfare, it is perfectly impossible to understand the nature of the conflict that now arose, and that culminated in the successive slaughter of each faction. We must turn, therefore, to the accounts of contemporaries in order to visualize the fearful scenes of confusion that took place in the Assembly, and the part played by the so-called " giants of the Convention." Even the toned-down official reports of the debates afford us glimpses of the strangest incidents—members making simultaneous rushes at the Tribune, frantically disputing who should have the right to speak—" 60 to 80 deputies advancing in a body on the President's desk,"—the President ringing his bell to obtain silence, breaking his bell in desperation, breaking three bells in succession,[1] putting on his hat to close the sitting—deputies drawing swords or brandishing pistols, threatening to blow out their brains, to stab themselves to the heart—roars from Danton, Legendre, David, of " Vile intriguer ! Monster ! Murderer ! Imbecile ! Pig ! "—Robespierre shrieking above the tumult, " Kill me or let me be heard ! "—Marat rushing about the hall like a maniac, crying, " Let the patriots speak ! " turning to the right and shouting, " Be silent, brigand ! " to the left, " Be silent, conspirator ! "—or, again, furious petitioners arriving at the bar of the Assembly, all talking at once, and all at cross purposes—the tribunes filled with brawlers and viragos hired by the opposing factions, shaking sticks and fists at the deputies, spitting on their heads, howling invectives.[2]

What was the reason for these continued dissensions ? If, as the Convention declared, every one wanted a Republic,—if, as they had asserted in the past, the King was the sole obstacle to the regeneration of France, why should the overthrow of monarchy and King have proved the signal for a further out-

---

[1] Moore, ii. 297.

[2] *Moniteur*, xiv. 80 ; Buchez et Roux, xxii. 461-464, xxiv. 296, xxv. 323, xxvii. 144, 145 ; Beaulieu, v. 126 ; *Mémoires de Mme. Roland*, ii. 304 ; Dauban, *La Demagogie en 1793*, p. 66.

break of revolution more violent than any that had preceded it ?
Why, as the Girondin Gensonné sensibly inquired, should the
opposing faction, that is to say, the Mountain, continue " to
declaim against the National Convention and provoke insurrections ? What do they want ? What is their object ? What
strange despotism threatens us ? And *what kind of government
do they propose to give to France?*"[1] English readers, indoctrinated by Carlyle, will answer : " The Girondins were now
reactionaries ; they wished to arrest the tide of progress ; their
schemes of social reform did not go far enough to meet the real
needs of the people." For, according to Carlyle, " all manner of
aristocracies being now abolished," the conflict that arose was
between " the Girondin formula of a respectable Republic for
the Middle Classes " and the " Liberty, Equality, and Fraternity "
of the Mountain, by which the " hunger, nakedness, and nightmare oppression lying heavy on twenty-five million hearts "
would be relieved. In these words Carlyle presents an imaginary
situation.[2] It is probably true that by 1793 the Girondins had
become genuine Republicans—henceforth we find no trace of
Orléaniste, Prussian, or English intrigue amongst them ; it is
also true that they desired an orderly Republic, but this was
to be no more in favour of the " Middle Classes " than of the
great mass of the people. The Mountain, on the other hand
—as represented by Marat, Robespierre and St. Just—no
doubt dreamt of a Socialist State for " the people " only,
but their immediate aim was still anarchy, by which " hunger
and nakedness " must be immensely aggravated. For Robespierre and Marat were surgeons, not physicians ; their only
remedy for all social ills was amputation ; they did not wish
to relieve present distress or to put down injustice by legislation, but only to annihilate all existing conditions, and to
exterminate all classes of the community except " the people "
over whom they hoped to rule supreme.

It was therefore the Gironde, not the Mountain, that now
came to the relief of hunger and nakedness ; it was Roland who
pointed out the real causes of the famine and proposed measures
for preventing it,[3] whilst Robespierre contented himself with

---

[1] Buchez et Roux, xxii. 391.

[2] Note Carlyle's inconsequence here, for whilst pouring sarcasms on
" the respectably-washed middle-classes," represented by the Girondins,
it is for Madame Roland, the soul of the Gironde and the embodiment of
pretentious middle-classness, that he reserves his deepest admiration, whilst
for Marat, the soul of the Mountain, and the apostle of unwashed Fraternity,
he has nothing but loathing and contempt. This instance goes to show
that Carlyle wrote mainly for effect regardless of truth or logic.

[3] See Roland's sensible report (published by Buchez et Roux, xxi. 199),
in which he points out that the price of bread being lower in Paris than in

vague theorizings and ignored offers of supplies.[1] Meanwhile Marat continued to urge the people on to pillage, a method which greatly aggravated the situation by terrifying the shop-keepers and peasants into concealing provisions. It seems, indeed, not improbable that the Mountain pursued the same system in 1793 as the Orléanistes in 1789—that of engineering famine in order to rouse the anger of the people against their political antagonists. Thus a contemporary states that, " at a sitting of the Comité de Neuf on September 2, 1793, it was decided by Jean Bon Saint André, Drouet, Cambon, and Robespierre, that an insurrection must be excited by means of the difficulty of supplies—and that the Municipality should direct accusations of monopoly against the party of the Giron-dins, Monarchists, and Brissotins." [2] It was this accusation of monopoly that in the hands of the Mountain served as a weapon against each rival faction in turn.

Such, then, were the men whom Carlyle represents as the protectors of the hungry and naked. The truth is that the people counted for very little in the great war between the Mountain and the Gironde ; it was not—as Kropotkin, following

---

the surrounding provinces, buyers are attracted to the capital ; he pro-poses, therefore, to raise the price of bread in Paris, and to assist the poor out of the public funds to meet the increased expense. Compare this with Robespierre's speech to the Convention of December 2, 1792 (Buchez et Roux, xxii. 178), in which he can find nothing more practical to say than that " everything which is indispensable for preserving life is common property," an axiom interpreted by the people, under the guidance of Marat, into laying violent hands on all foodstuffs that came their way. Undoubtedly there were still monopolizers as there had always been, and the succeeding revolutionary governments dealt with them less effectually than the Old Régime, but the methods of the Anarchists increased their number. " The dearness of bread," wrote Brissot in 1793, " is produced by the scarcity of the markets and the want of the circulation of grain. . . . What stops this circulation ? The eternal declamations of the anarchists against men of property, or against merchants, whom they mark out by the name of monopolizers ; the eternal petitions of ignorant men who call for a rate upon grain. The labouring man fears he will be plundered or have his throat cut, and he leaves his ricks untouched " (*J. P. Brissot à ses Commettants*).

[1] See the *Mémoires de Brissot*, note on p. 63, which mentions two letters from American corn-merchants written to Robespierre in October and November 1793 offering supplies of grain. *To these Robespierre did not reply*. Courtois in his *Rapport* says the offer was *refused* (*Papiers trouvés chez Robespierre*, etc. i. 21).

[2] *Fortescue Historical MSS.* ii. 457. The Socialist, Gracchus Babeuf, employed in the Supply Department of the Commune, formally accused Robespierre and the Comité de Salut Public of having organized a *Pacte de Famine* in order to starve Paris. For this Babeuf and all the *employés* in the Supply Department were thrown into prison at the Abbaye.

in the footsteps of Carlyle, falsely represents—such questions as feudal dues, the maximum price of bread, or communal lands that formed the subjects for heated debates at the Convention ; we have only to consult the *Moniteur* to find that the discussions that took place on these questions occupy a very small amount of space, and never became the occasion for tumultuous scenes. The great accusations levelled by one faction at the other related in no way to the needs of the people, but mainly to the form of government each wished to establish, the Gironde accusing the Mountain of wishing to establish a dictatorship under one of the Triumvirate—Marat, Danton, or Robespierre— the Mountain declaring that the Gironde aimed at a Federative Republic ; at the same time each hurled at the other the reproach of Orléanisme. Meanwhile the personal animosity existing between the members of the two factions, which found expression in recriminations of the most puerile description, made all hope of conciliation vain.

Whilst the politicians wrangled, the people bore their sufferings with admirable patience. Now for the first time at the bakers' doors were formed those long processions known as " queues " that grew in length as the year advanced, and were to continue for two years without intermission. Paris accepted the situation with its usual *insouciance*. " The French, who have always made merry over everything, even over their misery and their greatest misfortunes," says Beaulieu, " made merry over these gatherings at the bakers' doors, where they seemed rather to be asking for alms than for goods of which they paid the price. . . . I have seen women spend whole nights at these wretched doors for the sake of having an ounce or two of bad bread which dogs would not care for. Well, the Parisians laughed over these sad gatherings ; they called them *queues*. Since one was in want of everything one went in the queue for everything—in the bread queue, the meat queue, the soap queue, the candle queue ; there was nothing for which there was not a queue." [1]

Naturally, under these circumstances, when Marat proposed that the people should take the law into their own hands and pillage the shops, he endeared himself still further to the hearts of the tumultuous elements amongst the populace. " The capitalists, the stockjobbers, the monopolizers, the tradesmen, the ex-nobles," he declared in his *Journal de la République Française*, were to blame for the scarcity of provisions, and nothing but " the total destruction of that cursed breed could restore tranquillity to the State. . . . Meanwhile let the nation, weary of these revolting disorders, take upon itself to purge the

[1] Beaulieu, v. 117 ; Mercier, *Le Nouveau Paris*, ii. 92.

soil of liberty of this criminal race. . . . The pillage of a few shops, at the doors of which they hanged a few of the monopolizers, would soon put an end to these malpractices. . . ."

The call to plunder was received with enthusiasm, and in the morning of the 25th of February a troop of women marched to the Seine and, after boarding the vessels that contained cargoes of soap, helped themselves liberally to all they required at a price fixed by themselves, that is to say, for almost nothing. Since no notice was taken of these proceedings, a far larger crowd collected at dawn of the following day and set forth on a marauding expedition to the shops. From no less than 1200 grocers the people carried off everything on which they could lay their hands—oil, sugar, candles, coffee, brandy—at first without paying, then, overcome with remorse, at the price they themselves thought proper. In this they displayed a greater sense of morality than their leaders, who doubtless hoped that their enemies, the bourgeois, would be plundered without indemnity ; moreover, the crowd refrained from hanging any of the tradesmen at their shop doors as Marat had proposed. From the Anarchists' point of view the rising had, therefore, proved a failure.

Marat, when denounced at the Convention for provoking these disorders, retorted in his usual manner by calling his accusers pigs or imbeciles who should be shut up in asylums ;[1] and he could well afford to defy them, for he had the mob now whole-heartedly at his back.

The short-sighted Girondins, illusioned by the fact that the majority of the Convention was with them, under-estimated the force of this coalition. They could not realize that men who appeared in the eyes of all sane contemporaries so contemptible as Marat, so feebly vindictive as Robespierre, so addicted to empty noise as Danton, could end by carrying everything before them. They overlooked the fact that, as Danton himself afterwards expressed it, " in times of revolution authority remains with the greatest scoundrels "—that is to say, with the most unscrupulous ; and just as in the past it was the Orléanistes who had held in their hands the machinery of revolution, of which the Girondins had made use, it was now the Anarchists who alone knew how to frame that new engine of destruction—the second Revolutionary Tribunal—the Tribunal of the Terror.[2]

[1] Prudhomme, Crimes, v. 37.

[2] This Tribunal was at first known officially as the " Tribunal Extra-ordinaire," and not till later as the " Tribunal Révolutionnaire," but Beaulieu says it was habitually referred to in private conversation under the latter name, particularly by Robespierre and his friends, soon after its inauguration on March 10, 1793 (Essais de Beaulieu, v. 103).

The first Revolutionary Tribunal, created on August 17, 1792, had proved a failure; the populace were not yet ripe for wholesale executions; the spectacle of the guillotine had disgusted the humane portion of the people, and disappointed the sanguinary. The massacres of September had therefore been preferred as a method of extermination, and on the 29th of November 1792 the Tribunal was suppressed. But now that the Anarchists could make sure of support from the populace, and the restraining influence of the Girondins had been reduced to nothing, Danton resolved on a further venture. This time the Girondins were not to be spared; on the contrary, it was they who were to provide the principal victims of the new Tribunal.

As usual, the responsibility for this measure was to be laid at the door of " the people "; the same calumnies, the same futile pretexts that had done duty at the massacres of September were again employed.

On the 8th of March Danton and Lacroix, who had returned from a mission to the army in Belgium, appeared at the Convention with an alarming report on the military situation. The troops had been almost totally routed; treachery on the part of their officers could alone explain the state of affairs; the remedy lay in raising fresh forces, but before marching on the enemy the patriots must exterminate traitors at home.

That, as in September, no connection whatever existed between so-called " traitors " in Paris and the armies abroad is of course obvious, but Danton, like Mirabeau, excelled in rendering the flimsiest pretexts plausible, and in concealing sanguinary designs beneath a flood of high-sounding oratory. The great speeches of Danton that have gone down to posterity as trumpet-calls to patriotism were mostly delivered at a moment when he was meditating some fresh plan for slaughtering his fellow-countrymen. Thus, just as " audacity and yet more audacity " had been the signal for the massacres of September, another famous phrase heralded the inauguration of the Revolutionary Tribunal. " What matters my reputation ? Let France be free and my name for ever dishonoured ! (*Que la France soit libre et que mon nom soit flétri à jamais !*)." Stirring words truly in the ears of posterity, less stirring in those of contemporaries to whom such exclamations had by long use become familiar. The demagogy, says Mercier, had " created for itself a language to deceive and seduce the multitude. I have heard it shouted in my ear, ' Let the French perish as long as liberty triumphs ! ' I have heard another cry out at a section, ' Yes, I could take my head by the hair, I could cut it off and give it to the despot; I could say to him, Tyrant, this is the action of a free man ! ' This sublimity of extravagance was composed for the populace ; it was understood and it succeeded. . . ." [1]

The famous exclamation of Danton was a phrase of this order, and, in the sense in which it is usually accepted, meaningless. What connection can be found between the reputation of Danton and the success of French arms in Belgium ? Why should his name be dishonoured by France becoming free ? But when we understand the real intention that lay behind the words, we find them pregnant with meaning. Was not Danton's reputation to be for ever tarnished, his name for ever dishonoured, by the creation of that sanguinary Tribunal before which he himself was to be summoned only a year later ? was he not to cry out between his prison bars in an agony of remorse : " It was on this day I instituted the Revolutionary Tribunal, but I ask pardon for it from God and man ; it was not in order that it should become the scourge of humanity, it was in order to prevent a renewal of the massacres of September ! " ?

Always, to the end, the same calumny on the people ! The people at the time the Revolutionary Tribunal was inaugurated showed no symptoms whatever of wishing to massacre anybody —had they not refused to carry out the sanguinary suggestions of Marat only a fortnight earlier ? Danton was well aware of this ; he well knew that the thirst for blood existed not amongst the people, but amongst the leaders of the Mountain, the members of the Commune. Indeed, with his usual audacity of speech, he frankly acknowledged his own bloodthirsty intentions. The famous trumpet-call loses something of its splendour when quoted with its less lofty sequel : " What matters my reputation ? Let France be free and my name for ever dishonoured ! I have consented to be called a drinker of blood ! Well, let us drink the blood of the enemies of humanity ! "

Later in the evening, when the light in the hall of the Convention was growing dim, Danton sprang again into the tribune, and his great voice rolled out through the semi-darkness : " It is important to take judicial measures to punish the counter-revolutionaries, since it is on their account that this tribunal is to be substituted for the *supreme tribunal of the people's vengeance*. The enemies of liberty lift audacious heads . . . in seeing the honest citizen at his fireside, the artisan in his workshop, they have the stupidity to think themselves in a majority. Well, snatch them yourselves from popular vengeance ; humanity commands you ! "

Suddenly, whilst the thunderous tones of Danton still quivered in the air, another voice was heard ; one word, one only, but filled with terrible import, rang out through the stillness of the

---

[1] Mercier, *Le Nouveau Paris*, i. 25.

spell-bound assembly : " *September !* " It was again Lanjuinais, the one brave man who had dared to defend the King against the injustice of the Convention, who now arose in defence of the people against the calumnies of the great demagogue. The shaft had found its mark ; for a moment Danton faltered, became confused, then, quickly recovering himself, summoned more audacity to his aid, piled calumny on calumny :

" Since some one has dared," he shouted, " to recall those bloody days over which every good citizen has groaned, I will say, I myself, that if a tribunal had then existed, the people who have often been so cruelly reproached for those days would not have stained them with blood. . . . Let us profit by the mistakes of our predecessors . . . *let us be terrible to prevent the people from being terrible !* "

Never was hypocrisy more flagrant. Who had accused the people of responsibility for the September days but Danton and his colleagues of the Commune ? By every other party, by Girondins and Royalists alike, the people had been absolved from all complicity ; not a single reproach had been uttered against any but the real authors of the crime.[1]

The brazen effrontery of Danton won the day ; the Revolutionary Tribunal was decreed in spite of the protests of Lanjuinais and the Girondins, and on the 6th of April held its first sitting at the Palais de Justice. The Court was composed of five judges, ten jurymen—twelve had been ordained, but were not forthcoming—and the Public Accuser, whose name was to strike a deeper terror into the hearts of the Parisians than even that of Robespierre—Fouquier Tinville.

On the opening day of the dread Tribunal, Fouquier alone seems to have entered with zest into the proceedings ; the populace, whose ferocity it had been declared impossible to restrain, behaved with lamentable weakness. When the first victim, a gentleman of Poitou named Des Maulans, was summarily condemned to death for emigration, " the immense majority of the audience, particularly the women," says M. Lenôtre in his admirable description of the scene, " could not imagine that a man who had done no harm to any one should be condemned to death," and, as the fatal sentence was repeated

---

[1] " It is universally known," writes Dr. Moore, " that the Girondists exculpate the citizens of Paris from the horrid crimes of September ; whereas Robespierre, St. André, Tallien, Chabot, Bazire, and all that party, assert that the massacres were committed by the people. But as, at the same time, St. André always calls them ' le bon peuple,' Marat says ' he carries them in his heart,' and Robespierre declares ' he would willingly sacrifice his life for them,' the populace consider this faction as their friends, and look on Roland and the Girondists as their calumniators " (Moore's *Journal*, ii. 427).

by each judge in turn, the crowd burst out into weeping, "silently at first, then with much noise," and, their emotion communicating itself to the judges and jury, the whole court was shaken by a storm of sobbing, shoulders heaved, handkerchiefs were pressed to eyes and lips, men turned away their faces to hide their tears.[1]

Yet so potent was the spell cast over all minds by the authors of these tragic happenings, so skilfully had they impressed upon the multitude the necessity for " severity " towards the " enemies of the country," that no one seems to have thought of stopping the proceedings, and all resigned themselves to what followed as to the inevitable.

Day after day further victims were sent to the guillotine— an ex-Brigadier-General named Blanchelarde ; Gabriel de Guiny, a naval lieutenant; a young cabman called Mangot, who proclaimed himself a Royalist ; Bouché, a travelling dentist, who said that " the Convention were brigands " (sic) (*la Convention étoit des brigand*), and continued to call out " Vive Louis XVII. ! au f. . . . la République ! " after his condemnation ; an aged soldier who, under the influence of drink, had said that " France was too large for a Republic " ; a poor old cook called Catherine Clère, who had cried out " Vive le Roi ! " in the street at midnight, and had added in the hearing of passers-by that " all that rabble who dictated laws to decent people should be massacred."[2]

Truly a formidable band of conspirators ! That it was for such as these the Revolutionary Tribunal had been instituted no one could seriously imagine ; moreover, the leaders of the Mountain now showed their hand by publicly designating who were the real enemies of the country it was necessary to destroy.

At the same moment that the Revolutionary Tribunal began its sittings, Camille Desmoulins published his terrible indictment of the Girondins under the title of *Histoire des Brissotins, ou Fragment de l'Histoire secrète de la Révolution sur la Faction d'Orléans et le Comité anglo-prussien et les six premiers Mois de la République*. Revolutionary historians, to whom the facts revealed in this pamphlet are exceedingly unpalatable, have endeavoured to prove that Camille did not intend to be taken seriously, that he had allowed himself to be carried away by his whimsical imagination, that he was overcome with contrition when he discovered that taunts he had merely launched in sarcasm served as real grounds of accusation against his political antagonists. But there is not a shred of evidence to confirm this convenient theory.

Camille Desmoulins, original only in his style, was always

[1] Lenôtre, *Le Tribunal révolutionnaire*, pp. 84, 85.
[2] Wallon, *Le Tribunal révolutionnaire*, i. 93, 110, 133, 140.

the echo of a stronger mind. Once it was Mirabeau who had
served as his inspiration, now it was Robespierre and Danton,
later it was to be Danton only. In this *Histoire des Brissotins*
the influence of Robespierre is plainly visible, and indeed, in his
speech against the Brissotins only a few days later, Robespierre
followed precisely the same line of argument as his disciple
Camille.

To suppose that these accusations were suggested to Robespierre by Camille's pamphlet would be absurd; not to the
feather-headed Camille can we attribute the relentless logic, the
ingenious chain of evidence, by which the Brissotins are convicted
of complicity in the past with three of the great revolutionary
intrigues—the Orléaniste conspiracy, the intrigue with Prussia,
the intrigue with the Jacobins of England. In these illuminating
pages, perhaps the most brilliant Desmoulins ever wrote, the
workings of the first two revolutions are mercilessly unveiled—
the Orléaniste influence behind the so-called popular movement
on the 12th of July 1789, the collusion of Mirabeau with the
Duc d'Orléans at the march on Versailles, the accusations
brought against the King and Queen for holding " an Austrian
committee " by men who were themselves members of an Anglo-
Prussian committee, the visits of Pétion to London in order to
enlist the aid of his English allies, the support given to the
Brissotins by the Whigs, the proposal of Carra to place the
Duke of Brunswick on the throne of France, the persistent
attempts to form an alliance with Prussia, the gold received from
Frederick William, the negotiations with the Prussians at the
camp of La Lune that resulted in the retreat of the invading
armies after Valmy,—no Royalist has ever shown up the Revolution so completely. What wonder that revolutionary historians
prefer to dismiss the revelations of this *enfant terrible* as an
absurdity ?

It was not till much later that Camille realized that, in
giving away the secrets of the first two Revolutions, he had given
away his own share in the Orléaniste intrigue ; nor did he dream
that a year later Robespierre, through the mouth of St. Just,
would bring against Danton and himself precisely the same
accusations of Orléanisme that he had brought against the
Girondins. At present he thought only of destroying the rival
faction. " This work will send them to the guillotine ! I
will answer for it ! " he said to Prudhomme, giving him a
copy of the pamphlet. " That may be," answered Prudhomme
calmly ; " so much the worse for you. Your turn will come. . . ."
" Bah ! " said Camille, " we have the people with us ! "[1] He
had forgotten, as every demagogue in turn forgot throughout

[1] Prudhomme, *Crimes de la Révolution*, vi. 272.

the Revolution, that, in the words of Mirabeau, "it is but a step from the Capitol to the Tarpeian rock!" To-day the populace of Robespierre was with him, to-morrow they would be with Robespierre only, and he might scream to them in vain from the tumbril to save him.

To Robespierre the pamphlet of Desmoulins served a double purpose, for it helped to rid him of both the factions he detested —the Girondins and the Duc d'Orléans, with his few remaining supporters.   With his usual ingenuity he used one faction to destroy another, and we cannot doubt that it was owing to his influence that the Girondins on the 6th of April succeeded in obtaining the banishment of Philippe Égalité, the Marquis de Sillery, and Choderlos de Laclos, in spite of the protests of Marat. Three days later the whole Orléans family were sent to Marseilles and imprisoned.   Thus was the principal bone of contention removed from Paris, and Robespierre could concentrate all his energies on overthrowing the Girondins.   On the 10th of April he boldly demanded that they should all be summoned before the Revolutionary Tribunal ; at the same time Marat published an address, inciting the people to save the country by getting rid of "all traitors and all conspirators."   The Girondins retaliated by accusing Marat of "provoking disorders, and of attempting to destroy the Convention," and so great was the indignation of the great majority of the Assembly at Marat's incendiary proclamation that they actually succeeded in obtaining a summons against him to appear before the Revolutionary Tribunal.

But the movement was doomed to failure ; Marat had on his side all the turbulent elements of Paris, all the machinery of insurrection ; the jury, obedient to the dictates of Fouquier, declared Marat innocent, and the "Friend of the People," smothered in wreaths and roses, was borne triumphantly from the Palais de Justice on the shoulders of the crowd.

Of all the grotesque scenes of the Revolution this was perhaps the strangest—the malignant dwarf wrapped in a ragged coat of faded green, surmounted by an ermine collar yellow with age and dingy from long contact with his neck, the filthy handkerchief that usually bound his head for once discarded, and in its place a crown of laurels slipping down over the black and greasy hair, lending a still greener tint to the sickly pallor of his countenance.   And the smile of Marat—that was enough to strike a chill to the stoutest heart !   Dr. Moore has described the sensation of horror that overcame him in the Convention at the sight of "Marat attempting pleasantry" ; now he must have appeared more hideous still as, with withered cheeks creased into smiles, with mouth distended, he bent forward, holding out his arms to the people as if to press them to his heart.

The devotees presented an appearance worthy of the idol they carried ; all the *jupors gras* of Robespierre were there, nodding dishevelled heads in response to his greetings, throwing vinous kisses ; sans-culottes drunk with joy, cut-throats of September shouting, Vive Marat ! Long live the friend of the people ! " [1]

This time popular dementia had gone too far, and the result of the " triumph of Marat " was to produce a wave of reaction. When the Friend of the People " presented himself at his section he met with so hostile a reception that he was obliged to beat a hasty retreat. Nearly every evening crowds marched through the streets shouting, " Down with the Anarchists ! Long live the nation ! Long live the law ! " [2]

Good citizens, who had kept away from their sections on account of the anarchic schemes discussed there, now returned, to throw their weight into the scale of law and order ; a deputation from three sections arrived at the Convention to denounce " the brigands who have dared to raise the standard of revolt, and who under the perfidious mask of patriotism wish to kill liberty." [3] The speech was received with applause from a large majority of the deputies, and on the proposal of Barère, who had not yet thrown in his lot with the Mountain, the Convention decreed that an extraordinary committee should be formed, composed of twelve members, to inquire into the measures adopted by the Council of the Commune and the sections of Paris, and also into the operations of the Comité de Salut Public and its accessory, the Comité de Sûreté Générale. [4]

These two sanguinary committees—the great committees of the Terror—had only recently become a power. The former, which had originated in 1792 as the Comité de Défense Générale, took the further title " et de Salut Public "—under which name alone it was henceforth known—on the 6th of April 1793, the same day that the Revolutionary Tribunal

---

[1] Michelet, quoting *Le Publiciste de la République Française*, says that the women of the market were amongst the crowd, but this seems improbable in view of their attitude at the King's trial three months earlier, and on May 2 the Government agent, Dutard, reports to Garat that their attitude towards the Revolution is still the same : " It seems that these women, if they were not afraid of the guillotine for themselves, would cry in unison, ' Vive le Roi ! ' " (Schmidt, ii. 173).

[2] Mortimer Ternaux, vii. 215.

[3] *Ibid.* p. 237.

[4] I give the names of these committees in the original French, since there is no exact equivalent in English. The Comité de Salut Public is frequently referred to by English writers as the Committee of Public Safety, but this is misleading, for " safety " is the English for *sûreté*, not for *salut*. The nearest equivalent for *salut* would be " salvation," but this would not be an exact rendering of the French word.

began its sittings, whilst the latter, although subordinate to the Comité de Salut Public, had existed since 1789 as a Comité d'Information, assuming the name of Comité de Sûreté Générale in May 1792.

Hitherto the Comité de Salut Public had included men of all parties — Danton, Sieyés, Vergniaud, Guadet, Gensonné, Pétion, and others—but the restraint imposed on its operations by the Girondins exasperated Danton against the faction he had saved from the massacres of September, and he resolved on their destruction. Moreover, since seven out of the twelve members elected to the new Commission des Douze were Girondins, and the rest neutrals, it became evident that their inquiries into the workings of the two committees would act as a further check on the schemes of the Anarchists. For six months the Girondins had now held up the course of the Terror which, but for them, would doubtless have formed the sequel to the September massacres. Therefore the Girondins must not be simply overthrown, but put out of existence. It was this that in the eyes of the Anarchists necessitated the rising of the 31st of May.

That a massacre of the whole faction was now contemplated by the Commune cannot be doubted. Dutard, the secret agent of the minister Garat, records that "this moment is terrible, and much resembles that which preceded the 2nd of September."[1] And indeed, on the 23rd of May, a further deputation from the section of La Fraternité came to the Convention to reveal the fact that at a meeting of the Council of the Commune, to which several of their members had succeeded in gaining admittance, it had been proposed that thirty-two deputies of the Gironde should be "made to disappear from the face of the globe," or "Septemberized."[2] This, according to a deputy from Brittany to whom the plan had been confided, was to be followed by a further massacre of 8000 people.[3] Thereupon the Commission des Douze ordered the arrest of Hébert, the deputy attorney of the Commune, and author of the bloodthirsty journal, Le Père Duchesne; also of his two colleagues, Varlet and Dobsent. The same evening Hébert and Dobsent were imprisoned at the Abbaye.

The Commune retaliated with "a deputation from sixteen sections of Paris" demanding the release of the oppressed patriots ; meanwhile the women of the Société Fraternelle rushed through the streets armed with red flags, urging the people to march on the Abbaye and deliver Hébert—an appeal to which the people declined to respond.

The hall of the Convention at the Tuileries, which it had

---

[1] Schmidt, ii. 218.   [2] Ibid. i. 250.
[3] Beaulieu, v. 120 ; Letters of Helen Maria Williams (1795), p. 42.

occupied since the 10th of May, became again the scene of indescribable confusion ; deputations poured in continuously ; the petitioners, unable to find room in the places reserved for them, overflowed into the seats of the deputies, many of whom, overcome with fatigue, had retired for the night. Then, amidst the howls of the crowd, Hérault de Séchelles proposed the liberation of Hébert and his colleagues, and the suppression of the Commission des Douze. A few deputies, joined by the petitioners, voting as if they were the legal representatives whose places they occupied, succeeded in carrying the motion.

But the next day the Convention, restored to its normal conditions, reinstated the Commission des Douze by a majority of 259 votes.

" You have decreed the counter-revolution," cried Collot d'Herbois ; " I demand that the Statue of Liberty should be veiled ! "

This decision of the Convention gave the signal for battle, and immediately the Commune proceeded to put the revolutionary machine in motion—no easy matter, for Paris in general was singularly calm, and two days were necessary to prepare the rising.[1]

This is not the place to describe in detail the movement known as " the Revolution of the 31st of May," which was in reality simply a duel between the two opposing factions, and as such belongs to the history of the Convention, not to the story of the great popular outbreaks of the Revolution. No other great day of tumult was so completely artificial. When on the morning of the 31st Paris awoke to the sound of the tocsin, armed forces summoned from the sections assembled mechanically, women gathered on their doorsteps " to see the insurrection pass," but no one knew what all the stir was about.[2]

Throughout the day the Convention was surrounded with troops, who, for the most part, had no idea why they were there and whom they were protecting. Meanwhile deputations from the sections streamed into the hall, some to demand the suppression of the Commission des Douze and the arrest of the Girondins, others to protest in their favour. Amongst the latter was the section of the Butte des Moulins, and in retaliation for its spirited action the Commune despatched messengers wearing municipal scarves to Saint-Antoine and Saint-Marceau to rouse the inhabitants with the news that members of this section had formed a centre of counter-revolution at the Palais Royal, and were wearing the white cockade of royalty.[3] The

---

[1] Mortimer Ternaux, vii. 321.
[2] Ibid. p. 329 ; Mercier, Le Nouveau Paris, i. 164.
[3] Dauban, La Demagogie en 1793, p. 209 ; Mortimer Ternaux, vii. 351.

men of the Faubourgs who had been under arms for some hours, waiting for orders, marched off obediently with their cannon, and on arrival at the Palais Royal found indeed a battalion of the Butte des Moulins encamped there with detachments from other sections sent to their support—for what purpose no one seemed to know.

The folly of the whole proceeding now occurred to the men of the Faubourgs, who, after placing their cannon in position and ranging themselves in battle order, decided that before beginning to fire on their fellow-citizens it would be as well to discover whether there was any real *cause de guerre* between them. Accordingly a deputation was sent to verify the accusations of the agitators, and, as might be expected, the whole alarm was discovered to be needless—no white cockades were to be seen, the tricolour was flaunted everywhere, on hats and in the form of banners. Then amidst cries of " Long live the Republic ! " the gates were thrown open, and the opposing battalions fell into each others' arms, swearing eternal friendship.[1]

This sort of thing was always apt to occur when the people were left to themselves to settle matters, and no agitators were at hand to stir them up to violence. On this occasion Santerre, who excelled in the art of exciting revolutionary troops, was absent from Paris, and Hanriot, who had been illegally made commander-general by the Commune, was at the head of the forces that surrounded the Convention.

As an insurrection, therefore, the 31st of May had proved a failure just as the Affaire Réveillon, the first march on Versailles, and the 20th of June had proved failures for want of popular support. Always throughout the Revolution the same abortive movement before each outbreak, the same miss-fire preceding the explosion !

At the Convention the Commune had succeeded in again obtaining the suppression of the Commission des Douze, but had been unable to secure the arrest of the Girondins. So a further insurrection must be attempted, and all the following day was occupied in preparation. In the evening Marat appeared at the Commune and, after giving the order to the Council to begin the movement, proceeded himself to ring the tocsin. The same night the Anarchists struck their first decisive blow at the party of the Gironde by the arrest of Madame Roland, who, during the absence of her husband, was seized by emissaries of the Commune and led to prison at the Abbaye. The next morning, June 2, all Paris was again under arms, the tocsin rang out, an armed force of 80,000 men assembled, but amongst these 80,000,

[1] Mortimer Ternaux, vii. 352, 365; Beaulieu, v. 132,

says the deputy Meillan, "75,000 did not know why they had been made to take up arms,"[1] nor, owing to the skilful organization of the Commune, was it possible for them to discover.

For Hanriot, well aware that the honest citizens of Paris would not co-operate in the real purpose of the day—the destruction of the Girondins—had been careful to place the troops formed by the sections at a distance from the Château, some in the Place Louis XV. beyond the swing-bridge, which was closed between them and the garden, others in the Carrousel separated by a wooden barrier from the court of the Tuileries.[2] Meanwhile his picked force of four to five thousand insurgents— including a number of German mercenaries belonging to the legion of Rosenthal under orders to march on La Vendée, whose total ignorance of the French language rendered them docile instruments of the Commune[3]—formed a cordon immediately around the Château to which all the avenues were occupied by his officers or agents, "who had received orders to suffer no communication between the hall (of the Convention) and the court or garden."[4] By this means the troops of the sections were powerless to intervene, whilst the great mass of the people that had as usual assembled to look on was kept in complete ignorance of what was passing.[5] On the part of the people the 2nd of June was thus the same absolutely blind movement as the abortive rising that had preceded it two days earlier.

If only the Girondins had stood their ground on this critical day it is probable that the victory would have remained with them, but now that their own fate was at stake they displayed the same pusillanimity they had shown at the trial of the King. Instead of bringing their eloquence to bear on the situation, the leading members of the Gironde, including Brissot and Vergniaud, dared not venture into the Convention, but sought refuge at the house of Meillan near by. Meillan himself, and also Barbaroux and Isnard, remained at their post in the Assembly, but it was left to Lanjuinais, who was not a Girondin, to act as the principal defender of the faction with which during these days he associated himself as the champion of liberty. In the name of the people the courageous Breton now denounced the efforts of the factions to create disorders. "You calumniate Paris! You insult the people!" cried the Mountain. "No," answered Lanjuinais, "I do not accuse Paris; Paris is good-hearted, Paris is oppressed by a few scoundrels."

---

[1] Dauban, *La Demagogie en 1793*, p. 218.
[2] *Ibid.* pp. 214, 218; Mortimer Ternaux, vii. 391; *Letters of Helen Maria Williams* (1795), p. 41.
[3] Mortimer Ternaux, vii. 379.
[4] *Letters of Helen Maria Williams*, p. 41.
[5] *Ibid.*; Mortimer Ternaux, vii. 384.

Legendre the butcher, rushing upon Lanjuinais, attempted
to drag him from the tribune, but, quelled by the sang-froid of
his opponent, retreated discomfited, and only returned to the
assault when reinforced by Drouet of Varennes fame, the younger
Robespierre, and Jullien. A hand-to-hand struggle ensued, and
Lanjuinais remained master of the situation.

The craven Girondins, hearing of this momentary victory,
attempted to reach the hall of the Convention and rally around
Lanjuinais, but it was too late. A fresh deputation of the
Commune arrived on the scene to demand their arrest, and
departed shouting, " To arms ! Let us save the country ! "—
a battle-cry echoed with fury by the tribunes.

Meanwhile Hanriot's troops had closed around the Château
and the mob had taken possession of the halls, corridors, and
staircases ; the women - followers of Marat and Robespierre,
constituting themselves doorkeepers, forcibly prevented the
exit of deputies. At this Danton, who never believed in
allowing the *canaille* — particularly the female *canaille* — to
take command of the situation, grew indignant,[1] and when
at last the news reached the Assembly that armed sentinels
had been placed at the doors of the hall, it was on the proposal
of Danton's ally, Lacroix, that the Convention despatched an
usher to Hanriot demanding that the armed forces should be
withdrawn from the Château. Hanriot replied briefly, " Tell
your b—— president that he and his Assembly can be d——d
(*dis à ton f. . . . président que je me f. . . . de lui et de son
Assemblée*), and that if it does not deliver up the Twenty-Two
to me within an hour I will blast it with cannon."

Barère then proposed that the Convention should make
a display of independence by going out to face the army of
insurgents, and thereupon the whole Assembly, with Hérault de
Séchelles at its head, descended the great staircase by which
Louis XVI. had left the Tuileries on the 10th of August,
and filed out into the courtyard where Hanriot awaited them
at the head of his men. The half-drunken commander again
demanded that " the Twenty-Two " should be surrendered.
Hérault refused, and the deputies surrounding him, inspired
with sudden courage, cried out, " They want victims ! Let
them kill us all ! " Then Hanriot, grasping his sabre, turned
to his troops and shouted, " Cannoniers, to your guns ! " But
no one obeyed the order to fire. The men remained immovable—Hérault and a fellow-deputy who went boldly towards

---

[1] The rôle of Danton on this occasion is difficult to explain. He had
certainly co-operated in the movement to overthrow the Girondins, yet
now he seemed inclined to oppose it. Meillan accounts for his attitude by
saying he had begun to fear the Municipality.

them saw that "their eyes and attitude gave evidence of no evil design."

The truth is that the multitude was opposed to the insurgents; one of the sections of Paris actually pointed its cannon on the troops of Hanriot at the same moment that Hanriot's cannon were pointed on the members of the Convention.[1] It was therefore once again the people who ranged themselves on the side of law and order, and Hanriot, disconcerted by their attitude, was unable to carry out his sanguinary designs.

The troops, drawn up in the garden on the other side of the Château, whither the Assembly now made its way, seemed equally averse to bloodshed, and contented themselves with crying out, "Vive la Montagne! Vive la Convention!" and from time to time, "Vive Marat!" At this moment Marat himself, followed by the crowd of little ragged boys that his grotesque appearance frequently attracted,[2] appeared on the scene, shrieking imperiously to Hérault, "In the name of the people I charge you to return to your post, which you have basely deserted." And he added significantly, "Let the *faithful* deputies return to their posts!"[3] In other words, let the sheep be divided from the goats and the members of the Mountain retire into safety, whilst their opponents remain outside to be butchered. Hérault and his colleagues had evidently thwarted the designs of Marat by joining themselves to the Girondins who had been singled out as victims, but now, merged in the crowd of deputies, could not be distinguished by the insurgents. Such, however, was the authority the wretched dwarf had acquired that, obedient to the word of command, the Montagnards turned towards the Tuileries, leaving the Girondins to their fate, but the Girondins, seeing the snare, retreated likewise, and the whole Assembly, followed by Marat, re-entered the hall of the Convention and resumed the sitting.

Couthon, the friend of Robespierre, then proposed a decree against the Twenty-Two and the members of the Commission des Douze, but the parade round the courts and garden of the Tuileries had evidently convinced the leaders that violent measures would not meet with popular support, for it was no longer the imprisonment of the Girondins their opponents demanded, but simply their suspension, after which they were to be left in their own houses under supervision—a surprisingly mild conclusion to three days' insurrection!

The list of the proscribed deputies was then read aloud, and meanwhile Marat repeatedly intervened, adding certain names and ordering others to be removed without even consulting the

---

[1] *Rapport de Dutard à Garat*, Schmidt, ii. 11.

[2] Beaulieu, v. 145.   [3] Dauban, *La Demagogie en 1793*, p. 222.

Convention. " It was then," says Meillan, " that we understood all the power of Marat "—well for them if they had realized it earlier, and stood together as one man to resist it.

Now at the eleventh hour the Assembly made one expiring effort to assert its independence ; several members rose to declare that " they were not free, and that they refused to vote surrounded by bayonets and cannon "—a resolution in which no less than two-thirds of the Convention finally concurred.

The Mountain, not to be beaten, solved the difficulty by simply voting without them, and the majority, " thus becoming simple spectators, left the Montagnards to pass the decree, supported by a great number of strangers who, as on the 27th of May, had placed themselves in the seats of the legislators whose functions they had usurped." [1]

So, by a violation of law and justice as flagrant as that which had brought about the condemnation of the King, the Girondins fell victims to the Revolution they had helped to prepare. And just as Louis XVI. on the eve of his death had seen in one prophetic moment the future that awaited France, brave Lanjuinais, proscribed with the faction whose cause he had defended, foretold the terrible era of which this day was to be the prelude in his last words from the tribune : " I see civil war kindled in my country, spreading its ravages everywhere and rending France. I see the horrible monster of the dictatorship advancing over piles of ruins and corpses, swallowing you each up in turn, and overthrowing the Republic ! "

THE TERROR IN THE PROVINCES

Exactly as Lanjuinais had prophesied, the fall of the Gironde proved the signal for civil war. All over France a great wave of indignation arose, and within a few months the whole country was in a blaze from one end to the other.

In La Vendée, Royalist and Catholic to the core, the fire had broken out two months earlier ; the civil constitution of the clergy and continued persecution of all who remained attached to religion, the massacres of September, and finally the execution of the King, had each in turn roused the people's fury, and now 100,000 peasants, armed with forks and sticks, were marching in defence of the church and monarchy, led by the priests and few remaining nobles they had forcibly placed at their head. [2]

---

[1] Dauban, *La Demagogie en 1793*, p. 223.

[2] It is customary for revolutionary historians to make out that the priests and nobles incited the Vendéens to revolt ; this is absolutely untrue ; the movement was entirely a peasant rising—the nobles in certain cases showed reluctance to act as leaders. See Beaulieu, vi. 52.

Lyon likewise rose in revolt just before the final overthrow of the Gironde. The splendid city reduced to misery by the Revolution, its commerce ruined, its inhabitants starving for want of work, had nevertheless submitted to the Republic, but when an emissary of the Mountain, Chalier, a disciple of Marat, was sent to Lyon to propagate anarchy and set up a revolutionary tribunal, the sections of the town all combined against the Convention, and on the 29th of May a bloody battle took place in the streets between the National Guards of Lyon and the gunners enlisted in the service of the Mountain, which ended in the arrest of Chalier. Then came the news of the rising in Paris on June 2, and the victory of the Mountain. Thereupon Lyon boldly declared that it no longer recognized the Convention, and called its citizens to arms.

Meanwhile Bordeaux had risen in defence of its liberties, for with glaring injustice, when its deputies the Girondins were expelled from the Convention, the department had been invited to name no others in their places. Bordeaux was, therefore, now unrepresented in the Convention, and had every right to protest—indeed it had protested for some months before the 31st of May—against the treatment of its representatives by their adversaries of the Mountain.[1] Now on the 6th of June the Council-General of the city forwarded a threatening address to the Convention, and summoned Lyon and Dijon to combine in the fight for liberty.

Throughout the south-east of France the fire of revolt was spreading likewise: Toulon opposed a vigorous resistance to the dictates of the Mountain; Marseilles, once dominated by the most violent revolutionaries, had also turned against it, and, summoning Lyon, Normandy, and La Vendée to its aid, announced its intention of marching on Paris. Calvados, Caen, and Evreux, in Normandy, were organizing revolt; Dauphiné and Franche-Comté were in arms—altogether *no less than sixty departments had risen against the tyranny of the Convention.*[2] Such was the attitude of the twenty-five millions of France who, according to Carlyle, looked to the Mountain for salvation—as a matter of fact at least three-quarters of the population were violently opposed to it, and the remaining quarter was mainly terrorized into submission.

At the same time the people were by no means wholeheartedly on the side of the Girondins. Buzot, Pétion, Isnard, Barbaroux, and others of the faction, who escaped from Paris after their expulsion from the Convention and attempted to rally the provinces around them, failed entirely in their rôle

---

[1] Buchez et Roux, xxiii. 279.
[2] *La Demagogie en 1793,* by C. A. Dauban, p. 239.

of popular leaders. To the ruminating minds of the peasants, the aims of one Republican faction were indistinguishable from another; they were ready to oppose the bloodshed and anarchy advocated by the Mountain, but the ideal Republic offered them by the Girondins in no way roused their enthusiasm. The truth is that France remained at heart monarchic, partly by conviction and partly by habit. For in every country the characteristic of the true people is hatred of innovation, and against this prejudice the Republicans of both factions contended in vain. The correspondence of revolutionary emissaries to the provinces frequently breathes a spirit of despair : " The labourer is estimable, but he is a very bad patriot in general; " [1] and from Marseilles, " In spite of our efforts to republicanize the people . . . our trouble and fatigue are almost fruitless. . . . The mind of the public is still detestable amongst the proprietors, artisans, and day-labourers; " [2] in Alsace " Republican sentiments are still in the cradle, fanaticism is extreme and unbelievable ; the spirit of the inhabitants is in no way revolutionary. . . ." [3] No one, however, has described the utter failure of the Girondins to convert the people to Republicanism better than Buzot himself : " One must not dissemble ; the majority of the French people sighed after the monarchy and the Constitution of 1791. . . . Can one believe that the events of June 2 (1793), the misery, persecution, and assassinations that followed, made the majority of France change its opinion ? No, but in the towns they pretend to be ' sans-culotte,' because those who are not are guillotined; in the country places they obey the most unjust summons to serve (in the army), because those who do not go are guillotined. The guillotine, that is the great reason for everything. . . . *This people is Republican by blows of the guillotine.* But look closely at things, penetrate into the homes of families, sound all hearts, and if they dare open themselves to you, you will read there hatred against the government that fear imposes on them, you will see that all their desires, all their hopes, tend towards the Constitution of 1791." [4] And again : " The honest inhabitants of the countryside confound the crimes committed in the Revolution of 1793 with the Revolution itself; they abhor the Republic, and those who tyrannize over them in its name ; they regret and sigh for the return . . . of a gentler and more peaceable régime. . . . In the towns, where fear has withered all hearts, where commerce

[1] Legros, *La Révolution telle qu'elle est*, i. 366 (letter from Prieur de la Marne to the Comité de Salut Public).

[2] *Archives des Affaires Étrangères*, quoted by Taine, *La Révolution*, viii. 53.

[3] *Ibid.* p. 54.

[4] *Aux Amis de la Vérité*, by F. N. L. Buzot, pp. 32-34.

and industry are for ever annihilated, where it is a crime to live in any degree of comfort or to show any decency in one's tastes or manners . . . every citizen . . . in all classes . . . bitterly regretted the past." Indeed, Buzot himself is at last forced to arrive at this conclusion : " Amidst the abyss of evils into which this superb empire is precipitated by licence and misery one is almost reduced to desiring the return of ancient despotism, since it is uncertain whether the French could now bear the moderate régime of the Constitution of 1791." [1]

It was thus in La Vendée alone that real enthusiasm prevailed ; there the people, inspired by passionate devotion to cherished traditions, were at one with their seigneurs, whilst in the other provinces dominated by the Girondins the people took up arms in a cause that was not their own. Ostensibly they were fighting for the Republic, in reality they craved for the old familiar things the Republic had taken from them. What cared the peasants of France for the promise of a government modelled on Athens or Sparta that was to replace the antiquated monarchy, for the enlightened philosophy that was to compensate them for the destruction of their ancient faith ?

The Girondins themselves could not fail to perceive the failure of their efforts to inspire the people ; everywhere it was the Royalists who secured the largest following. Even in Republican centres Royalist generals led out the troops—at Lyon, Virieu and Précy ; at Bordeaux, De Puisaye ; even Wimpfen, beloved of the Normans, though avowedly a Republican, was believed by Louvet to be a Royalist at heart. The Girondins at Caen in Normandy—Louvet, Guadet, Buzot, and others—watched these symptoms with alarm and, rather than combine with their rivals to overthrow the Mountain, diverted their energies to opposing the progress of Royalism. Thus amongst the leaders of the people there was no co-ordination, and amongst the various elements that made up the population no unity of purpose that alone could have ensured success. Owing to these dissensions the movement was from the first doomed to failure, and the triumph of the Mountain seemed assured.

It was then that a girl who lived at Caen, Marie Charlotte Corday, resolved to take the law into her own hands and save the country by striking down the author of all the ills that were desolating France. For to Charlotte, as to many inhabitants of provincial towns, it was Marat who appeared as the incarnation of the Terror that now held France in its grip ; Marat once removed, she imagined that the other leaders of the Mountain might return to sentiments of humanity. If Charlotte had been

[1] *Mémoires de Buzot*, p. 19.

a Girondin, as certain writers have supposed, she would probably have thought otherwise, for to the Girondins Marat seemed merely a " loathsome reptile," far less to be feared than Robespierre, whom they regarded as their chief antagonist of the Mountain.   It is therefore improbable that when Charlotte went to request Barbaroux for introductions to some of his friends in Paris, she confided to him the object of her journey—" if," as Louvet said, " she had consulted us, would it have been against Marat that we should have directed her stroke ? " Undoubtedly no—Robespierre would have been the victim. Barbaroux, moreover, could have told her that in slaying Marat she was sacrificing herself needlessly, for Marat was already dying of a lingering disease, and had, indeed, only a short time to live.

This Charlotte did not know when she set forth for Paris on that morning of July 9, and all the way she pictured to herself the execution of the great deed as she had planned it.   The letter to Duperret, the friend of Barbaroux, was to procure her admittance to the Convention, and there in the midst of the Assembly, on the summit of the Mountain, she meant to deal the mortal blow that was to rid the world of Marat.

It was not until she reached Paris that she heard that the " Friend of the People " was too ill to attend the Convention. For some weeks already he had retired from public life, and the fearful irritation of his skin obliged him to sit perpetually in a bath with wet compresses around his head.   The precise nature of his malady is not stated by his biographers, but according to the delegates from the Jacobin Club who were sent to visit him it was simply an acute attack of " patriotism." The madness of Maratisme is nowhere better exemplified than in the following report published by the Society : " We have just been to see our brother Marat. . . . We found him in his bath, a table, inkstand, and newspapers around him, occupying himself unremittingly with public affairs.   It is not a disease . . . it is a great deal of compressed patriotism squeezed into a very small body ; the violent efforts of patriotism exuding from every part are killing him."[1]

This was the vision that confronted Charlotte Corday when, on the evening of July 13, she succeeded, in spite of the opposition of Marat's mistress, Simonne Evrard, in obtaining admission to the fateful bathroom.   If she had expected to see a monster she must have found her wildest imaginings surpassed now that she was brought face to face with the reality.   Out of the opening of the slipper bath appeared the withered neck, the misshapen shoulders, the puny arms of the People's Friend, and above them that monstrous head swathed in its compresses of vinegar

[1] *Journal des Débats,* July 16, 1793.

and cold water—truly an awful and a hideous sight. A fainter heart than Charlotte's must have quailed, a nerve of less tried steel than hers must have failed at this tremendous moment— have kept her rooted to the threshold, or driven her shuddering backwards through the door and down the narrow staircase, out—out—into the pure air of Heaven. But Charlotte, wholly concentrated on her purpose, had risen above such human weaknesses, and she went straight forward, calm as the summer evening outside the window, and sat down beside Marat.

Charlotte Corday did not kill Marat as Marat killed his victims, without a trial. She gave him now, at the last moment, a chance to prove that it was not he who had raised scaffolds all over France, that it was not by his orders that innocent victims were led daily to their death. So when he asked for news of Caen, she spoke of the Girondin deputies who had taken refuge there, mentioning them by name. And at that Marat croaked out with a frightful laugh :

" I will have them all guillotined within a week ! "

Then rumour had not lied—Marat was indeed the sanguinary monster he had been represented in the provinces ! Out of his own mouth he was convicted. Charlotte hesitated no longer, and grasping her knife she plunged it straight into his heart. The deed was done ; henceforth, as she said, she was to know peace.

The serenity she displayed at her trial amazed the world no less than the courage that had led her to carry out her enter- prise. " Who had inspired you with so much hatred against Marat ? " the President asked her. " I did not need the hatred of others, I had enough of my own." " In killing him what did you hope ? " " To restore peace to my country." " Do you think you have killed all the Marats ? " " That one dead, the others will perhaps be afraid."

Never for a moment does it seem to have occurred to Charlotte that her action could be regarded as murder. When Fouquier Tinville observed suspiciously, " You must be well practised in this kind of crime," she cried out in horror, " The monster ! He takes me for an assassin ! "

The truth is that Charlotte did not feel she had killed a human being, but rather that she had exorcised an evil spirit who had cast a spell over the capital. " It is only in Paris," she said to her judges, " that people's eyes are bewitched on account of Marat ; in the other departments he is regarded as a monster."

And, indeed, the more we study Marat the more we feel a sensation of unreality creeping over us. Can such a being really have existed outside the pages of a medieval legend ?

Robespierre, Danton, Billaud, even Carrier we can believe in as physiological possibilities, but Marat is a phenomenon to be explained by no natural laws: the shuddering repulsion he inspired in all normal beholders, the unholy fascination he exercised over those who fell beneath his power, the fearful rapidity with which immediately after death that hideous body crumbled to corruption, yet around which knelt crowds of worshippers, blaspheming Christ and crying out, "Oh, sacred heart of Marat!"—all these things belong surely to the region of the supernatural, and can only be accounted for by a belief in demoniacal possession. Exclude this hypothesis and Marat remains an insoluble mystery—unique in the annals of mankind.

At any rate, whether we believe in the powers of darkness or not, the phase on which the revolutionary movement now entered could not have been surpassed in devilry if evil spirits hitherto caged in the body of Marat had been loosed over France. Until now the atrocities committed have been traceable to perfectly tangible causes—to Orléaniste intrigue; to the personal ambitions of the leaders; to excitement, delusion, or drink on the part of the populace; but from the autumn of 1793 all political aims seem to be swallowed up in a wild rage for destruction; the scenes of horror taking place everywhere appear to serve no definite purpose, but, like the convulsions of a madman, to spring from a mind in delirium.

Yet if we examine the movement closely we shall find that there was nevertheless a method in the madness; that through this frightful period of the Terror there ran a system founded on the same political doctrines that had produced the massacres of September. This is what Collot d'Herbois meant when he said: "The 2nd of September is the Credo of our liberty"; in other words, the massacres in the prisons formed simply the prelude to a general scheme of destruction. At this earlier date, as we have seen, the idea of the leaders was to amputate the gangrened limb formed by the aristocracy and clergy; now that these two categories had been practically destroyed, the same operation must be carried out on those other portions of the body to which the gangrene had spread.

First on the list came, then, the prosperous *bourgeoisie*, the peculiar object of Marat's hatred—a hatred he had communicated to Robespierre and Hébert, who, after the death of Marat, were left to carry on the campaign against this obnoxious class. Thus we find Robespierre writing: "Internal dangers come from the *bourgeois;* in order to conquer the *bourgeois* we must rouse the people, we must procure arms for them and make them angry."[1] Hébert went further: "The virtue of the holy

[1] *Papiers trouvés chez Robespierre*, ii. 15.

guillotine," he wrote, " will gradually deliver the Republic from the rich, the *bourgeois*, the spies, the fat farmers, and the worthy tradesmen as from the priests and aristocrats. They are all devourers of men."

This campaign against commerce was again the direct outcome of Illuminism, for it was Weishaupt who had first denounced the " mercantile tribe " as capable of exercising " the most formidable of despotisms." [1] Accordingly war was now waged with particular ferocity on the manufacturing towns. In August the revolutionary troops surrounded Lyon, where the authorities, exasperated by the sanguinary propaganda of Chalier, had ended by condemning this disciple of Marat to death. The siege lasted until the 9th of October 1793, when, reduced by famine, Lyon was obliged to surrender, and it was then decided that the magnificent city, once the pride of France, must be demolished. " The name of Lyon," cried Barère at the Convention, " must no longer exist, you will call it Ville-Affranchie." On the ruins he proposed to erect a monument bearing the words, " Lyon made war on liberty ; Lyon is no more." Thereupon the Convention passed the decree : " The town of Lyon shall be destroyed ; every part of it inhabited by the rich shall be demolished, only the dwellings of the poor shall remain."

Emissaries were then sent to carry out the task ; the paralytic Couthon, borne on a litter about the city, struck with a silver hammer the buildings destined to destruction, saying as he did so, " In the name of the law I demolish you," and instantly masons set to work upon the task. Meanwhile orators incited the working-classes to violence : " What are you doing, pusillanimous workmen, in these industrial occupations by which opulence degrades you ? Come out of this servitude and confront the rich man who oppresses you . . . overthrow his fortune, overthrow these edifices, the wreckage belongs to you. It is thus that you will rise to that sublime equality, the basis of true liberty, the vigorous principle of a warrior people *to whom commerce and arts should be unnecessary.*" [2]

It will be seen, therefore, that there was no question of readjusting relations between employers and employed; the whole industrial system was simply to be destroyed whilst the workers were left to starve upon the ruins.

Yet even when commerce had gone the way of aristocracy, " and pride of wealth no longer violated the principles of ' sublime equality,' " yet another centre of gangrene still remained— the *educated classes.* It was here that Robespierre displayed

---

[1] *Histoire de la Révolution*, by Louis Blanc, ii. 91.
[2] Beaulieu, v. 405.

particular energy. Men of talent had always been abhorrent to him—hence his inveterate animosity towards the Girondins. Unable himself to rise out of the crowd of little lawyers amongst whom he had made his début in Paris, he could not forgive success achieved by eloquence or literary ability.[1] To the Incorruptible wealth offered little or no temptation; but superiority of talent roused in him an envy that bordered on insanity, and it was mainly owing to his influence that a campaign against intellect, art, and education was now inaugurated. " All highly educated men were persecuted," said Fourcroy later to the Convention; " it was enough to have some knowledge, to be a man of letters, in order to be arrested as an aristocrat. . . . Robespierre . . . with atrocious skill, rent, calumniated . . . all those who had given themselves up to great studies, all those who possessed wide knowledge . . . he felt that no educated man would ever bend the knee to him." [2]

This war on education was even carried out against the treasures of science, art, and literature. Manuel proposed to demolish the Porte Saint-Denis; Chaumette wanted to kill all the rare animals in the Museum of Natural History; Hanriot proposed to burn the Bibliothèque Nationale, and his suggestion was repeated at Marseilles; the other decemvirs, taking up the cry, added, " Yes, we will burn all the libraries, for only the history of the Revolution and the laws will be needed." And although the great National Library of Paris survived, thousands of books and valuable pictures all over France were destroyed or sold for next to nothing.[3]

Not only education but politeness in all forms was to be destroyed. By a decree of the Commune on the 21st of August 1792 the titles of " Monsieur" and " Madame" had been formally abolished, and the words " Citoyen " or " Citoyenne " substituted, and in order to satisfy the exponents of equality it had now beome necessary to assume a rough and boorish manner, to present an uncultivated appearance. A refined countenance, hands that bore no marks of manual labour, well-brushed hair, clean and decent garments, were regarded with suspicion—to make sure of keeping one's head on one's shoulders it was

---

[1] " Writers must be proscribed as the most dangerous enemies of the people " (Note in Robespierre's handwriting, published in *Papiers trouves chez Robespierre*, ii. 13). See also Pagès, ii. 19, and *Letters of Helen Maria Williams* (1794), p. 115.

[2] *Moniteur* for the 14th Fructidor, An II. ; also *Rapport de Grégoire* on same date : " Dumas said all clever men should be guillotined. . . . *The system of persecution against men of talents was organized.* . . . They cried out in the sections, ' Beware of that man, for he has written a book ! ' "

[3] Taine, viii. 206 ; Mercier, *Le Nouveau Paris*, ii. 141 ; *Mémoire sur le Vandalisme*, by Grégoire.

advisable that it should be unkempt. Thus, says Beaulieu,
" those who had been born with a gentle exterior . . . were
obliged to distort their faces, to quicken their movements, so
as to look as if they formed a part of those ferocious bands that
had been loosed against them. Our dandies had allowed their
moustaches to grow long : they had ruffled their hair, soiled
their hands, and put on repulsive clothes. Our philosophers, our
men of letters, wore large bristling caps from which hung long
fox-tails that floated on their shoulders ; some dragged great
wheeled sabres along the pavement ; they were taken for
Tartars. Paris was no longer recognizable ; one would have
said that all the bandits of Europe had replaced its brilliant
population." [1]

In a word, it was now not merely war on nobility, on wealth,
on industry, on art, and on intellect ; it was *war on civilization*.
France was to return to a state of savagery. Insane as the
project may seem, we must recognize it nevertheless to be the
logical outcome of the desire for *absolute equality*. But unfortunately, when the equalizing process reached this stage, an
unexpected difficulty occurred. The aristocracy of birth had
long since been humbled to the dust ; the aristocracy of wealth
was reduced to beggary ; the aristocracy of intellect concealed
itself beneath a rude exterior ; yet, after all, aristocracy still
survived triumphantly, for lo ! it had taken refuge amongst *the
people*. " Nowhere," says Taine, " are there so many suspects
as amongst the people ; the shop, the farm, and the workshops
contain more aristocrats than the presbytery or the château.
In fact, according to the Jacobins, the cultivators are nearly all
aristocrats ; all the tradesmen are essentially counter-revolutionary . . . the butchers and bakers . . . are of an insufferable
aristocracy." [2] " The women of the market," writes a government spy, " except a few who are bribed, or whose husbands
are Jacobins, curse, swear, rave, and fume ; but they dare not
speak too loud, because they are all afraid of the revolutionary
committee and the guillotine." " This morning," said a shop-
keeper, " I had four or five of them here. They do not wish to
be called ' citizenesses ' any longer. They say they spit on the
Republic." [3] In the provinces matters were still worse ; not only
had reverence for religion and the King survived, but everywhere
respect for superiority and successful enterprise prevailed—the
good bourgeois whose business had prospered, the worthy mayor
renowned for his benevolence, the working-man who had " got
on in the world," all these in the eyes of country-folk seemed

---

[1] Beaulieu, v. 281. [2] Taine, viii. 180.
[3] *Rapport de Dutard à Garat* (Minister of the Interior), June 24, 1793,
Schmidt, ii. 87.

more deserving of esteem than the drunkard or the wastrel. How was perfect equality to be achieved if the people themselves persisted in raising one man above another ?

It is easy to imagine the despair that seized on the surgeons who had embarked on the great scheme of eliminating gangrene when they discovered its existence in this most vital point of the body. Yet, nothing daunted, they grasped their instruments and set to work once more ; if "the people" themselves were gangrened, then the people too must come under the knife— the blade of the guillotine must fall alike on the neck of noble, priest, or peasant.

So on the 5th of September the word went forth from the Commune of Paris : " Let us make Terror the order of the day ! " [1] In order to carry out this system it was necessary to reconstruct the government. Already the first Constitution framed on the cahiers had been swept away and replaced by the anarchic code known as the "Constitution de l'An II." without further reference to the desires of the people. But now the Anarchists had recourse to a still more arbitrary measure, and on the 10th of October the Convention, entirely dominated by the Mountain, acceded to the proposal of St. Just that a " provisional revolutionary government " should be proclaimed, in which every department of the State was to be placed under the control of the Comité de Salut Public. The members of this committee—which included Robespierre, Couthon, St. Just, Barère, Billaud-Varenne, Collot d'Herbois, Jean Bon St. André, Carnot, Prieur de la Marne, and Lindet—were thus to be made the absolute rulers of France ; to their authority the " executive power, the ministers, the generals, and the constituted bodies " were to be subjugated ; [2] and since it was by the Incorruptible that they themselves were controlled, the reign of Robespierre may be said to have begun from this moment.

The Terror in the provinces was thus entirely the work of the Comité de Salut Public. Emissaries were now sent out by the committee to the towns and provinces that had risen against the Mountain, with instructions to show no mercy to the " counter-revolutionaries." The better to ensure a rigorous application of the new régime these men were usually chosen to act in couples, " one to check the other "—in reality to goad each other on to violence. Thus when at Bordeaux, Tallien, under the influence of the beautiful Térésia Cabarrus, showed signs of relenting, Ysabeau performed the office of denunciator ; [3] at Lyon, Collot d'Herbois urged on Fouché ; at Toulon, Fréron incited Barras,

---

[1] Buchez et Roux, xxix. 43.   [2] Ibid. p. 172.
[3] Mémoires de Madame de la Tour du Pin, ii. 345.

and so each emissary, terrorized by his colleague, attempted to outdo him in ferocity.

The atrocities that took place all over France from October 1793 onwards require volumes to be realized in their full horror, and can only be briefly summarized here.

At Bordeaux, then, owing to the intervention of Térésia, only 301 people fell victims to the guillotine, which took "patriotic journeys" to that city; starvation and terror were, therefore, the means by which it was finally reduced to submission. But at Lyon the population was literally mowed down in hundreds; carts filled with women, old and young, plied daily to the scaffold. But the guillotine proved too slow a method of extermination, and the method of "fusillades" was then adopted; young citizens tied together in couples were driven to the "Brotteaux" and blown into fragments by rifle and cannon fire. The Rhône, that received at least 2000 corpses, ran so red with blood that Ronsin, the general of the revolutionary armies, informed the Cordeliers in Paris of its utility in conveying a message of warning to the counter-revolutionaries all over the South.[1]

The South, however, needed no warning. Toulon, crushed and starved by the régime of Fréron and Barras, had opened its gates in desperation to the English on the 29th of August— a "treachery" never to be forgiven it. Yet there were certainly extenuating circumstances. "It was necessary," wrote Isnard, who was then at Toulon, "to yield either to the Mountain or to Admiral Hood. The former brought us scaffolds, the latter promised to shatter them; the former gave us famine, the latter offered us provisions; Fréron brought us the Constitution of 1793, written by the executioner at the dictation of Robespierre, Hood promised to put us under the laws promulgated by the Constituent Assembly. A few intriguers profited by these circumstances to tempt the multitude led astray by hunger and despair; it had the weakness to prefer bread to death, the Constitution of 1791 to the anarchic code of 1793."

Toulon paid heavily for its frailty when, on the 17th of December, the town was recaptured by the army of the Republic. Fréron, mounted on a horse, "surrounded by cannons, troops, and a hundred maniacs, adorers of the god Marat," ordered citizens selected at random to be lined up against the walls and shot. "Fréron gives the signal, the charge rings out from every side, the murder is accomplished. The ground is drenched in blood, the air resounds with cries of despair, the dying roll

---

[1] Prudhomme, *Crimes*, vi. 49, 50. Cadillot, a correspondent of Robespierre, placed the number of executions at Lyon at 6000 (Taine, viii. 126).

back upon the corpses. Suddenly, by order of the tyrant, a voice cries, ' Let those who are not dead arise.' The wounded raise themselves in the hope that help will be brought to them, a fresh discharge is made, and steel gathers those that fire has spared."[1]

After this Fréron complacently announced that 800 Toulonnais had perished in the fusillade, whilst at the same time 200 heads fell by the guillotine. These methods, repeated until the spring of 1794, resulted, according to Prudhomme, in the death of no less than 14,325 men, women, and children; and whether this figure is excessive or not the fact remains that by the 9th of Thermidor the population of Toulon was reduced from 29,000 to 7000 inhabitants.[2]

All over Provence men were hunted down like wild beasts; the prophecy of the Scriptures seemed now to be fulfilled—" for those that were in the cities fled into the mountains, crying to the rocks to cover them, and hiding in dens and caves of the earth."

At Marseilles the death-roll was comparatively light; only about 240 victims had mounted the scaffold by January of 1794, and the Comité de Salut Public in Paris found it necessary to issue a reprimand to the Public Accuser of that city : " In Paris . . . the art of guillotining has attained perfection. Sanson and his pupils guillotine with so much rapidity . . . they expedited twelve in thirteen minutes. Send, then, the executioner of Marseilles to Paris in order to take a course of guillotining with his colleague Sanson, or we shall never get through. You must know that we shall never let you want for game for the guillotine ; and a great number must be despatched."[3]

In the small town of Orange, however, 318 victims were disposed of in a very short space of time, whilst in the north at Arras and Cambrai, under the reign of the apostate priest, Joseph Lebon, between 1500 and 2000 perished. In the province of Anjou alone the number of people killed without a trial has been estimated at 10,000.[4]

La Vendée as the stronghold of Royalism, when finally vanquished in October, could not of course hope for mercy, and the plan of the Convention, " to transform this country into a desert,"[5] was adopted. " We are able to say to-day,"

---

[1] Description given by Isnard, who was amongst the wounded. Beaulieu, v. 449 ; Prudhomme, *Crimes de la Révolution*, vi. 157.

[2] Madelin, p. 335.

[3] Prudhomme, *Crimes*, vi. 128.

[4] Taine, viii. 131.

[5] Letter of the emissary Francastel to General Grignon (Taine, viii. 131).

wrote the Republican envoys, "that La Vendée no longer exists. A profound silence reigns at present in the land occupied by the rebels. One could travel far in these parts without encountering a man or a cottage, for we have left nothing behind us but ashes and piles of corpses." [1]

But of all the towns of France it was at Nantes in Brittany that the worst atrocities were committed, in spite of the fact that here the *bourgeoisie* had welcomed the Revolution with the greatest enthusiasm, " and, indeed, had actually taken up arms against La Vendée." [2] Unhappily, in the organizer of the campaign against Nantes the Comité de Salut Public had found a man after its own heart. Like " his divinity Marat," Jean Baptiste Carrier embodied in his person the whole principle of the Terror ; like Marat, physically abnormal with his lean misshapen figure, his long cadaverous face and bloodshot eyes, Carrier exhibited perpetually the same convulsive fury that had characterized the People's Friend—indeed it is probable that he too was the victim of homicidal mania. Carrier thought, spoke, dreamt incessantly of killing ; " I have seen him," a contemporary declared, " cutting candles in two with his sabre as if they were the heads of aristocrats." Even his colleagues trembled to approach him for fear of his " sudden angers, his bellowings like those of a famished wild beast."

In order to carry out the vengeance of this maniac upon the unfortunate city, three companies of bandits, selected for their ferocity, had been recruited. The first of these, which Carrier had named after his idol, " the company of Marat," consisted of sixty members who had sworn on enrolment to carry out the doctrines of the People's Friend ; the second, known as the " American Hussars," was composed of negroes and mulattos ; the third, which was called the " Germanic Legion," had been formed with German mercenaries and deserters. Thus, as Taine observes, " it was necessary, in order to find men for the work, to descend not only to the lowest ruffians of France, but to brutes of foreign race and speech. . . ." [3]

The services of the two last companies were utilized principally for brutality towards women and children ; an eye-witness related that on one occasion he saw the corpses of no less than seventy-five girls aged from 16 to 18 who had been shot down by the German legion. Carrier entertained a peculiar hatred for children — " they are whelps," he said, " they must be destroyed," and he gave orders that they should be butchered

[1] Mortimer Ternaux, viii. 196.
[2] *J. B. Carrier*, by Alfred Lallié, p. 57.
[3] Taine, viii. 110 ; Beaulieu, vi. 92, 93 ; *Les Noyades de Nantes*, by G. Lenôtre.

without mercy. The details of these massacres far surpass in horror anything that took place in Paris during the height of the Terror ; there young children at least were spared, but at Nantes they perished miserably in hundreds. The annals of savagery can show nothing more revolting—poor little peasant boys and girls thrust beneath the blade of the guillotine, mutilated because they were too small to fit the fatal plank ; 500 driven all at once into a field outside the city and shot down, clubbed and sabred by the assassins round whose knees they clung, weeping and crying out for mercy.[1]

Finally the executioner grew weary of the slaughter and declared he could go on no longer ; even the fusillades proved too slow a method of extermination, and it was then that Carrier embarked on the scheme which for all time has rendered his name infamous—the *noyades*, or wholesale drownings in the Loire.

The first experiment was made on about ninety old priests, who were placed on board a galliot in charge of several Marats—as the members of the Marat company were known— and when in mid-stream those men, obedient to orders, burst open the ports and sank the barge to the bottom of the river. This delighted Carrier—" I have never laughed so much," he declared, " as when I saw the faces those —— made as they died." [2] The incident, when reported to the Convention, met with no remonstrance ; Hérault de Séchelles, in fact, wrote to Carrier congratulating him on " his energy and talent in the art of revolution," [3] whilst Robespierre, we know, heartily approved.[4] Carrier, thus encouraged, set to work on a larger scale. The cargo-load of gangrene in the form of clergy had proved but the prelude ; now " the people " were to provide the victims. So through those bitter December nights crowds of poor women, armed with the little bundles of possessions that peasants in flight are wont to carry with them, some clasping babies to their breasts, some leading little children by the hand, were driven out into the cold and darkness, they knew not whither ; only when they found themselves on the bank of the river where the great barges waited the hideous truth dawned on them. Then all at once they burst into tears and lamentations, crying out, " They are going to drown us, and they will not bring us to trial ! " Many holding their babies

[1] Prudhomme, *Crimes de la Révolution*, vi. 314.

[2] *Ibid.* p. 323 ; *Procès de Carrier*, Buchez et Roux, xxxiv. 184.

[3] Beaulieu, vi. 98.

[4] See Lallié, *op. cit.* p. 230 ; also statement of Laignelot to the Convention that he informed Robespierre of the horrors taking place at Nantes, to which Robespierre replied : " Carrier is a patriot ; this was necessary at Nantes " (*Moniteur* du 3 Frimaire, An III. vol. xxii. 580).

closer refused to give them up to strangers, and bore them with them in their arms down beneath the dark waters of the Loire. These perhaps were wisest, for many of those poor children, whom stronger-minded mothers had placed in sympathetic arms held out to them, were seized by Carrier's agents and herded into the ghastly Entrepôt, or prison of the city, to die of cold and pestilence.

The noyades, which Carrier playfully described as " bathing-parties," offered a fresh field to his inventive genius, and by way of variety he now devised the plan of stripping men and women to the skin, tying them together in couples and throwing them thus bound into the Loire. Carrier called this " Republican marriages." [1]

Such was the Reign of Terror at Nantes, during which the number of victims that perished by drowning was estimated by one member of Carrier's committee at 6000, by another at 9000, whilst Prudhomme estimates the number of people killed by drownings, fusillades, the guillotine and pestilence, at the appalling figure of 32,000.

What must have been the death-roll for all France during the Terror ? Prudhomme places it at no less than 1,025,711 (including losses through civil war), Taine at nearly half a million in the eleven provinces of the West alone. But on this point it is impossible to speak with any certainty. We only know that the massacres were wholesale and, what is more important, *indiscriminate*. For not only were the victims of the fusillades and noyades almost exclusively taken from amongst the people —" creatures of no account," said Goullin, one of Carrier's *aides*—but no attempt was made to discover their political opinions. Some were Royalists, others Republicans ; the greater number probably held no views on politics at all, but lived like simple country folk, without a thought beyond their daily needs. The necessity for destroying gangrene cannot, therefore, have applied to them, and we must seek a further development in the scheme of the revolutionary leaders to explain this amazing paradox—*the massacring of the people in the name of democracy.*

THE SYSTEM OF THE TERROR

What, then, was the system that produced this later stage of the Terror ? Historians, weary of striving to solve the problem, have declared that there was none, that the Terror happened

---

[1] Prudhomme, *Crimes de la Révolution*, vi. 335 ; Beaulieu, vi. 100 ; Buchez et Roux, xxxiv. 149. And Kropotkin, that arch-calumniator of the people, dares to attribute the noyades of Nantes to the Breton peasants ! See *The Great French Revolution*, p. 458.

inevitably, or that the Terrorists were mad, or that they killed for fear of being killed, or that, as Thiers expressed it, they went on killing because of " the deplorable habit they had contracted." Such answers, however, are all unconvincing in view of the evident organization of the Terror and the character of the men by whom it was carried out. The members of the Trium-virate—Robespierre, Couthon, and St. Just—which had now become all-powerful, were men not of impulse but of cold calcula-tion, and it is impossible to believe that they struck out aim-lessly with no ultimate object in view. What, then, was the motive that inspired them ? Certain contemporaries, recog-nizing the indisputable fact that the movement had now turned not only against the people, but against many of the most ardent Republicans and the earlier champions of liberty, advanced the extraordinary theory that Robespierre was a Royalist agent employed by the emigrant princes to carry out their vengeances ; [1] and indeed, if the Old Régime had entertained a desire for revenge, it could not have satisfied it more effectually than by the reign of Robespierre. But that Robespierre, with his insatiable craving for power, should have wished to reinstate the Bourbons is impossible to believe. Still more absurd was the once accepted theory that the Terror was organized as a desperate measure of defence against " the coalition of kings," or in order to stimulate the ardour of the Republican armies.[2] What possible connection could there be between the massacring of peasant women in the extreme west of France and the success of French arms in Germany or Flanders ? What ardour was likely to be stimulated in the soldiers of the Republic when they returned from the field of battle to find their mothers, wives, and children murdered, their homes burnt to the ground ? Moreover, when the Terror broke out, the situation of the armies was in no way desperate ; on the contrary, at the very moment that " terror was made the order of the day "—that is to say, on the 4th of September 1793 — Robespierre at the Jacobin Club announced military successes everywhere : " the armies of the North . . . of the Rhine and the Moselle are in a brilliant situation." [3] The Terror, then, had nothing whatever to do with the question of national defence, but in its later as in its earlier stages was a measure of internal policy.

Now, although we may consult historians in vain for an explanation of this policy, we have only to study the writings of contemporaries who were behind the scenes in the Terror

[1] *Deux Amis*, xii. 411 ; *J. B. Carrier*, by A. Lallié, p. 379.

[2] Professor Moreton Macdonald has admirably refuted this legend in *The Cambridge Modern History*, viii. 372.

[3] Buchez et Roux, xxix. 25.

to discover a theory which, whether we accept it or not, provides the only clue to the mystery. According to these authorities a very definite system was at work in the Comité de Salut Public, which organized the Terror ; moreover, this system was the direct outcome of the political creed of its leading members. In order to understand this we must refer back to the theories of government propounded by the organizers of the Terror during the earlier stages of the Revolution. Amongst these we find the constantly recurring belief in the impossibility of transforming France into a Republic. Thus as late as 1790 Marat had written :

" In a large State the form of government must be monarchic, it is the only one that is suited to France ; the extent of the kingdom, its position and the multiplicity of its connections necessitate it, and we ought to keep to this for many powerful reasons, even if the character of its people admitted of any other choice." [1]

There is undoubtedly a good deal to be said for this theory. Whether the old aphorism was right or not in stating that " no democracy can hold an empire," it must be admitted that the history of the world so far has proved that democracy works most harmoniously on a small scale—as in Marat's native Switzerland —or in the thinly populated spaces of a colony. For since the essence of democracy is rule by the will of the Sovereign People, that will must be, as far as possible, unanimous ; the Sovereign must not be divided against itself if the system is not to lose its entire *raison d'être*. And obviously, the larger and more varied the population the more difficult it becomes to obtain unanimity.

This conviction of the impossibility of establishing a democratic form of government in so large and thickly populated a country as France seems to have prevailed amongst the revolutionary leaders of all parties ; hence, no doubt, Robespierre's earlier belief in monarchy and his later desire for a dictatorship.[2] As to the Girondins, although no definite evidence is forthcoming in support of Robespierre's accusation that they wished to establish a federal Republic, they undoubtedly realized the almost insuperable difficulty of achieving a harmonious democracy on so large a scale by means of centralized government. Thus Buzot himself wrote : " If there were a people of gods, says Rousseau, it would govern itself democratically. . . . As it is, men, who are not gods, must seek elsewhere the best

[1] *Plan de Constitution*, p. 17.

[2] See also Danton's remark to the Duc de Chartres, on October 1792, after the foundation of the Republic : " This country is not made for a Republic ; one day it will cry ' Vive le Roi ! ' " (M. de Barante, *Histoire de la Convention Nationale*, ii. 477).

form of government to suit them." And he went on to ask how, in a nation of 25,000,000, it would be possible to make sure that the wishes expressed by suffrage represented the real will of the nation

But with the proclamation of the Republic the situation of which Marat had foreseen the danger had been brought about, and the whole country was thrown into confusion ; differences of opinion sprang up on every side, and civil war was the inevitable result.

More than this, not only had France become a Republic, but, as we have seen, the further plan was evolved by Robespierre of transforming her into a Socialist State throughout which absolute equality and universal contentment should prevail.[1]

Under the influence of St. Just this plan had assumed definite proportions. The colony of workmen's dwellings, which might be said figuratively to represent Robespierre's conception of an ideal State, was *literally* adopted by St. Just in the "Institutions" he drew up for the government of France. The new Republic was to be founded on "virtue, if not on terror " ;[2] that is to say, when terror became no longer necessary, "virtue " was to be made the order of the day. Every one was to be sober, austere, incorruptible, laborious, and, above all, public-spirited ; for, according to the doctrine of the Illuminati, to whom Robespierre belonged, the only way to make men happy was to produce in them a "just and steady morality"—morality, that is to say, as interpreted by the Illuminati, which was simply civism.[3]

Now in the opinion of St. Just nothing tended so much both to happiness and morality as the profession of agriculture —" a cottage, a field, and a plough " [4]—these were to represent the summit of every man's ambitions. Accordingly France was to be turned into a vast agrarian settlement, in which there were

[1] The following explanation of the plan of Robespierre and St. Just is written on the hypothesis that these men were sincere—a point which is by no means proved. It is perfectly possible that, as M. Aulard suggests, Robespierre only professed Socialist doctrines as a matter of policy—in order to bring himself into power. Nor must we forget the letter found amongst his papers at his death addressed to him by a friend who urges him to join him at the place where he has " formed a sufficient treasure to be able to exist for a long time," and ending with the words : " I shall await you with great impatience so as to laugh with you over the rôle you have played in the troubles of a nation as credulous as it is eager for novelty " (*Papiers trouvés chez Robespierre*, ii. 157). Whether Robespierre was a consummate hypocrite or an honest fanatic is, therefore, an open question—for the purpose of this book I have assumed the latter.

[2] Dauban, *Paris en 1794*, p. 463.

[3] Robison's *Proofs of a Conspiracy*, p. 205.

[4] " Une charrue, un champ, une chaumière . . . voilà le bonheur " (*Rapport de St. Just sur les Factions de l'Étranger*).

to be no rich and no poor, no large properties and no cramped dwellings ; nothing but endless model cottages and small allotments tended by hard-working and virtuous cultivators. An admirable arrangement, no doubt, only unfortunately, in order to ensure its success, there was to be no personal liberty either. It is doubtful, indeed, whether liberty and equality can exist together, for whilst liberty consists in allowing every man to live as he likes best, and to do as he will with his own, equality necessitates a perpetual system of repression in order to maintain things at the same dead level. For this purpose, according to St. Just, every department of life must be placed under State control—perhaps the most inexorable form of tyranny it is possible to conceive. For to an individual autocrat some appeal may be made, but against the doors of a system one may batter in vain. Thus in St. Just's Republic every human relationship was to be regulated by the State. True, free love was to take the place of marriage, but the union thus contracted was to be dissolved at the end of seven years if no children were forthcoming, whether the contracting parties desired to separate or not. Parents were to be forbidden either to strike or to caress their children, and the children were to be dressed all alike in cotton, to live on " roots, vegetables, fruit, with bread and water," and to sleep on mats upon the floor. Boys were to belong to their parents only till the age of five ; after that they were to become the property of the State until their death. Every one was to be forced by law to form friendships, and " to declare publicly once a year in the Temple who were his friends." Any infraction of these laws was to be punished by banishment. Thus—

He who strikes a child is banished.
If a man commits a crime his friends are banished.
He who says he does not believe in friendship or who has no
    friends is banished.
He who being drunk shall have said or done evil is banished.
A man convicted of ingratitude is banished ; etc.[1]

It was an attempt to realize the ideal of Rousseau—" If there were a people of gods it would govern itself democratically." The French, so far, were not gods, but they were to be made so.

But could a nation of 25,000,000 be thus transformed ? To the regenerators of France it seemed extremely doubtful ; already the country was rent with dissensions, and any scheme

---

[1] " Institutions " of St. Just, Buchez et Roux, xxxv. 275 ; Dauban, *Paris en 1794*, p. 461.

for universal contentment seemed impossible of attainment. Moreover, the plan of dividing things up into equal shares presented an insuperable difficulty, for it became evident that amongst a population of this size there was not enough money, not enough property, not enough employment, not even at this moment enough bread to go round ; no one would be satisfied with his share, and instead of universal contentment, universal dissatisfaction would result. What was to be done ? The population was too large for the scheme of the leaders to be carried out successfully, therefore either the scheme must be abandoned or *the population must be diminished*.

To this conclusion the surgeons operating on the State had at last been brought. In vain they had amputated the gangrened limb of the nobility and the clergy, had paralysed the brain by attacking the intellectual classes, had turned (as in Æsop's fable) upon the stomach, that is to say, the industrial system, by which the whole body of the State was fed, and denied it sustenance—all these means to restore health to the State had failed, and they were now reduced to a last and desperate expedient : the size of the whole body must be reduced. In other words, *a plan of systematic depopulation* must be carried out all over France.

That this idea, worthy of a mad Procrustes, really existed it is impossible to doubt, since it has been revealed to us by innumerable revolutionaries who were behind the scenes during the Terror. Thus Courtois, in his report on the papers seized at Robespierre's house after Thermidor, wrote : " These men, in order to bring us to the happiness of Sparta, wished *to annihilate twelve or fifteen millions of the French people,* and hoped after this revolutionary transfiguration to distribute to each one a plough and some land to clear, so as to save us from the dangers of the happiness of Persepolis."

Another *intime* of Robespierre, the Marquis d'Antonelle, a member of the Revolutionary Tribunal, actually explained the whole scheme in print whilst the Terror was at its height. Beaulieu, who met him in prison, where he was incarcerated by Robespierre for giving away the secret of the leaders, thus describes the system as revealed to him by D'Antonelle : " He thought, like the greater number of the revolutionary clubs, that, in order to institute the Republic on the ruins of the monarchy, it was necessary to exterminate all those who preferred the latter form of government, and that the former could only become democratic by the destruction of luxury and riches, which form the support of royalty ; that equality would never be anything but a chimera as long as men did not all enjoy approximately equal properties ; and finally, that such an order of things could never be established until *a third of the population had been suppressed ;* this was the general idea of the fanatics of the Revolution." [1]

About two years later, that is to say in 1795, the Socialist, Gracchus Babeuf, employed at the Commune, gave a more detailed account of the scheme in his brochure, "Sur le Système de la Dépopulation, ou La Vie et les Crimes de Carrier." Of this system Babeuf declares that Robespierre was the principal author : " Maximilien and his council had calculated. that a real regeneration of France could only be operated by means of a new distribution of territory and of the men who occupied it " ; and he goes on to show the remorseless logic by which Robespierre reached his final conclusion : " He thought that, firstly, in the present state of things property had fallen into a few hands, and that the great majority of the French possessed nothing ; secondly, that in allowing this state of things to continue, equality of rights would only be a vain word in spite of which the aristocracy of owners of property would always be real, the smaller number would always tyrannize over the great mass, the majority would always be the slave of the minority . . . ; thirdly, that in order to destroy this power of the owners of property, and to take the mass of citizens out of their dependence, there was no way but to place all property in the hands of the government ; fourthly, that one could succeed without doubt only by immolating the great proprietors . . . ; fifthly, that, besides this, *depopulation was indispensable,* because the calculation had been made that the French population was in excess of the resources of the soil and of the requirements of useful industry, that is to say, that, with us, men jostled each other too much for each to be able to live at ease ; that hands were too numerous for the execution of all works of essential utility . . . ; sixthly, finally—and this is the horrible conclusion—that since the superabundant population could only amount to so much . . . a portion of *sans-culottes* must be sacrificed, that this rubbish could be cleared away up to a certain quantity, and that means must be found for doing it."

To this necessity Babeuf attributes not only the guillotinades, fusillades, and noyades in the provinces, but also the engineered famine to which he had drawn attention earlier, whilst the war, far from providing a reason for the Terror, was in reality part of the scheme of extermination. " What," he asks, " is this plan of eternal crusades, of repulsing peace, of universal conquest, of the conversion or subjugation of all kings and all peoples, if it is not the hidden intention to prevent any one coming back from amongst that important portion of the nation that armed itself so generously in order to chase the enemy from French territory ? "

The evidence of Babeuf is the more valuable since he declares himself to be heartily in agreement with the Socialistic schemes of Robespierre ; it is only the means employed to realize them that he disapproves. " On the subject of extermination," he naïvely concludes, " I am a man of prejudices ; it is not given to every one to rise to the heights of Maximilien Robespierre." But later on he came to see that Robespierre's plan alone could ensure success, and that if absolute equality was to be achieved the Terror must be revived. It was for the attempt to reinstate the régime of Robespierre that Babeuf finally met his end. However preposterous the *exposé* of Babeuf may seem, we must admit that it is the only one that explains the Terror. Moreover, that this was indeed the system on which it was founded does not rest on the authority of Courtois, Babeuf, and D'Antonelle alone, the very words " plan of depopulation " occur repeatedly in the writings and speeches of other contemporaries. Thus Prudhomme, in describing the massacres of September, explains the enormous proportion of " the people " amongst the victims as the first evidence of this scheme : " The plan of butchery did not end with the destruction of priests and nobles . . . but from that date there existed a *plan of depopulation* conceived by Marat, Robespierre . . ., etc., and this is what the method of the Terror has proved." [1]

Later on, at the trials of Fouquier Tinville and Carrier, several witnesses referred to the same scheme : Grandpré of the police declared that the most powerful means employed by Robespierre was " a vast system of depopulation " ; [2] Ardenne, Deputy Public Accuser, said the plan was " to clear out the prisons in order to *depopulate France*," [3] and in his summing up to the president and judges of the Revolutionary Tribunal stated that " Robespierre, St. Just, Couthon, and others, had expected *to depopulate France*, and above all to make genius, talents, honour, and industry to disappear " ; [4] Trinchard, member of the Revolutionary Tribunal, ended his evidence with the words : " Such was the *system of depopulation* organized by the last tyrants, and in order to make sure of its execution they employed the most immoral men " ; [5] indeed, Carrier himself admitted that " *this plan of destruction existed.*" [6] Carrier,

---

[1] Prudhomme, *Crimes de la Révolution*, iv. 112.
[2] *Procès de Fouquier Tinville*, Buchez et Roux, xxxv. 45.
[3] *Ibid.* p. 44.   [4] *Ibid.* xxxiv. 271.   [5] *Ibid.* p. 337.
[6] *Procès de Carrier, ibid.* p. 208. For other contemporary references to " the plan of depopulation " see Pagès, ii. 89 ; *Deux Amis*, xii. 238 ; *Mémoires de Senart*, edition de Lescure, p. 84 : " this great system of

Fouquier, Fréron, Lebon, and the other monsters were therefore only acting on orders from headquarters when they set out to decimate Paris and the provinces, and the terrible phrase of Carrier, " Let us make a cemetery of France rather than not regenerate her after our manner,"[1] simply epitomized the philosophy of Robespierre on which the system of the Comité de Salut Public was founded.

It was in the hall of the committee at the Tuileries that the great scheme of depopulation was discussed, and orders were issued to the revolutionary agents in the different provinces. Prudhomme has vividly described the scenes that took place nightly in the gorgeous salon at the end of a long dark corridor, where, amidst mirrors and bronzes, beneath gilded ceilings and glittering chandeliers, the " Decemvirs " took their ease on soft armchairs and luxurious sofas, whilst in the background sideboards laden with rare wines and delicate fare awaited them.[2] Around the great oval table, covered with a green cloth, the members of the committee—Billaud, Collot, Couthon, Barère—gathered merrily, " not precisely drunk, but spurred on by wine and good cheer, heated by liqueurs " ; only when the bilious face of the Incorruptible appeared amongst them a chill fell over the party, and there was less laughter whilst districts were marked out for destruction and human heads were counted up like scores at cards.

" It was at these times," says Prudhomme, " that they gave their secret orders to the chief scoundrels in their confidence. It was there that General Rossignol went to receive the plan for setting La Vendée in a blaze. It was there that Carrier organized the noyades of Nantes. It is there that Couthon said, laughing, before he started for Lyon, ' I have only a head and a body ; well, nevertheless, it is I who will give the first blow of the hammer to the second town in the empire of France, in order to destroy it.' It is there that they organized the conspiracies in the prisons, and that they drew up *that plan of depopulation* carried out during fifteen months. A map of France was spread out continually before the eyes of the Decemvirs as well as a table of the population of each Commune ; there they decimated towns and villages—' we must have so many heads in such and such a department.' . . . All the calamities of France, all the

---

devastation and of depopulation " (the *Résumé du Procès de Fouquier Tinville*, by Cambon de Gard) ; " the fearful system of depopulation de vised by the faction of Robespierre " (*Le Tribunal Révolutionnaire*, by E. Campardon, ii. 297) ; also Paganel, *Essai Historique*, ii. 350, 359, 381.

[1] Evidence of Lamarie, *Procès de Carrier*, Buchez et Roux, p. 204.

[2] Description confirmed by the contemporary Philippe Morice in his " Souvenirs," *Revue des Questions historiques*, for October 1892.

crimes of the Revolution, originated in the salon of the Comité de Salut Public." [1]

The precise proportion of the population it would be necessary to suppress formed the subject of calm mathematical calculation amongst the leaders. According to Larevellière Lépeaux, it was Jean Bon St. André who first openly admitted the existence of the scheme, and at the time that the Revolutionary Tribunal was instituted—that is to say, in the spring of 1793—declared in the tribune of the Convention that " in order to establish the Republic securely in France, the population must be reduced by more than half." [2] Beside this estimate D'Antonelle's proposal to reduce by one-third only seems comparatively moderate.

Other leading revolutionaries considered, however, that far more drastic measures were necessary; thus Collot d'Herbois held that twelve to fifteen millions of the French must be destroyed, [3] Carrier declared that the nation must be reduced to six millions, [4] Guffroy in his journal expressed the opinion that only five million people should be allowed to survive, [5] whilst Robespierre was reported to have said that a population of two millions would be more than enough. [6] Pagès and Fantin Désodoards assert, however, that eight millions was the figure generally agreed on by the leaders. [7]

The plan of the Terrorists was not, therefore, as is popularly supposed, to sacrifice a small minority for the happiness of the great majority, but to annihilate an immense proportion of the nation in order to ensure a contented residuum.

Such, then, was the system of the Terror, and however atrocious it may appear we must admit that it was founded on a perfectly logical premise—the conviction that the smaller the population the better for democracy.

It is not, therefore, the theory of the Terrorists that must be regarded as monstrous, but its application. For to admit that a certain end may be desirable of attainment is one thing ; to believe that any means are justifiable in order to attain it is quite another matter. The great criminals of history were not the people inspired by the worst motives, but the people for

---

[1] Prudhomme, *Crimes de la Révolution*, v. 111.

[2] *Mémoires de Larevellière Lépeaux*, i. 150.

[3] *Résumé du Procès de Fouquier Tinville*, by Cambon de Gard, Substitut de l'Accusateur Public, in *Le Tribunal révolutionnaire*, by E. Campardon, ii. 297.

[4] Mercier, *Le Nouveau Paris*, ii. 9.

[5] *Le Rougyff*, No. 8. (" Rougyff " is an anagram of Guffroy.)

[6] Letter to Robespierre from one who had been his friend : " What ? reduce France to two million men, and ' that is still too many,' you said ! " (*Papiers trouvés chez Robespierre*, ii. 153).

[7] Pagès, ii. 89 ; Fantin Desodoards, iv. 131.

whom this distinction did not exist. Catherine de Medici—to whom Robespierre bore a striking resemblance—undoubtedly thought it would be for the peace of France if the Huguenots ceased to exist, and therefore planned the Massacre of St. Barthélemy; Robespierre may have been actuated by precisely the same laudable intention in organizing the massacres of the Terror. In both cases the attitude of mind that made this action possible can be traced to the same cause—the doctrine that has produced all the worst atrocities in the history of the civilized world—namely, that " the end justifies the means." Whether it be under a Torquemada, a Medici, a Robespierre, or a Wilhelm II., the community or nation which accepts the belief that everything is justifiable—lying, duplicity, treachery, and murder—in order to benefit the cause it has embraced, sells its soul to the devil. To hold this doctrine is not only to repudiate Christianity, but to strike at the very root of all morality. It was therefore natural that the Terror, founded on this literally diabolical doctrine, should now enter on that hideous phase in its work of destruction—the desecration of the churches.

THE DECHRISTIANIZATION OF FRANCE

The leaders of the movement that was now directed against religion all over France belonged to a faction of the Cordeliers Club, led by Hébert. Hébert himself, who figured on the cover of his journal, the *Père Duchesne,* as a rugged stove-merchant with a large pipe in his mouth and a heavy moustache, was in reality a dapper young man, clean shaven, well powdered, and sybaritic in his tastes. The coarse language and oaths of the gutter that characterized his literary compositions were as foreign to his nature as the revolutionary frenzy he affected; for, although it was on Hébert that the mantle of Marat had descended when the *Ami du Peuple* ceased at the death of its author, Hébert had none of Marat's sombre ferocity. On the contrary, Hébert was filled with a riotous *joie de vivre.* During the " great angers " he depicted in the *Père Duchesne* he was enjoying " the sweetest and most peaceful of lives "; [1] his sanguinary tirades against the Queen, the Girondins, " la Reine Roland," were penned beside the cradle of his infant daughter. Hébert was an Anarchist by temperament rather than by policy; the prototype of the modern Apache, he would gaily have set Paris in a blaze for the excitement of seeing it burning. Revolutions inevitably bring these sort of characters to the surface—creatures endowed with the passion for destruction

---

[1] *Le Père Duchesne,* by Paul d'Estrée, p. 69 : " Je mène la vie la plus douce et la plus paisible " (Letter from Hébert written in 1792).

that human nature shares in common with the ape, who love to burn and spoil and desecrate without any ulterior motive. It was for this reason that Hébert ended by incurring the animosity of Robespierre. The Tiger Cat only desired a period of anarchy in order to establish his own domination, and naturally any one who, like Hébert, enjoyed anarchy for anarchy's sake could not be allowed to go on indefinitely wrecking everything ; the time must come when it would be necessary to suppress him. Already the green eyes were watching him suspiciously, and it was therefore not Robespierre who in the Comité de Salut Public supported the anti-religious movement of the Hébertistes, but the contemptible comedian Collot d'Herbois. Amongst the followers of Hébert were first and foremost Chaumette, once a cabin-boy, now procurator of the Commune and king of the Paris rabble ; Vincent, secretary to the Ministry of War, a creature of such extraordinary ferocity that in his fits of rage he was known to devour raw the flesh of animals ; Momoro, a printer ; Anacharsis Clootz, of whom more anon ; and Ronsin, a general in the Republican army who excelled in the raising of disorderly crowds. Ronsin's following inspired even its leader with disgust ; when some one complained to him of the excesses it committed in the streets and at the theatres, the outrages on women, the robberies and violence that marked its passage, Ronsin answered cynically, " What do you want me to do ? I know, like you, that it is a collection of brigands, but I have need of these rascals for my revolutionary army—find me decent folk who are willing to do the job ! " [1]

According to Prudhomme the Hébertistes were formerly Orléanistes ; at any rate their private life was far from consistent with the principles of Republicanism and equality that they professed. Whilst proclaiming the necessity of Spartan simplicity to counteract the famine they led a riotous Epicurean existence, and freely indulged their tastes for rare vintages and fiery liquors.[2] It was thus largely under the influence of drink that they now embarked on their scheme of dechristianization.

On the night of the 6th to the 7th of November, Hébert, Chaumette, and Momoro went to the " Constitutional " bishop of Paris, Gobel, and ordered him to abjure publicly the Catholic religion. " You will do this," they said to him, " or you are a dead man." [3] The wretched old man threw himself at their feet and begged to be spared this ordeal, but the Hébertistes were inexorable, and on the following day Gobel, terrorized into submission, presented himself at the Convention and declared that " the will of the Sovereign People " had now become " his

---

[1] Prudhomme, *Crimes de la Révolution*, v. 131.   [2] *Ibid.* v. 140.
[3] *Le Père Duchesne*, by Paul d'Estrée, p. 345 ; Beaulieu, v. 241.

THE REIGN OF TERROR

supreme law," and since the Sovereign so willed it there should be no other worship than that of " liberty and holy equality." Accordingly he now deposited his cross, ring, and other insignia upon the President's desk, and put on the red cap of liberty. Several of his vicars followed his example amidst the enthusiastic acclamations of the Assembly.

This grotesque scene gave the signal for the desecration of the churches throughout Paris and the provinces. At Notre Dame, stripped of its crucifixes and images of the saints, the Feast of Reason took place on the 10th of November. A temple was raised in the aisle on the summit of a mountain, from which shone forth the " light of truth," and amidst the strains of the " Marseillaise " and " Ça ira ! " the Goddess of Reason, personified by Mlle. Maillard, an opera-singer, dressed in a blue mantle and wearing the red cap of liberty, was borne in procession and solemnly enthroned to the cries of " Vive la République ! Vive la Montagne ! "

At the Church of St. Sulpice, during a ceremony of the same kind, Joachim Ceyrat, the director of the September massacre at the Convent des Carmes, ascended the pulpit and cried out, " Here am I in this pulpit, from which lies have so long been told to the sovereign people, making them believe that there is a God who sees all their actions. If this God exists, let Him thunder, and may one of His thunderbolts crush me ! " Then looking up to the heavens defiantly, he added, " He does not thunder, so His existence is a chimera ! " [1]

Another enthusiastic exponent of materialism was the famous Marquis de Sade, the moral maniac to whom we owe the adjective " Sadic." The atrocities this most vicious of all aristocrats had committed towards poor women of the people in no way precluded him from an honoured place in the ranks of " democracy." Sade was a follower of Marat and a member of the Section des Piques to which Robespierre belonged. An address from this section drawn up by Sade himself was now presented to the Convention, demanding that in all the churches the cult of the new divinities, Reason and Virtue, should be substituted for the worship of " the Jewish slave " and " the adulterous woman, the courtesan of Galilee." This petition was accorded " honourable mention " by the Convention, which ordered it to be sent to the Committee of Public Instruction.

But it was Clootz who played the leading part in the campaign against religion. Anacharsis Clootz, a Prussian baron, distinguished himself throughout the revolutionary movement by his plan of a " Universal Republic " and his hatred of Christianity. The apostle of " Internationalism " as developed

[1] *Journal des Lois*, du 14 Prairial, An III.

in the doctrines of the Illuminati, he said nearly everything that Internationalists propound to-day as the last word in modern thought. Briefly, all nations of the earth were to be welded into one as members of "the only nation" (*la nation unique*), which, by a play on the word *german*, that is to say, "closely allied," he suggested, with an ingenuity worthy of his race, should be known as "the immutable empire of Great Germany, the Universal Republic." [1] By way of illustration he had presented himself at the Legislative Assembly, under the title of "the orator of the human race," at the head of a strange procession composed of specimens from all available races—Germans, Swedes, Russians, Poles, Turks, and negroes—whom he had hired for the occasion, in dresses suited to the part, but, since he omitted to pay them as arranged, he found his own door next day beset by a furious crowd,[2] which seemed somewhat to disprove his theory that "the Republic of the human race will never have any dispute with any one since there can be no communication between the planets." [3]

In all this Clootz shows himself simply an amiable madman ; it is only on the subject of religion that he grows violent. The second title he had bestowed upon himself was that of "the personal enemy of Jesus Christ." Christianity filled him with an almost epileptic fury. "Religion," he wrote, "is a social disease which cannot be too quickly cured. A religious man is a depraved animal ; he resembles those beasts that are only kept to be shorn and roasted for the benefit of merchants and butchers." [4] "The People," he declared, "is the Sovereign and the God of the world ; France is the centre of the People-God ; only fools can believe in any other God, in a Supreme Being." [5]

It was in this strain that Clootz addressed the Convention on the 17th of November, and he ended his discourse by presenting the Assembly with a copy of a treatise he had written on the subject. The Convention thereupon passed a decree :

---

[1] Speech of Clootz to the Assembly, September 9, 1792 ; *Moniteur*, xiii. 660. See also *La République Universelle*, by Anacharsis Clootz.

[2] *Letters of Helen Maria Williams* (1795), p. 140.

[3] Speech of Anacharsis Clootz to the Convention, April 26, 1793.

[4] *La République Universelle*, p. 27.

[5] Clootz has obtained at least one panegyrist amongst posterity, and at the same time a convert to his theories of anti-patriotism. Thus at that most tragic date in the history of France—1871—a Frenchman could be found to write these words : " Clootz appears like the angel of the Revolution, the seal on the alliance between France and the nations. *The greatest figure of the French Revolution was a German.* Man of vast Utopias and limitless horizons, this apostle of universal fraternity was the first to pass over the Rhine with the olive-branch of peace" (*Les Hébertistes*, by G. Tridon).

"Anacharsis Clootz, deputy to the Convention, having paid homage with one of his works entitled *The Certainty of the Proofs of Mahomedanism*, a work that sets forth the nullity of all religions, the Assembly accepts this homage, accords it honourable mention, and orders it to be inserted in the bulletin, and to be sent to all the departments (of France)."

Everywhere in Paris and the provinces a perfect orgy of blasphemy and desecration now began; Bacchanalian feasts took place in the churches, triumphal cars carrying street-walkers dressed in chasubles, and donkeys laden with sacred relics, bénitiers, and church ornaments, passed through the streets ; crucifixes and breviaries were cast into bonfires amidst cries of " Perish for ever the memory of the priests ! Perish for ever Christian superstition ! Long live the sublime religion of Nature ! " [1]

But it was not by " the people " these revolting scenes were enacted ; the people everywhere bitterly resented them.[2] The closing of the village churches indeed caused so much indignation that the Convention began to fear revolt, whilst in Paris the women of the market overwhelmed the *Père Duchesne* with insults, and one of the hawkers of this journal complained to the " Society of the Friends of the Revolution " that he had been surrounded by these women, who covered him with mud, and seemed disposed to strangle him.[3] When by order of Chaumette the shrine of Sainte-Geneviève, the patron saint of Paris, was thrown into the flames on the Place de Grève, the outrage infuriated those whom the atheists described as the " ignorant and superstitious populace." [4]

The truth is, that the whole of the anti-Christian movement was the direct work of the Illuminati. Anacharsis Clootz, says Robison, " who was a keen Illuminatus, came to Paris for the express purpose of forwarding the great work, and, by in-triguing in the style of the Order, he got himself made one of the Representatives of the Nation. . . ." At the same time another German Illuminatus, Leuchtsenring, was also employed as secretary or clerk in one of the bureaux of the Assembly. The inscription put up by order of the Government in the cemeteries all over France, " Death is an eternal sleep," had always been the most cherished maxim of the Illuminati. There was nothing that the people abhorred more than this; to them the belief in immortality seemed the only consolation for the miseries of existence. " Yesterday," a government spy reported, " I talked for an hour with a Jacobin, a lemonade-seller, who begins

[1] *The Great French Revolution*, by Kropotkin, p. 523.
[2] Buchez et Roux, xxx. 42, 43. [3] *Ibid*. xxx. p. 182.
[4] *Ibid*. p. 142 ; Schmidt, ii. 63.

to feel the weight of years. He preached to me the doctrine of Christ . . . and explained . . . that it was very comforting for a man of a certain age to be able to see in the future another life awaiting him. The philosopher, he added, had other compensations, but for us poor folks . . . !"[1] All such hopes, all such beliefs, were now to be torn from the people; not content with destroying the body, the regenerators of France set out to destroy the soul.

THE TERROR IN PARIS

The campaign against Christianity heralded the Reign of Terror in the capital. In the same autumn of 1793 the series of executions began that was to continue without interruption, and in ever-increasing numbers, until the 9th of Thermidor. In order to carry out the great plan of depopulation the Revolutionary Tribunal had been reconstructed at the end of September and placed entirely under the control of the Comité de Salut Public and its subordinate, the Comité de Sûreté Générale, which dealt directly with the police of Paris.[2] Instead of twelve jurymen, sixty were now elected; amongst these figured three tailors, five carpenters, a seller of sabots, a bootmaker, etc.[3]—a fact that should be noted, since it marks the first appearance of men of the people in the Revolutionary Government. Hitherto it had been by aristocrats or middle-class men that the attacks on the aristocracy and *bourgeoisie* had been organized; now that the people were to become the victims, it was men of the people who were called in to carry out the work.

But the people were not the first to suffer. In Paris as in the provinces, as indeed in all revolutions, the task of demolition began at the top and descended by gradual stages to the lower strata of the population. At the head of the list of victims condemned by the Tribunal of Blood stands " the widow Capet." Her trial, which began on the 14th of October, does not, however, enter within the scope of this history ; Marie Antoinette, unlike Louis XVI., had played no part in the popular Revolution. Constantly depicted to the people as a " Messalina " or a " Medici," whilst to her the people were persistently represented by the revolutionaries as tigers thirsting for her blood, all understanding between them had become impossible, and so throughout the Revolution her attitude towards the people was merely passive.

Yet in reality the people did not hate her. During those last terrible weeks at the Conciergerie, poor women of the market

---

[1] Schmidt. ii. 10.   [2] Buchez et Roux, xxxiv. 467.
[3] *Le Tribunal Révolutionnaire*, by G. Lenôtre, p. 130.

came to the prison bringing her their finest peaches and melons, and recognizing her gaoler when he came to buy at their stalls, handed him their best fruits and poultry, saying with tears, " For our Queen ! " [1]

Others displayed still more energy on her behalf. Who at the last moment, asks M. Lenôtre, " were the Royalists who risked their lives to rescue the Queen ? A shoe-black, a pastry-cook, three hairdressers, a pork-butcher, several charwomen, two masons, an old-clothes seller, a lemonade-seller, a wine-merchant, a locksmith, and a tobacconist." Four of these heroic people—two men and two women—paid for their devotion with their heads.[2]

When at last Marie Antoinette appeared before the Revolutionary Tribunal, broken and white-haired, her eyes dimmed with long weeping, even the *tricoteuses* of Robespierre were stirred to pity, and it was for this reason that Hébert devised his infamous accusation concerning the little Dauphin. " A week after the Queen's trial," says Prudhomme, " I said to that monster Hébert, ' You must be a great scoundrel to have accused her of so horrible a crime ! ' He answered, ' Having noticed from the beginning of the trial that *the public seemed to take an interest in this woman,* and for fear she should escape us, I at once drew up my denunciation and passed it to the President, *in order to set the multitude against her !* ' " [3]

But Hébert and his kind had not succeeded in degrading the populace to their own level. The Queen's immortal protest produced so immense an effect on the women of the tribunes that for some moments the proceedings were interrupted.[4]

This *faux pas* of Hébert's infuriated Robespierre. The day after the Queen's trial, says Vilate, " Barère had ordered a dinner at Venua's to which he had invited Robespierre, St. Just, and me. . . . Seated around the table in a secret room well closed, they asked me for some features of the scene that took place at the trial of the Austrian. I did not forget that of outraged nature when, Hébert accusing Antoinette of obscenities with her son of eleven years old, she turned with dignity to the people : ' I appeal to all mothers present and to their consciences to declare whether there is one who does not shudder at such horrors ! ' Robespierre, struck by this answer as by an electric shock, broke his plate with his fork : ' That imbecile Hébert !

---

[1] *La Captivité et le Mort de Marie Antoinette,* by G. Lenôtre, pp. 244, 281.

[2] *Le Vrai Chevalier de Maison Rouge,* by G. Lenôtre, p. 97.

[3] Prudhomme, *Histoire des Révolutions,* vii. 203 (quoted by Granier de Cassagnac, *Causes de la Révolution,* ii. 56).

[4] *Le Tribunal Révolutionnaire,* by G. Lenôtre, p. 141.

As if it were not enough that she should be a Messalina, but he must make her out to be an Agrippina also, and provide her at her last moment with this triumph of public sympathy.' Every one appeared stupefied." [1]

Indeed, so thoroughly had popular feeling been aroused in the Queen's favour that Hébert found it necessary to warn his readers against the women who had planned to call out for mercy when she mounted the scaffold. But, as at the execution of the King, the revolutionary leaders were prepared for any attempts at rescue ; 30,000 armed men lined the streets, and cannons were placed all along the route between the Conciergerie and the Place de la Révolution. Beside the cart, drawn by one gaunt white horse, that bore the Queen to her death, rode Grammont, the miserable comedian employed by Philippe d'Orléans in the earlier outbreaks of the Revolution, he who had drunk the blood of the Swiss on the 10th of August at the Tuileries, and now with revolting brutality cried out to the people as the pitiable procession approached the scaffold, " Voici l'infâme Antoinette ! Elle est f. . . ., mes amis ! " Philippe had at last had his revenge. He was to follow the same road himself less than a month later.

On the whole the people showed themselves indifferent to the execution of the Queen, but they were not indifferent to the fate of the rest of the Royal Family—Louis XVII., his sister and his aunt, Madame Elizabeth, who remained in the Temple. It seems that Robespierre contemplated killing them all at this crisis, as the following significant passage in a letter addressed to him by one of his friends testifies. According to Robespierre's desires, says this naïve correspondent, his agents have " sounded the people on the subject " by means of circulating the rumour that both the little Capets had died. " But we had the grief to see our expectations disappointed in this direction. No one was taken in by our little ruse ; every one said, as if with one accord, ' Ah ! if those two children there are dead, they have been well helped (to die).' And all appeared—let us say the word—indignant. Leave there then, believe me, the little Capets and their aunt ; even policy demands it, for if you killed the boy the crowned brigands would instantly recognize as King of France ' le gros Monsieur de Ham ' (the Comte de Provence)." [2] It was thus really the people who stood between the poor children in the Temple and their murderers !

After the Queen followed the Girondins. On the last day of

---

[1] *Causes secrètes de la Révolution*, by Vilate.
[2] Letter from one who signs himself " Niveau," found amongst Robespierre's papers after his death (*Papiers trouvés chez Robespierre*, etc., i. 263).

October, Brissot, Vergniaud, Gensonné, Carra, Isnard, Ducos, and fourteen other members of the faction were brought before the Revolutionary Tribunal and charged with all the bygone intrigues enumerated by Camille Desmoulins in his *Histoire des Brissotins*. By way of emphasizing the accusation of Orléanism, old Sillery, the one-time boon companion of the Duc d'Orléans, was added to their number. Then to ensure their conviction, the same infamous device was adopted as in the case of the King, that of framing a law to fit the case, and on the fourth day of their trial the Convention passed the decree that when a trial had lasted three days the jury should be ordered to give their verdict without listening to further evidence. Thereupon the jury, obedient to the orders of the Comité de Salut Public, unanimously declared the accused to be worthy of death, and on the 31st of October the " Twenty-One " were executed in the Place de la Révolution.

The rest of the faction, with the exception of Louvet, perished later ; Condorcet took poison ; Guadet, Salles, and Barbaroux were guillotined in Bordeaux ; Buzot and Pétion, who attempted flight, were found dead, half devoured by dogs, in the fields of Médoc. A week later Madame Roland followed the men whom her thirst for vengeance on the Court had driven to their doom. To the end her hatred of the Queen knew no abating ; in her prison she heard of the terrible fate of that " proud woman who hated equality " without a stirring of compassion.[1] Manon's own conception of " equality " enabled her to confront the scaffold with composure. " Think," she wrote to Bosc, " how worthless is the *canaille* that feasts upon the spectacle ! "[2] Thus fortified by the consciousness of her own superiority, which in her case was almost a religion, she flung defiance at the Revolution, and from the platform of the guillotine her last words, addressed to the new statue of Liberty before her, were clearly heard by the wondering multitude : " O Liberty, how they have fooled you ! (*O Liberté, comme on t'a jouée !*) "[3] She forgot that she herself had played no small part in the fooling.

Poor old Roland, away at Rouen, hearing of the death of the wife who had long since ceased to love him, went out into a wood and stabbed himself, thereby proving that he was human after all, but, Girondin to the last, he did not forget to leave upon his body a note explaining that these were the remains of a man who had died as he had lived, " virtuous and upright."

[1] *Mémoires de Madame Roland*, ii. 389.   [2] *Ibid.* p. 411.
[3] *Letters of Helen Maria Williams* (1795), p. 102 ; Dauban, *La Demagogie à Paris en 1793*, p. 37.

So ended the famous Gironde. Within a month the Queen and her two bitterest enemies all met with the same fate on the same spot; for two days before the execution of Madame Roland, Philippe Égalité had paid the penalty for his crimes. All the way from the Conciergerie to the Place de la Révolution the wretched prince was overwhelmed with insults by the populace of whom he had been represented as the idol: " Scoundrel, it is you who are the cause of all our ills ! " " It was you who had the Princesse de Lamballe assassinated ! " " Wretch, you wished to be King, but Heaven is just, your throne will be a scaffold ! " Above all, it was as the murderer of Louis XVI. the crowd now taunted him : " You voted for the death of your kinsman ! " and mocking voices repeated the infamous words : " I vote for death ! " [1] Philippe listened to all these cries with perfect sang-froid; to him as to every revolutionary, once the game was up, the people were of no account whatever ; moreover he had taken the precaution to fortify himself with copious draughts of excellent champagne before leaving his prison cell, and it seems to have been this, rather than the ministrations of his confessor, that inspired him with courage to meet his end.[2]

Danton was away at his château in Arcis-sur-Aube when the death of Philippe Égalité occurred, and on his return to Paris at the end of November it became evident that he had undergone some surprising change. Was it the soothing influence of country life, or the society of the sixteen-year-old girl he had married three months after the death of his wife, or was it the loss of his patron the Duc d'Orléans that had moderated Danton's revolutionary ardour ? Or had Danton begun to fear for his own safety ? Where Orléans had gone, were all those suspected of Orléanisme to follow ? These and other theories have been put forward to account for the sudden cooling of Danton's revolutionary ardour. M. Madelin offers a fresh one by suggesting that Danton had become the victim of neurasthenia. Yet is Danton's change of front really so inexplicable ? Why, after all, should he have wished to continue the Revolution ? Everything that had inspired his diatribes — royalty, aristocracy, Girondisme—had been swept away; his career as agitator was done, and now he was ready to settle down comfortably on the profits of his labours.

It was thus that one day in this winter of 1794, whilst the cold and hungry people of Paris were waiting in ever-lengthening

[1] Montjoie, *Conjuration de d'Orléans*, iii. 286 ; *Fortescue Historical MSS.* ii. 462.

[2] *Mémoires de Monseigneur de Salamon*, p. 291 ; *Philippe d'Orléans Égalité*, by Auguste Ducoin, p. 294.

queues for the bread and meat doled out to them in miserable rations, Danton, well warmed and well fed after an excellent dinner at one of the best restaurants in Paris, expressed his attitude to the Revolution : " Well, at last our turn has come to enjoy life ! Delicate food, exquisite wines, stuffs of silk and gold, women one dreams of, all this is the prize of acquired power. For us, then, for us, all this, since we are the strongest. After all, what is the Revolution ? A battle. And shall it not be followed like all battles by the division of spoils amongst the conquerors ? " [1]

Under these circumstances it is hardly surprising that Danton should have failed to enter enthusiastically into that plan of depopulation which led only to the Spartan Republic wherein all these things would be denied him. At any rate, Danton and Camille Desmoulins—who had now become entirely his disciple —began to suggest tentatively that the Terror had gone far enough, and that a committee of clemency should be formed.

" You wish to exterminate all your enemies by the guillotine," wrote Camille on the 21st of December, " but was there ever a greater folly ? Can you cause a single one to perish on the scaffold without making ten enemies for yourself amongst his family or his friends ? Do you think it is these women, these old men, these dotards, these egotists, these laggards of the Revolution whom you imprison that are the most dangerous ? Of your enemies only the cowards and the sick have remained amongst you. The brave and the strong have emigrated. They have perished at Lyon or in La Vendée ; all the rest do not deserve your anger." [2]

Meanwhile Danton expostulated with Robespierre : " Let us limit our power to striking great blows profitable to the Republic. For that reason we must not guillotine Republicans." [3]

Robespierre, intent on his plan of depopulation, thought otherwise. He knew that amongst so-called Republicans there was, as yet, no hope of unity, that on one side the Hébertistes with their passion for destruction, on the other the Dantonistes with their schemes for self-enrichment, would never allow him to establish in peace that model colony of austere equality that was his dream. Therefore Hébertistes and Dantonistes must go, and according to his customary plan Robespierre set out to destroy one faction by another. He had used Hébert to bring about the final doom of the Queen and the Girondins, now he used Danton to rid him of the Hébertistes. In this order of

[1] Louis Blanc, *Histoire de la Révolution*, vii. 96 (anecdote related by Godefroy Cavaignac).
[2] *Le Vieux Cordelier*, No. IV.
[3] Prudhomme, *Crimes de la Révolution*, iv. 32.

campaign he showed his profound wisdom ; to have reversed
the process, that is to say to have attempted to demolish the
Dantonistes with the aid of Hébert, might have proved his
own undoing, for the people, drawn to Danton by his plea for
clemency, might have rallied round him, but for Hébert, since
his attacks on religion, the great majority of the people felt
nothing but contempt.

Robespierre, therefore, had the people whole-heartedly with
him when he now denounced the atheistic movement of the
Hébertistes. " Atheism," he said at the Convention, " is aristocratic. The idéa of a great Being who watches over oppressed
innocence and punishes crime triumphant is wholly popular."

In these words Robespierre had surpassed himself as a
crowd exponent—if the people wanted a God, well, he would
give them one, and thereby establish his power on an immutable
foundation. The Feast of the Supreme Being eight months
later formed the corollary to this design. Danton, quick to
see the advantage offered by this attitude, followed Robespierre's
speech a few days later with a further denunciation of the " anti-
religious masquerades " that had recently taken place, and the
two leading demagogues thus joining forces had no difficulty in
crushing the wretched Hébertistes out of existence.

On the 21st of March 1794 Hébert, Ronsin, Momoro, Vincent,
Clootz, and several foreign intriguers—Proly, Desfieux, Pereyre,
and others—were led before the Revolutionary Tribunal on a
charge of conspiring with foreign powers, notably with Pitt, to
overthrow the Republic. As far as Pitt was concerned, of course,
not a shred of evidence could be produced, but certainly, if foreign
powers had desired to destroy France, they could not have chosen
more effective measures than those adopted by this anarchic
gang. Clootz, as has been already said, had undoubtedly been
sent to France in order to create anarchy, but whether with
the collusion of the King of Prussia it is impossible to know.
Robespierre, at any rate, profoundly distrusted this Prussian
apostle of Internationalism. In vain Clootz had declared that
" his heart was French and his soul was *sans-culotte* " ; Robespierre
in demanding his expulsion from the Jacobin Club on the 12th
of December had observed drily, " Citizens, will you regard as
a patriot a foreigner who desires to be more democratic than
the French ? . . . Never was he the defender of the French
people, but of the human race. . . . Paris swarms with intriguers,
with English and Austrians ; they sit amongst you with the
agents of Frederick. . . . Clootz is a Prussian." [1]

[1] Buchez et Roux, xxx. 338. Mercier also regarded Clootz as the
agent of Prussia : " The Prussian, Anacharsis Clootz, paved the way for
Frederick William " (*Le Nouveau Paris*, ii. 91). And Brissot takes the

The exponent of universal brotherhood as expressed by the massacres of September—for it will be remembered that it was Clootz who had regretted that they had not " Septemberized " enough—had thus failed to inspire his French brethren with confidence, and now, arraigned before the Revolutionary Tribunal, was obliged to hear his system of a Universal Republic stigmatized as " a profoundly premeditated perfidy which gave a pretext for the coalition of crowned heads against France."

When finally the eighteen " conspirators " were condemned to death by the Tribunal, Clootz appealed in vain to the " human race " against the judgement ; the human race that filled the tribunes responded merely with frantic applause.

Paris went nearly mad with joy at the execution of the Hébertistes ; immense crowds collected as the criers went through the streets proclaiming the verdict ; the air resounded with shouts of " The Père Duchesne to the guillotine ! " Even the populace, whom Hébert, in the days when he held it at his command, had described as " the only good and pure element of the great Parisian family," rejoiced at the downfall of its former idol. Although by now it had begun to grow tired of the spectacle of the guillotine, it prepared on this occasion to assemble in force around the scaffold. The only fear was that the Place de la Révolution might not prove large enough to hold so vast a multitude. Every window in the Rue Saint-Honoré was let to see the procession pass.[1]

In the markets, at the street corners, people collected in groups, saying to each other, " It was the rascal Hébert and his clique who wished to make us die of hunger ; with the fall of this infernal faction we shall see once more peace and abundance." [2] Hébert's own bloodthirsty phrases were passed derisively from mouth to mouth : " Hé ! Hé ! the stove-merchant is going to put *his* nose out of the little window ! " " He is going to sneeze into the sack ! " [3] Some were of opinion that the guillotine was too gentle a mode of execution, and that something more lingering and painful should be devised for such scoundrels—conspirators " a thousand times more criminal than Capet and his wife." [4]

When at last, at four o'clock on the fine spring afternoon of the 24th of March, the tumbrils bearing their eighteen victims made

---

same view : " I accompany the name of Clootz with the epithet Prussian, not so much to recall his birthplace as to recall the fact that Clootz behaves here like a good and faithful subject of His Prussian Majesty, who, on his side, reserves his lands for him " (*J. P. Brissot à ses Commettants*, p. 52).

[1] Schmidt, ii. 163. [2] *Ibid.* p. 160.
[3] *Journal d'un Bourgeois*, by Edmond Biré, iv. 318.
[4] Schmidt, ii. 158, 163, 174 ; Dauban, *Paris en 1794*, p. 252

their appearance, so immense a crowd had collected that the procession was continually held up on its way to the scaffold. The pitiful spectacle of Hébert sobbing helplessly, and almost in a state of collapse, had no power to touch the hearts in which more than any one he had helped to kill all sentiments of humanity, and it was his own refrains that now echoed in his ears as the cruel mob surged around him singing in chorus, and with hands and feet drumming out the measure :

> Ran plan, ran plan plan-plan,
> Ran plan, ran plan-plan,
> Tambour, un ran !

or else with shrieks of ghoulish laughter :

> Drelin, drelin, drelin !
> A la guillotine ! [1]

The other Hébertistes listened to all this with disdain ; Clootz above all remained immovable, for if, as a contemporary relates, he was " dying of fright," it was only " lest any of his companions should believe in God, and he preached materialism to them until his last breath." [2]

As the tumbrils entered the Place de la Révolution a mighty roar arose from the assembled multitude, and thousands of voices began to chant the revolutionary " Complainte " of " Rougyff." One after another the victims ascended the scaffold. Hébert's head was the last to fall. As he lay tied to the plank the executioner playfully danced the blade of the guillotine over the wretched man's neck before allowing it finally to descend, and the populace, that only a few months earlier had adored Hébert, greeted this brutal jest with laughter and applause.

But if on this occasion the mob of Paris showed itself ferocious, it was the only execution, except that of Robespierre, at which such scenes took place. In general it will be noticed throughout the Revolution that the men the people ended by hating most were those with whom they had been most intimate, and who had promised them the most. They liked Marat, Robespierre, and Hébert as long as these demagogues promised them a millennial age and appeared to be, as they professed, true friends of the poor, living in Spartan simplicity and sharing their privations. But when the people discovered they had been deceived, when no millennium dawned, above all when they realized that their idols feasted whilst they themselves went

---

[1] *Anacharsis Clootz*, by Georges Avenel, ii. 147.
[2] *Mémoires de Riouffe*, i. 69.

hungry, they turned and rent them with all the fury of blighted hope and disappointed love.[1]

For this reason Danton did not end by incurring the animosity of the people; the "*grand seigneur* of the *Sans-Culotterie*" had always kept aloof from the crowd, had never promised to share the good things of life with them, never pretended to be one of them ; no draggled herd of *jupons gras* had followed in his wake, no adoring *tricoteuses* had hung upon his lips in the tribunes of the Convention. The people only knew him now from the distance as a great voice in the Assembly, as a great *bon-vivant* outside it ; they were well aware that he lived principally for women and good cheer, and being Parisians rather liked him for it.

The people, therefore, did not rejoice at the death of the Dantonistes which took place on the 5th of April. For now that Danton had served his purpose by helping to rid him of the " anarchic " gang, Robespierre lost no time in turning his attention to the remaining faction. Only one week after the execution of the Hébertistes, Robespierre hurled his thunderbolt at the head of Danton, and he hurled it by the hand of St. Just. This was really extraordinarily ingenious, for, as Danton's past connection with the Orléaniste conspiracy formed the chief ground of accusation against him, Danton might well have retaliated, if the charge had been made by Robespierre himself, with the reminder that he, " Incorruptible " though he was, had nevertheless worked with the conspirators in the early days of the Revolution. Against St. Just, however, no such insinuations could be made. This irreproachable young man, who moved through the scenes of the Terror like a marble Antinous " with his feet in blood and tears," [2] had only joined the revolutionary movement as a deputy of the Convention, and could not be suspected of complicity with previous intrigues. It was, therefore, to St. Just that Robespierre confided the materials for a great indictment of the Dantonistes on precisely the same lines as Camille Desmoulins' indictment of the Girondins a year earlier. It is impossible to read the pamphlet of Camille concurrently with the speech of St. Just and not to recognize that in both the chain of reasoning must have been evolved by the

---

[1] " The people cannot forgive Hébert for having deceived them. . . . ' Oh ! the hypocrite ! oh ! the scoundrel ! ' they cried on all sides " (Police report of March 21, 1794 ; Dauban, *Paris en 1794*, p. 288). " The women said that the more they had loved the Père Duchesne, the more horror they had of him . . . it is to be believed that the mass of the people will look on quietly at the trial of these men who had obtained their confidence " (*ibid.* p. 246).

[2] St. Just's own expression, see " Rapport de Courtois " in *Papiers trouvés chez Robespierre*, i. 20.

same brain, though in one it is expressed with the sprightly verve of the pamphleteer, in the other with the sober logic of the politician. And even more than the *Histoire des Brissotins* of Desmoulins, the " Rapport " of St. Just provides the most damning indictment of the Revolution.[1] No Royalist has ever exposed more remorselessly the workings of the great revolutionary intrigues ; Montjoie himself could not have penned a clearer résumé of the Orléaniste conspiracy and its subsequent ramifications than is contained in the following passages : " You have marched," St. Just said to the Convention, " between the faction of false patriots and that of the moderates you must overthrow. These factions, born with the Revolution, have followed in its course as reptiles follow the course of rivers . . . the party of Orléans was the first constituted ; it had branches in all the governments, and in the three legislatures (*i.e.* in the Constituent and the Legislative Assemblies and the Convention). This criminal party, lacking audacity . . ., always dissimulating and never boldly venturing, was carried away by the energy of the men of good faith and by the force of the people's virtue ; it followed always the course of the Revolution, shrouding itself continually and never daring. This is what made people believe at the beginning that Orléans had no ambition, for in the best prepared circumstances he lacked courage and resolution. These secret convulsions of the dissimulating parties were the cause of public misfortunes. *The popular Revolution was the surface of a volcano of extraneous conspiracies.* The Constituent Assembly, a senate by day, was by night a collection of factions which prepared the policy and artifices of the morrow. Affairs had a double intention ; one ostensibly and gracefully coloured, the other secret, leading to hidden results *contrary to the interests of the people.* They made war on the nobility, the guilty friend of the Bourbons, in order to pave the way to the throne for Orléans. One sees at each step the efforts of this party to ruin the Court, its enemy, and to preserve royalty, but the loss of one entailed the other ; no royalty can exist without a patriciate. . . .

" There was a faction in 1790 to place the crown on the head of Orléans ; there was one to maintain it on the head of the Bourbons ; there was another faction to place the House of Hanover on the throne of France. These factions were overthrown with royalty on the 10th of August ; terror forced all the secret conspiracies in favour of monarchy to dissimulate more profoundly than ever. *Then all these factions took the*

[1] " Rapport fait à la Convention Nationale . . . sur la Conjuration ourdie depuis plusieurs Années par des Factions criminelles pour absorber le Révolution française dans un Changement de Dynastie . . ." (Séance du 11 Germinal, An II.).

mask of the Republican party; Brissot, Buzot, and Dumouriez
continued the faction of Orléans ; Carra the faction of Hanover ;
Manuel, Lanjuinais, and others the party of the Bourbons."
Now, though the last passage displays some inconsistency—for
it will be remembered that during the Massacres of September
Robespierre had accused Brissot of being in league with Brunswick
—the preceding statements concerning the factions will be seen
exactly to coincide with those of Montjoie, Beaulieu, Pagès, the
"Deux Amis de la Liberté," and others quoted earlier in this book;
and thus, even in the opinion of Robespierre and St. Just, the
French Revolution was not, as is generally supposed, a struggle
between monarchy and republicanism, or between autocracy
and democracy, but simply a ramification of conspiracies by
various factions to usurp power *at the expense of the people.*

After this admirable preamble St. Just proceeded to describe
the rôle played by the Dantonistes throughout the Revolution—
he spoke of Danton's connection with Mirabeau, " who was
meditating a change of dynasty, and realized the value of his
audacity"; he referred to Danton's collusion with the petition
of the Champ de Mars in 1791, his nomination of Orléans to
the Convention, his intrigue with Dumouriez to ensure the safe
retreat of the Prussian armies after Valmy ; in scathing terms
he described his "cowardly and constant abandonment of the
public cause " at times of crisis, by invariably adopting the plan
of retreat, notably on the 9th of August, when he had betaken
himself to his bed whilst the revolutionary army was mustering ;
and he ended by denouncing the love of riches that distinguished
the Dantonistes, their " need of pleasures acquired at the cost of
equality."

As a matter of fact no one at the time doubted Danton's
venality, nor did this greatly injure him in the mind of the
public, since few of the revolutionary leaders had shown themselves proof against the seduction of money ; Robespierre would
not have won the title of " Incorruptible " if he had not been
almost unique in this respect. Danton himself had hitherto
made no secret of his greed for gold, only when charged with
it before the Revolutionary Tribunal did he attempt denial :
" I—sold ? Men of my stamp are not to be bought ; the seal
of liberty and Republican genius are stamped in ineffaceable
characters on their foreheads."

The trial of the Dantonistes—Danton, Desmoulins, Fabre
d'Églantine, Hérault de Séchelles, Lacroix, Philippeaux —
presented one of the strangest scenes of all the Revolution.
Danton, who had entered the court " like a furious bull plunging
into the arena with lowered horns," attempted to carry off the
situation with a high hand, now chaffing the judges or throwing

bread pellets at their heads, now breaking out into furious bellowings, but never refuting the accusations brought against him.[1] Again and again the President was obliged to call him to order, reminding him that his anger and his coarse invectives were damaging his case. Outside the hall of the Tribunal an immense crowd listened breathlessly whilst the thunder of Danton's voice rolled out through the open windows across the Seine, where further crowds had gathered ; and as each resounding phrase struck on their ears, the people passed it on till it reached the farthest limits of that vast multitude.

Finally the Tribunal, adopting the same illegal methods that had been employed at the trial of the King and of the Girondins, cut short the proceedings and pronounced sentence of death. Danton's fury now knew no bounds ; transferred to his cell at the Conciergerie to await execution, he continued to bellow incoherent phrases through his prison bars :

" It was on this day that I instituted the Revolutionary Tribunal ; but I ask pardon from God and men ; it was not that it might become the scourge of humanity, it was to prevent a renewal of the massacres of September. . . .

" I leave everything in a fearful muddle ; there is no one who understands government. . . .

" They are all my brothers Cain. Brissot would have had me guillotined like Robespierre. . . .

" I had a spy who never left me. . . .

" The f. . . . beasts, they will cry ' Vive la Republique ! ' as they see me pass ! "[2]

In the end Danton resigned himself and faced his end with courage. A few moments before starting for the place of execution he summed up his philosophy of life in a characteristic sentence : " What matter if I die ? I have well enjoyed myself in the Revolution ; I have spent well, caroused well, caressed many women ; let us sleep ! (*Qu'importe si je meurs ? J'ai bien joui dans la Révolution, j'ai bien dépensé, bien ribotté, bien caressé des filles ; allons dormir !*) "[3] As the three scarlet tumbrils made their way along the Rue Saint-Honoré, serried rows of spectators watched them pass in silence ; this time they did not rejoice, but neither did they dare to express disapproval. Camille Desmoulins, the one-time " procurer of the lantern," displayed pitiable weakness now that his own turn had come. In his despair he had so torn his clothes that his body was bare almost to the waist ; all the way he talked feverishly to his companions, laughing convulsively the while like one demented.

Only a year ago, in sending the Girondins to their doom,

---

[1] Buchez et Roux, xxxii. 164.   [2] *Mémoires de Riouffe*, i. 67.
[3] *Mémoires de Sénart* (edition de Lescure), p. 71.

Camille had said confidently, " We have the people with us ! "
now, like every demagogue in turn, he appealed vainly to the
people's pity. At one moment overcome with frenzy, Camille,
struggling madly, tearing at his clothes, shrieked out to them,
" People, it is your servants who are being sacrificed ! It is I
who in 1789 called you to arms ! It is I who uttered the first
cry of liberty ! My crime, my only crime, is to have shed tears ! "
     But the mob, always cruel to those who showed fear,
responded only with jeers and insults. At this Danton, rolling
his enormous round head contemptuously, said with a derisive
smile to Camille, " Be quiet, and leave alone that vile *canaille* ! "
     At the last moment the thought of his young wife, whom,
voluptuary though he was, he loved sincerely, wrung from
Danton one cry of agony, " My beloved, I shall see you no
more ! "   Then pulling himself together, " Come, Danton, no
weakness ! "   Turning to the executioner he said, " Show my
head to the people, it is worth it ! "   And amidst cries of
" Vive la République ! " that terrible head was held aloft.
     The execution of Danton has been frequently described as the
vengeance of Robespierre on a formidable rival. Undoubtedly
Robespierre's devouring envy was aroused by Danton's powerful oratory, as formerly it had been aroused by the eloquence
of the Girondins. At the same time it must be admitted that
the Dantonistes' philosophy of life was incompatible with the
schemes of Robespierre and St. Just. Long after the death of
the Dantonistes Fievée relates that he asked Voulland, a member
of the Comité de Sûreté Générale and the *intime* of Robespierre,
why the destruction of this party had been found necessary, to
which Voulland replied that as long as the Orléans faction
prevailed, that is to say, " the deputies who mingled pleasures,
luxury, and cupidity with proscriptions," it was impossible to
restore order. " Heaven knows what would have become of
France in their hands ! " As to Camille Desmoulins, Voulland
added, " who had ranged himself on their side as a dupe ratner
than as an accomplice, could we save him whilst attacking
Danton, the most dangerous of all Orléanistes, and Fabre
d'Églantine, even more immoral than Danton ? "
     It is not therefore, as certain historians would have us believe,
because the Dantonistes had become humane and " moderate "
that their fall was inevitable, but because they were Orléanistes,
because they were voluptuaries and reactionaries—reactionaries
in the true sense of the word ; that is to say, men who wished
to maintain the easy morals and the inequalities of the Old
Régime in an aggravated form. So whilst there can be no
excuse for their murder—and their trial was really nothing but
judicial murder—it was obviously impossible for Robespierre

to realize his plan of an austere Republic, founded on absolute equality, as long as they remained in power.

THE GREAT TERROR

The question has frequently been asked why, after the death of the Dantonistes, Robespierre did not immediately embark on his schemes of reconstruction. Why should the final overthrow of his most formidable rivals have proved the signal for a still more rigorous application of the Terror ? But when we have once grasped the theory on which the Terror was founded, the problem seems easier of solution. For in the spring of 1794 the process of depopulating Paris had only just begun, and to the triumvirate it seemed more than ever necessary to continue the operation with unremitting energy if a harmonious Socialist State was to result.

In order to understand this necessity to its full extent we must realize something of the state of Paris under the reign of Robespierre and his allies.

The truth is, then, that the populace whom these demagogues had made all-powerful had now become their terror ; no Sultan was ever watched more anxiously by trembling " wazirs " than was the Sovereign People by its courtiers of 1794. With a view to guarding against any ebullitions of popular feeling, agents were employed by them to go about the city and study the moods of the people—" listeners " and " observers " who stood beside the groups at the street corners, amongst the women in the markets and in the queues at the shop doors, or who mingled with the crowds watching the victims going to the guillotine. Everything the observers noticed ; everything the listeners overheard ; expressions of approval or murmurs of dissatisfaction at the existing régime, smiles, frowns, angry exclamations, or derisive laughter—all these were set down and conveyed verbatim to the revolutionary committees in detailed daily reports. These documents, which have been published both by Schmidt and Dauban, afford us the minutest insight into the mind of Paris at this moment, and at the same time throw a curious light on the mentality of the demagogues. The fact that they should have held this intricate system of espionage to be necessary shows how profoundly they distrusted the people they professed to worship, and how keenly they realized the insecurity of their own position. Nor were such fears groundless, for the result of all these observations was to reveal that beneath the apparent submission of the people there lay a deep undercurrent of discontent. This perhaps was not altogether surprising, for the famine was now worse than ever. All over France the inhabitants of the towns had been put on rations of the meagrest description; in the country districts, where even these were not obtainable, the unhappy peasants staved off the pangs of hunger with grass and acorns.[1] The queues at the shop doors had grown steadily longer; from three or four o'clock in the morning rows of starving men and women stood in the cold and rain, or, sinking from exhaustion, lay in heaps upon the pavement.[2] The law of the "maximum," by which a fixed price was set on all the necessaries of life, far from easing the situation as had been promised, immensely complicated it. The fishermen refused to put out to sea, the millers concealed their grain rather than sell it at a loss, the shopkeepers reserved their goods for favoured customers or disposed of them secretly at prices above the maximum to those who could afford to pay. The people, enraged by these manœuvres, and faithful to Marat's teachings, continued to waylay the peasants bringing supplies into the city, and pillaged the carts containing eggs, butter, or poultry. "Some paid; the others carried off the things without paying. The peasants in despair swore they would bring nothing more to Paris." [3]

Besides the want of food, the want of employment was still acute; bands of workmen gathered at the street corners complaining of the times. "How can you expect us to work when all the rich people, whether patriots or not, are imprisoned?" [4] Beggars, old men, women and children besieged passers-by for alms. Meanwhile the men who were still employed perpetually demanded higher pay; the masons and carpenters put up their prices every ten days, threatening not to work unless their demands were acceded to. "Everybody," writes a government agent, "cries out against the tyranny of the workmen." [5]

But even when the money they claimed had been paid they were not contented, for often they could buy nothing with it. What was the good of earning 100 sols a day instead of 20 sols [6] when neither bread nor meat, candles or firing were to be had? Moreover, owing to the bankruptcy of the State, the *assignats* or paper money they received had only a fictitious value. "A cab fare," relates Mercier, "cost 600 livres; that is to say, 10 livres a minute. A private person going home in the evening said to the cabman, 'How much?' '6000 livres.' He pulled out his pocket-book and paid. Every one was rich in imagination; they were unhappy only when they were disillusioned." [7]

---

[1] Speech by Tallien at the Convention, March 12, 1794. See also Buchez et Roux, xxxii. 423.
[2] Taine, viii. 255.   [3] Dauban, *Paris en 1794*, pp. 87, 173, 198.
[4] *Ibid*. p. 62.   [5] *Ibid*. p. 149.   [6] *Ibid*. p. 185.
[7] Mercier, *Le Nouveau Paris*. ii. 94.

The people were perpetually being disillusioned. This beautiful reign of equality which had been promised them had brought them nothing but misery ; yet they were continually assured that when a particular political faction had been overthrown all would be well, and the famine would miraculously disappear. Once it had been " the Court and aristocracy " who had monopolized the corn, but Court and aristocracy were long since swept away, and still the grain was not forthcoming ; then it was against the Girondins that the same charge had been brought, but the Girondins too were gone, and still the scarcity continued ; now the Hébertistes, to whom it had likewise been attributed, had followed the Girondins, yet the people were hungrier than ever.

Nothing had happened as they expected. Wealth still mocked at poverty, and those in power still drank and feasted whilst the struggling thousands starved. For at the butchers' shops, where the people waited from early dawn for a miserable scrap of meat, the best joints were reserved for the members of the revolutionary committees and their friends.[1] The restaurants too, where the " representatives of the people " forgathered, were still lavishly supplied with excellent food, as many as three or four meat courses being served at one meal.[2] It is hardly surprising, then, if the people grew indignant and cried out that, whilst " fathers of families could not put the pot on the fire in their homes when their wives were sick," and " honest citizens were eating only bread and potatoes, the wealthier citizens were making up parties for the restaurants. . . . It is only well-off people," they said, " who dine at restaurants, and they go there to regale themselves with light women whilst the poor sansculottes eat bread." [3]

Exasperated by their sufferings, the people cast about for remedies which varied according to the temperament of the malcontents ; thus, whilst some cried " Vive l'ancien Régime ! then we had abundance of everything ! " [4] others declared that things would go no better unless more victims were executed, and, nodding their heads in the direction of the guillotine, added, " It is only that saint there who can save us ! " [5]

The fact is that the people of Paris were now neither Royalist nor Republican, neither for their present rulers or against them ; their faith in all government had been shaken to its foundations.[6]

---

[1] Dauban, *Paris en 1794*, p. 126.   [2] *Ibid.* p. 181.
[3] *Ibid.* p. 65.   [4] *Ibid.* p. 202.   [5] *Ibid.* pp. 173, 253.
[6] " Everywhere the citizens are heard to say they have no great confidence in those in power after the arrest of several of them. . . ." (*ibid.* p. 269). " The people appear to repent of the ease with which they gave their confidence to men who have so cruelly deceived them. They wish now to go to the other extreme, for they will no longer trust anyone " (*ibid.* p. 271).

In consequence of seeing one faction after another led to the guillotine, they had come to regard this spectacle as the natural ending to a political career : " All these rascals of deputies will pass that way ! " they cried out in the popular assemblies.[1] A government agent, adopting an admirable simile, remarks : " The mass of the nation is a bear, and the political parties working it are turbulent monkeys who have climbed up and are playing on its back." [2] The question for every demagogue was thus, " Will the bear rise and throw us off ? " And, haunted by this apprehension, they played on in fear and trembling, now patting the great beast into good-humour, now terrorizing it into submission.

One thing was certain, the people were not to be depended on to support any faction or government consistently ; the needs of the moment were their only law. These same women who would fight each other to the death for a few ounces of butter,[3] and tear provisions furiously from the market-carts, would not raise a finger to save their idols from destruction— never once attempted to drag a victim—even one of their own kind—from his seat in the tumbril on the way to the guillotine.

How was it possible to make a " nation of gods " out of such elements ? Where amidst all this sea of human passions was the " virtue," the austerity, the " civism " necessary to the ideal Republic to be found ? Inevitably, therefore, the people of Paris must be subjected to the same process as the people in the provinces before the work of reconstruction could begin. It was thus that in April of 1794 Robespierre and his colleagues, now in sole possession of the field, set to work with redoubled energy on their great scheme—the depopulation of Paris.

From this moment the rôle of the people ceased entirely ; except as a hired and often recalcitrant *claque*, even the populace took no part in the scenes of bloodshed that followed. Once the people had been the tools of the demagogues, carrying out their vengeances ; now the people's own turn had come—as it must come in every revolution that does not stop half-way— and they had become the victims. No longer was the force of the people turned against themselves—demagogy had abandoned

---

[1] Dauban, *Paris en 1794*, p. 280.

[2] Schmidt, ii. 30.

[3] Dauban, *Paris en 1794*, p. 144. At this immense crisis, amidst the fearful bloodshed of the Terror, nothing seems to have stirred the women of Paris so deeply as the question of butter—" butter of which they make a god ! " (*ibid.* p. 231). Thus the Comité de Salut Public headed by Robespierre, writing to summon St. Just back to Paris on the 6th of Prairial, describes as one of the chief dangers of the capital " the crowds waiting for butter, which are more numerous and more turbulent than ever " (*Papiers trouvés chez Robespierre*, ii. 6).

" jiu-jitsu " and assumed the bludgeon. The Reign of Terror was absolute despotism.

" One must have seen," says Frenilly, " as I saw in 1793 and 1794, in the country and in the towns—which history will never tell—the entire population, good and simple peasants, tradesmen, artisans and owners of property, all trembling beneath the hauteur of a few lawyers formed into a Popular Society. Never did vassals submit more humbly to vexations ; never did barons exercise them with more arrogance." [1] The people were no longer merely paralysed, but absolutely crushed. Every vestige of liberty accorded by the first two Assemblies under Louis XVI.—personal liberty, liberty of the press, religious liberty, the sacredness of property—were utterly destroyed. Even speech was no longer free—a word sufficed to send one to the scaffold. " The worst thing under the rule of Robespierre," old men used to say long afterwards, " was that in the morning one could never be sure of sleeping in one's bed that night." [2]

Immediately after the death of the Dantonistes the condemnations passed by the Revolutionary Tribunal increased in number ; during the preceding month of Ventose the guillotine had claimed only 116 victims; in Germinal, on the 16th day of which the Dantonistes perished, the figure rose to 155, and in the following month of Floréal to no less than 354. These were still taken principally from amongst the Royalists, aristocrats, or bourgeois—on the 20th of April twenty-five Parliamentarians ; on the 3rd of May the Grenadiers des Filles-St. Thomas, who had remained loyal to the King at the siege of the Tuileries ; on the 8th of May twenty-eight farmer-generals ; on the 10th of May Madame Elizabeth and a number of aristocrats, both men and women. It was not until Robespierre had succeeded in obtaining the decree known as the " Loi du 22 Prairial " (the 10th of June) that the great indiscriminate butcheries began.[3] By this infamous law victims summoned

---

[1] Dauban relates that sixty years later the peasants of France had not recovered from their fright. When M. Vatel went to make historical researches in the provinces, and asked the old men for their recollections of the Terror, the whole country-side was immediately in a ferment ; the people asked anxiously, " Are they going to re-establish all that ? Are we to go back to the time of the bad paper (the worthless assignats) and the great fear ? " (La Demagogie en 1793, p. xii.).

[2] Taine, La Révolution, viii. 203.

[3] Robespierre seems to have meditated this law for three months before it was finally passed. As early as the month of the Ventose, D'Aubigny related at the trial of Fouquier Tinville, he attended a dinner at which he met Robespierre, who complained of the dilatoriness of the Revolutionary Tribunal in punishing conspirators. Sellier replied that the Tribunal merely observed the forms necessary to the protection of the innocent. " Bah ! bah ! " said Robespierre, " that is how you are

before the Revolutionary Tribunal were denied all rights of defence ; no advocates were to be allowed, no witnesses called, and the penalty imposed in all cases was to be death.

The " Loi du 22 Prairial " was undoubtedly Robespierre's bid for absolute power. Two days earlier he had presided at the " Feast of the Supreme Being," where he had thrown off his disguise of austerity and appeared before the people curled and powdered, in his pale-blue coat and nankin breeches, holding in his hands an enormous bouquet of flowers and wheat-ears. In order to make his entry more impressive, he had kept the immense crowd waiting for half-an-hour before he made his appearance, and as a storm of applause greeted his arrival a glow of triumph overspread the sallow countenance of the Incorruptible. At this moment, writes one who looked on, " he believed himself to be King and God." [1] The plaudits of the multitude mounted to his head like wine, and it was under the influence of this intoxication that he ventured on his great coup —the passing of the law that was to place in his hands the power of life and death.

Yet if it is to Robespierre that the system of the Terror in Paris must be mainly attributed, we should be mistaken in regarding him as the most sanguinary of the Terrorists. On the contrary, everything goes to prove that Robespierre and his principal ally, St. Just, did not love bloodshed for its own sake ; they regarded it merely as a means to an end—the establishment of a harmonious democracy on the plan they had devised. But, however exalted may have been the ideal at which they aimed, it was obviously impossible for them to find idealists exclusively to co-operate with them or to execute their scheme, and they were therefore obliged to throw in their lot with a band of men so atrocious that by comparison they themselves seem almost humane. These men were to be found amongst their colleagues in the Comité de Salut Public and their instruments in the Comité de Sûreté Générale and the Revolutionary Tribunal.

The Comité de Sûreté Générale had been created in 1789 by the National Assembly as a " committee of information," and only took its later name on the 30th of May 1792. Although supposed to be subordinate to the Comité de Salut Public, and in accord with it, the Comité de Sûreté Générale had in reality become its rival, and each committee was in turn divided into

---

with your forms ! Wait, before long the Committee will have a law passed that will clear the way for the Tribunal and then we shall see ! " (evidence of J. L. M. Villam d'Aubigny, ex-Adjoint au Ministre de la Guerre, etc., *Procès de Fouquier*, Buchez et Roux, xxxiv. 410).

[1] *Mémoires de Fiévée* (edition de Lescure), p. 162.

rival factions. These factions, and the mysterious names they bore, have been described by Sénart, and when tabulated in the following manner throw a strange light on the workings of the Terror :

COMITÉ DE SALUT PUBLIC

Robespierre		Barère		Carnot	
Couthon	Les Gens de la Haute Main.	Billaud	Les Gens Révolution- naires.	Prieur	Les Gens d'Examen.
St. Just		Collot		Lindet	

COMITÉ DE SÛRETÉ GÉNÉRALE

Vadier					
Voulland				Moïse Bayle	
Amar	Les Gens d'Expé- dition.	David	Les Écouteurs.	Lavicomterie	Les Gens de Con- tre-poids.
Jagot		Lebas		Elie Lacoste	
Louis du Bas Rhin				Dubarran	

By means of this table the really sanguinary authors of the Terror can be seen at a glance ; these were the " Gens Révolutionnaires " of the first committee, and the " Gens d'Expédition " of the second. For innate ferocity, for real bloodthirstiness— bloodthirstiness without any ultimate purpose—we must look, not to the triumvirate formed by Robespierre, Couthon, and St. Just, but to that infamous trio who afterwards overthrew them—Barère de Vieuzac, Billaud-Varenne, and Collot d'Herbois. Was it not Billaud who had presided at the massacres in the prisons, and urged the assassins on to violence ? Was it not Collot who had declared these same massacres of September to be the " Credo " of liberty, and who, as the ally of Chalier, had organized the atrocities that took place at Lyon ? And it was Barère, that miserable " chameleon," now Feuillant, now Jacobin, now aristocrat, now revolutionary, " atheist in the evening, deist in the morning,"[1] who in one atrocious phrase epitomized the plan of depopulation into which no one had entered more heartily than he. One day, Vilate relates, Barère, looking out of a window in the Tuileries towards the city, said, " Paris is too large ; it is to the Republic, by means of its monstrous population, what a violent rush of blood is to the heart of a man—a suffocation that withers the other organs and leads to death." And to Dupin he added : " Do you know, Dupin, that the idea of Nero, when he set fire to Rome in order to have the pleasure of re-building it, was a really revolutionary idea ? "[2]

The former phrase became current coin amongst the Terrorists ; it was continually on their lips, says Mercier, and they

[1] *Causes secrètes de la Révolution*, by Vilate (edition de Lescure), p. 224.
[2] *Ibid.* p. 262.

would observe that, in order to counteract this unhealthy rush of blood to the heart, one should have recourse to " phlebotomy." [1]

At his pleasure-house of Clichy, Barère met twice a decade [2] with his allies, the " Gens d'Expédition " of the Comité de Sûreté Générale, to plan fresh *fournées* for the guillotine.

It was these monsters—Vadier, Voulland, Amar, Jagot, Louis du Bas Rhin, names long since forgotten, yet in their day names of dread and horror—who lent to the Terror that spirit of ghoulish ferocity that makes the history of the period unique in the annals of mankind. This hideous band that Sénart describes with fearful realism in his *Mémoires* reminds one of nothing so much as a pack of jackals breaking the stillness of a Himalayan night with their dreary howling after blood. Thus Sénart relates :

" There had been one evening a great number of people guillotined ; Louis du Bas Rhin said :

" ' It is going well ; the baskets are filling.'

" ' Then,' answered Voulland, ' let us make a provision of game. . . .'

" Vadier said to Voulland : ' I saw you on the Place de la Révolution near the guillotine.'

" ' I went to laugh at the faces those rascals make at the window.'

" ' Ho ! ' said Vadier, ' it is a funny passage—the little window. They give a good sneeze into the sack. It amuses me, I have taken quite a liking for it. I often go there.'

" ' Go to-morrow,' resumed Amar, ' there will be a great show ; I was at the Tribunal to-day.'

" ' Let us go there,' said Vadier.

" ' I'll go for certain,' retorted Voulland."

Sénart declares that during this conversation he pinched himself to make sure he was not dreaming ; he felt as if he were between a tiger, a panther, and a bear.

Now it is remarkable that none of Robespierre's many enemies ever attributed to him sentiments of this atrocious kind, though had they done so they would have been readily believed. Yet amongst all the witnesses who afterwards came forward at the trial of Fouquier Tinville to testify to the system of the Terror, and Robespierre's share in it, none asserted that he had appeared to take delight in the sufferings of his victims or that he had even assisted at the spectacle of the guillotine. Indeed, all evidence goes to show that Robespierre took the first opportunity to disassociate himself from the men

[1] Mercier, *Le Nouveau Paris*, ii. 132.

[2] Decade = 10 days, the measure of time which in the Revolutionary Calendar was substituted for weeks.

he had set in motion ; and it was thus that five days after the passing of the " Loi du 22 Prairial " he ceased to attend the meetings of the Comité de Salut Public. But to argue from this, as Robespierre's panegyrists have done, that he now wished to arrest the course of the Terror is quite another matter. No, Robespierre did not wish to arrest the Terror—of this there can be no possible doubt. Was not the law that inaugurated those last terrible six weeks of his own making ? And if he no longer took part in the discussions of the Comité de Salut Public, were not the sanguinary Commune and the police of Paris entirely under his control? [1] If, therefore, Robespierre withdrew from the committee, it was either because he disapproved the manner in which his more ferocious colleagues carried out the system of the Terror, or, more probably, because he had begun to see in Billaud, Collot, and Barère a faction that threatened not only his supremacy but his life. After the " Loi du 22 Prairial," says Vilate, " Robespierre became more sombre, his scowling air repelled every one, he talked only of assassination, again of assassination, always of assassination. He was afraid that his shadow would assassinate him."

Already he believed that an attempt had been made to murder him. In the evening of the 25th of May Cécile Renault, the daughter of a small stationer, had entered the gloomy courtyard of the carpenter's house in the Rue Saint-Honoré and asked to see Robespierre. When told that he was out she showed temper and, evidently disbelieving the assertion, answered that a public functionary should be willing to receive all those who asked to see him. On these words she was led to the Comité de Sûreté Générale, and, by way of making her condemnation absolutely certain, observed that " under the Old Régime when one presented oneself to the King one was allowed to enter at once." " Then would you rather have a king ? " they asked her, and she answered boldly, " I would shed all my blood to have one. . . . That is my opinion ; you are only tyrants." She had gone to Robespierre, she told the Committee, " in order to see what a tyrant was like."

They found on her two little penknives, and in a basket she had left at a lemonade-seller's near-by a change of linen, which she explained she had brought with her, as she expected to be sent to prison and thence to the scaffold.

Before the Revolutionary Tribunal she declared that she had not intended to kill Robespierre, but persisted in expressing

---

[1] Schmidt, ii. 208 ; *Mémoires sur les Prisons,* i. 237. " Robespierre," says Michelet, " no longer went to the Comité de Salut Public, but he kept his power of signature, he signed at home ; a number of orders signed by his hand are still in existence " (*Histoire de la Révolution Française,* ix. 196).

her devotion to Louis XVI. : " I said I wept for our good King, yes, I said it, and I wish he were still living. Are you not five hundred kings, and all more insolent and more despotic than the one you killed ? "

This, of course, sealed the fate of Cécile Renault, and since on the same day a man named Amiral had really attempted to shoot Collot d'Herbois, the revolutionary committees seized the opportunity to proclaim that a " vast conspiracy " had been discovered. On the proposal of Louis du Bas Rhin of the Comité de Sûreté Générale, they further decided to represent this conspiracy as originating in England. Once again it was Pitt—solemnly declared by the Convention ten months earlier to be " the enemy of the human race "—who had instigated the papermaker's daughter to assassinate Robespierre. This ludicrous fable offered Barère an occasion to pour forth furious diatribes against the English [1]—" that treacherous and ferocious people, a slave at home, a despot on the Continent, and a pirate at sea " ; at the same time it afforded Robespierre a pretext for sending an enormous batch of victims to the guillotine. Amongst these were included, not only Cécile Renault's father, the paper-maker, her young brother, and an aunt who had been a nun, but all kinds of men and women, some belonging to the nobility, some to the people—the heretofore Prince of Rohan-Rochefort, the beautiful Émilie de Sartines, and her mother, Madame de Sainte-Amaranthe, four administrators of police, a grocer, a lemonade-seller, a concierge, and two domestic servants—sixty-one in all.

The most pathetic of these conspirators was a little seamstress of seventeen, known as "la petite Nicholle," too poor even to afford herself a bedstead, and when Sénart, secretary to the Comité de Sûreté Générale, sought her in her attic on the seventh floor, he found her lying on a straw mattress laid upon the boards. " Voulland," says Sénart, " wished for her death, because he said she took food to the woman Grandmaison "—an actress included in the same *fournée*—" ' and for that reason,' said the hypocrite Louis du Bas Rhin, ' she will go with her.' I was assured of her innocence. . . ."

It was also Louis du Bas Rhin who proposed that, in order to make the procession more imposing, all the victims should

---

[1] It was on this occasion that the Convention passed the decree that all English and Hanoverian prisoners should be shot. " Fortunately," says Taine, " the French soldiers feel the nobility of their profession, and on the order to shoot the prisoners a brave sergeant replies, ' We will not shoot them ; send them to the Convention ; if the representatives take pleasure in killing a prisoner, they can kill him themselves and eat him too, like the savages they are.' This sergeant, an uncultivated man, could not rise to the heights of the Comité or of Barère. . . ." (*La Révolution*, vii. 309).

be sent to the scaffold in the scarlet dress of assassins, " for," said he, " small things lead to great ones, appearances create illusions, and it is by illusions that the people are led." At this Vadier, fearing that his prey was to be snatched from him and the whole affair to end in a vain parade, cried out, " But we must have reality, we must have blood ! " Louis du Bas Rhin answered reassuringly, " Poets represent the sage to us as sheltered by a wall of brass ; let us raise a wall of heads between ourselves and the people." What despot, asks Sénart, had ever said, " Raise a wall of heads between myself and my subjects ? " On the day of execution the jackals were there to watch the procession pass, and it was then that Voulland, turning to his companions, uttered his famous *bon mot* : " Come, let us go to the high altar and see the celebration of the Red Mass." Fouquier, too, was determined not to miss the spectacle ; from a window in the Conciergerie he had watched the scarlet-clad figures ascending the tumbrils and, irritated by the sang-froid of Madame de Sainte-Amaranthe, exclaimed, " See how brazen they are ! I must go and see them mount the scaffold, even if I have to miss my dinner ! " [1]

The calm invariably displayed by the victims was a source of continual annoyance to the jackals of the Comité de Sûreté Générale and their allies in the Revolutionary Tribunal. One evening as they met at their favourite tavern—Chrétien, on the Place du Théâtre Favart—to drink punch and liqueurs, to smoke and laugh over the executions, and boast of the way they invented accusations against innocent people, Renaudin, one of the most ferocious members of the Revolutionary Tribunal, referring to a certain victim, remarked, " There was nothing against him." " When there is nothing," said Vilate, " one invents." " As for me," said Foucault, " I find nobles every-where, even amongst cobblers." Prieur then observed, " There is one thing that puts me in a temper, and that is the courage with which all these counter-revolutionaries go to their death. If I were in the place of the Public Accuser, I would have all the condemned people bled before their execution, so as to break down their insolent bearing." " Bravo, my friend," cried Leroy, known under the sobriquet of " Dix Août," " I will undertake to speak of it to Fouquier ! " [2]

After the great *journée* of the Chemises Rouges things moved faster, yet still not fast enough to satisfy the members of the two committees, and it was then decided to have recourse once more to the old device that had succeeded so admirably in

---

[1] Evidence of Robert Wolf, clerk of the Court at the Revolutionary Tribunal, *Procès de Fouquier*, Buchez et Roux, xxxiv. 447.

[2] *Histoire secrète du Tribunal révolutionnaire*, by Proussinalle, ii. 175, 181.

September 1792, and to announce that vast conspiracies were being formed in all the prisons. The pretext, which seems to have been concerted between Robespierre and Hermann, president of the Revolutionary Tribunal,[1] was, however, this time not so plausible, for the successes of the Republican armies made it impossible to represent the prisoners as a danger to the country through collusion with invading legions.[2] In order, therefore, to give some colour to the story, an attempt was made by means of systematic ill-treatment—by taking from them all their possessions, feeding them abominably, and waking them up repeatedly in the night—to drive the prisoners to form some plan of revolt which could be called a conspiracy.[3] But the unhappy captives bore all their sufferings with complete resignation ; not the faintest shadow of a conspiracy could be detected in any of the prisons. Yet in each prison in turn—Bicêtre, the Luxembourg, the Carmes, Saint-Lazare, and La Force—it was announced that a conspiracy had been formed, and on this pretext people of all kinds, men and women, deaf, blind, or paralysed, were condemned to death *en masse*. Many of these conspirators, accused of having conferred together, met for the first time in the tumbrils on the way to execution.

The hecatombs now became appalling. During the last six weeks before the fall of Robespierre, that is to say between the passing of the " Loi du 22 Prairial " on June 10 and July 27, the period which constitutes " The Great Terror," no less than 1366 victims perished, and amongst these by far the largest proportion was taken from amongst either " the people " or the *petite bourgeoisie*.[4] " One saw before this Tribunal of Blood," it was said later in the trial of Fouquier Tinville, " labouring men who tilled the soil, whose rags hardly covered their nakedness, ascending the rows of seats (of the Tribunal), and

---

[1] Evidence of Grandpré, chief of police, *Procès de Fouquier*, Buchez et Roux, xxxiv. 432.

[2] Evidence of Sauvebœuf : " Our victories no longer permitted of the renewal of this pretext " (*ibid.* p. 372).

[3] Evidence of Sauvebœuf and of Réal, counsel, *ibid.* pp. 372, 389.

[4] I have shown elsewhere (*The Chevalier de Boufflers*, p. 377) the proportion of victims amongst the middle- or working-classes to have been approximately 2110 out of the total of 2800. Mr. Croker places the total at 2730, and calculates that of these 650 were " rich people," rather over 1000 were middle-class, and *1000 working-class*. M. Louis Blanc (*Histoire de la Révolution*, xi. 155) accepts this statement, but endeavours to clear his idol Robespierre from guilt by saying that he protested against the massacre of poor people. This is a pure invention—Robespierre never once uttered such a protest. See his speeches against " indulgence " on June 10, July 9, 11, and 14, and especially his protest against showing sensibility on July 1 (13th Messidor) just after the execution of seventy-two victims, nearly all working-men (Michelet, ix. 196).

being led to the scaffold for having in a moment of anger, or perhaps of drunkenness, made some observation, or for having, through want of education (!), opposed the removal of their church bells." [1]

In order to swell the numbers of the condemned, poor people were dragged to Paris from all parts of France and butchered without any explanation being given them.[2] " Twenty women of Poitou," writes an eye-witness, " poor peasants mostly, were assassinated all together. I see them still, those unhappy victims, lying out in the courtyard of the Conciergerie, overcome with fatigue after a long journey—sleeping on the paving-stones. Their glances, which betrayed no understanding of the fate that threatened them, resembled those of oxen herded together in the market - place, looking around them fixedly and without comprehension. They were all executed a few days after their arrival. At the moment of going to death, some one tore from the breast of one of these unfortunate women the child that she was nursing. . . . Oh ! cries of maternal anguish, how piercing you were, but you were in vain. Some of the women died in the cart and they guillotined the corpses." [3]

In this case the victims were condemned all in a batch, without specific grounds of accusations being brought against them individually ; where men and women of the people were condemned singly some trumped-up charge was usually forthcoming. The following entries taken at random from Wallon's records of the Revolutionary Tribunal give an idea of the pretexts on which these poor creatures were done to death :

1. Françoise Bridier, widow Loreu, aged 72, domestic servant, accused of having hidden 12 ells of linen cloth required for the clothing of the volunteers.

2. Anne Thérèse Raffé, widow Coquet, denounced by the citizen Folatre to whom she had wished to give a note of 50 livres which he did not need.

3. Germaine Quetier, the wife of Charbonnier, who said that she wanted a *rouet* (spinning-wheel), which she pronounced like " roi." [4]

But it must be admitted that some of the victims brought their fate on themselves. " Aristocracy " was still rampant amongst certain classes of the people, and nothing could persuade them to keep silent. Thus Madame Blanchet, the old servant

[1] Notes by the reporter of the trial of Fouquier, Buchez et Roux, xxxiv. 487.

[2] Evidence of Grandpré, *ibid.* p. 427.

[3] *Mémoires de Riouffe*, i. 87 ; *Letters of Helen Maria Williams* (1795), p. 108. Helen Maria Williams, who had so rejoiced over the 10th of August, was now in prison, her revolutionary ardour considerably cooled.

[4] Wallon, *Histoire du Tribunal révolutionnaire*, iv. 402.

of the Abbé de Salamon—she who had turned over the corpses in the courtyard of the Abbaye in her search for her master during the massacres of September—still continued to speak her mind very freely. Blanchet was therefore imprisoned at the " Anglaises," where she found herself amongst a number of *ci-devants* who had sympathized with the Revolution. One of these ladies, the Duchesse d'Anville la Rochefoucauld, taunted Blanchet, saying, " Citizeness Blanchet, you will be guillotined like us ! " " I know that well," Blanchet answered, " but there is a difference between us. I shall die for your cause, which you yourself have abandoned, and you, you will die for having embraced the cause of the patriots. . . . It will be much more degrading to perish thus. . . . No one will be sorry for you, but for me all honourable people who learn of my sad fate will weep. . . . I have always been an aristocrat myself, and you, you were always the friend of that contemptible Condorcet about whom I could tell you fine things ! " [1]

But it was not only the " respectable poor " like Blanchet who entertained aristocratic sentiments. Some of the disreputable women of the people were violently Royalist. The Comtesse de Bohm has described a number of these poor creatures, mostly street criers, who were her fellow-prisoners at the Conciergerie, and " carried Royalism to excess." When, as frequently happened, they became noisily drunk, " their songs, their toasts, were constantly intermingled with cries of ' Vive le Roi ! ' " " These resounding exclamations," writes Madame de Bohm, " annoyed the gaolers, who, unable to make them keep silence, daily threatened and struck these drunken women. This bold, free, and exalted way of showing one's feelings, of preferring death to constraint, indicates a certain greatness of soul, a savage independence which contrasted strangely with the baseness, the coarseness, and the obscene habits of my neighbours. . . . I sometimes represented to them the dangers they were incurring. ' Oh well, my girl, we shall be guillotined ! One can only die once ! ' The turnkeys, tired of these vociferations, denounced them ; and after being judged and condemned they mounted the scaffold, crying deafeningly, ' Vive le Roi ! ' "

The temptation to commit suicide by uttering this fatal cry proved irresistible to certain women ; thus Marie Corrié, a young laundress of twenty-three, from sheer " gaiety of heart " opened her window and shouted loudly, " Vive le Roi ! " Before the Revolutionary Tribunal she frankly admitted the offence, declaring that she would always cry " Vive le Roi ! " and " Vive Louis XVII. ! " The guillotine silenced her at last.

[1] *Mémoires de Monseigneur de Salamon*, p. 206. Blanchet survived the Terror and died in her master's arms eleven years later.

It seems, indeed, that throughout this fearful period of the Terror some mysterious spirit of exaltation was abroad ; the utter uncertainty in which one lived, the breathless suspense that kept the nerves at concert pitch, the bridging over of the chasm that divides life from death effected by the daily spectacle of those slow-moving " hearses of the living " conveying youth and age, virility and beauty, to the other world, even the tropical heat of the weather, all combined to produce an abnormal state of mind which drove people of ardent imaginations to throw their lives recklessly away.

But whatever the cause, the courage displayed by the women of all classes during the Reign of Terror must eternally remain one of the most glorious episodes in the history of France. Amongst the hundreds that perished one alone, poor old Madame du Barry, showed weakness ; all the rest, without exception, faced the scaffold with unfaltering courage.

In the women of the aristocratic classes this heroism is the less surprising, for they were trained from infancy to hide their feelings and to live up to their traditions. To these bearers of great names, dying for a cause that was their own, the Terror must have appeared as a mighty drama in which each one felt herself called to play her part worthily, knowing full well that every word, every smile or glance or gesture would be noticed and recorded, her last words handed down from generation to generation, the lock of hair she gave preserved as a sacred relic amongst her descendants.

But for the women of the people, where was the incentive to courage ? To these poor souls, suddenly and roughly hurried out of life for no apparent reason, the Terror can have presented nothing in the least dramatic—merely a black horror they could not understand. The Revolution, they were told, was for the good of the people ; yet were they not the people ? Surely to be butchered in the name of democracy was a thousand times more maddening than to fall a victim to the tyranny of the Old Régime ! It cannot be too often repeated—the people were the chief sufferers in the Terror. Even in the prisons the aristocrats fared better than they. For there, as everywhere else during the reign of equality, money could buy alleviations, and the wealthier prisoners were able, by the payment of four or five livres a day, to secure cells and pallet-beds, wretched enough in truth, yet infinitely to be preferred to the dreadful *Souricière* or " Mouse-Trap " of the Conciergerie, where the unhappy members of the people were flung upon filthy straw to be devoured by rats and poisoned with pestilential odours.[1]

Why did the people submit to this régime ? How, in the

[1] *Paris Révolutionnaire*, by G. Lenôtre, p. 350.

words of Vilate, are we to understand " the blind docility of the most enlightened of nations in allowing itself to be taken piece-meal and butchered *en masse* like a stupid herd led to the shambles ?   History will ask this question."

The answer is surely that the despotism of the demagogues was organized, whilst the people were composed of solitary units that could not coalesce. To form an effectual opposition it would have been necessary to meet in consultation, to draw up some plan of campaign, and any such attempts would have been instantly crushed. The people, therefore, felt themselves helpless ; no one dared to break line, to take the first step, uncertain whether he would get a backing from his fellows or whether those very men who seemed most eager to rebel would not at the last moment bè stricken with panic and betray their allies.

Fear, indeed, held all hearts in its grip. *The Terrorists them-selves were terrorized.*   They lived in dread now less of the people than of each other.   The revolutionary committees were divided against themselves.   Robespierre had his spies in the Comité de Sûreté Générale ; meanwhile Vadier of this committee employed an agent to shadow Robespierre.   From this mutual distrust and suspicion arose much of the frenzy that characterized the Terror ; each man and each faction strove to outdo the other —" to kill in order not to be killed " became the plan of one and all.

Meanwhile the members of the Revolutionary Tribunal were driven onwards by the same haunting terror ; Fouquier Tin-ville himself trembled perpetually lest his zeal should be deemed unsufficing.   This was afterwards clearly proved at his trial, when all the workings of the Terror were laid bare.

Fouquier, it then transpired, was in the habit of going regularly every night during the time that he occupied the post of Public Accuser to receive his orders first from the Comité de Salut Public, then from the Comité de Sûreté Générale.[1]   It was then that the fate of the prisoners was decided and the *fournée* of the morrow arranged, after which Fouquier, armed with his lists, returned to the Conciergerie at one o'clock in the morning, or even later.   Against these decisions of the committees there was no appeal : " Do you not know," Fouquier said to Sénart, " that when the Comité de Salut Public has decided on the death of any one, patriot or aristocrat, no matter, he has got to go ? "[2]

That Fouquier knew exactly the number of the condemned

[1] *Mémoire* written by Fouquier in his own defence, Buchez et Roux, xxxiv. 234.

[2] Evidence of Villam d'Aubigny, ex-Adjoint au Ministre de la Guerre, *Procès de Fouquier*, Buchez et Roux, xxxiv. 412.

before they were brought to trial was proved conclusively. One day, Sénart related, he was waiting in an ante-chamber outside Fouquier's room at the Conciergerie, when one of the executioner's employés arrived, and Fouquier at this moment making his appearance the man said to him, " I have come, citizen, to ask you how many carts are wanted." Fouquier counting on his fingers murmured, " Eight — ten — twelve — eighteen — twenty-four—thirty—there will be thirty heads to-day." Sénart thereupon said to Fouquier, " What ? the trial has not yet begun, and you know beforehand the number of heads ? " " Bah ! bah ! " answered Fouquier, " I know what I am about, and besides, sir, that is none of your business. I know how to silence the ' moderates.' "[1] And he went off into his office saying suavely, " Au revoir, my fine gentleman ! "[2]

Fouquier at his trial, confronted with this incident, stammered out that the witness could not be relied on ; but whether Sénart is to be absolutely believed or not, the undeniable fact remains that the tumbrils arrived regularly in the courtyard of the Conciergerie every morning between nine and ten o'clock, before the trial began, and were found after it had ended to provide precisely the accommodation required.[3]

This detail, moreover, corresponds exactly with Fouquier's own repeated statement that he was merely " a cog in the wheel of the revolutionary machine,"[4] that he was perpetually goaded on to greater activity by the committees, threatened with dire consequences if he failed to provide a sufficient number of heads.

But that Fouquier was, as he also declared, an *unwilling* instrument in the hands of the committees it is impossible to believe ; overwhelming evidence goes to prove that, like his allies the jackals of the Comité de Sûreté Générale, Fouquier warmed to the work and, once put on the scent, followed it up with all the fury of a beast of prey. " Heads are falling like tiles," he said exultingly to Héron, who answered him, " Oh, things will go still better—do not worry ! "[5] Sometimes during the so-called trials Fouquier would enliven the proceedings with jests; thus when a woman, paralysed even to her tongue, appeared before the Tribunal, he observed gaily, " It is not her tongue, but her head we need."[6]

---

[1] At the trial Sénart said that Fouquier added, " Do you think I do not know the number of those who will be condemned ? "

[2] *Mémoires de Sénart.*

[3] Evidence of Grandpré, *Procès de Fouquier*, Buchez et Roux, xxxiv. 427.

[4] *Ibid.* p. 293.

[5] Evidence of Sénart, *ibid.* p. 307.

[6] Evidence of Retz, *ibid.* p. 135.

Yet it seems that there were moments when Fouquier, like Charles IX. on his death-bed, was overcome with horror at the thought of the innocent blood he had shed. One night as he passed over the Pont Neuf with Sénart he looked down at the Seine and cried incontrollably, " Ah, how red it is ! How red ! " Then turning to Sénart he said, " I live unquietly; I am tormented by the shades of those whom I have had guillotined—yet they had to die ; the political system required it." Sénart took this opportunity to ask him why he condemned victims without proof instead of making inquiries, to which Fouquier replied, " That would be the way to get myself guillotined." [1]

Spurred on by this fear Fouquier redoubled his activities. Often after his interviews with the committees he would go into the tap-room of the Conciergerie to nerve himself for his fearful task with copious draughts of beer. It was then that he confided to his colleagues of the Revolutionary Tribunal the instructions he had received for further *journées* : " Things are not going fast enough. . . . We must have 200 to 250 heads a decade ; the Government wishes it." [2] Then when this figure had been achieved—exceeded—" We are not keeping up the pace. . . . The last decade was not bad, but this one must go to 400 or 450. . . . *Il faut que cela aille.*" [3]

And it *went*—with fearful rapidity. During the month of Messidor the number of victims had risen to 796 ; in the first nine days of Thermidor alone it reached no less than 342. At this rate Fouquier's 450 a decade would speedily be attained. Plans, indeed, had been made on a far larger scale ; the size of the guillotines was to be increased so that four heads could be severed at a blow ; an amphitheatre capable of containing 150 victims was to be erected at the Revolutionary Tribunal, and of this number each *journée* for the guillotine was to be composed.[4] Already an immense *sangueduct* had been constructed in the Place Saint-Antoine, to which the guillotine had been removed on the 21st of Prairial, in order to carry away the torrents of blood that flowed from the scaffold, and an operation of the same kind was in progress at the Barrière du Trône, which had now become the place of execution.[5]

For as a spectacle the guillotine had long since lost its

---

[1] *Mémoires de Sénart* (edition de Lescure), p. 114.

[2] Evidence of Auvray, usher to the Revolutionary Tribunal, of Bucher and of Tavernier, clerks of the court, *Procès de Fouquier*, Buchez et Roux, xxxv. 9, 12, 15.

[3] Evidence of Robert Wolf, *ibid.* xxxiv. 448 ; of Tavernier, *ibid.* xxxv. 2.

[4] *Mémoires de Riouffe*, i. 84 ; Taine, viii. 133.

[5] *Mémoires de Riouffe*, ii. 196.

popularity; none but the *tricoteuses*, the hired "furies of the guillotine," now applauded the executions ; even the populace of Paris were sickened with the sight of bloodshed.[1]

Directly after the passing of the "Loi du 22 Prairial" the inhabitants of the Rue Saint-Honoré petitioned for the removal of the guillotine from the Place de la Révolution near-by, for not only had the spectacle of the tumbrils daily passing under their windows become intolerable to the dwellers in this street, but the whole neighbourhood had become infected with the odour of carnage—the very oxen drawing country-carts refused to pass over the blood-soaked soil of the Place de la Révolution. Accordingly the scaffold had been erected in the Place Saint-Antoine, but Saint-Antoine too had complained of its propinquity, and again it was found necessary to remove the instrument of death—decidedly La Sainte-Guillotine had lost favour with the public.

Sanson, the executioner, himself was growing weary, and declared that "the immense and unremitting work" to which he and his aides were subjected was enough "to lay low the most robust of men," consequently he now desired to end his term of service.[2]

At the Conciergerie, too, the officials were beginning to find the strain unendurable ; one entering the office cried out to his comrades, "It is finished, no one is being judged any longer ; we shall all go the same way, we are all lost ! " and a porter of the prison, named Blanchard, bursting into tears, declared that he could bear it no longer, that he "was not the sort to occupy such a post, and that it made him ill."[3]

Everywhere throughout the city the same sense of horror prevailed; the Palais Royal, once the hotbed of revolution, was silent and deserted—the courtesans that had filled its arcades had retired into hiding, the taverns were empty, the booksellers displayed no pamphlets ;[4] people moved fearfully about the streets, afraid to speak, to smile, even to whisper. In a word, Paris was once more on the verge of a *crise de nerfs*.

[1] "We must say that for more than six months before the 9th of Thermidor the public no longer applauded condemnations, but loudly manifested its joy and satisfaction at all acquittals. If furies of the guillotine, led astray, corrupted and *paid* by the faction of the murderers, often insulted the victims who walked to death with the calm of innocence, we must declare it was never the people of Paris ; this people never asked for blood. . . ." (Notes of reporter at trial of Fouquier, Buchez et Roux, xxxiv. 488). [2] *La Guillotine*, by G. Lenôtre, p. 181.
[3] *Le Tribunal Révolutionnaire*, by G. Lenôtre, p. 280.
[4] "Nothing was published. In the enormous collection of revolutionary pamphlets we find this interval (between the Fête du l'Être Suprême and the fall of Robespierre) almost a blank " (Croker's *Essays on the French Revolution*, p. 404).

As usual, at nearly every great crisis of the Revolution, the weather was hot to suffocation. From the 4th of Thermidor the temperature rose steadily until by the 8th Paris had become a furnace—men and animals dropped dead from the heat. So physically and morally the storm gathered, then burst with a mighty thunderclap over the affrighted city on that momentous day—the Neuf Thermidor.

LE NEUF THERMIDOR

Ever since the Feast of the Supreme Being Robespierre had understood that the time was approaching when he must engage in a life-and-death struggle with his rivals of the Comité de Salut Public, and it was in preparation for this contingency that, after ceasing to frequent the meetings of the committee, he allied himself more closely with the Commune and the Jacobin Club. By this means he had succeeded in organizing a formidable opposition, and it seems probable that he had planned a rising for the 10th of Thermidor, by which the revolutionary committees were to be overthrown and the triumvirate of Robespierre, Couthon, and St. Just left in sole possession of the field.

On the 8th of Thermidor (the 26th of July) Robespierre judged that the moment had come to open the campaign against his enemies. Ascending the tribune of the Convention he embarked on a denunciation of the two revolutionary committees—the Comité de Sûreté Générale must be purged and subordinated to the Comité de Salut Public ; the latter committee must likewise submit to purgation, the traitors must be punished. In other words, both committees were to be entirely subordinated to that virtuous and incorruptible trio—Robespierre, Couthon, and St. Just. The rival faction, instantly taking up the gauntlet, retorted with accusations against the Incorruptible. " One man only," cried Cambon, " paralyses the will of the Convention—that man is Robespierre ! "

Robespierre, undismayed, went on after the sitting of the Convention to the Jacobin Club and delivered a further oration, this time openly attacking Billaud and Collot, who were present at the meeting and found themselves obliged to escape for their lives amidst the angry howls of the Jacobins. Encouraged by this demonstration Robespierre retired peacefully to bed, whilst St. Just spent the night at the Comité de Salut Public, writing out the act of accusation which was to be brought against the opponents of the triumvirate on the morrow.

The 9th of Thermidor dawned sultry and lowering—no sun, and a sky of molten lead. But Robespierre and St. Just appeared

at the Convention dressed as for a gala—Robespierre in the light-
blue coat which had made its début at the Feast of the Supreme
Being, St. Just in a coat of chamois colour with an immense
and carefully arranged cravat, white waistcoat, and breeches of
delicate grey. The tribunes, still Robespierriste, greeted these
apparitions with frenzied applause.

Then St. Just ascended the tribune to deliver his speech of
indictment, and once again reverted to the surgical simile which
ever since the massacres of September had haunted the imagination of each revolutionary leader in turn : " I had been charged
to make a report to you on the scandalous deviations that for
some time have tormented public opinion, but the remedies I
wished to propose to you were powerless to heal the ills of the
Republic ; a little balm will not suffice for so difficult a cure, we
must carve down to the quick and cut off the gangrened limbs." [1]

At these words Tallien rose indignantly, and rushing at the
tribune thrust aside St. Just : " I demand that the curtain
be drawn aside ! " Tallien was quickly followed by Billaud-
Varenne, crying out that a plot had been formed to murder the
Convention : " The Convention will perish if it shows weakness ! "

Then from all sides a tremendous uproar arose ; members
waved their hats, the audience shouted, " Long live the Convention ! Long live the Comité de Salut Public ! "

Collot, the president on this day, pealed his bell to restore
order ; Tallien flourished a dagger—sent him, it was said, by
Térésia Cabarrus, now in prison awaiting death—and threatened
to pierce the heart of " the new Cromwell " if the Convention
did not decree his arrest ; Robespierre dashed frantically at the
tribune, but his voice was drowned in cries of " Down with the
tyrant ! "

Then one after another, Tallien, Fréron, Billaud, Collot,
Barère, once the servile accomplices of Robespierre, now his
cowardly assailants, rose to denounce him : he whom they had
hailed as the " Incorruptible " had become " the new Catilina " ;
with St. Just and Couthon he had intended to establish a
triumvirate after the manner of Sylla ; one accused Robespierre
of befriending Danton, another of murdering him. Meanwhile
the wretched Vadier interposed perpetually with his story of
Catherine Théot, the crazy old woman who called herself the
mother of God, and under whose mattress a letter to Robespierre
had been found addressing him as the Messiah.

Amidst all this wild medley of accusations Robespierre and

---

[1] This last phrase, given by Beaulieu and by Fantin Désodoards, which
alone explains the uproar created in the Convention, is omitted by Buchez
et Roux, who give the speech of St. Just as it was written, not as it was
delivered. The *Moniteur* does not report it at all.

his allies vainly strove to obtain a hearing ; once the thin voice of the Incorruptible raised itself above the tumult in a despairing appeal : " For the last time will you let me speak, president of assassins ? " But the words he would have spoken died away in his throat : " The blood of Danton chokes him ! " cried Garnier de l'Aube. " Ah, then, it is Danton you wish to avenge ? " began Robespierre, but again his voice was drowned in angry clamour. An obscure member named Louchet called out for his arrest, and the proposal being put to the vote was unanimously adopted. Other members followed, demanding the decree to be extended to his brother, Augustin Robespierre, to St. Just, Couthon, and Lebas, and these demands again met with unanimous approval. So at half-past five, as the sitting ended, the police entered the hall and led away the five arrested deputies to the prisons assigned to them.

But the Commune, which still remained faithful to Robespierre, prevented the execution of this project ; word had already been sent out by Fleuriot Lescot, the mayor of Paris, to the concierges of the different prisons forbidding them to admit the Robespierristes, who were then—again by the order of the mayor—conveyed triumphantly to the Hôtel de Ville. Meanwhile Fleuriot Lescot ordered the tocsin to be sounded, and summoned the Jacobins to the rescue of " the martyrs."

But now that the moment for-action had come Robespierre displayed the same fatal irresolution that had characterized the leaders of each party in turn at the moment of crisis. Like Louis XVI. on the 10th of August, the Girondins on the 2nd of June, Danton on the 5th of April, Robespierre could find no stirring words wherewith to inspire his supporters, could decide on no heroic course of action that might have rallied the hesitating multitude around him.

There were no great men in the Revolution, contemporaries declare ; amongst the many leaders of the people was not one Cromwell,[1] and when we consider the end of all these men whom historians have magnified into giants, and observe the total inability of one and all to play a losing game, we are forced to the same conclusion. Whilst still on the crest of the wave— whither they had been carried by circumstances rather than by personal ability—they could display vigour, audacity, resolution, but the moment the tide turned forcibly against them, they allowed themselves to be engulfed almost without a struggle.

---

[1] *Mémoires de Frénilly*, p. 166. And Mounier : " Nature in giving us for this Revolution so many men with the heart of Cromwell did not produce one with his head " (*Appel au Tribunal de l'Opinion publique*, p. 291). And Madame Roland : " France seemed exhausted of *men* ; it is a really surprising thing the dearth of them in this Revolution, there have been hardly anything but pigmies " (*Mémoires*, i. 235).

As late as seven o'clock on that evening of the 9th of Thermidor the day was not lost for Robespierre and his adherents—Hanriot that afternoon had triumphantly escorted " a batch " of forty-two to the guillotine—nearly all obscure and humble members of the *petite bourgeoisie* or the people—ruthlessly cutting down the crowd with his sabre when for the first and last time they attempted to intervene and save the victims ; [1] and since still at the head of his troops, the Commune had reason to hope that he would repeat his success of the 31st of May by keeping the Hôtel de Ville in a state of siege.   But Robespierre, instead of concerting with Hanriot on the measures to be taken, left the commander to his own devices, which, on this fateful day, consisted in getting gloriously drunk and galloping about Paris shouting, " Kill the policemen ! "

Hanriot's wild career was brought to an abrupt conclusion in the Place de Palais Royal, where he fell from his horse and was seized by the police, who placed him under arrest.   Later in the evening, Coffinhal, vice-president of the Revolutionary Tribunal, came to his rescue with 200 gunners and delivered him, but the wretched man had now completely lost his head, and instead of rallying the crowd merely succeeded in terrifying it by his maniacal aspect and behaviour.

All this time the Faubourgs were waiting for orders.   Accustomed throughout the Revolution to march only at the word of command, they were now quite incapable of independent action, and had no idea whether they were to support the Commune or the Convention.   Sainte-Antoine at last wrote naïvely to the magistrates of the Commune explaining the dilemma, and if Robespierre or any of his supporters had only gone in person to rouse the district, they could undoubtedly have mustered the men of the Faubourg around them.[2]   Instead of this Robespierre could do nothing but talk, leaving the field open to his adversaries, who thereupon circulated a rumour in Saint - Marceau that he was a Royalist conspirator, for a seal with a *fleur de lys* had been found in his possession.[3]

The Faubourgs, thus left without a leader, abandoned the Commune and went over to the Convention.

Meanwhile the crowd collected on the Place de Grève outside the Hôtel de Ville showed no more decision than the Faubourgs, and only awaited events in order to throw its weight into the scale on either side.   Already, however, its confidence in the Commune had been shaken by the deranged behaviour of Hanriot,

---

[1] Beaulieu, v. 497 ; Dauban, *Paris en 1794*, p. 446.   This incident provides further proof that Robespierre did not disapprove of the butchery of poor people, for Hanriot was absolutely under his orders.

[2] Buchez et Roux, xxxiv. 58.

[3] *Ibid.* pp. 59, 84.

and to this Paris populace that always worships strength the news that Robespierre and his party had been outlawed by the Convention served finally to alienate any lingering sympathy it entertained for the defeated faction. When at midnight the storm that all day had been gathering burst over the city in a torrent of rain, the crowd, damped both in mind and body, took the opportunity to disperse, leaving the Robespierristes to their fate.

It was thus that Barras, placed by the Convention in command of the troops, was able to advance through the deserted Place de Grève without encountering any resistance, and Léonard Bourdon at the head of the armed police went forward into the Hôtel de Ville to re-arrest the five deputies.

Then Hanriot, losing his head completely, rushed into the Salle de Conseil where Robespierre and his party were assembled, crying out that all was lost, whereupon Coffinhal overwhelmed him with reproaches, and finally seizing him round the body hurled him out of the window into the courtyard below. There a manure heap broke his fall, and the besotted commander was able to crawl into a sewer, where he remained until the following day.

Close on the heels of Hanriot, Léonard Bourdon and his policemen entered the Salle de Conseil, and at this sight the Robespierristes gave way to despair. A scene of wild confusion followed. Maximilien Robespierre, seated at a table where he had begun to write out an order summoning the Section des Piques to his rescue, fell forward suddenly shot through the jaw —whether by his own hand or by that of the policeman Merda, who afterwards boasted of the deed, is uncertain;[1] his brother Augustin climbed out of the window, and running along an outside ledge flung himself down on to the steps of the Hôtel de Ville, where he lay, mutilated and bleeding ; Couthon dragged his paralysed limbs beneath a table, whence he was dislodged and brutally flung down the staircase by the commissioners of the Convention. St. Just, according to certain contemporaries, alone remained immovable ; according to others, he asked Lebas to shoot him, but Lebas responded, " Coward ! I have other things to do ! " and forthwith blew out his own brains.

Early in the morning of the 10th of Thermidor a part of this human wreckage was gathered up and carried to the Tuileries, where the Convention still remained sitting : first of all Maximilien Robespierre borne on a stretcher, his eyes closed, his

---

[1] On this point opinions are almost equally divided. Merda (or Méda) declared he shot Robespierre ; others present at the scene declared that they saw Robespierre shoot himself. See the conflicting evidence collected by M. Biré in the *Journal d'un Bourgeois de Paris*, v. 387-392.

naturally bilious countenance wearing the livid hue of death, and so apparently lifeless that the Assembly refused to admit "the corpse of the tyrant," and the stretcher-bearers were obliged to go on to the Comité de Salut Public and deposit their burden on a table—according to Barras, the famous green-covered table around which the committee gathered nightly to draw up their lists of proscriptions.

Here, then, on the very spot where he had ordained the slaughter of countless human beings, Robespierre lay himself, a piteous object now, with his head resting on a wooden box, and the blood flowing from his fractured jaw over the white frilled shirt and the pale-blue coat. For seven hours, racked with agony, the man before whom all France had trembled endured the jeers and insults of the soldiers and policemen he had believed to be devoted to his cause. At one moment a working-man approached and, looking long and closely into the shattered face of the tyrant, murmured in awe-struck tones, " Yes, there is a God ! " [1]

After a while St. Just, still erect and impassive, was led in with Dumas, their hands tightly bound, and later more stretchers arrived at the foot of the staircase leading to the committee-room on which lay the mangled forms of Couthon and Augustin Robespierre.

At ten o'clock, whilst the criers went through the streets calling out, " The Great Arrest of Catilina Robespierre and his accomplices ! " the prisoners were all transferred to the Conciergerie—" the ante-chamber of death." No trial was to be accorded them, for with the downfall of each faction the revolutionary government took a further step in illegality, and, the Robespierristes having been declared outlaws, the Convention held it necessary only to bring them before the Revolutionary Tribunal for purposes of identification, a process that occupied a bare half-hour. The whole band, to the number of twenty-two, including, besides Robespierre and his accomplices, the miserable cobbler Simon, to whom the little Dauphin had been confided, Fleuriot Lescot, and twelve members of the Commune, were sentenced to be executed the same afternoon on the Place de la Révolution. For on this great day no fear was enter-tained of wounding the susceptibilities of the dwellers in the Rue Saint-Honoré and the surrounding district by the spectacle of the guillotine, and the Place de la Révolution alone could accommodate the crowds that hastened from all quarters of Paris to celebrate the death of the tyrant.

When in the late afternoon the four tumbrils emerged from the courtyard of the Conciergerie, all Paris had turned out to

[1] Toulongeon, iv. ; *Moniteur*, xxi. 385.

see them pass, and to the wondering multitude the sight presented by the men who had so long held them under the sway of the Terror seemed awe-inspiring evidence of " the justice of God." [1]

So had the mighty fallen ! Robespierre the all-powerful, a crushed and broken thing, the livid countenance swathed in its bloodstained bandages, the sky-blue coat torn and discoloured ; Couthon lying helplessly on the straw of the tumbril trampled by the feet of his companions ; Hanriot, who but yesterday had cleared the way for the forty-two poor victims, cutting down the people with his sabre, now a ghastly spectacle, with one eye falling from its socket, his face bleeding, his clothes tattered and covered with filth from the sewer whence he had been dragged. St. Just alone retained his habitual calm. The voluminous cravat was gone, leaving his neck bare for execution, but the delicate chamois-coloured coat still remained unspotted, the wide expanse of white waistcoat still fresh and uncrumpled, whilst in his buttonhole there glowed a red carnation. So with head erect St. Just, that strange enigma of the Terror, passed to his death, a marble statue to the last.

As the procession slowly made its way along the Rue Saint-Honoré it was not only joy that greeted its progress but fury —the long-pent-up fury of a crushed and suffering people. The tyrant had fallen, but could his downfall give them back their dead ? Everywhere in that vast crowd were men and women who had lost their all, in whose hearts was no room for rejoicing, only for reviling. One such grief-racked creature—a woman— sprang on to the back of the cart that held Robespierre and, clinging to the bars, cried out in a voice of agony :

" Monster vomited by Hell, thy torment intoxicates me with joy ! I have only one regret—that thou hast not a thousand lives so that I might enjoy the spectacle of seeing them torn from thee one by one ! Go, scoundrel, go down to the tomb with the curses of all wives and of all mothers ! "

Thus amidst the maledictions of the people, whose servile courtier he had been, Maximilien Robespierre passed to his death. Those amongst the crowd around the scaffold who desired to see him suffer—and they were many [2]—were gratified by the horrible scene that took place on the platform of the guillotine when the executioner, roughly tearing off the bandage that bound the head of Robespierre, loosed the fractured jaw, which fell, leaving a gaping chasm, and wrung from the tortured

---

[1] *Journal d'un Bourgeois de Paris*, by Edmond Biré, v. 399.

[2] Beaulieu, v. 502 : " The greater number of those who were present at his execution would have liked to see him suffer the tortures of Damiens, to whom he was said to be related."

victim a roar of agony "like that of a dying tiger which could be heard in the furthest extremities of the square."

As at the death of Hébert, the brutality of the executioner delighted the spectators, and when a moment later the mutilated head was raised aloft, the vast multitude that filled the Place de la Révolution and overflowed into the Tuileries and the Champs Élysées broke into a perfect thunder of applause that rose and fell and rose again, whilst men and women fell into each other's arms crying out, "At last we are free! The tyrant is no more!"

But this time it was no sudden madness such as had seized a part of the crowd gathered around the scaffold of the King, and which had been immediately succeeded by reaction; on this 10th of Thermidor the people really did go home rejoicing with a joy that throughout the days that followed grew in intensity, transforming Paris from a place of gloom and mourning into a gala city of new-found delights. Only to be able to walk abroad at liberty, to hold one's head up in the sunshine, to greet one's fellow-men, to speak one's thoughts aloud—what strange and wondrous happiness! At the street corners, in the public squares, the theatres, the cafés, long-lost friends whom terror had kept apart clasped each other's hands, embraced with tears of joy—it was a delirium, an ecstasy of bliss!

Why had the death of Robespierre brought about this marvellous transformation? Robespierre and his allies were, as we have seen, by no means the sole authors of the Terror—nor indeed the most ferocious. Barère, Billaud, Collot, Fréron, Tallien—henceforth to be known as the Thermidoriens—still remained; Fouquier still sat making up his lists in his tower at the Conciergerie; the jackals of the Comité de Sûreté Générale still prowled at large about the city. Until the 10th of Thermidor it does not appear that one of these men had any thought of ending or even modifying the Terror. It was certainly not from any disapproval of the system they had attacked Robespierre. For amongst all the accusations brought against him at the Convention by the Thermidoriens, not one related even remotely to the matter of bloodshed; on the contrary, he had been reproached for not loving Marat or Chalier, the author of the atrocities at Lyon and the object of Collot's ardent admiration.

These facts have given the panegyrists of Robespierre a further opportunity to declare that he wished to end the Terror, and that the Thermidoriens were alone to blame for its continuance. But to suppose this is to deny Robespierre any motive in originally organising it. If, as we have seen, he had embarked on it with a purpose—a system of depopulation which was to produce a harmonious democracy—why should he wish to arrest it at this stage ? The execution of 2800 people could not be said to have sensibly diminished the population of Paris, nor could the death-roll for all France—even if it amounted to the figure of 1,025,711 given by Prudhomme—be considered as more than a step towards the reduction of the French nation to the eight millions generally advocated by the leaders. There is, therefore, every reason to suppose that by the 9th of Thermidor the Terror was really only beginning, and that if the division had not taken place on this day between the Terrorists the hecatombs would have reached colossal proportions.

With this scheme, however, the Thermidoriens were heartily in accord. How, then, did it come to pass that the downfall of the Robespierristes resulted in the ending of the Terror ? The simplest explanation seems to be that the system of the Terror gave way under the weight of public opinion. For to the people of Paris, who always identified each régime with a personality, Robespierre and the Terror were synonymous, and consequently to their minds the end of Robespierre meant the end of the Terror—hence their outburst of rejoicing.

The Thermidoriens realizing this, and finding themselves greeted on the morning of the 10th of Thermidor by a rapturous crowd as the deliverers of France, were quick to see that their best chance of popularity lay in accepting the rôle assigned to them. If the people thought that in overthrowing Robespierre they had intended to overthrow the system of the Terror, well, they would stop the Terror and shift all the blame for the past from their own shoulders by making Robespierre the scapegoat of the whole Terrorist party. For the purpose that had inspired the Robespierristes to reduce the population these Opportunists cared nothing, and they were ready to fall in with any régime provided only they themselves could cling to place and power.

The Thermidorien reaction was thus not the work of a political party, but a really popular movement brought about by the force of the people's will, which, for the first time since the beginning of the Revolution, triumphed over the designs of the demagogues.

Although the 9th of Thermidor had removed only a portion of the Terrorists, the growing force of public opinion rendered the downfall of the remainder inevitable. On the 27th of November, Carrier, the " depopulator of Nantes," was summoned before the Revolutionary Tribunal, where he protested his innocence and declared that he had acted only from motives of the purest patriotism. A more plausible line of defence consisted in his plea that his methods had received the approval both of the

Comité de Salut Public and of the Convention,[1] and that no reproaches had been addressed to him until after the Terror had ended.[2] The apologists of Robespierre have attempted to prove that Carrier was recalled from Nantes on account of the atrocities he committed there ; the truth is that he incurred the displeasure of the Incorruptible, not by his fearful cruelty towards the people, but by his corrupt and vicious manner of life, and also by his threatening attitude towards Robespierre's protégé, young Jullien, who, terrified for his own safety, wrote to the Comité de Salut Public to complain. Moreover, in the letter from the Comité summoning him back to Paris not the faintest disapproval was expressed, and Carrier was merely informed— amidst assurances of fraternal good-will—that his arduous labours had entitled him to a little rest and that another mission would be given him. It was, therefore, in no way a chastened or repentant Carrier who returned to Paris on February 16, 1793—that is to say, more than three months after he had inaugurated the noyades. On his arrival he received the compliments of the Jacobin Club, and met with not a word of remonstrance from the Convention, where he resumed his place as a respected member and of which he was elected secretary three months later. But to the people Carrier, like Robespierre, embodied the system of the Terror, and he was condemned to death amidst universal applause. On the 16th of December 1794 an immense crowd once more assembled to watch the passage of the cart containing Carrier and two of his accomplices —Grandmaison, a member of the revolutionary committee of Nantes, convicted of having sabred the drowning victims of the noyades as they struggled in the water, and Pinard, leader of the negro legion that had outraged and murdered women and children. If the people had expected a wild-beast show they were not disappointed, for although Carrier, fortified by the conviction that he was a martyr dying for his country, faced his end with serenity, and Grandmaison only sobbed with helpless rage, Pinard presented a terrifying spectacle as, with flaming eyes and foaming lips, he spat upon the crowd, or when the jolts of the tumbril threw him against Carrier attempted to tear him with his teeth, overwhelming him with invectives for the

---

[1] Campardon, *Le Tribunal Révolutionnaire*, ii. 118 ; *J. B. Carrier*, by A. Lallié, p. 258. In a memoir presented to the Comité de Salut Public by Lequinio (another emissary to the provinces) on the 12th of Germinal, An II., the question is asked whether it would be advantageous to continue *the plan of total destruction* ; Carrier, quoting this letter at his trial, remarked that it proved this plan of destruction to have existed (Campardon, ii. 122). As M. Lallié points out, he was therefore only one of the agents ordered to execute it.

[2] Campardon, ii. 121.

fate he had brought on them all. It is said that as Carrier lay strapped to the plank of the guillotine a clarionet struck up the air of the " Ça ira! " and at this last insult the wretched man raised his head and darted a look of fury at the jeering multitude. The musician continued to play gaily until the blade had fallen.

On the 1st of May 1795 the Public Prosecutor of Paris followed the same road to the Place de Grève. Fouquier too protested his innocence : " I acted only in accordance with the laws passed by an all-powerful Convention." If he, the instrument, was brought to justice, should not the authors of the system, the remaining members of the revolutionary committees, be summoned before the Tribunal? True, and the subsequent condemnation of Collot, Billaud, and Barère to mere transportation for life was only one more miscarriage of justice in the history of the iniquitous tribunal.

The spirit that animated the multitude around the tumbrils which bore Fouquier and his accomplices to the scaffold was less one of " ferocious joy," says a police report, than of " curiosity to see extraordinary monsters "; the truth is, perhaps, that Paris was now too hungry to rejoice uproariously at anything. But when the carts approached the Place de Grève there burst forth shouts of fury : " Go and join your victims, scoundrel! " " Give me back my brother, my friend, my father, my wife, my mother, my children! " As at the execution of Robespierre, a woman, half demented with grief, clung to the bars of the tumbril cursing the murderer of her husband. Fouquier, looking forth with bloodshot eyes at the starving people, returned insult for insult, jeered at their misery in incoherent words of which the following only were distinguishable : " Vile rabble, go and look for bread! (Vile canaille, va chercher du pain !)."

Fouquier, reserved to the end as the pièce de résistance of the day, heard the blade descend fifteen times whilst in an agony of terror he waited his turn at the foot of the scaffold. As each head was held up to the wondering gaze of the multitude a mighty sigh of relief rose from amongst them like the moan of a troubled sea, but when that last frightful trophy was raised aloft the people, struck with horror as at a Gorgon's head, were frozen to silence.

RESULTS OF THE TERROR

The Terror, then, had ended, and what had it done for the people? It is to Carrier that we owe the famous phrase, " France was saved by the Terror," [1] a phrase eagerly adopted

[1] *Procès de Carrier*, Buchez et Roux, xxxiv. 208.

by revolutionary historians, and that by force of repetition has almost come to be believed.

But from what was France saved by the Terror? From hunger? From misery? From oppression? Alas, no, all these evils, which, as we have seen, flourished more luxuriantly during the Terror than ever before it, increased steadily after it had ended. Throughout the lean years that followed Paris was reduced to the lowest pitch of wretchedness ; people fainted in the streets for want of food,[1] or in desperation threw themselves into the Seine; women, maddened at the sight of their starving children, cried out for death to end their sufferings ; [2] and when at last bands of women invaded the Convention as they had once invaded Versailles clamouring for bread, they were met this time with no tears of compassion, but were driven out with whips.[3]

What wonder, then, that the people "incessantly compared their condition with that of 1788,"[4] that the women said to each other in the streets : "We need a good father of a family to feed us as we had before ; how can we love the Republic that makes us die of hunger ? "[5]

Not only did the people suffer from official mismanagement and indifference, but from the lack of all private effort to relieve distress—benevolence had vanished with the Old Régime. "Every day offers the proof of a sad truth," says the *Républicain Français*, "which is that the *parvenus*, the new rich, have harder hearts than those born in affluence. The latter used to share their superfluity with the poor, and nothing was commoner in this town than to see delicately bred women carrying soup, money, and consolations into garrets and prisons. To-day one dies of hunger and grief amidst these new millionaires enriched by our spoils ; one dies without experiencing a single moment of pity."

It will be urged that it was from external danger that the Terror saved France ; that if the people suffered the State prospered, the defences of the country had been made secure. To judge of the truth of this statement let us refer to the descrip-

---

[1] Schmidt, ii. 337.

[2] " The 6th of Germinal (An III.) several women asked for knives with which to stab themselves." The 30th of Brumaire " a woman in a frenzy came to ask a baker to kill her children as she had nothing to feed them with " (*ibid.*).

[3] On the 12th of Germinal, and again on the 1st of Prairial, An III. (April 1 and May 20, 1795), Schmidt, ii. 308, 327.

[4] Schmidt, ii. 462.

[5] *Ibid.* p. 481. See also p. 298 : " The public said loudly, ' We are going to have a king and we shall be much happier ; we shall not suffer so much.' "

tion of the condition of France at the end of the Terror, given
by one of the revolutionaries themselves—Larevellière Lépeaux,
a member of the Directory :

" The National Treasury was entirely empty ; not a *sou*
remained. *Assignats* were without value . . . public revenues
were nil, no plan of finance existed. . . . Enfuriated stock-
jobbing had taken the place of loyal and productive commerce ;
it corrupted all classes of society . . . there was not a sack of
corn in the granaries nor even a single grain of wheat. . . .
Hospitals were without revenues, without resources or administration ; public relief of every kind was reduced almost to nothing.
The canals were ruined, many bridges broken down, the roads
impassable . . . communications of all kinds had become
extremely difficult. . . . Public instruction, so to speak, no
longer existed. . . . The insolent cynicism of the leaders of
anarchy had created oblivion to all decency . . . what was
the state of the army ? Disorganization was complete . . .
in a word, the army, whether in the interior or on the frontiers,
was without discipline, without provisions, without pay, without
clothing, without equipment. As a climax of misfortune these
beaten and discouraged armies had lost all the fruit of their
successes beyond the Rhine. . . . As to the navy . . . our
fleets were humiliated, beaten, blockaded in our ports, tormented
by insubordination . . . ruined by desertion."

Such, then, was the state to which France was reduced by the
Terror. Can we doubt that if it had continued she must eventually have fallen a prey to a stronger power ? And what prevented this ? One thing only—the advent of the strong man
for whom during ten long years she had waited in vain ; the
man who put down with an iron hand the tyranny and corruption of the Directory and rallied the French around the standard
of the Empire. The truth is then that France was saved from
dismemberment, not by the Terror, but by *Imperialism*, whilst
she was saved from internal ruin and disruption, *in spite of the
Terror*, by the indomitable spirit of her *people*.

THE COURSE OF THE INTRIGUES

Whilst France was brought to the verge of ruin, and her
people were dying of starvation, the great intrigues continued
their course with unabated ardour. Orléanisme, though momentarily checked by the execution of Philippe Égalité and the
banishment of his sons, was to see its efforts rewarded thirty-
six years later ; Prussia, rid of the most formidable obstacle
to her power—the Franco-Austrian alliance—could afford to
bide her time in spite of military defeats in order to realize her

dreams of European domination; Anarchy, which had already triumphed under Marat and the Hébertistes, had become a force that has never since ceased to threaten the peace of the world. These consequences must be dealt with more fully in a concluding chapter amongst the results of the Revolution as a whole.

Alone of the four great intrigues, that of the English Jacobins received a serious check in the Reign of Terror. This was, however, not owing to any modification in the sentiments of our revolutionaries; the frightful period of bloodshed and horror that had overtaken France served merely to stimulate their ardour for revolutionary doctrines, and right up to the 9th of Thermidor they never relaxed their efforts to bring about the same order of things in our own country. True, the outbreak of war between England and France, followed by Pitt's timely introduction of the Traitorous Correspondence Act, considerably hampered their relations with the French Jacobins, and open addresses of congratulation were rendered impossible; nevertheless the intrigue between the Subversives in both countries was still clandestinely carried on, and mutual support was given throughout the Terror: Danton, by means of his connections in London, actively co-operated in the attempt to overthrow the British monarchy; [1] Fox assured the Comité de Salut Public of his sympathy and approval,[2] and later publicly applauded British reverses; whilst Lord Stanhope continued to maintain an affectionate correspondence with Barère, the archenemy of his country,[3] and to applaud the atrocities committed in France. This last flagrant betrayal of the interests not only of the English people but of the human race roused even the indignation of men who had formerly sympathized with the Revolution, and in April 1794 we find William Miles, once a member of the Jacobin Club in Paris, writing these words of remonstrance to Lord Stanhope:

"In the name of Heaven, my Lord, what frenzy is this that stimulates you to qualify as improvement what has proved fatal to millions? Whichever way you direct your attention you find affluence and content, freedom and happiness. In France every tree is a gibbet and every other man you meet a hangman. Yet your Lordship stands forth avowedly an admirer of crimes which desolate the earth and dishonour humanity." [4]

But the people of England expressed their disapproval in a

[1] *Danton Émigré*, by Dr. Robinet, p. 90.

[2] See remark of Vergniaud to Mrs. Elliott at the Comité de Salut Public: "Mr. Fox is our friend . . . he loves our revolution, and we have it here under his own hand-writing" (*Journal of Mrs. Elliott*, p. 146).

[3] *The Life of Charles, third Earl of Stanhope*, by Ghita Stanhope and G. P. Gooch, p. 134.

[4] *Ibid.*

more emphatic manner, and on the night of the 10th to the 11th of June, whilst London was celebrating Lord Howe's victory over the French, the crowd, enraged by Lord Stanhope's revolutionary sentiments, set fire to his house, and the unhappy peer was obliged to escape for his life over the roofs. The same thing had happened three years earlier at Birmingham, when the so-called Constitutional Society of that town, headed by Dr. Priestley, had issued " inflammatory handbills of Republican tendency." When on the 14th of July the Society met at a dinner to celebrate the fall of the Bastille, an angry crowd assembled and burnt down both the meeting-houses of the sect ; Dr. Priestley's house was attacked and he himself had to fly from door to door for refuge. The riots went on for three days, and the magistrates were powerless to interfere. It is, therefore, as much of an error to imagine that the failure to produce revolution in England was owing to the uninflammable character of the English as it is to attribute its success in France to the inflammable character of the French. It was precisely because the great majority of the French people were *un*inflammable, because they passively submitted to the domination of a handful of demagogues, that the Revolution was able to assume such frightful proportions. And it was because the English people beneath their apparent calm were in reality highly inflammable, were ready to oppose an active and even violent resistance to subversive doctrines, that the revolutionary movement could make no headway amongst them. Nor was this the result of servile submission to the existing order of things ; the people of England were well aware that great and drastic reforms were needed, but because they understood the meaning of true liberty it was not to Jacobinism that they looked for salvation.

Thus England at this supreme crisis in her history was saved from anarchy and ruin, not only by the statesmanship of Pitt and the eloquence of Burke, but *by the sound common sense of the British people.*

EPILOGUE

EPILOGUE

IN the foregoing chapter we have seen the results of the great revolutionary climax, the Reign of Terror; and although at the close of this frightful epoch the Revolution was not yet ended, it is impossible within the limits of this book to follow it throughout its final convulsions. To judge of the ultimate results of the movement by the state of France in 1795 would, however, be inconclusive; at this date, it might reasonably be urged, the country was still in a transition stage; a period of chaos was bound to follow on the great upheaval before matters could readjust themselves and the beneficial effects of the Revolution become apparent. To this argument the only reply is a brief summary of the succeeding régimes in France during the century that followed; it will then be seen, not as a matter of opinion but of fact, how far the new order proved permanently satisfying to the nation.

The *Directory* that succeeded to the Convention lasted four years, from 1795 to 1799, during which period two *coups d'état* took place. The Directory was then abolished on account of its tyranny, corruption, and mismanagement.

In 1799 the *Consulate* was formed, with Napoleon Bonaparte as First Consul, but five years later the Republic was declared a failure as " unequal to the exigencies of the country."

Accordingly in 1804 Napoleon was made *Emperor*, and by re-establishing despotism—a rigorous system of conscription, the abolition of the liberty of the press, etc.—he succeeded in restoring order. It is needless to enumerate the disasters that followed on this brief spell of glory—the retreat from Moscow during which thousands of Frenchmen perished in the snows of Russia; the invasion of France by Russians, Austrians, and Prussians; the overthrow of Napoleon for " having violated the rights and liberties of the people and the laws of the Constitution."

Then France, sickened with anarchy, republicanism, and imperialism all in turn, reverted to *monarchy*, and in 1814 Louis XVIII. was called to the throne only to be driven away by Napoleon six months later. Fresh disasters followed — the

485

defeat of Waterloo, the second entry of foreign armies into Paris, the payment of an indemnity of twenty-eight millions.

Once more Louis XVIII. was recalled, and the nine years of " legitimist " monarchy that followed was the only government since the Revolution that did not come to a violent end, but ceased with the death of the King in 1824.

The reign of Charles X., the unpopular Comte d'Artois, was foredoomed to failure, and the Legitimist dynasty was overthrown in 1830 by a fresh rising of the Orléanistes.

But now that at last the conspiracy had achieved the purpose for which forty-one years earlier it had plunged France into the horrors of revolution, and the succession was transferred to the *House of Orleans*, it became apparent that Louis Philippe firmly seated on the throne of France was a very different person from the Duc de Chartres sitting in the tribune of a revolutionary assembly and calling out for " lanterns." The liberty that the change of dynasty was to confer proved, like all the other visions of liberty offered by the Revolution, only a mirage, and after eighteen years of unrest Louis Philippe was driven from the throne he had usurped.

In this third revolution of 1848 fresh scenes of bloodshed took place; led by Socialists the workmen of Paris broke out into violent insurrection, the national workshops were suppressed, and finally a *Second Republic* was proclaimed.

Let us leave it to a Frenchman who lived through that time to tell the rest of the tragic story.

" We see this ephemeral Republic," says M. François St. Maur, " perishing beneath an audacious *coup d'état*; France hungering for rest and order, throwing herself at the feet of a representative of a great name (Louis Napoleon); the *Second Empire* established and soon shattered; a series of wars ending with the most terrible of all; Napoleon III. conquered and a prisoner, and the *Third Republic* proclaimed without having been asked or desired by the nation; anarchy, despotism, and licence under the name of liberty . . . a bold and incapable dictatorship profiting by the disasters of the country to seize the reins of power . . . a frightful insurrection holding Paris for two months under the sway of the Terror, living and dying in murder, pillage, and burning; the grossest instincts glorified and triumphant, the most odious crimes evading just repression, *the Revolution always armed*, right trampled under foot . . . such is the history of that mournful period." [1]

In spite of such incidents as the Affaire Boulanger, the Affaire Dreyfus, frequent strikes of workmen, the strife of factions, this Third Republic, the Republic of to-day, has nevertheless held

[1] Preface to the *Mémoires de Hua*.

her own for nearly fifty years, and now, after gloriously retrieving the disasters of 1870, we fervently hope will at last give peace to France.

The sequel to the great French Revolution was thus eighty years of unrest. That this unrest was the direct outcome of the Revolution it is impossible to deny. To attribute it to the unstable character of the French people is as illogical and unjust as to attribute the crimes and follies of the Revolution to their passions. The French people had not proved fickle or unstable under their former government ; were they not the same people who had proved passionately loyal to their kings during fourteen centuries ? If after the Revolution they became restless and unstable, it was simply that the Revolution itself had produced this change in the national character. For by that gigantic demolition France lost the habit of stability, the power of remaining content with any form of government ; the spell exercised by the monarchy once broken she lost faith in all rulers, and through eight succeeding forms of government never found one to satisfy her permanently. As M. de Loménie has expressed it : " The persistence of subversive Utopias is at the same time the cause and the natural consequence of all those abortive strokes that make up our history since 1789 ; a vicious circle in which France turns and mentally exhausts herself." [1]

Yet, if the century that followed had proved a millennial age of contentment, if the Republic established in 1792 had never been overthrown but had continued to this day to satisfy the desires of the French people, the panegyrists of the Revolution could not have pronounced it a more unqualified success. For in spite of subsequent upheavals, they hasten to assure us, great and lasting reforms were brought about by the Revolution— reforms so immense as to atone for all the crimes and follies that attended their birth. Contrary to all previous experience in the history of the world, this time, we are asked to believe, men did gather grapes of thorns and figs of thistles, and from the hatred, the lust, and the corruption that marked the whole revolutionary period there sprang up a harvest of love and liberty and justice.

If this were so, morality might well be proclaimed a fraud, and the divine ordering of the universe a delusion. Mercifully it is as untrue as all the other deductions of revolutionary sophists.

The immense reforms brought about during the revolutionary era were not the result of the Revolution. It was to the King and his enlightened advisers, as I have shown in this book, that the reforms in government were primarily due; it was the noblesse that dealt the death-blow to the feudal system ; it was the Royalist Democrats, abhorred of the revolutionary leaders, who drew up

[1] *La Comtesse de Rochefort*, by L. de Loménie, p. 288.

the Declaration of the Rights of Man and framed the Constitution. The work of the Revolution was to destroy all these reforms—to abolish the liberty of the press, liberty of conscience, personal liberty, to replace the comparatively mild feudalism of the Old Régime by the most frightful tyranny the world had ever seen, and finally to annul the Constitution demanded by the people in favour of a Constitution that could never be enforced, that lasted exactly twenty-six months, and was followed by no less than six others in the eighty years that followed.

Of all the measures passed by revolutionary legislation one alone can be quoted with some show of reason by historians to have resulted in permanent benefit to the people ; this was the law passed in 1793 conferring a greater proportion of the land on the peasants by the sale of " national goods "—that is to say, property formerly owned by the nobility and clergy. Thus although, as M. Louis Madelin points out, " the workman was the principal victim of the Revolution," [1] the peasant proprietor profited by it. " The peasant alone," writes a contemporary, " is happy ; he alone has gained."

But how far was this happiness a reality, or did it, like his pre-revolutionary " misery," exist largely on paper ? To judge of this we must refer to the accounts of eye-witnesses who record their impressions after the revolutionary storm had subsided. Thus, for example, we may compare the following passage in the journal of an Englishwoman who travelled through France in 1802 with the descriptions given by Dr. Rigby of dancing French peasants quoted at the beginning of this book :

" Breteuil, *July* 8.—Where is the gaiety we have heard of from our infancy as the distinguishing characteristic of this nation ? Where is the original of Sterne's picture of a French Sunday ? I have seen to-day no cessation from toil, no intermixture of devotion, and repose, and pleasure. I have seen no dance, I have heard no song. But I have seen the pale labourer bending over the plentiful fields, of which he does not seem, if one may judge by his looks, ever to have enjoyed the produce ; I have seen groups of men, women, and children working under the influence of the burning sun . . . and others giving to toil

---

[1] Not only did the working-classes suffer from unemployment and the suppression of their trades unions, but when employed they were obliged to work much harder than before, owing to the fact that all the feasts of the Church (Easter, Christmas, etc.), and all the saints days which, with the day following each, were holidays under the monarchy had now been done away with, whilst Sunday had been replaced by *décadi* that occurred once in ten days instead of seven. See the amusing article in the *Moniteur* for September 9, 1794, congratulating the Revolution for putting an end to " national idleness " by " consecrating to work at least 120 days " that the Old Régime devoted to " unemployment "—*i.e.* to rest and recreation—thus leaving the people only thirty-six holidays in the year.

the hours destined to repose, even so late as ten o'clock at night,"
etc.[1] By dint of this capacity for unremitting labour, combined
with his inherent thrift, the peasant of France has contrived to
make a living out of the soil, but certainly not under the millennial
conditions promised him by the revolutionary leaders. A still
more striking comparison might be made between the accounts
given by Arthur Young of the peasant's lot in 1789 and that
of his successor in agricultural lore, Mr. Rowland Prothero,
in his *Pleasant Land of France*, written precisely one hundred
years later. After describing in detail the wretchedness of the
French peasant's food and dwelling which he witnessed during
a tour through France in 1889, Mr. Prothero concludes with
the words : " The position of the peasant thus miserably lodged
and poorly fed is said to be precarious and perilous. He is a
proprietor only in name. The real owner is the money-lender,
and the peasant proprietor is a veritable serf." [2]

If this, then, was all that the one purely revolutionary reform
did for the peasant of France, we may well ask whether it was
worth the seas of blood shed to effect it.

But whilst the benefits resulting to France from the Revolution may be comprised in so small a compass—peasant pro-
prietorship on an increased scale—the evils of which it was the
cause are immeasurable.

" The Revolution," wrote Hua, who had lived all through it,
" was terrible because it was neither in the interests nor in the
character of the people . . . it had a million soldiers killed, 200,000
to 300,000 citizens butchered. . . . I shall be told : ' You are
wrong, confused . . . one must not place on the score of the Revolution all the errors, the mistakes, or even the crimes of which it was
the occasion, not the cause. . . .' But what is this idea of separating the Revolution from the ills it produced ? To what other cause
must they be attributed ? It is to it, to it alone, that they are
due ; these effects were not accidents but consequences. The
tree has borne its fruits. This is what many people will not see." [3]

We are told that it was with the Revolution that ideas of
liberty originated in France. Nothing is further from the truth.
France had a far clearer conception of liberty, even of democracy,
during the years that preceded the Revolution than in those
that followed after, in the days when Rousseau said that " liberty
would be too dearly bought with the blood of one French citizen "
than when Mirabeau demanded that " liberty should have for
her bed mattresses of corpses," or when Raynal declared that
" a country could only be regenerated in a bath of blood." No,

---

[1] *The Remains of Mrs. Richard Trench*, edited by her son, the Dean of
Westminster (1862).
[2] Exactly confirmed by Prince Kropotkin, *Paroles d'un Revolté*, pp.
325-327 (1882).   [3] *Mémoires de Hua*, p. 46.

it was not ideas of liberty that the Revolution bequeathed to France, but a legacy of bitterness, of envy, and of strife.

I am convinced that the day will come when the world, enlightened by the principles of true democracy, will recognise that the French Revolution was not an advance towards democracy but a directly anti-democratic and reactionary movement, that it was not a struggle for liberty but an attempt to strangle liberty at its birth ; the leaders will then be seen in their true colours as the cruellest enemies of the people, and the people, no longer condemned for their ferocity, will be pitied as the victims of a gigantic conspiracy. It was this conspiracy, or rather this combination of conspiracies, that alone triumphed in the Revolution ; it was the same great intrigues at work amongst the people in 1789 that survived all the storms that followed after and that now once again threaten the peace of the world.

THE FINAL TRIUMPH OF THE INTRIGUES

Of the first great intrigue of the French Revolution—the Orléaniste conspiracy—little more remains to be said, for although it was the cause of the Revolution of 1830, and again made itself felt as recently as 1889 in the Affaire Boulanger, it claims at the present day so few supporters that it may be described as dead. It is therefore with the other three intrigues, now more alive than ever, that we need concern ourselves.

That the French Revolution proved a triumphant success for Prussia might be proved in half-a-dozen ways—the severing of the Franco-Austrian alliance, the alarm created amongst the smaller German sovereigns that caused them to rally around Prussia, the overthrow of the Bourbons who had constituted the chief rivals to the ambitions of the Hohenzollerns and the removal of whom enabled Germany to place the offspring of her royal houses on all the thrones of Europe, the destruction of the French Court which, as the centre of art and learning, formed the greatest safeguard of civilisation and the strongest antidote to militarism, and, on the other hand, the rise to power of Napoleon I., who in the rôle of an aggressor alienated from France the sympathies of all Europe, the decline in the population [1] which weakened the

---

[1] It should be noted that this decline in the birth-rate dates from the Revolution. Before 1789 France was the most thickly populated of all European countries ; since that date the rate of increase in the populations of France and England offers this striking contrast :

	1789.	1918.
France	25,000,000	40,000,000
England and Ireland	12,000,000	45,000,000

Thus England under a monarchy has nearly quadrupled her population, whilst France under a Republic has increased hers by only three-fifths.

EPILOGUE

military strength of France,—these are only a few of the benefits
reaped by Prussia from the harvest of sedition she had sown.

But perhaps the principal advantage that Prussia gained by
the Revolution was the propagation of those doctrines of socialism and anti-patriotism that, first circulated by the revolutionaries
of France, have paralysed the resistance of Prussia's enemies.
Before 1870 it was the Socialists of France who opposed the re-
organisation of the army ; it was Michelet, the great panegyrist
of the Revolution, who, on the very eve of the Franco-Prussian
war, hailed the rising power of Germany, and in the great war
that has just ended it was the Radical Socialists of France and
the corresponding factions in all the countries of the allies who
have displayed the least resentment of Prussian aggression. Thus
the immense paradox has been created that amongst the so-
called democrats of Europe Prussian autocracy has found its
most valuable allies.

From the eighteenth century onwards Prussia has never
relinquished the policy of Frederick the Great—that of encouraging social unrest in the countries she wishes to subdue. The
first experiment was made in France, the second in Belgium
during the same period, the third, at an interval of a century and
a quarter—during which period German philosophers and writers
ceaselessly disseminated those subversive doctrines so rigorously
suppressed in the land of their birth—was to have taken place
in Ireland during the spring of 1914. This effort proving temporarily abortive Germany concentrated all her energies on
Russia, and by the fearful cataclysm that ensued very nearly
succeeded in turning the tide of the war irretrievably against
the Allies.

But it would seem that Prussia had played with fire too long,
that the fire she had fanned so assiduously abroad had all the
while been smouldering within her own borders, and now
threatens to envelop her in the general conflagration. If indeed
the present revolution in Germany is genuine and the power of
the Hohenzollerns has been finally overthrown, it is surely the
most amazing case of being " hoist with one's own petard " in
the history of the world.

For side by side with the intrigue of the Hohenzollerns that
other intrigue has gone forward—the scheme that, originating
with the Illuminati of Bavaria in 1776, is now being actively
carried out by their successors. The plan of world revolution
devised by Weishaupt has at last been realised. Can we believe
that it is by mere coincidence that the Spartacists of Munich have
adopted the pseudonym of their fellow-countryman and pre-
decessor, Spartacus-Weishaupt, the inaugurator of class warfare ?
Is it a mere coincidence that their doctrines are the same as his ?

We have only to study the course of the revolutionary movement in Europe during the last 130 years to realise that it has been the direct continuation of the scheme of the Illuminati, that the doctrines and the aims of the sect have been handed down without a break through the succeeding groups of revolutionary Socialists. Thus, for example, if we compare the confession of faith issued by Bakunin in the name of the International Social Democratic Alliance of 1866 with the creed of the Illuminati quoted on page 20 of this book, they will be found to be almost identical :

" The Alliance professes atheism ; it aims at the abolition of religious services, the replacement of belief by knowledge and divine by human justice, the abolition of marriage as a political, religious, and civic arrangement. Before all it aims at the definite and complete abolition of all classes and the political, economic, and social equality of the individual of either sex, the abolition of inheritance. All children to be brought up on a uniform system so that artificial inequalities may disappear. . . . It aims directly at the triumph of the cause of labour over capital. It repudiates so-called patriotism and the rivalry of nations, and desires the universal association of all local associations by means of freedom."

Indeed Prince Kropotkin, one of the leading spirits of the " Internationale," admits that there was " a direct filiation between this association and the ' Enragés ' of 1793 and the secret societies of 1795." Now, since we know that ever since 1866, and still at the present day, it is in secret societies and at meetings of spurious Freemasons [1] that revolutionary doctrines have been propagated, can we doubt that these associations are also the direct continuations of the Illuminati, and that it is on the doctrines of Weishaupt, the inventor of " world revolution," that the thing we now call " Bolshevism " is founded ? Can we doubt, moreover, that many of the terrible secrets of engineering popular tumults have been handed down to these societies from those that organised the first experiments in France ? The art of working on the public mind by calumny, corruption and terror, the seduction of the soldiery by women in the pay of the agitators, the fabrication of pretexts by which the people were made to carry out the designs of the leaders, the holding up or destruction of food supplies in order to drive them by hunger to violence, and at the same time the distribution of fiery liquor to inflame their passions, the hiring of foreign assassins to lead them on to

---

[1] Notably the " Grand Orient " of France, an order in no way to be confounded with British freemasonry, by which it was repudiated in 1885 in consequence of its rejection of the fundamental doctrine of true masonry —a belief in God, " the Great Architect of the Universe," and in the immortality of the soul.

bloodshed,—all these diabolical methods employed by the Jacobins of France, indoctrinated by the Illuminati, have been repeated in Russia with terrible effect. Moreover, not only in its secret organisation but in its outward manifestations the Russian Revolution has obviously been inspired by the French—the September massacres in the prisons of Petrograd by those in the prisons of Paris, the drownings in the Black Sea by the *noyades de Nantes*, the desecration of the Kremlin by the desecration of Notre Dame; the very phraseology of the leaders is the same, the Bolshevik tirades against the *bourgeoisie* are copied almost verbatim from the diatribes of Robespierre.

The danger that threatens civilisation is therefore no new danger but dates from before the French Revolution. The blaze kindled by Weishaupt has never ceased to smoulder ; France was only the place of its first conflagration. The same doctrines again put into practice must inevitably lead to the same result as surely as the fusion of the same gases must produce the same explosion. For the Terror, as I have shown, was not a frightful accident but the logical consequence of attempting to establish by force a system of equality not demanded by the nation. It matters not how averse to violence the leaders of such a movement may be, or how exalted the ideals which inspire them, they will find themselves obliged to resort to violent methods in order to maintain themselves in power, firstly, because by no other means can resistance be overcome, and secondly, because a period of anarchy is unavoidable for the destruction of the existing order, and this must inevitably rally round them men who are not Idealists at all but simply criminals whose ferocity they will be unable to control. " Whoever stops half-way in revolution," said St. Just, " digs his own grave." So just as Robespierre, who in 1791 had proposed the abolition of capital punishment, and later still had shuddered at the sanguinary schemes of Marat, found himself obliged to adopt the system of depopulation and to ally himself with Collot, Billaud, Barère, and the Jackals of the Comité de Sûreté Générale in order to carry out his scheme of equality and to save his own head ; just as Babeuf, who had denounced the atrocious methods of Robespierre, came to see that the triumph of Socialism could be ensured by no other means ; just as Lenin, who has likewise been described as an Idealist, is forced to permit—if not to ordain—wholesale massacre, and to associate himself with the dregs of the Russian underworld in order to make his position and his system secure, so in any country the attempt to establish Socialism by means of revolution must inevitably be accompanied by a Reign of Terror, not merely for the subjugation of the people as a whole, but as a means of defence against rival revolutionary factions.

For with the sweeping away of the Old Order the conflict will only have begun and must then enter on its further phase —the war between the factions that from the outset has divided the forces of revolution. The quarrel that took place between "Spartacus" and "Philo" was repeated in the perpetual dissensions between the disciples of the Illuminati throughout the whole French Revolution, and recurred again continually between the various revolutionary groups during the last century. Broadly speaking these groups have been divided into two opposing camps—the State Socialists and the Anarchists, that is to say, on the one hand the faction which aims at the supremacy of the State and the subjugation of the individual, and on the other hand the faction that would do away with the State and proclaim the complete liberty of the individual—policies which, of course, are diametrically opposed. It was this difference of opinion which in its embryonic stage caused the feud between the Robespierristes and Hébertistes, which broke out later between the revolutionaries of 1869—the State Socialists, Karl Marx, Engels, and Louis Blanc, violently separating themselves from the Anarchists, Proudhon and Bakunin—and that finally led to the rupture in the "Internationale." So still to-day the same feud rages in Russia, for it is towards Anarchists such as Kropotkin that the State Socialist Lenin has displayed the greatest severity. The hatred entertained by the believers in these opposing creeds has throughout been even fiercer than that of either party for the upholders of the Old Régime; the same furious animosity that led Robespierre to ordain the death of Hébert flamed out again in Proudhon's denunciations of Robespierre, in Marx's diatribes against Proudhon, in Bakunin's detestation of Marx. In Marx it would seem that not only the policy but the very spirit of Robespierre lived again. " His vanity," wrote Bakunin, " knew no bounds, a veritable Jew's vanity. . . . This vanity, already very great, was considerably increased by the adulation of his friends and disciples. Very personal, very jealous, very susceptible and very vindictive, like Jehovah, the God of his people, Marx cannot suffer one to acknowledge any other God but himself. . . . Proudhon . . . became the *bête noire* of Marx. To praise Proudhon in his presence was to offer him a mortal affront deserving of all the natural consequences of his enmity, and these consequences are at first hatred, then the foulest calumnies. Marx has never recoiled before falsehood, however odious, however perfidious it might be." [1]

Such, in the opinion of one of his most intimate associates, was the prophet now held up by the exponents of revolutionary

[1] *Michael Bakunin, eine Biographie*, by Max Nettlau, p. 69. See also *L'Anarchia*, by Ettore Zoccoli, pp. 107, 108.

Socialism to the admiration of the English people, and such is the conflict on which they are invited to enter at the very moment when real and far-reaching reforms are actually within their grasp. Could they but realise the true character of the men whose gospel is offered them as their one hope of salvation, could they but study the history of the revolutionary movement in Europe, the miserable quarrels that took place between the leaders, the grotesque failure of every attempt to put their theories into practice—notably in such experiments as " the New Harmony " and " the New Australia " carried out by Lane and Owen— it is inconceivable that they could lend an ear to such counsels. But all these things are unknown to the working-classes in our country—the true history of revolution has very carefully been kept from them by the propagandists on whom they depend for instruction, and who, in no way blind leaders of the blind but guides endowed with the clearest powers of vision, will lead them not into a ditch but over the brink of an abyss.

For whichever revolutionary party succeeds in establishing its domination over the people it will be all over with democracy, since neither in the plan of the State Socialists which entails autocratic control of every department of life—that is to say, Prussianism of the most intolerable kind—nor in the scheme of the Anarchists which consists in the absence of all control, and must necessarily end in rule by the strongest, can any element of liberty be found. The ideal of true democracy, rule by the will of the majority, must then in either case be finally abandoned, and the people must submit to the domination of bureaucratic minorities or return to a state of savagery.

Naturally this is not the programme placed before the nation, for, just as in the French Revolution, the people are invited to co-operate on some perfectly plausible pretext—the redressing of their real grievances and the improvement in the conditions of labour—but are not admitted to the secrets of the leaders. Indeed it is probable that those of the extremists amongst the leaders who are of British birth and origin little realise whither they themselves are being led. It is on these supposed leaders, mainly middle-class men posing as representatives of labour, that the makers of world revolution have founded their hopes. The " extraordinary simplicity and want of acquaintance with Continental thought " which the German, Karl Hillebrand, long ago detected in the attitude of " the rising Radical school " in England towards the French Revolution,[1] which characterised the correspondence of their prototypes the " English Jacobins " with their brethren in France, and that is still to be found in the

---

[1] Karl Hillebrand, *Aus und über England*, p. 339.

utterances of our Pacifists and Internationalists to-day, makes them the ready dupes of subtler Continental minds. For it is not they but their allies of foreign blood who are the real directors of the movement—Prussian exponents of democracy who entertain the secret hope of building up their shattered military machine once more on the ruins of civilisation, German merchants who see their chance to corner the markets of the world by paralysing industry in the countries of their rivals, Cosmopolitan Jewish financiers who hope by the overthrow of the existing order to place all capital beneath their own control, Anarchists from the east of Europe animated solely by a passion for destruction— who have all adapted Weishaupt's scheme of world revolution to their own particular purpose. Of all these conspiracies it might be said, as Robison said of the Illuminati : " Their first and immediate aim is to get the possession of riches, power, and influence, without industry ; and to accomplish this they want to abolish Christianity ; and then dissolute manners and universal profligacy will procure them the adherence of all the wicked, and enable them to overturn all the civil governments of Europe ; after which they will think of further conquests, and extend their operations to the other quarters of the globe, till they have reduced mankind to the state of one undistinguishable chaotic mass." Over this helpless mass each conspiracy hopes to estab- lish its ascendancy, thereby bringing the peoples of the world under an iron tyranny unequalled in the annals of the human race. With each conspiracy, moreover, militant atheism forms an integral part of the scheme. Beginning with Weishaupt, continuing with Clootz, with Büchner and with Bakunin, hatred of religion, above all of Christianity, has characterised all the instigators of world revolution, since it is essential to their purpose that the doctrine of hatred should be substituted for the doctrine of love. We have only to replace the old word Jacobinism by its modern equivalent Bolshevism in this prophetic warning written by the Abbé Barruel in 1797 on the " universal explosion " devised by " Spartacus-Weishaupt " to understand the danger that now threatens the whole civilised world :

" To whatever government, to whatever religion, to whatever rank of society you belong, if Jacobinism wins the day, if the projects and oaths of the sect are accomplished, it is all over with your religion, with your priesthood, with your government and your laws, with your properties and your magistrates. Your riches, your fields, your houses, even to your cottages, all will cease to be yours. You thought the Revolution ended in France, and the Revolution in France was only the first attempt of the Jacobins. In the desires of a terrible and formidable sect, you have only reached the first stage of the plans it has formed for that general Revolution which is to overthrow all thrones, all altars, annihilate all property, efface all law, and end by dissolving all society."

It rests with the people to prevent the execution of this project in our country. Can we believe that at this hour they will fail to play their part as the champions of liberty? Can we believe that the working-men of England who put down with an iron hand all attempts to establish Jacobinism in their midst throughout the French Revolution, amongst whom Marx himself for more than thirty years laboured in vain to obtain a following, whom Kropotkin left in anger and disgust after his failure to win them over to his schemes of anarchy, will now be persuaded by the agents of Lenin to accept that which their sturdy forefathers rejected and to become the instruments of their own ruin? Is it possible that the " English Jacobins," so ignominiously defeated in 1793, will now triumph over the good sense of their fellow-countrymen? Will that " isle of serenity," whose soil the *émigrés* fell on their knees to kiss when flying from the horrors of their own unhappy country, after another century and a quarter of civilisation become the scene of kindred disorders? Shall we, the freest people on earth, whose laws and Constitution have been for countless generations the envy and the admiration of the world, now consent to be taught liberty by men nurtured under Kaiserdom and Tsardom, or by a race without a country of its own on which to experiment in government? Shall we, in the words of Arthur Young, " imitate the example of France, and by tampering with that Constitution to which we owe all our prosperity hazard so immense a stake of happiness"?

APPENDIX

APPENDIX

THE DUC D'ORLÉANS ON THE 6TH OF OCTOBER

At the Procédure du Chatelet the following witnesses came forward to testify to the presence of the duke amongst the crowd during the invasion of the Château on the morning of October 6 :

The Vicomte de la Châtre, witness cxxvii., and two men-servants (Eudeline and Gueniffey, witnesses cxxxiii. and cxxxvi.), who were with him, swore to having seen the Duc d'Orléans amongst the crowd in the courtyard of the Château in the morning of the 6th whilst the Guards were being massacred, adding that the duke had a switch in his hand and " never ceased laughing."

De Guillermy of the bodyguard, witness cxlix., testified to seeing the duke in the crowd at the same moment.

The Chevalier de la Serre, witness ccxxvi., brigadier in the King's army and a *chevalier de Saint-Louis*, stated that " at six o'clock in the morning of the 6th he went to the Château by the Place des Armes, where he perceived a great movement of the people . . . that he then ran to the Cour Royale, there he joined the people and with them ascended the great staircase (the Escalier de Marbre), that these people were uttering imprecations, saying, ' Our father is with us, let us march ! ' that he asked one of these men who was this father ? This man answered him, ' Ah, Sacredieu, do you not know him ? It is the Duc d'Orléans ? ' that he asked this man, ' Where is he ? Is he here ? ' The witness had then reached the first flight of the great staircase ; this man answered him by indicating with a gesture of his arm that he (the duke) was at the top of the staircase. ' Eh ! f. . . ., do you not see him ? He is there, he is there ! ' Then the witness raising his head and rising on tip-toe saw *the Duc d'Orléans at the head of the people making a gesture with his arm to indicate the hall of the Queen's bodyguard*, and that the Duc d'Orléans then turned to the left to reach the King's apartments."

The Marquis de Digoine du Palais, witness clxviii., stated that just after the rush of the crowd up the Escalier de Marbre he went down the Escalier de Princes leading to the King's apartments, and at the foot of this staircase he met the Duc d'Orléans.

Morlet, witness ccclxxxiii., the sentinel on guard outside the King's apartments, related that the duke presented himself at this door and that he refused him admittance,

After this, that is to say between seven and eleven in the morning, the duke was seen amongst the crowd in the courtyards of the Château by six other witnesses—De la Borde (cxcv.), Quence (ccliv.), a coachman, Jobert (cclvi.), a valet and hairdresser, Mme. Tillet (ccclxv.), wife of a restaurant-keeper, Brayer (ccxvii.), an upholsterer, and De Frondeville (clxxvii.), King's Councillor and deputy of the Assembly. The duke was described by these witnesses as being dressed in a grey frock-coat, carrying a switch in his hand and smiling at the people who followed him crying out, " Vive notre Roi d'Orléans ! " [1]

It is true that in the published report of the Procédure du Châtelet the Chevalier de la Serre was the only eye-witness who testified to seeing D'Orléans actually on the staircase pointing to the Queen's rooms, but De Nampy (witness lxxxviii.), captain in the Régiment de Flandre, stated that he had heard Degroix, one of the bodyguard, say that he saw " the Duc d'Orléans in a grey coat pointing out to the people the great staircase of the Château, and signing to them to turn to the right, and that he heard the people cry, ' Vive le Roi d'Orléans ! ' "

Moreover, according to Madame Campan, several other witnesses at the Procédure du Châtelet declared that they had themselves seen the duke at the head of the staircase pointing the way to the Queen's apartments, and the English contemporary Robison asserts that the most important evidence on the duke's complicity was not printed.[2]

But the obvious answer to these accusations would have been to prove an alibi. If, as revolutionary historians would have us believe, all the witnesses above quoted were not only liars but perjurers— for their evidence was given on oath—when they declared that they had seen the duke in the courtyards or on the staircase, then where was he ? According to his own statement he was at the Palais Royal and did not start for Versailles till just on eight o'clock in the morning, but the only witnesses he could produce were some of his own servants and three obscure people (whose names only were given but whose identity was not stated), who said that they had passed him at Auteuil at 7.30, *i.e.* half-an-hour before the time at which he himself said he had left Paris. Yet one other alibi was afterwards provided by his friend Mrs. Elliot, and since it is on this evidence that certain historians have founded their exoneration of

---

[1] This evidence was recently confirmed in the *Mémoires* of Madame de la Tour du Pin, who was in the Château at Versailles on the 6th of October, and relates that early in the morning her *bonne* Marguerite rushed into her room and told her that on going down into the courtyard where the guards had just been massacred she had seen a *monsieur* arrive on the scene " with very muddy boots and a whip in his hand, who was no other than the Duc d'Orléans, whom she knew quite well from having often seen him, that also the wretches surrounding him showed their joy, crying out, ' Vive notre Roi d'Orléans ! ' whilst he signed to them with his hand to be silent " (*Journal d'une Femme de Cinquante Ans*, i. 229).

[2] Robison's *Proofs of a Conspiracy*, p. 392.

the duke, it should be compared with the duke's own account of his movements given in his *Exposé de la Conduite*, drawn up by him in London :

The Duke's Account	*Mrs. Elliott's Account*

There was no Assembly on Sunday the 4th, and I had started off according to my custom on Saturday evening for Paris, intending to return on Monday morning to Versailles, but I was kept by work which certain people of my household had to do with me. I learnt in succession throughout the day (*i.e.* the 5th) of the effervescence taking place in Paris, of the start for Versailles of a considerable quantity of the people with arms and even with cannons, and at last the departure of a great number of the Parisian Guards. I knew nothing else of what was going on at Versailles until the following morning, when M. le Brun,[1] Captain of a company of the National Guard . . . and Inspector of the Palais Royal, had me awoken and came to tell me that an express of the National Guard had come to bring his bodyguard news of Versailles. . . . The same day (*i.e.* the 6th), *towards eight o'clock in the morning, I started for the National Assembly.* . . . Between Sèvres and Versailles I met some carts laden with provisions and escorted by a detachment of the National Guard. . . . The officer in command of the detachment . . . gave me two men as escorts. . . . These two cavaliers escorted me in fact to my house (*i.e.* the Hôtel de Vergennes at Versailles). . . . I left again immediately to go to the National Assembly. I found a number of deputies in the Avenue. They told me the King would hold the Assembly in the Salon d'Hercule; I went up to the Château and to his Majesty (*Exposé de la Conduite de M. le Duc d'Orléans* redigé par lui-même à Londres (June 1790), pp. 17-19).

Soon after came the 5th of October, a memorable and dreadful day. But I must here do justice to the Duke of Orleans. He certainly was not at Versailles on that dreadful morning, for he breakfasted with company at my house when he was accused of being in the Queen's apartments disguised. He told us then that he heard the fish-women had gone to Versailles with some of the Faubourgs, and that the people said they were gone to bring the King again to Paris. He informed us that he had heard this from some of his own servants from the Palais Royal. He said that he was the more surprised at this, as he had left the Palais Royal at nine o'clock of the night before, and all then seemed perfectly quiet. . . . He stayed at my house till half-past one o'clock. *I have no reason to suppose that he went to Versailles till late in the day when he went to the States,* as everybody knows. I have entered into this subject that I may have an opportunity of declaring that I firmly believe the Duke of Orléans was innocent of the cruel events of that day and night, and that Lafayette was the author and instigator of the treatment the August Royal Family then met with. . . . The Duke of Orléans was even tried on this account, but the proofs were so absurd that it was dropped. And indeed it was clear to everybody that Lafayette and his party were the only guilty people (*Journal of Mrs. Elliott*, pp. 37, 38).

---

[1] Note that Le Brun did not appear as a witness at the Châtelet to substantiate this statement.

It will be seen that between these two accounts there is no resemblance whatever. In the first place, the Duc d'Orléans says nothing about breakfasting with Mrs. Elliott either on the 5th or 6th ; on the contrary, he distinctly states that he was in his own house, the Palais Royal, early in the morning of both days. Mrs. Elliott says he breakfasted with her on the 5th, " when he was accused of being in the Queen's apartments disguised " ; but he was never accused of being there on the morning of the 5th, for the mob did not start for Versailles till the middle of the day ; and if this was a mere slip of the pen, and Mrs. Elliott really intended to say the 6th, this does not tally either, for the Duke says he left the Palais Royal at eight o'clock and went straight to Versailles, where he remained till the Assembly met, which was about eleven o'clock in the morning.   Nor was he ever accused of being disguised as were his followers, and all eye-witnesses were agreed in their description of his dress on that morning.   Mrs. Elliott's story, like several other passages in her journal, is evidently a tissue of inaccuracies, or of deliberate mis-statements, but the accusation against Lafayette can only be attributed to Orléaniste influence.   No one at the time thought of accusing Lafayette of complicity with the events of October 5 and 6 ; this charge was brought against him only by the real authors of the day—the members of the Orléaniste conspiracy.[1] Yet it is on this obviously trumped up story that revolutionary historians found their exoneration of the duke !   In the absence, therefore, of any convincing alibi, and in the face of the overwhelming evidence brought forward at the Procédure du Châtelet, it seems to me impossible to doubt that the Duc d'Orléans was actually with the crowd at Versailles when they invaded the Château on the 6th of October.

ROTONDO AND THE PRINCESS DE LAMBALLE

The document preserved amongst the Chatham Papers at the Record Office (where it has been wrongly dated in pencil 1791) consists of a series of questions and answers in French written by two different hands, and accompanied by a letter signed only L., saying that the sender has the honour of forwarding the answers to Mr. Pitt's questions.   The inquiry concerning Rotondo runs thus :

(Question) " Qui est Rotondo ?   Est-ce son nom de guerre ou de famille ?   A-t-on quelques notions sur ce qu'il faisait avant la Révolution ?   Depuis quand est-il ici ?   [i.e. evidently in London]. A-t-il avec lui quelque autre chef connu des Travailleurs ? "

---

[1] See the letter of Laclos to Latouche quoted by Montjoie (Conjuration de d'Orléans, iii. 72), in which this phrase occurs in connection with the events of October 6 : " Remember above all that it is only by the discredit and degradation of M. de Lafayette that Monseigneur (the Duc d'Orléans) will triumph."   The democratic historian Fantin Désodoards quotes this same letter (Histoire Philosophique, i. 287), of which he declares that he has seen the original.

(*Answer*) " Rotondo est un maître italien, c'est son nom de famille : il mourait de faim avant la Révolution. Il est arrivé ici le 24 ou le 25 8bre, il a remplace Chevy (?), que l'on a envoié au Portugal : son assesseur est un nommé tillaïe (sic) an^ien avocat ; beau-frère de la femme de Danton. Rotondo est l'ami de Barbaroux, le fameux marseillais qui vendait des Bas dans la cour de l'hôtel de Penthièvre et mari d'une fille de cuisine de Madame de Lamballe qui l'a eventrée après qu'on lui eut coupé la tête."

This reveals a curious web of revolutionary intrigue—Rotondo, the friend of Barbaroux, who first sent for the Marseillais ; Barbaroux, a lawyer by profession, selling stockings in the courtyard of the Duc de Penthièvre,[1] father-in-law of the Princess de Lamballe and with whom she lived ; Rotondo sent officially to London—by whom ? Evidently by the leaders of the Orléaniste conspiracy. Incidentally, this correspondence provides further proof of Pitt's non-complicity with the revolutionary movement ; if he had encouraged sedition is it possible that after three years of revolution he would have known nothing of Rotondo, a leading agitator who was frequently in London, and, as we see, officially employed there ? The Travailleurs referred to were evidently an association for watching the movements of the revolutionaries and reporting them to Pitt.

---

[1] A fact confirmed by Peltier, *La Révolution du 10 Août*, i. 121.

INDEX

INDEX

135, 139, 142 *note*, 176, 184
Lameth, Charles de, 15, 45, 120,
135, 139, 176
Lane, William, 495
Lanjuinais, Jean Denis, 369, 370,
371, 393, 401, 402, 404
Lansdowne, Henry Petty, 1st
Marquis of, 198 *note*, 380, 384
Larevellière Lépeaux, Louis Marie
de, 428, 479
La Serre, Chevalier de, 135 *note*,
142, 148
Lasource, Alba-, 179, 221, 222
Latouche-Tréville, Louis Réné de,
135, 148
La Tour du Pin, Mme. de, 43
Latude, 380, 384
Lauderdale, Earl of, 380, 384
Launay, Marquis de, 42, 80-92, 96 ;
murder of, 92
Lauzun, Duc de. *Vide* Biron
Lavaux, 71
La Vendée, rises against Conven-
tion, 404-407 ; Terror in, 416, 439
Lavicomterie de Saint - Sanson,
Louis Thomas Hébert, 454
Lazowski, 250, 252, 261, 273
"League of perpetual peace," 383
Lebas, Philippe François Joseph,
454, 469, 471
Le Bon, Joseph, 279, 416, 427
Lebrun-Tondu, Pierre Marie, 350
Le Chapelier, Isaac René Guy, 184
Lecointre, Laurent, 129, 144
Legendre, Louis, 228, 336, 358, 386,
402
Legislative Assembly, inaugurated,
190 ; elections for, 191 ; char-
acter of, 192 ; superseded by
Convention, 356
Lehardy, Pierre, 370
Lemonnier, 279
Lenin, 493, 494, 497
Leopold II., Emperor of Austria,
177, 188, 201 *note*, 214, 245, 246,
382
Lepeletier St. Fargeau, Marquis
de, 374
Lequinio de Kerblay, Joseph Marie,
476 *note*
Leroux, 266, 267
Leroy, "Dix-Août," 458
Leuchtsenring, 433
Liancourt, Duc de, 144, 184
Limon, Marquis de, 246, 247
Lindet, Robert, 414, 454

Lindsay, Mr., 347
Linguet, Nicolas Henri, 78, 99
Losme - Salbray, Antoine Jerôme,
Major de, 82
Louis XIV., 3, 9, 383
Louis XV., 3, 18, 79, 289, 291
Louis XVI., 9, 21, 28, 46, 56, 79,
107, 112, 119, 122-124, 196, 198,
270, 301, 304, 349, 359, 386, 393,
402, 404, 434 ; character of, 53,
102 ; marriage of, 24, 26 ; his
death planned by German Freemasons, 21 ; his reforms, 6, 7,
45, 49, 77, 289, 452 ; and the
famine, 18, 164, 478 ; and the
Duc d'Orléans, 12, 33, 105 ;
holds Séance Royale, 48 ; dis-
misses Necker, 57 ; and the
revolution of July, 58, 66, 67,
69, 70, 83, 99, 100 ; visits Paris
on 17th of July, 100-103 ; proclaimed " Restorer of French
liberty," 118 ; and the march
on Versailles, 126-158, 160-162 ;
comes to Paris, 159 ; sends the
Duc d'Orléans to England, 164 ;
his attitude to Revolution in
1790, 175 ; appeals to foreign
powers, 176, 177, 201 ; starts
for St. Cloud, 181 ; flight to
Varennes, 181 ; accepts Constitution, 186-188 ; his opinion
of Constitution, 187, 188 ; restored popularity of, 189 ; and
the Legislative Assembly, 192 ;
and the Brissotin ministry, 202-
218 ; and the 20th of June, 220-
241 ; deposition of, demanded,
245, 249-256 ; negotiates with
Danton, 257 ; on the 10th of
August, 261, 263-269, 273, 275-
277, 285, 469 ; imprisoned in
Temple, 283 ; people against his
death, 362-366 ; his trial and
condemnation, 366-373 ; his
death, 374-378 ; news received
in England, 378-380, 383 ; Pitt
and the death of Louis XVI.,
379, 380
Louis XVII. (the Dauphin), 100,
104, 128, 149, 157, 160, 195, 229,
234, 235, 268, 269, 301, 435, 436,
461, 472
Louis XVIII. (the Comte de Provence), 187, 436, 485, 486
Louis du Bas Rhin, 454, 455, 457,

THE END